ISBN 978-1-334-67700-7
PIBN 10759805

English
Français
Deutsche
Italiano
Español
Português

www.forgottenbooks.com

Mythology Photography **Fiction**
Fishing Christianity **Art** Cooking
Essays Buddhism Freemasonry
Medicine **Biology** Music **Ancient
Egypt** Evolution Carpentry Physics
Dance Geology **Mathematics** Fitness
Shakespeare **Folklore** Yoga Marketing
Confidence Immortality Biographies
Poetry **Psychology** Witchcraft
Electronics Chemistry History **Law**
Accounting **Philosophy** Anthropology
Alchemy Drama Quantum Mechanics
Atheism Sexual Health **Ancient History**
Entrepreneurship Languages Sport
Paleontology Needlework Islam
Metaphysics Investment Archaeology
Parenting Statistics Criminology
Motivational

MEMOIRS

OF

THE ADMINISTRATION

. OF THE RIGHT HONOURABLE

HENRY PELHAM,

COLLECTED FROM THE FAMILY PAPERS,

AND OTHER AUTHENTIC DOCUMENTS.

By WILLIAM COXE, M.A. F.R.S. F.S.A.

ARCHDEACON OF WILTS.

IN TWO VOLUMES.

VOL. II.

LONDON:

LONGMAN, REES, ORME, BROWN, AND GREEN,

PATERNOSTER ROW.

1829.

T. C. Hansard,

MEMOIRS, &c.

VOL. II.

CONTENTS

ILLUSTRATIVE CORRESPONDENCE.

CONTENTS:

c 2

MEMOIRS, &c.

CHAPTER XVIII.

1748.

Increasing embarrassments of the Duke of Newcastle—Sudden departure of the Dutch minister, Bentinck, from Aix, and dissatisfaction of lord Sandwich, at the new orders conveyed to him—Sir Thomas Robinson, in conjunction with lord Sandwich, opens a friendly communication with count Kaunitz—Return of the Dutch minister to the Congress, and acquiescence of lord Sandwich—The Duke of Newcastle differs in opinion with his brother, and the Cabinet in England, on the expediency of concluding without Austria—Correspondence on these topics.

WHILE the duke of Newcastle was perplexed by the answer of the ministers in England, and the representations of his brother, he was involved in farther difficulty by the precipitate conduct of lord Sandwich and count Bentinck. It cannot be doubted, that lord Sandwich, aware that a majority in the cabinet felt anxious for peace, at all hazards, was mortified at the contradictory orders which he had just received. He consequently did not fail to manifest his dissatisfaction to the duke of Newcastle himself, and even deferred the execution of that part of his instructions, which enjoined a change of deportment towards the Austrian minister. Count Bentinck partook of this feeling, in a still stronger degree, and abruptly quitted the Congress, with the connivance, at least, of the English plenipotentiary. On his arrival at the Hague, he wrote to the duke of Newcastle, explaining the motives for his departure, and warmly maintaining, that the foreign and domestic circumstances of the Republic, as well as those of England, Austria, and Sardinia, would not permit a protracted negotiation. He requested permission for lord Sandwich to repair to the Hague, that he might come to an understanding with the Dutch government; adding, that, for his own part, he could not negotiate with the Austrian and Sardinian ministers jointly, and that, to treat separately with either, would throw the whole affair into confusion. He concluded, by announcing his resolution, not to return to the Congress, until the orders sent to lord Sandwich, for conciliating Austria, should be recalled.*

These incidents threatened an immediate rupture of the negotiation; for lord Sandwich himself seemed disposed to follow the example of count Bentinck. In this dilemma, the duke of Newcastle appealed to his brother, bitterly complaining of the conduct of both the plenipotentiaries, and inclosing copies of his correspondence with them, in justification of his own proceedings.

" DEAR BROTHER,   " *Hanover, August 7th-18th,* 1748.

" On Wednesday night, Lucas, the messenger, brought me your kind letter of the 29th of July, O. S. It was, in every respect, so proper, so honest, and so sensible a one, that I shewed it immediately, both to the king and the Duke, which has had an extreme good effect: they were both prodigiously pleased with the contents of it. The Duke said, that it was like yourself, honest, plain, and sensible; and yesterday morning he sent me word by *Yorke,* that he never saw the king so pleased, as he was with your letter. Believe me, dear brother, as much as I like to be commended, I had infinitely more satisfaction in this, than if it had happened to myself.

" The king has ordered the Duke to stay until the end of the week, at the request of the poor princess of Hesse. I am glad of it, for a thousand reasons, particularly at this time.

" The king shewed me, yesterday, the Duke's plan of reduction, and talked it over with me. As well as I can understand it, the number to be reduced amounts to about 40,000 men; that to be kept in England, I am positive, is 18,900, with the addition of 4,000 in Ireland; all the marines to be broke; but the king said, 'William would keep the other young regiments: I dare say you will not differ about them.' Your letter gave occasion to a great deal of serious conversation, in which the king shewed the greatest tenderness and regard for the Duke. In our late conversations, we have had much discourse upon the extravagancy of the household. I have ventured to promise, that no man ever was more ready than yourself, to set your face against the abuses of the Civil List, in every shape. I had

* Count Bentinck to the Duke of Newcastle, Hague, August 17th, 1748, MS.

my *reasons* for saying it. It was very rightly taken, and I *hope will be put in execution.*"   *   *   *   *   *

After alluding to the appointment of Mr. Münchhausen the younger, as Hanoverian minister in England, instead of baron Steinberg, who had resigned, he continues :—

" I come now to a very disagreeable affair, in the conduct of my friends, lords Sandwich and Bentinck. Was there ever any thing like it! Sure I have not deserved this treatment from either of them. The Duke, with all his partiality to Sandwich, entirely gives him up. I wish you would consider it thoroughly, and I am sure you will think it insufferable. I am convinced they are engaged farther to St. Severin, than they own ; and are afraid of being disavowed, and therefore they act in this manner, in order to frighten us. Can any thing be righter, more reasonable, or more innocent, than my letter of the 6th? The case is plainly thus : lord Sandwich gave us reason to hope, that all, or certainly the greater part of Flanders, might be put provisionally into our hands ; and, on condition of the possession of the whole, he is told, that he should be authorised to sign without the court of Vienna. If France does not accept the proposal, then he is directed, which indeed he should have done in all events, to endeavour to do every thing to get Kaunitz to concur; which Sir Thomas Robinson, who is just come from Vienna, thinks may be done. This, his lordship thinks, is sufficient to tell the king : *Mr. Bentinck is of another opinion ; and will not return to the Congress, if these orders are executed.* This is the true state of the case. I hope you will approve my short letter to Sandwich. I am sure you will, my long one of this date, to the two Plenipoes. I have endeavoured, by that, to prevent any ill consequences from lord Sandwich's ill humour or ill turn, upon St. Severin's coming back.

      *   *   *   *   *   *

" The king is very angry, and said, ' *My Lord, this man would not have done for Secretary of State.*' To which I answered, ' *Your Majesty always thought so.*' The king says, ' Sir Thomas Robinson *will set all right.*' He is a great favourite, both with King and Duke. In order to enable Sir Thomas Robinson to do it, I have written, as you will see, in the most pressing manner I could to him."

      *   *

* From Compiègne.

The noble secretary inclosed the copy of an indignant letter to lord Sandwich, which is here inserted, as conveying the strongest expression of his feelings, in his own language.

"MY LORD,   "*Hanover, August 7th-18th,* 1748.*

"Your Lordship will easily believe, that it is with great concern, that I send away this messenger. I will say as little as possible, as to the letters which Collins brought. I did not think, that either my public or private conduct deserved them. I have, however, the comfort of his Royal Highness's entire approbation of every thing that I have done, or writ; and have taken no one step, since he has been here, without previously consulting with his Royal Highness. I always thought my situation difficult; but did not expect, the attack would come from the quarter, it has done. It is, however, an additional comfort and satisfaction to me, in my present distress, to find, that my friends in England, with whom I formerly differed, when I had the pleasure to agree with your lordship, seem to think entirely in the same way, that the king's orders have been given; viz. that there are but two safe methods of signing a definitive treaty, without the concurrence of the empress queen. I believe his Royal Highness has very clearly expressed his thoughts upon that point. I will dwell no longer upon this disagreeable subject; but conclude, with the assurances of my being," &c.

The reply of lord Sandwich contains an apology for suspending the execution of his orders; with a manly vindication of the principles, on which he had acted; but announces his resolution to obey implicitly his future instructions.

"MY LORD,   "*Aix, August* 19th, *N. S.* 1748.

"It is so new to me to write to your Grace, in answer to a letter, in the style of that, which I received with your Grace's last dispatches, that I never in my life was so much at a loss what to say; and though my heart is full, I own I know not how to express to you the half of what it contains. Surely, my lord, it is a little unkind, to call the substance of my last dispatches an

---

* Pelham *Papers*.

attack upon your Grace's measures. I should think myself the last of men, if, after the favours I have received from your Grace, I was ever capable of such a design. I meant no more, than to say all I could think of, to shew you, that there was no going on in perfect concert with the court of Vienna, or at least, with count Kaunitz. I thought it my duty to endeavour to shew it you, in every light it would bear. But I have most scrupulously avoided throwing my reasoning into the channel of public business. And I give you my word and honour, that I have wrote no letter of any sort, since I was at the army, to any of the king's ministers, except two to Mr. Pelham, the one of which I sent your Grace a copy of; and in the other, which I think was wrote about the 15th or 16th of last month, I entered into business no other-wise, than to tell him, in general terms, that I was very well pleased with the orders I had received. Nay, my lord, I can go farther, by assuring your Grace, that I think it very probable, that I may have disobliged a great and sincere friend,* by avoiding a secret correspondence, which I think there was some disposition to enter into with me. If this is true, (I have the proofs in my hands of what I say,) where is it that I can have formed my *attack?* Or, in what channel do I propose to carry it on? In public, I have confined myself barely to the answering of your Grace's dispatches ; but even in that point, now I know your final resolution, I will alter my style, and consider only how I may repair any damages, that you may think I have already occasioned. For, my lord, let what will happen to me, your Grace never shall have reason to say, that I have left you in any distress, much less that I have ever had a thought of acting against you.

" As to the representations against the late orders which I have received, I own it is my own opinion that they were founded ; and I wish my appre-hensions may not prove true in the end. But be that as it will, you, nor no one else, shall hear any more of that opinion; and I shall go on upon the system you have laid down. But, my lord, if I had thought otherwise, the representations would have been the same, and my delay in executing the orders, just as it was on the late occasion ; for you may judge, by Bentinck's paper and his subsequent letter to your Grace, how much he took this affair to heart; and I am sure, if I had not complied with his request, in suspending the execution of my orders, it would have come to a much greater *éclat* than it did on the late occasion.

* The duke of Bedford.

" I do not mean by this to throw the whole upon my friend Bentinck. I own I think as he did : but still I say, that if I had thought otherwise, the difficulty your Grace is under, in this matter, would have been the same. However, as I have already said, all this, with regard to me, is at an end ; and I shall consider only how to set things again to rights, in the very way you would wish to have them.

" I am excessively at a loss, how to bring Bentinck back. If he does not return, the negotiation is in the hands of Van Haaren, who will soon throw every thing into confusion, and can be trusted in no instance whatever ; and I own I much doubt, whether he will be prevailed on, at any rate, to recede from his late resolutions. I will write a softening letter to him, this evening ; but I much fear whether writing will do ; or, indeed, whether, if I saw him, I should carry my point ; though I know, I shall be more likely to succeed there, than any other person whatever. Your Grace is, I dare say, too much convinced of the importance of his continuing to act with us, both here and at the Hague, to think any thing ought to be neglected to regain him. I shall write to him to that purpose, as often as I can write to any effect. But I dare not stir from hence, without your Grace's leave ; though I think, nothing would be so likely to bring him in again, as an interview with him, before he has taken his final resolution.

" I could write much more, but I am not willing to detain the courier one moment longer than is absolutely necessary ; so I shall conclude with desiring your Grace to put me to any proof that you shall think proper, to try my attachment to you, and to be assured, that I shall never persevere in an opinion that differs from your Grace's, however I may be convinced, in my own mind, that that opinion is founded ; and that I am what I have been, ever since I had the honour of being known to your Grace, and I shall ever be," &c.

Reply of the Duke of Newcastle.

" My Dear Lord,   " Hanover, Aug. 23rd, 1748.

" I received, yesterday morning, the honour of your private letter of the 19th, N. S., in your own hand : and you must allow me to say, that every word that has come from you, either jointly or separately, has confirmed me in the necessity of the king's orders, which his Majesty at first thought proper to send, and has since been pleased to adhere to. We do not want to convict, or force the court of Vienna; we want to gain them; and the only way of doing that, is by the method proposed, at least in my poor opinion. St. Severin, I do not doubt, is of another mind. He now enjoys the separate confidences of both parties; and will make his own use of them. If he can knock our heads together, he will; and he is in a fair way of doing it. Had what I long ago humbly advised from London, which the king was afterwards pleased to approve from Hanover, been followed; viz. had we then prepared a plain, simple draught of our own, of a definitive treaty, upon the foot of the preliminaries, all this, or, at least, the greatest part of it, would, in all probability, have been avoided. But I will say no more, in support of my own thoughts; but, in justification of them, you will not wonder if I send you a copy of his Royal Highness's letter to count Bentinck. That is an authority, which will have weight with you. If you are hurt, I am sure I am so. Think of the situation I was in, and where I may be! What has lately passed has already confounded things in Holland, and may possibly do the same in England; where every thing, before, was quiet and approved.

"I must say one word. His Royal Highness's letter is a full answer to all charges of inconsistency and want of concert. For God's sake, let us look forward, and endeavour, if possible, to redress our past mistakes on all sides. I am," &c.

"P. S. His Royal Highness has seen and approved this letter, and that to you and Sir Thomas Robinson. He went from hence last night, and, I hope, will contrive to see Bentinck soon."

In the midst of these proceedings, Sir Thomas Robinson reached his destination at Aix. In obedience to the orders he had received, he opened a friendly communication with count Kaunitz, and laboured to soothe the irritation of lord Sandwich, that he might act in the same spirit of conciliation. In a letter to the duke of Newcastle, he thus describes the state of affairs at the Congress.

"MY LORD, "Aix, August 20th, 1748.

"I was honoured this morning with your Grace's most private letter of the 7th-18th instant, and have only time, such are the extremities lord Sandwich runs into, to write these few lines, without letting him perceive, that I am writing what he will not see. Finding things here in the confusion your

Grace imagines, I gained a good deal, in bringing about our talking to
Kaunitz, as we did on Sunday.   What has been done to day, your Grace will
see, by our joint letter. I must have acted alone, if I had managed otherwise
than I have done.   For, I must, in the utmost confidence, acquaint your
Grace, that his lordship let drop, more than once, that he might be reduced
to follow M. Bentinck's example, that is to say, refuse to go on.

"Bentinck has sent a copy, to his lordship, of his letter to your Grace,
from the Hague.   God knows whether Bentinck will come back ! If that
happens, what shall we do with these Dutchmen here ?   What I cannot but
guess from the whole, is, *that Bentinck, at least, is too far engaged with St.
Severin ; whose game it certainly is, to divide us and the court of Vienna, and
to divide that court and the court of Turin.*

" I humbly hope, that the full and candid communication made to Kaunitz,
this morning, will have a good, and, as far as I can see, can have no bad effect,
at Vienna, whatever it may have with M. Bentinck and M. St. Severin. We
shall not have an answer from Vienna, before twelve or fifteen days.   In the
mean while, we will go on, if my opinion is founded, in communicating
to him our proceedings, even though he refuses to concert them with us.   I
will be preparing a full letter, in secret, against the next courier. I lay
myself at the king's feet, for his Majesty's most gracious opinion ; but I
heartily thank your Grace, for rather wishing only, than expecting, that it
may be in my little power to set every thing right. Lord Sandwich is strong
and obstinate in his opinions; but, I see, it hurts him to think he is ill in your
Grace's.   He has only shewn me the public dispatch, and the inclosed from
the duke of Bedford, but not that from his Royal Highness. I must gain
his confidence ; or, between us, we shall spoil all. I have a delicate commission. I will do for the best; that is, do my duty, which will be ever
agreeable to that most profound respect, with which I have the honour
to be," &c.

From the public dispatch of both plenipotentiaries, it appears, that their
first joint step, as mentioned in this letter, was an earnest appeal to obtain
the cooperation of count Kaunitz.   On the two great points at issue, however,
they found him still inflexible.   He pertinaciously adhered to his original
proposal of separate treaties, while he maintained his former intractability
on the subject of the barrier, and strongly contended for the sovereign rights
and privileges of his imperial mistress.   On no point could they prevail on

him to make the smallest concession, without an appeal to his court. A courier was therefore dispatched to Vienna, with a new communication, which was rendered more necessary, because Kaunitz, in his project of a definitive treaty, had omitted all mention of the guaranty of Silesia to the king of Prussia, and of the cessions in Italy to the king of Sardinia.

Even at this period of the negotiation, the duke of Newcastle did not relinquish his hopes of obtaining the concurrence of Austria; and used every exertion in his power for that purpose. He exhorted the court of Vienna, in terms of friendship and confidence, to agree to the conditions proposed; but he threatened, that, if they should refuse their consent, the king would be reduced to the necessity of signing without them. As his object could not, however, be effected, so long as count Bentinck continued absent from the Congress, he endeavoured to regain his good will. This resolution he communicated, in an interesting letter to Mr. Pelham, in which he gave a long and able detail, in justification of his own conduct, and explained the motives which induced him to press so earnestly for the accession of the empress queen.

"Dear Brother, "Hanover, August 14th-25th, 1748.

"My public letters, with their inclosures, will inform you of the present state of the negotiation at Aix. The contrary winds have prevented my hearing any thing from you, since my last letter; so, you may imagine, I must be very impatient to know your opinion, upon the late most extraordinary behaviour of my lord Sandwich and Mr. Bentinck. I hope you will not, I think you cannot blame what I have done. The Duke, who wishes peace as much as you do, is strongly of my opinion; and indeed was I of opinion, that we could, nay, that we should conclude a definitive treaty, without the queen of Hungary or Flanders, I would have been more for this communication to Kaunitz than I am now; for nothing could justify such a separate conclusion, but the having tried all previous means to avoid it.

"But I beg you would consider, what shall we get without Flanders. Be assured, the queen of Hungary, in that case, would not come in, till next spring. She would have the whole winter to negotiate. She would think to gain some point for herself. She would try France, and tempt France; and nobody can tell, what that might produce. I am persuaded, that the effect of such a measure would be, either the total destruction of the House of Austria, which is the worst of all; or the queen of Hungary's gaining, during the winter, some more advantageous conditions for herself, either against the king of Sardinia, or with regard to the Barrier Treaty ; for we should all be so weary of *that* war, and so desirous of getting Flanders, that, I am afraid, either of the two points above mentioned, would not stand in the way of it. And, in the mean time, the alliance with the House of Austria is destroyed, and we obliged to keep up all our expenses, to secure, at last, the restitution of Flanders, and what is worse, to force the queen of Hungary into the definitive treaty. A demand of parliament, for that purpose, would be a bad end of the war.

"Lord Sandwich is clear that St. Severin does not think of the restitution of Cape Breton, of sending orders for it, or giving hostages, until the restitutions in Italy or Flanders are made ; which, in other words is, until the queen of Hungary has acceded. I own, I cannot conceive that France will make the restitution of Cape Breton, and of the conquests, if any, in the East Indies, depend upon the accession of the queen of Hungary, to the definitive treaty. Sure I am, that, until now, that never was the intention ; and my lord Sandwich has not appeared to be so correct in his remarks, as to make me sure that it would be the intention, upon concluding the definitive treaty. But, if that should be so, it only comes to this point. Would such a definitive treaty be any thing more than the renewal of the preliminaries ; or what advantage, in point of security and reduction of expense, would be got by it, this winter, with a sure foundation laid, of a breach with the House of Austria ? But I still insist, that even in that case, the method I have taken is the only right one. Every thing is now in confusion. Reduce the several projects into one draught of a definitive treaty ; see what each party will accept, or object to, and then finally determine ; and, in the mean time, act an honest, open, confidential part, with your allies : shew them all you have done, (and there is nothing they may not see,) shew, you desire to have them, are unwilling to act, much less to conclude, without them ; and then leave them without excuse, if they do not finally concur with you.

"This is so evident, that I am amazed how any two men, who mean the same thing, can be of different opinions. But the case is plainly this. My lord Sandwich's vanity, and desire of concluding the material part of the negotiation before Sir T. Robinson came, hurried him on, in this strange undigested way, with St. Severin ; and then he blew up Bentinck, to think their honours were concerned not to depart from that method. If it is a point of honour, which is to carry it : the honour of the king, or the honour of his plenipotentiary ? Or, which of the two is to recede ? If they are engaged to St. Severin, to communicate nothing to the king's ally, why are they ? Who gave them authority to make such an engagement ? As long as I have the honour to serve the king, in this station, the foreign ministers in the several courts shall obey the orders I send them, in my own department, if these orders are legal, and thought, by the king, to be expedient.

" Thus much of this letter, you may, if you think proper, read to the duke of Bedford ; but the rest is for yourself and my lord Chancellor, to whom I beg you would send it, for I have not time to write to him.

" I now send you two private letters from Sir T. Robinson, and one from my lord Sandwich, the last of which, you will see, the duke of Bedford must not be acquainted with. I also inclose to you my answers to the former. I have wrote nothing in answer to the latter, being in constant expectation of another courier from Aix, with an account of what shall have passed with St. Severin. I also inclose to you, copies of my private letters to the Duke, and to the two Bentincks. You see we do all we can, to get Bentinck back. Lord Sandwich is thoroughly hurt, though I do not apprehend, as the king does, that there is any danger of his quitting. He will talk to Robinson, stronger than he will *act*, or write to me. I have no objection to the shewing every thing to the duke of Bedford, if you think proper, except my lord Sandwich's letter, which immediately concerns his Grace.

" I come now to give you an account of the particular occurrences here. The Duke left us on Thursday night, in the best disposition imaginable, though very uneasy, at the public appearance of things. He seems to despair of being able to conclude, before the winter, from the absolute refusal, on the part of France, to give the provisional possession of Flanders ; and from the danger and little utility of concluding definitively without Flanders, in some shape or other, which, his Royal Highness thinks, no English minister will advise. I am sure you will be glad to hear, that, during his stay, his Royal Highness has been treated by the king, with the utmost marks of affection, attention, and esteem ; and he let drop that he had some notion he might make us another visit here, before our return to England.

" To-morrow fortnight is the day appointed for the Göhrde.* The stay there is supposed to be a month. How long the stay here, afterwards, will be, I cannot pretend to say ; but it is whispered that the birth-day is to be

A hunting seat in the electorate of Hanover, belonging to the king.

kept here. As to that, I am all submission. I work like a horse : I have scarce a quarter of an hour in the whole week to myself. I will go through it as well as I can, with cheerfulness; and I hope, with the approbation of my friends. I will act honestly, and take care not to expose myself, and that is all I can answer for. The king continues extremely good to me. I have scarce ever once made him wait, and do not trouble him with long audiences.

" The best news I can send you is, that the king enjoys, God be praised, the most perfect health; is in extreme good spirits; and I really think, disturbed at nothing, but the awkward appearance of things at Aix ; and God knows, that is bad enough ; and I really think we may, in great measure, thank our ministers for it. I hope you will own, that I have acted with moderation. Put yourself in my situation, and you must think I have been greatly provoked. Would my lord Townshend have been as moderate as I have been, in these circumstances ? He would have complained of Bentinck to the Prince of Orange, demanded his recal, and have immediately recalled my lord Sandwich ; but I have acted otherwise. There was a design to bully me ; but that design has not taken place. I am," &c.

The following note to count Bentinck, of which the Duke sent a copy, in the preceding letter, displays his anxiety for the return of the Dutch plenipotentiary.

"DEAR SIR,   " *Hanover, August* 14*th*-25*th,* 1748.

" Since writing my other letter, I have received, from Aix-la-Chapelle, an account of the farther proceedings of our ministers, which I have sent in my letter to the Greffier, as well as a copy of the orders, with which Mr. Keith set out, last night, for Vienna. I am grieved to my heart to think, that you and I should differ in opinion, who have hitherto agreed in almost every step that has been taken. For God's sake, let us come together again as soon as possible. I do not apprehend, that any inconvenience can arise, from the communication made to count Kaunitz. He will see, that even St. Severin has been more reasonable, in the points that related to the empress queen, than in those which immediately concerned us; and he will also see, how very careful the king has been of his mistress's interest. This communication, and the measures to be taken upon it, will leave the queen of Hungary without excuse, if she finally refuses to concur in the definitive treaty ; and, without this communication, I think, we could not have been justified in proceeding farther. But it is the court of France, that has made that very hazardous, if not impracticable. How can we conclude a definitive treaty of peace, and leave France in the possession of the Low Countries? That is the point with the king, the Duke, and myself. However I may have flattered myself formerly, with a belief, that I might have prevailed upon you to take a step which appeared to me so necessary, for the good and salvation of the whole, as your return immediately to Aix-la-Chapelle, I can now depend only upon the king's and Duke's weight with you, to induce you to do it. His Royal Highness will desire an interview with you; and, I hope, send for lord Sandwich to meet you; and I doubt not, but you will together, set every thing right. Do not, for one single difference of opinion, in which, at least, I have great authorities on my side, at once decline cooperating in that great work, in which you and I have of late been jointly engaged.

" Nobody has more deference for his Royal Highness than yourself; and, I am sure, you cannot oblige him more than by returning to Aix, and going on with your old faithful friends and servants. I dare say, you will like Sir Thomas Robinson. His principles are the same with ours, and his temper and manner will make him very agreeable to you. Give me leave only to add, what triumph will it be to some we know, if you should decline returning to the Congress, on account of orders sent to the king's plenipotentiaries. But I must beg, that you would take no resolution, till you have seen the Duke. I am and shall ever be," &c.

The remonstrances of the duke of Newcastle, aided by the representations of the duke of Cumberland,* induced count Bentinck to change his sentiments, and to admit, that a longer secession from the Congress would create a breach between the two Maritime Powers, and retard the conclusion of peace. He even candidly confessed his error; and acknowledged, that since France had refused the provisional surrender of the Netherlands, a concert with Austria was become absolutely necessary, as the only expedient to avoid the heavy expenses of an armed inactivity. He expressed the fullest approbation of the counter-orders sent to lord Sandwich, as well as of the concurrent instructions to Mr. Keith, who had succeeded Sir Thomas Robinson at

* Letter from the duke of Cumberland, dated Eyndhoven, August 21st-September 1st, 1748. Newcastle Papers, MS.

Vienna, and was gratified with the decisive resolution of the king, not to make peace with France, unless it was expressly stipulated, that the Netherlands should be restored to the House of Austria. The return of the Count accordingly produced the most favourable effect; and the proceedings of the Congress were resumed.

During this intricate negotiation, it is not surprising that the two brothers should differ essentially, in their views of the questions at issue. The duke of Newcastle, deeply impressed with the danger, that would arise from the retention of the Netherlands by France, was anxious to conciliate the court of Vienna; while Mr. Pelham, from a feeling of despondency, in regard to the financial embarrassments of England, combined with his unceasing anxiety for a reduction of the public burthens, was convinced of the pressing necessity for an immediate conclusion of peace. Instead, therefore, of disapproving the conduct of lord Sandwich and count Bentinck, Mr. Pelham was inclined to regret every obstruction to the arrangement of a definitive treaty; and disposed, by a demonstration of firmness, to extort, rather than propitiate the acquiescence of the Austrian court, whose conduct he attributed to pride and selfishness. He, therefore, importuned his brother, to persist in the resolution of concluding, without the court of Vienna, if they refused or delayed their concurrence. His arguments on this subject are repeated and inforced, in several successive letters, which were written to his brother, after he had been informed of the new instructions sent to lord Sandwich.

"August 4th-15th, 1748.

  *   *   *   *   *

* " We had a long evening at the lord Chancellor's, yesterday. We read both St. Severin's and lord Sandwich's draughts of a definitive treaty. Could I flatter myself the queen of Hungary would come in, after the great pains which are now taking to convince her, that we will not, and cannot act without her, I should be exceedingly easy. But the infatuation of that court is so great, that I have been, you know, always of opinion, and am so still, that nothing will bring them to their senses but a conviction, that we will act without them, if they do not concur in our most reasonable propositions. I doubt, too, that France, when she sees that we are so tied

---

  * See the first part of this letter in chap. xvi. v. 1. p. 447.

down, to whatever the Austrians shall demand of us, will recoil, and turn their politics another way. I may, possibly, be quite mistaken in this reasoning ; but in another I am sure I am not, which is, that we cannot carry on the war another year ; and that, if this treaty goes off, France is not only master of the Low Countries and Holland, but will, in a short time, do what she will with the rest of Europe. Can the queen of Hungary see this, and still persist in her obstinacy ; and can she think, and hear, and not see it ? I own, Brother, I am most terribly afraid, that our too great scrupulosity will lead her and ourselves into this fatal dilemma.

" I would fain have her think, we are determined to finish without her, if she will not comply ; and, to carry her farther into that belief, I could have wished some friendly negotiation had been encouraged at Berlin : not that I would have advised you to enter into any offensive engagements with that Court ; but to have given some credit to the supposed scheme of looking out another way, in order to have driven her into the only measures that can prevent it. I have also one selfish consideration in this whole affair, but I hope not a dishonourable, or a dishonest one.

" You know, I have had very little comfort in the great scene of business, I have long been engaged in. I have no court ambition, and very little interested views ; but I was in hopes, by a peace being soon made, and by a proper economy in the administration of the government, afterwards, to have been the author of such a plan, as might, in time to come, have relieved this nation from the vast load of debt. it now labours under ; and, even in my own time, had the satisfaction of demonstrating to the knowing part of the world, that the thing was not impossible. Here, I own, lay my ambition ; but very little more delay will render it impracticable. For me, I am sure it will ; and I am apt to fear, no one else will be better able to bring it about.

" You now see what it is that affects my spirits, on all these occasions. I doubt you do not sufficiently think of the consequences, in case we should not finish soon. The transactions of this summer will then, instead of being approved by all sensible men, be animadverted upon, by all wicked ones. They will then see our inferior land-force, grown still more so ; France, by our cessation of arms at sea, recovering her trade, restoring her marine ; and the riches of Spain brought home to their own ports unmolested. Forgive me for saying so much upon this subject. It is not to find fault with what you have hitherto done ; for, till within this post or two, I have differed in nothing, excepting your cold reception of the Prussian offer. But now I fear, you are going a little back again. I hope I am mistaken; for, believe me, I can never suffer more, than when I am obliged to differ in essentials with you; which, excepting in peace or war, I have no apprehension can ever materially happen.

"The duke of Bedford has written at large to you, upon this subject. The Chancellor was as forward in this way of thinking as any of us; and, therefore, wished, all our endeavours should be used, either to drive the queen of Hungary into our definitive treaty, since we cannot lead her, or else use all our art and industry with France, to persuade them to accept the act of mutual cession and restitution, from the court of Vienna; and we ourselves enter into a definitive treaty with France and her allies, without her, as proposed in the duke of Bedford's former letter.

Reply of Mr. Pelham to the Duke of Newcastle's letter,
dated August 3rd-14th.

"DEAR BROTHER,   "*August 11th-22nd*, 1748.

" On Tuesday night, I had a long conference with the Chancellor alone, and yesterday with his lordship and the duke of Bedford, from half an hour past seven, till a quarter past one. We read over all your letters and papers; and, at the end, put down in writing, heads for the duke of Bedford to turn into a letter for you, which will go by the messenger to-morrow. I think our opinions are sufficiently seen, as far as we are capable of giving any. But as I desired the Chancellor to read your letters carefully, having taken care that he should have them, one whole day, in his custody, I doubt not but he will very amply supply what is deficient in mine. When I was at Powis-house he seemed entirely of my opinion; exceedingly anxious that this treaty should not go off; and somewhat apprehensive that it would, from the different ways of thinking and acting, between lord Sandwich and Mr. Bentinck at Aix, and yourself and greater men at Hanover.

" The particulars of the projects are sufficiently animadverted upon, in the duke of Bedford's several letters. All I shall say is, that I am far from thinking our ministers have shewn themselves able, in their *precis.* Their object I like, because it tends to finishing their work soon; but the expedient for passing the second article, in St. Severin's project, is really ignorant. It answers no objection at all; leaves the force, as well as the indecency, of that article subsisting; and, indeed, I think that it is such an article,* that if the French insist upon its standing, they cannot mean peace. I doubt not, therefore, if the rest of the treaty is properly adjusted, that article, as far as it relates to his Majesty's rebellious subjects, will be waived.

" As to Kaunitz's project, it is, to my understanding, very complaisant to our enemies. It grants every thing to France and her allies, that can be desired. Why then does she refuse to come into a general treaty? Plainly, because she will not give the same security to our ally, the king of Sardinia, and the king of Prussia, as she is willing to do to France and Spain. Is this acting upon the old system, or is it decent with regard to the king, and this country? It is this behaviour of the court of Vienna that provokes me. How is it possible to think they are ignorant of the orders sent to prince Repnin,† by the Czarina? Is not the court of Petersburg absolutely theirs at present? Have they not the same aversions, and the same partialities? Do they not both make a property of us, without returning the least civility or complaisance to our opinions? I have so often written upon this subject, that it must appear to you troublesome. I shall, therefore, sum up the whole with this melancholy reflection :—

" If France does not mean to finish, she will find out a thousand cavils to break upon. They have us in their power: we may upbraid, but cannot compel. But, if she does not mean to deceive us, by keeping up a proper confidence with their ministers, I should hope we might come to a conclusion soon, as it is her interest, as well as our own. But, if the queen of Hungary should mean foul play, she has no right to cavil; and, if gratitude has no influence on great powers, she must see, linked as we are together, her Imperial Majesty is full as much in our power, as we are in hers. Strong words and resolution, therefore, may have some influence with that court; whereas, too great an attention to their pride and passions, has, by fatal experience, almost ruined us, as well as themselves.

" I own, Brother, it has given me great concern, to see you run so fast into declaring, that we will do nothing without the court of Vienna, let them be never so obstinate. How will your friend, Bentinck, like your sending

---

* This article related to the demand of France for the pardon and restoration of persons engaged in the late Rebellion.

† Commander-in-chief of the Russian forces.

all the papers to the Greffier, to be laid before the prince of Orange, before you know, what he has thought proper to say, or do, himself? I am apprehensive you will think I am grown fond of this gentleman, as well as of lord Sandwich, just when you seem to be less pleased with them. I am not a quick changer, and dislike those that are, as much as you do ; and, therefore, am not in love with these two great men ; although I am free to own, that I like them much better, when they pursue ends, which I think necessary and practicable, than when I see them blinding the eyes of my best friends, giving them expectations of events, which, either they have never tried to be rightly informed of, or else must have seen not one of those things could or would happen, which they promised.

" You say my letter of the 26th, was a scolding one : upon my honour, I did not write with that temper of mind. Perhaps you may not like the subject of this letter neither ; but, if ever I wrote from cool reflection, not of days and weeks, but years, I have written, and do write so to you now, and ever since you went abroad. I feel the weight that lies upon you ; I am sensible of your honest intentions ; but I do not think that the reflection, which you often resort to, will be sufficient to carry you through, which is, ' You know you act honestly ; you do for the best.' If the obstinacy of one court, the falsehood of another, the coldness of a third, or any other unforeseen reason, should break off this affair, you will undoubtedly be called upon ; and then you will see, though perhaps too late, who are, and have been your true friends.

" I would not have you rest upon the fidelity alone of any of your foreign fellow labourers. Perhaps I could go farther; but that I leave for future conversations. It is success must do your business : this country has too long been taught, that both ability and integrity depend on success. It is that opinion has reduced the characters of those who attempted to rise upon the fall of their inactive predecessors ; and it is from that experience, I heartily wish you were extricated out of impracticable pursuits, though in the theory never so wise and honest.

" I have said all I can, upon the great political question. Details require more experience than I have, and more time than I am at present master of. After the regency, I set out for Halland.* To-morrow and Saturday are the Lewes races. I did suppose, you would think it right I should be there,

---

* The family seat in Sussex.

though I go with a heavy heart, and that assembly is not, as you know, likely to raise my spirits.

" When I have the honour to see his Royal Highness here, I shall, with submission, open my mind freely to him. I do not think we shall differ in opinion materially, as to the manner of reduction. I have so bad an opinion of the strength and abilities of those powers abroad, who call themselves our friends, and I know the sentiments of those who must direct our foreign affairs too well, to think we shall long keep well with France ; and therefore, we must have an army within call, at least, to protect us from any sudden attempt of our enemies. Let us have it upon as cheap a foot as we can, for the necessary expences must be very great."

      *   *   *   *

" DEAR BROTHER,   " *August* 19*th*-30*t h*, 1748

" I told you in my letter of Tuesday last, that I would write a long private letter to Stone, by this messenger ; but, as I am at present a little out of order, and have tired myself with writing letters of compliment to M. Munchausen, the University of Gottingen, and my good friend the Baron, I am afraid, I shall not be able to go so far, as I once designed. I have seen your *friend*, and talked over there, the apprehensions I have upon the present state of our foreign negotiations. I knew you had no secret in that quarter ; and, as I wanted to unburthen myself, I chose rather to trust my secret with a friend of your own, than mine. I shall not lay any claim to others' opinions ; but this I must always call upon the party for, to testify to you, when we meet, that I have no partialities nor prejudices, but for your sake. I may err, but I am sincere. I therefore heartily wish, you had kept count Bentinck's paper to yourself. It is written with spirit; and, though I agree in the doctrine, with an acrimony I did not expect, from that quarter. If it had gone no farther than amongst yourselves, I should have hoped accidents and the public interest might have set things right again ; but now that it is in the duke of Bedford's office, we do not know who sees it, or what will be said of it. His *commis* are new ; and his clerks have all of them served many masters, some of whom they are very partial to, and I believe with reason.

" I hear, Charles Bentinck is gone to Hanover ; probably, upon his brother's coming to the Hague, it was thought advisable to send him. I long to hear from you, how things were upon his arrival; for, let me like or dislike the people, I know the consequence of any misunderstanding between you and them, at this time; though, to speak the truth to you, which I shall always do, I never had an ill opinion of the Bentincks; but I did not conceive the elder to have had either the parts or passions, which he shews on this occasion. I remember the short turn he took with lord Chesterfield, and though *you* thought him then in the right, *lord Chesterfield* did not. Possibly, he may think himself in the right now; and if he does, he appears to me a gentleman, who, in these circumstances, will stick at nothing. I am still in hopes, this paper will not be of that moment, which in some circumstances it may; for, by letters which came from Aix-la-Chapelle, since St. Severin's return, and which arrived here last Wednesday, I find our Plenipoes in good hopes, all will end well. But that appears to be by a separate signature. They send over a copy of a treaty, prepared by themselves and Chavannes; they make no mention of Kaunitz, which, I suppose, is owing to the absolute refusal he gave them, to join in drawing any definitive treaty. Are they mad at Vienna? Or have they any subterfuge which we cannot find out, and no one, abroad, has ever suspected?

" You see, my thoughts are bent on nothing but finishing. Every thing that tends to that, gives me pleasure; and every thing that delays it, gives me pain. I will venture to foretell this. We shall have a peace, but not so good a one, as we might have had, the week after the preliminaries were signed. The allies will all accede; and take up with less than they might have had at first. We shall be a million more in debt; and this country will, in all probability, not only owe that debt to the weakness and want of good faith, in a certain power, but, by their obstinacy, be rendered incapable of extricating itself out of every part of that debt, for some years to come.

" I will not dwell upon that disagreeable subject, but desire you not to laugh at my Latin letter to the University of Gottingen. I thought, as I received a very high one from them, it was incumbent upon me to make a return. I got Roberts, therefore, to muster up his academical talents; and I think, upon the whole, we have said enough, and not so much as to make it ridiculous. My letter to the Baron,* was in my own strain; and that to Munchausen, I got Roberts to put into French.

* Baron Steinberg.

" I shall be glad to hear, the duchess of Newcastle goes abroad into company; they say here, she is a great deal better. Lady Frances goes to Allerton next week ; I do not, therefore, expect the old gentleman until the meeting of parliament. By-the-bye, if your expenses continue, we shall want a money-bill before Christmas. The extraordinaries of this *no campaign* are prodigious.

" My compliments as due, and believe me, dear brother, ever most affectionately, yours."

It appears, also, that the lord Chancellor fully coincided in opinion with Mr. Pelham; for, in a letter to Mr. Walpole, dated August 11th,* his lordship observes : " Difficulties, as usual, have arisen with the court of Vienna; but they must soon either be untied, or cut through ;" and we also find, that in his correspondence with the duke of Newcastle, he had frankly conveyed his sentiments on this subject. In a letter to Mr. Pelham, dated August 22nd-September 2nd, he details the arguments which he had previously used to the Duke, and expresses his full conviction, of the necessity of concluding a separate treaty with France, if the empress queen should still continue intractable.

" DEAR SIR,   " *Wimpole, August 22nd-September 2nd,* 1748.

" I return you my sincere thanks for your kind letter, and for the communication of the several letters and extracts, which are herewith returned. I am extremely sorry that you have been indisposed of late ; but hope that it was but slight, and is now entirely removed, by the precautions you have taken. Mr. Roberts was so good, as to acquaint me with what you had instructed him, particularly as to the time when the Duke is expected, which agrees with the account I have from my son. I have wrote to the secretaries to the lords justices, to let me know, by a messenger, the moment his Royal Highness arrives, and I will come away immediately.

" I see, with the utmost concern, the *embarras* under which things are at present ; and think you observe very justly on the authorities, whereby the duke of Newcastle, all along, supports his opinion. You know what I always thought, the effects the journey to Hanover would probably produce. We must now look forward ; and, as the communication has been made to count

Kaunitz, (which Monsieur St. Severin has not attempted to resent in the manner expected,) I really think we must try to close that scene there; and, if the answer which is to come soon from Vienna, is either negative, or plainly dilatory and amusing, endeavour to conclude, in some reasonable way, upon the foot of the new project, last sent out by my lord Sandwich, which the duke of Bedford sent to me from Woburn on Friday evening, and which I returned to him next morning, with some few remarks, chiefly on the penning.

"I observe, the duke of Newcastle's letters were writ before he had received that project, which, I should hope, with paring off some things, which we cannot flatter ourselves to carry, might in general do. As to Bentinck, I should hope that the Duke, by a personal conference, might be able to bring him back.

"In my last letter to the duke of Newcastle, I writ as fully, and as strongly, upon the principles we agreed in, as possibly I could. The letters by that messenger he had not received, when his Grace wrote last. I laid down two principles as essential : 1st. To prevent the court of Vienna from being master of the negotiation, and to preserve *that* (so far as the allies can have the direction) in the hands of England and Holland : 2nd. Not to insist upon, or start points, not essential, which cannot be carried. I then endeavoured to shew, that it is impossible to resume the war ; and, if that is made necessary, we are undone. That so long as the court of Vienna adhere to their two previous objections, of not concluding in one treaty, and not yielding to accept the possession of the Austrian Netherlands, on the foot of the barrier, it is vain to have any farther communication with them. I then went through the several methods of concluding, without the court of Vienna, and added this paragraph—'If this will not do, all that remains is, to proceed on the plan, concerted between my lord Sandwich, Mr. Bentinck, and Monsieur St. Severin ; and to assign the empress queen a term to accede. If this is done, no cession, and consequently no resti-tution will be made, except, possibly, as to the king of Sardinia ; and we shall remain in possession of Cape Breton. It is true, this is not in sub-stance much more than the preliminaries ; but, however, the entire general plan will be ascertained and settled ; and it will be getting one step farther before the winter ; and, in my opinion, the court of Vienna will take the other step. If the preliminaries had been delayed to be settled with the ministers of that court, they would not have been signed at this day ; and yet they afterwards acceded, in a very little time. So, in my apprehension, they will do, if England, France, and Holland sign a definitive treaty, inviting them, at the same time, to come in. They will not carry the weight of finally standing out, when their hopes of making a better market are over.'

"At the time I writ this, I saw the objection, which my lord Duke mentions in his letter, that a definitive treaty, so made, would not immediately enable us to reduce our expenses, in the manner we wish. But, if some part of it could be reduced, it would point out the period of reducing the rest; and it would throw the blame on the court of Vienna, for not completing the work to which they themselves had agreed, by acceding to the preliminaries, when, by so doing, they might have back their dominions.

"I observe, by Sir Thomas Robinson's letter, that they expected an answer from Vienna, either this day, or on Wednesday. May not the time of the Duke's beginning his journey hither, be calculated with some view to that?

"The Archbishop, who has been here since Saturday noon, desires me to make you his best compliments. His Grace proposes to be at Kensington, the latter end of this week.

"I agree with you, that our situation requires all the ability, consideration, and temper possible. I am sensible of my own incapacity for affairs of this nature, but shall never fail in good will, fidelity, and attachment; being ever," &c.

The duke of Newcastle was extremely chagrined, to find that the sentiments of the Chancellor and Mr. Pelham differed so much from his own. He did not affect to conceal his concern; but in several letters justifies the measures which he had recently adopted, to conciliate the House of Austria, and strongly represented the danger of signing without that power, as long as France retained possession of the Netherlands.

We have already observed, that the duke of Newcastle had transmitted to the lords justices two questions,* relative to the conduct to be observed towards the court of Vienna, should France agree to the provisional surrender of the Netherlands to the Maritime Powers; but, on the positive refusal of France to accede to that measure, he deemed it necessary to lay

---

* These two questions were submitted to the lords justices, in a letter from the duke of Newcastle to the duke of Bedford, dated August 7th–18th. This letter is missing; but, in a letter dated Aug. 28th–Sept. 8th, these questions are repeated. Grantham Papers, MS.

before them, two other questions for their consideration, and to request advice in this critical emergency.

"1st. Whether it be advisable for his Majesty to direct his plenipotentiaries at Aix, to sign the definitive treaty, or, indeed, any definitive treaty, which should leave France in possession of all the Austrian Low Countries?

"And 2ndly. If it should be their opinion, that such a separate definitive treaty should be made, whether they would think it advisable, that his Majesty should depend so much upon the faith of it, as to send back his German forces; discharge the Hessians in his Majesty's pay; and recall the British troops then in Flanders?"

He farther wished that their lordships would consider, whether the cession of Cape Breton, the sending hostages for its immediate restitution, or the concession respecting the Asiento, should in any event take place, except upon the immediate restitution of all the Low Countries.

The lords justices suspended their reply, until the majority of them could attend; and Mr. Pelham, in a letter dated September 5th-16th, to his brother, justifies this delay, observing, that his questions were of that momentous nature, that they could not venture to answer them, without consulting all the lords justices that were in or near town; "for, although," he adds, "I am not at all shy of speaking my mind, yet I do not think it is very decent, for some few of us to give an opinion, upon a national question, when we are all equally intrusted by his Majesty here. Private advice, such as a minister gives to the king, in his closet, is of one nature; but a formal opinion, in writing, possibly to be transmitted to the plenipotentiaries at the Congress, is of a very different one." The lord Chancellor, also, in the same tone, vindicated the silence of the lords justices, and observed, "that they must defer their answer, until farther accounts were received from Vienna."

The duke of Newcastle was much disappointed at this delay; but was enabled, by a favourable change of circumstances, to continue the negotiation, without waiting for the opinion of the lords justices, which they seemed so unwilling to give, and which, indeed, was rendered unnecessary by subsequent events. We shall find him, also, gradually adopting the pacific sentiments of his brother, and ultimately concluding the definitive treaty, with the full approbation of his colleagues.

CHAPTER XIX.

1748.

*Illness and Recovery of Mr. Pelham—Affectionate anxiety of the Duke of Newcastle—
Firmness of Mr. Pelham, in pressing the reduction of the Army, and the dimi-
nution of the Public Expenditure—Continuation of the Negotiations at Aix, and
difficulty of accommodating the pretensions of the different Powers—Opposition on
the part of Austria and Sardinia, in particular, to the proposed terms of Peace—
Efforts of the Duke of Newcastle to obtain the concurrence of Austria—Project of
Du Theil, the French Minister, sent to act in conjunction with St. Severin—
Private understanding between Austria and France—The Austrian and Dutch
Forces withdrawn from the Netherlands.*

AT this period, Mr. Pelham was attacked by an inflammatory disorder,
to which he was constitutionally subject, and which was aggravated by
anxiety of mind, and the pressure of public business. He gives a minute
account of his illness, in a letter to his brother.

" DEAR BROTHER,   " *Greenwich, Aug. 26th-Sept. 6th,* 1748.

" I write to you by this mail, more to satisfy you that my disorder has
been of no ill consequence, than for any other purpose. It would be too
much for me, to enter into the particulars of your letter of the 19th; I give
it no epithet, though I think it entitled to many. The duke of Bedford
was at my bed-side, when it came, which I am sorry for, as I could not
avoid reading some parts of the contents to him, though I concealed the
greatest.

" I have been ill, about a week, and, the greatest part of that time, in bed
eighteen hours out of the twenty-four, which has reduced me low in flesh
and spirits. But this day, notwithstanding I have taken a dose of physic,
I find myself much better; so that I am satisfied, the disease has had its
force; and that I shall be able to attend my duty in London, the middle

of next week. As I know, when you have leisure, you love to hear the
particulars of any illness, which your friends have been troubled with, I will
give you a short account of mine; otherwise I do not love talking of myself,
even to you. When I came out of Sussex, I found I had got a great cold,
but was in hopes it would have gone off, with sack-whey, &c. But, when
I came here, I found strong muscular pains, almost all over me, which I
conceived to be rheumatic, till, on Monday night, I was taken with a violent
shivering, and that got over, I went into a warm bed, and the morning, or
rather noon, we perceived an eruption gathering almost in all the places
where the pain was. I sent to Wilmot, who immediately determined (as
indeed Dr. Harrington had said before) that it was what the learned call
the *herpes*, and the old women, the *shingles*. I have been kept very low.
It was, and is exceedingly painful; but I am certain, all is over, nor was
there ever any the least danger, after the eruption appeared. I believe I
was the worse, apprehending the Duke would come whilst I was confined;
but by a letter he wrote to the duke of Bedford, I find he has put off his
journey *sine die*, that is, till he has seen Mr. Bentinck in his way to
Aix. I believe this is the most agreeable letter you have had from me a
great while; but I solemnly declare, not wrote by me, with half the affection
and concern that those have been, which seem to have given you offence.
I will rest till I hear from you again, before I say any more upon that
subject."

Although the indisposition of Mr. Pelham was not made known to the
duke of Newcastle, until the danger had subsided, it deeply affected his
sensitive mind; and, in a very affectionate reply, he reproached himself for
having aggravated the disorder, by the warmth with which he had supported
his own opinions.

"DEAR BROTHER,   "*Hanover, September* 4th-15th, 1748.

" I know you will think me sincere, when I assure you, that your illness
gives me the greatest concern, though I hope in God, by your account, as
well as by Mr. Roberts's, that the worst was then over. I happened to
receive a letter from Greening first, which alarmed me extremely. He
told me you had been very ill; and afterwards I had your letter, and Mr.
Roberts's to Stone. I should have been very uneasy indeed, if I had not
had a very particular account, and should have been extremely frightened

with the symptoms, had I seen, or heard of them, without hearing, at the same time, that the violence of them was over.

" I certainly love to hear the particulars of all cases, where my friends are concerned. But where your health is in question, nobody can be more interested, from all the causes of love, tender affection, and unfeigned regard. I doubt not, but my friend Wilmot has done as well as man can do. He is particularly good, where discipline and evacuations are wanted. That is a method I always like, and I am sure was necessary upon this occasion.

" For God's sake, my dear brother, take care of yourself; exercise and some temperance in eating, will be to be observed. Believe me, I am the more touched upon this occasion, as I am sensible the situation of affairs, and possibly the part I may have had in them, or at least some warmth I have used, in justifying them, has been in a great measure the cause of the continuance, if not of your original illness. This good effect it has had, that you shall never more have one disagreeable word from me.

" I am extremely impatient for the arrival of the messenger, which I hope in God will bring me an account of your perfect recovery, and of the pains being quite gone, and your rest and appetite returned.

" I do not flatter, when I assure you, the king was most extremely alarmed and concerned, and shewed all the tenderness imaginable. I sent the duke of Bedford's private letter, which mentioned your illness. I met the *Grosvoigt* as I went to Court, who told me, that the king was under the greatest concern and apprehension for you; that he had spoke to him upon it, and, indeed, all the Court was alarmed. When I came, the king, who is a bit of a doctor too, made me give him an account of the whole. He said, he knew the disorder, as I described it to him, that he was under great concern, till I had assured him, that you had wrote me word, that all was over.

" Finding the king in that tender, kind disposition, I took that opportunity of talking to him of the time of his return to England; stating the necessity there might be to have money bills passed before Christmas. He received it with great goodness, and much better than I could have expected. He said, the parliament might meet the end of November. I told him, that was as soon as we would propose; but that his Majesty's presence in England, would be necessary some time before, to prepare for it.

He thought not; said all his servants, except myself, were there; and that that would be sufficient. I very truly told him, 'how much his subjects interested themselves in every thing that concerned his health; that the season of the year would make them impatient for his return. He said, had he gone sooner, he would have returned, the end of October. I told him, *that was* the time that every body wished he would return; that his Majesty went, the hour the parliament rose. He slightly mentioned, that "the duke of Bedford was always in the country; my lord Chancellor, at present; your brother, indeed, I cannot say it of; and yet he might not stay where he was." I urged the season of the year; the danger of the passage, which had been severely felt by his subjects. The king seemed in very good humour, and was so yesterday; but did not say things positively.

"I should imagine, that the parliament might certainly meet, the end of November; and that the king will either come before, or immediately after his birth-day. As soon as ever I can discover any thing with certainty, you shall know it. But I must beg, it may not be known, that I have ever said any thing upon the subject, or that any thing has yet passed, or is known, relating to the time of his Majesty's return.

"I will not trouble you about our public affairs. I think they are far from desperate. If France is sincere, I verily believe, all the other difficulties will be got over; and then, I think, the present method cannot be blamed. Wassenaer has assured me this morning, that they will conclude; and I begin to think they will, in earnest. But time presses, and the delay of producing Du Theil's counter project has a bad appearance. You have now the Duke with you, who, I dare say, will have cleared up many points to your satisfaction. I think you will like all my letters to Keith.

"I am sure you will be sorry to hear, that the poor duchess of Newcastle has been very bad for this last week; and particularly yesterday morning; and was attended by Dr. Hugo and Dr. Werloff, with Dr. Shaw. She grew better in the afternoon, and in the evening seemed as well as ever she was in her life. I go, to-morrow, to the duke of Wolfenbuttel, and shall lie at Zell on Thursday night, and purpose to be at the Göhrde on Wednesday. I am afraid, I shall have but little time to hunt. You can have no notion, how constantly I am employed. I shall be very happy, if, in any shape, I shall be able to contribute to the conclusion of the peace before winter. I think we must now have Flanders; and that has been the only point I have laboured."

After stating that the duchess of Newcastle was better, he adds, " For God's sake, dear brother, make yourself as easy as you can about our foreign affairs. If they are not so well as we could wish, I hope they are better than you fear. I will do more than is possible, to conclude. My heart is set upon it, for my country's service; for my own honour; to recommend myself to the king; and believe me, I speak truth, to remove the only possible point of difference, that can ever be, between you and me. I love you; I esteem you; and I pray God grant good news of you, by the messenger I expect. I can say no more."

Before Mr. Pelham received the preceding letter from the duke of Newcastle, he wrote another to him, bearing date September 2nd-13th, in which he related his conferences with the Duke of Cumberland on the reduction of the army, and expressed his hopes that he should ultimately persuade his Royal Highness to agree to his arrangements.

After mentioning, that he was gradually recovering from his recent illness, he continues, " What gave me concern at this trifling disorder, at this time, was, the Duke of Cumberland's arrival in London, last Monday morning. I could not possibly stir out that day, nor the next; but his Royal Highness had the great condescension, to come to me at Greenwich, on Tuesday, in the afternoon, when we had a very full conversation upon that point of business, which his Royal Highness seems to have most at heart; or, at least, which he thinks material to talk to me upon.

" The next day I went to London ; and have had the honour of two conferences more with him, yesterday and this day. The Duke will write, himself, to Hanover, by the messenger that goes this evening : it is unnecessary for me, therefore, to forestall any thing you shall hear from his Royal Highness. I shall only say, that I flatter myself the Duke does not think me unreasonable in what I have offered; and I have the pleasure to see his Royal Highness disposed to make his military partialities as little burdensome to the public as is possible.

" I will not trouble you with animadversions and reasonings upon the several papers and letters, which I have received since I wrote to you last. Let lord Chancellor reply to the answer you sent him, upon his lordship's and my weak, but I still think, not improper representations. You know my thoughts as well as if I was to write them over once a day. You do not like to hear them. Why should I then trouble you with them? They have no weight, and therefore, if right, can do no good; and if erroneous, they tend only to put you out of humour, and provoke not very agreeable letters for me."

After alluding to some appointments in the Household, he recommends Dr. Blackwall, author of the "Life of Homer," and other learned works, to be Principal of Marischal College, Aberdeen. He then adds, "since writing what is above, the mail has come in. I have, as yet, only read your Private* to me; and one that Mr. Stone sends me also. As they chiefly relate to what is past, it is not material for me to say any thing upon them, only this, that I most heartily wish, the measures you have adopted may have the desired effect. Whatever turn they take, it will not be my part to find fault. If a happy one, I shall rejoice; if the contrary, I shall lament; desiring only that you will remember, I have always told you, that if the expenses of the public are to continue, in any great degree, another year, I never did, nor do now promise for success, at least not in my hands.

"You say the Duke is entirely of your mind, in every thing. I do not doubt it. You say, also, that the Bentincks have assured his Royal Highness that they are convinced, or to that effect: I am glad of it, if they are so. The Duke having said nothing to me upon the subject; I know nothing of his sentiments but from you; and as to Charles Bentinck, I never heard what his opinion was. The last letter I saw, of the elder brother's, does not look to me, as giving up his own opinion.

"I expect the duke of Bedford and lord Chancellor, every minute. I suppose they will bring with them your public dispatches. I doubt by the turn of your private letter, I have not much to flatter myself with, from your public ones. We shall, I fear, be brought to a terrible dilemma; but we have no choice. It is the work, or rather no work, of former years, that has brought us to this terrible situation. But, what is worse, if any thing can be so, than the situation itself, is to be in it, and not to know it. Dear brother, we are conquered; we have little strength of our own, and less of other people's: you act with as great spirit and resolution as any man can do; but all that will not change the nature of things."

In another letter, dated September 5th-16th, Mr. Pelham expresses his wish, that he could flatter himself so far as to think, that nothing existed to

---

* This letter is dated August 28th, September 8th. MS.

obstruct the execution of that necessary scheme of reduction, except the difference of opinion between his Royal Highness and himself.

The following is the reply of Mr. Pelham to his brother's affectionate letter, of the 4th-15th September, on occasion of his illness.

"DEAR BROTHER, "*September* 9*th*-20*th*, 1748.

" I received your kind letter of the 4th-15th this morning, and cannot avoid returning you my cordial thanks for it. I never doubted of your concern and affection for me ; and therefore took care to give you the earliest notice of my illness proving a thing of no consequence, and only a little painful and troublesome. I am, however, now, by pretty severe discipline, and great abstinence, in a manner free from any complaint.

* * * * * * *

" I have had the honour of several conferences with his Royal Highness, and I hope we have at last settled the reduction, in a manner not quite disagreeable to him. The Duke thought we should want more troops than the number I had allotted for Great Britain; which, if we have any disturbances from abroad, or formidable insurrections at home, we certainly shall ; but that we should do, even upon the numbers his Royal Highness proposed. So that, to tell you the truth, I think the Duke's great object was to keep up all the new regiments, except the Marines, and Loudon's Highlanders. We have contrived to save five, by adding them to the Irish establishment ; in which, I must do lord Harrington the justice to say, he has contributed every thing in his power, by preparing the government of Ireland to expect something of this nature. We were obliged to keep it also within the number of 12,000 men; for, both the Chancellors of England and Ireland are clear in the opinion, that the act in king William's time is obligatory to Ireland even now. I have left the number of effectives in England and Scotland 18,990 men, which is more than we have ever had in times of peace. The other particulars the Duke will acquaint you with, and with the reasons which induced me humbly to advise his Royal Highness, to be contented with this scheme.

" I shall trouble you with no more, on this head, at present. I heartily wish, we may be able to put in execution any project of reduction yet awhile; for, on perusing the letters from Vienna, and the account our plenipotentiaries give of their conference with count Kaunitz, I much doubt whether his Court intends to come into the measure, proposed by his Majesty. I cannot conceive from whence you form a doubt of the sincerity of the French plenipotentiaries. As they found a new plan of a treaty prepared by our ministers, upon St. Severin's return, it was natural for them to take some time to consider of it, and to prepare one of their own, to come to a clear understanding of what we were to do. Their proposal of evacuating the Low Countries, in a month or six weeks, according as the season will permit, seems to me a symptom of their sincerity; besides, what should they carry on this farce for, if they did not mean peace? All they want is done, unless it is to finish well.

" You see, the latter part of your instructions to Keith had its effect; and whatever good disposition they * have shewn, arises purely and simply from the strong manner in which they were told, that the king could no longer forbear concluding separately, if they did not come in thoroughly to our measures. I suspect much, that this new project, of the Russians quartering this winter in Upper Silesia, arises from M. Bartenstein; and that we shall at last be found to have paid the Court of Vienna, through Russia, a subsidy, for keeping the troops of Muscovy, where the Empress Queen desires they should be, for reasons that perhaps may give us future trouble. Otherwise, to get rid of the unreasonable demand, which that foolish treaty has left us liable to, I do not know whether the proposal may not end in economy, though made in a very indecent and unbecoming manner. As to our moiety of the 150,000 dollars, I have already ordered the remittance of that sum to Belitz; and Mr. Thornton, who is consul Woolfe's correspondent, assures me the money shall be there in a very short time. Mordaunt wrote to me for it, and count Czernichew also. I see, by the memorials of the elector Palatine, Bishop of Liege, &c. every prince in Germany, through whose country our troops have passed, in any year of this war, is preparing to bring in his bill of damages. You have ordered these papers to be referred to Hunter. I like it well, for he can allow none of them. His rule must be, Contracts and Treaties; and, as I am satisfied, there are none, that can justify these demands, his answer will be short and clear. The Duke goes to-morrow morning, or in the evening, as the wind will permit; it is at present full against him. I think I never saw his Royal Highness look better; and, if you can finish, so as to get the restitutions and cessions made soon, I believe his Royal Highness will find himself happy, even in peace.

* The Court of Vienna.

"Chavannes must lower his sails; he is not in a condition to threaten; we are his master's only support. He ought therefore to be contented with the security we can get him, especially as we profess the Treaty of Worms sacred, as to what concerns his master. I cannot finish without thanking you again, for your great kindness, expressed in your last letter; and, most heartily wishing that I may hear of the duchess of Newcastle's perfect recovery, I am," &c.

So anxious, indeed, was Mr. Pelham, for a general reduction of the national burthens, that he repeatedly urged his brother to avoid every step in the least degree likely to delay the conclusion of peace, on which, of course, his plan of reduction entirely depended. He experienced, however, great difficulty in combating the wishes of the Duke of Cumberland, who was desirous of retaining a larger number of troops, than was consistent with his views. His Royal Highness was also particularly unwilling to disband a favourite regiment of dragoons. However, by the respectful firmness, with which Mr. Pelham adhered to his resolution, he finally prevailed on his Royal Highness to consent to the intended limitation of the military establishment.*

In the mean time the negotiation proceeded; though many of the impediments, arising from the conflicting claims, which had delayed the signature of the preliminaries, still remained. But the principal obstacle to the conclusion of a definitive treaty, arose from the pertinacious conduct of the Empress Queen; for, notwithstanding a pure and simple accession to the preliminaries, count Kaunitz persisted in refusing to concur in a general arrangement, and in objecting to the barrier treaty, as well as to the establishment for Don Philip, and to the mode of confirming the guaranties demanded by the kings of Prussia and Sardinia. Finding him thus inflexible, the ministers of England, Holland, and Sardinia, formed a new project,† which they communicated to him and to St. Severin, as the latter was preparing to set out for the French Court, then at Compiègne, to obtain farther instructions.

* See Mr. Pelham's letter to the duke of Newcastle, dated October 25th–November 5th, 1748. Illust. Corresp.

† Letter from lord Sandwich and Sir Thomas Robinson to the duke of Newcastle, dated August 24th N. S. 1748. Grantham Papers, MS.

Both Kaunitz and St. Severin expressed a general approbation of this project, but declined giving an explicit answer, until they had consulted their respective sovereigns; and Kaunitz, in particular, declared that he would use his utmost endeavours, to obtain a favourable decision from his Court. The project was accordingly dispatched to Vienna; and, on the day of its arrival, Mr. Keith received from the duke of Newcastle, instructions* conformable to those, which had been forwarded to the British plenipotentiaries at Aix. By these he was commanded to represent to the Empress Queen, the necessity of an immediate peace; to insist, first, on the formation of a general treaty according to the preliminaries; secondly, on the specific confirmation of the Barrier Treaty; and lastly, to declare explicitly, that if her Imperial Majesty refused her concurrence in those two measures, the king of England must and would, though reluctantly, enter into a separate engagement with France.

The court of Vienna, however, remained obstinate, and sent orders to Kaunitz to object specifically to three points† contained in the project:

1st. To the article regarding the Barrier Treaty.

2ndly. To that, by which the king of Sardinia peremptorily demanded farther securities from Austria, for the possessions which had been ceded to him by that power, and for which it was proposed to substitute the seventh article of the preliminaries.

And 3rdly. To the formation of a general treaty.

Soon after his return from Compiègne, St. Severin proceeded to discuss, with the English minister, the project which had been delivered to him; and evinced a much more favourable disposition, than he had shewn before his departure. He even declared, that, if the questions relating to the Asiento, and the establishment for Don Philip, could be adjusted, no obstacle would arise to the conclusion of peace, from France and her allies. ‡ He also promised to prepare an answer to the project, on the arrival of M. Du Theil, who was to act with him, as joint plenipotentiary, and to assist him in maturing the plans, for a speedy conclusion of the treaty.

* Dispatches of the 18th-29th August, from the duke of Newcastle to Mr. Keith. Keith Papers, MS.

† Letter from the duke of Newcastle to the duke of Bedford, dated August 28th-September 8th, 1748. Grantham Papers, MS.

‡ Letter from Sir Thomas Robinson to the duke of Newcastle, August 28th N.S. 1748. Grantham Papers, MS.

On the 5th of September, the arrival of Du Theil gave a new impulse to the negotiations ; and a lively expectation was excited by his appointment, because he was not only remarkable for frankness and sincerity, but was expected to be perfectly acquainted with the views of his court, from the situation which he held, as principal *commis* or clerk, in the office of foreign affairs.

Without entering into a tedious detail of the proceedings, it is sufficient to observe, that England and France made reciprocal concessions; and the progress of the treaty was accelerated by the private negotiation which Spain was carrying on in London, through the agency of general Wall. The king of England consented to the renewal of the Asiento contract, for the four years interrupted by the war ; and reserved for future discussion, his claim of exemption from the right of search, as well as that of indemnification, for the depredations committed by the Spaniards, and his demand for other commercial regulations. He also agreed to the expedient, suggested by the Bourbon courts, relative to the establishment for Don Philip. France, on the other hand, consented to ratify the article in the preliminaries, relating to the fortifications of Dunkirk, to withdraw the demands in favour of the Scottish rebels, and to renew the guaranty of the Protestant Succession.

In consequence of these mutual concessions, Du Theil framed a new project of a definitive treaty. As it was intended for an ultimatum, he earnestly laboured to reconcile the conflicting interests, which so much retarded the peace, and endeavoured to render it palatable to all the powers, especially to the court of Vienna, whose concurrence he deemed most essential. With this view he omitted many points, which had been found objectionable in the former draughts, and adhered, as closely as possible, to the tenour of the preliminaries. Indeed this new project appeared in so favourable a light to Kaunitz himself, that, notwithstanding his habitual caution, he almost ventured to promise the concurrence of his Court.

But the crisis was hastened principally by the extraordinary conduct of the Empress Queen. Indignant at the rejection of her demand for the £.100,000, and at the convention between England and France, for the return of the Russian auxiliaries, she authorised Kaunitz to enter into an adjustment of a similar nature with St. Severin. By this compact, which was signed on the 25th of September, she agreed to withdraw thirty thousand of her troops from the field, on condition that the same number should be recalled from the French army; thus abandoning, not only the Netherlands, but even the Dutch frontier to the enemy, while the Duke of Cumberland was left with a very inferior force, exposed to insult, and even to serious danger, should hostilities be renewed.

Accordingly, the Austrian troops were withdrawn, without any notification, direct or indirect, to the British Court, and even without any formal announcement to the Duke of Cumberland, until the order for their march was imparted to him by marshal Bathiani. The Duke, extremely mortified at this information, expressed his surprise that such a resolution should be taken, without reference either to his Majesty or his ministers. But he obtained from the marshal only the cool and disrespectful reply, that he had no knowledge of the order, until he received it, and did not consider that it deserved the least blame, since it was only an imitation of what had been before done, in remanding the Russian troops.* "The campaign," he added, "had been extremely expensive to the Empress Queen, and all the subsidy due to her imperial Majesty, by the last convention, had not been paid." Actuated either by fear or economy, the Dutch likewise ordered their troops into winter quarters. A renewal of war was thus rendered impracticable; and peace became absolutely necessary for the allies.

Mr. Pelham manifested great indignation at this indecorous precipitancy of the court of Vienna, and at the insult offered to the Duke of Cumberland; yet he did not conceal his exultation, in a procedure so likely to accelerate the peace, and urged it as an argument for instantly recalling the British forces, and dismissing the German auxiliaries.

The lord Chancellor fully concurred in opinion with Mr. Pelham, on the good effects, which would result from the convention between France and Austria, and on the necessity of terminating a war, which could not be carried on, without involving the country in ruin.†

The duke of Newcastle was no less offended than his brother, with the conduct of the Austrian cabinet, and was moved by his earnest representations on the state of public credit: he saw, also, the expediency of acce lerating the conclusion of the treaty, and acknowledged the necessity of obtaining the concurrence of the empress queen, either by conciliation or

* Letter from Sir Everard Fawkener to Sir Thomas Robinson, October 6th, 1748. Grantham Papers, MS.

† See Letters from the Chancellor to the duke of Newcastle, and from Mr. Pelham to the duke of Newcastle, dated September 23rd, 26th, and October 4th, 1748. Illust. Corres.

menaces. We find him, therefore, declaring his resolution to renew his expostulations in a more peremptory manner, and observing, that if the court of Vienna should continue so obstinate as to withhold their assent, after the attention and regard which had been shewn to them, the king would be justified before God and man, in signing the definitive treaty without them.* With this determination Mr. Pelham was highly gratified, and had soon the satisfaction to find that these spirited remonstrances produced the desired effect.

Numerous letters continued to pass between the two brothers, as well as between the Chancellor and the duke of Newcastle, on the subject of the negotiations; but as they are too voluminous to be inserted in the narrative, some of them are introduced in the Illustrative Correspondence, to which we refer the reader.†

* Letter from the duke of Newcastle to Mr. Pelham, dated September 19th-30th, 1748.
† See letters from September 13th-24th to Nov. 1st, in the Illustrative Correspondence.

CHAPTER XX.

1748—9.

Objections of the courts of Austria and Sardinia to the proposed plan of the Treaty, overcome by the firmness and prudence of the British cabinet—Signature of the Definitive Treaty, by England, France, and Holland, and accession of the other belligerent Powers—Articles of the Treaty—Restoration of harmony between England and France—Removal of the young Pretender from France—Differences of opinion, between the duke of Newcastle and Mr. Pelham, on various questions of policy—Their reconciliation promoted by the friendship of the lord Chancellor.

THE project of Du Theil was considered by the king, as including terms more advantageous than could have been expected, in the actual state of affairs; and was likewise sanctioned by the lords justices. Mr. Pelham, in particular, rejoiced in the prospect of a speedy conclusion of peace, and urged his brother not to delay the signature. " For God's sake," he emphatically exclaims, in a letter Sept. 20th-Oct. 1st, 1748,* " do not let us delay ; every day is material ; and I think experience shews us, we are not likely to better our terms by standing out. My spirits," he adds, " rise and fall, as the pacific plan gains or loses ground." In another letter, dated Sept. 23rd-Oct. 4th, 1748,† he observes, credit sunk, and the stocks fell, during the temporary pause which had occurred in the proceedings at Aix ; but, as soon as it was known, that the project of Du Theil was likely to be approved by the belligerent powers, the funds rose two per cent.

Considering, therefore, the pressing necessity of peace, and the lateness of the season for the restitutions and cessions, his Majesty concurred in opinion with Mr. Pelham, that it would be imprudent to postpone the conclusion of the treaty; and the duke of Newcastle, who was now as anxious for peace as his brother, had the satisfaction of dispatching the royal orders, for the Plenipotentiaries to sign, provided the project of Du Theil experienced

---

* Illustrative Correspondence.   † Ibid.

that favourable reception at the court of Vienna, which they were led to anticipate, from the language of count Kaunitz. In this expectation, however, they were again disappointed.

The Empress Queen, thinking that her interests had not been sufficiently consulted, was extremely dissatisfied with the project, and declared, that it was not formed by the French alone, but that its most objectionable stipulations had been suggested by England. She still protested against the article, which required her, more fully to guaranty her cessions to the king of Sardinia, as well as against those which implied her specific confirmation of the Barrier Treaty, and the renewal of the guaranty of Silesia and Glatz to the king of Prussia.

Her plenipotentiary at Aix was consequently instructed to declare, that if such articles stood in the treaty, she could never engage to concur. In making these remonstrances, however, Kaunitz added, that if the obnoxious points were rescinded or amended, he believed that he might still promise the acquiescence of his sovereign.

The question with regard to the king of Prussia was easily adjusted, as his consent to give a reciprocal guaranty to Austria, for all her remaining possessions, was obtained by the urgent representations of the king of England; and the empress was contented with the proffered security.

The difficulty created by her Imperial Majesty's refusal to confirm the Barrier Treaty, as it existed before the war, seemed almost insurmountable; for, the States-General had given positive instructions to count Bentinck, not to sign without that condition; while by England it had been considered as an ultimatum, throughout the negotiation; and it was accordingly settled in the project of Du Theil, that the Low Countries should be restored, *as well to the Empress Queen, as to the States-General.* This stipulation was strongly resisted by the court of Vienna, as implying that the sovereignty of those countries belonged jointly to the two Powers; whereas the empress queen possessed the sole sovereignty, while the Dutch had only the right of placing garrisons in the barrier towns, and received a subsidy from her Imperial Majesty for their maintenance.

Admitting the validity of this objection, and finding that a specific confirmation of the Barrier Treaty could not be extorted, the duke of Newcastle prudently yielded; and authorised Mr. Keith to propose a modification, by which that treaty, though not expressly mentioned, might be virtually confirmed. An article, to that effect, was transmitted from the Austrian cabinet to count Kaunitz, with orders to introduce it into the treaty. It contained the stipulation, "That the towns and places, of which the *sovereignty belonged to the Empress Queen, and in which the States-General had right of garrison*, should be yielded to the troops of the republic, six weeks after the ratification." In a conference, which took place on this subject, the British plenipotentiaries, in conjunction with Kaunitz, made such representations, as induced count Bentinck to agree to the proposed modification, in direct opposition to his instructions; and it was accordingly substituted, for the objectionable clause in the project of Du Theil.

The last remaining obstacle arose, from the difficulty of arranging the claims of the king of Sardinia on the Empress Queen. While her Imperial Majesty refused to give a more specific guaranty of her cessions to that sovereign, than was contained in the preliminaries, the king of Sardinia required still farther securities, for those cessions, as well as for the eventual reversion of Placentia. On this occasion, the king of England had a difficult part to act. He had to decide between two of his allies, both of whom he was anxious to gratify. As a guarantee of the Treaty of Worms, he was however more inclined to support the claims of the king of Sardinia; and he continued to favour them, until he found that his plenipotentiaries were left to contend, not only with the Austrian, but with the French and Dutch ministers, who considered the conduct of his Sardinian Majesty as unreasonable, and deemed his interests to be sufficiently secured by the twelfth article. The English plenipotentiaries, therefore, informed those of Sardinia, that if they did not yield, the treaty would be signed without them; and by this menace, extorted their consent.

All impediments being at length removed, the Treaty of Aix la Chapelle was signed by the plenipotentiaries of England, France, and Holland, on the 18th of October; and the ratifications were exchanged, the following day. On the 20th, the accession of Spain took place; that of Austria was withheld no longer than till the 23rd; Modena acceded on the 25th; Genoa on the 28th; and lastly Sardinia on the 7th of November.*

The only belligerent power that refused to accede, was the king of Naples, who objected to the articles securing the reversion of Parma and Guastalla to the House of Austria, and of Placentia to the king of Sardinia,

---

* I have fallen into an error, in my History of the House of Austria, in stating that Sardinia acceded on the 7th of December.

if Don Philip inherited the crown of Naples; because he considered it as derogating from his own right of transferring that crown to one of his younger sons, should he himself ascend the throne of Spain.*

The following is an abstract of the articles of the definitive treaty, in which the reader will recognize a general conformity with the preliminaries.

Article I. Renewal of peace between all the contracting powers.

Art. II. Restitution of all conquests, and the *Status quo ante bellum*, with the exceptions herein mentioned.

Art. III. Renewal of the treaties of Westphalia, 1648; of Madrid, between England and Spain, 1667, 1678, and 1679; of Ryswick, 1697; of Utrecht, 1713; of Baden, 1714; of the triple alliance, 1717; of the quadruple alliance, 1718; and of the treaty of Vienna, 1738.

Art. IV. Mutual restoration of prisoners, six weeks after the ratification.

Art. V. Mutual restitution of conquests, and specification of the cessions assigned by Austria, to Don Philip, according to the preliminaries.

Art. VI. All the restitutions in Europe, specified in this treaty, to be made within the term of six weeks after the ratifications, and in particular all the Low Countries to be restored to the Empress Queen, and likewise those Barrier Towns, the sovereignty of which belonged to the House of Austria, to be evacuated, for the admission of the troops of the States-General.

Art. VII. Parma, Placentia, and Guastalla, to be delivered to Don Philip, at the time that Nice and Savoy are restored to the king of Sardinia.

Art. VIII. Measures to be adopted for insuring the restitutions, within the period appointed.

Art. IX. The king of England engages to send two hostages of rank to Paris, until Cape Breton, and all his conquests in the West and East Indies, shall be restored.

Art. X. The revenues and taxes of the conquered countries, to belong to the powers in possession, until the day of the ratification.

Art. XI. All archives to be restored within two months, or as soon afterwards as possible.

Art. XII. The king of Sardinia to retain possession of all the territories, conceded to him by the treaty of Worms, excepting Finalé and Placentia; namely, the Vigevenasco, part of the Pavesano, and the county of Anghiera.

---

* This right he afterwards exercised, when, on the death of his brother Ferdinand, without issue, he inherited the crown of Spain, and his younger son, Ferdinand, became king of Naples.

Art. XIII. The Duke of Modena to be restored to all his dominions.

Art. XIV. Genoa to be reinstated in all her possessions and rights, and her subjects in the enjoyment of all the funds belonging to them, in the Austrian and Sardinian banks.

Art. XV. All things in Italy to remain, as before the war, with the exceptions contained in the preceding articles.

Art. XVI. The Asiento Treaty, and the privilege of sending the annual ship to the Spanish colonies, confirmed for four years, according to the right possessed before the war.

Art. XVII. Dunkirk to remain fortified on the side of the land, in its existing condition; and, on that of the sea, to be left on the footing of antient treaties.*

Art. XVIII. Certain claims of money, by the king of England, as elector of Hanover, on the crown of Spain; the differences concerning the abbey of St. Hubert, and the boundaries of Hainault; and the courts of justice recently established in the Low Countries, as also the pretensions of the elector-palatine, to be amicably adjusted by commissaries.

Art. XIX. Confirmation of the guaranty of the Protestant Succession of the House of Brunswick, in all its descendants, as fully stipulated in the fifth article of the Quadruple alliance.

Art. XX. All the German territories of the king of England, as elector of Brunswick Lunenburg, guarantied.

Art. XXI. All the contracting powers, who guarantied the Pragmatic Sanction of the 19th April, 1713, now guaranty the entire inheritance of Charles the Sixth, in favour of his daughter, Maria Theresa, and her descendants, excepting those cessions previously made by Charles the Sixth, or by Maria Theresa herself, and those included in the present treaty.

Art. XXII. Silesia and Glatz guarantied to the king of Prussia.

Art. XXIII. All the powers interested in this treaty, jointly guaranty its execution.

Art. XXIV. Exchange of the ratifications to be made at Aix la Chapelle, by all the contracting powers, within a month after the signatures.†

Thus peace was restored; and when we consider the victorious career of France in the Netherlands, the dangerous situation of Holland, the financial

* These words implied, that the port and harbour should remain in a state of demolition.

† The articles of this memorable treaty are found in all the general collections of Treaties, and are abridged in the Continuation of Rapin, Vol. xxi. p. 357.

embarrassments of England, the absence of the king, the divisions in the cabinet, and the jealousy which existed between Austria and Sardinia, it must be admitted, that the conditions obtained for England and her allies, were, in general, more favourable, than their situation entitled them to expect. Many points, at issue, which could not be satisfactorily adjusted, were however prudently reserved for future discussion.

The absolute necessity of a cessation of hostilities, induced the majority of the nation to approve the peace. This reason operated with Mr. Pelham, in pressing its immediate conclusion; and furnished the principal argument in his justification of the treaty, when it was vehemently arraigned in parliament.

Among the points reserved for adjustment, was one, which though of minor importance, had created great embarrassment, in the course of the negotiation with the court of Vienna. This was, the payment of the £.100,000, arrears of subsidy, to which we have repeatedly alluded. On acceding to the treaty, Kaunitz delivered a letter to the English plenipotentiaries, in which he insinuated, that the exchange of the ratifications might depend on the liquidation of these arrears; and, in fact, it was delayed on that account, until the duke of Newcastle indirectly gave some hopes, that means might ultimately be found, for gratifying the Empress Queen, in that particular. The ratifications were then exchanged, without any farther declaration or protest.*

Strong objections had been raised, by the two brothers, as well as by the lord Chancellor, and other ministers in England, to the humiliating article of the treaty, which contained the stipulation, that hostages should be given to France, for the restitution of Cape Breton. Accordingly, every endeavour had been used, to obviate the necessity of its execution. But as no other alternative could be devised to satisfy France, it was punctually fulfilled by the British Court; and, that no pretence might be afforded, for delaying the evacuation of the Netherlands, the earls of Cathcart and Sussex, who had been selected as hostages, repaired to Paris, where they were honourably received. This voluntary choice of two noblemen of distinguished rank, was considered as a mark of personal respect towards the French

* These facts are taken from the duke of Newcastle's dispatches to Mr. Keith, Oct. 18th-29th, 1748, Keith Papers, MS; a letter from Mr. Pelham to the duke of Newcastle, dated Nov. 11th, 1748; and a letter from the duke of Newcastle to the Chancellor, Nov. 14th-25th, 1748. Newcastle Papers, MS.

monarch, and as a clear indication of the sincere disposition of the king of England, to fulfil his engagements.

A similar inclination, on the part of France, was no less strongly evinced, by the measures adopted for removing the young Pretender. He had formally protested against the conditions, established at the congress of Aix-la-Chapelle, as injurious to the interests of his family; but his remonstrance was indignantly rejected, and, on the conclusion of the treaty, intimations were conveyed to him, that his longer residence in the French dominions could not be consistently permitted. The high-spirited prince received this intelligence with undisguised resentment; nor was he soothed by a conciliatory letter, on the part of Louis himself, or by the endeavours used to secure him a proper asylum in Switzerland, accompanied with the offer of a liberal pension. On the contrary, he set the French court at defiance; insisted on the distinctions due to his rank; and evinced a resolution to repel force by force, should any attempt be made against him, derogatory to his dignity. Even after the arrival of the British hostages, he affected to court public notice; and wrought so powerfully on the sympathies of the people, that apprehensions were seriously entertained of a tumult in his favour.

Finding remonstrances vain, the French monarch reluctantly adopted more decisive measures. In the beginning of December, the prince was arrested, while entering the Opera-house in state; and was conveyed to the castle of Vincennes. Soon afterwards, he was privately escorted, under a strong guard, to the frontiers of Switzerland.* This decisive act of severity against the son of the Pretender, strengthened the feelings of amity between the two courts; and their pacific relations were speedily established, by the mission of embassadors extraordinary, from the respective monarchs. At the same time, the most effectual means were adopted, in both countries, for the general fulfilment of the treaty.

Within the period prescribed, France restored all the Low Countries, in full sovereignty, to the Empress Queen, and admitted the Dutch troops into those towns, in which they had right of garrison. The Hanoverians and Germans marched to their respective countries; and the duke of Cumberland, with the British troops, returned to England. Similar arrangements took place in Italy: the king of Sardinia relinquished Finalé, and the territories

* Continuation of Rapin, vol. xxi. p. 376. Hénault, Abrégé, 1748.

wrested from Genoa, and retained quiet possession of all the cessions, which had been made by the court of Vienna, in the treaty of Worms, excepting the city of Placentia. The dominions of the duke of Modena were, in the same manner, restored. The Spaniards evacuated Savoy, and the other countries which they had occupied; and, in return, Don Philip received the establishment of Parma, Placentia, and Guastalla. The restitution of Cape Breton took place, with as little delay as possible; and the conquests of the English and French in the East Indies were respectively relinquished.

Mr. Pelham was much gratified by the conclusion of peace, as it tended to facilitate the execution of his intended plan, for reducing the interest of the national debt. He had the farther gratification of knowing, that his views were generally approved by the king, who bestowed on him distinguished marks of favour and approbation, and characterised him as the most able and willing minister, that had ever directed the affairs of his government.* The duke of Newcastle, also, testified his satisfaction at the judicious arrangements, by which his brother proposed to effect his object, which he described as " the greatest work that ever was done," avowing, that it would complete his political wishes, because it would be done by him. In a letter to the Chancellor, he mentions it in still stronger terms of approbation. " The king, and the Duke," he writes, " tell me, my brother has great national views now in his thoughts : no less than the reducing the whole debt of the nation, to three per cent, and the keeping the current expense within the land and malt, and paying, yearly, a million of the sinking fund, to the lessening the debt of the nation. It is a great and glorious design, worthy of him ; and I have told the king and every body I speak to, that no man is, or I verily believe ever was, so willing and so able, to do this great service to his country, as my brother is. I will assure him two things : that this will make my happiness in public affairs complete, and, secondly, that all I can possibly do to contribute towards it, shall be done, by never proposing any measure that does not appear to me to be absolutely necessary, that can in any way delay the execution of this great design. And, lastly, I never will hear any body talk, who will pretend to let any body else share in the merit." †

Although the two brothers agreed in this particular instance, yet we cannot but observe, that while the negotiations were depending, a difference

* Letter from the Duke of Newcastle to Mr. Pelham, dated Oct. 19th-30th, 1748.

† Letter from the Duke of Newcastle to the Lord Chancellor. Newcastle Papers. See, also, part of a letter from Mr. Pelham to the duke of Newcastle, dated August 4th-15th, 1748,

of opinion occasionally arose between them, which was not wholly removed, even by the conclusion of the definitive treaty. For, the duke of Newcastle still persisted in his suspicion, that the course which he had pursued towards Austria was indirectly disapproved by the British cabinet; because the testimonies of satisfaction, which he received from his friends, were less warm and cordial than he had expected. We find him, in a confidential letter to the lord Chancellor, renewing his complaint, that he was left without advice or assistance, as long as affairs were in agitation, and censured when they were concluded, on his own responsibility; adding, that he had deplored to the king, his unhappy situation, in being blamed at home, and disobeyed abroad. He also particularly lamented, that his services were not sufficiently appretiated by his brother, nor even the lord Chancellor* himself.

Mr. Pelham, though he occasionally manifested some warmth at these reproaches, yet omitted no affectionate argument or profession, of a soothing tendency; and, in his turn, gave way, in several instances, to the wishes of his brother. On financial points of importance, he however continued inflexible. Accordingly, on the Austrian demand for the £.100,000, he displayed the same firmness which he had hitherto shewn; and persisted, in opposition to the importunities of the duke, in his refusal to issue the money, without the consent of parliament.

We find Mr. Pelham also evincing his firm resolution to disband several regiments, even in contradiction to the desire of the Duke of Cumberland; expressing the greatest anxiety for the diminution of the public expenditure; and repeatedly declaring, that the nation could be saved, only by the speedy adoption of a well-judged system of economy. These, and other subjects, are minutely detailed in the letters, which passed between the two brothers, and which are inserted in the Illustrative Correspondence. †

chap. xviii. p. 15, in which he alludes to his plan of reduction; and see, particularly, an extract of a letter, dated November 15th-26th, 1748, from the duke of Newcastle to Mr. Pelham, in the Illustrative Correspondence. By the perusal of these documents, it will be evident to the reader, that Mr. Pelham had already formed the plan for reducing the interest of the national debt, the merit of which, we shall find, was afterwards unjustly claimed by others, who endeavoured to deprive him of the praise, due to this important and beneficial regulation.

* Letter from the duke of Newcastle to the lord Chancellor, October 9th-20th, 1748. Newcastle Papers, MS.

† See letters, from October 9th-20th to November 15th-26th, 1748. Illust. Corres.

From the same principle of economy, Mr. Pelham objected to every project, however plausible in appearance, which tended to increase the public expenditure, without exhibiting indisputable proofs of national utility. On one occasion, in particular, we find him opposing the wishes of the king, and the views of his brother, for extending the influence of England abroad, and for counteracting the ascendancy of France; on account of the expense, with which the execution of the design must necessarily be attended.

The plan was, to form a grand alliance, by means of subsidiary treaties, in time of peace, in order to retain, in the interest of the Maritime Powers, those princes and states, who could most readily supply military aid, in case of a rupture.

Of this extensive system of alliance, England, Holland, Austria, and Russia, were to be the principals; and to these the duke of Newcastle hoped to add Denmark, and the minor princes of the Empire. He proposed to begin, by taking a certain number of Danish troops into British pay, and by appropriating for this purpose, an annual subsidy of about £.45,000.

Mr. Pelham objected to this proposal, as unnecessary. He deprecated, also, the impolicy of subsidizing foreign powers in time of peace, because such powers, in case of a war, might desert the alliance of England for that of France, if allured by the offer of greater advantages. His chief reason, however, was grounded on the principle of economy. To the petty subsidy of £.45,000, he observed, he was inclined to offer no decided opposition, if it did not lead, as he feared it would, to other demands, which would considerably increase the national expenses, and counteract his intended plan for the reduction of the public debt.

Influenced by his brother's opinion, the duke of Newcastle, with great reluctance, postponed his design, until a more favourable opportunity should occur; and the king was afterwards induced, by the minister of finance, to issue a declaration, that he would enter into no subsidiary treaties, during the continuance of peace.*

In conclusion, we deem it proper to remark, that although the two brothers thus widely differed in opinion, upon some particular points, and were occasionally so irritated, as to express their feelings in querulous language; yet their fraternal affection for each other was rather interrupted,

---

* These circumstances are alluded to in several letters of the duke of Newcastle and the ord Chancellor, in August and September, 1749. Newcastle Papers, MS.

than diminished.   The restoration of harmony was effectually aided by their common friends, the lord Chancellor and Mr. Stone ; the former of whom convinced the duke, that the principal causes of his brother's uneasiness were derived from his extreme anxiety to lessen the public burthens, and to realise his meditated plan of finance.   In fact, their quarrels, if we may use so strong an expression, were invariably followed by a better understanding ; and, as the duke himself aptly observes, in one of his subsequent letters, seemed to verify the adage of the poet ·—

"Amantium iræ, amoris integratio est."*

* The quarrels of lovers are the renewal of love.

CHAPTER XXI.

1748—9.

ON his return to England, the 23rd of November, the king participated in the satisfaction produced among all classes of his subjects, by the restoration of peace. He was greeted on his arrival, with a loyal address from the lord mayor and aldermen of London, who were ambitious to be foremost, in exhibiting to the country an example of duty and allegiance.

Mr. Pelham was fully sensible of the defects of the Treaty of Aix-la-Chapelle; but, regarding it as the offspring of imperious necessity, he employed all practicable means to render it beneficial to the country. In expediting the discharge of the auxiliaries, and the return of the British troops from Flanders, as well as in providing for the reduction of the national expenditure, he proved the sincerity of that zeal, which he had recently testified for the restoration of peace. He had also the gratification of meeting his brother, with renewed cordiality, and of finding him perfectly disposed, to cooperate in his plans for the public welfare.

On the meeting of parliament, Mr. Pelham had to devise means for liquidating the multifarious expenses of a disastrous and protracted contest; to protect and encourage those branches of national industry, which had languished during its continuance ; to form new expedients for conducting the public service ; to facilitate the change, in the habits and pursuits of the people, required by a transition from war to peace ; and to defend the government against an opposition, recently strengthened by the direct accession of the prince of Wales,* and his restless but able partisans.

The prince of Wales, by the advice of his adherents, had been induced to hold a Court of Stannary, in quality of duke of Cornwall ; and had attempted to revive some claims attached to that dignity, which, if admitted, would have greatly augmented his influence among the Cornish boroughs. His pretensions were consequently opposed by the whole weight of the ministry, who had always considered those boroughs, as dependent on the Crown. Hence, the misunderstanding between the Prince and the administration was increased ; and the hostile feelings of his Royal Highness were still farther inflamed by the intrigues of lord Bolingbroke, who had returned from France, and was impatient to avenge on the ministry, his own exclusion from political power.†

The principal adherents of his Royal Highness were lord Percival, who had now succeeded to the title of earl of Egmont, Dr. Lee, an able civilian, and Mr. Nugent, a confident and fluent orator. The Prince had also regained Mr. Dodington, who relinquished the treasurership of the navy, to resume a station in his establishment ; and his Royal Highness had given appointments to lord Middlesex and lord Archibald Hamilton, who had recently resigned their posts under government. His party was strengthened by many members of the former opposition,‡ as well as by others, who like Sir John Hinde Cotton, and Sir John Philips, had deserted the Court. In this phalanx, which, from the residence of the Prince, was called the party of Leicester House, were found many eloquent and acute debaters. Lastly, his Royal Highness was also supported by the earl of Bath, who was displeased with the Pelhams, not only for his own exclusion from power, but also for the recent

---

* See a Letter from the Prince of Wales to Sir Thomas Bootle, in June, 1747. Illust. Corres. v. i. p. 492.

† Lord Bolingbroke, soon after the death of queen Anne, entered into the service of the Pretender, and acted as his prime minister, for which he was attainted. In 1725, his attainder was reversed, and he was permitted to reside in England, being restored to his estates and honours, but excluded from his seat in parliament, and from holding any office under government. For the motives, which occasioned his banishment and recal, see Memoirs of Sir Robert Walpole, chap. xxv.

‡ Lord Melcombe's Diary.

dismissal of his friends, lord Sandys and Sir John Rushout, from their official situations. Indeed that peer had zealously assisted the Prince in the late parliamentary elections; and had expressed his readiness to attend the House of Lords, at the shortest notice, and to support, on all occasions, the interests and views of his Royal Highness.*

Parliament was opened on the 29th of November, 1748, by a speech from the king in person. It was the production of the Chancellor, and had been composed in perfect accordance with the feelings and views of the minister.

In announcing the conclusion of the definitive treaty, with the full concurrence of his allies, his Majesty expressed his satisfaction, at the attainment of this important object, on the best terms that the state of affairs would admit; and anticipated, from the harmony prevalent among the contracting parties, a long continuance of peace.

Great reductions having been made in the public expenditure, his Majesty required only supplies for the current service of the year, and for the completion of engagements already made known to parliament. He then recommended, as the most effectual means for reducing the debt, and providing against future dangers, the improvement of the revenue, and the maintenance of the naval force in proper strength and vigour.

After thanking both Houses for their liberal support, during the war, and approving the constant bravery of the British troops, his Majesty adverted to the naval operations, and exultingly observed, " Our signal successes at sea must ever be remembered, to the glory of the British fleet, and entitle it to the particular attention and support of this nation." In conclusion, he earnestly recommended the advancement of commerce, and the cultivation of the arts of peace, which, he said, should ever claim his hearty concurrence and encouragement. "It shall be my endeavour," he added, " to continue these blessings, by a punctual execution of the engagements now taken, and by maintaining the most perfect harmony and good correspondence with the friends and allies of Great Britain."

In the House of Peers, an address, moved by lord Powis, congratulating his Majesty on the peace, and repeating the usual assurances of fidelity to his sacred person, and zeal in support of the Protestant Succession, was carried unanimously.

* Letter from the Prince of Wales to Sir Thomas Bootle, in June, 1747. MS.

In the lower House, the address was moved by lord Barrington, who had recently been placed at the Board of Admiralty, and seconded by Mr. Charles Yorke, son of the lord Chancellor. After offering their congratulations on his Majesty's happy return, the Commons warmly acknowledged his constant attention to the welfare of his people, and his successful exertions for restoring peace to Europe. They recognized, with the same feelings, the prompt reduction of the public charges ; and promised to pursue most zealously, the wise plans recommended by his Majesty, for economizing and improving the revenue, that the burthens of the people might be diminished, while provision was made against future contingencies. After concurring in the approbation bestowed on the army and navy, they assured his Majesty, that they would grant the supplies, necessary to secure the peace and tranquillity of the government, and to maintain the honour of the nation, by making good its engagements. In deference to the wise and gracious injunctions of his Majesty, they declared that their earnest attention should be directed to the improvement of commerce, the support of public credit, and the cultivation of the arts of peace.

This address was vehemently assailed by the opposition, who were eager for an opportunity to arraign the whole conduct of the war, and to condemn the terms on which peace had been concluded. Dr. Lee and Mr. Nugent, as leading orators of the party, denied that the Dutch were reduced to such a state, either of weakness or of peril, as the ministers had represented; and affirmed that they had numerous resources, which might have been called into action. They contended, that if the strong fortress of Maestricht had at length been reduced to capitulate, others remained, which might have checked the career of the enemy, until the arrival of the Russians ; when the duke of Cumberland might have met the enemy on equal terms, and headed an army, inspired with full confidence, by the remembrance of his success at Culloden. They censured the articles of the treaty, as obscure and indefinite ; denounced the restitution of Cape Breton, the only conquest England had made, as dishonourable in itself, and rendered still more degrading, by an acquiescence in the demand of the enemy for hostages. So little care had been taken, they added, to reconcile conflicting interests, and promote the welfare of our allies, that the treaty had been concluded in direct opposition to the queen of Hungary, and the king of Sardinia ; while every expedient was sanctioned, which, at their expense, might gratify the allies of our antient rival. Lastly, they complained, that the question concerning the right of search, in which the contest with Spain originated, had been scandalously passed over in silence. In support of these arguments, they expatiated on the weak and distracted state of France, the ruin of her trade, the destruction of her navy, the failure of her revenues, the general discontent of her people, and her consequent incapacity for prosecuting the war. They also contended, that France could not have continued her conquests, either in Holland or in Italy, without alienating her allies; for by attempting to retain the Netherlands, she would have provoked the hostility of the king of Prussia, and of the princes of Germany; and by making similar incroachments in Italy, would have forfeited the friendship of Spain and Naples.

While the situation and means of France were thus depreciated, those of England were placed in advantageous contrast. Mistress of the ocean, she might easily, it was urged, have appropriated the whole trade of the world; and, on the strength of such resources, her vast credit must have continued to flourish. While France had little to expect and all to fear, Great Britain had small cause for apprehension, and every ground of hope and confidence.

The observations in the royal speech, relative to retrenchment of expenditure, improvement of the revenue, and cultivation of the arts of peace, were treated with derision; and the plans of the minister, condemned by anticipation. It was therefore proposed, to omit the expressions, relative to the concurrence of the allies in the treaty; to qualify the encomiums on the troops, with the intimation of a hope, that an inquiry would be made into the causes, which had rendered their bravery unavailing; and to disparage the services of the navy, by omitting the congratulatory clause, on the successful operations of the fleets. The opposition finally protested with great energy, against any pledge for fulfilling the engagements arising from the late treaty, until those engagements should have been laid before the House, and deliberately examined.

These arguments were ably combated by the Solicitor-general; but the best and most effectual vindication of the peace, occurs in the speech of Mr. Pelham.

He began by observing, that the propriety of voting the customary homage to the throne, had been tacitly acknowledged; and that as those who disapproved the address, proposed by his noble friend, had not offered another, or moved any amendment, he would not take up much of their time; for he thought that the best advice, that could be given upon this occasion, would be in the well-known words of the poet—

> "——— Si quid novisti rectius istis,
> Candidus imperti, si non his utere mecum."

But as great pains had been taken, during the debate, to excite a prejudice against what had always been deemed a blessing, he hoped to render an acceptable service, by offering an antidote. " Peace," he continued, " has ever been deemed especially desirable, for a nation subsisting chiefly by commerce ; and that peace must be truly bad, which can be worse than an unsuccessful war. The peace, now concluded, must therefore be considered as a relative good ; for the late war was not only unsuccessful, but disastrous. As to the prospect of continuing it with advantage, which some gentlemen have described in such glowing colours, I am afraid, that the result would have shewn it to be vain ; nor shall any oratory persuade me, that of two contending parties, that antagonist has not most to fear, who has been most frequently defeated."

Adverting to the argument, that France and her allies had the greatest reason to deprecate a continuance of hostilities, he declared it to be founded on the mere supposition, that the Russian troops might have arrived, before the French could have penetrated into Holland, or forced the Dutch to a separate peace. "This is a postulate," he observed, " which no one I think will grant, who considers the situation of affairs at the time, and the terms offered by France, even as they appeared in our public gazettes, the only authorities from which we are at present competent to speak. From those gazettes, though generally too favourable to our own cause, it appears that the French would have been masters of Maestricht, by the middle of May ; and, as the Russians had not reached the neighbourhood of Silesia, when the preliminaries were signed, their arrival could not have been expected until the end of July ; so that, after the fall of Maestricht, the French would have had ten weeks, to force their way into Holland, before we could have collected an army sufficient to risk a battle.

" What obstructions had the French to expect in prosecuting a march to the Hague ? The little fortified towns of Stevenswaert, Roermond, Venloo, and the Graave ; for, as to the city of Nimeguen, its fortifications were so much dilapidated, and it would have required so large a garrison, that the attempt to defend it must have been madness. Of these four little towns, the French would soon have been masters, if we may judge from the fate of Menin, which they took on the sixth day after opening the trenches. Indeed, with their numerous and well-appointed artillery, they would have made their way to the Hague, in four weeks. Then, if they had not forced the Dutch to a neutrality, they might have occupied the seat of government, and this they might have effected, without giving alarm to any prince in Europe ; for, on entering the United Provinces, they would doubtless have published a manifesto, disclaiming all views of conquest, or permanent occupation, and professing a design to restore the Commonwealth, and protect the liberties of the Dutch, against the Stadtholder and his party, supported by the English. A powerful faction, under French influence, would thus have been created, which, after seizing the government, would probably have joined the enemy against us.

" In either of these cases, what advantage could we have reaped from the arrival of the Russians ? If the Dutch had agreed to a neutrality, they must have withdrawn their troops from our army, which after the arrival of the expected auxiliaries, would have remained as inferior to the French as it was before ! Nay, they must have warned our army to evacuate their territory'; and I much doubt, whether any of the princes of Westphalia, or of the Lower Palatinate, would have permitted it to sojourn in their dominions. In my opinion, then, it would certainly have been reduced to a most unfortunate situation, if the preliminaries had not been accepted ; for if the terms offered by France had been rejected, even the government of Holland would have consented to a neutrality, pleading in excuse, the refusal of the queen of Hungary to cede the little duchies of Parma and Placentia, and the obstinacy of England, in withholding the barren and useless isle of Cape Breton. Barren it naturally is, and useless it must ever be to us, though not to the French, so long as they possess Canada, or have fisheries on the coast of Newfoundland.

" Considering the state of affairs, I hope gentlemen are now convinced, that the terms of the preliminaries were as good as could then be expected ; and I believe the French were extremely sorry, that we did not reject them ; as in that case, the Dutch would have consulted their safety in a separate treaty ; and, to regain their own territories, with the addition of some parts of Flanders and Brabant, as a barrier, would have agreed to leave the French in possession of all the rest of the Austrian Netherlands. After such a compact, I believe, that with the single aid of the House of Austria, we could

not have expelled the French from Flanders; and I need not expatiate on
the danger that would have ensued, if they had been left in undisturbed
possession of the whole range of coast, opposite to the south-eastern and
southern shores of England, from the mouth of the Thames, to the Land's
End in Cornwall.

" I can, therefore, see no reason, why so many objections should be raised
against the very general expressions, in our address, regarding the late
peace ; and, if ever the honourable and learned gentleman * should be in my
place, which probably he may soon fill, he will then appretiate the difficulty
of raising supplies, for such a war, or of giving general satisfaction, by any
terms of peace. Few men know the circumstances and views of foreign
nations ; but those who have duly considered them, will allow, that conjunc-
tures may occur, in which any nation will find it more prudent to accept bad
terms of peace, than to wage an unequal war ; for, as circumstances are ever
changing, a new conjuncture may enable the injured nation to commence
hostilities with advantage, or procure the redress of all its wrongs, without
risking an appeal to arms.

" As to the proposed inquiry into the causes which frustrated the bravery
of our troops, I am sure it would be very improper, on an occasion of
this kind. Without positive information, it would be contrary to all parliamentary precedent, to decide, whether such an inquiry be necessary; and
without some necessity, no inquiry should be instituted by this House. I
shall readily acknowledge, that we owe much to the royal commander of our
armies. To him we owe, that we are this day once more assembled. To
him the nation owes the preservation of its liberties, its religion, and every
thing that can be dear to a people. But no obligation to him, can impose
on us, the duty of instituting such an inquiry ; because no man, at home or
abroad, ever blamed, or even suspected his conduct. The causes of our
misfortunes are well ascertained. Almost every man is aware, that they were
solely attributable to the preponderating force of the enemy ; and it is
equally apparent, that our inferiority was not the consequence of any
neglect, or remissness, in this nation. On every occasion, we furnished
more than our contingent of troops, of money, and of all other requisites
for insuring victory. I cannot therefore perceive any useful purpose, which
such an inquiry would answer ; and shall make no farther observation on this
head, unless it become the subject of a specific motion.

* Dr. Lee.

" The other amendments that have been suggested, though not moved, are rather criticisms than objections ; and as I do not like to deal in criticism, I shall leave the House to form their own judgment upon them. But before I sit down, I must notice the learned gentleman's paradoxical distinction,* between the king and his ministers, as if a disunion could exist between the parliament and the ministers, without any disunion between the king and his parliament. According to this doctrine, no disunion can ·exist between the king and his parliament ; for the parliament never expresses any disunion with the king. Even in the time of Charles the First, the parliament always expressed a great regard for their sovereign, though, at last, when properly modelled for the purpose, they severed his head from his body. Therefore, all foreign nations, when they see a disunion between the parliament and the king's ministers, will suppose it to be a disunion between his Majesty and his parliament, and will treat both him and · the nation accordingly ; for they have the highest authority to conclude, that a kingdom divided against itself cannot stand.

" For this reason, we should carefully avoid giving occasion for foreign courts to imagine the possibility of disunion between the parliament and the king's ministers. While a cordial union is apparent, I believe that every court in Europe will be cautious not to inflict on us a real injury. Though Spain, in particular, may be as unwilling expressly to renounce her right of searching, and of seizing all ships suspected of illicit trade on the coasts of her American colonies, as we should be to relinquish our right of searching, and of seizing all ships on our own coasts, which we suspect to be concerned in the contraband exportation of our wool ; yet, while we are united among ourselves, I am persuaded that Spain will not allow her *guarda costas* to abuse this right. If she should, I am convinced, that whatever forbearance may hitherto have been practised, the present administration will not allow that abuse to be perpetrated with impunity ; and, until a contrary policy be apparent, the parliament ought not to manifest any disunion even with the king's ministers ; therefore, I hope that the address, now proposed, will be agreed to."

* The Solicitor General having, in the conclusion of his speech, asserted, that if the House should be less dutiful in the language of the address, than usual, it would argue a disunion between his Majesty'and his parliament ; Dr. Lee contended, that it would imply a disunion, not between his Majesty and his parliament, but rather between the parliament and the ministers. This distinction, which Mr. Pelham calls paradoxical, he ably refutes in this speech. See the speeches of the Solicitor General and Dr. Lee, in Hansard, vol. xiv. p. 331.

This speech seems to have closed the debate ; for so little confidence had the opposition in the force of their arguments, or the strength of their party, that they did not venture to press a division on their amendment. The original address was in consequence voted.*

During the session, however, a question arose, which was calculated to widen the breach between the Pelhams and the friends of lord Granville ; and at the same time to create an invidious distinction, between the minister and some of his colleagues. On the 31st of January, lord Doneraile moved for the production of papers, relative to the convention of Hanau, and took occasion to observe, that the misfortunes which led to the late disadvantageous peace, might have been avoided, if the proposals offered by Charles the Seventh, in 1743, had been accepted. He dwelt on the advantages that might have been obtained, by detaching so valuable an ally from France ; and even asserted, that the French, expecting those offers to be accepted, had proposed to desert their allies the Spaniards, and agree to a peace upon the basis of *uti possidetis*. He added, that if a peace had been made on such terms, the Spaniards, deserted by the French, and disappointed in their views on Italy, would have thrown themselves entirely into the arms of England. In exculpating, therefore, the king and lord Granville, he bitterly censured those members of the cabinet, through whose influence the overture was rejected. He imputed this rejection to a mean jealousy of the ex-secretary of State, who had framed the articles of the treaty, and engaged for their acceptance. Founding his remonstrances on common rumour, as a sufficient basis for parliamentary inquiry, he demanded that the people should either be convinced, that their complaints were futile, or that the blame should be laid on those, by whom it was merited. In conclusion, he artfully inferred, that ministers would either accede to the motion, in the confidence that the treaty was justifiable, or, by rejecting it, would furnish additional evidence of their own guilt.

Notwithstanding these insinuations, Mr. Pelham, though reluctant to advert to the contentions with lord Granville, which had so much affected the feelings of the king, did not shrink from the question. He observed, that common rumour, however substantial, was not always an eligible foundation for parliamentary inquiry ; that the discussion of questions relating to foreign policy, generally tended to offend some of our allies, to disturb negotiations, to impede public business, and to interrupt the deliberations of parliament on affairs of the highest moment; and therefore an inquiry of that nature ought never to be instituted, unless strong presumptive evidence existed, of some weak or wicked measure.

After citing several antient laws, for preventing the diffusion of false reports, he adverted to the subject of debate; and in reference to the late treaty of peace, demanded, if terms so reasonable could have been expected from the enemy, in the midst of their triumphant career. He maintained, that there was no reason to blame the conduct of the negotiators; and, calling to remembrance the dismal forebodings of those who now censured the treaty, reminded them, that during the war, whenever an arrangement was suggested, their exclamation had been, "a peace indeed we may have; but it will leave the French in possession of the Netherlands, and transfer to Spain, almost all the Austrian dominions in Italy." He rejoiced, that their predictions had been falsified; and he believed, that their chagrin arose from their disappointment.

In objecting to the proposed inquiry, he observed, that, during so complicated a negotiation, in which so many European powers were concerned, many conferences must have been held, and much correspondence have taken place, which it would be imprudent, and even dishonourable, to make public; that such disclosures would alienate the confidence of foreign states, and at the same time diminish the influence of our ministers, in regard to the articles concerning our commerce and colonies, which still remained to be settled with France and Spain.

An inquiry, he continued, into the proposed treaty of Hanau, in 1743; or into any other negotiation during the war, would be still more imprudent. "With regard to that particular treaty, in which," he said, "I had no concern, because I was not then of the cabinet council, the terms have ever been described to me, as merely evincing a desire, on the part of the emperor Charles VII. to temporise, until he could regain his ascendancy, through the aid of a subsidy from England, much larger than she could spare, while at war with France and Spain. Had the emperor been thus enabled to effect his object, the ulterior consequences might have been easily foreseen. We might have maintained the contest against France and Spain; but in two or three years, the emperor, with the whole Germanic body, except the Houses of Brunswick and Austria, would have declared against us, unless we had accepted such terms, as he might have been pleased to prescribe. We should then have been accused of subsidizing the emperor, to accomplish the ruin of ourselves and our allies. But, supposing it true, that the French, likewise, at that time, offered to desert their allies the Spaniards, though I never before heard it asserted ; and, also, that the Spaniards had agreed to such terms of peace, as we might think reasonable, can we suppose that such a peace would have been lasting ? While the king of Spain has such a near view to the crown of France, we cannot imagine that the two Courts will long continue disunited ; and therefore our only security against such a formidable union, is to preserve the sincere friendship of the emperor and empire. Could we expect such an advantage, from an emperor chosen by French influence ? Could we expect any sincere coalition, between the Houses of Bavaria and Austria, while the former has such unbounded pretensions on the latter ? A peace on such terms would soon have proved treacherous ; for, when the emperor had gained a majority in the diet, and the French and Spaniards, relieved from danger on the side of Germany or Italy, had recruited their marine, a war would have arisen, in which this nation must have contended alone, against France, Spain, and Germany. Therefore I must ever believe, that the very existence of this nation depended on her success, in preventing the secure establishment of the late emperor ; and I must approve the policy which rejected the treaty of Hanau."

Repelling the insinuation, that invidious motives had actuated those who recommended that policy, he declared, that if any man, having the honour to sit in the king's council, should act on so unworthy a principle, he would be dismissed from the royal presence with indignation ; and, as his Majesty had shewn no such resentment, it must be concluded, that he accepted the advice, as proceeding from a sincere and honest concern, for the honour and interest of the country.

He concluded by declaring, that as the production of papers would afford no remedy for any evil, which was imputable to the rejection of the convention of Hanau, and, as no man ought to be punished for giving sincere advice, even supposing it to have been erroneous, he should decidedly oppose a motion, tending to no national advantage, and likely to occasion much national mischief.

Lord Egmont, in reply, observed, that though proper information had been withheld by the government, it was evident that the terms of the rejected treaty of Hanau were favourable, from the proofs afforded by the manifesto of the emperor himself, which had never been contradicted. He then vindicated the sincerity of the emperor, and of the French court, who were at that time interested in the termination of the war. He repeated the remark of lord Doneraile, that ministers, if innocent, would have made the proposed communication ; and by refusing it, would virtually admit, that the rejection of the treaty proceeded from the most egregious weakness, or from wickedness the most perfidious.

Mr. Walpole argued against the general principle, of making popular fame a ground for public inquiry. Lord Strange earnestly supported the motion; but frankly owned, that he himself had erred, in opposing the continuance of the Hanover troops in British pay, and admitted, that the peace of Aix-la-Chapelle was rendered necessary, by the threatened defection of the Dutch.

The motion was rejected by 288 against 138.*

The attack was renewed, on the 7th of February, by lord Egmont, who moved for the communication of all the papers and documents, relating to the different overtures and negotiations for peace, from the year 1744, to the final overture in 1747, which led to the peace of Aix-la-Chapelle. He was seconded by Sir Edmund Thomas, in a brief but able speech.

After construing the former refusal of papers, into a proof of conscious guilt, he argued, that ministers, by their reserve, in relation to subsequent negotiations, afforded additional reason to infer, that the terms originally rejected, and characterised as inadmissible, in the speech from the throne, the preceding November, were more favourable than those finally accepted. He then censured the treaty itself; and particularly complained of the vague stipulations concerning the trade with Spain, notwithstanding the unanimous resolution of parliament, that no peace should be signed with that power, until the right of search, claimed by her, had been specifically renounced. He concluded, by calling on the House to resent the contemptuous conduct of ministers, in withholding the communication of the preliminaries, during the last session, and in sending to Madrid Mr. Keene, the same agent, who a few years before, had signed the infamous and detested convention with Spain.

Mr. Pelham, relieved from the restraint which he had felt on the former occasion, now made a judicious and decisive reply. He expressed his surprise, that after the rejection of a similar motion, by a large

* Hansard's Parl. Hist. vol. xiv. p. 354. Journals of the Commons.

majority, this should have been proposed, for which he could trace no other cause, than a desire to excite popular clamour against the peace of Aix-la-Chapelle. That peace, he allowed, was not such as ministers could have wished; but it was rendered necessary, by the misfortunes of the war; and on a treaty so recent, it would be highly impolitic and dangerous, to lay any papers before the public, because even should the assertion be true, that terms deemed inadmissible, were before the end of last session admitted, might not this admission be rendered expedient, by a change of circumstances? He maintained, that this consideration would alone be conclusive against the communication required, which might be of infinite detriment to our natural allies, and of which our natural enemies might take great advantage.

Adverting to the commercial stipulations with Spain, he denied that a general treaty of peace afforded the proper occasion for regulating the trade between two particular nations; as it was usual to make commercial regulations, the subject of a subsequent and specific arrangement. "Therefore," continued Mr. Pelham, "if our trade with Spain be exposed to high duties, and our ships be subjected to search, which I am far from admitting, these very circumstances afford an argument against any call for papers, concerning the late negotiations; since such a disclosure might retard, if not frustrate, the adjustment of points relating to that trade, and to the freedom of our navigation."

After noticing the insinuation, that every pledge, calculated to induce the compliance of Spain and France, had been relinquished, and that some future sacrifice would be required, to gain that compliance, he said, " While Great Britain retains her invincible navy, she will possess an argument more cogent than any pledge, and will never have to make a sacrifice for any compliance, which she can reasonably demand. But we ought never to employ that invincible navy, to inforce an unjust claim, lest it should incur the only peril which it has to apprehend, the vengeance of the Almighty. Therefore, the argument supplied by our maritime force, should be exercised only in the last resort; and we should avoid every thing, that may tend to make that resort necessary, which, I think, is the direct object of the motion under consideration.

"The right of inquiry," he continued, " inherent in the Legislature, ought solely to be exercised for the benefit of the nation; and none of the advocates for the address now proposed, has attempted to justify it on that principle.

National resentment against insult has been urged as a motive for its adoption ; but by whom have we been treated in a contemptuous manner ? Surely not by his Majesty ; and yet no minister would dare to communicate the preliminaries to parliament, without his Majesty's order. But it may be alleged, that ministers acted contemptuously, in not advising the king to make that communication, before he ratified them. This may be an argument for an address to the king, to ascertain, who gave that advice; but it can be no argument for inquiry into the late treaty, or into the preceding negotiations. The address, proposed by those in whom this motion originated, will, I contend, be a flagrant incroachment on the prerogatives of the Crown, which include the power of making peace and war, that our designs may be kept secret, until the moment of execution. Even in making peace, if our motives were disclosed to the enemy, we might be disappointed in our views ; and, if the negotiations anterior to the treaty of Utrecht, had been better concealed, they would have led to better terms of accommodation. No inducement, therefore, can exist, for a minister to advise, or for a wise parliament to desire the communication of preliminaries of peace.

" With regard to those signed at Aix-la-Chapelle, I assert, that if circumstances rendered their acceptance necessary, prudence required that they should be ratified by the king, without a previous communication to parliament; because, if rejected, they could not have been ratified ; and, to ensure their approval, the circumstances inducing our acceptance of them, must have been publicly explained. On ascertaining these circumstances, our adversaries might have receded from their offers ; it being well known, that until the exchange of the ratifications, either party to a treaty is at liberty to recede from terms already offered, or to qualify them in such a manner, as entirely to alter their tendency. I, therefore, hope, that no farther mention will be made of contempt shewn to parliament, with regard to the late preliminaries, as it can afford no ground for agreeing to the motion proposed.*

The arguments of Mr. Pelham were controverted by Sir John Hinde Cotton. In denying, that the unfavourable terms of peace were justified by necessity, he censured ministers for creating that necessity, by their misconduct in the prosecution of hostilities. He indirectly characterized

* Hansard's Parl. Hist. vol. xiv. p. 386.

them, as alike incapable of conducting a war, and of negotiating a peace ;
alienating their best allies by their ignorance, and converting neutrals into
enemies ; alternately extravagant and penurious, and constant only to one
principle, that of enriching their friends, in order to strengthen their own
influence, and set their sovereign at defiance.   After exclaiming, " Is it not
better to be governed by able rogues, than by such weak fools?" he laboured
to prove, that by the terms of accommodation with Spain, and particularly
by omitting in the general treaty, all mention of the right of search, the
national honour was degraded, the commercial interests of the country
sacrificed, and every example and precedent disregarded.

No reply was made to an effusion so replete with the rancour of party,
aggravated by personal invective ; and, on a division, the motion was
negatived, by 181 against 120.

But the proceedings which excited the greatest interest, were the new
regulations brought forward, for the army and navy ; the most remarkable
of which was the proposal for making all half-pay officers subject to
martial law. With regard to officers of the army, it was reasonable to infer,
that they had formerly been amenable to the articles of war ; but no proof
was exhibited, that such subjection was common to naval officers. The
extensive reductions, however, both in the sea and land service, having
greatly increased the number of officers on half-pay, government deemed it
expedient, that they should all be placed under proper discipline. No
sooner was this purpose known, than the greatest efforts were made, to
excite alarm, not only in the army and navy, but among the people in
general, against a regulation, which was denounced as unconstitutional and
dangerous. It was censured also, as tending to increase the power of the
Crown, by obliging the half-pay officers, many of whom were of good
family and fortune, to exert their extensive influence in favour of ministers.

The subject was first brought into discussion, on the 1st of February, when
lord Barrington, as a lord of the Admiralty, proposed a bill for incor-
porating all the laws relative to the sea service. On this occasion, many
naval officers hastened to the Admiralty, and avowed their determination
to resign their commissions, on the passing of the bill ; against which a
petition was presented to the Commons, by Sir John Norris, and supported
by Sir Peter Warren. It was signed by three admirals and forty-seven
captains, not members of the House. The petitioners firmly remonstrated
against the measure, on the ground that the navy had been hitherto

well-governed, under the existing laws, and that the proposed regulations tended greatly to increase their hardships. A motion, that they should be heard by counsel, at the bar of the House, was warmly supported by Sir John Norris, admiral Vernon, lord Strange, and general Oglethorpe; but being opposed by Mr. Pelham, Mr. Pitt, Mr. Fox, and Mr. Lyttelton, it was negatived by 227 to 121.

During the discussion on the bill in the committee, the first clause that encountered any material objection, was that which imposed on all members of a court-martial, an oath not to disclose any of its proceedings, unless required by lawful authority. This clause was opposed, as an unconstitutional innovation, and several amendments were offered; but, after the words " act of parliament" had been substituted for " lawful authority," it was finally carried, by 111 against 67.

The clause subjecting naval officers to martial law, was still more vehemently opposed; and, although on each division in the committee, the influence of the ministers secured very considerable majorities, yet on the report, it was silently withdrawn, and after a series of discussions, which had lasted for upwards of a month, the bill, with that omission, was enacted.

Though liable to some objections, this law had a beneficial tendency; as it not only introduced a better discipline, but simplified the regulations established by various statutes, for the naval service.

We are not able to lay before the reader, any of the speeches of Mr. Pelham on this bill; but, from his observations in a subsequent debate, on lord Barrington's proposal, relative to a plan for obviating the necessity of impressment, we learn that he was favourable to the clause originally suggested, and only consented to its omission, in consequence of the alarm excited in the nation.

When the mutiny bill was brought forward for renewal, it was found to contain some provisions, analogous to the obnoxious innovations in the navy bill, and excited long and vehement discussions. The clauses relative to the oath of secresy in courts-martial, and to the revision of sentences passed by them, were after several divisions carried unanimously. The article subjecting military officers, on half-pay, to martial law, was strongly opposed as unconstitutional; and great efforts were made to excite an alarm against it, in the army. But, as proofs were adduced, that half-pay officers, though not in actual service, had originally been held subject to that law, ministers succeeded in carrying the clause, and the bill finally passed without a division.

In the House of Peers a debate arose on the general tendency of the bill. In all its bearings it had the especial support of the duke of New-castle, the lord Chancellor, the duke of Bedford, and lord Sandwich; and it was opposed by lords Westmoreland, Bathurst, and Bath. The judges, when consulted whether half-pay officers were then by law subject to the articles of war, were divided in opinion; but the provisions and purpose of the measure appeared so beneficial, that, in one instance, the small number of 15 divided against 72, and in another against 88. After a few trifling amend-ments, which were agreed to by the Commons, the bill received the royal assent.*

The minister took a prominent share in another discussion, relative to naval affairs, which involved a constitutional principle. Considerable difficulty having been experienced in manning the fleets during the war, a plan was devised for effecting this object, on any emergency, without having recourse to the unpopular usage of impressment. This plan received the approbation of Mr. Pelham, and was introduced on the 25th of April, 1749, by lord Barrington, who moved for leave to bring in a bill, to provide seamen for his Majesty's navy, without distressing trade. After expatiating on the necessity of maintaining such a body of mariners, as might be competent, both for the purposes of commerce, and the supply of the navy, he gave a brief exposition of his design, which was, to retain a force of twenty thousand seamen, at the disposal of government, by allotting an annual pension of ten pounds each, to three thousand, to be raised in addition to the seventeen thousand, then on the peace establishment. Conscious, however, of the delicacy of the subject, and of the difficulty of obtaining the immediate consent of the House, he declared that, although he had received the unanimous approbation of the Board of Admiralty, and was convinced of the reasonableness and utility of the plan, his intention was, not to propose passing the bill into a law, before the end of the session; but merely to introduce it, for the purpose of affording an opportunity to those without doors, as well as to those within, to deliberate, seriously upon its provisions, and then to leave it to the consideration of the House, whether it ought to be presently adopted, or

* Continuation of Rapin, vol. xx. pp. 387–390.

left until the ensuing session. He concluded by moving for leave to bring in the bill.

The plan was severely criticized by lord Egmont. After some sarcastic allusions to schemes and projects in general, he characterized this, as the result of a regular design to circumscribe public liberty, and augment the number of those, whom ministers desired to reduce to a state of slavery. He ridiculed the provisions, as futile and inefficient; declared that, in three years, these pensioned seamen would either enter into the merchant service, or become useless for that of the navy; and inveighed against the bill, as an expedient to enlarge the overgrown influence of the cabinet, by introducing corruption into the few remaining cities and boroughs, which were not already subject to the *congé d'élire* of a minister. He ironically suggested, as an amendment, that such pensioners, if retained, should be trained and regimented as soldiers, and employed on the military service, as substitutes for the same number of regular troops.

Mr. Pelham repelled these sarcasms, by observing, that the charge against ministers, of assuming false appearances with an intention to deceive, might, with equal justice, be levelled against those professed patriots, who affected to be zealous for the preservation of public liberty, with no other design than to distress the servants of the Crown, in order to force themselves into their places. After appealing to the sense of the House on the question, whether any government could be conducted without adequate powers, he proceeded to shew the necessity of adopting some method, for manning the navy, on the eve of a war, without inflicting that distress on trade, to which, in similar emergencies, it had hitherto been exposed. No project, he said, could be devised for this purpose, so effectual as that of constantly maintaining, at a certain allowance, a greater number of seamen than the navy required in time of peace. As to the objection, that in a few years the supernumeraries would become mere landsmen, it might be obviated, by a clause for making them take their turn in actual service, which would keep them inured to the sea, and preserve them from the *dreaded contagion* of ministerial influence.

"It has been urged," he continued, "that the bill is a scheme, for increasing the number of those intended to be made slaves. But who ever dreamed that the three thousand seamen, thus to be maintained, at a small yearly allowance, would be rendered subject to the mutiny-bill? And, while they are on land, they can be subject to none of the regulations of

the naval service, except that which renders them amenable to punishment
as deserters, should they abscond, and refuse to appear, when summoned
to enter on duty.

" I deny that attempts have recently been made, to introduce a military
government, and inforce a blind and slavish obedience among the officers
and men, both in the navy and army. The mutiny-bill, even in its original
form, differed little from those of past years ; and no addition to the navy
bill is now proposed, that can endanger the public liberty. In both those
bills, some little variations, tending to the maintenance of order and discipline, were indeed introduced ; but was any attempt made in either, to
subject any man in the nation, to martial law, except such as properly
belonged to the army and navy ? On the contrary, the provisions of each,
as originally framed, would have secured to each soldier and sailor, who
did his duty, equal protection of life, liberty, and property, with any of his
Majesty's subjects. Besides, every amendment, which the fears of gentlemen, rather than their reason, could suggest, was readily adopted ; and
perhaps these concessions will prove to have been made, to an extent
incompatible with the subordination requisite in the service. The insinuations against the present plan, appear therefore, more like rhetorical
flourishes, than solid arguments ; and, with respect to the proposal of training the seamen to military discipline, it surely cannot have been seriously
offered. Whenever war begins, those men must be sent to serve in the
navy; and, in case of an invasion, which implies actual war, we shall
have a force of infantry ready for action ; for cavalry, as every military
man must acknowledge, would be totally useless in a close country. Should
this motion pass, and a bill be consequently introduced, the noble lord may
offer any expedient he chuses ; but, if he can devise none better, it will be
difficult to obstruct its progress. At all events it seems proper, that the
motion should be agreed to."

Some pointed remarks of Mr. Walpole, on the clamorous opposition of
pretended patriots, again drew up lord Egmont. After retorting on his
assailant, with equal severity, he complained of the late dissolution of
parliament, as precipitate ; and of the changes in the mutiny bill, as
indicating a systematic design, for subjecting the nation, imperceptibly, to
military law. He then recapitulated his objections to the plan in agitation,
declaring that the number of registered seamen would be indefinitely
increased, and that the entire scheme would prove inefficient.

Mr. Henry Bathurst remarked on the irregularity of proposing a grant of money, without a specific object, or reference to a committee of supply; and as the force of this objection was admitted by Mr. Speaker Onslow, lord Barrington, conforming to the temper of the House, repeated his declaration, that the plan was not intended to be carried into effect, immediately, but merely to be digested for future consideration.

Observing the course which the debate was taking, Mr. Pelham made a judicious and temperate appeal to all parties. He urged that the House might the more readily receive the bill now proposed, because even if it should be passed, no money would be wanted for the service, during the current year, which would be more than half expired, before the reduction of seamen, to the number intended for the peace establishment, could be effected; and that the money required by this bill, could not be expected to exceed £.15,000, which sum might be raised, by savings from other disbursements for the navy, particularly from the half-pay. In reference to lord Egmont's animadversion on the dissolution of parliament, he observed, that complaints against the long duration of parliaments were not unusual; but that no one ever blamed the king, for dissolving a parliament, too soon, except the dissolution was intended to prevent the redress of some grievance, or an inquiry into some misconduct; and it could never be supposed, that his Majesty was actuated by such motives, in dissolving the last parliament. Adverting to the alterations in the articles of war, and other amendments of the laws, relating to the army and navy, which had been so severely censured, he remarked, that they were thought necessary by those who proposed them, and who being far from entertaining any design against the liberty of the subject, had abandoned most of them, *from deference to the opinion of such, as deemed them dangerous.* He declared, that nothing had been proposed, which could give any commander a greater influence over courts-martial, than he already enjoyed; that it had never been intended to subject any man to martial law, who did not belong to the army or navy; and that when differences arose, respecting the necessity of new statutes, or of amendments to existing laws, he recommended gentlemen to judge more charitably, than to cast infamous imputations on each other. Reasoning on this liberal principle, he concluded, that no gentleman could ascribe the present motion to any evil design.

After some farther objections from Mr. Henry Bathurst, on points of form, the debate was closed, by Sir John Barnard, with a proposal for the nomina-

tion of a committee, to digest the most practicable plan for the intended
law. This expedient, which was calculated to gratify all parties, being
approved, if not suggested, by Mr. Pelham, was unanimously agreed to.
The committee so appointed, met on the 3rd of May, and the result of their
deliberations was a resolution, that the engagement of supernumerary
seamen, by a proper allowance of pay, would be a means of more speedily
manning the navy, on any future occasion, without distressing trade.
Although this resolution was carried by 110 to 47, the plan itself was afterwards silently relinquished; the persons best acquainted with naval affairs being
of opinion, that it would not answer the end proposed. Mr. Pelham, however,
anxious to remove the evils of impressment, acquiesced in the sentiments of
those whom he considered as better judges than himself. Whatever were its
merits, the attempt to substitute a more constitutional mode of recruiting the
navy, than the severe, and often cruel resource of impressment, evinced a
laudable regard for the liberty of the subject.   But the efficiency and
practicability of such a reform are alike doubtful ; and in manning the navy,
the state is still obliged to sanction a practice, which necessity alone can
justify.*

We now advert to the financial measures of the session.   As the land
forces were reduced to eighteen thousand men, and the seamen to seventeen
thousand, the whole expenses of the army and navy, for the year 1749, did
not exceed £.2,374,333.   Small as this amount was, the opposition omitted
no opportunity of censuring such items, as appeared to them in any
degree exceptionable.   They objected specifically to the grant of £.285,873,
for the ordinary of the navy, and half-pay of naval officers; to that of £.16,000
for the pay of general and staff officers ; and to that of £.67,226 for reduced
officers of land forces and marines.   These sums, however, were voted,
without a division, in the committee ; on the report, by 171 against 93 ; and
on the third reading, by 147 against 70.†

A more unpopular task remained for the minister, in the arrangements
requisite for liquidating the unfunded debt, which had been accumulating
for nearly ten years.   It consisted, 1st. Of the navy, victualling and trans-
port debts ; 2ndly, Extraordinary expenses, for the land forces and ordnance ;

---

* Journals of the House of Commons, from April to May 1749, and Hansard's Parl. Hist.
vol. xiv. p. 538 to 563—Cont. of Rapin, vol. xxi. p. 395.

† Journals of the Commons, Jan. 14th-April 14th, 1748-9.

3rdly, Deficiencies in taxes and other charges, including £.10,000 to the city of Glasgow, amounting in the whole to £.5,685,567.*

So large an arrear alarmed the unreflecting part of the nation, who imagined that the burthens of war would have been instantly removed by peace, and did not take into consideration, expenses for which no provision could previously be made. The loyal and considerate, however, admitted that this accumulation of debt was unavoidable, in such a protracted contest; and in the debates concerning its liquidation, the opposition received so little encouragement, that they at last limited their objections to two articles, the payment of the £.100,000 claimed by the empress queen, and the petty grant of £.10,000 to the city of Glasgow, for losses sustained in the rebellion.

The grant to the city of Glasgow occasioned a discussion in the committee on the 21st of April, when it was supported by Mr. Pelham; and another on the report, in which he took no share. The arguments against the grant were grounded on the undue preference shewn to Glasgow, over other towns, which having equally suffered by the rebellion, might advance similar claims; and on the injustice of exacting from the public a compensation chargeable on the civil list, or on the forfeited estates in Scotland, if not indeed recoverable by assessment on the city itself. Mr. Pelham urged, that the loss and expense incurred by that loyal city, justly entitled it to the remuneration proposed. He observed, that the civil list had suffered severely by the rebellion; that the forfeited estates being sequestered, were not available; and that an assessment would increase, rather than diminish, the evil; and therefore the claim could not be satisfied, except by a parliamentary grant. He also remarked, that the peculiar circumstances of the case would prevent it from becoming a precedent for similar demands on the public. The grant passed without a division.†

The question relative to the arrear of the subsidy claimed by the empress queen involved the minister in great perplexity. He had, as we have seen, invariably opposed the pretensions of the House of Austria, during the war; and on this point in particular, had strongly manifested his disappro-

---

* This account is taken from the History of the Revenue, by Postlethwayte, who may be considered as more accurate than any other writer on finance. The Continuator of Rapin, however, makes the unfunded debt amount to £.6,952,915, but he erroneously includes many items provided for in the current service of the year, and consequently not belonging to the unfunded debt, and, among others, the £.100,000 claimed by the court of Vienna.

† This sum was not included in the current service of the year, but formed part of the extraordinary supply; see Table 2nd. p. 74.

bation even after the termination of hostilities.   But as the king and the
duke of Newcastle were induced, by the incessant expostulations and
reiterated demands of the court of Vienna,* to urge the discharge of this
arrear, for the sake of maintaining the alliance, Mr. Pelham, with the concurrence of the cabinet, at length consented to refer the claim to the decision
of parliament.   On the 6th of March, he accordingly presented a message
from the king, communicating a memorial from the court of Vienna, for the
payment of that arrear ; and submitted the reasons contained in it, without
any expression tending to bias the opinion of the House.   In this document,
which was more conciliatory than former memorials, the empress queen,
after expressing a lively sense of the aid of Great Britain, in the late troubles,
pressed for the payment of the £.100,000, as stipulated by the convention of
the Hague.   She argued, that the lists exhibited on her part, ought to be
admitted as equivalent to an official certificate of the number of her troops,
of which the full contingent had been raised, at a vast expense, and was on
its march, when the preliminaries were signed.   After representing, that
notwithstanding the liberal subsidies furnished during the war, her efforts
and cessions had disabled her from paying the troops so raised, she added;
that this sum was to be appropriated, for discharging the arrears of the
generals, officers, and soldiers, who had defended the Netherlands.   She
concluded by adducing the sacrifices she had already made, as an indication
of her constant readiness to concur with Great Britain, in maintaining the
peace restored by the treaty of Aix-la-Chapelle. †

Against this demand, the opposition argued, that as the empress queen
had never fulfilled the convention, by bringing her stipulated contingent into
the field, she had no right to the arrear; and that the sum claimed might be
better applied to national purposes.   The friends of the minister admitted
the force of this argument; but represented the expediency of the grant, in
consideration of the sacrifices made by her Imperial Majesty to maintain peace,
and of the good disposition which she had lately manifested towards
England.   They also stated, that as Austria was our natural ally, we ought
not to grudge so trifling a sum, when the affairs of Sweden threatened to
rekindle war among the northern powers, and when the dominions of the
empress queen might again be exposed to invasion; while she was endea-

* Letter from Mr. Keith to the duke of Newcastle, Jan. 1st. 1749. MS.
† Journals of the Commons, March 17th, 1748.

vouring, at a great expense, to prevent hostilities, in which Great Britain might be ultimately involved.

Mr. Walpole, the friend of Mr. Pelham, had intended to oppose the grant; but, on mature consideration he supported it, though, in an energetic speech, he strongly protested against the right on which it was claimed; and we can find no proof that the minister himself spoke, though he certainly voted in its favour. After being adopted in the committee, by 200 voices against 82, the grant was passed by 129 against 49.*

Without vindicating the inconsistency of Mr. Pelham in this instance, it may be observed, that his prejudices against the House of Austria were often carried too far; and that the policy of the duke of Newcastle was justifiable, in the existing posture of continental affairs, when it was necessary to conciliate the sovereign who held the Netherlands, and when too great a mistrust might, as it subsequently did throw that sovereign into the arms of France.

In a letter to Mr. Keith, dated March 3rd-14th, 1748-9, the noble secretary exultingly directs him to inform the court of Vienna, that the question had been carried, by his sole influence, against all the other members of the cabinet. He also desires him to inform baron Wassenaer, that the grant of this hundred thousand pounds had cost him more trouble than the definitive treaty of Aix-la-Chapelle.†

The arrangements of the minister for liquidating the unfunded debt, amounting to £.5,685,567, encountered no farther opposition. Of this sum £.3,072,472 was discharged by transferrable annuities, at four per cent, and £.1,000,000 by a loan at three per cent; the interest on both sums being made payable from the unappropriated monies of the sinking fund.

Thus, in one year, was liquidated the greater part of those expenses, for which no provision had been made by parliament; and it is observable that this was done, without a single additional tax : a fact which proves at the same time, the financial skill of the minister, and the reviving prosperity of the country. The remainder, £.1,613,095, was provided for by subsequent arrangements.

* Cont. of Rapin, vol. xxi. p. 381-2.—Hansard's Parl. Hist. vol. xiv. p. 491. This sum of £.100,000 does not appear in the tables of supply for this year, because it was part of a grant of £.400,000 in the previous session, [chap. xiii.], of which only £.300,000 had been paid; the remaining £.100,000 being retained, because the empress queen had not completed her contingents; but, in consequence of this decision, it was now issued.—Postlethwayte's Hist. of the Revenue.

† Letter from the Duke of Newcastle to Mr. Keith, Keith Papers, MS. Memoirs of lord Walpole, vol. ii. p. 267.

The regulations for the current service of the year, are exhibited in the following tables.

ORDINARY SUPPLY.

NAVY. — Maintenance of 17,000 seamen; Greenwich Hospital, including arrears of wages and other payments on the debt of the navy, £.1,000,000 ....£.1,179,878

ARMY.—Maintenance of 18,857 men, including ordnance, guards, garrisons, and half-pay, extraordinary expenses, pensions, &c...	1,163,892
Payment to the Elector of Bavaria	44,744
——————— Duke of Brunswick Wolfenbuttel	30,548
——————— Landgrave of Hesse	30,078
——————— Elector of Mentz.	8,620
For supporting the African trade.	10,000
Improving the Colony of Georgia	5,304
Settling Nova Scotia	40,000
Compensation for the loss of horned cattle......................	7,400
For building Westminster Bridge	12,000
For making good deficiencies, interest, &c....................	327,032
	2,859,496
Balance..................	734,194
	£.3,593,690

£.3,593,690

Extraordinary Supply for the year 1749.

UNDISCHARGED DEBT.		WAYS AND MEANS.	
Navy debt.....................£.4,779,708		By transferrable annuities, at four per cent, chargeable on the unappropriated monies of the sinking fund	3,072,472
Transport debt................	77,435		
Victualling debt	12,472	By loan at three per cent, the interest charged on the unappropriated monies of the sinking fund	1,000,000
Extraordinary expenses of the army and ordnance, compensation for services in the Colonies, and the East Indies	805,951		4,072,472
Grant to the city of Glasgow, for losses during the rebellion	10,000	Balance, or deficiency provided for, by subsequent arrangements....	1,613,094
	£.5,685,566		£.5,685,566

Among the beneficial regulations, adopted during this session, for the improvement of trade, may be distinguished, the acts for prohibiting the importation and wear of foreign embroidery, brocade, and other fabrics of gold, silver, or lace; for more effectually preventing frauds and abuses in the manufacture of woollen, linen, cotton, hemp, flax, iron, leather, and silk; for punishing illegal combinations among journeymen, and for securing the better payment of their wages.

A bill was also passed, for encouraging and extending the whale-fishery, and for naturalizing foreign Protestants, employed as seamen, in that branch of national industry. By another enactment, officers, mariners, and soldiers, who had been in service, since the accession of the king, were empowered to exercise any trade or handicraft, without the obligation of a regular apprenticeship.*

On the 13th of June, the king closed the session, by a speech from the throne. After acknowledging the desire, manifested by all the powers concerned in the late treaty, to preserve the peace, so happily established, his Majesty professed his own anxiety to promote the welfare of the country, and the general tranquillity of Europe, by steadily adhering to his engagements, and by cultivating the good-will of other states. He applauded the solicitude shewn by parliament, for the advancement of trade and navigation; expressed his thanks for the supplies voted by the Commons; and concluded with the usual exhortation, that the members of both Houses would employ their personal efforts, in promoting such principles and dispositions, among their fellow subjects, as might contribute to the stability of the government, and to the happiness of the people.

Stedfastly contemplating the removal of all the burthens imposed by the war, Mr. Pelham discountenanced every proposal, which was likely, in the remotest degree, to interfere with his views. The king of Poland, elector of Saxony, had applied for a loan of £.500,000; but notwithstanding the support of the king and the duke of Newcastle, this loan was withheld, in consequence of the judicious and manly representations of the minister. His reasons for that advice, are stated in a letter to Sir Charles Hanbury Williams, envoy at Dresden, and deserve to be submitted to the reader.

---

* Journals of Lords and Commons.

"*Feb.* 28*th*, 1748-9.

" I desired Mr. Fox to send you my opinion without delay, which I dare say, he did. Legge has, or will write to you upon the same subject; but I cannot forbear telling you, myself, why I think it both improper, and impracticable. —The first arises from the plan I have laid down, with regard to our affairs here. If we were to borrow money for our own services, it would naturally keep down the public stocks; all the spare money would be reserved, for a new subscription; and of consequence, our present public annuities would go to market at a disadvantageous price. The good effects of this scheme, are already seen; for the four per cents, are at par, and the three per cents at ninety-five. I resolved, therefore, to raise what we wanted, within the year, which has cost the land another four shillings in the pound. By this, you will easily perceive, that if a loan was opened, for half a million, to go abroad, all the good effects of this measure, would fall to the ground; under the inconvenience, which would arise, from so large a sum of money going out of the kingdom, when we have little enough to circulate our vast capital debt, with the other necessaries of government, which require money."*

* Hanbury Papers.

CHAPTER XXII.

1749—50.

Views of Mr. Pelham for the reduction of interest, and the diminution of the public burthens—Debts of the nation—Opening of Parliament—Opposition from the party of the Prince of Wales—Speech of Mr. Pelham, in which he supports the Address, vindicates the peace, and lays before Parliament, his plan for diminishing the interest of the national debt—Debates on the reduction of the naval establishment—Discussions on the Mutiny Bill—On the question concerning Dunkirk— Measures relative to commerce and domestic policy—Speech of the King, at the close of the Session—Embarrassment of Mr. Pelham, in consequence of the attempts of the duke of Newcastle to remove the duke of Bedford, from the office of Secretary of State—Departure of the King for the Continent—Domestic administration, during his absence—Colonization of Nova Scotia, and foundation of Halifax.

AS no transaction, worthy of particular notice, occurred, relative to foreign affairs, during this summer, and as the English cabinet were employed in prosecuting the negotiations for carrying into full effect, the articles of the late treaty, which will be recorded in the next Chapter, we shall advert to that measure of domestic policy, which reflects so much honour on the administration of Mr. Pelham, namely, the reduction of the interest on the national debt.

After the close of the war, at the latter end of the year 1748, the amount of the national debt, funded and unfunded, was £.78,293,313, and the annual amount of interest £.3,005,325.

Anxious to diminish this charge with all practicable expedition, Mr. Pelham, immediately after the signature of the Definitive Treaty, had commenced a rigorous reduction of both the military and naval establishments. Thirty-four thousand men, including the marines, were discharged from the navy, and twenty thousand from the army. These important retrenchments were effected, notwithstanding the wish of the king and the

Duke of Cumberland to retain a larger military force, in which several members of the cabinet manifested a disposition to concur. They are interesting proofs of the sincerity, with which this upright minister laboured to remedy the evils, arising from a protracted and unfortunate war.

The most obvious expedient for relieving the country, was the reduction of the interest on the public debt. This interest had been diminished, at two different periods, by means of the sinking fund. The first reduction took place in 1717, when the interest was lowered from six to five per cent average. The second in 1727, when it was again reduced from five to four per cent average. Mr. Pelham, however, contemplated a still farther reduction; and, for this object, the course of events had long prepared a way; as the accumulation of capital, since the accession of George II, had so far diminished the value of money, that at this time, the natural rate of interest was lowered to three per cent.*

Mr. Pelham was aware, that the measure would be opposed by the Bank, the South Sea Company, the East India Company, and the fund-holders in general. He also knew, that the unpopularity of such a project, had influenced Sir Robert Walpole,† in his opposition to the scheme of Sir John Barnard, in 1737, for a gradual abatement of interest to three per cent, commencing with the stock of the South Sea Company. At that juncture, however, a war was hourly expected, and a powerful opposition existed in the House of Commons; but now the nation was at peace, and the opposition comparatively small. Justly estimating these advantages, Mr. Pelham confidently prosecuted his design, availing himself of the advice of Sir John Barnard; ‡ and it will be found, that he accom-

* I am informed by Edward Roberts, esq., late clerk of the Pells, that at this period, his friend, the late Dr. Gisborne, purchased stock, in the three per cents, at the enormously high price of 109¼.

† See chap. xlvii. of the Memoirs of Sir Robert Walpole, which relates the motives of his conduct on this occasion.

‡ Glover assumes the merit of this reduction to himself, in conjunction with Sir John Barnard, and Mr. Brogden, adding, that Mr. Pelham adopted the measure with great reluctance. The falsehood of this assertion is proved, by the correspondence of Mr. Pelham, the duke of Newcastle, and the lord Chancellor, in 1748, from which it is evident, that Mr. Pelham himself, before the conclusion of the peace, had formed that plan of reduction, which he was now about to carry into execution.

Several other persons have also asserted, that Mr. Pelham adopted the scheme proposed by Sir John Barnard, in 1737, of which the conditions were, that the proprietors of South Sea

plished this important undertaking, with equal prudence, firmness, and integrity.

The session of parliament was opened on the 16th of November, 1749, by a speech from the throne. After congratulating both Houses on the restoration of peace, and on its beneficial results, to the commerce and credit of the country, the king acknowledged the favourable disposition of all the foreign powers, concerned in the late treaty.

To the Commons he expressed his desire for the grant of such supplies, as might be found necessary for the security and welfare of the nation; recommended the maintenance of the navy in its full strength; and urged them to improve the opportunity, for reducing the national debt, with a strict regard to public faith, and private interests. He concluded with an exhortation to unanimity and dispatch; and an assurance, that such laws as might be devised, for the advancement of trade, and the encouragement of industry, should receive his approbation; since the glory of his crown, and the stability of his government, were, in his estimation, inseparably united with the happiness and prosperity of his people.

In the House of Lords, an address was passed unanimously, conveying a hearty concurrence in the different topics of the speech.

In the Lower House, an address was moved by the Honourable Charles

---

stock, consenting to the reduction of their interest, from four to three per cent, should be entitled to hold irredeemably their capital, charged with that interest, during a term of fourteen years; and that his Majesty should be enabled to raise, at three per cent, sufficient money to redeem the debts of those who refused their consent to the reduction. Another condition was, that after the interest, payable to the holders of South Sea stock, should have been reduced to three per cent, the surplus of the sinking fund, arising from this reduction, should be applied to the redemption of the stocks belonging to the Company of the Bank of England, and to the East India Company, until the whole incumbrances of the nation were successively removed. Sir John Barnard inferred, that as soon as the redeemable debt should be diminished to an interest of three per cent per annum, parliament might annihilate one half of it, by repealing the taxes on coals, candles, soap, leather, and other commodities, essential to the comfort of the labouring classes. His scheme evidently implied the appropriation of the sinking fund, during forty-seven years, the utmost term of the short annuities.

To this appropriation Sir Robert Walpole and Mr. Pelham alike objected; and they both disdained to court popularity, by acceding to the inexpedient proposal of diminishing the taxes.— See Memoirs of Sir Robert Walpole, chaps. xvii and xlvii. Sinclair's History of the Public Revenue, chaps. iv. and v., p. 109. Speech of Sir John Barnard, in Chandler's Debates. Continuation of Rapin, vol. xx. p. 348. Smollet, vol. ii. p. 521; and Glover's Posthumous Memoirs, p. 38.

Townshend,* in terms corresponding with the speech, and laying particular stress on the great financial measure, now in contemplation.

The address, as well as the speech, appeared so temperate and unexceptionable, that the moderate part of the opposition were unwilling to injure their cause, by offering captious objections. Even among the prince's adherents, we find Mr. Dodington actuated by this feeling, which was doubtless participated by many others. Such, however, was the antipathy of the Prince to the ministry, and such the mortification he felt, in consequence of his recent failure, in the struggle for the high office of chancellor† of the University of Cambridge, that some of his more violent partisans were induced to oppose the address. The earl of Egmont, in particular, resumed his wonted strain of invective, notwithstanding the expostulations of Dodington.‡

He began by censuring the pliancy of parliaments to the will of ministers; and complained that, by this shameless servility, they had lost the confidence of the people. He then reiterated his objections to the peace, as indefinite and dishonourable; contended that no improvement had ensued in the trade or prosperity of the country; and argued, on the contrary, that both must materially suffer, from the competition of foreign powers, favoured by the unequal terms of the recent treaty. He concluded, by adverting to the constant drain of wealth, for paying the interest on that part of the public debt which was due to foreign creditors; and contended that, as the balance of trade, in our favour, was progressively declining, we should at length be deprived of our stock of the precious metals, and finally reduced to utter ruin.

These intemperate remarks afforded Mr. Pelham a favourable opportunity for vindicating his whole system of policy. He availed himself, also, of the complaint, relative to the drain of money by foreigners, to explain his plan for the reduction of interest, and to develop views of political economy, superior to the prejudices of the age.

In controverting the assertion, that the people had become disgusted with parliaments, he reminded the House, that two successive prime ministers,

* Son of Charles, third viscount Townshend.

† The duke of Somerset, the late chancellor, died, the beginning of February, 1748-9, and the duke of Newcastle, who was supported by the friends of the king, against the heir apparent, was chosen chancellor on the 6th of July, in the same year.

‡ Dodington's Diary.

had been recently dragged from behind the throne, by the declaration of parliament against them, which he considered a sufficient proof, that the nation in general had no reason to be dissatisfied with parliaments. He then noticed two classes of people, who despaired of experiencing any public benefit from parliament, the Jacobites, and the friends of a late minister, expelled from the closet, by the voice of the legislature; but he asserted, that the people in general manifested a high opinion of parliament; and that this body had never shewn more complaisance to ministers, or even to the king, than the constitution required. That opinion, he contended, would not be altered, if the motion for the address was adopted; because it involved no approbation of the Treaty of Aix-la-Chapelle, though every impartial man in the kingdom would have acquiesced in such a sentiment; for, considering our own dangers, and those of our allies, that treaty was rather better than could have been expected.

The noble lord, he contended, had denied that peace was re-established, because our dispute with Spain, on what should be deemed illicit trade with South America, had not been adjusted. He might as well have urged that denial, because the limits of the French and English territories in North America were not expressly defined. Such minor arrangements were always reserved for commissioners; yet no one ever imagined that peace was not fully restored, as soon as a general treaty was signed and ratified, by all the parties concerned. " I could adduce," he said, " examples from every treaty of peace, for above a century past; but I shall mention only the Treaties of Ryswick and Utrecht. By the Treaty of Ryswick, the affair of Hudson's Bay was left undecided, and commissioners were to be appointed on both sides, for adjusting the respective claims, and agreeing on the reciprocal restitutions. By that of Utrecht, many of us must remember, that the limits between Hudson's Bay and Canada, as well as other boundary lines, between the French and English colonies in that quarter, were reserved for adjustment by commissioners. Yet no one ever doubted that peace was completely re-established by both those treaties.

" But to leave pending the dispute concerning illicit trade, has been denounced by the noble lord, as an unpardonable omission; because parliament had resolved that no treaty with the crown of Spain should be admitted, until our exemption from the right of search, claimed by that power, should be acknowledged, as a preliminary. On this point I have to observe, that parliament is not competent to determine what terms of peace ought to be required; because this determination must depend on the chance of war, which the supreme power cannot foresee. For example, during the war in queen Anne's reign, parliament resolved, that no safe or honourable peace could be concluded, while any branch of the House of Bourbon remained in the possession of Spain; yet a peace was afterwards concluded, by which a Bourbon was established in possession of that monarchy; and parliament, notwithstanding its former resolution, approved that peace. Such negative resolutions were objectionable, because they arrogated a superhuman control over events.

"Supposing, however, that an article, exactly conformable with the declaration concerning right of search, had been inserted in the treaty, it would have been of no force, without explanatory clauses, in the settling of which, the merchants and ship-owners, on both sides, must be consulted. An affair so delicate and complicated, could not have been adjusted in a general treaty of peace, without depending in a great measure on the good faith of the parties concerned. If the Spanish guarda-costas occasionally exceed their duty, we must rely on the court of Spain for reparation; and, if that be refused, his Majesty, it is to be hoped, will always have the power, as he certainly has the will, to see justice done to his subjects.

"On the good disposition of foreign states, of which human sagacity cannot judge, except by external indications, no rational doubt can be entertained. The allies have evinced it, by readily agreeing in the stipulations; the French by evacuating all their conquests; and the Spaniards by quitting the duchy of Savoy, and the county of Nice. With respect to arrangements requiring time, both the French and Spaniards have shewn an inclination to complete them as soon as possible.

"Every thing, therefore, justifies the hope of future tranquillity. No dispute now exists between any of the powers of Europe, of sufficient consequence to occasion a rupture. The expressions in the address appear rather modest than over-sanguine; and, with respect to commerce and manufactures, I have evidence to warrant a very different inference, from that of the noble lord. Accounts from the north and west, shew that the high wages of labour arise, not from the high price of provisions, but from the great demand for our manufactures, and the great scarcity of hands. Indeed, it is hardly possible to suppose, that the provisions necessary for the poor can be dear in this country, which has produced such a superabundance of corn, that incredible quantities have been lately exported. From the

Custom-house books, it is proved, that in three months, above £.220,000 has been paid in bounties, on corn exported. Our other exports, since the peace, have been more considerable than during many preceding years. That the consumption, also, has increased, is evident, from the produce of the sinking fund. In the first three quarters of the past year, that fund yielded more than a million ; and the produce of the last quarter, though not yet ascertained, cannot be estimated at much less.

" From the consumption, as well as from the exports, therefore, it is to be concluded, that the people in general are in a prosperous state ; and I will say, that there is no country in the world, where a poor man may more easily, and certainly support himself, and even become rich, than in this : nor is there. any other country, where poor and rich can more securely enjoy the fruits of their industry, or accumulate a capital by their economy.

" As to our duties, excises, and customs, I am sorry that they are so heavy, and that we cannot give immediate ease to the people. I shall grant, that they might be detrimental to our commerce and manufactures, if we had for rival, any nation paying no taxes. But where shall we find such a rival ? not in Europe, I am sure. In France the taxes, though not apparently, are in reality heavy ; at least the public burthens fall more grievously, both on the poor and rich, especially that onerous imposition, by which soldiers are quartered on the people. The dearness of the wages of labour, in England, cannot proceed from our taxes ; it must arise from the greater abundance of the currency ; for the price of gold and silver, as well as of every other commodity, must depend on their abundance or scarcity. Therefore in a country where money is abundant, labour, as well as commodities, must bear a higher price, than in a country where money is scarce.

" Manufactures and commerce will always move by degrees, into those countries where labour is cheapest, if not obstructed by other causes. No human regulation can prevent such a transfer ; and therefore we must maintain, as long as we can, their free circulation from one part of our own dominions to another ; and the best method for effecting this, is to repeal every law, tending to establish a monopoly, in any quarter of the realm.

" If, however, our gain upon the general balance of our trade, be inadequate to supply the demand, for paying the interest to foreign fundholders, resident abroad, we shall certainly be drained of our currency, and consequently the prices of labour and of commodities in this country will be reduced. As the exhaustion of our circulating medium is an evil greatly to be dreaded, I hope the noble lord himself will acknowledge the wisdom of his Majesty, in recommending to us the reduction of the national debt; and as the rise of public credit, consequent on the peace, has afforded an opportunity for lessening the interest, payable to the public creditors, which is equivalent to the discharge of a portion of the principal, I think we ought to avail ourselves of it, without delay.

"We cannot execute this measure, without offering payment to those creditors, who will not accept the reduced interest; nor can we make any payment, without giving twelve months' notice. We ought therefore to proceed in it with the utmost dispatch. I shall now mention generally, the result of my thoughts on this important subject. We know that some of our public debts bear an interest of only three per cent, others of three and a half; but by far the greater part bear an interest of four per cent. The first two cannot, I think, admit of reduction at present; but as the three per cents sell at par, and the three and a half per cents are above par, I think we may venture to reduce all the four per cents to three and a half, after Christmas twelvemonth, provided we secure to them that interest, and guaranty their continuance for seven years; after which time they are to yield but three per cent, until redeemed by parliament.

"Therefore, I shall very soon move, that the whole House do resolve itself into a committee, to take into consideration that part of his Majesty's speech, which relates to the national debt. In that committee I shall propose a resolution, that such proprietors of our four per cents, as shall consent to accept an interest of three per cent, to commence from the 25th of December, 1757, shall, in lieu of their present interest, have an interest of four per cent, until the 25th of December 1750, and after that day, an interest of three and a half per cent, until the 25th of December 1757, without liability to redemption, before the arrival of that period.

"If some such resolution be agreed to, a bill will accordingly be prepared, which may be expected to pass before next Christmas, and from which the proprietors of our four per cents may learn, that the three branches of the legislature concur, in resolving to pay off such creditors as shall not accept the reduced interest. Thus, time will be allowed for consideration before the day appointed by the act, for the proprietors to make their election. If

we appear nearly unanimous in this resolution, I believe that so great
a proportion of the holders of four per cent stock, will accept the terms
offered, that it will be easy to raise money at three per cent, for paying off
those who refuse; and I hope no gentleman will oppose a measure so
obviously beneficial; since, if we do not embrace every opportunity
of diminishing the public debt, or the interest, the nation must at last
be undone. Those gentlemen who despond, will, I hope, keep their
fears to themselves, and refrain from propagating a groundless panic,
remembering the axiom of a late honest and sensible writer, no less celebrated
as a poet, that " fear, admitted into public counsels, betrays like treason."*

Sir John Hinde Cotton offered an ingenious reply, to that part of the
minister's speech, which related to the conclusion of peace, against the
express resolution of parliament, that no peace should be concluded with
Spain, unless the right of search was abandoned. He maintained, that the
resolution and address of parliament, in the reign of queen Anne, against
leaving any part of the Spanish dominions in the possession of a Bourbon
prince, was not implied in the original terms of the grand alliance; but was
produced by the instances of the Dutch, in the exultation of success. When
that address was passed, the emperor Joseph was alive, and his brother
Charles had been declared by us king of Spain, and was in possession of
a great part of that monarchy. But in 1711, Joseph died, and Charles
then became the sole representative of the House of Austria, succeeded him
in all his dominions, and was chosen emperor. This produced an entire
change in the system of affairs; and justified the ministers, who negotiated
the treaty of Utrecht, in departing from the resolution of parliament; otherwise such a power would have been vested in Charles, as must have destroyed
the balance of Europe. But the ministers who negotiated the treaty of Aix-
la-Chapelle, could plead no such necessity; since the right of search,
claimed by Spain, was a primary cause of the war; and to leave it subject
to future discussion, was to admit its validity. He concluded by asserting,
that Spain had no such right; and that a declaration to that effect, ought
to have been inserted in the treaty. He also reproached the ministers for
omitting to communicate the preliminaries of the peace to parliament, as had
been done by the negotiators of the treaty of Utrecht.

These remarks drew from Mr. Pelham a reply, which placed the question

---

* Hansard's Parl. Hist. vol. xiv. p. 586.

in a true point of view, " The honourable gentleman," he said, " had overlooked a circumstance, which must annihilate all the material differences he
had been labouring to establish, between the treaty of Utrecht and that of
Aix-la-Chapelle. Admitting our disputes on the right of search, to have
been the sole cause of our war with Spain, they could not be said to have in
any degree excited the war, which subsequently broke out on the continent,
and the termination of which was the chief design of the treaty of Aix-la-
Chapelle. Those disputes were doubtless of some consequence to this
nation ; and had it not been for the death of the emperor Charles the Sixth,
at such a critical time, we should probably have compelled Spain to settle them
to our satisfaction, in a more summary way, than had been proposed in the
address ; because, while Germany remained united under its head, France
would not have ventured openly to take part with Spain against us. But
when the union of the empire was dissolved, by the death of Charles the
Sixth, and the House of Austria was attacked by France and her allies, to
the imminent danger of our own independence, then our disputes with Spain
became of secondary importance, when compared with the war, in which we
were engaged upon the continent ; since if we succeeded in reuniting the
empire, and securing the balance of power, we might soon find means to
settle those disputes, either by negotiation, or by force of arms.

As the protection of the House of Austria against France, so essential to
the equilibrium of Europe, was the cause for which we engaged in the war
on the continent, consequently it was our chief concern in the negotiations,
at Aix-la-Chapelle, in which we had all the success, that could be expected,
after so disastrous a conflict. But to this, the resolution of parliament, not
to make peace with Spain, unless the right of search was abandoned, had no
manner of relation. And, if a change of circumstances furnished the
negotiators at Utrecht, with a pretext for departing from the declared sense
of parliament, respecting the Spanish monarchy, surely the negotiators at
Aix-la-Chapelle were equally authorised, by a change of circumstances, to
deviate from the rule laid down by parliament, for treating with Spain.
Will any one, indeed, say, that the strong confederacy, which was formed, and
the war, which soon afterwards broke out, against the queen of Hungary, was
not a most material alteration in the posture of affairs ; and such as might exculpate our ministers, for acting contrary to a previous resolution of parliament?

Thus we may see, that in every case, which will admit of a comparison,
the treaties of Utrecht and Aix-la-Chapelle are upon a perfect par, except in

that of the communication of the preliminaries to parliament, and its approbation of them, before they were ratified by the sovereign. In this respect,
the plenipotentiaries at Utrecht derived so little benefit from their precaution,
that subsequent ministers had good reason for disregarding such a precedent.
The very caution of those plenipotentiaries proved them to be conscious of
having acted inconsistently with the true interest of the nation; for no
minister, having a due regard for the prerogatives of the Crown, will ever
court the interference of parliament, in any treaty, before it be concluded.
Precedents are dangerous things; and if often repeated, may be used as
a pretext for depriving the Crown of the prerogative of making peace
and war, which would be a dangerous innovation on our constitution.

"I disclaim any intention to derogate from the right of parliament, to
inquire into any treaty after its conclusion; and to censure it, or even punish
its advisers and negotiators, if it should be found, that the honour, the
interests, or the rights of the nation have been wantonly, or unnecessarily
sacrificed. That right operates as a salutary check on the conduct of
ministers, obliging them for their own sakes, to maintain the honour and
interests of the country. But, if parliament should incroach upon the
prerogatives of the Crown, by assuming a right to make peace or war,
and to inquire into foreign transactions, under negotiation, our affairs
will be reduced to a dangerous predicament; for no foreign state will
negotiate with our ministers, or conclude any treaty with them, either
political or commercial.

"For the same reason, parliament cannot constitutionally assume a right,
to prescribe rules to the sovereign, for his conduct in any future negotiation
or treaty. Either House is competent to offer its advice; but if it be
coupled with the condition, that it must in no case be departed from,
without the consent of the House, it will cease to be advice, and become
a rule or law, which parliament has no right to prescribe to the sovereign,
and which no faithful minister would advise him to consider as such. Hence
there is no reason to suppose, that in not ordering the preliminaries of the
late treaty to be laid before parliament, his Majesty entertained the slightest
contempt or disregard of its authority; nor can there be any pretext for
calling into question the conduct of his Majesty, or of his ministers, in
this respect. But if there be, let any gentleman move, that those ministers
be called to a strict account, who negotiated or advised the late treaty of
peace, and I shall readily concur in the motion.

" Supposing, however, that after such inquiry, it had proved unjustifiable, what has their conduct to do with the present question ? Is there any thing in the words objected to, which can be construed into an approbation of the treaty, or anticipate the opinion of any gentleman in its favour ? And if there be, is not an address of this nature always regarded as an act of mere homage to the sovereign, leaving every gentleman at liberty to form his opinion, when affairs are particularly investigated ? This being the acknowledged rule of parliament, the very objections urged against the present address, include a strong argument in favour of its adoption ; because foreign states form their opinion of this nation, from the apparent concord between the king and his parliament. When that concord seems well-established, this nation can never fail to possess a commanding influence in the deliberations of all continental states ; but when symptoms of dis-agreement are manifested, the nation itself is despised, and the interposition of the sovereign disregarded.

" Suspicions of such disagreement must be excited by the rejection of any part of the proposed address. Supposing the peace not to be com-pletely re-established, would the desired result be hastened by the excite-ment of such suspicions ? Would it have a salutary influence on any of the contracting powers, who might hesitate to fulfil their engagements ? Would it revive commerce and public credit, if on the decline ? Would it not rather tempt our commercial rivals to encroach on our trade, in every part of the world ? Would it not discourage our own people, as well as foreigners, from vesting their money in the public funds ? And in such a case, would it be possible to reduce the interest on those funds ? Therefore, since every objection, when duly considered, presents strong reasons for concluding in favour of the address, I must hope that it will be unanimously approved."

The debate was closed by admiral Vernon, who censured the ministry for the levity with which they treated the war with Spain, and repeated the trite arguments against the conditions of the peace. He then laboured to prove the intention of the French, to attain a naval superiority, and alluded to a dispute, which had arisen with the officers of that crown, relative to the occupation and supposed appropriation of Tobago, and some of the smaller West-India islands, which had been declared neutral, in the treaty of peace.

Notwithstanding the warmth thus manifested by some of the speakers in opposition, they felt themselves so faintly supported by their adherents, that they did not venture to call for a division; and the address passed unanimously.

Duly impressed with the importance of his financial plan, Mr. Pelham suffered no avoidable delay to intervene, before he submitted it to the House. By this promptitude, he manifested the decision of a great minister; for, the proposal was at first so unpopular, or so little understood, that, even on the very day before the resolutions were brought forward, some of his friends endeavoured to dissuade him from his purpose; but their remonstrances were ineffectual. He persevered in his determination,* and the event fully justified his expectations. On the 28th of November, a motion was made for a committee of the whole House, to take that part of his Majesty's speech into consideration, which related to the national debt. The expediency of reducing the interest had been so clearly demonstrated by Mr. Pelham, that his plan was unanimously approved, and the following resolutions were sanctioned :—

1st. That such proprietors of those parts of the national debt, which bore an interest of four per cent, as should subscribe their names before February 28th, 1749-50, should be intitled to an interest, on their respective shares, of four per cent, until December 25th, 1750; of three and a half per cent, until December 25th, 1757; and of three per cent afterwards, subject to the established provisions, and clauses of redemption. No part of this stock was to be redeemable, until December, 1757, except such as was due to the East India Company.

2ndly. That the funds appropriated to the payment of the said interest, of four per cent, should still be applied to the same purposes; and that the surplus arising from the reduction, should be added to the sinking fund.

Lastly. Books were to be opened for receiving subscriptions, at the Exchequer, the Bank of England, and the South Sea House.

A bill having been prepared by Mr. Fane, the Lords Commissioners of the Treasury, and two secretaries of that Board, in conjunction with the Attorney and Solicitor General, and Sir John Barnard, pursuant to the said resolutions, it was presented to the Commons by Mr. Fane, as chairman of the committee, on the 4th of December; and having passed through both Houses, received the royal assent, on the 20th of the same month.

---

* Continuation of Rapin, vol. xxi. p. 410.

Notwithstanding the promptitude with which this plan was sanctioned by the legislature, some obstructions occurred in its execution. The three great corporations of the Bank, the India, and the South Sea Companies, by the resolutions of a majority of proprietors, were restrained from subscribing ; and some reluctance was also evinced by individuals, who either misunder-stood the nature of the bill, or considered that its operation would be retarded or frustrated, by the uncertain duration of peace.

To counteract these prejudices, several pamphlets were published, under the direction of Mr. Pelham, and by Sir John Barnard ;* in which the utility of the reduction, and the advantages which would accrue, even to the subscribers themselves, were so clearly pointed out, that the public opinion took a favourable turn. Accordingly, on the 28th of February, the appointed day, all the holders of Bank-stock, and the principal part of the South Sea and Bank Annuitants, and of the Annuitants on the Plate Act, had subscribed, to the amount of £.38,806,496, being almost three-fourths of the debt, bearing four per cent interest ; although the holders of East India and South Sea Stock refused to subscribe.

Encouraged by this success, Mr. Pelham proceeded in the execution of his scheme. The proper returns of the state of the subscription, having been laid before the Commons, were referred to a committee of the whole House, on the 19th of March. The speech delivered by Mr. Pelham, on that occasion, will develop his farther views, and at the same time display his justice towards the country, and liberality towards those creditors, who were now inclined to offer that acquiescence, which they had before withheld.

Adverting to the state of the subscription, he said, that the amount unsubscribed was not above eighteen or nineteen millions,† the proprietors

---

* The mutual confidence between Mr. Pelham and Sir John Barnard reflects equal honour on both : on Mr. Pelham, in cordially accepting the assistance of Sir John Barnard, whose dictates, however, he did not blindly follow ; and on Sir John Barnard, in affording that assistance, although his original plans were not adopted by Mr. Pelham. Among the principal pamphlets, published on this occasion, was one by Sir John Barnard, intitled " Considerations on the Proposal for reducing the Interest of the National Debt."

† This speech of Mr. Pelham is given from the London Magazine for July, 1750, which was copied by Debrett, in the second volume of his Debates, 1745 to 1750, and the sum remaining unsubscribed is therein erroneously said to be not above eight or nine millions ; but in the tables given by Postlethwayte and Sir John Sinclair, the deficiency is evidently near nineteen millions.

The funds bearing four per cent per annum amounted to £.57,703,475 ; the first subscription amounted to £. 38,806,496, consequently there remained unsubscribed £.18,896,989. As

of which had forfeited the advantages offered by parliament. "As, however, many of these may have been influenced by evil advisers, who design to distress the government, rather than serve their friends; and, as many are foreigners, who have had no time to consult their correspondents in England, it may be deemed cruel to take advantage of the lapse. Many of the proprietors, also, in the great companies, though willing to subscribe, as individuals, may have been restricted by the decision of the majority; yet the mode of voting by ballot renders it impossible to distinguish them. For these reasons, I recommend that a farther time be allowed to the companies, and the holders of unsubscribed annuities, to come in, and subscribe their several properties; but, to preserve the authority of parliament, I think it proper, that they should not obtain the advantageous terms granted to those who have already subscribed. I therefore propose, that the time should be extended to the 30th of May; but that such subscribers shall not be intitled to an interest of three and a half per cent, for a longer period than until December, 1755. .

This proposal being adopted, the Speaker was authorised on the 1st, to give notice, that the different annuities, not subscribed before the 30th of May, would be paid off at various periods, in the year 1751. The bill for this purpose, like the former, passed both Houses without opposition, and, at the close of the session, received the royal assent.[*]

On these terms, £.15,606,937 was subscribed on the 30th of May, and the remainder, which amounted only to £.3,290,041, was paid off in 1751.[†]

The following statement[‡] exhibits the amount of the different kinds of

---

another proof of the error in the London Magazine, we may adduce the amount of the second subscription, £.15,606,937. Now, had only eight or nine millions remained unsubscribed, when the time for the first subscription expired, there would have been, when the time, allowed for the second subscription should have expired, an excess of more than six millions, instead of a deficiency of £.3,290,041. The error undoubtedly arose from a mistake of the reporter, as it is impossible that Mr. Pelham could make a statement so contrary to fact. We have, therefore, ventured to correct the error in the speech.

•[*] The Journals of Parliament.—Hansard's Parl. Hist. vol. xiv. p. 619.—Periodical publications of the time.—Anderson's History of Commerce, vol. iii. p. 372.—Sinclair on the Revenue.—Chalmers's Estimate, p. 272.—Continuation of Rapin, vol. xxi. p. 409.—Debrett's Debates from 1745 to 1750, vol. ii. p. 347.—Postlethwayte's History of the Revenue, p. 230.

† See chap. xxvi. Table of Supply.

‡ See Sir John Sinclair's History of the Public Revenue, quarto edition, p. 113.

stock, subscribed at the successive periods, and the sums that were finally paid off, to those who did not accept the conditions.

	First Subscription.			Second Subscription, and posterior acts.			Unsubscribed.		
1. Bank Stock ....£.	8,486,800	0	0 £.			£.			
2. East India Stock				3,200,000	0	0			
3. South Sea Stock				3,662,784	8	6½			
4. South Sea Annuities	15,335,740	5	0	6,026,785	0	5	2,276,893	11	7
5. Bank Annuities	14,857,455	18	4	2,714,117	18	0	830,898	4	6
6. Annuities on the Plate Act..	126,500	0	0	3,250	0	0	182,250	0	0
First Subscription	38,806,496	3	4	15,606,937	6	11½	3,290,041	16	1
Second Subscription, &c. ..	15,606,937	6	11½						
	54,413,433	10	3½						
Unsubscribed............	3,290,041	16	1						
	£.57,703,475	6	4½						

Thus, then, the first subscribers received three and a half per cent, from December 25th, 1750, to December 25th, 1757, with a promise, that their principal should be irredeemable during the interval; the second subscribers were to receive the same interest, coupled with the same promise, until December, 1755, and the non-subscribers were paid off, by a loan, raised at three per cent.

The annual saving of interest, by this reduction, for seven years after 1750, was £.288,517; and after 1757, it amounted in the whole to £.577,034, which was to be applied for the same purpose as the Sinking-fund, namely, the discharge of the national debt.*

The unexpected success of this measure raised the public credit of England abroad, in a surprising degree, as may be inferred from a letter of count Bentinck to the duke of Newcastle, dated March 25th, 1750.†

"I write to-day to Mr. Pelham, to wish him joy on the great subscription, and do the same to you most sincerely. I am persuaded that this affair, having succeeded, contrary to all expectation abroad, and notwithstanding all that has been done to oppose it, will have a much greater effect, than any of us can yet foresee. It will certainly make France, who may boast of her resources, but who has none like England, more moderate in her language and behaviour to other powers, and more cautious in her under-

---

* London Magazine for 1749, vol. xix.   † Newcastle Papers.

takings, for fear of drawing, on her commerce and navigation, new losses, before the old ones are repaired, which will not be for a long time. And if France is resolved to be quiet herself, it is not even probable that those who depend on her, will stir, without being sure of her succour and assistance."

The plan for reducing the interest has ceased to excite curiosity; but we cannot dismiss it, without citing the praise bestowed on its accomplishment, by an historian in no degree partial to a Whig Administration.

" The capital measure which distinguished this session of parliament, was the reduction of the interest on the public funds, a scheme which was planned and executed by the minister. By this measure, the national burthen was comfortably lightened, and the Sinking-fund considerably increased, without producing the least perplexity or disturbance in the Commonwealth, a circumstance which could not fail to excite the admiration and envy of all Europe, the different nations of which could not apprehend, how it would be possible for the government, at the close of a long expensive war, which had so considerably drained the country, and augmented the enormous burthen of the national debt, to find money for paying off such of the public creditors, as might choose to receive their principal, rather than submit to a reduction of the interest."*

Having concluded, without interruption, our account of the parliamentary proceedings, relative to the reduction of the interest on the national debt, we shall now advert to the other debates in their regular order.

Mr. Pelham was so zealous for retrenchment in all branches of the national expenditure, that notwithstanding the recommendation in the royal speech, to retain the navy at its actual complement of seventeen thousand men, he fixed the number of seamen at ten thousand. This diminution of so popular a force, could not be expected to escape animadversion. When the supplies for the navy were moved by lord Barrington, on the 27th of November, Mr. Nugent declaimed against the imprudence of ministers, in proposing the reduction, accused them of abandoning the national bulwark, through preference of a standing army, the engine of absolute governments; and contended, that the land forces should be diminished, in order to maintain the navy in its full efficiency. He then descanted on the inadequacy of the reduction of interest, to produce a prompt alleviation of the public burthens, and to extinguish a sufficient proportion of the public debt. The conse-

* Smollett, vol. iii. p. 260, et seq.

quences which he anticipated, from the protracted operation of the taxes for this purpose, were the decline of trade, the decrease of population, and eventual but inevitable ruin.

He was followed by admiral Sir Peter Warren, who, after insisting on the necessity of a large naval establishment, contended that the peace had neither restrained the usurpations, nor abated the hostility of our former foes. He expatiated on the continued insults, offered by both Spain and France, and particularly adverted to the incroachments of the French in the West Indies and America. These he construed into unequivocal indications, that the peace would speedily be broken; and argued, that the only expedient for preventing that evil, was the maintenance of our maritime power.

Notwithstanding these objections, no amendment was offered to the motion, and it passed without a division.* It must, however, be admitted, that the economical views of Mr. Pelham were in some instances, carried to excess; and that he acted on this occasion, in direct opposition to the recommendation of the king, and to the opinion of his brother, who, in many of his letters, advises that no farther reduction should be made in the naval establishment.

While, however, Mr. Pelham thus diminished the number of seamen, he consented to retain the amount of land forces voted in the last session; but when the motion of supply for 18,859 men, was made in the committee, it was strenuously opposed, with the usual argument, grounded on the danger of standing armies in time of peace. A proposal for reducing the number to 15,000 was made by Mr. Prouse, seconded by lord Egmont, and supported by the other adherents of the Prince of Wales; but being opposed by Mr. Fox, lord Coke, Mr. Horace Walpole, sen., and Mr. Pelham, it was negatived by 211 votes against 81.†

The mutiny bill,‡ as usual, excited warm and protracted discussions, in which the principal speakers on both sides took an active share. The most obnoxious clauses were those relative to the revision of sentences passed by courts martial, to the oath of secrecy administered to the members of such tribunals, and to the punishment of non-commissioned officers.

The minister evinced great moderation, in regard to this annual bill, by allowing its rigours to be essentially mitigated. Among other alterations,

---

* Hansard's Parl. Hist. vol. xiv. p. 610.   † Journals of the Commons. Lond. Mag. p, 221.
‡ Rapin, vol. xxi. p. 411.

was a dispensation from the oath of secrecy, in particular cases, by which members of courts martial were enabled to give evidence, if legally required, in any court of judicature. And whereas, by the former bill, a general was empowered to order the revisal of any sentence, by a court martial, as often as he pleased, and consequently to retain the accused soldier in custody, under pretence of such revisal, after he had been fairly acquitted, it was now proposed by the Secretary at War, "That no sentence, given by any Court Martial, and signed by the President, shall be liable to be revised more than once." Lord Egmont moved, by way of amendment, to leave out the words, "more than once," in order to prevent any revisal whatever; but this amendment was negatived, and the original clause carried by 177 against 125.

Collaterally with their efforts to modify the Mutiny bill, the opposition suggested a change in the constitution of the army. An act for limiting to a fixed period, the service of non-commissioned officers and soldiers, was introduced on the 17th of January, by Mr. Thomas Pitt, and read a third time on the 16th of February. The servants of the Crown opposed it, on the ground, that it would at once increase the public expense, and by relaxing the discipline, diminish the efficiency of the military force. Being but faintly supported by the leaders of opposition, it was negatived by 154 votes against 92.

Scarcely any of the articles of peace had occasioned more perplexity in the negotiation, than that which related to Dunkirk.* Involving a question, which affected the honour of both Nations, it is no wonder that the original stipulation in the treaty of Utrecht should have been unsatisfactorily executed, or that France should now manifest a reluctance to fulfil the conditions, to which she had recently agreed. The advisers of the Prince of Wales were not ignorant of the feelings of ministers on this delicate point; and an early opportunity was taken, to bring it before the notice of parliament. On this, as on other topics, however, they were divided in sentiment; and, according to the avowal of Dodington,† they failed, through their eagerness

---

* It is necessary to remind the reader, that, by the treaty of Utrecht, all the fortifications of Dunkirk, both by land and sea, were to be destroyed. By the treaty of Aix-la-Chapelle, the port and harbour were to remain on the footing of former treaties, which implied their demolition; but the fortifications, which had been erected during the war, on the side of the land, were to continue in their actual condition.

† Dodington's Diary.

to bring forward a charge, without being able to adduce the evidence requisite for its support.

On the 5th of February, lord Egmont moved an address to his Majesty, for a perfect account of the present state of the port and harbour of Dunkirk, and for copies of all the memorials, letters, and other papers, which had passed between the courts of England and France, relative to the article on that subject, in the treaty of Aix-la-Chapelle.

He introduced this motion, by an exaggerated contrast of the terms of the treaty, as affecting the two countries ; inveighed contemptuously against the complaisance evinced by ministers in the fulfilment of them, notwith-standing the delays and chicanery of the French ; and expatiated on the indignity, to which they had exposed the nation, by giving hostages for the performance of conditions, to be executed antecedently to those, stipulated on the part of France. He then criticized the articles relating to Spain, reproached ministers for their imputed servility to that power ; and bitterly commented on the tardiness of the court of Madrid, in fulfilling the only stipulation to which they were bound, namely, the renewal of the term limited for the Asiento.

In conclusion, he animadverted on the indefinite construction of the article relative to Dunkirk. The expression, " according to antient treaties," he denounced as furnishing the French with a plea, to evade the engagement included in that of Utrecht; and insinuated, that such was obviously their intention, since they kept the port and harbour of Dunkirk, not only in the state to which they were restored before the rupture, but even in the improved condition, to which the works had been raised during the war.

In reply to this harangue, Mr. Pelham expressed his regret that the motion had not been made, for a general inquiry into the peace, instead of an address respecting a particular article. He did not deny the right of the House to institute such specific investigations ; but experience had convinced him, that parliamentary scrutiny into foreign transactions, had oftener proved prejudicial, than advantageous to the nation. Such interference, he de-clared, had driven us into a war with Spain, which might, and should have been prevented ; and by this motion, if adopted, we might be precipitated into a war with France, at a time, when every consideration ought to render us solicitous for peace.

" It is, I know," he said, " an ungracious duty, to inform a people, that they are not in a state to contend with their enemies ; but from this duty no minister ought to shrink, who perceives in them an eagerness for war, or for measures tending to war. If the minister of Sweden had given this salutary admonition to his countrymen, before their late hostilities with Russia, they would have avoided the disgrace of engaging in a contest, which they were utterly unable to maintain. For this reason, I think it my duty to declare my opinion, that in our present condition, when the people are all so burthened with taxes, mortgaged for the payment of debts, we are in no wise able singly to withstand the whole House of Bourbon; and that in the present circumstances of Europe, it would be impossible for us to form a continental confederacy, which would not be an incumbrance to us, rather than an advantage.

"In these circumstances, would it be wise in us to provoke a war? Would it not be wiser to dissemble our sense of wrong, to delay the inforcement of our just demands, and to wait with patience a convenient opportunity for redress? The present motion has a contrary tendency; for it implies a mistrust in the good faith of France. Will the manifestation of such a feeling be an inducement for the French to execute any of the conditions of the late treaty, not already fulfilled? And if they refuse, can we compel them, without commencing a new war? Should we not, then, examine our resources; and if we find them defective, pause before we determine upon hostile proceedings? At this unpropitious juncture, such ought to be our conduct, even supposing that France and Spain had refused, or unreasonably delayed, to comply with any of the terms of the late treaty. But neither of those powers has thus acted. The Court of France dispatched an order for restoring Madras, long before they heard of the restitution of Cape Breton. They have likewise directed the evacuation of Tobago, and have publicly announced their determination at Paris, to prevent settlers from going to that island. With respect to Dunkirk, if they have not already sent orders to demolish the works, erected during the war, for the defence of the harbour, the omission is of very little consequence; a few months sooner or later can make no difference; for in time of peace, the works can be of no prejudice to us, and of no advantage to the French, nor will it be proper at present, to insist on rendering the harbour useless, even for small trading vessels. With regard to the limits of Nova Scotia, a long discussion will be requisite, before commissaries who are already appointed. In reference to Spain, many disputes existed between that court and the South Sea Company, anterior to the commencement of the war; and all these must be adjusted, before

the Company can expect permission to send out the annual ship, stipulated
by the Asiento treaty, which is an affair of so much intricacy, as to excite no
surprise, that it has not yet been settled.   It is to be doubted, whether the
Company will find that trade still worth their notice, unless they can obtain
it for a much longer term than the four years ; because they must incur great
expense in establishing factories, at the several Spanish ports in America,
where the trade is to be carried on ; and in four years the profits of that trade
will not yield an equivalent for the expense.   Neither France nor Spain
has hitherto given any just cause of complaint, by the non-performance of
the stipulations in our favour ; and they have so punctually performed all
their engagements towards our allies, that we may expect to be treated with
the same good faith, as soon as the nature of things will allow, if we can
avoid manifesting unreasonable suspicions.

"The objections incidentally made to the treaty itself, I consider as
irrelevant to the question, and improper on any occasion, unless followed by
a motion for inquiry into that treaty, and the conduct of its advisers.   But,
as a digression of that kind has been made, I hope for the indulgence of the
House, in briefly answering those objections.   Our acceptance of the treaty
was rendered obligatory, by our own disasters, and by the imminent danger
of our allies, the Dutch.   There are other inducements, of a nature not proper
to be divulged ; but one may be mentioned ; the perilous state of our public
credit.   The tides of public or private credit, are not equal, like the tides
of the ocean, and are directly contrary to those which we observe in
this river ; they are slow in their flood, but extremely rapid in their
ebb.   Just before the conclusion of peace, it will be remembered, our
public credit had taken a turn.   The ebb had begun, and how far it might
have receded, no one can calculate.   It might have left us without ability
to send an army into the field, or a squadron to sea; and in such a dangerous
situation, would it have been prudent for us to insist on high terms of
peace ?

"Let us consider, that the large and extensive conquests made by France
and Spain, were all, except Madras, on the continent of Europe ; whereas
neither we nor our allies had made any conquests in America, except Cape
Breton, which is of no value to us, but of so great importance to France,
that in order to recover it, she offered to restore all her conquests in the
Austrian Netherlands, and in Dutch Flanders and Brabant.   Supposing that
we had laid aside all consideration for our allies, can it be denied, that the

interest of this nation, was more concerned in restoring Cape Breton to France, than in leaving her mistress of Hainault, Flanders, Brabant, and Namur, with the whole range of coast from Zealand to the extremity of Bretagne, and an accession of territory, that would have supplied her with a great number of seamen and a large revenue ?

"The restitution of Cape Breton, on this consideration, was essential to the interests of England, without any regard to her allies, or to the balance of Europe. But as France was forthwith to restore her conquests in the Netherlands, without waiting for our restitution of Cape Breton, it was necessary that she should insist on hostages for that restitution ; and as we were thus to be the last in performance, it was reasonable for us to comply with her demand. We had no occasion to require hostages ; because the restitution of the Netherlands was to be immediately performed, and Madras was of so little moment, that we might safely depend for its recovery, on a solemn engagement, especially as we had then a superior force in the East Indies.

" Thus, the articles concerning Cape Breton, and the hostages to France, against which so much popular clamour has been raised, will be found perfectly justified, by the necessity of the case, and strictly consistent with prudence, and a regard to the true interests of the nation. Our present inability, therefore, to dispute with France, must be ascribed to the fate of the last war, and not to the treaty which, in terminating it, rescued us from the danger of being reduced to a lower degree of incapacity, and prevented France from acquiring absolute control over all the seventeen provinces of the Netherlands.

" To provoke a war with France, by insisting peremptorily on all that we have a right to demand, would be censurable as an act of imprudence ; not from the actual power of that monarchy, but from the close connection now subsisting between the several branches of the House of Bourbon, and from the present divided state of Germany. These divisions may be healed ; those connections will certainly cease, in the very next generation ; and then we shall have a much better opportunity than at present, for insisting on the redress of all our grievances.

" If, however, the existing circumstances of Europe be favourable to France, I must say that the noble lord has furnished her with a pretext for taking advantage of them, by his present motion, and his comment on the article relative to Dunkirk. The brevity of that article has been strangely represented as an objection; for, surely, if the sense be full and plain, the more concise an article is, the less liable it is to misconstruction. And as to the term 'antient,' it must certainly comprehend all former treaties, in contra-distinction to that recently concluded, which moreover, makes express mention of that of Utrecht."

He then vindicated the omission of any stipulation against the right of search, claimed by Spain, and concluded with an able and perspicuous exposition of the nature and principle of this right, as applicable to the general intercourse of nations. " In visiting ships at sea," he said, " the common rule is, for the men-of-war, guard-ships, or privateers, to remain out of cannon-shot, and to send a boat to the merchant-ship, with only two or three men, to go on board, and examine her passports and certificates, to which they are to give entire credit, without attempting to search the ship, to detain, or turn her from her course, unless in time of war it shall appear, that she is bound to a port of the enemy, and has contraband goods on board.

" But if this rule were at all times strictly adhered to, notwithstanding the strongest suspicion of fraud, it would be impossible for the Spaniards to prevent an illicit trade with their American possessions; and it would be equally impossible for us to restrain the contraband export of our own wool. Nay, it would often be impossible to discover a pirate ship at sea, or even to ascertain whether a ship, seen at sea, belonged to an enemy, or was carrying contraband goods to an enemy. Therefore in all such cases, a certain discretion must be exercised by naval commanders, who, if they transgress this rule, transgress it at their peril; and, if no just cause of suspicion exist, nor any fraud be discovered, they ought to incur severe punishment, besides compensating the damage.

" For the regulation of maritime search, in time of war, many precedents exist, both in treaties and in practice; but for conducting a similar search, in time of peace, we have no precedent whatever; and, any new regulation on this point, must demand, from both parties, the most deliberate caution. The Spaniards should be careful not to render the prevention of illicit trade impracticable; and we should as vigilantly guard against the admission of any thing, that might in time tend to encroach upon, or interrupt the freedom of our own commerce and navigation, in the American seas. These reasons ought to diminish the surprise of those, who affect to wonder why the dispute is not yet settled.

"I think the only objection now remaining, is that relating to the South

Sea Company's annual ship. The noble lord has observed, that instead of four years, the term should have been ten or eleven ; and that by not insist-ing on such an extension, we tacitly admitted, that the interruptions encountered by us, were justly merited. If any such admission was ever made, it was not by the late treaty, but by those of Madrid in 1721, and Seville in 1729 ; for, as no prolongation of the Asiento contract was then stipulated, in compensation for the interruptions experienced by us, the point was certainly understood to be relinquished, and could not be resumed in any subsequent negotiation. All that we could desire, therefore, in the late treaty, was the revival of the contract for four years ; and as we obtained this, it must be allowed, that notwithstanding the misfortunes of the late war, we gained more from Spain, by the treaty of Aix-la-Chapelle, than by those of 1721 and of 1729. And if, in not procuring a prolongation of that contract, in either of the last mentioned treaties, we admitted on both those occasions, that we had been in the wrong towards Spain, the grant of the prolongation now, is an admission on the part of Spain, that in the disputes which occasioned the late war, she had been in the wrong towards us ; and this concession affords a sort of earnest of her future good behaviour.

"No just cause of complaint being discoverable, concerning either omissions or commissions, in negotiating the late treaty, or concerning any unnecessary delay, in the execution of its articles, I consider the proposed address to be useless, and hope that it will be either withdrawn or rejected."

The debate was ably maintained by other speakers. Lord Strange, in particular, replied to the minister in a speech, containing the best argument, that could be offered, in favour of the motion. He began by observing, that as the motion had been made and seconded, the question before the House was, not whether it would be wise or prudent to make such a motion, but whether it would be wise or prudent to dismiss it by a negative. After asserting, that such a negative would be most derogatory to the honour of the nation, and to the dignity of the House, he continued, "It is with nations as with individuals ; misfortune or debility affords no reason for the tame endurance of insult. A weak state may be affronted by a potent enemy ; but if it manifests a proper resentment, and resists manfully, some of its neighbours will be encouraged to come to its aid. Without proving this truth, by the example of the Romans, in the second Punic war,

we may cite the recent instance of the queen of Hungary. When that
undaunted princess found herself obliged to retire from Vienna, and appeal
to the fidelity of her brave subjects, the Hungarians, she addressed them
with these memorable words : ' Abandoned by my friends, persecuted by
my enemies, attacked by my nearest relations, the only resource I have
left, is to stay in this kingdom, and commit my person, my children,
my sceptre, and crown, to the care of my faithful subjects.'* At that
time, I say, could any one have anticipated that she would withstand the
multitude of her enemies? Yet she resolved never to submit to the disgraceful terms imposed upon her; and Providence, it seems, approved her
resolution ; for, contrary to all human calculation, a few months not only
restored her to her own capital, but put her in possession of the capital of
her enemies. The ultimate consequence is, that her family has recovered
the imperial diadem, without any great loss of power or dominion. Had
she practised the rules of prudence, inculcated by the right honourable
gentleman, another family would have been established on the imperial
throne, whose protection she must have solicited, to preserve the remnant
of her dominions from the Turks.

   " This memorable example shews, that a nation ought to hold nothing so
dear as its character ; and should never, in any extremity, submit to
insults, tending to create a mean opinion of its courage, resolution, or
power. But if we put a negative on this motion, what will be the
consequence ? All the world knows, and the French themselves confess,
that we have a right to see the port of Dunkirk absolutely demolished.
But is it not equally notorious, that since the peace, not one step has been
taken to demolish even the works erected during the late war? Will not,
then, our rejection of this motion, induce our neighbours to think, that we
have not courage to vindicate our right? Will not the French consider it
as a surrender of the right, or at least as a demonstration of the indifference
prevailing in the British parliament, relative to the demolition of the port
of Dunkirk? And after such a demonstration, will the French court listen
to any instance from his Majesty, on that point ? They know perfectly well,
that his Majesty will never proceed to declare war, on the refusal of a
demand, which parliament had disregarded as of no moment. The
question, then, is, whether it be the opinion of this House, that the

---

* See an account of this animated appeal in the History of the House of Austria, chap. xxii.

fortifications of the port of Dunkirk ought to be demolished ; and I shall be sorry to see that question decided in the negative.

"But it has been observed, that the delay of a few months, in executing this condition, will be of no consequence, because in time of peace, the works can neither be prejudicial to us, nor advantageous to the French. Will they demolish them, after the commencement of a new war? And if they will not, we are deeply interested in having the works demolished as soon as possible ; for it is difficult to say how soon hostilities may be renewed ; and the French will take that opportunity to add new works, and perhaps to make the port and harbour of Dunkirk as complete and as defensible, as they were at the peace of Utrecht.

"It has been urged, also, that by agreeing to this motion, we shall manifest a mistrust towards France, and a disposition to find objections to the late treaty. Can our desire to have the terms fulfilled, be imputed to such a disposition? Is it not, on the contrary, a proof of our determination to abide by the treaty? And if we manifest a suspicion of the French, they have deserved it, by delaying to execute what might and should have been performed, twelve months ago. Surely we are not, by the management of the right honourable gentleman, and of his former and present friends, reduced to a condition so wretched, that we dare not even ask for what is due to us. If we are, we have abundant reason to reject the motion. But would it be consistent with the dignity of the House, to admit the validity of such a reason, without inquiring into the means by which the country had been so miserably degraded? Could such an inquiry be detrimental to the nation, unless some amongst us had been guilty of something worse than misconduct? Therefore, if by putting a negative on this motion, we expose our country to contempt, I hope that, in vindication of our own honour and character, we shall institute an inquiry into the present state of the nation, and the conduct and conclusion of the late war."

Mr. Pitt spoke twice in this debate, with great spirit and animation. In reply to lord Strange, he censured the motion as wicked, because it was intended to inflame the minds of the people ; and as absurd, because no nation ought to provoke a war, when it was conscious of being the weaker party : "nor," added he, in allusion to a figure employed by lord Strange, "would any man in his senses, provoke another to combat, when he is but just recovered from a violent fever, and his adversary is in full strength and vigour."

His second speech was in answer to one from lord Egmont, who not only insisted on the necessity of demolishing the fortifications of Dunkirk, but censured Mr. Pitt's application of the word " wicked" to the motion, as malignant and $_{o}ppr^{o}bri^{o}us$; and derided him for supporting measures, which he had formerly opposed, with such violence and acrimony.

The temperate language employed by Mr. Pitt, not only did great credit to his candour and feeling, but produced a decisive effect, both on the House, and on the public in general.

" I must confess," he observed, " that upon some former occasions, I have been hurried by the heat of youth, and the warmth of debate, into expressions, which, upon cool recollection, I have deeply regretted ; and I believe the same thing has happened to many gentlemen in this House, and especially to the noble lord. In designating the motion as *wicked*, I qualified the term, to guard it against misconstruction ; for I must observe, that the only point in debate has been overlooked by the noble lord, and by all who have spoken on that side of the question. Our right to have the port and harbour of Dunkirk destroyed, is not denied or doubted. On the other hand, it has been universally admitted, that if it were restored to its former state of perfection, it would, in the event of war, be highly detrimental to this nation. But no one can assert, that the French are attempting that restoration ; nor will they, I believe, make the attempt while peace continues ; and, after war is declared, our maritime force will frustrate such an undertaking.

" The question before us, therefore, does not concern our right to insist on the demolition ; neither does it embrace the consequences to be apprehended, from the restoration of the works. The only point in dispute is, whether, in existing circumstances, it would be wise in us to risk a war with France, by insisting on a right, which we may vindicate when we please, without any detriment from delay, so long as peace continues between the two nations. If the French were now beginning to repair the port, then indeed the vindication of our right would become daily more difficult, and delay would be prejudicial ; but, as there is no complaint of that kind, we may safely and prudently wait a more favourable conjuncture ; for no conjuncture can be more unfavourable than the present.

" Nations, as well as individuals, must sometimes forbear from the rigorous exaction of what is due to them. Prudence may require them to tolerate a delay, or even a refusal of justice, especially when their right can no way suffer by such acquiescence; and that this is our case at present, there are abundant proofs. Until a more favourable opportunity occurs, this affair should be left in the hands of ministers, whose acquiescence in the non-fulfilment of this article, would be merely a ministerial acquiescence, in no degree affecting the credit or the character of the nation. But should parliament once interpose, and afterwards acquiesce, it would be a national acquiescence, which would compromise our right; and we could never expect the article relating to Dunkirk to be fulfilled, without entering into a new war. I think that no gentleman, after due consideration of the question, whether it would be prudent in us to declare war against France, in case she should not, on the first demand, instantly begin to demolish the port of Dunkirk, can agree to this motion." With this speech the debate was closed, and the motion was rejected by 242 against 115.[*]

It has been remarked by a firm friend[†] of Mr. Pelham, that, in the House of Commons, his language was often timid and desponding; and that the candour and openness of his temper, led him occasionally to depreciate the resources of the country, and to magnify the strength of the rival power. On no occasion was this remark more strongly verified, than in this debate; for, though his general arguments against any intemperate provocation of France, while the two states seemed to be in perfect amity, were sound and unanswerable, yet it cannot be denied that he made too many concessions in favour of France, and said, what it did not become a British minister to admit, that England was unable to cope single-handed with the House of Bourbon.

Mr. Pelham was too warm an advocate for our maritime and commercial interests, not to regret, that in the last session, the motion relative to the encouragement of the British White Herring and Cod Fishery had been rejected by the Peers. He was, therefore, induced to bring it forward at an early period, by the general voice of the nation; and the subject was considered in a committee of the whole House. Petitions from Lowestoffe and Southwold, against the encroachments of the Dutch, on their respective fisheries, were immediately presented, but were prudently passed over, as tending to excite unnecessarily the spirit of national jealousy. On the 14th of February, the deliberations of the committee were embodied in a series

[*] Journals. Hansard's Parliamentary History, vol. xiv. p. 723.
[†] Mr. Yorke, in his Parliamentary Journal.

of resolutions, of which the principal were, the recommendation of a bounty of thirty shillings per ton, to all vessels from twenty to eighty tons burthen, employed in the White Herring and Cod Fisheries ; and a proposal for the formation of an open Company, to be called the Free British Fishery, with power to raise a capital of £.500,000. For the farther encouragement of such an undertaking, an interest of three and a half per cent was to be granted out of the Customs, for fourteen years, on such part of the Company's capital, as should be áctually employed in the said fisheries. On these principles, a bill was introduced on the 26th of February, and, after various amendments, was sent up to the Peers. Here it encountered considerable opposition ; but was finally passed, without essential alteration, and received the royal assent, at the close of the session.

Many beneficial acts were passed, for the improvement of trade and manufactures. Among them may be specified, those for reducing the duties on raw silk, imported from China ; for encouraging the growth and culture of raw silk, in the American colonies ; and for facilitating its importation from Persia, through Russia, as tending to improve the silk manufacture in the British dominions. A bill was also sanctioned to promote the importation of pig and bar iron from America ; and to prevent the manufacture of that article into locks, bars, and various other utensils, in order to favour the manufactures of the mother country. The same consideration suggested a law for prohibiting the abduction of artificers into foreign states, and the export of implements, used in the British woollen and silk manufactures.*

Collaterally with these acts, were introduced various bills for the improvement of the metropolis, for the formation of turnpike roads, and for other objects, connected with the administration of justice, and with domestic policy.

The supplies, arranged by the minister, previously to the completion of his plan for the reduction of the interest, are exhibited in the following table.†

* Journals of Parliament.—Anderson's History of Commerce, vol. iii.—Gent. Mag. vol. xx.—London Magazine, for 1750.

† From Postlethwayte's History of the Public Revenue.

| SUPPLY. | | WAYS AND MEANS. |

NAVY.—Maintenance of 10,000 seamen, building and repairing ships, ordinary, half-pay, and Greenwich Hospital..........£.1,021,521			....................£.1,430,510	
ARMY.—Maintenance of 18,857 men, ordnance, extraordinary expenses in the year 1749, Chelsea Hospital, half-pay and pensions, and garrisons in Gibraltar, Minorca, and the Plantations ..	1,324,667		.... ———	594,115 900,000 17,553 29,856 71,116
Subsidy to the Elector of Bavaria .	22,372			
——————— Duke of Brunswick Wolfenbuttel	29,993			
————— Elector of Mentz	8,620			
For the Forts on the Coast of Africa	10,000			
For improving the Colony of Georgia	3,304			
For defraying the charges of transporting the new colonists to Nova Scotia, and other expenses connected with that settlement	76,225			
For Westminster Bridge	8,000			
For the loss of horned cattle	13,370			
For making good deficiencies, payment of interest, &c.	320,386			
	2,838,458			
Balance..........	204,692			
	£.3,043,150		£.3,043,150	

This important session was closed on the 12th of April, 1750. In the speech from the throne, the king expressed his thanks to both Houses, for their zeal in the dispatch of public business ; and for the laws, which had resulted from their deliberations relative to the improvement of public credit, the promotion of trade, and the encouragement of national industry. He, at the same time, alluded to the sincere disposition manifested by foreign powers, to maintain the general tranquillity ; and testified an anxious desire that his own dominions, as well as Europe, should long continue to enjoy the blessings of peace.

To the Commons he addressed his acknowledgments for the supplies, and for their patriotism, in taking so early an opportunity to reduce the interest of the national debt, without the least infraction of public faith. He concluded with congratulating them, on the encouraging proof of general confidence, which the success of this plan afforded; and on the strength and reputation, which it was calculated to give to the government, both at home and abroad.

In addition to the difficulties which Mr. Pelham experienced in conducting the measures of government, in the House of Commons, against a violent opposition, supported by the influence of the Prince of Wales, he had to encounter farther obstructions, from the political rivalry subsisting between his brother and the duke of Bedford, and the endless bickerings, which arose from their discordant tempers.

John, duke of Bedford, was born in 1710, and succeeded to his paternal honours and estates in 1732, on the death of his elder brother, Wriothesley, without issue. He distinguished himself in the Opposition, as an eminent debater; but, on the formation of the Broad Bottom administration, he coalesced with the Pelhams, and accepted the post of first lord of the Admiralty. His tried integrity, energetic eloquence, and parliamentary influence, rendered him a valuable auxiliary; for he was no less frank and zealous in his friendship, than open and decided in his enmity. From his elevated rank and affluent fortune, as well as from the course of his education, he was imperious, irritable, and tenacious of his opinions, though liable to be swayed by flattery and deference. Mr. Fox, who knew him well, describes him as " the most ungovernable governed man in the world." Although he had now reached his thirty-eighth year, he still retained his youthful fondness for cricket matches, and other rural amusements, and was greatly attached to theatrical representations. These propensities, together with his social habits, rendered him impatient of restraint, and negligent in the discharge of his official duties.

As he accepted the office of Secretary of State, contrary to the views and wishes of the duke of Newcastle, it could not be expected that the two noble colleagues would long continue to act with perfect cordiality. Indeed, the independent spirit and impatience of control, which marked the character of the duke of Bedford, soon produced such discordance, that the duke of Newcastle made some ineffectual attempts to liberate himself from so intractable an associate in office.

At this period, the duke of Bedford was principally influenced by the earl of Sandwich, who, to great classical acquirements, and qualifications for business, united talents for wit and humour, a frank and lively temper, and an insinuating address. He gladly cultivated an intimacy with the duke of Bedford, which was founded on congenial tastes and pursuits ; and, as he was confined in his circumstances, he omitted no effort to preserve the affection of his noble friend, to whose patronage he looked for the means of acquiring the power and emoluments of office.

Lord Sandwich was born in 1718, and took his seat, as a peer, in 1741, in the 24th year of his age. He soon distinguished himself as an able orator, in the ranks of opposition, and rendered himself obnoxious to the king, by his sarcastic invectives against Hanoverian influence.

In 1744, lord Sandwich, under the auspices of the duke of Bedford, obtained the second place at the Board of Admiralty. In this situation he ingratiated himself, also, with the duke of Newcastle, through whose favour he was sent to conduct the secret negotiation with France, after the battle of Lauffeld, and to arrange with M. Puisieulx, the preliminaries of peace, under the duke of Cumberland. This delicate trust he discharged so satisfactorily, that he was appointed sole negotiator for England, in the conferences at Breda ; and was soon afterwards constituted embassador at the Hague. Indeed, the duke of Newcastle entertained so high an opinion of his talents and docility, that he was desirous to place him, as we have already observed, in the office of Secretary of State, when it was vacated by lord Chesterfield. On the acceptance of the Seals by the duke of Bedford, lord Sandwich was promoted to the head of the Admiralty,* and appointed plenipotentiary at the Congress of Aix-la-Chapelle.

In the course of that negotiation, lord Sandwich deeply offended the duke of Newcastle, by deviating from his instructions ; and, on his return to England, he increased the alienation, by manifesting undiminished attachment to his patron, the duke of Bedford.

Mr. Pelham had the mortification to find, that this disagreement contributed to deprive his brother of that favour and support, which he had hitherto received from the Duke of Cumberland and the Princess Amelia, whose influence with the sovereign gave great weight to the administration.

In the course of the negotiations for the peace of Aix-la-Chapelle, lord Sandwich had so far acquired the favour of the Duke of Cumberland, that

* See Chapter xii.

his Royal Highness exerted himself to effect a reconciliation between his lordship and the duke of Newcastle; but the latter abruptly rejected the mediation of the Royal Duke, to whose proposals of accommodation he did not even return an answer. It might naturally be expected, that this conduct would excite the high displeasure of the Duke, who, on his return to England, supported both lord Sandwich and the duke of Bedford, against the duke of Newcastle. The Princess Amelia, also, who had been offended with the duke of Newcastle, for discontinuing his wonted attentions. and for paying court to lady Yarmouth, fully participated in the feelings of her brother. The consequence of such a change of sentiment was evinced by the conduct of all parties. The Princess and the Duke concurred in accusing the duke of Newcastle of coolness and disrespect; while his Grace, on his part, ceased to treat them with that consideration, which was due to their elevated rank.*

The mortification, which the duke of Newcastle endured from this diminution of his interest with these members of the royal family was aggravated by the marked attention, which the duke of Bedford received from the king himself; and he frequently complained of the constant presence of his

---

* The truth of these facts is proved by a letter from Mr. Fox to Sir Charles Hanbury Williams, and also by the avowal of the duke of Newcastle himself, in a letter to Mr. Pelham, and in one to Mr. Stone.

Mr. Fox. in his letter to Sir C. H. Williams, dated December 4th-15th, 1751, observes, "You want, you say. in one of your letters, to know the truth of the quarrel between his Royal Highness and the duke of Newcastle, and why the latter goes no more to Princess A——. Sandwich and his Grace differed in the summer of 1748. The Duke had a mind to make them friends. Sandwich gave his Royal Highness a *carte blanche*. His Royal Highness proposed an accommodation. His Grace never honoured the Duke with any answer; left him off; grew cool, impertinent, and inveterate. In the same summer, a letter from the duke of Newcastle to the Princess A——, had pert, not to say impertinent, expressions in it, which, instead of explaining, he aggravated, when he came home; and a breach ensued."

The duke of Newcastle, in his letter to Mr. Pelham, dated June 9th-20th, says, "The not taking my lord Sandwich into the same degree of confidence as before, is the original cause with the Duke, from whence all the rest has proceeded. And the intimacy and supposed attachment to my lady Yarmouth, is undoubtedly the only reason of the Princess's behaviour, which, from coolness. is worked up to aversion.

In another letter, to Mr. Stone, dated December 26th, 1751, he observes, "The conduct of my lord Sandwich, during the negotiation at Aix-la-Chapelle (which was then equally disapproved and resented by the Duke), made such a breach between his lordship and me, as could not be made up; and there can be no doubt, but my refusal to be thoroughly reconciled to lord Sandwich (for every thing short of that I was willing to do) was the sole cause of his Royal Highness's the Duke's displeasure with me."

colleague in the closet, declaring the utter impossibility of transacting any material business, either in his presence, or without his being present.*

In the course of the preceding winter, the duke of Newcastle had attempted to procure the dismission of his rival ; and when he ventured to hint his wishes, the king appeared not entirely averse to the change.   But in a conversation, which he held soon afterwards with lady Yarmouth, he was surprised to discover, that she had formed a sudden intimacy with lord and lady Sandwich, with whom she had no previous acquaintance. This circumstance excited his suspicion, that she indirectly supported the duke of Bedford ; and he was confirmed in that opinion, by the advice which she gave him, not to attempt the removal of his Grace, because he was of too great consequence to be hastily dismissed ; adding, that it would make the king uneasy.   The duke of Newcastle could not refrain from expressing his surprise at this sudden change in his Majesty's sentiments : and on inquiring the cause, the lady replied, " the king did not then know that Mr. Pelham was averse to the measure."   This declaration extremely disconcerted the duke of Newcastle.   He bitterly complained of his brother's opposition to his wishes, and even accused him of combining with the two royal personages and lady Yarmouth, to lessen his influence in the closet, by assisting to prevent the dismissal of his colleague, which he was so anxious to accomplish.

Although Mr. Pelham was much affected by this unjust accusation, yet in exculpating himself, he did not conceal his sentiments with respect to the duke of Bedford.   He frankly declared, that the only motive, which induced him to oppose his removal, was the firm conviction, that the attempt at this crisis, would be not less impolitic and dangerous, than it was impracticable ; and therefore he would neither directly nor indirectly enter into any scheme for that purpose.†   Discouraged by this declaration, the noble secretary had no alternative but to submit, and announced to the countess of Yarmouth, his intention of leaving England, without pressing the affair any farther. With this promise the lady appeared much gratified, and he observes, in a letter ‡ to his brother, that she behaved with great good humour towards

---

* See Letter from the Duke of Newcastle to Mr. Pelham, dated Sept. 2nd-13th, 1750. Illust. Corres.

† See Letter from Mr. Pelham to the Duke of Newcastle, Aug. 12th-23rd, 1750.   MS.

‡ Letter from the Duke of Newcastle to Mr. Pelham, dated Dec. 26th, 1751. MS.

him, and was seemingly as well satisfied with him, and he as much in her confidence as ever. He added, that she also repeated to him assurances of her friendship, with promises of doing every thing that was agreeable to him, during their residence at Hanover. Mr. Pelham was relieved from much anxiety, by the suspension of this political feud; and having soothed the irritated feelings of his brother, exacted a promise, that during his stay at Hanover, he would make no new attempt against the duke of Bedford, without his approbation.

On the departure of the king for Hanover, at the close of the session, the government was vested, as usual, in lords justices; and the details of domestic policy were principally confided to Mr. Pelham. This branch of administration required equal vigilance and firmness; for the reduction of the army and navy had thrown on society, a vast body of men, unfitted for the habits and pursuits of ordinary life; and the transition from war to peace, had been attended with a considerable increase of crime, and with outrages of various kinds. But, by a firm execution of the laws, tempered with judicious forbearance, this turbulent spirit was gradually repressed, and the country soon resumed its pacific character. Although these and other salutary regulations afforded no opportunity for a brilliant display of talent, they reflected high credit on the minister, by whom the authority of government was so steadily and temperately exercised.

Mr. Pelham had now leisure to attend to the leading principles of his policy, the economical management of the public expenditure, the gradual execution of his scheme for reducing the interest of the national debt, and the improvement of foreign and domestic trade. Nor did the remote possessions of the crown fail to derive their share of the advantages, resulting from the provident spirit of amelioration, which pervaded every department of the state.

Among the transactions of this period, we cannot refrain from noticing one, which eventually produced the most important consequences, with regard to the British possessions in North America.

Although the circumstances of the peace would not permit the ministry to provide against the collision of interests likely to occur in that quarter, by any specific stipulation in the treaty of Aix-la-Chapelle, the care required by those distant territories was not relaxed, nor were proper precautions omitted for their security and improvement.

The attention of government had been already called to the province of Nova

Scotia, by the celebrated captain Coram, projector of the Foundling Hospital; and so fully did the subject occupy public attention, that in March 1749, proposals were issued by authority, for encouraging the officers and soldiers, dismissed from the army and navy, to settle in that province, by the grant of lands, and other benefits. The proposed settlement was so attractive, that 3750 individuals, and many families, availed themselves of the invitation; and in May, a body of these new colonists sailed in transports provided by the state. In the latter end of June, they reached their destination, under the most favourable auspices. For their protection, two regiments of foot had accompanied the convoy; and a farther military force was immediately drawn from the garrison of Louisbourg, in the island of Cape Breton, which had been recently restored to France. The necessary operations attending a new colony commenced with the utmost zeal and alacrity; and, before the middle of October, a regular settlement was formed, and fortified with a palisade. From this foundation arose the present town of Halifax, so named in honour of the earl of Halifax, first lord of the Board of Trade; and, in the course of a few years, the wisdom of the scheme was manifested, by the increasing population and abundant resources of a province, which is now ranked among the most valuable dependencies of the British Crown.*

---

* Journals of the Lords and Commons. Continuation of Rapin, vol. xxi. p. 400. Anderson's History of Commerce.—Gent. Mag. 1749.—Winterbotham's America.

CHAPTER XXIII.

1750.

Difficulties attending the conclusion of a new treaty of Commerce with Spain—Negotiations with Austria—Change in the views of the Austrian cabinet—Interminable disputes respecting the Barrier Treaty—Anxiety of the king and the duke of Newcastle, to secure the Imperial Crown in the Austrian family—Overtures for obtaining the election of the archduke Joseph, as king of the Romans—Opposition of Prussia and France—Subsidiary treaty with Bavaria, and attempts to obtain the other electoral votes—Sentiments and conduct of Mr. Pelham on this occasion—Negotiations with Sweden, and designs of France to effect a change in the constitution of that country prevented—Attempts of France to incroach on the limits of Nova Scotia, and to acquire the neutral islands in the West Indies—Embarrassments of Mr. Pelham, from the misunderstanding between his brother and the duke of Bedford, and from the refusal of the king to confer any favour on the earl of Harrington.

IN his visit to Hanover, the king was, as before, accompanied by the duke of Newcastle; and, during his residence abroad, his Majesty was anxious to consolidate the system of German politics, and complete the arrangements arising out of the peace. Among the subjects reserved for future discussion, in the treaty of Aix-la-Chapelle, the negotiation with Spain claimed the earliest attention.

Ministers had been generally blamed, for the indefinite arrangement of the disputes with Spain; but the difficulties, which they had to surmount, were little appreciated, or even known in England. The establishment of a Bourbon prince on the Spanish throne, had led to an essential change in its political system; and though the caprice, resentment, and private views of Philip the Fifth, occasionally produced an alteration in his conduct towards England, yet in all its leading principles, his government retained an unfavourable character. The cabinet of Madrid had at length become sensible of the value and importance of the American colonies, and had sedulously encouraged manufactures and commerce, as the means of rendering those possessions more available, and of increasing the resources of the mother country. The impulse which had been first given by Alberoni and Ripperda, was still felt; and the mercantile maxims introduced by foreigners, were now adopted and reduced to practice, by native Spaniards, with the more zeal and perseverance, as their nature and tendency were better understood.

To the jealousy, arising from this source, were to be ascribed the depredations of the Spaniards on British commerce, and the interruption of the privileges enjoyed by the South Sea Company; and therefore the causes which had produced the war, still subsisted at the conclusion of peace. By the accession of Ferdinand, a prince born and nurtured in Spain, the Spanish councils lost much of that national rivalry against England, which had been excited by his father; and the impression produced by the favourable disposition of the new monarch, was strengthened by the powerful influence of his consort Barbara, a Portugueze princess, attached to England, and averse to France. But this patriotic prince could not consent to sacrifice what he deemed the vital interests of his country, to inferior considerations; and this honourable predilection was equally felt, by his favourite minister, Don Joseph Carvajal. The other minister, the marquis of Ensenada, and the chiefs and subordinate members of the different departments of state, formed a powerful body, deeply imbued with the principles of Ripperda and Alberoni, and jealous of all foreign encroachments on their colonial trade and possessions. This party, secretly encouraged by the French court, made great exertions to decoy Ferdinand into a renewal of that system of policy, which had generally governed the actions of his father; and so far succeeded, as to fortify him in his resolution of advancing the trade and commerce of his subjects. To counteract such obstructions, required no ordinary abilities; nor was it to be hoped, that the most practised diplomatist could entirely succeed, in restoring the British trade to the state in which it existed after the peace of Utrecht. Mr. Keene, the British envoy, however able in fulfilling the duties of his official situation, and, however favourably regarded by the king, the queen, and the prime minister, was unequal to the task; and might indeed be considered as fortunate, in his endeavours to soothe the jealousy which he could not conquer, to detach Ferdinand from France, and to procure the reestablishment of certain privileges, by the sacrifice of others. After a long negotiation, he obtained from the Spanish court a treaty,*

* On the 5th of October 1750.

Q 2

restoring the privileges possessed by the British nation, in the time of Charles the Second, king of Spain, and equal advantages in trade, with those which native Spaniards, or the most favoured nations enjoyed. In return, the remaining term of four years of the Asiento treaty was renounced; the claims of the South Sea Company were compromised, for the sum of £.100,000; the treaty, called Dodington's Treaty,* was not renewed; and the right of search, by mutual consent, was passed over in silence. Notwithstanding this conciliatory arrangement, no human power could obviate the innumerable causes of dissension, arising from commercial jealousy; or establish a permanent system, capable of satisfying the ministers of Spain, on the one hand, and the merchants of England, on the other. The question therefore remained undecided; and supplied a theme of fruitless reproach, against every subsequent administration in England.†

While these political discussions occupied the cabinet, the attention of the king was engrossed by others, in which he felt himself personally concerned. On resuming his residence at Hanover, one of his first cares was, to complete the arrangements in Germany, arising out of the peace, and to settle the protracted disputes with Austria, relative to the Netherlands, and to the renewal of the Barrier Treaty. He was also anxious to give farther stability and extension to the political system of the empire, in which he was deeply interested both as king and elector.

For a long series of years, the House of Austria had been considered as the chief counterpoise to the increasing ascendancy of France; and in the war of the Spanish Succession, had united with the Maritime Powers, to preserve the liberties, and maintain the independence of Europe. The impolitic termination of that contest, by the peace of Utrecht, had, however, left a Bourbon prince on the Spanish throne. Although the disadvantages flowing from such an accession to the power of France, had been partially counteracted by the transfer of the Italian territories and the Netherlands, to the emperor Charles the Sixth, as sole head of the House of Austria, yet the

---

* The objections to Dodington's Treaty, which was concluded in 1715, were not grounded on its general tenor, as affecting the commercial privileges enjoyed by the English, but related to the confirmation it contained of a private agreement with the magistrates of Santandér, concluded in 1700. This agreement was considered as affording great facilities for contraband trade, and as derogatory to the dignity and prerogatives of the crown. The British cabinet prudently desisted from urging its renewal.—See Memoirs of the Kings of Spain, ch. 24 and 50.

† Memoirs of the Bourbon Kings of Spain.

effects of that arrangement had not ceased ; for Naples and Sicily had been appropriated by the infant, Don Carlos, during the war of the Polish Succession, while Parma, Placentia, and Guastalla, had recently been alienated, to form the establishment of his brother, Don Philip. The Netherlands, also, instead of proving a source of strength to their sovereign, and a bond of union with the Maritime Powers, had furnished a perpetual subject of dissension, in consequence of the shackles imposed on their trade, by the Barrier Treaty, and the complicated system of civil and military government, derived from the same source. Indeed, the empress queen herself complained to Mr. Keith, that, from the weak and defenceless condition in which they had been restored, those territories were rather an incumbrance than an advantage.

An essential change had also been produced, in the situation of Austria, and in the Germanic system, in general, by the elevation of the Brunswick family to the throne of Great Britain, and by the rapid aggrandizement of the House of Brandenburg. On one side, therefore, the influence of Austria in the empire had been abridged, by that which the king of England acquired as elector of Hanover ; and, on the other, its possessions had been curtailed, and its views defeated, by the policy and arms of Frederick, king of Prussia, whose predecessors had quietly filled a sub-ordinate station.

The members of the Germanic body, who had so long recognized one leading principle of union against France, now beheld a second power arise, under the direction of a prince, whose military talents, and increasing resources, rendered him no less efficient as an ally, than formidable as an enemy. Personal antipathy to his nephew, sufficed to render George the Second averse to a connection with Prussia ; and, as it was impossible to unite two such rivals as Maria Theresa and Frederic, in one common cause, his Majesty adhered to the antient connection with Austria, without, however, overlooking his own interests and views, as elector of Hanover, increased resources, as king of England.

The sentiments of Maria Theresa towards England, had also undergone a change, since the commencement of the war. In the crisis of her fate, the chivalrous sympathy, and generous aid of the British nation, had excited the most grateful emotions in her ardent mind ; but, in the prosecution of the contest, she keenly resented the sacrifices which she was constrained to make, first to detach the king of Prussia from France, and afterwards to purchase the assistance of the king of Sardinia. The additional cessions, in favour of a Spanish prince, at the peace, proved a farther source of chagrin; and the means employed to extort her acquiescence, so far increased her indignation, that when the British envoy, Mr. Keith, requested permission to offer his congratulations on the event, she haughtily replied, " It is rather a subject of condolence than of congratulation," and requested to be spared an interview, which must be painful to both.*

After the restoration of peace, farther causes of dissatisfaction arose. Anxious to repair her losses by the war, she directed her first cares to the improvement of her revenue, the increase of her military establishment, and the amelioration of her domestic policy. In the extensive circuit of her dominions, she found no portion so susceptible of improvement, or so rich in advantages for trade, as the small but valuable territory of the Netherlands. She had, therefore, meditated the deliverance of those provinces, from the shackles of the Barrier Treaty, which had obstructed the commercial enterprise of the natives, and diverted the revenues, in support of a complicated and inadequate system of defence.

During the late negotiations, she had kept this purpose steadily in view; and, by omitting to specify the Barrier Treaty, in the definitive arrangements for the peace, and refusing to accept the Netherlands, on the former tenure, she hoped that she had prepared the way for the accomplishment of her object. In fact, one of her earliest regulations, soon after the recovery of the Netherlands, was a decree, abolishing the old tarif,† or list of duties, and establishing a new one, by which she secured to her subjects, equal advantages with those of England and Holland, and thus partially abrogated the Barrier Treaty. She also withheld the arrears of the annual subsidy, due to the Dutch, and declared her resolution to diminish its amount, on the plea that it could not be justly claimed, for the towns of which the fortifications were demolished; and that it would be far more appropriately employed, in the repair of the works, and the maintenance of an efficient military force. Such proceedings were naturally opposed by

---

* History of the House of Austria, chap. xxix.

† This tarif had been regulated by England and Holland, as soon as the Netherlands were recovered from France, in the war of the Spanish Succession, and was calculated to restrain the trade of the people of the Netherlands, by continuing the imposition of heavier duties on them, than were paid by the Dutch and English traders. It was confirmed by the 26th article of the Barrier Treaty, and though that article contained an agreement for the formation of a new tarif, such a regulation had been constantly evaded. History of the House of Austria, chap. xxx.

the Maritime Powers, who refused to acknowledge her right, to issue this decree, in violation of the Barrier Treaty, the twenty-sixth article of which could not be altered, except by common consent, and therefore remained in full force, until the three contracting parties should concur in forming a new treaty of commerce. Pretensions so discordant admitted of no compromise; and, although projects for an amicable arrangement were reciprocally offered, the question not only remained undecided, but furnished new causes of disagreement, at every discussion.

This misunderstanding produced feelings by no means favourable to the establishment of an efficient political system in the empire, which was a leading object with George the Second. As a German prince, he was anxious to avert the recurrence of those changes, which had placed his electorate at the mercy of France; and even as a British sovereign, he was sensible that the predominant interest of the empire could be placed in no hands, so safely, as in those of the sovereigns of Austria. The unfavourable terms of the recent peace, and the uncertainty of its duration, rendered this system an object of the most urgent importance. Hence, notwithstanding the disputes on the Barrier Treaty, the king endeavoured to secure the imperial dignity in the Austrian family; and was anxious to prevent the evils, likely to result from a vacancy in the Imperial throne, by obtaining the election of the archduke Joseph, as king of the Romans. This expedient had been occasionally adopted, when the heir of the reigning sovereign had attained his majority; but the young prince being only in his tenth year, the attempt to elect a minor, was not justified by any precedent, since the accession of Rodolph of Hapsburg, the founder of the Austrian dynasty.

The proposal was at first warmly approved, both by the emperor and empress queen, who felt a natural solicitude for the interests of their family; but, in its execution, innumerable difficulties arose. Directly thwarted by Prussia, and indirectly by France, it was but faintly supported by the electors and subordinate princes, who were less anxious for prospective and general security, than for immediate and personal advantage. It was, however, stedfastly pursued by the king, who found, in the duke of Newcastle, a minister fully disposed to promote its accomplishment.

The grand purpose was, to gain eight of the electoral votes, and thereby extort the consent of the king of Prussia, who, it was conjectured, would not venture singly to oppose the election. With this view, the king granted, as elector of Hanover, an annual subsidy of

100,000* florins to the elector of Cologne ; but, as he could not subsidize
any of the other electors, from his own private resources, it became necessary
to appeal to England.   Mentz and Treves being considered certain, the
duke of Newcastle urged the policy of subsidizing the electors of Bavaria,
Palatine, and Saxony ; but Mr. Pelham, deeming this scheme subversive of
his own plans of economy, refused his consent to any subsidy, excepting
that of Bavaria.

In compliance with his brother's representations, the duke rejected the
pecuniary demands of the electors Palatine and Saxony ; but at the same
time he flattered himself, that he should ultimately obtain their votes, without
subsidies.

A negotiation was accordingly opened, with the elector of Bavaria,
whose cooperation was purchased, by the promise of an annual payment
of £.40,000, for the term of six years,† of which England was to advance
two-thirds, and the Dutch one-third.   But the empress queen having signed
a declaration, rendering herself responsible for one-fourth, the payment of
England was reduced to £.20,000, and that of the Dutch to £.10,000.
This compact was vested with the semblance of a subsidiary treaty, by
which the elector agreed to maintain six thousand infantry, at the disposal
of the Maritime Powers, with the reservation, that they should not be
employed against the emperor or empire ; while, in deference to the forms
of the Germanic constitution, the real purpose, that he should give his vote
to the archduke Joseph, was implied in a general engagement, to support
the views of his Britannic Majesty, in promoting the interests of the
empire.‡

A political measure of such importance soon excited the opposition of
those sovereigns, who were interested in its failure.   The king of Prussia,
in particular, protested against it, as contrary to the fundamental laws of
he empire, which, he declared, required the previous consent of the college
of princes, and the unanimity of the electoral body.   He also objected to
the choice of a minor, as premature ; and contended, that no necessity

---

* See letter from the duke of Newcastle to Mr. Pelham, dated September 29th–October 10th,
1750.   Illust. Corres.

† The original term was four years, but the two years were added, in compensation for the
claims of the elector to Mirandola and Concordia.   See letter from the duke of Newcastle to
Mr. Pelham, dated June 23rd–July 4th, 1750.   Illust. Corres.

‡ See copy of the treaty, in the Journals of the House of Commons, January 31st, 1750-1.

existed, to warrant such an anomaly. He was countenanced by the king of France, who, while he affected unwillingness to interfere in the affairs of Germany, and promised to offer no opposition to a majority, that should consist of six votes; yet announced his resolution to support the German princes, if required, as a guarantee of the treaty of Westphalia, which was interpreted as militating against the proposed election.

The duke of Newcastle was, however, deceived in his expectation of gaining the elector Palatine, without a pecuniary sacrifice; for, while the treaty with Bavaria was pending, the elector, at the instigation of Prussia, advanced the most exorbitant demands. He required territorial grants and privileges from the court of Vienna, and a subsidy of, at least, £.40,000 per annum, from the Maritime Powers, as a compensation for arrears due to the Palatine House, during the war of the Spanish Succession.* Although the duke of Newcastle rejected these claims, yet he was subsequently led to believe that he had regained the elector Palatine, without a subsidy,† and that his success was accordingly certain.

From these favourable appearances, Mr. Pelham himself entertained hopes that the election would be speedily accomplished; and sincerely congratulated his brother on the prospect of this happy event. "I hope and believe," he says, in a letter dated Sept. 21st-Oct. 2nd, 1750, "the great end for which you have laboured, will also be brought about soon. I hope it will at least be put in motion, and possibly be in such forwardness, as to leave no room for doubt, before you leave Germany. If so, you may come with a light heart, and cheerful countenance."‡

But, at the very moment when Mr. Pelham was anticipating the accomplishment of the scheme, without any farther expense, he was disconcerted by the information of its probable failure, which was communicated to him by his brother, in a sad tone of disappointment. "I have," he writes, in a letter dated Sept. 29th-Oct. 10th, 1750, "the mortification to see the great system, the great object of my life, in foreign affairs, that I thought as good as concluded, that I know the king of Prussia gave up, now upon the point of miscarrying, from the ignorance, if not worse, of our negotiators at the

---

* See letter from the duke of Newcastle to Mr. Pelham, dated Aug. 1st-12th, 1750.

† See letter from the duke to Mr. Pelham, in the Illust. Corres. dated Aug. 23rd-Sept. 3rd, 1750.

‡ See the letter in the Illust. Corres.

court of Bonn.* The hope of retrieving it, has put me upon writing the letter, that goes by this messenger. In justice to what I think right; in justice to myself; I could not avoid laying it before you, and there I leave it, without any promise or engagement whatever." †

The cause of this failure was a farther pecuniary demand, made by the elector of Cologne, for an increase of the former subsidy, paid by the king, as elector of Hanover.

Notwithstanding, however, the defection of the elector of Cologne, and the refusal of Saxony to support the measure, without a subsidy, the duke of Newcastle calculated on the concurrence of the elector Palatine, with whom he had continued his negotiations; and still deemed himself secure of six votes,‡ even should the elector of Cologne persist in his determination. He therefore pressed the court of Vienna to issue the usual letters of convocation; and the elector of Mentz, to whom, as chancellor of the empire, that office belonged, so far entered into the design, as to publish a circular address, on the necessity of assembling the diet.

But, as the elector of Cologne still continued refractory, as the elector Palatine resumed his unreasonable demands, and as the king of Prussia persisted in his opposition, the king of England, on his departure from Hanover, was compelled to leave this favourite project in a state of suspense.

The correspondence between the two brothers, shews the progress of this complicated negotiation, and displays the motives which induced, on one side, the duke of Newcastle to propose the grant of additional subsidies, for the purpose of securing what he considered so important an object, and on the other, those which influenced Mr. Pelham, to refuse his consent, to any farther extension of the subsidizing system; § especially as he was endeavouring by every expedient in his power, to lessen the public burthens.

A negotiation on the affairs of Sweden proved more successful. France, being anxious to augment the power of the king of Sweden, had exerted her influence with the aristocracy, to effect a change in the constitution. The empress of Russia had marched a body of troops towards Swedish Finland, to counteract these machinations; and the troubles of the North seemed likely

* The residence of the elector of Cologne.
† See the letter in the Illust. Corres.
‡ Viz. Bohemia, Bavaria, Mayence or Mentz, Treves, Cologne, and Hanover. See letter of the duke of Newcastle to Mr. Pelham, dated June 23rd-July 4th, 1750. Illust. Corres.
§ See the Illustrative Correspondence, passim.

to recommence. The king of England, however, interposing his mediation, France was induced to desist from her intrigues, and Russia to withdraw her forces. Thus, by the firmness and address of the British cabinet, a change in the constitution of Sweden was prevented, and with it a renewal of hostilities with Russia, which might have led to a continental war. This negotiation was opened with great ability by Mr. Pelham, and conducted with equal address by the duke of Newcastle at Hanover.*

The disputes with France, relative to the fulfilment of the definitive gave rise to another delicate negotiation. Notwithstanding the stipulation, that all things should remain on the same footing as before the war, the French not only evinced an intention of appropriating the islands of St. Lucia, St. Vincent, and Dominica, which had hitherto been regarded as neutral, but had actually taken possession of Tobago, which was considered as belonging to England. Proceedings so detrimental to the British colonies in the West Indies, produced a lively sensation in the cabinet; and pressing representations were made against this violation of the peace. But, notwithstanding the declaration of the French court, that these encroachments had been made by the marquis de Caylus, governor of Tobago, without their knowledge, and though the copy of an order sent to the marquis, for the evacuation of those islands, signed by the king of France, had been transmitted to London in December 1749,† yet that order had not been obeyed. The forcible remonstrances, however, of the duke of Newcastle, induced the French to abandon their settlements in Tobago, after having destroyed the forts;‡ but the fulfilment of their promise to evacuate the islands of St. Lucia, and St. Vincent, was still delayed, under various pretences.

Similar attempts in another quarter, created still greater alarm. The indefinite stipulations in the treaty of Utrecht, relative to the limits of Nova Scotia, had neither been rectified nor explained, in that of Aix-la-Chapelle; and consequently furnished a plea to France, for impeding the growth of a colony, daily rising into commercial importance. Advantage was taken of

* See particularly Mr. Pelham's letter to the duke of Newcastle, April 25th, 1750, relating the circumstances of a conference with the duke de Mirepoix, the French embassador, on the affairs of Sweden, in the Illust. Corres.

† Cont. of Rapin, v. xxi. p. 396, and abstract of the duke of Newcastle's letter to Mr. Pelham, dated Sept. 4th-15th, 1750. MS.

‡ Gent. Mag. 1751.

the vague expression in the treaty, "according to its antient limits," to appropriate, as belonging to Canada, an extensive and valuable district, which would have reduced to insignificance the territory ceded to England.

On this subject Mr. Pelham endeavoured to effect an amicable accommodation with the court of Versailles; while the duke of Newcastle, appreciating the value of the colonies, and the necessity of resisting encroachment, proposed to require the immediate acquiescence of France, in the demands of England, even at the risk of a rupture. He also drew up a memorial in terms too likely to excite the indignation of the French court, and produce a renewal of hostilities; but, by the earnest representations of his brother, he was persuaded to modify it,* and to continue the negotiation on a friendly footing.

The appeals continually made to the judgment of Mr. Pelham, during these foreign negotiations, greatly perplexed him; and he occasionally found it difficult to divert the king and his brother from the prosecution of some of their favourite schemes, which he considered, either as chimerical, or as inimical to his plans of economy. But, in the domestic administration, he encountered still greater embarrassments, from the increasing misunderstanding between his brother and the duke of Bedford, and from the behaviour of the king towards the earl of Harrington.

We have already observed, that before the departure of the king from England, the duke of Newcastle had agreed to suspend the attempt to procure the removal of the duke of Bedford.† He was, however, far from relinquishing his purpose. Being intrusted with the principal management of foreign affairs, he laboured to exclude his colleague, as much as possible, from participating in the pending transactions. This reserve drew from the duke of Bedford complaints, that he was reduced to a mere cipher, while the real business of administration centered in the two brothers and the lord Chancellor. He occasionally manifested his disgust, by a haughty silence, even when his advice was requested, on matters belonging to his own department, and by a frequent disregard of his official duties. Mr. Pelham, although much dissatisfied with the negligence and procrastination of the duke of Bedford, yet beheld with pain the increasing dissension

---

* See Illust. Corres. passim, and particularly a letter from the duke of Newcastle to Mr. Pelham, dated June 17th-28th, 1750.

† See the end of the preceding chapter, p. 111.

between the two Secretaries; because he dreaded the loss of a noble-man, possessing such powerful influence in parliament, and was appre-hensive, that it would be difficult to find a successor, who would prove equally agreeable, both to the king and to the cabinet. He therefore laboured to soothe his brother, and pressed him to conciliate his colleague, by unequivocal marks of confidence.

A political rivalry, once begun, is continually increased, by the most trifling circumstances. Indignant at the proceedings of his brother secretary, the duke of Bedford more sedulously cultivated the favour, which he had acquired with the Duke of Cumberland, and the Princess Amelia. He was a frequent attendant, with his duchess, and lord and lady Sandwich, at the parties given by the Duke and Princess, and was honoured with a visit by their Royal Highnesses, at his magnificent mansion at Woburn. On these occasions, the duke of Grafton, Mr. Arundel, and other friends of the duke of Newcastle were present; Mr. Pelham was also invited, though he seldom accepted the invitations.*

The intelligence of this intercourse increased the disquietude of the duke of Newcastle, who, aware of the secret dispositions of the two royal personages, regarded it as the indication of an intrigue to supplant him. In his letters to his brother and the Chancellor, he bitterly complains that their Royal Highnesses, who were under the king's inspection, and ought to be under his command, had opposed many measures of government, and that they had endeavoured, by every art and insinuation, to pervert and silence those associates, with whom he had been connected for thirty years, by all the ties of friendship. He even declared, in the strong language of resentment, that they had excommunicated him from all society, and set a species of stigma upon him.

In vain did both the Chancellor and his brother endeavour to convince him, that these complaints were ill founded, and that their Royal Highnesses still spoke of him, in terms of esteem and confidence. In vain they urged, that he had provoked their displeasure, by his coolness and neglect, but that he might easily recover their favour, if he would condescend to pay them more attention, and make proper acknowledgments for any mark of disrespect, which might have escaped him. No arguments, however, could

* See letter from Mr. Pelham to the duke of Newcastle May 25th-June 5th, 1750. Illust. Corres. In the early part of the month of May, Mr. Pelham dined with their Royal Highnesses at Windsor Lodge; and they dined with him at Esher in July.

appease his irritable spirit, or induce him to renew his court to the Duke
and Princess, who so strongly supported his rival in the cabinet. On the
contrary, he even accused his particular friends and adherents, of apathy ;
and complained that his brother, though aware of the hostile sentiments entertained by the two royal personages towards him, had paid
assiduous court to them, and was not sufficiently vigilant, in counteracting
the machinations of his adversaries.

While harassed by these suspicions, he was much mortified at perceiving
an evident change in the conduct of lady Yarmouth.

Although she had promised to continue her usual support, during their
residence at Hanover, and in public had behaved in the most gracious
manner towards him, and the duchess of Newcastle ; yet, for three months
after their arrival, she carefully declined all private interviews, and, in particular, avoided holding any conversation on the subject of the duke of
Bedford. Hence he was convinced that she continued her cabal with his
rival ; and he was not ignorant, that she received large packets from England,
of which she carefully suppressed the contents. At the same time, he had
the mortification to perceive, that the king withdrew those marks of
confidence, with which he had hitherto distinguished him. His Majesty
received him coldly, gave him short audiences, conversed solely on English
affairs, and concealed from him many details of the pending negotiations
with the German courts.

He accordingly became so impatient of his irksome situation, that he
hastily adopted the resolution of taking the post of President of the
Council, which was likely to become vacant by the removal of the
duke of Dorset to the lord lieutenancy of Ireland, if the duke of Bedford
could not be induced to resign the seals, in exchange for that office, and
thus give place to a more eligible colleague, as Secretary of State. This
design he imparted in the most confidential manner to his friend the Chancellor, to whom he related all the real or supposed grievances, which had
induced him to form it, and requested his advice, as to the time and mode of
its execution. To his brother, he also made a similar communication ; but
with this difference, that he withheld the account of the coolness of the
king, and the altered demeanour of lady Yarmouth. The principal motive,
which he assigned for relinquishing the seals, was his aversion to the duke
of Bedford ; with whom, he said, it was impossible any longer to act ;
because in consequence of his great quality, and the support which he

received from the Duke of Cumberland and the Princess Amelia, he could not be treated with that freedom, which would certainly be used towards a person of inferior consideration, who fulfilled the duties of his office so negligently. With regard to himself, he added, that daily opportunities were taken by the Duke of Cumberland, and the Princess Amelia, to mortify and depress him, by the countenance shewn to the duke of Bedford. He then pointed out three persons, as eligible for the office of Secretary of State, Sir Thomas Robinson, lord Chesterfield, and even lord Granville, against the latter of whom, he said, the prejudices of his friends had begun to subside. He also expressed great uneasiness at some animadversions on his management of foreign affairs, contained in his brother's late letters. These communications were accompanied with many expostulations, and with exaggerated complaints of the embarrassments with which he was surrounded.*

The lord Chancellor, with candour and firmness, laboured to dissuade him from so hasty a determination, which must occasion a breach in the cabinet, and render the conduct of affairs impracticable. He assured him, that the suspicions which he had conceived against his friends, were unfounded; that Mr. Pelham, to whom he advised him to be more frank and open in his communications, had declared his general approbation of foreign measures. He added, that he equally blamed the contemptuous and dilatory behaviour of the duke of Bedford; and was ready to assist in obtaining his resignation, if practicable; but that, having sounded the Duke of Cumberland and the Princess Amelia, and having found that the duke of Bedford would not resign, unless lord Sandwich should be nominated his successor, he was decidedly of opinion, that it would be better to leave things, at present, as they were. His lordship finally urged many forcible arguments, to prove that his Grace would experience more uneasiness and disappointment, in his proposed change of office, than in his actual situation, however irksome it might appear.

Mr. Pelham, also, in several friendly letters to his brother, combated his resolution; and in acknowledging the offensive negligence of the duke of Bedford, repeated his conviction, that any plan for his immediate removal would be impracticable, though it might easily be effected, by taking

---

* See letter from the duke of Newcastle to Mr. Pelham, dated July 4th-15th, 1750. Illust. Corres.

advantage of accidents, at some future period. He declared, that he had used all the means in his power, but ineffectually, to procure his voluntary resignation. He lamented that his brother should suspect him of partiality to his colleague; and to promote his wishes, he asserted, in the language of fraternal affection, that he would walk barefoot to Hanover.* He also earnestly advised him, to take an opportunity of renewing his correspondence with their Royal Highnesses. At the same time he complained of the irksomeness of his own situation, and avowed that he himself had long wished to retire from office.

In his turn the duke of Newcastle expressed his concern at his brother's uneasiness, and endeavoured to rouse him from his despondency, by announcing that the king, from a knowledge of his integrity, ability, and influence, had expressly said, he would do nothing without him.†

Fortunately, these reciprocal expressions of kindness and affection, aided by the representations of their common friends, the Chancellor and Mr. Stone, had a due effect. The two brothers ultimately relinquished the rash resolution of dissolving their united administration; and the duke of Newcastle was persuaded by the Chancellor and Mr. Pelham to forego his intention of resigning the seals.‡

The duke was, however, still so much embarrassed, by the coolness of the king, and the change in the conduct of lady Yarmouth, that he deemed it necessary to comply with the Chancellor's exhortations, and confide those particulars to his brother, which he had previously withheld. In making this communication, he expressed his full conviction, that lady Yarmouth was caballing with the duke of Bedford's party in England, and was using all her efforts to prevent his removal. He also mentioned, that the king was continually changing his sentiments and resolutions, with respect to his rival. At one time, he observes, his Majesty said to Mr. Stone, who informed him that no letters had been received from the duke of Bedford: "What would you have him write about? there is nothing to do;" and another time his Majesty remarked, "He never

---

* See letter from Mr. Pelham to the duke of Newcastle, dated July 13th-24th, 1750, in the Illust. Corres.

† Abstract of the duke of Newcastle's letter to Mr. Pelham, dated Sept. 15th-26th, 1750. MS.

‡ See in the Illustrative Correspondence the interesting letters of the duke of Newcastle to the lord Chancellor, and Mr. Pelham, July 3rd-14th, and July 4th-15th, with their replies, July 13th-24th, 1750.

troubles his head about business : never man had an easier place than he has." Having himself spoken to the king of the silence of the duke of Bedford, his Majesty replied, " It is not to be borne ; he never writes ;" and then said, " He has an easy office, and he receives his pay easily."

From these indications of dissatisfaction, the duke of Newcastle inferred, that the king was inclined to remove the duke of Bedford ; but, in a subsequent audience, he had the mortification of receiving a very cold reply, to an observation, which he again made, respecting the silence and negligence of his colleague. " He has nothing to write about," said his Majesty, " he is a mere subordinate minister. His office is a sinecure, and he may as well fill it as any other." The king then added, in the very words of the duke of Bedford himself, " You and your brother, and the Chancellor, are the only real ministers : the rest are ciphers."

Soon after this audience, the king again appears to have resumed his displeasure against the duke of Bedford ; on account not only of his negligence, but of his obstinate silence, on the pending negotiation, for the election of a king of the Romans. Actuated by this feeling, he spontaneously testified an intention to remove him, from the office of Secretary of State, though to soften his fall, he was disposed to appoint him President of the Council. Lady Yarmouth was chosen to communicate this change of sentiment, to the duke of Newcastle ; but before the interview took place, an event happened, which gave a new turn to the affair. This was the death of the duke of Richmond, who had held the post of Master of the Horse. The vacancy appears to have furnished the king, or at least the lady, with a new expedient for retaining the duke of Bedford in office, should he be inclined or compelled to relinquish the seals of Secretary of State.

Accordingly, in the course of the interview, having imparted to him the king's resolution to appoint a new Secretary, she cited some expressions of contempt, used by his Majesty towards the duke of Bedford, adding, "His Grace thinks he does much business, by riding post from Woburn to London, and from London to Woburn,* as I see by the newspapers." She then said, " will not this *facheux* accident furnish a means of accommodation ?" evidently alluding to the death of the duke of Richmond, and the consequent vacancy in the office of Master of the Horse. To the observation of the duke of Newcastle, that there were two vacancies, namely

* The duke of Newcastle to the lord Chancellor, Aug. 19th-30th, 1750. Illust. Corres.

those of Master of the Horse, and President of the Council, the lady quickly replied, " No, the latter he will not take ; and I will speak to the king on the subject."

The duke of Newcastle was greatly surprised by this communication, particularly as he noticed a degree of confusion in lady Yarmouth, which led him to suspect, that it was made with reluctance on her part. Soon afterwards she informed him, that the king had consented to confer the Mastership of the Horse on the duke of Bedford ; and, in another interview, he remarked that her behaviour was still more embarrassed, than on the former occasion. She did not deny that the king persisted in his resolution, to make the proposed change in the cabinet; she even affected to know the sentiments of the duke of Bedford, and observed, that he certainly would not take the post of President of the Council, but would accept that of Master of the Horse. Notwithstanding this remark, the countess evidently endeavoured to prevent his removal; and was anxious to preclude the duke of Newcastle from holding any direct communication with the king, on the subject. After the lapse of a few days, however, a letter from lord Poulett, applying for the Mastership of the Horse, rendered such a communication necessary. The king read the letter with good humour, and then observed, " I am aware, your brother sees that things cannot continue as they are; and he will be proposing disagreeable changes to me, in order to prevent a rupture, or to keep things quiet."

The duke exculpated Mr. Pelham from the slightest intention to distress the feelings of his Majesty ; and the king turned the conversation to the subject of the duke of Bedford. After praising the talents and character of lord Waldegrave, his Majesty approved the removal of the noble secretary to the post of Master of the Horse. He then added, " I see plainly, that things go on lamely ; and do not think that I have not seen it, for some time ; but they went well in parliament ; and you and I, my lord, cannot do it alone ; we must have the Council with us." This, the duke clearly understood as a hint, that the king expected an application from Mr. Pelham himself. The conversation then turned on other arrangements, arising from the change ; and his Majesty expressed a wish, that the seals held by the duke of Bedford, should be transferred to lord Holdernesse, and that lord Waldegrave should be deputed embassador to Paris, in the room of lord Albemarle, in order to qualify him eventually for the office of

Secretary of State. In subsequent conversations, both the king and lady Yarmouth explicitly mentioned the necessity of a formal application from Mr. Pelham, to sanction the proposed alteration in the cabinet. The duke of Newcastle imparted these conferences to his brother and the lord Chancellor, exulting in the prospect of so desirable an event, which he said entirely originated with the king, and therefore obviated the blame of his personal interference. He added a request, that his brother would write an ostensible letter, to be submitted to the king, inforcing the expediency of the change. To urge his compliance, he expatiated on the irksomeness of his own situation, and intreated him not to forego so favourable an opportunity of attaining an object, which they both deemed so desirable.

Mr. Pelham was thus placed in a delicate situation. He saw, that in existing circumstances, the odium of the change would fall on his brother and himself. He was apprehensive, that the duke of Bedford would acquire merit with the king, by submission ; and that either of the posts offered to him, would furnish more dangerous opportunities for cabal, than that which he then held. Lord Holdernesse seemed to him, unfit for the seals, from inexperience and want of interest. He objected to Sir Thomas Robinson, because the presence of a Secretary of State, in the Lower House, might occasion considerable embarrassment ;* and he was still more averse to lord Granville, on account of his unabated influence in the closet, and his known devotion to German politics. For these reasons, he declared, that if lord Granville was appointed Secretary of State, he would himself no longer remain in office. These objections he stated with considerable warmth ; and, while he declared that, should the king ask his advice, he would give his decided opinion, in favour of the proposed change, he declined writing the ostensible letter, as he could not venture to trouble his Majesty on so delicate a subject. He also requested his brother to assure the king, that he was far from interfering, in the least, with any disposition his Majesty should think proper to make, in relation to the appointment of a Secretary of State, in the place of the duke of Bedford. He then observed, that as they could not change their natures, nor add to their understandings, they must be satisfied with each other, and be convinced, that if they did differ, it was what they could not avoid ; but that they should endeavour,

---

* See letter from Mr. Pelham to the duke of Newcastle, dated August 3rd-14th, 1750, in which he says, " the new secretary must not be a member of the House of Commons." Illust. Corres.

that those differences should have as little effect upon the public, and be as little known as possible. He concluded this expostulatory letter, by reprobating the unjust suspicion of his brother, that he was a supporter of the duke of Bedford's party ; and declared that, as he saw the present state of things could not last long, he should rest contented, whatever his fate might be, provided he was not obliged to act contrary to his principles, in public measures.

He again conjured his brother not to press the subject, until the return of the king, representing that if the resolution should be previously adopted, he, as the only minister attending his Majesty, must incur the whole blame.

This diversity of sentiment again produced mutual irritation ; and the letters which passed at this season, are filled with complaints and recriminations. But, by the interposition of the lord Chancellor, harmony was in some degree restored, and Mr. Pelham agreed to take any step, which would satisfy his brother, consistently with his duty to the sovereign, and his own feelings of propriety. He candidly assured him, that he had refrained from paying his former attentions to the Duke of Cumberland and Princess Amelia, and that when he did visit them, it was merely for the sake of form. He repeated his willingness to declare in favour of the proposed change, if his Majesty should be induced to ask his advice.

As the crisis approached, the duke of Bedford, who evidently resolved, not to leave the disposal of the seals to his rival, contrived to raise new difficulties. He explicitly avowed his intention, not to accept any office, unless, as Mr. Pelham had before surmised, lord Sandwich should be appointed his successor, in which resolution, he was strongly supported by the Duke of Cumberland and the Princess Amelia. This determination disconcerted the whole design ; for, as the king would by no means accept lord Sandwich, who was equally obnoxious to both the brothers, no alternative remained, but the absolute dismissal of the duke of Bedford. Such a procedure, Mr. Pelham was by no means disposed to risk, from a conviction that, whichever party should prevail, neither would be able alone to carry on the king's affairs in parliament. He, therefore, again intreated his brother to tolerate his present inconveniences ; and renewed his assurances of earnest assistance, on the first favourable opportunity.

* We abstain from farther details on this subject, and refer the reader to the Illustrative Correspondence for 1750.

The sanguine temper of the duke of Newcastle, however, still led him to calculate, that his noble colleague might possibly be induced to exchange the seals, for the Mastership of the Horse, without any stipulation, in favour of lord Sandwich ; and he hoped that his removal might be effected on the return of the king to England ; though, at the same time, he was aware, that the interposition of Mr. Pelham would be absolutely necessary, to attain his object.

In a letter to the lord Chancellor, he observes : " The king will certainly never be easy, in keeping the duke of Bedford ; and, if he is kept, it must be by a force, upon the principle (at least) of that which has been so long complained of, without the same cause, and consequently without any justification."* Mr. Pelham, however, was far from entertaining such sanguine expectations of the speedy and successful accomplishment of the change ; and being aware that no accommodation could be effected, by an epistolary correspondence, relative to a subject on which they so essentially differed, he was anxious to have a private interview with his brother, before the arrival of the king in London, when he hoped to settle the affair, in an amicable manner.

He was, therefore, much disappointed, at receiving a letter from the duke, expressing an intention to remain a few days at Dover, as he did not intend to be in London, until after the arrival of the king, who had testified his desire, through lady Yarmouth, that he should not reach the metropolis before him. His Grace farther added, " I should be glad to know your final thoughts upon our great question : what you yourself think would be right for you to do, and what you can advise me. Something must be done. For God's sake, let us agree what, and in what manner." In reply to this request, Mr. Pelham having testified his regret, that his brother had deferred his journey to London, until after the king's arrival, observes, " Had you been here any time before the king came, we could have talked amongst ourselves, coolly and temperately, upon it ; but to say any thing by letter, after what I have said, and been so ill understood, I hope you will excuse me from. I most heartily wish every thing may end to your satisfaction ; and, if that can be done, without breaking us all to pieces, I shall be very happy.—I know nothing ; I see nobody ; and I ask no questions."

* Dated October 23rd–November 3rd, 1750.—Newcastle Papers, MS.

Thus the affair remained in suspense; and, as Mr. Pelham would not interfere, unless the king expressly required his advice and aid, the absence of his brother afforded an opportunity to the friends of the duke of Bedford, to redouble their exertions in his favour, and, consequently, to prevent his dismissal.

The other affair, which deeply affected the feelings of Mr. Pelham, was the case of lord Harrington. We have already noticed the displeasure of the king against that nobleman, his consequent resignation, and the great difficulty, which occurred in procuring his appointment, as lord lieutenant of Ireland. That high office was usually retained only for three years; but, at the expiration of this term, the king was reluctantly induced, by the Pelhams, to continue him another year; after which, the minister hoped, that in reward for his services, he would be nominated lord President, or Secretary of State, or be appointed to some other efficient situation in the cabinet. But, notwithstanding repeated solicitations, the king persisted in his refusal to confer on him any other post, and spoke of him in the most indignant terms.* Mr. Pelham was much hurt at the king's inflexibility, and equally affected by the moving appeals of his friend; nor was he fully satisfied with his brother's efforts, to procure some mark of favour for a nobleman, whose disgrace he attributed to his fidelity, in their struggle with the. earls of Bath and Granville. He seems, however,. to have unjustly accused the duke of Newcastle of lukewarmness, and not to have sufficiently considered the difficulty of urging a claim, which militated so strongly against the prejudices of the king.

In September, the post of General of Marines became vacant, by the death of lord Stair; and Mr. Pelham entertained a hope, that this appointment, which was of no official consequence, might be obtained for his noble friend. The duke of Newcastle requested it from the king; but was answered by an unqualified refusal. Among other angry expressions, his Majesty observed, that the generalship of Marines was to be the reward of all who flew in his face; that this was the case with lord Stair; and when the duke endeavoured to soothe him, he said, " I will do nothing; I will not be troubled about it. Lord Harrington deserves nothing; and shall have nothing. As to the generalship of the Marines, he shall not have it, if I can hinder it."† In reply to this information, Mr. Pelham writes,

* See the duke of Newcastle's letter, of September 2nd–13th, 1750.
† Abstract of the duke of Newcastle's letter to Mr. Pelham, dated Oct. 10th–21st, 1750, MS.

October 16th, 1750, " Your letter about lord Harrington is as cruel and melancholy, as can be. I have done saying any thing more upon the subject. I shall write to the poor man, and tell him the truth, leaving out the coarse expressions. You may depend upon my saying every thing from you, that I possibly can. I fear this measure will do the king no service. His Majesty is, however, the best judge of his own actions, and I know my duty and situation too well, to interfere any more."

From this time, no farther attempt was made, to overcome the repugnance of the king. Soon afterwards, lord Harrington returned from the government of Ireland, but was disappointed in his hope of obtaining an official situation ; and the duke of Dorset was declared Lord Lieutenant, on the 6th of December, by his Majesty in Council.*

* Gent. Magazine, vol. xx. 1750.

CHAPTER XXIV

1750—51.

*Return of the King to England—State of the Cabinet—Ineffectual attempt to remove
the duke of Bedford—Misunderstanding between the two brothers—Opening of
Parliament—Royal Speech—Addresses of both Houses—Censure of the " Constitutional Queries," a libel on the Duke of Cumberland—Debate on the Naval
establishment—Reduction of the number of Seamen to eight thousand, supported by
Mr. Pelham, and opposed by Mr. Pitt.—Reconciliation between Mr. Pelham and
the duke of Newcastle—Motion to reduce the military power of the Duke of
Cumberland—Discussion on the Bavarian subsidy—Debate arising from the Mutiny
bill; and affair of general Anstruther.*

WITHOUT having concluded any of the pending negotiations, except
the treaty with the elector of Bavaria, the king landed in England, on the
4th of November, when the usual preparations were made, for opening the
session of parliament.

At this critical period, the feud in the cabinet, on the subject of the
duke of Bedford, increased to an alarming height, and threatened a dissolution of the ministry.

From conversations with the king at Hanover, and from the latest communications of lady Yarmouth, the duke of Newcastle still flattered himself,
that his Majesty would desire the duke of Bedford to resign the seals as
Secretary of State, and accept the post of Master of the Horse, for which he
was persuaded nothing more was necessary, than an application from Mr.
Pelham.* By incessant importunities, he prevailed upon his brother to
apply to the king; but his hopes were again disappointed, for his Majesty
gave a mild, though peremptory refusal. Mr. Pelham, who had made the
attempt with undisguised reluctance, respectfully submitted to the royal

---

* See Chap. xxiii. p. 130.

decision,[*] and used his utmost endeavours to persuade his brother to desist from any farther attempt against his rival, until a more favourable opportunity should occur.

This change in the royal mind, and the refusal of Mr. Pelham to renew his solicitations, deeply affected the duke of Newcastle. In a letter to the Chancellor, he gave vent to his feelings, observing, " I find myself in a condition, where no man ever was before. I have nobody but your lordship in the ministry, to avow me; and had my friends adopted a different conduct, the mischief which they and I now labour under, would have been prevented." In another letter to the Chancellor, we find, that his agitation of mind was so great, as to induce him to declare, that he could no longer bear his present situation, and that he would take the office of President, as he had formerly intended, or wholly retire from business, unless some alteration could be speedily effected. He was indeed so anxious to remove his colleague, that he actually proposed, either to open a negotiation with earl Granville, for settling a new administration, or to conciliate the Duke of Cumberland, without the interposition of Mr. Pelham, by agreeing to sub-stitute lord Sandwich, in the room of the duke of Bedford. He also suggested, that the Chancellor, or some other friend, should declare in the closet, " that the king could not be easy, or have any administration, whilst things remained as they were;" and should endeavour to prevail on his Majesty to extort the consent of the duke of Bedford, to the meditated arrangement, which he still imagined might easily be effected, with the assistance of Mr. Pelham.

These threats of resignation were not, indeed, carried into execution; but his displeasure against his brother was increased to such a degree, that all private intercourse between them was suspended.

A train of unpleasant feelings resulted from this contention; and at no period of his administration, did Mr. Pelham encounter more perplexity, or experience greater difficulty, in directing the House of Commons. His influence was weakened by many causes, besides the misunderstanding with his brother. The visible decline of their favour with the Duke of Cumber-land and the Princess Amelia, abated the zeal of many of their adherents ; while the hostile feelings of the duke of Bedford, even during his ostensible

---

[*] Letter from the Chancellor to the duke of Newcastle, dated Dec. 10th, 1750, and also a letter from Mr. Pelham to his brother, dated March 16th, 1750-1. MS.

support of government, were manifested by the apathy, and occasionally even by the indirect opposition of his adherents. The increasing power of the Prince of Wales, also, was felt with double effect, in this temporary collision of interests; for the countenance of the heir apparent was an essential support to many, who were tempted to take advantage of the difficulties of administration. Lastly the rivalry, which had always subsisted, between Mr. Fox and Mr. Pitt, proved an additional source of embarrassment. Both were of too independent and aspiring a character, to act consistently with their subordinate situation; and, during the coolness which subsisted between the two brothers, they respectively took a part, which was not likely to restore harmony; Mr. Fox attaching himself to Mr. Pelham, while Mr. Pitt courted the favour of the duke of Newcastle. Lord Cobham, and his party, who perhaps at no time had perfectly identified themselves with administration, were, at this juncture, likewise labouring to aggravate the dissensions in the cabinet, and secretly caballing with the Prince of Wales.*

These elements of discord were particularly injurious at a season, when union had become so desirable, from the unpopularity of the German negotiations, and the obloquy excited by the recent arrangement with Spain.

The session of parliament was opened on the 17th of January. In the speech from the throne, the king, after expressing his satisfaction at the continuance of tranquillity abroad, announced the conclusion of the convention with the court of Madrid, for the adjustment of such differences, as could not be decided in a general treaty. He represented this arrangement as the more gratifying, because it had been effected, without the intervention of any other party; and not only declared, that he had succeeded in re-establishing the commerce with Spain, on the most advantageous foundation; but adduced the friendly disposition of his most Catholic Majesty, as a presage of the complete restoration of amity between the two nations.

He also spoke of the subsidiary treaty with Bavaria, as the commencement of a system, for securing the tranquillity of the empire, and for preventing the recurrence of events, which had involved Europe in calamity, and drained the blood and treasure of his subjects.

Finally, in requesting the requisite supplies, he congratulated the Commons on the progress they had made, in reducing the interest of the national debt.

* See Chap. xxv.

The address of the Peers, which was voted without opposition, conveyed their full approbation of the policy pursued by the king.

In the lower House, an address was moved by Mr. Horatio Walpole, jun. and seconded by Mr. Proby, applauding in every point the communications of the speech, and professing the readiness of the Commons, to gratify the wishes of his Majesty, and assist in fulfilling his engagements.

This motion was ably opposed by lord Egmont. He protested against the approbation of measures, concerning which the House was held in utter ignorance. He questioned the existence of general tranquillity, and alluded to the continued depredations of Spain upon our commerce, as well as to the encroachments of France on our settlements in North America, and her detention of the neutral islands, as indicative of hostile purposes. He censured the treaty with Spain, as derogatory to the national honour; complained that the right of search had been tamely admitted; and that for such a trifling sum as £.100,000, the demand of the South Sea Company on Spain had been sacrificed, to the amount of nearly a million, exclusive of claims from private merchants, for depredations, estimated at half a million more. Adverting to the treaty with Bavaria, he condemned all subsidiary engagements during peace, as useless and unprofitable; and denounced the proposed system of continental policy, as more likely to provoke war, than to maintain peace. He stigmatized the whole address, as the most servile ever offered, and resembling the homage of a Turkish divan to their sultan, rather than that of a British House of Commons to the sovereign. In conclusion, he proposed to omit all those clauses which conveyed any expression of approbation.

As Mr. Pelham took no share in this debate, the task of defending the address devolved chiefly on Mr. Pitt. He vindicated the Spanish treaty, with great spirit; contended that the losses of the South Sea Company were far more than counterbalanced, by the amount of captures during the war; that the unexpired term of the Asiento was too short to be of any real value; and that by the conditions of the treaty, British commerce had acquired greater advantages than had been enjoyed for many years. The principle of *no search* he condemned, as incompatible with the existing system of national law; and, alluding to the celebrated address of the House of Commons, praying the king not to make peace with Spain, until that right should have been relinquished, he unequivocally censured it, as an improper interference with the royal prerogative. He frankly acknowledged

T 2

his own error, in having seconded such advice, and excused himself solely on the ground of youth and inexperience; adding, that as he was now ten years older, he had more maturely considered the demand, and found it to be unwarrantable.

He then applauded the care of his Majesty for the preservation of tranquillity; expatiated on the danger, which must arise from a new vacancy in the imperial throne; and argued that the Bavarian treaty was justifiable, on every principle of sound policy, as a proceeding subservient to that end, and to the important purpose of detaching Bavaria from the French interest.

After a debate, in which the same arguments on either side were repeated by other speakers, the address was carried, by 203 votes against 74.

The attention of parliament was soon afterwards directed to a recent libel, containing a violent attack on the Duke of Cumberland, and probably occasioned by the unfortunate misunderstanding between the king and the Prince of Wales.

This misunderstanding had been aggravated by time; and though suspended on the establishment of the Broad Bottom administration, it now broke forth with renewed animosity. The contention naturally recoiled on the ministers, and still more on the Duke of Cumberland, whose superior favour was a perpetual source of mortification to the Prince. The court of Leicester House became therefore the focus, not merely of opposition, but even of disaffection; for the Prince was led into every selfish scheme or imprudent connection, which could supply the means of distressing or weakening the government of his royal father.

On the opening of the session, the libel, which bore the title of "Constitutional Queries, earnestly recommended to the serious consideration of every Briton," was insidiously circulated among the members of both Houses, and through the cities of London and Westminster. Its object was, to expose the Duke of Cumberland to popular odium, by comparing him with Richard the Third, and exciting a suspicion, that he would employ his military power, to violate the birthright of his brother, and usurp the throne.

This inflammatory address produced so strong a sensation, as to attract the immediate notice of Parliament. On the 22nd of January, it was formally denounced in the House of Peers, by the duke of Marlborough; and a resolution was instantly passed, that it should be burnt by the common hangman. After a conference with the Commons, the same resolution was proposed in the Lower House, by Sir John Strange, master of the Rolls, and seconded by the Attorney-general, Sir Dudley Ryder. Some quibbling objections from Sir Francis Dashwood and colonel Richard Lyttelton, were ably refuted by Mr. Pelham,* who said, that the impression which the libel had already produced on honest minds, was an additional reason for its condemnation.

Lord Egmont, though he disapproved generally the interference of parliament, on such subjects, yet frankly joined in condemning the paper; and declared that no censure could be too severe, for so flagrant an attempt to sow dissension between two brothers of the blood royal. The resolution was carried unanimously; and an address presented to the king, requesting him to use effectual means for the discovery of the authors, printers, and publishers.

In arranging the naval and military estimates, for the current year, Mr. Pelham consented that the army should still consist of eighteen thousand effective men; but from an excessive regard to economy, he unwisely determined to reduce the number of seamen, from ten, to eight thousand. This determination was not cordially approved, either by his brother, or by several of the ablest adherents of government, who regarded the navy, with a natural and national partiality.

The reduction was proposed in the committee of supply, on the 25th of January, by lord Barrington, as a Lord of the Admiralty, who justified it on the plea, that the former amount had been rendered necessary, by the fear of piracy, which was now no longer to be apprehended, and by the employment of ships in the East Indies, which had been since recalled. For these reasons he asserted, that eight thousand seamen would be fully adequate to the service of the year.

Mr. Nugent condemned the proposal, as impolitic and unjustifiable. He urged, that if economy was necessary, it would have been better shewn, in diminishing unmerited salaries and useless expenses, than in reducing the naval force, which might be considered as the palladium of the state. He accused the minister of a design to rule by military power; and drew a striking picture of the dangers to which the country was exposed, by the

* "Memoires," &c. by lord Orford, who says [vol. i. p. 9.] that Mr. Pelham answered in a very fine speech; but he does not give the substance of it.

maritime exertions of France. Then, adverting to the proposed extension
of martial law, by the Mutiny act, and to the expedient for superseding
impressment, he invidiously added, " But one enslaving scheme was defeated,
and the other shewn to be ridiculous; and now, since the minister finds that
he cannot make slaves of our seamen, he is for retaining as few of them as
possible in the public service. Soldiers are his only darlings; and therefore
we must maintain twice as many of them as we need, in time of peace;
though we may thereby lose that superiority at sea, which has cost us so
many millions of money, and so many thousands of lives."

He was followed by Mr. Oswald, who, quoting the speeches of the king,
and the addresses to the throne, of the two last sessions, for maintaining the
naval establishment, in the most efficient state, noticed the inconsistency of
the minister in the present proposal, and ridiculed the pretext of economy,
at a time when the public money was squandered on foreign princes, who
might declare against us, in case of a war.

Mr. Pelham advocated the reduction, with as much ability, as a measure
so injudicious would admit. In urging the necessity of economy, he
deprecated any comparison between the army and navy, and contended that
the smallest savings must be considered, whenever they could be securely
effected. He declared, that in the judgment of experienced persons, eight
thousand seamen were fully sufficient for the service of the year; and in
reference to the exertions of France, for extending her marine, he observed,
that naval superiority consisted, not in the mere number of ships and men,
in actual service, but in the number of effective ships, and in the proportion
of able seamen, placed at the disposal of government, by the extension of
commerce and fisheries. No power in Europe, he added, had eight thousand
mariners in actual service; while this country, by resorting to the indispensable
expedient of the impress, might collect ten thousand men, without distressing the merchant service, and in a few weeks, man a larger fleet, than any
other state could equip in several months. He ridiculed the alarm concerning
the power of the French by sea; and argued that past reverses would
discourage them from lightly measuring their strength with us, on that
element. Even if they made such an attempt, he trusted they would find
themselves mistaken, while England preserved such alliances, as would
expose them to an attack by land. On this ground, he justified the
connections formed with the electoral courts, from the conviction that
France would cautiously abstain from disturbing the tranquillity of Great

Britain, so long as she should be unable to entertain a well-grounded hope of exciting, at the same time, intestine war in Germany.

He admitted, that the proposed reduction would not produce a saving of more than £.80,000; but, he contended, that even this sum was important, in the actual situation of the country. Lastly, he repelled the charge of inconsistency, deduced from the royal speeches and addresses of the preceding session, by asserting, that the navy was as much an object of care to his Majesty and his servants, at the present, as at any former period. In proof of this assertion, he mentioned the perfect state of equipment, in which the ships were maintained, and added, that nearly a million had been expended during the last year, on the naval service alone.

The proposal was violently resisted by Mr. Potter and lord Egmont, and as strongly supported by Mr. Fox. But it was remarkable, that Mr. Pitt and his friends, Mr. Lyttelton and Mr. George Grenville, though holding offices in the administration, voted in the minority. The resolution was, however, carried by 167 against 107.*

In the debate on the report, Mr. Pitt and his friends renewed their objections, with increased vehemence. Mr. Pitt, in particular, affected great concern and reluctance, in opposing the views of Mr. Pelham. He protested, that he did not even know it to be his measure, and he added, "my fears of Jacobitism alone, have induced me to differ upon this only point, with those, with whom I am determined to lead my life." He called the fleet the standing army of the country; and praised the army, also, for its high state of discipline, which he said was alone worth five thousand men. He concluded, by declaring his conviction, that the majority of the House really preferred an establishment of ten thousand seamen.

The harangue of Mr. Pitt produced a singular scene. Mr. Hampden attacked him and his friends, with the most poignant ridicule; and after piteously bewailing the mischiefs, which rhetoric had brought on the nation, sarcastically alluded to the advantages, which it had produced to the great orator himself, by raising him to offices of high trust and emolument. These personalities provoked an indignant reply from Mr. Pitt; and the quarrel was assuming a serious character, when Mr. Pelham interposed. With his usual good nature, he endeavoured to soothe the irritated disputants;

* Journals of the Commons. Hansard, v. xiv. p. 828.

defended Mr. Pitt, notwithstanding his opposition; and discountenanced the zeal, which Mr. Hampden had displayed, in behalf of government, though in defence of his own measure. The Speaker was at length obliged to exert his authority, and prevent an appeal to arms, which the spirit of both parties might otherwise have occasioned. The proposal for recommittal having been negatived by 189 against 106,* the original resolution finally passed without a division.

The conduct of Mr. Pitt and his friends produced a considerable sensation, both in and out of parliament, and strengthened the report, previously circulated, that a misunderstanding had arisen between the two brothers, and that Mr. Pitt would either join with the duke of Newcastle, or re-enter the lists of opposition. There is no doubt that this open hostility to a favourite plan, deeply affected Mr. Pelham; but, to such an extent had the unfortunate alienation really proceeded, that we find the conduct of Mr. Pitt warmly approved by the duke of Newcastle. In a letter to his relative, colonel Pelham, one of his confidential friends in the House of Commons, he thus expressed his feelings.

"DEAR JEMMY,   "Newcastle House, Jan. 30th, 1750-1.

"As you can be no stranger (if you have attended the late debate) to the able and affectionate manner, in which Mr. Pitt has taken upon himself, to defend me, and the measures which have been solely carried on by me, when both have been openly attacked with violence, and when no other person in the House opened his lips, in defence of either, but Mr. Pitt, I think myself bound, in honour and gratitude, to shew my sense of it, in the best manner I am able. I must, therefore, desire, that neither you nor any of my friends, would give into any clamour or run, that may be made against him, from any of the party, on account of his differing as to the number of seamen. For, after the kind part he has acted to me, and (as far as I am allowed to be a part of it), the meritorious one to the administration, I cannot think any man my friend, who shall join in any such clamour, and who does not do all in his power to discourage it. I desire you would read this letter to Sir Francis Poole, Mr. Thomas Pelham, Mr. Watson, Mr. Hay, Mr. Butler, and to Mr. Nathaniel Newnham, and Mr. Sergison, if you have a proper opportunity. I am sorry to be obliged to

---

* Lord Orford's Memoires, vol. i. p. 10-16.—Journals of the Commons.

take this method, in order to have my friends know what are my thoughts, when they might judge of them, by what they naturally ought to be.

" P. S. As I mean this only for the information of the persons above-named, I must desire that you would communicate this letter to no one else ; and that you would let them know, that I wish they would not mention my having written such a letter, though I can have no objection to any body's knowing my thoughts upon the subject."

This letter brought the misunderstanding between the two brothers to a crisis. Mr. Pelham, who could not be unacquainted with its contents, saw that no alternative remained, but a perfect reconciliation, or an open rupture. Both his affection and interests inclined him to the former ; and he accordingly made an overture, through his son-in-law, the earl of Lincoln. The proposal was candidly and readily accepted ; and the duke, in his reply to the earl of Lincoln, dated February 6th, stipulates certain conditions, as essential to their future harmony.

1st. That no allusion should be made to what had previously passed ; 2ndly, That they should determine to overlook any cause, which might have excited differences between them, either as ministers or as brothers ; and, 3rdly, That they should mutually endeavour to promote each other's views, and should publicly avow the satisfactory renewal of their good understanding.*

By the cordial reconciliation which ensued, Mr. Pelham was enabled to encounter, more successfully, the difficulties of his situation, and carry his plans of economy through parliament.

On the 4th of February, a vote of 18,850 men was proposed as the military establishment for the year. Lord Limerick moved an amendment, limiting the number to fifteen thousand. He was supported by Mr. Martin, who skilfully employed the trite arguments against standing armies ; but, on a division, the original resolution was approved by 240 votes against 117. On the report of the Committee it produced a new debate ; but was finally carried by 175 against 75.†

Notwithstanding the formal condemnation of the infamous libel against

* Letter from the duke of Newcastle to the earl of Lincoln, Feb. 6th, 1750-1. Newcastle Papers, MS.
† Journals of the Commons.—Lord Orford's Memoirs, vol. i. p. 21.

the Duke of Cumberland, at the commencement of the session, the adherents of the Prince took every opportunity to mortify his Royal Highness, by attempting to abridge his power, or by exciting suspicions of his character and principles. The question which they particularly selected for this purpose, was that relating to the establishment of the military staff. On the 11th of February, the sum of £.16,000 being reported from the Committee of Supply, for the payment of the general and staff officers, lord Egmont moved an amendment, for reducing it to £.11,000. In the discussion of this subject, he principally confined his objections to the office of Captain-general, which he declared to be unnecessary, in time of peace ; and, by the power and influence attached to it, no less dangerous to the Sovereign, than to the Constitution. He compared it with that of Lord High Constable, in the early periods of our history, and represented it as less circumscribed, and more fraught with peril to the country.

After inveighing against the dangerous effects, which the post of Captain-general was calculated to produce, he adroitly disclaimed any reference, either to the reigning sovereign, or to the Duke of Cumberland, as Captain-general, grounding his objections on the general principle, and on the dangerous precedent which it would establish. He, however, introduced an ideal comparison, which was intended to set the characters of the king and the Duke in an odious light ; and to shew, that the adoption of the principle would endanger the succession, or subject the heir apparent to the control of the younger brother. " In what a condition," he exclaimed, " would such an heir apparent be on his accession, with not an officer in our army or navy, on whom he could depend ; nay, most of them jealous of having offended him, and consequently his secret, if not avowed enemies ! Must not he, through necessity, allow himself to be as much governed by his younger brother, as his father had been through choice ? If he attempted to take into his own hands the reins of government, a civil war might ensue, which would, of course, raise a new pretender to the crown ; and we have had so much trouble with the last, that I think we ought cautiously to guard against any precedent, tending to create another. This caution every man will exercise, who does not purposely endeavour to set up a new pretender, in order to make way for the old." He concluded with reprobating the affected economy of ministers, who, after professing a disposition to curtail every expense, had confined their retrenchments to the reduction, which had doomed two thousand brave seamen to beggary.

In a manly and able reply, Mr. Pelham refuted these objections. He observed, " It was well known, 'that ever since we had an army, the Captain-general, who commanded in chief during war, always had his commission continued in time of peace. The duke of Ormond, for having commanded but one sorry campaign, enjoyed not only the commission, but the pay, during the life of queen Anne ; and, after the accession of his late Majesty, the duke of Marlborough was most justly restored to his commission of Captain-general, which he held during life, though he liberally gave up the pay, in order to save money to the public. These two instances, the only ones that occur, since our armies were continued during peace, establish the precedent ; and would it not be a most glaring affront, to make an exception, in disparagement of his Royal Highness, who has done so much service to his country, even at the peril of his life ? Admitting that his foreign campaigns were unfortunate, yet that ill success was not owing to any failure in him. His conduct and courage were acknowledged in every part of Europe, and were both manifested in a signal manner, on British ground. At a time when the enemy had occupied a great part of the island, and despair sat brooding on every countenance, he flew to our aid, and by his presence and example, revived the courage of the troops, after they had been twice defeated by the rebels. This very assembly owes its existence to him ; and shall we offer a manifest insult to our preserver ?

" If our gratitude militates against such an affront, our very security is concerned, in adopting the resolution now proposed. He must either have no connection with the army, or he must act as Captain-general. As such, and he can hold no inferior station, he must have officers under him, whom the efficiency of that command requires. The preservation of discipline in our army, demands that his Royal Highness should retain his commission as Captain-general ; for, without him, no inferior general would possess authority sufficient to inforce that discipline, which is so necessary to render the troops serviceable against an enemy ; and, to prevent that laxity and sloth, which peace would engender among them, requires great power and authority in the commander. For it is congenial to the nature of Englishmen, that soldiers should be held to their duty, by the principle of honour, rather than by the fear of punishment. Good order among private soldiers must depend on the strict and constant attention of the inferior officers ; and this cannot be easily maintained, unless the command of the army be entrusted to a person, highly eminent by his birth, or by his

character as a general. As these qualities are united in his Royal
Highness, it would be extreme folly, to deprive him of all influence with
the army.

"If the noble lord had moved for the commission and instructions given
to the Captain-general, much of the trouble which he has taken on this
occasion,' would have been spared. As to the dangers, which he has been
pleased to depict in such alarming colours, most gentlemen must have seen,
that they were altogether imaginary. He might as well have compared the
post of Captain-general to that of Grand Vizier, as to the antient office
of Lord High Constable. There is not the least analogy between our
present constitution, and that which existed in former ages; nor would it
be possible for us to return to the old form of government. The king
then held absolute power over the military; and that power was intrusted
to the Lord High Constable. The marshal, it is true, sat with him, in that
court of judicature called the Court of Chivalry, but had no control over the
orders issued by him, concerning the military. In this respect he was sole
and absolute; and almost every man in the kingdom was then reckoned
among the military, and of course subject to his orders. The power possessed by him, therefore, was materially different from that which a
Captain-general now has, or indeed can have, unless with the sanction of
an act of parliament.

"The post of Captain-general, as now constituted, is, in time of peace, and
within the kingdom, rather a post of dignity than of power. All commissions
in the army, and all general orders, must be signed by his Majesty, and
counter-signed by the Secretary-at-War, who is an officer quite independent
of the Captain-general, and answerable to parliament for every thing which
he countersigns. As to courts-martial, it is well known, that to serve upon
such courts, either regimental or general, is part of a duty devolving by
rotation, which every officer must perform in his turn. Besides, their sentence, especially if affecting life or limb, must be confirmed by his Majesty,
before it can be executed. How then can it be said, that the life of any
officer is placed at the disposal of the Captain-general? Is it to be supposed,
that a court-martial would, at his desire, condemn a brother officer, whom
they knew to be innocent; or that the king, duly informed, would confirm
the sentence? The Captain-general, then, can have no power over the life
of any soldier, much less of any officer, under his command. As he cannot
promote, so neither can he break any officer in the army, without his

Majesty's approbation. He may indeed order the arrest of an officer, or suspend him, until his Majesty's pleasure be known, or until he be tried by a court-martial. As to his power of dispensing rewards, he may promote officers when vacancies occur; but this promotion may be confirmed or annulled by the sovereign, who, at his own pleasure, may bestow the commission on another. This is all the power, either of rewarding or punishing, which a Captain-general enjoys, during peace, and this power can never, I think, be dangerous to king or people.

" I therefore infer, that neither sovereign nor people can have any thing to fear from the power of a Captain-general over the army. But both sovereign and people may expose themselves to great danger, by dealing unjustly and ungratefully with a brave and beloved commander; because such treatment would urge him, in self preservation, to attach to his own interest, the army, and a great part of the people. Ingratitude like this, provoked and enabled Julius Cæsar to overthrow the liberties of his country; for, if the leading men in Rome had not offered such provocation, he would never have conceived the design, nor could he have calculated on the support of the army. But we need not look so far for examples. Many of us may remember the indignation excited against queen Anne, for her ingratitude to the duke of Marlborough; indignation which, notwithstanding the love of the people, might have proved fatal to that sovereign, had not the general himself exhibited a rare example of loyalty and constancy. Let a just return of gratitude, therefore, be made to a commander, who has performed eminent services; and neither king nor people need fear, that the army will support him, in any unprovoked attack, either on the dignity of the crown, or the liberties of the country.

" As to the hypothetical case, adduced by the noble lord, that the king's younger son might, in some future time, have the chief command of the army, while the elder was excluded from all the councils of his father, it is, like many other suppositions, a case that can never happen, in the manner contemplated; for whatever dislike or indifference a king may entertain towards his eldest son, no minister, I believe, and most certainly no officer, will, either from interest or inclination, disoblige the heir apparent. All would behave towards him with the respect consistent with their duty to the sovereign; and on his accession, he might expect, at least as much fidelity from them, as from those who, during the life of his father, had flattered him, at the expense of their allegiance. And, allow me to observe, that no man who truly values our present happy establishment, will endeavour to sow discord between any two branches of the royal family. On the contrary, if an accidental misunderstanding should arise, it is the duty of those who have access to either, to employ every method of reconciliation, and not to widen the breach, by setting up one in opposition to the other.

" Lastly, in regard to the economy of the measure, I think the noble lord has admitted, that what he calls the civil part of the staff, exceeds £.10,000 a year ; therefore the whole amount that we could save, by dismissing the great Prince, who has so high a claim on our gratitude, would not amount to six thousand a year, a pitiful sum, even supposing that the whole could be saved. This would not be the case ; for while we maintain regular troops during peace, we must have them inspected and reviewed by general officers, to ascertain their efficiency and state of discipline, and to inquire if the people of the country where they are quartered, have any just ground of complaint against their behaviour. When you keep such officers in pay, their duty is to go upon the service, as often as his Majesty shall think necessary, without any extraordinary allowance ; but, if you keep no such officers in pay, a specific expense must be incurred, which experience has shewn to be nearly equivalent to any saving, that could be effected, by abolishing this military part of the staff.

" I hope I have now placed this affair in such a light as will prevent farther discussion ; for it is of so delicate a nature, that it really gives me inexpressible pain to hear it debated. Therefore, if the noble lord will insist on his motion, I think the question should be put as soon as possible." *

This reasoning was not invalidated, by the replies of Dr. Lee and Mr. Potter, who reiterated with great spirit, but with equal acrimony, many of the arguments advanced by lord Egmont. Indeed, the factious temper of the Prince's adherents was so little restrained, that it gave offence to the sober-minded members of all parties ; and the invidious tendency of the amendment being generally perceived, it was negatived by 205 against 88.†

The motion for the supplies ‚brought into discussion the critical question of the Bavarian subsidy. Notwithstanding the aversion of Mr. Pelham to

---

* Hansard's Parl. Hist. vol. xiv. p. 910.
† Hansard's Parl. Hist. vol. xiv. p. 930.—Journals of the Commons.

subsidize foreign powers, in time of peace, we have seen, that he consented to that of Bavaria, on the supposition, that the election of a king of the Romans would be effected, without farther pecuniary sacrifices. On this condition, he had obtained the consent of the duke of Bedford ;* and had induced Mr. Walpole, and many of his friends, in the House of Commons, not to oppose the motion. Accordingly, in the committee of supply, on the 22nd of February, he moved for a grant of £.30,000,† to make good his Majesty's engagements with the elector of Bavaria, and supported the proposal, with the most judicious arguments that could be adduced in its favour.

After adverting to the documents relative to the treaty, which had been long in the possession of the House, he proceeded to vindicate the policy of that engagement. As a commercial people, he said, the British are at all times interested in the preservation of peace, and especially at this period, when war could not be carried on, without adding to a load of debt already excessive. One beneficial result had accrued, in the reduction of interest, which afforded the means of liquidating annually a large portion of that debt ; and if the peace should continue only a few years, the accumulation of ready money in the country, would facilitate a farther reduction, with the full consent of all parties concerned. Whether it might be possible to pay off the whole debt, before another war became necessary, he would not pretend to decide ; but he insisted that it would be highly dangerous, to engage in a new war, before a great part of the existing debt was liquidated. " For," he continued, " until the whole be discharged, we cannot expect to maintain war, except on credit, and the events preceding the close of the last contest have fully proved how precarious was that support. Credit, either public or private, supposes a two-fold ability : the borrower must be deemed competent to repay ; and the party willing to lend, must be in such circumstances, that he can afford to lend. A landed proprietor might possess an unincumbered

---

* See the duke of Bedford's speech on the Saxon subsidy in 1752, chap. xxvi.

† Journals of the Commons. Ways and Means in the Gent. Mag. vol. xxi. p. 247. We cannot explain Mr. Pelham's motion for a grant of £.30,000 ; because, had England even paid two thirds of the £.40,000, as stipulated by the treaty between the Maritime Powers and the elector of Bavaria, the sum would not have exceeded £.27,000 ; but, as the empress queen had agreed to one fourth, or £.10,000, the sum to be paid by England was reduced to £.20,000 ; and we find that, excepting this first year, England only paid annually, £.20,000, until the term expired. Possibly the additional £.10,000 might be the empress queen's proportion, which was paid for her, the first year, by England.

estate, so large as to leave no doubt of his ability to repay, and yet he could not borrow a shilling, on mortgage, unless he could find one who had that shilling to lend. Such might be our case, if forced to engage in a new war : we might, perhaps, though not easily, devise new funds, but the greatest difficulty would be, to find people who had money to lend.

" We are bound, therefore, to neglect no expedient calculated to preserve the peace ; for, in my opinion, Europe is now so circumstanced, that no war can arise, in which we can avoid being involved. But that peace must be precarious, which depends on the will of a single prince or state; and to control the will, we must restrain the power. How is this to be accomplished ? Certainly by forming such a defensive confederacy, among the European states, most likely to remain well disposed towards us, as may render it dangerous for any power to disturb the general tranquillity, by attacking one of its neighbours. Of the disposition of the Dutch we are certain ; of that which prevails in Germany, we can hardly entertain a doubt ; for I believe that scarcely an instance is on record, in which that empire has been the aggressor. A defensive alliance, therefore, between the States General, the empire, and this nation, should be as strongly cemented as possible ; and, that the empire may be an efficient ally, we should adopt all practicable methods, to prevent disunion among the members constituting that great and formidable body ; for, while it remains united, and in close confederacy with the Dutch and us, no power, I believe, will venture to break the peace of Europe. Should differences arise, the parties concerned will terminate them amicably, through our mediation, rather than incur our resentment by an appeal to arms.

" To prevent disunion in the Empire, we must consider what are the circumstances most likely to produce it ; and we shall soon find, that the two principal contingencies to be apprehended, are the formation of a powerful French party in Germany, and a vacancy in the imperial throne. All the European states, therefore, who are inclined to preserve peace, must labour to diminish the French interest in Germany, and to provide against a vacancy in the throne, by that method which the laws of the Empire sanction, and which repeated precedents have authorised ; I mean by the election of a king of the Romans. These were the views of his Majesty, in concluding the treaty now under consideration ; and I do not think that any more effectual expedient could have been devised to realise them.

" For more than half a century, the House of Bavaria has been devoted to the French interest, through which it has twice brought the House of Austria, and I may say the empire itself, to the brink of perdition. On both occasions, we had the honour of contributing mainly to their preservation, first by the glorious victory of Blenheim, and secondly by that of our most gracious sovereign, at Dettingen. By these victories, the empire, and the House of Austria, were twice saved from ruin; and I trust that by this treaty his Majesty will have prepared the means of shielding them from similar danger.

"If its sole object had been, to attach the House of Bavaria to the true interests of Germany and Europe, the treaty would have been well worth the small expense which it has imposed on the nation; especially when we consider that the immense sacrifices for preserving the House of Austria, in the reign of queen Anne, and during the late war, were rendered necessary, by the subserviency of Bavaria to France. Deprived of the access into Germany, afforded by that subserviency, France would have conceded to Austria a reasonable satisfaction for its claim to the Spanish Succession, and a sufficient barrier to the Dutch; and again on the death of the emperor Charles the Sixth, can any one imagine, that the old cardinal * would have engaged his country in a war, or that Prussia would have attacked Silesia, if a perfect union had subsisted between the Houses of Austria and Bavaria? Both those wars, which have cost us so many millions, would have been prevented, if so wise a measure as this had been adopted before the death of king William; and, that he conceived it, I do not doubt, but there was at that time so strong a party against him, and so violent an opposition to all his measures, that he despaired of obtaining the sanction of parliament, and therefore relinquished his intention.

"On the single consideration, which I have stated, the treaty would have been well worth the stipulated amount. But when we calculate its tendency to secure the other object, by preventing a vacancy in the imperial throne, we cannot sufficiently admire the wisdom of his Majesty, in contriving the measure, or his ability in bringing it to perfection, on such easy terms. From the large subsidies paid by France to some other princes of the empire, it might have been apprehended, that she would outbid us. But his Majesty, through his ministers, placed the circumstances of Europe, and particularly of Germany, so clearly before the court of Bavaria, and

---

* Cardinal Fleury.

exhibited in so strong a light, the consequences of their continued adher¬
ence to France, that they at length accepted a smaller subsidy from us,
than probably might have been obtained, and perhaps was offered, by the
court of Versailles. The ulterior object of this treaty will doubtless be
admitted to be most essential to the public peace ; for, should the
reigning emperor happen to die, before the election of a king of the
Romans, a general war must ensue. The Treaty of Aix-la-Chapelle
terminated, as conclusively as was then possible, all the disputes existing
among the princes of Europe ; but no treaty can extinguish the ambitious
designs entertained by some of those potentates. Such designs are
suspended, only until an opportunity shall occur, for carrying them into
execution. A vacancy in the imperial throne would afford such an opportunity ; we should then hear again of armies marching, either for attack or
defence, from every corner of Europe ; and this nation would again be
obliged to drain its manufactures for soldiers, and its commerce for sailors,
and to incur an annual expenditure of millions. The life of the present
emperor I admit to be a very good one, and I hope it will long continue ;
but no certain dependence can be placed on human existence, and no wise
man would risk the peace and happiness of his country, on so precarious
a tenure as a single life. It is, therefore, absolutely necessary to add
another life, by electing a king of the Romans, during the reign of the
present emperor. The archduke Joseph, eldest son of the emperor, is the
only eligible person, for two incontrovertible reasons : the concurrence of
his Imperial Majesty cannot be expected for any other candidate, and the
equilibrium of Europe requires, that the imperial diadem should remain
with the House of Austria.

" The first of these propositions will be evident to any one, who understands the Germanic constitution ; and, with respect to the second, as a
merely trifling revenue is annexed to the high office of Emperor, no prince
legitimately eligible, except a prince of the House of Austria, can defray
the expense of supporting its dignity, without a pension, or in modern
phrase, a subsidy from France ; and to establish in Germany a stipendiary
emperor is an object at which that politic court has long been aiming, as
the means of securing incontestable sway in Europe. Against such an
ascendancy, the vigilant exertions of this nation are especially required ;
not only because we have most to lose, but because the French are naturally
more inveterate enemies to us than to any other people ; for their hostility

to us proceeds from difference in character and manners, as well as from the many sanguinary wars, formerly waged between the two nations.

"It will be urged, I am well aware, that if the continental states will not defend their own liberties, we have only to retire within our wooden walls, and bid defiance to all the powers of Europe. This refuge is easily prescribed, but it was never thought practicable, by any man of common understanding; for even the French alone would soon render themselves superior to us by sea, if they had no apprehension of an attack upon the Continent. What might they not then achieve against us, if supported by the Dutch, and by the other Maritime Powers? Besides, if they were incontestably predominant, at the continental courts, they would command them to close all their ports against the ships of Great Britain, and to prohibit all our manufactures. Thus would our navy be ruined; for ships of war, without seamen, are useless; and, without an extensive commerce, it is impossible to have a sufficient number of seamen. Had we adopted this selfish and foolish maxim, at the commencement of the late war, what would have been the consequence? The House of Bavaria would have been established on the Imperial throne, and would have acquired, at least the Austrian Netherlands; Spain, or the Spanish House of Bourbon, would have possessed the Austrian dominions in Italy; and thus the French would have been absolutely secured against attacks by land. In these circumstances, they might perhaps have tolerated our war against Spain, for a year or two, until they had augmented their navy, especially as they knew that in attempting any conquest on Spain in America, we should have more to fear from the climate than from the enemy. Having sufficiently augmented their navy, they would then have dictated the terms of our submission to Spain; and, had we refused, they would have ordered all the maritime powers of Europe to join them, in chastising the insolence of the English.

"This view of the consequences to have been apprehended, from our adoption of such selfish policy, at the commencement of the late struggle, may convince us, that notwithstanding our insular situation, we are vitally interested in preserving the House of Austria, and in securing the imperial diadem to that family. The election of the archduke Joseph, therefore, as king of the Romans, is an object which we ought to promote, with all practicable vigour and expedition; and nothing could have tended more effectually to its accomplishment, than the treaty under consideration. It does not indeed, nor could it include an express stipulation, binding the elector of Bavaria to give his vote for the young archduke ; for that would have been contrary to the fundamental laws of the empire. But the intent of the treaty is generally known ; and no one doubts, I believe, that the elector of Bavaria is resolved to concur with his Majesty in that election, which I hope will take place before our next session ; for, to all appearance, a majority is secured, and any existing delay can only arise from the endeavour to obtain unanimity, which may perhaps be successful.

"We have no reason to apprehend, that we shall be led into an increase of expense on this account ; for the present aspect of European affairs affords ground to hope, that the election will be speedily accomplished, without opposition. But, whatever may be its result, this treaty, as a preliminary, must be allowed to be wise and necessary. Even if we should be disappointed, the separation of the House of Bavaria from France, and its reunion with Austria, is a change in favour of the common cause of Europe, which might well deserve a higher price than that at which it has been purchased. Without farther observations, therefore, I move, ' that the sum of £.30,000 be granted to his Majesty, to enable him to make good his engagements with the elector of Bavaria, according to treaty.' "

The arguments of Mr. Pelham were first combated by Mr. Martin, an adherent of the prince. To shew the utter inefficiency of all subsidies in time of peace, he alluded to the conduct of the Hessians, the Danes, and even of the deceased emperor, Charles the Seventh, who, after accepting pecuniary aids from England, had deserted, or opposed her cause. "In a new war," he observed, " princes are guided by their actual interests ; and, therefore, instead of exulting, that we have detached Bavaria from France, we ought rather to apprehend, that the elector will take the earliest opportunity of resuming the connection." He then recapitulated the reasons alleged by the king of Prussia against the election ; and entered into a detail of historical facts, to prove that it might eventually be set aside, as informal, or, if carried by a majority only, might produce the very evils which the subsidy was intended to prevent.

He farther argued, that, if the proposed election were essential to the interests of Germany, the princes of the empire would need no bribe to carry it into effect. But, if they retained their former jealousy of the House of Austria, they could not fail to be alarmed, by the intimate connection of England with that power; and would take an early opportunity of resenting our efforts to render the imperial dignity virtually hereditary in the Austrian line.

He justly inferred, that this subsidy was only the first step of an extended system; and that if we gained the support of one elector by purchase, we must offer our contributions to the others, and even to many of the States, who were enabled to influence the election. He adroitly turned against Mr. Pelham his own argument, that the public burthens ought to render us anxious for the prevention of war, by insisting that such a reason presented an additional motive for husbanding our resources, in order to lighten the pressure of those burthens, and to afford more liberal subsidies when really needed.

The Solicitor General controverted, with great acuteness and learning, the arguments grounded on the manifestos of Prussia and France; and proved by historical evidence, that the proposed election was not contrary to the practice of the empire, nor the means employed for its promotion, at variance with the principles of the Germanic constitution. He justified it as a measure of economy, by maintaining that the attendant expense was trifling, compared with that which would be imposed on the nation, if the Imperial throne should become vacant, and troubles arise, without proceeding to actual war.

Jealousy against the overgrown power of Austria did not, he contended, prevail, except among those who fostered selfish views of increasing their own strength and importance, at the expense of that family. He considered that France possessed more formidable means than Austria, for injuring the liberties of Europe; and complained that she never interfered in the affairs of Germany, except to foment troubles, by which she might profit; while the interposition of England was prompted solely by a desire to maintain the union, and consequently the welfare of the empire.

The discussion was prolonged by lord Egmont, who, in reprobating the means employed for securing the election, admitted the wisdom of the scheme itself. He was answered by Mr. Pitt, who availed himself of this concession; and, in vindicating the means, principally recapitulated the arguments already used by Mr. Pelham, and the Solicitor General, which derived new force from the characteristic energy of his eloquence.

The opposition did not risk a division in the Committee; and, though they renewed the discussion on the report, the grant was finally carried, by 197 against 74.*

It might have been expected, that after the mitigation of the Mutiny Act, in the last session, the renewal of this annual bill would have produced no serious opposition. An individual case, however, presented itself, which occasioned an attempt to extend the powers of general, to regimental courts-martial. This was a dispute between general Anstruther, formerly lieutenant governor of Minorca, and Sir Henry Erskine, nephew of John, late duke of Argyle. General Anstruther was extremely unpopular in Scotland, as being the only Scottish member, in the House of Commons, who had voted for the demolition of the Netherbow Gate at Edinburgh, soon after the murder of captain Porteous. Sir Henry Erskine, who was quartered in Minorca, with his regiment, and had imbibed all the prejudices of his countrymen, concerning this unhappy event, had, by most severe animadversions, led general Anstruther to suspect, that he was engaged in a conspiracy to undermine his character, which had already suffered by imputations of tyranny and oppression, from some inhabitants of the island. General Anstruther accordingly brought Sir Henry Erskine before a court-martial, but he was acquitted ; and the misunderstanding, thus suspended, continued to rankle in the minds of both, until it was revived, by the discussion on the Mutiny bill.

On the 19th of February, in the committee, lord Egmont, who considered the conduct of general Anstruther, in the court-martial on Sir Henry Erskine, as an offence against the Mutiny Act, proposed, as an amendment to the clause, enabling general courts-martial to administer oaths to witnesses in any trial, and obliging officers present at any court-martial, to take a prescribed oath, that regimental courts-martial should have the same power, to administer oaths to witnesses, and that the oath† prescribed for the officers, should be administered in regimental, as well as in general courts-martial. In support of this amendment, Sir Henry Erskine, after complaining of the exorbitant power of general officers in courts-martial, took occasion to adduce his own case, and recounted, in violent language,

---

* Hansard's Parl. Hist. vol. xiv. p. 939.—Lord Orford's Memoires, chap. i.—Journals of the Commons.

† "You shall well and truly try, and determine, according to your evidence of the matter now before you, between our sovereign lord the King's Majesty, and the prisoner to be tried."—Hansard, vol. xiv. p. 972.

many instances of the rigorous treatment, which he had experienced from general Anstruther. The facts produced so strong a sensation, that on the following day, general Anstruther appeared in his place, and made a formal defence, in which he not only attempted to exculpate himself, but brought forward many charges against Sir Henry Erskine, tending to justify his own suspicions of a conspiracy, and to represent himself as the victim of persecution.

Sir Henry Erskine, in reply, stated that he had forgiven the ill usage of the general, as sincerely as he now pardoned his suspicions; and concluded, by earnestly requesting the House, that the dispute might be buried in oblivion. Here the affair seemed to terminate; but, on the 4th of March, it was brought forward in another shape. Mr. Townshend, eldest son of viscount Townshend, moved for the production of all the papers relating to courts-martial, during general Anstruther's government, and complained that the general was still permitted to retain his regiment, though he had been found guilty in 1748, by the privy council, of oppressing the inhabitants of Minorca, and had been ordered to make compensation to the parties aggrieved. Sir Henry Erskine again disclaimed vindictive motives, but intimated that he had heavier charges in reserve, and accused government of partiality, to the disadvantage of the Scots, in the disposal of military promotions.

This invective called up Mr. Pelham, who said, " I know little of military promotions, but I see in the newspapers as many Erskines and Dalrymples promoted, as any persons of English families." Then, alluding to the question before the House, he continued, " I dislike proceeding parliamentarily in this business, but if it should be the opinion of the House, I will engage to have general Anstruther tried by a court-martial." Lord Egmont threw out threats of an impeachment. Mr. Pitt strongly supported a parliamentary inquiry, which Mr. Fox as strenuously opposed, on the ground, that it was improper to bring to trial any person, though guilty, for offences committed previous to the act of grace. In this opinion all the lawyers in the House, except Mr. Fazakerley, concurred; and at length the debate was closed, by a motion of Mr. Fox, for reducing the number of papers demanded, and for allowing Sir Henry Erskine two days to prepare his charges.

On the next day, Mr. Townshend presented a vehement petition, from a gentleman of Minorca, complaining of barbarous treatment from general

Anstruther, stating that the sentence against the petitioner had been rescinded by the privy council, and, that having incurred considerable debts during his suit, he had applied ineffectually to the Treasury, for money to carry on the prosecution. Mr. Townshend moved that this petition should lie on the table.

Mr. Pelham owned, that he had refused to issue money to the petitioner from the Treasury, and condemned as improper, the reception of such petitions, as it would encourage similar claims from all our colonies. He declared that, for his part, he should not singly oppose it, but if any other member spoke against it, he should vote for its rejection.

Mr. Pitt, with a singular spirit of contradiction to Mr. Pelham, justified the grant of two or three thousand pounds, to a poor petitioner of such high rank; and declared, with his usual energy, that he would support the petition, to the last drop of his blood.

Mr. Fox ridiculed this warmth with great humour, and questioned the allegations of the petition. He then attributed the persecution against general Anstruther to national inveteracy, of which he cited conspicuous proofs, and urged that his conduct in the affair of Porteous's murder, deserved the applause, not the censure, of all good men. During the warm debate, which ensued, lord Egmont, in an inflammatory speech, argued in favour of the petition, and declared that no man who voted for its rejection, would dare to shew his face. This illiberal remark roused Mr. Pelham, who said that he would faithfully serve his king in place and out of place, without opposing measures from motives of resentment, and then he should dare to shew his face any where. The petition was rejected, by 97 against 58.

On the 11th, Sir Henry Erskine brought forward his charge against general Anstruther, in the form of a statement of his own case, which appeared very trifling, after the parade of his first accusation. In the opinion of a member, who was present,* his grievances simply amounted to a confinement of six weeks, before, and during the court-martial, and of a few days after the termination of the trial. The debate dwindled into a desultory conversation, respecting the propriety of preserving the records of courts-martial, even in cases of acquittal, and the House adjourned, without coming to any conclusion.

---

* Lord Orford's Memoires.

A copy of the proceedings of the court-martial, and an answer to the charges, were presented by a friend of general Anstruther, who was confined to his house through age and infirmity. The answer was plain and simple; it acknowledged the facts, but denied the aggravating circumstances.

The charges against general Anstruther were now considered so trivial and exaggerated, that the partisans of Sir Henry Erskine could not venture to make them the basis of a parliamentary inquiry; and therefore the assailants of the general pursued a different course. On a subsequent day, Mr. Townshend moved an address, praying his Majesty to inforce the sentence of the privy council, and oblige general Anstruther to make compensation to those whom he had oppressed and despoiled. The question was adjourned to the 24th, when several witnesses attended to prove the charges. Sir Henry Erskine having proposed that brigadier O'Farel should be called in, as a witness, Sir William Yonge objected to the motion, and said that the honour of the House was concerned, in previously ascertaining whether the crimes specified were not comprehended within the late Act of Grace.

Though both the accuser and the defendant expressed their anxiety, that the cause should be heard, the proposition of Sir William Yonge was adopted; and it appeared as the opinion of all the lawyers, that the offences, being anterior, were included in the Act of Grace; that the conduct of general Anstruther, in the court-martial on Sir Henry Erskine, was not, as some had insinuated, an offence against the Mutiny Act; and that, therefore, the proceedings should be discontinued. Lord George Sackville resisted the motion for calling in the witness, and proposed that general Anstruther should be tried by a board of general officers. Lord Strange, in conformity with the opinion of the lawyers, moved a resolution, declaring that the Act of Grace was the reason for not proceeding; and added that, if the House would take no cognizance of the affair, it might still be heard before a board of officers. Mr. Pitt declared that he never had entertained a thought of infringing the Act of Grace; but was anxious to scrutinize the tyranny of the general, merely with a view to new-model the Mutiny-bill, if necessary; that he desired to see the minutes of the court-martial for information, and not for the foundation of a criminal charge; that, without the restraint arising from the Act of Grace, he should have opposed the examination of O'Farel, because the business of the House was, not to hear causes beyond their jurisdiction, but to find remedies for deficiencies in the laws. After some farther observations, he remarked, that to send this affair before a board of officers, would be to constitute the crime anew; and concluded by saying, " It is my sole desire, that governors in our plantations and foreign garrisons may know, that the prosecution of this affair was stopped by the Act of Grace, and may tremble for the future.".

Mr. Pelham, gratified to perceive that this embarrassing debate was drawing to a close, merely added, " If I were disposed to try the general by a board of officers, I should not consider the Act of Grace as an impediment; this being, in my opinion, the proper way of carrying the cause before the king. But the affair must now rest here; as all the lawyers are agreed, that such a course would violate that act. So far from concurring in a wish, which has been expressed, that the king may remember it, I sincerely hope that the whole case may be obliterated."

' Apprehensive that the high words which had passed between the parties might lead to an affair of honour, he intreated them to suppress their private resentments, as the House was obliged to extinguish those of the public. This judicious advice was inforced by the Speaker; and, after some altercation, general Anstruther and Sir Henry Erskine, mutually pledged their honour, to proceed no farther in the quarrel. Lord Strange having withdrawn his motion, the question was dropped, and no alteration was made in the original clause of the Mutiny Act.* Foiled in the attempt to extend the powers of general, to regimental courts-martial, the Opposition made another effort to prevent a revision of the sentences of courts-martial, a motion to that effect having been lost in the preceding session ;† but it was warmly opposed by the ministerial party, and finally negatived by 137 against 74.

---

* It is remarkable, that parts of the debates on this dispute are not mentioned, in any of the reports of parliamentary proceedings on the Mutiny-bill. For the account here given, we are wholly indebted to lord Orford, who was present on the occasion.—See Memoires of the Last Ten Years of the Reign of George the Second, vol. i. pp. 36, 55, 82, 91, 98.—Hansard, vol. xiv. p. 972.

† See chap. xxii. p. 95.

CHAPTER XXV

1751.

Increasing jealousy between the dukes of Newcastle and Bedford—Suspended by the interposition of the King—The Cobham party continue to tamper with the Court of Leicester House—Disputes between Mr. Fox and Mr. Pitt—Death of the Prince of Wales—Its immediate effects—Reconciliation of the King and Princess—Formation of the new Household—Weakness and division of the Prince's party—Difficulties and discussions on the Regency-bill—Embarrassments of the Pelhams—Conversation of Mr. Fox with the King, on the subject of the Regency-bill—The King opposes the wish of Mr. Pelham to retire.

THE misunderstanding between the two Secretaries of State continued during the session ; and many circumstances occurred, which increased their mutual irritation. The duke of Newcastle even again made an attempt to liberate himself from his colleague ; but was mortified by the peremptory declaration of the king, that he would sanction no present change in the cabinet, and that whoever should importune him upon that subject, would incur his royal displeasure, as the aggressor.*

This collision of interests led to several unpleasant discussions ; particularly on the dispatch of a naval force, to protect Nova Scotia from the vexations of the French and Indians. On this point, the duke of Bedford, lord Sandwich, the duke of Marlborough, and lord Gower, divided against the Pelhams ; the duke of Bedford unequivocally construing the proceedings into an act of hostility against himself.† In the debates, also, on the bill for the naturalization of foreign Protestants, which was promoted by Mr. Pelham, the adherents of the duke of Bedford evinced the feelings of their leader, by quitting the House before the division.

At this period the strength of the administration was likely to be diminished

---

* Letter from Mr. Fox to Sir Charles Hanbury Williams, dated Feb. 7th-18th, 1750-1.
† Memoires of lord Orford, vol. i. p. 59, 60.

by the defection of lord Cobham and his partisans, who had manifested their views on various occasions, by feebly supporting, and in some instances even by opposing the measures of Mr. Pelham, in the House of Commons. They were also making secret overtures to the Prince of Wales.*

The feud in the cabinet, the displeasure of the king against the duke of Newcastle, the enmity of the Duke of Cumberland, the increasing strength of Opposition, and the probable defection of the Cobham party, portended an important change in the political drama; and indeed the union of the ministry, could scarcely have subsisted, even during the session, had not an event happened, which absorbed all inferior considerations.

In the beginning of March, the Prince of Wales was seized with a sudden indisposition. The disorder, which arose from a common cold, was at first thought trifling, but it unexpectedly changed to a pleurisy. No danger, however, was apprehended; and his royal consort, as well as his friends, were struck with consternation, by his instantaneous death, which happened on the 20th of March, in consequence of the rupture of an imposthume in his breast.

The impression produced by this melancholy event, is well described in the letters of Mr. Fox and Mr. Harris, to Sir Charles Hanbury Williams.

Mr. Fox to Sir Charles Hanbury Williams.

"Dear Sir Charles,   "*March 22nd-April 2nd, 1750-1.*

"At the lower end of the Council-table, Legge and I are beginning to write to you. Curiosity has brought me hither, to hear the physicians and

---

* Lord Orford, in his posthumous Memoirs, relates an anecdote, which proves that Mr. Lyttelton and his friends had been tampering with the prince.

"After the death of his Royal Highness, Mr. Lyttelton wrote a letter to his father, lamenting that event, as having defeated a scheme for a coalition with the prince's party, negotiated through his brother-in-law, Dr. Ayscough, preceptor to prince George. The letter being directed to Sir Thomas Lyttelton, without any mention of the place of his abode, and put into the Post-office, by a careless servant, who ought to have delivered it in person, at Hagley, was opened, and sent to Mr. Pelham. He would have honourably suppressed the secret, though aimed against himself; but from the imprudence of those employed in the Post-office, it transpired, and at length came to the ears of the king. His Majesty questioned Mr. Sherlocke, Secretary to the Post-office, on the subject, who was injoined by the minister to avoid a direct answer; but the incident was afterwards avowed by Mr. Lyttelton himself."—Lord Orford's Memoires, vol. i. p. 174.

See also Mr. Fox's letter to Sir Charles Hanbury Williams, dated March 22nd-April 2nd, 1750-1, in a subsequent part of this chapter.

surgeons give an account of the illness, death, and appearances, on opening the body of the Prince of Wales ; and I propose to close this letter with a short account of what they say.   *   *

"The great event, which we are going to inquire after the cause of, you may be sure has given great apprehensions, and will have great consequences. Disappointment and despair appear on many faces, belonging to ambitious heads. My lord Drax, my lord Colebrook, earl Dodington, and prime minister Egmont, are distracted ;* but nobody more than lord Cobham, who *cum suis*, has been making court, and with some effect, all this winter. * * * But do not name this from me. I fear they will not be dealt with, as I would deal with them. Adieu.

"I have learnt nothing but what I knew before. The prince died of an imposthume in his breast, which, after ten days' illness, and when he was thought out of danger, broke, and suffocated him instantly. There was another large bag of matter appeared, when he was opened, on the right side, which is supposed to have been of long standing, and imputed to a blow or a fall. He died at a quarter after nine on Wednesday night. His Majesty was surprised, and is infinitely affectionate towards the princess, and the children, and has sent and wrote to her every day. The sons, the eldest at least, will come to St. James's ; and his Majesty has the Duchy of Cornwall reverted to him. Poor Tom Pitt ! "

Mr. Harris to Sir Charles Hanbury Williams.

"*London, March* 22*nd*, 1750-1, *O. S.*†

"I told you that the Prince of Wales was just mending, from a very dangerous pleuritic fever, as it was then styled. The folks of physic, and every body, thought him to be in a fair way. Wednesday the 20th, in the afternoon, lord Bathurst was sent for, with his *agreeable chat;* the people of his family all dispersed in the several diversions of the town : in short, no doubt made of his recovery. A pain came on suddenly ; and while the page assisted to turn him in bed, the prince said, "*je meurs*," and expired instantly, before the princess, upon the cry of the page, could get from the feet to the

---

* These were some of the principal officers of the Prince's household, who looked forward to titles and honours on his accession to the throne.

† Hanbury Papers.

head of the bed. This happened about half an hour after nine in the evening. He was opened yesterday ; and the true cause of his death, was a
gathering imposthume in the breast, which is now carried back to a hurt
done him by a fall at trap-ball, full two years ago at Clifden. The king
sent, in writing, a very affectionate message, in the tenderest terms, to the
Princess.

" The Land-tax and Mutiny-bills are passed, this day, by commission ; and
the House adjourns to the middle of next week. What an event! how many
dreams of greatness ended at once! Their imagined splendours, and their
meditated vengeance hereafter, all undone and vanished ! . Well, I will only
say, that *worthy honest* men may now do what is right, and meet with no
thwartings and difficulty, in making the latter part of his Majesty's life and
reign, easy, happy, and glorious to him."

*　　　*　　　*

The melancholy death of the prince revived all those kindly feelings,
which had so long been suppressed in the royal family. The king instantly
wrote and dispatched a letter of condolence to the widowed princess ; and in
two subsequent visits, treated her and her children, with all the tenderness
and sympathy of a parent. The princess, herself, deeply affected by these
tokens of paternal regard, not only acknowledged them, with fervent
respect and gratitude ; but, by the advice of Dr. Lee, who acted with great
uprightness on the occasion, she determined to abandon all views of separate
interest. She placed herself and her children, entirely under his Majesty's
protection ; and not only submitted implicitly to his will, but seemed to
have totally renounced that spirit of opposition, which had set the son at
variance with the father. This unexpected, yet cordial union in the royal
family, disconcerted all the ambitious schemes, conceived by the partisans of
the late prince. On the morning after his death, they assembled, indeed,
at the summons of lord Egmont, to form a plan of future conduct ; but the
meeting was cold and formal ; whispers were substituted for discussion,
and they separated in doubt and alarm, without having adopted, or even
proposed any system of action.* Many of them afterwards attempted to
make their peace with the ministers ; others vacillated, and even the most
strenuous in opposition were afraid to take a decisive part. Pitt, Lyttelton,

---

* Lord Melcombe's Diary.

and the Grenvilles, who had been tampering with the prince, now felt that their desertion would be disadvantageous only to themselves, and again became zealous supporters of administration. In consequence of the satisfactory arrangement in the royal family, £.50,000 a year was settled on the princess, with a liberal allowance for the younger children.

The new regulation of the household was facilitated by the good understanding between the king and princess. His Majesty was indeed advised to take prince George under his immediate control, by removing him to the palace ; but partly from aversion to so troublesome a charge, and partly from a wish to gratify the princess, he confided to her the care and education of his grandson ; and thus unconsciously laid a foundation for future dissension. In April, the heir apparent was created Prince of Wales and Earl of Chester ; and the places appointed for his residence were Leicester House, and the royal palace of Kew.

In the arrangement of the new household, it was natural that the Pelhams should be inclined to place their own adherents about the person of the prince ; but, from the indulgence shewn to the princess, they were far from carrying their purpose to the extent that has been generally imagined. Jealous of the Duke of Cumberland, and desirous to prevent him from acquiring influence over his nephew, which, they were fearful, would have been the case, had the royal children been domiciliated in the palace, they forbore to oppose the king's wish, that they should be consigned to the care of their mother ; and consequently committed to her a greater share in their education, than was consistent with their own interests, and even with the tranquillity of the administration.

Dr. Ayscough, the tutor, was the first removed ; and his place was supplied by a gentleman of the name of Scott, who had been recommended to the deceased prince, by lord Bathurst, at the suggestion of lord Bolingbroke, and who was favoured by the princess. The appointment of preceptor, was conferred on Dr. Hayter, bishop of Norwich, who was considered as attached to the duke of Newcastle. Lord North was removed, to give place to the earl of Harcourt, as governor, on the recommendation of lord Lincoln. The post of sub-governor was filled by Mr. Stone, long the confidential secretary of the duke of Newcastle, who had conciliated the favour of the king at Hanover. Dr. Lee, the personal friend of the deceased prince, was appointed treasurer to the princess. The post of secretary, having been resigned by Mr. Potter, was restored to her confidential dependent, Mr.

Cresset, who was remotely related to the royal family, through the consort of George the First,* and who had essentially promoted the harmony now subsisting, between the king and the princess.   This gentleman had an additional claim to the gratitude of the princess, as the agent who had facilitated her union with the Prince of Wales ; and, like Scott, he was intimately connected with lord Bolingbroke.   Lord Sussex, lord Robert Bertie, and lord Downe were appointed lords of the Bedchamber ; and Mr. Selwin, a veteran adherent of Sir Robert Walpole, was nominated treasurer to the young prince.   Lord Bute, who had filled the office of lord of the Bedchamber, to the late prince, although he no longer continued in that post, was frequently consulted by the princess dowager ; and, on the establishment of the prince's household in 1752, was constituted one of the lords of the Bedchamber.   In this situation he laid the foundation of that high favour with the princess and the heir apparent, which he afterwards attained.

In consequence of these changes, the political party of Leicester House was dissolved ; for those who received appointments, imitated the example of the princess, in their devotion to the court, and others either sunk into insignificance, or like Dodington, opened a negotiation with Mr. Pelham for a restoration to royal favour.†

Notwithstanding these auspicious appearances, the crisis itself was pregnant with difficulty.   The establishment of a regency, in the event of a minority, became the subject of immediate deliberation ; and only two courses presented themselves, either to vest the regency in the princess, as mother of the heir apparent, or to intrust it to the Duke of Cumberland, who, as first Prince of the blood, of mature age, considered himself intitled to that high office.   The first expedient was contrary to all precedent ; as no instance had occurred of a female regency, unless that usurped by queen Isabella, during the minority of Edward the Third, could be so regarded.   But against the appointment of the Duke of Cumberland, a reason existed, much stronger than want of precedent.   The recent efforts of the prince's adherents had propagated a suspicion, however unjust, that the king was disposed to alter the succession, in favour of a son, who seemed to possess all his affec-

---

Sophia, daughter of William, duke of Zell, by Eleanor d'Emiers, of the French family of d'Olbreuse, to which Mr. Cresset was distantly related.—See an account of the unfortunate Sophia of Zell, in the Memoirs of Sir Robert Walpole, vol. ii. p. 258.

† Lord Melcombe's Diary.

tion and confidence. On the death of the prince, this popular apprehension had been unequivocally manifested; for the chorus, added to the public ballads, sung in the streets, was " Oh ! that it was but his brother ! Oh ! that it was but the butcher !" Nor was he obnoxious only to the lower orders. The severity of his military government had alienated many of the higher ranks; and his German reserve, and unconciliating manners, toward those who were not immediately attached to his person, were far from inspiring affection or regard. His unpopularity, indeed, was such as to render it probable, that his appointment as regent, would scarcely be sanctioned by the House of Commons, or admitted by the nation. It was aggravated also by the dislike, which had subsisted between him and his deceased brother, and which had created a violent prejudice against him, in the minds of the princess and the heir apparent.

The wishes of the king were strongly inclined towards the nomination of his favourite son; but the ministers were not disposed to brave the odium attached to such an arrangement, and they prevailed on his Majesty to sacrifice his own partiality to public opinion. The Duke of Cumberland, with unfeigned reluctance, acquiesced in this decision.

The alternative was, to adopt a middle course, which would in some degree reconcile the wishes of the king with those of the people. It was proposed, that the princess should be nominated regent, with the care of the young sovereign; and that her authority should be circumscribed by a council, over which the Duke of Cumberland was to preside. In maturing the details of this arrangement, the Pelhams encountered very serious difficulties; for, while the king insisted on the closest restrictions, many members of administration were averse to a division of the regal functions, which was so likely to render them inefficient. The preparation of the bill was confided to the lord Chancellor, with the assistance and advice of the crown lawyers; but many alterations were made in the draught, both at private meetings of the ministry, and in the privy council. Perhaps not a single clause was unanimously adopted; and the duke of Bedford, though he had recommended the nomination of the princess, notwithstanding his regard for the Duke of Cumberland, yet vehemently opposed all restrictions on her authority. Mr. Speaker Onslow likewise controverted many regulations laid down by the lord Chancellor; and Mr. Fox, from attachment to the royal Duke, was hostile to the very principle of the bill, and inclined to question its provisions, though he could not openly venture to oppose it.

At length the plan was deemed sufficiently mature to be submitted to parliament; and on the 26th of April a royal message was conveyed to the House of Peers by the duke of Newcastle, and to the House of Commons, by Mr. Pelham.

After earnestly recommending this important measure to the most serious consideration of parliament, his Majesty proposed that when the Crown should descend to any of the issue of his son, the late Prince of Wales, who should be under the age of eighteen, the Princess dowager of Wales, their mother, should be guardian of the person of such successor, during his or her minority, with such powers and limitations, as should appear necessary and expedient for that purpose.

In reply to this message, the two Houses unanimously voted an address, warmly acknowledging the paternal care of his Majesty, for the future welfare of his dominions, approving the recommendation in favour of the Princess dowager of Wales, and testifying their intention to take the matter into immediate consideration.

In pursuance of this resolution, the House of Peers assembled on the 7th of May, when the duke of Newcastle presented the draught of a bill, to provide for the administration of government in case of a regency. It was read a first time, and the second reading was fixed for the following day.

Previously to the second reading, the duke of Newcastle delivered another royal message, suggesting the appointment of a Council to the Regent, with such powers as should be deemed necessary and expedient, and recommending that the members of that council should be, the Duke of Cumberland, and the persons who should, at the time, respectively hold the offices of Archbishop of Canterbury, lord Chancellor, lord Treasurer, or first lord of the Treasury, lord President, Keeper of the Privy Seal, lord High Admiral or first Lord of the Admiralty, the principal Secretaries of State, and the lord Chief Justice of the Court of King's-bench.'

The bill was then read a second time, and committed for the 10th of May. The acquiescence of the Princess dowager in its provisions, was communicated by lord Bath ; though some of her violent partisans had advised her to object to the restrictions.

The recommendation conveyed in the royal message was literally adopted ; and a clause was added, empowering his Majesty to appoint by will, four additional members of the council. The Duke of Cumberland was constituted president; and the decision of at least five members was declared necessary for the validity of any act whatever. The consent of a majority was requisite for all creations, pardons, gifts, grants, instructions, or orders; for making war, or concluding peace; for adjourning, proroguing, or dissolving parliament; and for giving the royal assent to any bill affecting the succession. Vacancies in the council by death, were to be filled up by the regent, with the consent of the majority; and the same consent was indispensable to sanction the marriage of the sovereign while a minor. It was provided, that on the demise of the king, the parliament then existing, or if dissolved, the preceding parliament, should continue for three years, unless the sovereign should, in the interim, attain his majority, or unless it should be dissolved by the regent, with the consent of the council. In case of an equality of suffrages, the regent was to be intitled to the casting vote; and persons concurring to change the form of government, thus established, by commission, letters patent, or otherwise, were to incur the penalties of *præmunire.**

In the committee on the bill, some opposition was manifested. The appointment of a council, with any restrictive power, was opposed by earl Stanhope, but he was supported only by a few peers. The clause extending the duration of parliament for three years, excited the animadversions of lord Talbot; but was defended with equal warmth by lord Granville, who approved all the restrictions, and declared that this clause gave stability to the whole, being calculated to preclude the enemies of the country from profiting by the confusion invariably attending a general election. Lord Bath, among others, pronounced a high panegyric on the princess, and strongly objected to the limitation of her powers, in the appointment to offices. Similar arguments were employed by the bishop of Worcester; but all these objections were over-ruled by a large majority, and, on the third reading, the bill passed unanimously. It was said that the duke of Bedford had intended to repair to the House, for the purpose of opposing the restrictions, but was discouraged by the smallness of the minority, and dissuaded by his friends. Lord Sand-

---

* The original purpose of what are called the statutes of *præmunire* was to repress the power of the popes; and the designation is derived from the first words of the writ used in the process, " *Præmunire facias,*" a corruption of *præmonere.* The penalties were, outlawry, or exclusion from the protection of the crown, forfeiture of lands and goods, and attachment of the body, to answer to the king and his council. The term appears in many statutes; but the penalties were so severe, that the process itself was seldom resorted to.—Blackstone, vol. iv.

wich, with the approbation of the Duke of Cumberland, who publicly professed great moderation, gave his unqualified assent to every clause.

On the 13th of May, the bill was transmitted to the Commons. It was offered to the consideration of the House by Mr. Pelham, and encountered at first little opposition. Dr. Lee and Mr. Nugent both warmly approved it; and the few observations made on the first and second readings, appeared to be chiefly directed against the authority vested in the Duke of Cumberland.

The principal struggle occurred in the committee, when Mr. Pelham, being called to the chair, was precluded from participating in the debate. The various provisions of the bill occasioned a desultory conversation, in which the adherents of government seemed to be totally at variance in their sentiments. The Regency clause, after some objections, passed without a division; but an animated debate arose on the question concerning the appointment of a council with restrictive powers. Among the opponents of the bill, no one was more conspicuous than Mr. Speaker Onslow, who solemnly protested against it, as establishing a division of the royal functions, inconsistent with the principles of the constitution, and who reprobated the privileges assigned to the council, as favourable to the formation of an oligarchy, which might usurp the authority of the regent herself, and even assume absolute power. He also arraigned the *præmunire* clause, as excessively severe, and as tending, by the discretionary latitude of some of its provisions, to encourage acts of oppression.

His arguments were answered by the Attorney-general, who, in admitting that the royal authority ought not to be divided, except in extreme cases, contended, that as a minority was liable, either to faction, with a council, or to usurpation, with an unlimited regency, the least of the two evils should be chosen, and usurpation prevented, by proper limits to the regent's authority. Mr. Charles Yorke, in support of this line of argument, observed, that on the first Regency-bill after the Revolution, ten of the judges maintained, that the royal authority might be delegated, and even divided. He farther asserted, that no precedent existed of a regency without limitation. In the course of the debate, Mr. Fox, though affecting to approve the bill, severely censured the clause of *præmunire* as indefinite, and contended that the person who framed it, if aware of its injustice, merited its penalties. He therefore proposed to substitute in its place, impeachment, or a trial in the ordinary courts of justice. In this strain of reprobation, he was called to order by Mr. Pelham, who declared that the *præmunire* clause was not the subject of debate.

After some farther discussion, Mr. Pitt, with great energy, defended the nomination of a council, with restrictive powers. He denied that any record of an unrestricted regency existed ; and, after eulogizing the late prince, to whom he avowed his obligations, he adverted to the dangers which might have been apprehended, if a great person (meaning the Duke of Cumberland) had become sole regent, who might have been excited by ambition, to think less of protecting, than of wearing the crown. Mr. Fox repelled this imputation on his princely patron, with some asperity. An altercation ensued, and he indignantly quitted the House, before the division. The council clause was carried by 278 against 90, and the debate was adjourned to the ensuing day.

After some preliminary discussion, the clause for the prolongation of parliament was warmly debated, but was carried by 258 against 81. That which regulated the marriage of the sovereign, if a minor, occasioned some scrutiny, but was adopted without a division. The opposition, in fact, had reserved their strength for the debate on the *præmunire* clause.

On this occasion, Mr. Fox renewed his objections, and again proposed the substitution of impeachment, or trial in the ordinary courts of justice. The Attorney-general, in defending the clause, admitted that the words, "unlawfully, and without consent of parliament," might render the provision more distinct. In this amendment Mr. Fox acquiesced ; and the words were inserted in the bill. The discussion, however, continued, and on the suggestion of Mr. Pitt, the expression, " without consent of parliament," was excluded. At length the debate degenerated into a mere grammatical dispute, and after various insignificant amendments, the clause was passed by 126 against 40.

The bill was read a third time on the 20th of May; when Mr. Beckford appears to have been its sole remaining opponent. Mr. Pelham, released from his duties, as chairman of the committee, gave it his entire support. He expressed his surprise at so much debate on the subject of a royal message, recommending restrictions, which had been approved, with addresses of thanks, by both Houses. Objections had been made, not merely against a particular restriction, but against any restriction at all. " Yet I must ask," he continued, " how the appointment of a council for the regent, can be considered a breach of the constitution? I approved the council, because I would not expose the princess to temptation. I was willing to give her all the agreeable part of authority ; and the

council will not impede her in the exercise of grace and favour : it will
operate as a check only, where points of importance may introduce
difficulties. A regent may be encompassed with favourites, as well
as a king; and, therefore, her security requires, that she should have
a responsible council. When the settlement of the Crown was made,
in favour of the House of Hanover, greater restrictions than these
were proposed ; restrictions somewhat stronger than in temporary
regencies. The regent will be limited only in those important acts, in
which the Crown itself is limited, except on the subject of peace and war.
Is there any person here wise enough to tell me, who can be answerable
for the acts of the regent ? She herself is ; and, as this provision relieves
her from that responsibility, it is an act of respect towards her Royal
Highness."

In justification of the clause, for prolonging the parliament, he observed,
that ever since the Revolution, a dissolution or suspension of government
had occurred, during general elections, the contagion of which for a time
disunited all connections of friendship, and confounded all notions of right
and wrong, so utterly, that an elector, after giving his vote to one candidate,
would leave the care of his children and property to the antagonist of that
very candidate. He declared, farther, " that the constitution sanctioned
that bad spirit of disaffection, which made our enemies lie in wait, until
they saw how elections were likely to terminate.

" On the clause of *præmunire*, which has been so fully explained by the
lawyers, I have only to observe that, as Englishmen want no better safeguard, than trial by jury, little fear may be entertained of constructive
abuses. I must, however, declare, that the bill cannot be too strictly
observed. The objections are not made against the whole bill ; and the
committee has adopted amendments of the parts most liable to exception.
Indeed, I lament that the approbation of the House has not been more
general, though I impute no blame to any one, and have spoken without
prejudice, passion, or partiality. No one, I am persuaded, will suspect me
of any aim at personal power, in this bill ; and I should be indeed a wretch,
were I capable of entertaining views of aggrandisement, from an event,
which I must regard as a misfortune that would shake the state to its
foundations."

The arguments of the minister were ably supported by Mr. Pitt; and,
notwithstanding the various objections raised in the committee, no division

took place. The adherents of the late prince mostly voted for the bill, without reserve; even lord Egmont only argued against the clause for the prolongation of parliament. The lords adopted these trifling amendments, and on the 22nd of May, the bill received the royal assent.[*]

Mr. Pelham was particularly chagrined by the opposition offered to this bill, and especially by the objections of the Speaker. He was also surprised and vexed at the part taken by Mr. Fox, whom he reproached with not having spoken like himself, adding a commendatory remark on the speech of Mr. Pitt. He was, however, of too placid a temper to foster any resentment; and he heard, with his usual good-nature, the spirited reply of Mr. Fox, "Had I indeed spoken like myself, I should have said ten times more against the bill."

But Mr. Pelham was still more mortified at the indignation expressed by the Duke of Cumberland. Attributing to the Pelhams, his exclusion from the office of regent, his Royal Highness received the first communication of the contents of the bill, through their friend, the lord Chancellor, in an ungracious manner. His sole reply was, " Return my thanks to the king, for the plan of the regency. As for the part allotted to me, I shall submit to it, because he commands it, be the regency what it will." That this reply might appear the more pointed, he afterwards desired Mr. Fox to repeat it to Mr. Pelham, and charged him not to leave out the word *submit*, adding, " It is a material word, and the lord Chancellor will remember it, however he reports it." His displeasure had doubtless been inflamed, by the insinuations of his adherents, representing that his patronage of the duke of Bedford and lord Sandwich, had provoked the Pelhams to exclude him. We shall find that this impression was never effaced from his memory,

---

[*] The account of these debates is principally taken from the Memoires of Lord Orford, who was present, and who has left a copious, though desultory record of the speeches. Some particulars have been supplied from Dodington's Diary, p. 18–121, and from Hansard's Parliamentary History, vol. xiv. p. 992.

It is worthy of observation, that George the Third, in 1765, on his recovery from a serious indisposition, went in person to the House of Lords, and proposed to the consideration of parliament, the expediency of vesting in him the power of appointing, from time to time, by instruments, under his sign manual, either the queen, or any other person of the royal family, usually residing in Great Britain, to be guardian of his successor, and regent of the kingdom, until the successor should attain the age of eighteen, subject to the like restrictions and regulations, as are specified in this Act of Regency.—Journals of the Lords and Commons.— History of England, by Adolphus, vol. i. p. 197.—Thackeray's Life of Lord Chatham, vol. ii. p. 51.

for that he afterwards even accused the minister of a want of candour, honour, and sincerity.

Although the wishes of the king had been fully gratified by the restrictions imposed on the princess, the exclusion of the Duke of Cumberland from the office of regent, proved a source of regret. A conversation of his Majesty with Mr. Fox, which is recorded by lord Orford, strongly manifests his real feelings. He asked Mr. Fox, whom he would have made regent? " I never thought I should be asked," replied Mr. Fox, " and, therefore, never considered it as impossible, that the Duke should." The king said, " My affection was there," but made no allusion to the impossibility. After speaking with complacency of the share which Mr. Fox had taken in the discussions, his Majesty added, " I have a good opinion of the princess, but I do not quite know her." He strongly approved the restrictions, and said, " A council is necessary for her, even in cases of treason. Women are apt to pardon : I myself am inclined to mercy. It is better to have somebody to refuse for her. As to the power of peace and war, I would never declare either, without consulting others. And, as to the objection, that the council is immoveable, who knows if it will be composed of the present people? It will be the ministers whom I shall leave. Would you rather have those I shall leave, or have the princess at liberty to put in lord Cobham, or lord Egmont?"

He then asked, " What did you say against the bill? Do you like it? Tell me honestly." Mr. Fox answered, " If your Majesty asks me, Sir, No. What I said against it, was, because what was said for it was against the Duke." The king replied, " I thank you for that; my affection is with my son. I assure you, Mr. Fox, I like you the better for wishing well to him. The English nation is so changeable; I do not know why they dislike him. It is brought about by the Scotch, the Jacobites, and the English that do not love discipline; and, because all this is not enough, discouraged by the ministry.† "

Soon after the death of the Prince of Wales, Mr. Pelham was so harassed with the feuds in the cabinet, the contentions in the House of Commons, and the fatigue of his official duties, that, on the death of lord Orford, auditor of the Exchequer, on the 30th of March, he is said to have intimated

* Memoires of Lord Orford, vol. i. pp. 89, 90, 304, 305.

† Lord Orford's Memoires, vol. i. p. 137. Doubtless lord Orford received the account of this interesting conversation from Mr. Fox himself.

a wish to retire to this sinecure post. The king, apprehensive that such a change would be followed by an immediate dissolution of the ministry, earnestly pressed him to forego his purpose. In deference to the sovereign, he at length consented to retain his eminent, though irksome situation; and his Majesty graciously conferred the vacant office on the earl of Lincoln, his son-in-law.*

* See Lord Orford's Memoires, vol. i. p. 78.—Gent. Mag. for 1751.

CHAPTER XXVI.

1751.

Reformation of the Calendar—Bill for the naturalization of foreign Protestants—Supported, and afterwards abandoned, by Mr. Pelham—Gin Act—Contested election for Westminster, and case of the Hon. Alexander Murray—Supply—Acts for the improvement of trade, and other measures of domestic policy—Changes in the Cabinet—Dismission of lord Sandwich, and retreat of the duke of Bedford—Appointment of lord Granville, as President of the Council, and of lord Holdernesse, as Secretary of State—The displeasure of the King against the duke of Newcastle, gradually subsides.

AMONG the remarkable proceedings in this session, was the bill for abrogating the Julian, or Old Style, in the Calendar, which had been pertinaciously observed in England, long after it had been abandoned by the chief states of Europe.

The principal honour of introducing this reformation is due to the earl of Chesterfield. During his frequent residences abroad, that nobleman had noticed the numerous inconveniences in diplomatic affairs, resulting from the confusion of dates, and clearly perceived the chronological inaccuracies, which must arise from the same cause. After consulting the most eminent mathematicians, he communicated his design to the duke of Newcastle, for the sanction of the ministry. The noble Secretary was too deeply impressed with the favourite maxim of Sir Robert Walpole and his royal master, *tranquilla non movere,** to relish a proposal, which was likely to shock the civil and religious prejudices of the people. Lord Chesterfield, however, was not discouraged by his scruples, and had the satisfaction to find, that Mr. Pelham and the lord Chancellor concurred in the resolution to favour his purpose. He prepared the public for the intended change, by

---

* Not to disturb things at rest.

several essays in the " World," and other periodical papers, equally replete with wit and good sense; and the requisite scientific demonstrations were supplied to him, by the earl of Macclesfield, president of the Royal Society, and one of the ablest mathematicians of the age. After these judicious preparations, he brought forward the bill, on the 25th of February; and, on the second reading, March 18th, he made an elegant and perspicuous speech, chiefly occupied with historical disquisitions, and calculated both to prepossess, and to convince. The earl of Macclesfield afterwards pronounced an erudite discourse, in favour of the bill, which passed without a dissentient voice. Having undergone some trifling amendments, in the House of Commons, it was read a third time on the 17th of May, and being returned to the Lords, received, on the 22nd, the royal assent.

By this act it was determined, that the new year should begin on the first day of January, and not on the 25th day of March; and that, in order to obliterate the accumulated errors of the old calendar, eleven intermediate nominal days, between the second and fourteenth of September, 1752, should be, in that year, suppressed; so that the day succeeding the second, should be denominated the fourteenth of that month.

In practice, however, this innovation was strongly opposed, even among the higher classes of society. Many landholders, tenants, and merchants, were apprehensive of difficulties, in regard to rents, leases, bills of exchange, and debts, dependent on periods fixed by the Old Style. But the perspicuity and provisions of the act soon obviated these objections, and experience proved its utility. Greater difficulty was, however, found in appeasing the clamour of the people against the supposed profaneness, of changing the saints' days in the Calendar, and altering the time of all the immoveable feasts. At the period when the bill took effect, the populace marked their dissatisfaction, by exclaiming, " Give us back our eleven days !" and by other tumultuary indications. This spirit was slow in subsiding; and years elapsed, before the people were fully reconciled to the new regulation.*

In the course of the session a considerable sensation was excited, by the proposal of a bill, for the general naturalization of foreign Protestants. An act for that purpose, had been obtained by the influence of the Whigs,

---

* Continuation of Rapin, vol. xxi. p. 436.—Lord Orford's Memoires, vol. i. p. 44.—Anderson, vol. iii. p. 233.—Maty's Life of Lord Chesterfield. Hogarth, in one of his satirical prints, humorously commemorates these popular ebullitions.

in 1708; but it was repealed by the Tory parliament in 1711. It still, however, continued a favourite object with the Whig party; and, in consequence of the drain on population occasioned by the war, a motion for its revival had been made in the House of Commons, during the session of 1747. From party principle, as well as from a patriotic wish, to enrich the country with the arts and industry of other nations, Mr. Pelham at first encouraged it; but, as it was very unpopular in the city of London, he suffered it to be withdrawn. The same considerations still operating in its favour, it was again introduced on the 5th of February, 1751, by Mr. Nugent, with the cordial concurrence of Mr. Pelham. After some debate, in which Mr. Pelham strenuously supported the motion for leave to bring in the bill, it was carried by 152 against 69. The bill was read a first time, on the 14th; and, although a strong petition against it was presented by the city of London, the influence of the minister prevailed, and it was read a second time on the 28th. A motion, then made for its committal, was carried by 146 against 81. The bill was strenuously opposed in the committee; but when the report was brought up, the question that it should be engrossed, and read a third time on the 20th of March, was carried by a considerable majority. The death of the Prince of Wales on that day, occasioned its postponement, until the 23rd; and, as public opinion appeared to militate strongly against it, the third reading was farther deferred to the 16th of April. Deprecatory petitions poured in from all quarters during the interval; and Mr. Pelham, unwilling, at so critical a period, to persist in this unpopular measure, again withdrew his support. Accordingly a motion that the bill should be then read, was negatived by 129 against 116, and it was ordered to be read a third time on that day two months; but it was not again brought forward, though the session continued beyond that period.*

The licentiousness prevalent among the people, awakened the anxious attention of the legislature; and a committee was appointed, to inquire into the best means for suppressing vice and crime among the lower orders. On the suggestions offered in the report of this committee, various expedients were framed, for inforcing the penal law against the depredations on public and private property, which had recently been carried to an alarming extent. Acts were passed for regulating trials by jury, for protecting justices of peace in the execution of their duty, and for indemnifying peace officers,

* Journals of the Commons.—Hansard, vol. xiv. p. 970.

acting under their orders ; also for extending the operation of warrants from county to county, for preventing rapine and piracy on the northern coasts, for punishing persons wandering about armed and disguised, as well as those guilty of cutting or destroying the banks of rivers, of firing mines, and of other similar offences.

One great source of crime, which had been long regarded with pain, was the destructive habit of dram-drinking, which within a few years had made the most alarming progress. The distillation of British spirits, first allowed about the year 1723, extended to the lower orders, a temptation to which only the higher classes, who could afford to pay the price of foreign spirits, had hitherto been exposed. The consequence was, a rapid increase of drunkenness, which was strikingly marked by the excessive consumption of British spirits. In 1727 the quantity distilled amounted to 3,601,000 gallons, and in 1735 to no less than 5,394,000.

With the patriotic view of rescuing the lower orders from their brutal degradation, an act had been passed in 1736, for subjecting the sale of the commodity to conditions almost amounting to a prohibition, by a duty of twenty shillings per gallon, on the spirits, and a tax of fifty pounds annually on retail licences. But so vitiated were the habits of the people, that the law was openly braved, and the penalties rendered unavailing. The consumption of British spirits increased so rapidly, that in 1742 it amounted to 7,161,000 gallons. Accordingly, soon after the dismission of Sir Robert Walpole, his successor in office, conceiving that the severities of this act defeated its purpose, substituted a milder regulation, by lowering the penalties and duties, with the hope of diminishing an evil, which, as experience had shewn, no legislative restriction had hitherto been powerful enough to eradicate, or even to restrain.

Notwithstanding such a modification, this reigning vice of the age extended its ravages. According to a contemporary statement, the number of persons convicted of selling spirituous liquors, without licence, in the single year 1749, amounted to upwards of four thousand, and the number of private gin-shops, within the bills of mortality alone, exceeded seventeen thousand.

New efforts were therefore deemed necessary, to eradicate this cause of national degeneracy ; and, in consequence of a petition from the city of London, a bill was proposed by Mr. Nugent, for restraining the consumption of gin. Mr. Pelham appears at first to have apprehended, that the regulation might have no better result, in a moral view, than those which had already been tried, and that it would injure the revenue, by encouraging illicit distilleries. On mature consideration, however, and from a regard to the real welfare of the people, he adopted it, among the ways and means for the year. The bill seems to have passed, without much discussion, and to have received the royal assent at the close of the session. It prohibited distillers from retailing spirituous liquors, or vending them to unlicenced retailers, under the penalty of ten pounds; pronounced as irrecoverable all debts contracted for spirituous liquors, by the purchase of any quantity, not amounting in value to twenty shillings at one time; and restricted the retail sale to victuallers, innkeepers, and other authorised venders, occupying houses of at least ten pounds annual rent, within the bills of mortality, or liable to certain parochial rates elsewhere. In addition to the pains and penalties, attached by former acts to the illegal sale, or possession, of spirituous liquors, the second offence was to be punished by three months' imprisonment, and whipping, and the third by transportation. Small additional duties were also imposed on each class of spirits; and jailors, masters of Bridewells, and overseers of work-houses, were restricted, by special penalties, from trespassing against the statute. These wise regulations realised the expectations of their authors, and formed the foundation of the present efficient system.[*]

A very interesting proceeding in parliament during this session, arose from an election contest, of which the incidents exhibited a memorable lesson on the effects of personal resentment, combined with party animosity.

Lord Trentham, son of earl Gower, having in 1749 vacated his seat for Westminster, by the acceptance of a place at the board of Admiralty, again offered himself as a candidate; and the usual writ was issued the 16th of November.

The party hostile to the Gower interest were however zealously supported by the Prince of Wales; and an opposing candidate was speedily found, in the person of Sir George Vandeput, Bart., whose claims were promoted, against the views of government, by a faction, professing to vindicate the independence of Westminster. During the election, extraordinary violence was displayed on both sides. The poll finally closed on the 8th of December; when the votes reported in favour of lord Trentham were

---

[*] Journals of the Lords and Commons.—" Memoires," &c. by Lord Orford.—Documents and Papers, in the Gentleman's Magazine for 1751.

4,811, and for Sir George Vandeput 4,654. But a scrutiny being demanded, the whole affair was subjected to a tedious revision. On the 22nd of February, as no regular return of the writ had been made, the High Bailiff was summoned to the bar of the House of Commons, to account for the delay. He pleaded the difficulty of the scrutiny, and received from the House an admonition to proceed with all diligence, and a promise of protection, if required. The scrutiny was, however, protracted, by every possible act of violence and chicanery ; and at length, on the 15th of May, after the prorogation of parliament, the High Bailiff declared lord Trentham to be duly elected, by a majority of 170 votes.

The disappointment of the vanquished party was evinced by increased outrages. The returning officer was exposed to the utmost danger, in the execution of his duty; and the passions of a misguided mob were exasperated by persons, whose station ought to have inspired them with respect for the laws. Among these, the most conspicuous was the honourable Alexander Murray, a brother of lord Elibank, who had been long suspected by government, of being implicated in the plots of the Jacobites.

On the 20th of January, 1750-51, soon after the opening of the session, petitions were presented to the House of Commons, by Mr. Cooke, from the unsuccessful candidate, and from a considerable body of the burgesses, reflecting in the strongest terms, on the conduct of the High Bailiff. The affair was thus brought under the cognizance of the House of Commons, in opposition to the wishes of many of the more moderate opponents of administration.

Lord Trentham, who had taken his seat, vindicated the choice of his constituents, with great spirit, and complained of the unwarrantable expedients which had been employed to defeat his election. In justification of the High Bailiff, he read a letter, written by Mr. Cooke himself, to that officer, on the very eve of the return, commending, in the strongest terms, his impartiality and integrity.

After an angry discussion, on the 28th, the petitions were ordered to be taken into consideration on the 5th of February; and lord Dupplin immediately moved, that the High Bailiff should be summoned, to render an account of the manner in which he had obeyed the orders of the House, issued on the 23rd of the preceding February, for the execution of the precept of election. As this motion was preconcerted, it passed without opposition ; and the High Bailiff, who was already in attendance, and was immediately ordered to the bar, ascribed the delay of the return to the obstructions he had experienced during the scrutiny. He was then asked, by whom, or by what means, he had been obstructed ; but strong objections being offered to this question, as informal and improper, a debate ensued, in which several members, particularly Dr. Lee and lord Egmont, strenuously opposed the proceeding as unjust. But, although the Speaker himself concurred in these objections, and some of the moderate Whigs discountenanced the motion, the younger and more violent members carried the point by 204 against 106.

The interrogatories having recommenced, the High Bailiff, after some hesitation, charged Mr. Crowle, counsel for Sir George Vandeput, with obstructing the scrutiny, and using disrespectful language towards the House of Commons. In reply to farther questions, he accused also the honourable Alexander Murray, of exciting the mob to an attempt against his life, and finally included in his charges an upholsterer, named Gibson. Orders were instantly issued, by the Speaker, requiring the attendance of the accused persons.

On the 31st of January, Crowle was placed at the bar, and was dismissed with the usual reprimand, which he received on his knees. On the following day, Gibson, after the examination of witnesses, was committed to Newgate. But the chief vengeance of the Whigs was reserved for Mr. Murray, who had rendered himself peculiarly obnoxious, by his political opinions, as well as by his furious zeal for the unsuccessful candidate.

Mr. Murray being placed at the bar, was charged by the High Bailiff with riotous behaviour when the scrutiny was terminated ; and with committing other acts of violence, after the return was made. He desired to be heard by his counsel, which was granted. In the mean time, a motion was made, for committing him to the custody of the Serjeant-at-Arms, with liberty to give bail. Several of lord Trentham's friends, and Mr. Pelham in particular, considered this motion as contrary to equity ; because it was in fact punishing a person by confinement, before he was proved to be guilty, or had even been heard in his own defence. It was, however, carried ; and Mr. Murray being taken into custody, gave surety for his appearance.

On the 6th of February, the charge of the High Bailiff was read and supported by the testimony of witnesses; and counsel having been heard in defence of Mr. Murray, a resolution was proposed, declaring the facts to be clearly substantiated. A discussion ensued, which lasted until midnight; and a motion for committing Mr. Murray a close prisoner to Newgate was carried by 210 against 74. An opposition to the words "close prisoner," having occasioned another debate, the vote, that those words should remain, was passed by 169 against 52.

The triumphant party, who had received intimation, that Mr. Murray had declared he would not submit to kneel at the Bar of the House, were now determined to move, that he should receive his sentence on his knees, in the hope that his refusal would be considered as a proof of contempt, and thus increase the severity of his punishment. Mr. Pelham, from whom Mr. Murray's determination had been carefully concealed, reluctantly consented to this petty revenge of his violent adherents, supposing that Mr. Murray would not object to comply with the usual form. The motion was, therefore, carried by 163 against 40.*

Mr. Murray, on being placed at the bar, refused to submit to the ignominy prescribed; and exclaimed, "When I have committed a crime, I kneel to God for pardon; but knowing my own innocence, I can kneel to no one else." This refusal at once disconcerted the moderate, and exasperated the violent members. The Speaker, hitherto inclined to lenient measures, now exhorted the House to maintain its dignity; while Mr. Pelham, in the hope of allowing time for reflection, proposed the appointment of a committee, to examine precedents. At length, on the motion of Sir William Yonge, a vote was passed, that Mr. Murray should be committed to Newgate, under the closest restrictions, that he should be debarred from the use of pen, ink, and paper, and that no person should be allowed to have access to him, without leave of the House. The offender, irritated rather than humbled by this order, departed for his place of confinement, with an air of triumph. Meanwhile the petitions against the return were withdrawn, and the House was left completely at issue, with the refractory prisoner.

In the course of the proceedings, some violent members had proposed, that Mr. Murray should be confined in that dungeon of the Tower, called "Little Ease," so named because it was too small for a person to stand

* Continuation of Rapin, vol. xxi. pp. 426, 427.

upright, or lie at length. But Mr. Pelham censured even the mention
of so cruel and disgraceful a mode of torture ; and his objections to any
increase of severity were confirmed by the report of the committee, which
was presented on the 18th of February, stating that the House had no power
to inflict any farther punishment than that of close confinement.

Gibson was now permitted to avail himself of the indulgence of the
House ; and, submitting to a reprimand on his knees, obtained his discharge.
Even the restrictions, to which Mr. Murray had been subjected, were so far
relaxed, that he was allowed the society of his sister, and the attendance of
a physician, in consequence of his complaint of illness.

At the interposition of his brother, lord Elibank, the House evinced a
still farther disposition to relax ; and issued an order for his removal into
the custody of the Sergeant at Arms, with a view to the benefit of his
health. The reputation of a martyr was, however, too attractive to be
readily relinquished ; the proffered indulgence was respectfully, but firmly
declined ; and Mr. Murray did not hesitate to accuse his brother of meanness, in presenting a petition on his behalf, without his knowledge. The
House then revoked its order, on the representation of the physician, that
Mr. Murray's health was improving. His friends now made an attempt to
remove him, by writ of *habeas corpus ;* but the Court of King's Bench,
recognizing the undeniable privilege of the House of Commons, to commit
for contempt, he remained in confinement, until the close of the session.
His liberation was signalised by the acclamations of the populace ; and he
passed through the city, in a species of triumph, attended by the sheriffs of
London and Middlesex, and a numerous train of partisans.*

In a season of profound peace, and when so many reductions in the
various branches of the public service had created a well-founded confidence in the economy of the administration, Mr. Pelham had no difficulty
in obtaining the necessary supplies for the year, which are enumerated in
the following table ·

---

* Journals of the Commons, passim.—Memoires, by Lord Orford, vol. i. p. 12-27.—Cont. of
Rapin, vol. xxi. p. 443.—Accounts in the London and Gentleman's Magazines, and other
periodical publications.

The reader will find the issue of this unpleasant affair in the ensuing chapter.

SUPPLY.

NAVY.—Charge of 8,000 seamen; rebuilding and repair of ships; Ordinary of the navy, &c.		
ARMY.—Charge of 18,857 men; ordnance, guards, and garrisons; and extraordinary expenses of the forces for 1750	1,155,769	....
Subsidy to the Elector of Bavaria, by treaty concluded at Hanover in 1750.....................	30,000	
For the support of the Forts on the Coast of Africa	10,000	
For transporting colonists to Nova Scotia, and other charges on account of that settlement	111,510	
For loss of horned cattle	23,904	
Extraordinary charge of the Mint.	3,000	
Making and repairing a road between Newcastle-on-Tyne and Carlisle....................	3,000	
For making good deficiencies, and payment of interest	290,739	
	2,484,481	
Balance..........	211,048	
	£.2,695,529	£.2,695,529

Besides these grants, the government was empowered to raise the sum of £.3,290,041 for the redemption of the unsubscribed South Sea and Bank Annuities. The Ways and Means for this purpose, consisted of a loan from the Bank, of £.1,400,000, for the purchase of annuities, at three per cent, £.700,000 by a lottery, £.176,893 by Exchequer bills, and another loan from the Bank, of £.1,013,148. The interest of all the above sums was charged on the surplus monies of the sinking fund. Hence the whole supply for the year, exclusive of the appropriated taxes, amounted to £.5,985,570.

The commerce and manufactures of the country continued to occupy the attention of the minister. Among the plans adopted for their improvement, during this session, may be noticed, the acts for extending and facilitating the trade to Africa; for encouraging the manufacture of pot-ash and pearl-ash in the American colonies; for restricting paper credit in those colonies; for continuing the premiums on the importation of masts, yards, tar, pitch, and other naval stores; and for preventing theft or rapine in any port, harbour, or haven, of Great Britain.

The public business being at length dispatched, the king in person terminated the session, on the 25th of June. He thanked both Houses for their diligent application to public affairs; expressed the usual sentiment on the continuance of peace; and acknowledged the promptitude of the House of Commons, in granting supplies, and in completing the arrangements, for reducing the interest on the national debt. He concluded, by recommending to the members of the legislature, the preservation of tranquillity and good order, that by their personal exertions and example, the laws enacted by parliament, might not prove inefficient.*

The opposition being disunited by the death of the Prince of Wales, the king and ministers were enabled, towards the close of the session, to proceed in the accomplishment of that change, which had been long in agitation.

During the progress of this transaction, Mr. Pelham had a delicate and difficult part to act. He was not inclined to thwart the wishes of the king; nor was he disposed to offend the Duke of Cumberland and the Princess Amelia, both of whom warmly protected lord Sandwich, and espoused the cause of the duke of Bedford. He was also unwilling to strengthen the opposition, by the accession of the adherents of that nobleman, which his removal would occasion, particularly at a time when lord Cobham, Mr. Pitt, and their friends, were tampering with the Prince of Wales, and when their coalition would have rendered the party adverse to government extremely formidable. He therefore declined, as we have already shewn, to exert his influence in the closet, notwithstanding the earnest solicitations of his brother. But when the death of the Prince of Wales diminished or neutralised the opposition, the determination of his brother to retire, if the duke of Bedford continued in office, induced him to make another application to the king.

Although his Majesty disapproved the duke of Bedford, as Secretary of State, he hoped to retain him in office, as Master of the Horse, and positively refused to sanction an order for his dismission. But, as the Pelhams were well aware that the disgrace of lord Sandwich would cause the duke of Bedford to resign, Mr. Pelham suggested to the king, the expediency of that

* Journals.—Hansard's Parliamentary History, vol. xiv. p. 1057.

nobleman's removal, to which his Majesty readily assented. Accordingly, on the 13th of June, the duke of Newcastle formally notified to lord Sandwich, that the king had no farther occasion for his services.

On the following day, the duke of Bedford repaired to Kensington, and resigned the seals to the king, in person. During the audience, he entered into a long and bitter invective against the duke of Newcastle, accusing him of haughtiness and treachery. He told the king, that every measure relating to his Majesty's service was so concerted, as to serve the interests of the duke of Newcastle, and increase his power, as he could prove by an hundred instances, but would mention only one. " Your Majesty," he continued, " will find, that as soon as I am out of the Secretary's office, one considerable part of it will be lopped off, and thrown into the hands of the first Commissioner of Trade, lord Halifax. This is an affair, settled without the knowledge of your Majesty. I mention it, not from hostility to lord Halifax, with whom I am not now intimate, but to shew your Majesty, that persons are to be ill treated and removed, and the chief offices of the state are to be mangled, altered, and lowered, at the pleasure of the duke of Newcastle and his party, in order to promote their scheme of ingrossing all power to themselves and their creatures."* He also charged Mr. Pelham with mischievous interference in the family of lord Gower; and declared that the persecution directed against himself and lord Sandwich, was provoked by their firm attachment to the Duke of Cumberland.

The king received the seals, with many gracious expressions; acquiesced generally in the observations on the duke of Newcastle; but testified his doubts concerning the facts imputed to Mr. Pelham; and concluded with observing, " As to lord Sandwich, I know not how it is, but he has very few friends."† His Majesty also gratefully acknowledged the attachment of the duke of Bedford to the Duke of Cumberland; and not only treated him with kindness and regard, but pressed him, though ineffectually, to accept the vacant post of Master of the Horse. On the 15th, lord Trentham, much to the displeasure of his father, earl Gower, followed the example of the duke of Bedford, by resigning his seat at the Board of Admiralty.

The vacancies were immediately filled. Lord Holdernesse, whose foreign connections and docility of temper rendered him acceptable to his Majesty,

* Postscript of a letter from the lord Chancellor to the duke of Newcastle, Aug. 13, 1751. MS.
† Lord Orford's Memoires, vol. i. p. 168.

was nominated Secretary of State, to the satisfaction of the duke of New-castle. ' The king was farther gratified by the appointment of lord Granville, as President of the Council; in the room of the duke of Dorset, then lord Lieutenant of Ireland ; and, notwithstanding his transcendant abilities, ambitious views, and superior favour, that distinguished statesman accepted a subordinate post, under the ministers to whom he owed his former disgrace.

On the 23rd, a new commission was passed for the Admiralty. Lord Anson, son-in-law of the lord Chancellor, was selected to preside at the Board, and the other two vacant places were assigned to admirals Boscawen and Rowley, whose naval services entitled them to such advancement. Lord Albemarle, at the recommendation of the Duke of Cumberland, was appointed Groom of the Stole. The marquis of Hartington, son of the duke of Devonshire, received the post of Master of the Horse, and was raised to the peerage. This mark of favour was highly gratifying to Mr. Pelham, who had been long and intimately connected with the duke of Devonshire, whom he regarded as one of the most distinguished members of the Whig party. He appretiated this favour the more highly, because in some of the appointments, especially in that of lord Granville, he had acquiesced solely in deference to the king, and in compliance with his brother.* In making these changes, however, his Majesty did not affect to conceal his reluctance to part with the duke of Bedford ; and indirectly rebuked the duke of Newcastle, when, on delivering the seals to lord Holdernesse, in his presence, he enjoined the new Secretary to confine himself to the business of his province, and not to render it, what it had lately been, a mere office of faction.† The king likewise manifested both to the lord Chancellor and Mr. Pelham, much displeasure against the duke of Newcastle, of whose impracticable temper he warmly complained, and did not even condescend to honour him with his usual attention, for several weeks.‡

Deeply affected by this coldness, the noble Secretary addressed an expostulatory letter § to his Majesty, in which he vindicated his own conduct with great spirit and freedom. He expressed a hope, that no misrepresentation had been suffered to influence the royal mind to his disadvantage ; and declared that his behaviour to the duke of Bedford, had been as unexception-

* Letter from lord Granville to the duke of Newcastle, June 16th, 1751. MS.
† Lord Orford's Memoires, vol. i. p. 172.—Dodington's Diary.—Memoirs of lord Walpole.
‡ Lord Orford's Memoires, vol. i. p. 172.
§ See this letter in the Illustrative Correspondence.

able, as that of his Grace to him. He also denied, that since the return of his Majesty from the continent, he had urged the subject more than once. He concluded by observing, that the dismission of lord Sandwich had been the immediate cause, which occasioned the resignation of the duke of Bedford.

This manly address, and the unequivocal determination evinced by Mr. Pelham, not to desert his brother, contributed to allay the resentment of the king. His Majesty was also farther soothed, by the zeal with which the duke of Newcastle promoted the project, for securing the election of the archduke Joseph, and by the consideration, that his advice and assistance would be requisite, in completing the treaty with Saxony, to which Mr. Pelham was known to be adverse, but which was rendered an object of immediate concern, by the arrival of count Fleming, the Saxon envoy, in England. These various motives induced the king to receive the faithful and noble Secretary again into favour; and in a letter dated July 28th, the lord Chancellor congratulates the duke on the change in the closet, which, he says, "I never doubted would come about in time." *

* Letter from the lord Chancellor to the duke of Newcastle.—Newcastle Papers, MS.

CHAPTER XXVII.

1751—52.

Prosecution of the negotiations for electing a King of the Romans—Subsidiary treaty with the Elector of Saxony—Attempts made to gain the Elector Palatine—Indifference of the Austrian Court—Session of Parliament—Revival of the affair of Mr. Alexander Murray—The order for his recommittal renewed, and supported by Mr. Pelham—Mr. Murray withdraws to the continent—The publisher of a seditious pamphlet, in his favour, tried and acquitted—Discussions on the naval and military establishments—Bill for rendering the militia more efficient, not passed— Opposition to the continuance of the Land-tax, at three-shillings in the pound— The Salt-tax rendered permanent—Mr. Pelham proposes the grant of the Saxon subsidy—Discussions in both Houses—Bill for vesting the forfeited estates in Scotland in the Crown—Naturalization-bills, qualified by a restrictive clause—Consolidation of the funds—Result of measures for reducing the interest—Supply— Regulations of internal policy, and laws for promoting commerce and manufactures —Close of the Session.

WHILE the collision of interests in the cabinet and in parliament, occasioned so much domestic embarrassment, the aspect of foreign affairs was far from affording hopes of external tranquillity. The disputes with France, relative to the limits of Nova Scotia, and the neutral islands in the West Indies, were still maintained with unabated warmth. The contentions between the rival East India Companies had at length led to open hostilities in the Carnatic. Lastly, the intimacy of France with Prussia, and the intrigues of the French court, indicated a purpose to revive the troubles in Germany. Denmark had been detached from the alliance with England, by a liberal subsidy from the Court of Versailles ; and in Sweden a wider career had been opened to the French and Prussian influence, by the recent accession of Adolphus Frederic,* lay bishop of Lubec, who had espoused the princess Ulrica of Prussia. No endeavour was spared to strengthen that interest at the court of Dresden, which had been derived from the marriage of the Dauphin, with the eldest daughter of the king of Poland, elector of Saxony; and even the minor princes of the empire were not overlooked, in the various machinations for consolidating an extensive system of alliance.

The king of England observed these proceedings with anxiety, accompanied as they were, with the dispatch of troops to America, with attempts to gain the native tribes of that continent, and with extensive preparations in the ports and arsenals of France. The duke of Newcastle, ever jealous of the French power, fully participated in the feelings of the sovereign, and strenuously endeavoured to establish some counterpoise, against the dangerous ascendancy meditated by the court of Versailles. The project, therefore, for securing the Austrian Succession in the empire, not only now became of paramount importance, but was identified with an extension of the general system of foreign policy.

We have before observed, that the negotiation for the election of a king of the Romans, was suspended at the time of the king's departure from Hanover, in October 1750; and we find, that before the prorogation of parliament, on the 25th of June, 1751, it had taken an unfavourable turn. The demands of the electors Palatine and Cologne being rejected by England, the latter not only withdrew his promised vote, but even accepted a subsidy of 270,000 florins from France, and they both concurred in issuing a strong protest against the proposed election.

The king of Prussia, emboldened by their defection, as well as by that of Treves, hastened to publish a counter-memorial,† to the circular address, issued by the elector of Mentz, in which he reiterated his former arguments, against the legality and expediency of the election. As it was evident, that

---

* Adolphus Frederic succeeded to the Swedish throne, on the death of Frederic the First. He was descended from Catherine, daughter of Charles the Ninth, being the son of her granddaughter, by Christian Augustus, of the House of Holstein Utin, cousin of Ulrica Eleonora, wife of Frederic the First. The real heir was Peter, son of Hedwige, eldest sister of Eleonora, by Frederic, duke of Holstein Gottorp; but he renounced his right to the crown of Sweden, to become emperor of Russia.—See Geneological Table of the Kings of Sweden, in Coxe's Northern Travels, vol. iv.

† London Mag. for 1751, p. 191.—This memorial was probably issued about the beginning of 1751.

he was assured of the support of France, the fear of creating a civil war in the empire induced the court of Vienna and the king of England again to suspend their design; and consequently the elector of Mentz desisted from his intention of convoking an electoral diet.

The emperor and empress-queen also issued two public declarations, announcing that they had gratefully acquiesced in the overture of his Britannic Majesty, for promoting the election of their son, but were determined to adopt such measures only, as might be conformable to the Golden Bull, and to the fundamental laws of the empire.

Between the empress of Russia and the king of Prussia, disputes now arose. which led them to recall their respective embassadors, and to make active preparations for war. Russia appealed to England and Austria; while the king of Prussia concluded a treaty with France, by which he obtained a considerable subsidy,* and the promise of 40,000 troops, should such an auxiliary force be required. He also expected to be joined by Denmark and Sweden.

On the other hand, the king of England and the empress-queen hoped that the disputes between the courts of Berlin and St. Petersburgh would afford means to restrain the ambition of the Prussian monarch, and made overtures for a subsidiary treaty between the Maritime Powers and Russia. The demands of the empress Elizabeth were, however, deemed too exorbitant; but the duke of Newcastle still trusted, that a grand confederacy might be formed against France, by the Maritime Powers, in concert with Austria, Russia, the electors of Bavaria and Saxony, and some of the minor princes of Germany. As the French influence at Madrid was at this period diminished, he also flattered himself that he should include Spain in this confederacy; and made overtures to the Spanish ministry, for establishing a concert with the court of Vienna. But this plan was not carried into effect, because Ferdinand manifested no disposition to adopt any decisive step, and absolutely refused to involve himself in the chaos of German politics.

Amidst these negotiations, the scheme for the election of a king of the Romans was resumed; and, as soon as the affairs in parliament left the king of England at liberty to attend to foreign transactions, attempts were made to gain the king of Poland, elector of Saxony, by a subsidiary treaty. His

---

* See the Chancellor's letter to the duke of Newcastle, dated Sept. 10th, 1751. Illust. Corres.

concurrence was deemed the more important, because, in conjunction with the elector of Bavaria, as a vicar of the empire, he was entitled to a share of the government, in case of an Interregnum, and consequently his rights would have been affected, by the proposed election of a minor. A collateral negotiation was also opened with the elector Palatine, whose vote would have completed the requisite majority. On the other hand, the courts of Versailles and Berlin were not idle; and while the king of France still affected to disclaim all interference, he secretly encouraged the king of Prussia, in his open resistance to the election, and favoured his intrigues with the minor German powers.

The French ministry continued to make professions of amity towards England, but their real sentiments did not long remain equivocal. The attainted Jacobite, Keith, who still designated himself as earl mareschal of Scotland, was suddenly sent as embassador from Berlin to Paris, and as promptly received; and on the remonstrance of the British Chargé d'Affaires, colonel Yorke, against this public recognition, as a glaring mark of disrespect to his sovereign, the offence was aggravated, by the harsh reply of the French Secretary of State, who said that the king his master was much displeased with the British court, for not making a suitable return to his offers of friendship, and not believing his declaration, that he would not concern himself in these matters. The counter mission of the exiled Jacobite, Lord Tyrconnel, from the court of Versailles to Berlin, furnished a confirmatory proof of a deliberate and concerted purpose to insult the British Crown. Soon afterwards, the disinclination of the French cabinet, to adjust the points at issue with England, was evinced by the disgrace of M. Puisieulx, who, as one of the principal negotiators of the treaty of Aix-la-Chapelle, might have been considered as interested in its fulfilment, and by the nomination of M. de St. Contest, who was known to be adverse to the British claims.*

The king and the duke of Newcastle were deeply affected by these proceedings, and were still more mortified by the numerous obstacles, which continually occurred, to prevent the success of their endeavours, for consolidating the projected confederacy. They found much difficulty in contending against the influence of France at the court of Dresden; because Augustus the Second, availing himself of the competition for his vote, rose

* This account is principally taken from a letter of the duke of Newcastle to the Chancellor, and the Chancellor's reply, dated Sept. 6th and 10th, 1751. Illust. Corres.

in his demands, and attempted to evade any engagement for furnishing troops, while he declined to give, even an indirect promise, to promote the election of the archduke. Nor were the negotiations with the elector Palatine more successful ; for he did not confine himself to the demand of a subsidy, but at the instigation of Prussia and France, reiterated his claims on the Austrian court, for territorial acquisitions and privileges, and even required compensation from the Maritime Powers, for the ravages committed in the Palatinate, during the war of the Spanish Succession. These obstructions again frustrated the design ; the court of Vienna not only declining any contribution to the Saxon subsidy, but peremptorily refusing to gratify the elector Palatine with a grant of the territories and privileges which he required. When pressed by England to make some sacrifice for the attainment of an object so important, the empress queen treated the election of her son, as a measure scarcely practicable, and not worth the price at which it was to be purchased. She recommended its suspension, and urged that a subsidiary engagement with Russia and Saxony, would be the only effectual expedient, for defeating the hostile purposes of France and Prussia, and for preserving the tranquillity of the Empire.

The duke of Newcastle did not scruple to resort to threats as well as expostulations ; but both were alike unavailing with the court of Vienna. Sensible, also, that the high demands of Russia would be discountenanced by his brother, he suspended the negotiation with that power ; and, as Spain could not be led into a German alliance, he relinquished his project for a grand confederacy, and contented himself with securing the cooperation of the king of Poland. Accordingly, the subsidiary treaty, which had been so long pending, was concluded at Dresden, on the 13th of September, 1751, by Sir Charles Hanbury Williams, the British envoy, and was ratified, as the only expedient to advance the election, and to prevent Saxony from uniting with Prussia and France. By this engagement, the king of Poland was to receive an annual subsidy of £.48,000, for four years, of which sum England was to pay £.32,000, and the States General £.16,000. In return he was to furnish six thousand troops, should the Maritime Powers be attacked, and his ministers were to act in concert with those of Hanover, in the diets and assemblies of the empire, according to the fundamental laws of the Germanic constitution.* This treaty, like that with the elector

---

* Copy of the Treaty, in the Journals of the House of Commons, January 16th, 1752.

of Bavaria, was construed as implying an obligation, to concur in the choice of a king of the Romans.

For the accomplishment of that object, the king of England still persisted in his efforts, notwithstanding the supineness, or aversion of the cabinet of Vienna. Disregarding the insults offered to him, he earnestly appealed, even to the court of Versailles; and, from its ambiguous answers, was encouraged to hope, that France would abide by the promise of acquiescing in the election, if six votes could be procured. With the same constancy of purpose, he forbore to resent the violent protest and opprobrious taunts of the king of Prussia, who had characterised his interference, as unbecoming the youngest of the electors; and he even expected to conciliate his good will, by obtaining the guaranty of Silesia from the emperor and the diet of the empire, which, though solemnly stipulated in the twenty-third Article of the Treaty of Aix-la-Chapelle, had been hitherto eluded. This expedient also failed; for the king of Prussia was no sooner gratified, than he renewed his public remonstrances against the election.

It was, therefore, judged advisable to postpone the negotiations to another year, rather than risk the chance of intestine troubles in the empire, by pressing a design, which was likely to encounter the open resistance of Prussia, and the secret, if not public opposition of France.*

While this affair was pending, Mr. Pelham had been principally engaged in perfecting his grand scheme for the reduction of interest, and the diminution of the public expenditure. He interfered little in foreign transactions, and chiefly employed his efforts, in soothing the anxieties of his brother and the king, and in preventing a rupture with France. Though, in conformity with his previous declarations, he objected for a long time to the Saxon treaty, he finally acquiesced in it, as tending to the preservation of tranquillity, by curtailing the influence of France on the continent. He did not cease, however, to protest against the farther extension of the system of subsidizing foreign powers, during peace, as an addition to the burthens of the country, and a waste of the public money.†

---

* Continuation of Rapin, vol. xxi. p. 440.—History of the House of Austria, chap. cix.— Protests and Memorials, in the periodical publications.—Letters between the duke of Newcastle and the lord Chancellor, in September, 1751. Illust. Corres.—Also correspondence of the duke of Newcastle with Mr. Keith and Sir Benjamin Keene, for the same period. MS.

† Letter from the lord Chancellor to the duke of Newcastle, dated July 28th, 1751, MS., and letter from the duke of Newcastle to the lord Chancellor, September 6th, 1751. Illust. Corres.

Parliament assembled on the 14th of November, 1751 ; and, it may truly be said, that no session commenced under more tranquil auspices. To adopt the expressions of an author, who was intimately acquainted with the state of parties, "The miscarriage of the rebellion had silenced Jacobitism ; the death of the Prince of Wales had quashed opposition ; and the removal of the duke of Bedford and lord Sandwich, had put an end to feuds in the cabinet."* The general result of the session certainly did not disappoint the expectations, founded on this favourable posture of affairs.

After congratulating both Houses on the national prosperity, resulting from the continuance of peace, the king adverted to the treaty with Bavaria, presented during the last session, as part of a series of measures, to be adopted for the security of the empire, and the promotion of the common cause. He now announced that, in conjunction with the States General, he had concluded a treaty with the king of Poland, elector of Saxony, which he should order to be communicated. In adverting to the death of his son-in-law, the prince of Orange, he observed, that this event had produced no change in the government or disposition of Holland ; that, on the contrary, the quiet of the country had been secured, the foundations of its political system preserved, and its connection with England confirmed and strengthened, by the unanimity of the States General.

After the usual expression of his reliance on the Commons, for the requisite supplies, he concluded with an earnest recommendation, that effectual precautions should be adopted, to suppress that spirit of robbery and violence, which unfortunately prevailed throughout the country, and which his Majesty ascribed to the increase of irreligion, idleness, gaming, and extravagance.

The peers unanimously voted an address, in which, after testifying their zeal for his Majesty's person and government, they applauded his foreign plans, as not merely establishing present security, but as providing against future dangers. In this light they regarded the recent treaty with Saxony, from which they augured effects answerable to the salutary views of his Majesty. In offering their condolence on the death of the prince of Orange, they added their congratulation on the tranquillity and friendly disposition of the States General, whose security as a Protestant republic, they considered as intimately connected with that of Great Britain. They

* Lord Orford, Memoires, vol. i. p. 209.

concluded, by gratefully acknowledging the firm and effectual measures of his Majesty, for maintaining domestic tranquillity, and for improving the moral character of the people.

The Commons, in their address, expatiated on the flourishing condition of the kingdom; and cheerfully promised such supplies as might enable his Majesty to fulfil the engagements, and carry into effect the several plans, which he deemed necessary for the public good. After a solitary objection, by Sir John Hinde Cotton, to the words "flourishing condition," which was disregarded, as a cavil unworthy of notice, the address was voted unanimously.

On the very first day of the session, the case of the Honourable Alexander Murray again occupied the attention of the House, and created fresh embarrassment. Soon after his liberation, a pamphlet had been published, entitled, "The Case of Alexander Murray," in which the proceedings of the Commons were stigmatized as unjustifiable, arbitrary, and oppressive. It being deemed dishonourable to suffer such an insult to pass unnoticed, for a single day, lord Coke brought the subject before the House, and not only dwelt with great emphasis, on the circumstances attending Mr. Murray's liberation, as constituting a farther proof of his contempt; but adduced this pamphlet, as a heinous aggravation of his offence. He concluded by moving for the rigorous infliction of the former punishment, and for again committing him a close prisoner to Newgate.

A debate ensued, in which lord Egmont strongly objected to the proposal, as unnecessarily severe, and moved an adjournment. Although Mr. Pelham had consented to the former proceedings with reluctance, yet he now felt that the House could not refrain from vindicating its privileges; and, therefore, denounced the conduct of Mr. Murray, as an aggravation of his offence, which called for signal chastisement.

He avowed, that he was glad to be informed, on such good authority as that of the noble lord, who had moved an adjournment, that the people were peaceably disposed. They had no reason to change that disposition, nor would any such reason occur, during the reign of his present Majesty. But however tranquil might be the general state of the people, there would always be turbulent persons, inclined to molest the government, and foment discord among their neighbours. Against such offenders, who had of late

* Journals.

become numerous and daring, the laws ought to be inforced, and perhaps
a little severity would be indispensable. "The gentleman, whose case is
now under consideration," continued Mr. Pelham, "has plainly shewn his
contempt of the laws, in his behaviour to our returning officer, at the last
election for Westminster; and his contempt of this House has been still
more audaciously evinced, from the beginning to the end of a very long
session. His triumphant exit from Newgate has been properly adduced,
as a strong argument in favour of my friend's motion. That triumph, I will
say, was something more than audacious; it was really seditious; and if he
cooperated, in composing or publishing that infamous libel, which was
afterwards so industriously circulated, he has, by that act, manifested a
fixed resolution to excite insurrection against the established government
of his country. But, on this point, I shall say no more, because it requires,
and will, I trust, receive particular attention; and, because, from what is
notoriously known, every gentleman interested in the honour and dignity
of this House, ought to be convinced, that the order for the committal of
the offender, must be renewed, if pardon be not asked for the offence. If we
do not commit him, every future offender will hold our orders in contempt,
and deem himself at liberty to abscond, in the confidence, that the power
of the House will not be exercised against him in another session.

"That the privilege of parliament extends to the renewal of such orders,
is indubitable. The question, however, at present, is not whether we have
the power, but whether we shall use it, or suffer an opinion to go forth,
that such a power does not exist, or that, if we possess it, we never will
exert it; an inference which would induce every man to disregard our
orders, at his own discretion.

"It has been fully proved, that Mr. Murray behaved in a very menacing
and illegal manner towards our returning officer; because, forsooth, he
would not follow that gentleman's directions, in making his return. For
this offence, he has not yet undergone the slightest punishment. His
imprisonment, last session, was for contumacy, in refusing that ceremony
which has always been observed, by persons receiving any sentence at our
bar; and if such imprisonment proved a grievous punishment, the fault
lay in his own obstinacy, for he might have shortened the term, if he had
chosen.

"I admit that, during the last session, he could not expect to be discharged
from prison, without petitioning to express his contrition; and perhaps some

acknowledgment of the justice of his sentence might have been demanded. But, supposing that he had refused this concession, and of course had continued in prison till the separation of parliament, he would then have suffered the punishment inflicted by the House, for the offence of which he had been guilty towards our returning officer ; and, I am persuaded, no gentleman would, in this session, have thought of moving for his recommittal. If any had, I am fully convinced the motion would have been rejected by a great majority. But the offence he has now to answer for, is an act of disrespect against the House itself, which cannot be forgiven, unless pardon be asked in the humblest manner. Therefore I cannot doubt that the question for adjournment will be negatived, and that the motion of my noble friend will be carried by a great majority."

This anticipation was fulfilled, by a resolution for the recommittal of Mr. Murray ; and the pamphlet was then taken into consideration. It was not only declared an impudent, scandalous, and malicious libel, but an address was voted, requesting his Majesty to give the proper orders for the prosecution of the publisher.

In the mean time, Mr. Murray had retired to the continent, to avoid a second imprisonment ; and the deputy Serjeant-at-Arms, having reported his flight to the House, the king, at the instance of the Commons, issued a proclamation, offering a reward of five hundred pounds for his apprehension. When the publisher of the obnoxious pamphlet was prosecuted by the Attorney General, and brought to trial, the jury, notwithstanding its inflammatory and seditious tendency, returned a verdict of acquittal, which was received by the populace with unusual exultation. After this decision, the House wisely abstained from any farther notice of Mr. Murray or his case.[*]

On a review of this transaction, it is to be inferred, that party prejudice and personal resentment may have impelled the Prince of Wales and his adherents, to take so violent a share in the Westminster election, and to unite with the Jacobites, for the purpose of carrying a favourite point ; and to party feelings also may be ascribed, the vindictive conduct of the Whigs, in rendering a petty election squabble the subject of serious deliberation. Without however wishing to vindicate the obstinacy of Mr. Murray, we cannot but blame the imprudent facility of Mr. Pelham, in suffering his better

---

[*] Journals of the House of Commons.—Continuation of Rapin, vol. xxi. p. 443.—Hansard's Parl. Hist. vol. xiv. pp. 1063 and 1083.—Lord Orford's Memoires, vol. i. pp. 183-4.

judgment to be over-ruled, by the impetuosity of those, who, in their zeal for the privileges of the House, exposed its dignity to insult, and invested an obstinate individual with that popularity, which usually attends the object of violent persecution.

From the general aspect of affairs, and especially from the exertions of the French, to augment their navy, and increase their power in America, Mr. Pelham was convinced, that he had the last year carried his economy too far, in reducing the naval establishment to eight thousand men. He now purposed to restore it to its former complement of ten thousand. As the Opposition had then argued against the decrease in the number of seamen, little objection was anticipated; and when the measure was brought forward, on the 25th of November, it merely called forth a remark, that the augmentation might have been larger. The only speakers were Mr. Thornton and Mr. Beckford, and the original motion passed without a division.*

The military establishment occasioned considerable debate, though no increase was proposed. It was discussed on the 28th of November, when Sir John Hinde Cotton offered an amendment, for reducing the proposed number of men to fifteen thousand, which was seconded by Mr. Beckford. Dr. Lee now appeared on the side of the ministry, and to justify his change of opinion, expatiated on the crisis, occasioned by the deaths of the Prince of Wales and the Prince of Orange, and by the birth of a duke of Burgundy, which he considered as increasing the influence of the French crown. He adverted, also, to the undiminished strength of the Jacobites, and to the dangers which might arise in case of a minority.

His arguments were ably combated by his former colleague, lord Egmont, who ironically animadverted on his change of opinion, as well as on the conduct of those who, like him, had deserted their party. Adverting then to the argument in favour of a standing army, he observed, that those by whom it was maintained, on the ground of historical precedent, would find the experience of ages to be wholly against them, and in favour of the contrary proposition. "A civil government," he continued, "must always derive its main support from the civil power, in aid of which, a small subservient military force may be allowed; but, if you raise this force to an equality with the civil power, or render it superior, it will cease to be subservient, when it has obtained a chief, who possesses ambition and

* Hansard's Parl. Hist. vol. xiv. p. 1085.

ability, to appropriate the civil power. Such a man may, like Julius Cæsar, tolerate the form or shadow of civil institutions ; but, from that moment, the government will be a military government, which is always absolute, and often tyrannical. Of this evil we seem to be in danger, from the policy now exercised, in the executive part of the government. Our military force, I know, cannot legally be maintained, without the consent of the civil power, that is to say, without the consent of parliament ; but, if this consent should be refused, and if the military force should at the same time deem itself preponderant, would it not resolve to dispense with that consent? Are we sure that a majority of the officers would resign their commands and their pay, notwithstanding the tempting solicitations of a favourite general, and an ambitious sovereign? Of this, I confess, I am far from being convinced ; and, therefore, I shall never vote for maintaining more troops, than are just sufficient to guard us against any sudden, unexpected invasion, and to support the civil power, upon some extraordinary emergencies."

For the sake of economy, however, he avowed his readiness to enter into a compromise with the ministry, if they would as readily consent to reduce the staff, as he would agree to continue nearly the actual number of troops. He proposed the dismission of the staff, which, he contended, was useless, the reduction of the guards, the diminution of officers, and the increase of private soldiers. He urged that this plan would produce a saving of £.140,000 ; while the numerical amount of the army would scarcely be diminished nine hundred men. In conclusion, he sarcastically alluded to the disappointment of the ministry, in their foreign negotiations ; augured no better success from his own proposal ; and, deploring the weakness of the opposition, protested that he offered this suggestion, merely to preclude any improper construction on his silence, adding that he should probably, in future, abstain from disturbing that unanimity, which was likely to prevail.

In reply to these observations, Mr. Pelham declared that he never entered on the discussion of any subject, with more concern than on that now under consideration. He did not deny, that a standing army, in time of peace, had always been unpopular in this country, from the attendant expense and inconvenience. He observed, that many plausible arguments might be adduced, to represent it as inimical to public liberty ; and that these would always have great weight with the vulgar, who cannot easily distinguish, between an army maintained against law, and one maintained according to

law. . He admitted the perilous nature of an army maintained against law ;
but. insisted, that an army sanctioned by law, could never endanger the
liberties of the people, . and might be supported at much less expense than
would be incurred, if no such force existed. " A rebellion, or an insurrection," he said, " would, in one year, occasion greater expense and loss to
the people, than would be incurred, in maintaining our present army for
seven years ; not to mention other misfortunes, incident to a civil war ; and
I am persuaded that we should never be, for seven successive years, free from
some such commotion, if we had no regular troops in the kingdom.
Gentlemen may now display their wit, in ridiculing Jacobitism and defying
disaffection ; but no. one present can forget the time, when a handful of
malcontents spread terror through the country, and when the wittiest
among us generally appeared the most alarmed. Therefore, however disposed gentlemen may be to exercise their wit, in speaking on this subject,
I hope they will evince their judgment in voting ; for it should be remembered, that no great reduction was ever made in the regular troops in this
island, without occasioning insurrection or conspiracy among the disaffected.

" The great reduction at the end of queen Anne's reign, was, I believe,
by some designed to afford to the disaffected, an opportunity for overturning
our established government ; and, as it would have been very unpopular in
his late Majesty, to commence his reign, by an increase of our army, we
were exposed to a most dangerous rebellion, which broke out, the very same
year. Again in 1718, when his Majesty, for the relief of his subjects,
reduced the army, an invasion from Spain was menaced, and an insurrection
actually broke forth, among the malcontents in the north of Scotland. In
1722, though our army then scarcely exceeded the number to which some
gentlemen would now reduce it, a plot was formed, which would have been
of most dangerous consequence, if not opportunely frustrated. The last
unnatural rebellion, I need not mention ; because every gentleman must
remember, that it was incited by the absence of a large proportion of our
force, sent to assist our allies on the continent. The perils then encountered
will, I hope, ever operate as a warning ; for, if the arrival of our troops
from Flanders had been retarded by contrary winds, even for three or four
weeks, the crown of these kingdoms, and with it our liberties, religion, and
property, must have been at stake, in a battle at the very gates of our
capital, much to our disadvantage, considering the amount of raw soldiers

in our available force, the panic among them, and the number of Papists in London and Westminster, who would probably have joined the rebels.

"Thus from late experience we may learn, that a standing army, even during peace, is absolutely essential to our tranquillity; and I am convinced, by the events of the year 1722, that fifteen thousand men are not sufficient. So far from being dangerous, our standing army, while maintained according to law, is indispensable for the support of our liberties; and for no other purpose can it be lawfully maintained, since parliament on the first suspicion, would undoubtedly withhold its sanction; and, at the expiration of the Mutiny-bill, the soldiers, however their officers might act, would certainly disband themselves, and join with the parliament, in bringing to condign punishment, all who attempted to force them to serve contrary to law."

Adverting to the civil uses of the army, he argued, that a respectable military force was requisite, for the suppression of riots and commotions, the prevention of illicit traffic, and the collection of the revenue. He admitted, that the expense of an army was far greater in England than in foreign states; but observed, that the troops of those states, by their quarters and exactions, were far more oppressive to the people, than our troops were to our own nation, because in reality the respective countries were compelled to bear the principal part of the expense.

After proving that the value of military pay was much depreciated, by the rise in the price of provisions, he thus stated his reasons for resisting the proposed reduction. "No gentleman, I believe, will think that the pay, either of our officers or soldiers, can be diminished; and, in the reform proposed for our troops his Majesty has gone to the utmost practicable extent, for the relief of his people. The foot-guards cannot be reduced below their present number; the remaining troops of horse-guards, are really not sufficient for the service of the royal family, without detachments from the Blues; and hence it is impossible to reduce that regiment to dragoons, in common with the other cavalry regiments." Having stated the numerical proportions fixed for the marching regiments, he animadverted on the various schemes of economy proposed, which, on examination, had been found partially, and at length wholly objectionable, and had been renounced by their projectors. "Even the saving upon our marine, voted last session, we have this year been forced to abandon; because other nations are endeavouring to deprive us of our trade, and may succeed, if we do not protect it with our navy. A squadron has been found requisite on the coast of Africa, and we have now another in the East-Indies.

"In conclusion," he said, " I have the satisfaction to know, that the nation is at present in a very prosperous situation. From the accounts of our imports and exports, but especially from the latter, it appears that our trade improves daily. The late reduction of interest will enable us to discharge, annually, a considerable part of the public debt ; and this liquidation will regularly increase, if we be not engaged in foreign war. The tranquillity of Europe is not likely to be disturbed for several years ; since, though some nations may be disposed for war, others must continue to restrain their inclinations. In this state of affairs, can we wonder at the unanimity that prevails, within doors and without ? Has any thing been recently attempted, that can afford a pretext for opposition ? Let us therefore hold ourselves well, while we are so, without engaging in new projects, which may be attended with consequences, that no human prudence can foresee. Of this character I consider the proposed reduction of our army to be, and shall therefore most heartily give my vote against it."

The debate was closed by a violent speech from Mr. William Thornton, who argued, that the army, though nominally eighteen thousand men, was so constituted as to form a real force of fifty thousand ; that its mechanism was devised for the oppression of a free people ; and that it could only be used for the support of an arbitrary ministry, because his Majesty reigned absolutely in the hearts of his subjects, and needed no force to ensure their obedience and affection. This philippic produced little impression, and the question was decided by 108 against 43.*

Of those who had formed the party of the late prince, only three joined the minority ; Lord Middlesex, Mr. Martin, and lord Egmont. Mr. Speaker Onslow voted with them ; thus availing himself of the opportunity, which a Committee of the whole House could alone afford him, of manifesting his continued dissatisfaction with ministers.

The result of this debate, and the state of parties in the House, are thus mentioned, in a letter from Mr. Fox to Sir Charles Hanbury Williams.

" *Dec. 4th*, 1751

"The division against the army, last Wednesday, was 43. Dr. Lee spoke for us, and gave his true reason, the prince's death ; which, he said, makes

* Hansard's Parl. Hist. vol. xiv. p. 1086 to 1127.—Lord Orford, vol. i. p. 187.

us much worse than we were. It makes our side much stronger in parliament, I am sure; for, except lord Egmont (who spoke with great
moderation), lord Middlesex, and Mr. Martin, no one of the late prince's
family voted against us. I do not foresee a debate this session, nor any
difficulty to the ministers, but that of getting forty every day to make a
House." *

At a subsequent period of the session, another attack on the standing
army, was made by Mr. Thornton, who brought in a bill, to render the
national militia more useful. He expatiated on the necessity and efficiency of
a well-constituted militia, as capable of protecting the country, at a far less
expense, than even a limited regular army. He adduced the examples of
Germany and Switzerland, in support of his assertion, that a force of at
least 260,000 men, might be kept armed and ready, at a charge not exceeding
£.10,000 a year. Such propositions being, at this period, regarded as
covert attacks on the regular army, his reasoning did not obtain the attention
which it deserved. The bill was introduced on the 16th of February, read
a second time on the 18th of March, and amended in a committee; but its
progress was checked, by successive adjournments, until the session was
closed, by a prorogation,† on the 26th of March, 1752.

The principal article of the ways and means, was the Land-tax, which the
minister entertained hopes of reducing, to the ordinary rate of two shillings
in the pound. He discovered, however, that this reduction could not be
effected, without trenching on the sinking fund, and thus depreciating the
public securities; and therefore he resolved to continue the tax at three
shillings. This resolution was resisted by some violent members, whom
lord Orford sarcastically terms, "the sad refuse of all the last Oppositions,"
who contended, that the land was already too much burthened, to admit
of the continuance of the Land-tax at three shillings. Mr. Pelham, and
his adherents, in reply, alluded to the great rise in the value of land,
which, they said, rendered a reduction unnecessary. The arguments and
influence of the minister prevailed, and the resolution was carried in the
committee, by 176 against 50. On the report, the opposition was still more
feeble; and Mr. Sydenham concluded a speech, which closed the discussion,
by a ludicrous parody of the well-known epitaph on Sir John Vanbrugh,
which he applied to Mr. Pelham:—

* Hanbury Papers.   † Journals.—Hansard's Parl. Hist. vol. xiv. p. 1271.

> " Lie heavy on him, *land*, for he
> Laid many a heavy load on thee."

The resolution was finally adopted, by a majority of 58 against 19.*

Notwithstanding the weakness of Opposition, and the general strength of the ministerial party, Mr. Pelham felt some embarrassment, in proposing the grant, for a subsidy, to the elector of Saxony, conformably to the recent treaty.

When the expedient of purchasing the votes of the German electors was adopted, he had acquiesced with undisguised reluctance, in a proceeding so contrary to his political principles, and to his views as a minister of finance. His consent to the Bavarian subsidy had arisen, solely from the hope, that the election of the Archduke would be accomplished without delay. He therefore witnessed with grief and disappointment, the prosecution of nego-tiations for purchasing the votes and influence of other electors and princes, particularly of the elector of Saxony. In the cabinet, he remonstrated against this measure ; made strong representations on the subject to his brother ; and even, in a moment of irritation, expressed to his friend Mr. Walpole, who had delivered to the king a memorial against subsidiary treaties in time of peace, his purpose of seconding the opposition to the proposed subsidy, in the House of Commons. But the mediation of friends, and their just repre-sentations, that a separation from his brother, would ruin their party, and involve the country in confusion, induced him to change this hasty resolu-tion.† He therefore ceased to oppose the Saxon subsidy, though he naturally felt some scruple in submitting it to the sanction of parliament ; because, in the debate on the Bavarian treaty, he had suffered an opinion to be entertained, that no farther grant of the kind would be required.

On the 22nd of January, 1752, in fulfilment of his official duty, he called the attention of the House to this subject, and adduced the sanction already given to the Bavarian subsidy, as an argument for complying with the present proposal. He candidly admitted the reasonableness of a hope, formerly entertained, that the Bavarian subsidy would be the only expense to be incurred by the nation on this account; " and this expectation," he added, " would perhaps have been realized, had it been deemed prudent to

---

* Lord Orford's Memoires, vol. i. p. 190.—Journals of the Commons.—Hansard's Parl. Hist. vol. xiv. p. 1127.

† Memoirs of Lord Walpole, chap. xxxv.—This fact is given on the authority of Etough, who received it from Mr. Walpole himself.

proceed to the election, after securing a bare majority in the diet. But it must be evident, that to render it secure and indubitable, the concurrence of the whole electoral college must be obtained, or at least the utmost possible majority of votes. Hence it became an object of the first necessity, to gain the elector of Saxony, as not only as one of the most powerful princes, but, in case of an interregnum, as one of the two vicars of the empire.

As a farther reason for approving the treaty, he adduced the example of the Dutch, and added, that we had greater cause, than even that cautious and economical people, to be anxious for the preservation of public tranquillity; since, if the States General were attacked, the princes of Germany would concur in supporting them, from motives of private interest; whereas, if France and Spain should combine to wrest from Great Britain the whole of her distant colonies and possessions, the attempt would create little sensation among the friendly powers abroad, particularly if we had previously manifested an utter indifference to their interests. " I know," he continued, " it is an unpopular and invidious office, to call in question the power or resources of our country; but I disdain to flatter, even my native country, at the expense of my sincerity; and therefore I must say, that in my opinion, it would be impossible for us, singly, to support a war of any duration, against the united strength of France and Spain, and probably of the whole House of Bourbon. In such a contest, they would certainly compel Portugal to exclude our ships of war from all her ports, and might perhaps oblige her to declare against us; for Portugal is exposed to an attack from Spain, by land, against which we could contribute little or no assistance. If then Portugal were forced to submit to the House of Bourbon, what must be the condition of our ships, when in time of distress or danger, they had no port of refuge, from the Land's End to the Straits of Gibraltar? In the event of such a war, also, how greatly must our navy, formidable as it is, be divided, and consequently weakened! For, we must always have one squadron stationed in the Mediterranean; another no less efficient in the West Indies; a third, superior to either, on our own coast, besides others of smaller force, on the coast of Africa, in the East Indies, and in the Baltic. These squadrons, I say, must be constantly maintained, in their respective stations, for the protection of our trade and colonies; and might it not, after all, be possible for the navies of France and Spain to elude our vigilance, and attack us with a superior force, on one or other of these stations?

" All circumstances duly considered, it must be evident that, while France and Spain continue united, and while both are forming projects against our commerce and colonies, to be executed when a favourable opportunity shall occur, we ought to have a confederacy on the continent, always ready to attack them, if they should attack us by sea or in America. Should an intestine war break forth in Germany, how is such a confederacy to be formed? and what is so likely to create such an intestine war, as a vacancy in the imperial throne? Therefore, in existing circumstances, no nation, not even Germany itself, can be more deeply interested than we are, in preventing, by means consistent with the Germanic constitution, the possibility of such a vacancy. Consequently, we ought not to grudge any expense, that may appear absolutely necessary, for averting so dangerous a contingency.

" But that is not the only misfortune, against which we have to guard. France, we know, makes great exertions, and incurs vast expense, to attach to her interests, as many of the German princes, as she can induce to accept her terms ; and, since most of those princes maintain a larger number of regular troops than their own revenues can support, they must receive subsidies from some foreign state or other. The empress queen, ever obliged to maintain a large defensive force against the Turks, cannot afford any subsidy ; the Russians are in the same predicament ; consequently the German princes can expect no pecuniary aid, except from France and Spain, or from the Dutch and us. I have good reason to believe, that most of them will accept a smaller subsidy from us, than may be offered from France ; but if we should parsimoniously withhold any subsidy, they would be obliged to accept one from France and Spain, and would accordingly be compelled to join with those two powers, perhaps against the interests of their native country, as well as against those of Europe in general.

"His Majesty, therefore, has effected two important purposes, in concluding this subsidiary treaty with the king of Poland. He has prevented that prince from being reduced to the necessity of making any compact with France ; and has secured, as far as is consistent with the constitution of the empire, his vote and interest, for the election of the Archduke, as king of the Romans. This condition, indeed, could not be expressly stipulated in the treaty ; because such an article would have been contrary to the Germanic constitution ; but it was implied, and will, I am convinced, be faithfully performed, not so much in deference to the tacit understanding between the contracting parties, as from its conformity with the particular interest of Germany, and the general interest of Europe.

"Thus, I may venture to say, we have secured, not only the two vicars of the empire,* but two thirds of the electoral college; and I entertain a confident hope, that the Archduke Joseph will be chosen before the next session. Nothing, I think, can retard it, except the laudable design of rendering the election unanimous, which I am disposed to consider as not impracticable, and of which the good effects would well compensate for the delay of another year, if that should appear necessary. I still hope, however, that this will be the last expense, which the nation will have to incur, for securing the tranquillity of Germany, and of course our own tranquillity, together with the free and undisturbed possession of our trade and settlements, in every part of the world. If advantages so important be procured, at so trifling an expense, I am sure it will not be denied, that we have made a cheap purchase therefore I shall conclude by moving, 'That a sum not exceeding £.32,000 be granted, to enable his Majesty to make good his engagements with the king of Poland, elector of Saxony, pursuant to treaty.''

This proposition was strenuously opposed by persons of all parties. Mr. Walpole was the first to enter his protest against the expenditure of the public money, in prosecution of a scheme, which he represented as doubtful, at least, if not fruitless. He reminded Mr. Pelham of the pledge given at the time of the Bavarian subsidy, that no farther application of the same nature would be made; a consideration, by which he declared, that he and many other members had been induced to give their reluctant assent to that grant. He ironically hinted at the eagerness of the ministers, in the pursuit of this object, and concluded by saying, "I shall vote for the present question, notwithstanding all I have said against it : and for this reason ; because the treaty is signed ; the treaty is ratified ; and, should we give a negative, or take a step to disappoint the performance of it, such a procedure would affect his Majesty's honour, and lessen the influence and respect, which he has so justly obtained abroad." Appealing then to the party of the old Whigs, he added, " If I may be so vain as to suppose, that I have influence or weight with them, I must intreat and exhort them to join with me, notwithstanding what I may have said to the disadvantage of this treaty, in sanctioning it, for this time, under the persuasion, that the door will not only be shut, but barred and barricadoed for the future, against the dangerous system of granting subsidies to foreign powers, in a time of profound tranquillity."

* The electors of Bavaria and Saxony.

2 E 2

A désultory discussion ensued, in which the Solicitor General, Sir William Yonge, Mr. Fox, and others, defended the grant, and Sir Walter Blacket, Mr. Beckford, lord Strange, and lord Cobham,* spoke against it. The declaration of Mr. Pelham, that he hoped it would be the last proposal of the kind, appears to have induced many to give it their support; for it was carried by a very large majority, namely 236 against 54.

When the report was presented, several members spoke, who had taken no share in the former debate. Mr. Viner strongly censured the king, for loading with such expense the nation, which had so liberally provided for his Majesty and his royal family. This attack drew from Mr. Pelham, a reply glowing with gratitude and loyalty,† which produced an impression so effectual, that no division was proposed.

In the upper House the same result was anticipated, because the duke of Bedford, who was regarded as alone likely to oppose the grant with effect, could not be deemed capable of offending a sovereign, whose past kindness seemed to require a grateful return. Influenced, however, by several enemies of the Pelhams, particularly by Mr. Horace Walpole, junior, he disappointed the hopes, both of his family and his dependents. After apologising for his opposition to a measure, instituted by so good and gracious a sovereign, he declared, that he could not conscientiously content himself with giving merely a silent vote. He scrutinized the treaty, article by article ; condemned it as equally useless and improvident; indirectly censured Mr. Pelham, for surrendering his better judgment to his brother's partiality for German politics, which he called extravagant imbecility ; and expatiated on the mixture of penury and prodigality, which the administration had manifested, in the domestic concerns of Great Britain and her colonies. He concluded with proposing an address to the king, disapproving all subsidiary engagements, in time of peace, and stigmatizing the Saxon treaty as peculiarly impolitic and unnecessary.

In repelling this attack, the Duke of Newcastle justified the treaty, with the same general arguments, which had been used by his brother, in the House of Commons. He commended it as a wise provision for preventing war, and

---

* On the death of his uncle, lord Cobham, Mr. Grenville succeeded to the Irish barony of Cobham, and afterwards, on the death of his mother, to the title of earl Temple.

† Lord Orford, vol. i. p. 218, alludes to this speech as glowing with gratitude and loyalty, but there is no specific account of it, either in his " Memoires," or in any of the periodical publications.

for securing allies, should a war occur. If it effected either of those objects, he said, it must deserve praise even as an act of economy ; for, since the peace of Utrecht, no interval of four years had elapsed, without greater foreign expenses than had been now incurred. He emphatically recounted the advantages, which would accrue from these engagements with the electors of Bavaria and Saxony, the two most probable candidates for the imperial throne, and the two princes, in whom the vicariate of the empire was vested. He also reminded the Opposition, that by securing those princes, his Majesty had removed the chief objection raised by the king of Prussia. Far from imitating the reserve of his brother, he avowed that six votes must be gained, to secure the election ; and that the scheme was yet to be carried to a farther extent.

It was expected that lord Sandwich would concur with the duke of Bedford ; but in deference to the Duke of Cumberland, he opposed the motion for the address, though he accused the administration of imbecility and extravagance.

The President of the Board of Trade, lord Halifax, after defending the policy of ministers, imprudently taunted the duke of Bedford, with the change in his sentiments, since he approved the Bavarian treaty. This charge had been anticipated, and was ably rebutted. The duke of Bedford owned that he had hitherto refrained from vindicating his own conduct, though fully pre-pared to maintain its consistency. He had always wished to detach Bavaria from France, but not merely with a view to secure an electoral vote. He had, however, strongly remonstrated against the grant of subsidies, in time of peace ; and, having particularly disapproved the Bavarian subsidy, he had received the strongest assurances from *one*, who had inclination to prevent, and power to hinder, that the subsidy to Bavaria should be the last that would be given. He was prepared to authenticate this assertion, by a letter from the Chancellor of the Exchequer himself.*

Lord Granville deprecated the proposed address, as inflammatory in itself, and as an unconstitutional infringement on the royal prerogative. He hinted that France was lavishing her favours, to conciliate and gain the princes of Germany ; and that it would be impolitic for England to remain inactive, while a powerful rival was taking such steps to usurp the ascendancy.

* Memoires, &c. by lord Orford, vol. i. p. 220.

The address, though urged by the duke of Bedford, was regarded as of such dangerous tendency, that it was negatived without a division.

This debate, however, afforded a plea for bringing the question in a new shape, before the House of Commons. On the 29th of January, a motion for an address to his Majesty, deprecating any subsidiary treaty in time of peace, was made by lord Harley, and seconded by Mr. Northey. Most of the principal speakers entered into the discussion ; and on the part of government, it was particularly resisted by Mr. Pelham, and Mr. Horace Walpole, senior. The general arguments urged in favour of the address, were founded on the impolicy of subsidiary treaties in time of peace ; while, on the other hand, the machinations of France were alleged, as creating abundant cause for precautions, to secure the German princes, whose necessities compelled them to depend on the favours and largesses of the greater powers. On a division, the motion was negatived by 182 against 52.* The termination of these unpleasant discussions must have been a grateful relief to Mr. Pelham, who deeply felt the charges of inconsistency brought against him, by his friend Mr. Walpole, and the duke of Bedford.

Towards the close of the session, another discussion arose, which gave pain to Mr. Pelham. By an act, passed after the Rebellion, the forfeited estates of several Highland chiefs had been directed to be sold ; but as the former owners might possibly purchase them, on trust, and again foment the spirit of disaffection, the sale was suspended, as long as the law would permit. A plan was now projected, for rendering this property subservient to the civilization of the Highlanders, as well as to the diffusion of loyal principles, and industrious habits among them. By this plan, which was supported, if not suggested, by the duke of Argyle, to whom the interests of government in the Highlands had long been intrusted, it was proposed, that these estates, after paying off the mortgages on them, should be vested inalienably in the Crown, with power to lease them, for the term of twenty-one years, in small farms, upon a reserved rent of not less than three fourths of the real annual value, and in portions, of not above twenty pounds yearly, to any one person. The lessees were to take the oaths of allegiance, and to reside upon, and cultivate their farms. The income accruing from the rents, was to be employed by the Crown, in civilising the inhabitants of those districts, and of other parts of the Highlands and isles of Scotland ;

* Hansard's Parliamentary History, vol. xiv. p. 1192.—Journals of the Commons.

in diffusing among them Protestant principles, and in training them to arts and manufactures. The management was to be intrusted to a certain number of commissioners, acting without salaries, but authorised to appoint stewards, with an allowance of five per cent on the rental, and to nominate clerks and other officers, with reasonable emoluments.

The bill was brought into the House of Commons on the 23rd of February ; and, from its peculiar character and beneficial tendency, Mr. Pelham could scarcely apprehend any serious opposition. But he had not sufficiently considered the strong prejudice then prevailing against the Scots, and the insinuation artfully circulated, that this was a job, devised to gratify the duke of Argyle, and to afford the means of providing for some of his numerous dependents. Nor could Mr. Pelham conceive the slightest suspicion, that the antipathy of the Duke of Cumberland against the natives of that country would prompt him to encourage any indirect attempt to defeat a regulation, so. clearly calculated to increase the stability of the government, and preserve the future tranquillity of the realm.

In its early stages, the bill was attacked only by the usual speakers in opposition ; and being warmly defended by the lord advocate for Scotland, Mr. Pelham, Sir William Yonge, and Mr. Oswald, it was read the first and second times, without a division.

On the 4th of March, when the bill was reported from the committee, it encountered vehement resistance. Sir John Mordaunt contended that its execution was impracticable ; that the comparative cheapness of land was not a sufficient inducement for Englishmen to settle in so wild a country ; and adduced instances to prove, that such settlers would be exterminated by the natives. From government they could alone hope for protection ; and what protection, he asked, could be expected from the supineness of a government, which suffered one of the most active agents in the rebellion, to remain safely on his estate, and to triumph over the loyal and well-affected. Mr. Northey strenuously arraigned the conditions on which the payments were proposed to be made ; and entered into calculations to prove, that the amount of the pretended claims was merely collusive. The friends of government renewed their vindication of the bill ; and, after declaring that the military force stationed in the country, was sufficient to protect the colonists, they justified the result anticipated, by adducing the success of a similar experiment in Ireland. The motion for bringing up the report was

carried by 171 against 34,* and the bill passed triumphantly, without
another division.

In the House of Lords, it encountered an opposition of a different
character.   To turn on the ministers the prejudice prevailing against
the Scots, the Duke of Cumberland, through the agency of Mr. Horace
Walpole, junior, privately furnished the duke of Bedford with various
instances of connivance, on the part of government, in permitting guilty
participators in the rebellion, to retain the official situations which they had
previously held.   These instances, though trifling in themselves, were
calculated to fix on ministers the invidious imputation of favouring the
private views and partialities of the duke of Argyle.

On the first reading, the duke of Bedford, after recapitulating the general
objections to the plan, employed with equal skill and effect these implements of attack. "With reference to Scotland," he observed, "such is
the encouragement given to that country, by this and ·other bills, that I
apprehend they will in time produce another rebellion.   The great lords
have obtained funds and resources for new commotions, which they could
have acquired in no other way ; and, though particular towns and persons
are pretended to be relieved, money is through them circulated over the
whole kingdom, and we deprive ourselves of the advantages which might
accrue even from treason, when the disaffected have contributed to despoil
and impoverish their own country.   I fear that rebellion will become a
national malady.   Danger is even to be apprehended, in reducing the
scheme to practice ; for, should the commissioners not act, the bill is
needless ; if they be willing to act, what is to encourage them ?   In my
apprehension of new commotions, I am but too strongly warranted, by the
favour shewn to the disaffected, and the discouragement given to the loyal.
I have in my hands a long and crying catalogue of facts, to verify my
assertions ; and these facts I am ready to prove.   I will select two examples.
The first is the case of John Cummings,† who at the time of the late
rebellion, being a collector at Montrose, assisted the rebels in seizing the
Hazard sloop, for which service the titular duke of Perth appointed him

---

* Lord Orford's Memoires, vol. i. p. 228.

† It appears from a letter of Mr. Pelham to the duke of Newcastle, dated May 8th, 1752.
Illust. Corres. that this case was misrepresented ; but that the case of Hume was truly stated,
is candidly admitted by Mr. Pelham ; and the man was accordingly discharged.

collector for the Pretender. This Cummings, on the Duke of Cumberland's arrival in Scotland, was imprisoned by command of his Royal Highness, and carried to Inverness. Escaping from thence, he was again imprisoned; but, at the desire of lord Milton, was released by Mr. Bruce, who was then empowered to detain or to release prisoners. This Mr. Cummings is now collector of Excise at Aberdeen, an appointment almost double in value, compared with that which he formerly held at Montrose! The other case is that of Hume, of Munderson, a man engaged in the earlier rebellion, or, as the Scotch call it, "in the fifteen." His brother was executed for participating in the last rebellion, but he himself has been made a general supervisor of Excise. These, my lords, are among the many flagrant instances of the favour, I may truly say, of the rewards, bestowed on rebels. I can, if required, produce a greater multitude of equally striking, and perhaps more alarming, instances of punishment inflicted, or permitted to be inflicted on individuals, well affected to his Majesty's government and person; but I will not now recapitulate them."

After a pause, the duke proceeded: " My lords, these, and facts like these, call for inquiry; but my farther objection strikes at the bill itself, which various concurrent indications denote to be but a more extensive job. Is it proper to present a bill of this nature, at the close of a session, when so far from having leisure to examine it, we have barely time to pass it? That this delay must have been intentional is manifest; since the report of the barons of exchequer, who were to examine into the nature and state of the forfeitures, was given so long ago as December, 1749. The money to be raised is a most unjust burthen upon England. The commissioners, at least, for carrying this act into execution, ought to be Englishmen. If they are not, we are warranted in surmising, that this money will be as much perverted, as taxes have been fallaciously collected. Let us notice, for instance, the produce of the coach tax, in that part of the United Kingdom. To what does it amount? For the first year to one thousand pounds. For the second to . . . . nothing! Must we suppose that this burthen was so heavily felt, that the whole nobility and gentry of Scotland at once concurred to lay down their equipages? In those years England paid, on the same account, £.60,000 and £.58,000. If such be the partialities of the Scots, is it not allowable for Englishmen to have some? Be that as it may, my lords, let us know what grounds there are for these complaints, for these accusations. I, therefore, move, that your lordships do defer the farther consideration of this bill, until we have had time to inquire into facts."*

The lord Chancellor ably defended the principle of the bill, in a series of historical and legal deductions, and clearly pointed out the beneficial tendency of its different provisions. He also frankly admitted, that the complaints of partiality adduced by the duke of Bedford, deserved a prompt and effectual inquiry.†

Lord Bath, pursuing the line of argument adopted by the duke of Bedford, recommended as indispensable, a previous examination of the claims on these forfeited estates, and vehemently censured the partiality manifested towards Scotland, in the levy of taxes, and in the encouragement of persons who had taken a part in the rebellion. He concluded with proposing the enactment of a bill for punishing frauds relative to forfeitures.

The duke of Argyle, against whom so many imputations had been levelled, felt it necessary to make some reply ; but, notwithstanding the animation which he had formerly displayed in debate, his speech was short and confused. He principally confined himself to a positive disavowal of any private view or personal interest in the bill.

The duke of Newcastle combated the arguments advanced for a previous examination of the claims, by insisting that the evidence already before the House was sufficient, and that farther information, if necessary, might be elicited from noblemen and gentlemen of Scotland, in both Houses, who were equally willing and competent to afford it. He contended, that no more delay on that account ought to be allowed, and that the provisions of the bill were framed to prevent, as much as possible, the realization of fraudulent claims. On its tendency to weaken the spirit of clanship, he observed, that if a disaffected chief were dispossessed of his estate, and that estate vested in the Crown, and leased out to individuals of the clan on long terms, at an inferior value, the self-interest of every such lessee would operate directly against his clannish spirit. "Instead of following their chief," he added, "in any future rebellion, the cheapness and the certainty of their leases will induce all, and probably prevail with most of them, to assist the government in opposing his return ; and a spirit

* " Memoires," &c. by lord Orford, vol. i. p. 230.
† Hansard's Parl. Hist. vol. xiv. p. 1235.—" Memoires," &c. by lord Orford, vol. i. p. 224.

of industry and improvement will be propagated among them, not only by the certainty of holding their estates, for a longer term of years, but by all the methods that the managers under the Crown can devise.

" The improvement of the forfeited lands, therefore, is expected to arise, not from the commissioners or managers for the Crown, but from lessees for long terms, under the Crown ; and it is by such lessees, under ground-landlords, that the lands in England, and indeed in all countries, have been improved. But other great improvements, in every part of the Highlands, are to be expected from this bill. By introducing industrious strangers among the inhabitants, by erecting public schools, and dividing parishes, it is to be hoped that a new direction will be given to the spirit of the people. By making highways passable in winter, as well as in summer, and by improving some of the many natural harbours on the coast, so as to render them safe and accessible at all seasons, it may be expected that towns and villages may in a few years arise, in regions now presenting only barren mountains and inaccessible valleys. The rents of the estates will, I hope, be sufficient for the whole expense of these improvements ; and, besides establishing a security against future rebellion, it will be money profitably invested by the public, as the increase of wealth and industry in the Highlands will redound to the augmentation of the revenue, in a much greater ratio, than the interest of the money paid by the public for those estates.

" I hope I have now demonstrated, that this bill is likely to answer both the salutary ends, proposed by the legislature, and steadily pursued ever since the last rebellion. But whatever doubts may exist, concerning its beneficial tendency, the necessity of passing the bill, before the end of the session, is unquestionable ; for you cannot now alter the act of the 20th of his Majesty's reign ; and, unless that act be altered, or this bill be passed in the present session, some of the forfeited estates, if not all, must be sold before parliament again assembles. If any of them be sold by public sale, it is certain, that some trustee of the forfeiting family will be the highest bidder, and of course the purchaser. Thus the disaffected chief will recover his family estate, contrary, I am persuaded, to the unanimous disposition of your lordships ; and, as not even a suggestion has been offered, that any ill effect can ensue from the enactment of this bill, before the next session,

2 F 2

I trust, that the question for its committal will be carried in the affirmative, without a dissentient voice."*

In concluding his speech, he alluded to the charges of partiality ; and having taken minutes of the cases mentioned by the duke of Bedford, he expressed his hopes, that such recommendations would be no more allowed to operate ; and declared, that he had sent orders for the apprehension of several rebels, who were still lurking in Scotland.† This sensible speech produced a due effect; and, on a division, the motion for the second reading was carried by eighty against twelve ; and the bill passed through the subsequent stages, without farther obstruction.

This success did not however alleviate the mortification which Mr. Pelham felt, at the unexpected charges advanced against the government; or his disappointment at the languid and inefficient defence offered by the duke of Argyle. It was an additional source of concern, to find that the attack thus aimed at himself and his brother, was secretly directed and encouraged by the Duke of Cumberland. ‡

We have seen that Mr. Pelham twice endeavoured to introduce an act for the general naturalization of foreign Protestants, but desisted from his purpose, in compliance with public feeling. We now find him, from the same principle, not opposing the introduction of a general restrictive clause into all private bills of naturalization.

On the 11th of March, a petition was presented from the city of London, complaining that many foreigners had lately repaired to England.; and, having procured advantages in trade, by private naturalization bills, had returned to their own countries, where they were exempted from contributing to our public burthens. The prayer of the petition was, that this abuse might in future be prevented, by confining the benefit of naturalization to the time during which such foreigners should reside within the realm. This request was deemed reasonable ; and the facts alleged were so satisfactorily proved, that the proposed restrictive clause was inserted in a private naturalization bill then pending; and it still

---

* The substance of this speech is drawn from Hansard's Parl. Hist. vol. xiv. p. 1235.

† Lord Orford's Memoires, vol. i. p. 239.

‡ Hansard's Parl. Hist. vol. xiv. p. 1235.—Continuation of Rapin, vol. xxi. p. 446.—Smollett, vol. iii. p. 305.—Lord Orford's Memoires, vol. i. pp. 224, 228, et seq.—London Magazine for 1752, p. 270.

continues to be a permanent provision in all acts of that description.*

In justice to the liberality of the minister, it should be recorded, that during this session, an order was passed, for printing the Journals of parliament; and that the requisite advances, to the amount of £.5,000, were made to Mr. Hardinge, late clerk of the House, to whom the task was assigned. The accuracy with which it was executed has been universally acknowledged; and the advantage accruing from this publication of the Journals, to every cultivator of our national History, deserves to be warmly and gratefully commemorated.

In this session, also, Mr. Pelham prosecuted his plan for that financial reform, which he had commenced, by the reduction of interest. Hitherto a considerable portion of the public debt had been divided into no less than fourteen different stocks, established at different periods, and under different acts. Those bearing an interest of three per cent, consisted of eight, and amounted to £.9,137,821. Those at three and a half per cent, reducible to three per cent in January, 1758, consisted of six, and amounted to £.17,701,323. As the necessary accounts were thus rendered not only complicated, but expensive, an expedient was devised by Mr. Pelham, for their simplification. Accordingly, a committee, appointed for the purpose, presented a series of resolutions,† on the 22nd of February, which were approved by the Com-

---

* Continuation of Rapin, vol. xxi. p. 449.—Journals of Parliament.

† The several classes of annuities at three per cent, established in 1731, 1742, 1743, 1744, 1745, and 1750, were to be consolidated into one joint stock of annuities, payable out of the sinking fund, until redeemed by parliament, and transferrable at the Bank and South Sea House respectively; thus forming the largest portion of the public funds, technically denominated the *three per cent consols*. The holders of orders and tallies, bearing an interest of three per cent, payable at the Exchequer, might subscribe the same to the said annuities, and the duties charged with the payment of the interest, were to be carried to the sinking fund. The same power was given to the holders of orders issued from the Exchequer, instead of St. Nevis' and St. Christopher's debentures. The first and second subscriptions of 3½ per cent annuities, were converted into one joint stock of annuities, payable from the sinking fund, and transferrable at the Bank. The holders of orders and tallies, bearing 3½ per cent interest, on the duties on wrought plate, were empowered to subscribe the same to the said stock of annuities, and the revenue, charged with the interest, was to be carried to the sinking fund.

The joint stock of the first and second Bank annuities was to be consolidated into one joint stock of Bank annuities.

Finally, the joint stock of the first and second Old South Sea annuities, was formed into one joint stock of South Sea annuities, transferrable at the South Sea House, and the same change was proposed, with regard to the first and second subscription of New South Sea annuities, transferrable at the same place.—Journals of the Commons.

mons, and embodied in a bill. It was read a first time on the 28th of February, passed through both Houses with little alteration, and received the royal assent. By this act, the several classes of annuities were consolidated into five stocks,* chargeable on the sinking fund, and made transferrable at the Bank and South Sea House respectively. Thus a great cause of perplexity, both to individuals and the public, was effectually and permanently removed.† The consolidation of these stocks may be regarded as the completion of Mr. Pelham's financial system, for the simplification of the public funds, and the reduction of interest.

The different regulations for the service of the year are exhibited in the following table :

SUPPLY.

NAVY.—Charge of 10,000 seamen; building and repair of ships; Ordinary, half pay, &c. ......£.	894,561		
ARMY.—Charge of 18,857 men;		......	649,666
ordnance, guards, and garrisons;		..	500,000
and extraordinary expenses, &c..	1,112,048		
Subsidy to the Elector of Bavaria .	20,000		
————— Elector of Saxony .	32,000		1,000,000
For supporting the Settlements on the Coast of Africa	10,000		
Compensation to the African Company, for their charter, forts, settlements, &c.	112,142		
For supporting the colony of Nova Scotia	61,493		
For the colony of Georgia ..	4,000		
For the loss of horned cattle	6,600		
Extraordinary expenses of the Mint	4,000		
For the road between Newcastle and Carlisle	3,000		
For making good deficiencies, interest, &c..................	368,512		
	2,628,356		
Balance.........	972,787		
	£.3,601,143		£.3,601,143

* One, of the 3 per cent annuities; one, of the 3½ per cent; one, of the first and second subscription of Bank annuities; one, of the first and second Old South Sea annuities; one, of the first and second New South Sea annuities.

† Continuation of Rapin, vol. xxi. pp. 447, 448.

Besides these provisions, £.900,000 was granted towards discharging the debt of the navy, and £.400,000 for paying off the three and a half per cent annuities, charged on stamped vellum, which were not included in the current service of the year; the first item having been previously carried to account, under the head of naval services, and the second having been discharged by Exchequer-bills at three per cent.

From the different measures adopted in this session, it is manifest that the attention of government was still directed to the promotion of trade, and the improvement of the colonies, as well as to the establishment of an efficient police. Acts were passed for protecting the commerce of the sugar colonies, and for encouraging the growth of cotton in the American plantations; for restricting insurances on ships bound to and from the East Indies; and for permitting the importation of wool from Ireland, into the ports of Lancaster and Great Yarmouth. Others also received the sanction of the legislature, for remedying abuses in the collection of turnpike tolls, and for exacting proper sureties from persons intrusted with the disposal of the funds thence arising; for preventing thefts and robberies; for regulating places of public entertainment; for punishing the keepers of disorderly houses; for preventing the crime of murder; for the more effectual employment of the poor; and for securing mines of black lead from theft and robbery.

As the contagious disorder still continued to rage among horned cattle, the preventive regulations adopted in the preceding session were amended; and, under the vigilant care of the magistracy, in executing the directions of the legislature, this evil was gradually subdued.

Parliament was prorogued on the 26th of March. In the speech from the throne, the king, after thanking both Houses for the great application and promptitude with which they had dispatched the public business, observed, "You have not only shewn your just satisfaction in the measures I have pursued in foreign affairs, but have also given me your support in carrying them on, with that zeal and cheerfulness which I had reason to expect, from so dutiful and affectionate a parliament, who are entirely convinced that those measures are calculated to maintain the essential interests of the nation, and to render the present peace durable and lasting." He then distinctly approved the bill for purchasing and colonizing the forfeited estates in Scotland. To the Commons, he testified his satisfaction at their readiness in voting the requisite supplies, and at the plans adopted by them, for consolidating the funds and reducing the interest. "Nothing in this world," he concluded, "can give me so much pleasure, as to see you a flourishing and happy people. Exert yourselves in your several stations, to do your parts; and you may depend on my unwearied endeavours to secure this great blessing to ourselves, and transmit it to posterity."*

The mortification to which Mr. Pelham had been subjected, during the discussions on the bill relative to the forfeited estates in Scotland, was aggravated by an additional proof, that the attack against him and his brother was still pressed by the Duke of Cumberland. On the 21st of March, the king delivered to him a private report of the state of Scotland, and a list of the Jacobites, holding offices under government, furnished by his Royal Highness. This communication was accompanied by an order to attend the Duke, and enter into an examination of every case. Aware that many were false, and all exaggerated, Mr. Pelham at first resolved to decline the task;† but, on farther consideration, he felt it his duty to obey the commands of the sovereign; and the correspondence with his brother at this period, shews that he entered into the investigation with as deep and continued an interest, as if it had originated in his own choice.

* Journals of Parliament.—Hansard's Parl. Hist. vol. xiv. p. 1271.

† The duke of Newcastle to the lord Chancellor, March 21st, 1752.—Illust. Corres. Also, correspondence between the two brothers, in April and May, 1752.

CHAPTER XXVIII.

1752.

Disputes between the King, as Elector of Hanover, and the King of Prussia, relative to East Friesland—Continuation of the Negotiations for the election of a King of the Romans—Demands of the Elector Palatine, and opposition of the Court of Vienna —Anxiety of the Duke of Newcastle for the attainment of this object—Conditional treaty adjusted between the King of England, and the Elector Palatine—Preparations for convoking an Electoral Diet—Opposition of Prussia and France—Silent abandonment of the design—Aversion of Mr. Pelham to the grant of farther Subsidies—Critical state of Foreign affairs—The King approves Mr. Pelham's management of the Revenue—Result of the inquiry relative to the affairs of Scotland.

THAT part of the Royal Speech, which related to foreign affairs, clearly indicated, that the king was determined to persevere in his system of policy, and that he calculated on the full concurrence of parliament. His views were, as usual, promoted by the duke of Newcastle; who, on many occasions, boasted of the affair of the election, as his darling child; and even Mr. Pelham so far relied on the professions of the French Court, as to entertain hopes of final success.

Accordingly, on the arrival of the king, at his Electoral capital, on the 10th of April, the duke of Newcastle zealously resumed his negotiations; and ministers from several German princes repaired to Hanover. The French monarch also sent thither M. de Vergennes,* envoy at the court of Treves, ostensibly authorised to promote the wishes of the king of England, but secretly furnished with instructions to defeat them.†

At this period new difficulties had arisen, from a serious dispute between

---

* Subsequently so well known as prime minister of France.

† See letters from the duke of Newcastle to the Chancellor, and Mr. Pelham, on the subject of M. de Vergennes. Illust. Corres.

the king, as elector of Hanover, and the king of Prussia, concerning their
respective pretensions to East Friesland, which on the extinction of the
ducal line in 1744, had been occupied by Prussia, in virtue of an expectative or eventual reversion, granted by Leopold the First, to the House of
Brandenburg, in 1694. The king of England, as elector of Hanover, at the
same time, claimed the duchy, in consequence of an hereditary union, concluded by the House of Brunswick Luneburg, in the year 1691, with Duke
Christian Eberhard. This dispute, which had been suspended, during the
struggle for more important interests, now assumed a new and serious character.
The king of England insisted, that the question should be submitted to the
Aulic council; while the king of Prussia not only denied the competency
of that tribunal, but manifested a determination to vindicate his rights
by force of arms. To gratify his resentment, and also to involve the interests
of England, in a German quarrel, Frederic availed himself of certain British
property, subjected to his power, by a loan of £.250,000, for which the late
emperor, Charles the Sixth, had pledged certain mines in Silesia, to British
subjects. This mortgage had been transferred to the king of Prussia, on the
cession of Silesia, and guarantied by public treaties; but, on the plea that
depredations had been committed by British cruizers on Prussian ships,
carrying contraband goods to France, during the late war, he suspended the
payment of the interest, until compensation should be made.

Under such unfavourable auspices, the negotiation with the electoral
princes was resumed. As Bavaria, Saxony, and Mentz, were already gained,
and as the accession of the elector of Cologne was expected, through the
influence of his nephew, the elector of Bavaria, every effort was again tried
to secure the elector Palatine; and pressing applications were made to the
Courts of France and Prussia. Those courts affected a willingness to
acquiesce, provided satisfaction were given, for the demands of the elector
Palatine, on their Imperial Majesties, as well as on the Maritime Powers;
and the election conducted according to the laws and institutions of
the empire. The demands appear to have varied, according to the suggestions of France and Prussia; but at length, in addition to his former claims,
for the damages committed by the Austrian troops, during the war of the
Spanish Succession, and the reversion of the fief of Ortenau, with the privilege *de non appellando*, for the duchy of Deux Ponts, the elector required a
compensation for the supplies of forage, furnished to the English and Dutch
troops, before the battle of Dettingen. After a series of discussions on these

points, through the intervention of the Court of Versailles, the French minister affected to leave the question to the decision of the king of England himself; and in this reference, the king of Prussia apparently acquiesced. Accordingly, the pecuniary demands of the elector were reduced from 3,000,000 florins to 1,200,000 (£.120,000), with the consent of France. Of this sum, England and Holland agreed to pay 500,000 florins; and nothing seemed wanting, to render the election successful, but the acquiescence of the court of Vienna, in the discharge of the remainder, and in the grant of the territorial demands of the elector Palatine.

An application was now made to the Austrian cabinet, to procure their assent to the arbitration of the king of England, and the fulfilment of their promise to convoke an electoral diet, as the requisite majority of votes was fully secured. But the king had the mortification to encounter the most obstinate resistance, from the very court, which he was labouring so assiduously to serve. All the representations of Mr. Keith, the British envoy, proving fruitless, lord Hyndford was deputed as embassador extraordinary to Vienna, with the hope, that such a proof of respect would produce a due impression. The expedient, however, tended only to strengthen the objections of the Austrian cabinet; for, the answers returned, both to Mr. Keith and to lord Hyndford, were in so ungracious a style, that even the duke of Newcastle himself, could not refrain from denouncing them, as arrogant, ungrateful, and even impertinent.*

The king, resenting this unmerited treatment, declared, that the affair of the election was at an end; that he would instantly recal lord Hyndford, and would not make the slightest pecuniary sacrifice, for the interest of so unthankful an ally.

The duke of Newcastle, though equally incensed, was unwilling to risk an open breach with the House of Austria. He therefore prevailed on the king to defer the recal of lord Hyndford; and at the same time transmitted to the court of Vienna an ultimatum, which was, that they should contribute 700,000 florins towards the liquidation of the elector Palatine's claims, and convoke the electoral diet, the refusal of which, he said, would dissolve the union of the Maritime Powers with the House of Austria, and force them to form a connection with France and Prussia.†

* See the duke of Newcastle's letter to Mr. Pelham, May 20th–31st, 1752. Illust. Corres.
† Letter of the duke to Mr. Pelham, dated June 9th–20th.

Mr. Pelham also strongly censured the court of Vienna; and in a letter to his brother, observes, " I shall be glad to see the day, when you have done negotiating with them; for never any good came of their counsels. You certainly do all you can, in the present circumstances; but an angel from Heaven cannot effectually serve some people, against their wills." * Notwithstanding this burst of indignation, he coincided in opinion with his brother; and, though highly displeased at the conduct of Austria, he deprecated an open rupture with that power, in existing circumstances. He, however, recommended, that a good understanding should be maintained with France, as the best expedient for obviating any imprudent proceeding on the part of Austria and Prussia. He advised the adoption of conciliatory language; and urged, that no reasonable means should be spared, to accomplish the election, and thus establish the Germanic system, on a basis calculated to secure a durable peace. Finally, he did not disapprove the subsidy to the elector Palatine, provided his vote would render the election unanimous, and insure the consent of France; for he reflected that the sum payable by England was in itself inconsiderable, and was to be supplied by such distant instalments, that the election, if attainable, would take place, before any payment was required.

He insisted, however, on the necessity of unanimity; being apprehensive, that a partial election would involve England in a war, as principal; since she would be bound in honour to support the House of Austria, and those princes who favoured the election, should they be attacked on that account. He also emphatically observed, that such a war would be attended with the most disastrous consequences, should it occur at a time when the parliament was on the eve of expiring; when a new one was to be called; and no fruit of the last peace enjoyed, except the taking from individuals one fourth of their income, the better, as it would be said, to enable ministers to carry on new and greater expenses.†

Farther instances proving ineffectual, orders of recal were dispatched to lord Hyndford; and this decisive measure made a considerable impression on the court of Vienna. In the audience of leave, the emperor, after strong expressions of regret and gratitude, offered in his own person, to place 500,000 florins at the disposal of the king of England, towards the

* See letter from Mr. Pelham to the duke, dated June 26th, 1752. Illust. Corres.

† See letter from Mr. Pelham to the duke of Newcastle, dated July 1st-12th, 1752. Illust. Corres.

liquidation of the Palatine claims; but, at the same time, repeated his objections to the concessions exacted from himself, as head of the empire. Before the departure of lord Hyndford, it was understood, that the court of Vienna would advance 500,000 florins, in the expectation that the Maritime Powers would discharge the remainder.

The king still persisted in his resolution not to consent to any farther advance; and in this dilemma, the duke of Newcastle ventured to make a new and private appeal to the court of Vienna, through Mr. Keith. In this letter,* after repeating his former declaration, that the failure of the election would produce so much resentment, as to cause a change of system, break the connection of England with Austria, and induce her to unite with Prussia and France, he instructed Mr. Keith to press for an increase of the advance, offered by the empress-queen; and not to desist from his remonstrances, until he had obtained at least 700,000 florins. The arrangement of the German points was left to the management of the Hanoverian ministers.

The court of Vienna, with the utmost reluctance, consented to pay an additional 100,000 florins, making 600,000; but insisted, that the Maritime Powers ought to advance the other 600,000, and repeated their determination not to grant the territorial concessions and privileges, required by the elector Palatine. The manner of this refusal was scarcely less offensive than the refusal itself; for, although the emperor and some of the ministers endeavoured to preserve a conciliatory tone, those counsellors who were considered adverse to the English interest, did not scruple to complain that England patronized and supported every claimant, who was desirous of stripping the empress-queen. In foreign courts, also, the Austrian ministers represented the project of the intended election, as originating solely from the wishes of the king of England; and hints were not spared, that her Imperial Majesty considered it an indignity, to owe the advancement of her family to the influence of a foreign power.

The repugnance of the court of Vienna, which was not concealed from the German princes, gave double effect to the machinations of Prussia, and the intrigues of France; and the intention of proceeding to an immediate election was again necessarily suspended. Yet it appears, that the duke of

---

* The duke of Newcastle to Mr. Keith, Hanover, Aug. 20th-31st, 1752, MS. Also a letter from the duke of Newcastle to the lord Chancellor, dated Aug. 5th-16th, 1752. Illust. Corres.

Newcastle still adhered to his purpose, notwithstanding these multiplied objections; for he thus expresses his feelings, in a letter to the lord Chancellor, dated Aug. 21st-Sept. 1st.

"If you do not send a thorough strong opinion, for making up whatever shall be wanting of the 700.000 florins, I shall be much disappointed; my credit and reputation greatly disgraced; but, what is of much more consequence, the honour of the king our master, and the reputation of England, reduced extremely low, in every court in Europe; and we shall soon become a province of France. Consider maturely my letters to Holdernesse and my brother."

At the period, when the court of Vienna were quibbling on the demands advanced in favour of the elector Palatine, and when France and Prussia were indirectly thwarting the negotiation, the duke of Newcastle encountered an unexpected mortification from the king himself. The answer of Mr. Pelham to his brother's letter, having announced his approbation of the proceedings, and his consent to the proposed payment of the additional sum of 200,000 florins, the king appeared highly gratified. But notwithstanding this gracious approbation, his Majesty suddenly changed his language. Being desirous of protracting the negotiation, that he might remain at Hanover until the end of the year, he positively objected to the payment of the 200,000 florins, and expressed the utmost indifference, as to the success of the election. While the duke was labouring to remove this unforeseen impediment, he had the farther mortification of learning from the Hanoverian minister, baron Münchhausen, that the king, in his capacity of elector, had privately dispatched a formal memorial,* to the court of Vienna, requiring some fief or expectative for himself, should the elector Palatine obtain his territorial demands; thus furnishing that court with an additional argument for rejecting them. In consequence, however, of the manly expostulations made by the duke of Newcastle, on the impolicy and impropriety of such pretensions, a change was soon manifested in the royal mind; for, in a subsequent audience, the king rejoiced in the prospect of a speedy and successful conclusion, and appeared to have entirely forgotten his objections to the pecuniary demands on England.†

In the same letter, the duke also mentioned an incident, which equally

---

* See letter from the duke to Mr. Pelham, dated Sept. 28th, 1752. Illust. Corres.
† See the duke's letter to Mr. Pelham, dated Görhde. Oct. 3rd, 1752. Illust. Corres.

disconcerted and afflicted him. From the information of baron Münchhausen, he found, that his Majesty had objected to the additional sum required for the elector Palatine, with the view of obtaining an annual subsidy of £.40,000 in favour of Russia ; that he deemed himself secure of the duke's acquiescence ; and hoped that he should cajole and manage Mr. Pelham, and thus obtain his consent. On this occasion Mr. Pelham, in a letter to his Grace, observed, that he was not easily cajoled, and that he never yielded on any occasion, excepting where his brother was concerned, and when the part he must have taken, had he not yielded, would have been more dangerous than the thing itself. This occurrence, though of no public import, yet occasioned considerable uneasiness to both the brothers, who plainly perceived the intention of the king, to manage them separately, and thus obtain the acquiescence of both, in measures upon which they materially differed. They consequently now felt it more necessary than ever, carefully to preserve their good understanding, and to act in perfect concert, and without the least reserve, notwithstanding their difference in opinion on some particular points in agitation. * Indeed, there was no period from the commencement of the Pelham administration, in which they were more cordially united ; and we find their letters no longer conveying mutual reproaches and recriminations, but filled with warm expressions of confidence and affection.

It was not to be expected that a negotiation, prosecuted under such circumstances, and obstructed by so many conflicting interests, could ultimately succeed. Farther attempts were indeed made, to gratify the elector Palatine ; and at length, in the beginning of October, his demands were reduced into the shape of a treaty, which was regularly concluded, between him and the king of England, and was to be ratified, as soon as the acquiescence of Austria could be obtained. The terms were, an allowance of 1,200,000 florins, for his various demands of compensation, of which sum 500,000 were to be advanced by the empress queen, and 700,000 by the Maritime Powers, according to the proportions established in former treaties, namely, two thirds by Great Britain, and one third by Holland. The payment was to be made in three instalments : the first of 600,000 florins, which was not to be advanced until the election was concluded ; and the two

* For farther details on this interesting subject, see the following letters in the Illust. Corres. for 1752 :—From the duke to Mr. Pelham, Oct. 3rd. From the lord Chancellor to the duke, Oct. 10th-21st. From Mr. Pelham to the duke, Oct. 13th-24th.

others of 300,000 each. From the emperor, he was to obtain an exemption from appeals, for his duchy of Deux Ponts, and the expectative, or reversion of the fief of Ortenau, or an equivalent. In return, he was to concur in the election of the Archduke Joseph ; and to join with the other electors, in settling the articles of capitulation. At the same time, it was stated, that this engagement was only conditional, and dependent on the fulfilment of the articles, by their Imperial Majesties.*

Notwithstanding this arrangement, the objections of the court of Vienna continued insurmountable. The treaty, therefore, became a mere nullity ; and the king and the duke of Newcastle, however unwilling to forego their favourite object, were compelled to leave Germany, without having fulfilled the promise held forth in parliament, that the election would be accomplished, during the king's stay abroad.

Mr. Pelham could not contemplate the unsatisfactory result of this long negotiation without regret ; but, in one of his latest letters to his brother, he appears to have derived consolation from the idea, that if, as was likely, the scheme should eventually fail, a war at least would be avoided, which, notwithstanding the increase of wealth in the kingdom, nothing but absolute necessity could justify ; and that necessity must, he said, be very apparent to enable them to carry it on. At the same time, he observed, " While we take no steps that will aggrandize our great rival, France, we should do all in our power, by friendly communications, and pacific measures, to conciliate all parties, and thus prevent another rupture."

During the period spent by the duke of Newcastle at Hanover, in arranging foreign affairs, and in forwarding the project for the election of a king of the Romans, Mr. Pelham was engaged in conducting the domestic concerns, and in the exercise of his financial duties. He was likewise employed in an inquiry into the affairs of Scotland, in consequence of the orders, from the sovereign himself, for a minute examination of the long list of cases, which had been furnished by the Duke of Cumberland.

Mr. Pelham was the more interested to undertake this examination, because the king, in a conversation with the duke of Newcastle, had expressed his conviction, that many of the cases adduced were true ; and, that if no inquiries were made, or proper measures taken, the accusations

---

* The abatement of the 100,000 florins in the contribution of the empress-queen, was made with the view of obtaining her more ready acquiescence in the German points.

would be renewed the ensuing session. His Majesty also added, that if the duke of Argyle was suffered to do wrong, by recommending improper persons, the blame would ultimately fall upon the ministry in England.* Mr. Pelham, therefore, wrote in the strongest manner, upon the complaints relative to his department, to the Commissioners of the Customs and Excise, and to the Barons of the Exchequer;† and the duke of Newcastle gave strict injunctions to lord Holdernesse, as Secretary of State, to assist in the investigation.‡ We find, from the correspondence between the two brothers, that the inquiry was no less humanely, than judiciously and strictly carried into execution. Most of the cases, however, were exaggerated; some were false; and but few were well founded. These were remedied, and a few of the accused persons discharged. Mr. Pelham also declared, that since the Union, so complete an investigation had not been prosecuted in Scotland; and expressed his conviction, that there never was a time, when the officers of the revenue were so little liable to the charge of Jacobitism, as at the present.§

The king was highly satisfied with the conduct of the two brothers ; and not only exculpated them from all blame, but expressed his full approbation of their prudence and loyalty. . He particularly praised Mr. Pelham for his activity, and observed, that he would never fail to do right, when he was rightly informed. ||

At the departure of the king from the continent, the aspect of foreign affairs by no means indicated a continuance of tranquillity. The misunderstanding between Sweden and Russia still subsisted ; and symptoms of hostility again appeared between Russia and Prussia. Frederic had also evinced the most hostile disposition towards England, by erecting courts of his own, to overthrow the sentences of our Admiralty Court of Appeal, and by appropriating the interest due to the creditors of the Silesia Loan, for the payment of such sums as were adjudged, in this unjust and irregular manner. He was even suspected of endeavouring to excite the Turks to declare war

---

* Letter from the duke of Newcastle to the Chancellor, dated April 29th-May 10th, 1752. Newcastle Papers, MS.

† Letter from the lord Chancellor to the duke of Newcastle, dated May 1st, 1752. MS.

‡ Letter from the lord Chancellor to the duke of Newcastle, dated April 29th-May 10, 1752. MS.

§ See letter from Mr. Pelham to the duke of Newcastle, dated May 8th, 1752. Illust. Corres.

|| See letter from the duke of Newcastle to Mr. Pelham, dated May 15th-26, 1752. Illust. Corres.

against Russia and Austria, that while they were engaged in this contest, he might wrest from the Republic of Poland, Dantzic, and part of Polish Prussia, to which he revived some obsolete pretensions. He also seemed to meditate some aggression against Holland and the electorate of Hanover.

The empress queen, foreseeing new troubles, had strengthened her connections with Russia, by an alliance, nominally defensive, to which she endeavoured to gain the accession of England. France likewise seemed to be preparing for war, not only by exertions to augment her navy, but by intrigues and machinations in every European court, where she had a prospect of consolidating, or extending her interest. She had even successfully availed herself of the coolness that existed between the courts of London and Vienna; and obtained considerable influence among the ministers of the empress-queen, by encouraging their zeal for the improvement of commerce in the Low Countries, and by fortifying their opposition to the renewal of the Barrier Treaty.

Such was the critical situation of foreign affairs, when the king returned to England; and, as we have repeatedly observed, it required all the caution and prudence of Mr. Pelham to maintain that tranquillity, which was so necessary to complete the execution of his plans for diminishing the national debt, the interest of which he had already so considerably reduced.

He had the satisfaction to obtain the concurrence of his brother in these pacific views; and they acted with harmony and concert. He also experienced the gratification of knowing that his financial measures were highly approved by his sovereign, who preferred his management of the revenue to that of Sir Robert Walpole, and warmly commended him as being far more frugal than his predecessor in the domestic expenditure.*

---

* See letter from the duke of Newcastle to Mr. Pelham, dated July 1st-12th, 1752. Illust. Corres.

CHAPTER XXIX.

1752—53.

Feuds in the Household of the young Prince of Wales—Resignation of lord Harcourt, and the Bishop of Norwich, and appointment of the earl of Waldegrave, and the Bishop of Peterborough—Jealousy excited by this change among the Whig party —Opening of Parliament—Addresses of both Houses—Discussion on the Military establishment—Bill for the Naturalization of the Jews—Favoured by Mr. Pelham —Strenuously opposed.

THE King returned to England on the 18th of November; and soon afterwards a schism, of the most serious kind, occurred in the household of the Prince of Wales.

This establishment was of too heterogeneous a nature to be tranquil or permanent ; for, while the nominal authority was vested in the governor and preceptor, the tutelage and education of the young prince were engrossed by subordinate officers, who enjoyed the patronage of his royal mother, and were his companions in the hours of amusement and relaxation. The governor and preceptor, therefore, soon found themselves reduced to insignificance ; and their mortification was aggravated, by the open preference shewn to Messrs. Stone, Scott, and Cresset. In fact, while lord Harcourt had been obliged to hire a house at Brentford, and of course to cross the Thames, twice a day, for the fulfilment of his duties, Mr. Stone had been accommodated with a residence near the palace of Kew. He also enjoyed the confidence of his royal charge ; and on various occasions was supported by the princess, in opposition to the governor and preceptor.

Mr. Scott continued likewise to rise in favour ; while Mr. Cresset, having conciliated, not only the good will of the princess, but that of the king, had recently been nominated Treasurer to her Royal Highness, on the promotion of Dr. Lee, to the office of Dean of the Arches, and Judge of the Prerogative Court.

Two contending parties, were thus formed in the prince's household ; the one including the governor and preceptor, and the other, the three subordinate agents. The governor, laying claim to the entire superintendance of the prince's conduct and manners, neglected. to manifest the deference towards Mr. Stone, to which that gentleman considered himself intitled, by his connection with the duke of Newcastle, and his favour with the king and princess. The bishop of Norwich, also, who was a prelate of profound learning, and conscientiously zealous for the mental improvement of his pupil, disgusted the young prince by his dry and pedantic manners, and offended the princess, by persevering in the discipline, which he deemed necessary to remedy the gross, neglect of her son's education. He was mortified by the obtrusive behaviour of Mr. Scott, the sub-preceptor, whom he accused of assuming a greater share in the instruction of the prince, than became his station ; and on more than one occasion repressed his boldness, in an authoritative manner. These bickerings were aggravated, by the interference of Mr. Murray, the Solicitor-general, who was much consulted in the prince's education, and who, from intimacy with Mr. Stone, and high favour with the princess, enjoyed great influence in the household. Mr. Murray even complained to the bishop, of the want of attention manifested towards his friend Mr. Stone ; and in answer to the remark, that Mr. Stone was subordinate to the governor, lord Harcourt, in whom the principal trust was reposed, he is said to have exclaimed, " His lordship is a mere cipher, must- be- a- cipher, and was intended to be only a cipher." Cresset also inflamed the feud, by his disrespectful reflections on the preceptor and governor, the latter of whom, he declared, had only the manners of a groom.

As the princess countenanced this triumvirate, lord Harcourt adopted towards his royal pupil a dignified but imprudent reserve, and disclosed his grievances only to lord Lincoln. The bishop, on the other hand, presumed to remonstrate ; but experienced from her Royal Highness, a reception neither gracious, nor encouraging.

These jealousies not only created much confusion in the household, but frustrated any regular system of instruction for the prince. Accordingly, in the preceding September, the king himself had been obliged to interfere. Having summoned lord Harcourt and Mr. Stone into his presence, he expressed his dissatisfaction with those who superintended the education of his grandson; and delivered a plan in writing, which he ordered to be followed in future. We learn, from a letter of the duke of Newcastle to the lord Chancellor,[*] that in addressing them, his Majesty made no distinction in the authority of the governor and sub-governor, declaring, "that he placed confidence in both;" and adding, "that he desired to see both of them frequently, either together, or separately, as they pleased."

Although the interposition of the royal authority suspended the feud, it was renewed with increased violence, during the residence of the king at Hanover; and, from the superior means of communication enjoyed by Mr. Stone and Mr. Cresset, the information conveyed to his Majesty was not to the advantage of either the governor or preceptor. In several conversations with the duke of Newcastle, the king severely condemned the indiscreet behaviour of the bishop of Norwich.[†] He was likewise so dissatisfied with earl Harcourt, that on his return to England, he did not deign to notice him, when he presented himself at court.[‡]

In this agitated state of the Prince's household, the most trifling subject was sufficient to provoke an open quarrel. The bishop having discovered in the hands of the prince, " L'Histoire des Revolutions d'Angleterre," was indignant that any book should have been offered to his pupil, without his sanction, especially this work, which was regarded as fraught with improper principles, having been compiled by father d'Orleans, the chaplain and confessor of James II, in vindication of that monarch's unconstitutional proceedings.

The introduction of this book was at first imputed to Mr. Stone, who was suspected of fostering principles adverse to those of the Revolution. But, on his absolute denial, the suspicion was successively transferred to Scott and Cresset, from whose habits and connexions it was surmised, that they had adopted this expedient, for infusing into the mind of the young prince, the well-known maxims of their patron, lord Bolingbroke. At length, after a minute inquiry, the book was said to have been lent to the heir apparent by his brother, prince Edward, who had borrowed it from the princess Augusta.

Notwithstanding this exculpation, lord Harcourt and the bishop resolved to relinquish their trust, if they could not obtain the dismission of Stone

* Dated Sept. 27th, 1751. MS.
† Letter from the duke of Newcastle to Mr. Pelham, July 1st-12th, 1752.—Illust. Corres.
‡ Lord Orford's Memoires, vol. i. p. 252.

Scott, and Cresset. Accordingly, his lordship, in a message to the king, represented, that expedients had been employed to implant improper principles in the mind of his royal charge, and that continual efforts were made to obstruct him in the fulfilment of his duty. The lord Chancellor and the archbishop of Canterbury were deputed to hear his complaints; but he refused to communicate them, except to his Majesty in person. Having obtained an audience for the purpose, he detailed the motives which induced him to offer his resignation; but, as he failed in establishing one of his most material charges, which was, that Cresset had acted as secretary to lord Bolingbroke, while in the service of the Pretender, the king, offended by an accusation, which he knew to be false, permitted his lordship's retirement from office, without expressing any concern.

The bishop of Norwich tendered his resignation, at the same time, through the archbishop of Canterbury; and the king accepted it, without vouchsafing to grant him an audience, declaring he wished to hear no more on the subject.

This change was highly gratifying to the princess, who was eager to monopolize the management of her son; and the king not only testified his displeasure at the conduct of lord Harcourt and the bishop, but expressed his conviction that their charges were frivolous. The duke of Newcastle and his brother were too much attached to Mr. Stone, to give credence to the accusations against him; and of course espoused his cause, although the appointment of the governor and preceptor had been chiefly owing to their recommendation.

The vacant places were soon filled by persons expressly selected by the king. Lord Waldegrave reluctantly accepted the office of governor; and that of preceptor was conferred on Dr. Thomas, bishop of Peterborough, who had acquired the favour of his Majesty, before his accession to the throne. The courtly manners and prudent reserve of lord Waldegrave, and the mild and unassuming character of the prelate, were probably considered by the king, as the best pledges of future concord in the prince's establishment; and the Pelhams, even had they been inclined, could not so far venture to oppose the royal will, as to object to their appointment.

The Whigs, however, were far from approving a change, which strengthened their former suspicions, arising from the marked favour shewn to Scott and Cresset. Lord Waldegrave, though a nobleman of high integrity and constitutional principles, was regarded with unmerited distrust; because his grandfather had accompanied king James abroad at the Revolution, and had espoused his natural daughter, Henrietta; and, because his father, though subsequently employed in the highest diplomatic offices, had not renounced the Catholic religion, until he had attained the age of thirty-eight. The new preceptor was also charged with a strong propensity to High Tory principles.

These transactions, therefore, produced a deep sensation in the public mind, and especially among the zealous Whigs, who are said to have transmitted anonymous letters to several popular preachers, in the hope that the charge of Jacobitism against the subordinate agents, would be made the subject of alarm from the pulpit. The feeling was still more strongly evinced, by a paper, intitled, "A Memorial of several Noblemen and Gentlemen," which was sent to different persons, particularly to general Hawley, the favourite of the Duke of Cumberland, through whose hands it was conveyed to the king. This Memorial contained a series of complaints, on the improper principles infused into the mind of the young prince, and the dangerous course pursued in his education. It strongly impugned the supposed Jacobite principles of Stone, Scott, and Cresset, and particularly of Mr. Murray, who was so often suffered to interfere in the education of the prince, although known to be of a disaffected family, and most nearly related to the earl of Dunbar, the first minister of the Pretender. It also censured with great acrimony the undeserved indignities offered to the late governor and preceptor;* and intimated, that the minister who had advised the king to refuse an audience to the bishop of Norwich, was either desirous of governing by a faction, or was himself the instrument of a more dangerous faction, which intended to overthrow the government.†

Parliament met at the moment when this unfortunate feud was the topic of general discourse. Hopes were, however, entertained that, as the question appeared to be purely personal, the ferment would gradually subside, and excite no public discussion.

The Session was opened on the 11th of January, by a speech from the throne. The failure of the negotiation with the elector Palatine, precluded,

---

* Anonymous Life of Lord Chatham.—Dodington's Diary.—Cont. of Rapin, vol. xxi. p. 455.
—Lord Orford's Memoires, vol. i. p. 249-55.—MS. documents of Mr. Etough.—Supplement to lord Hardwicke's Parliamentary Journal, in Hansard, vol. xiv. p. 1294.

† This paper is printed in the Anonymous Life of Lord Chatham, and in Lord Orford's Memoires, as well as in most of the periodical publications.

indeed, the necessity of any specific proposition to parliament; but the purpose of the king to persevere in his system of foreign policy, was indicated by the expression, "that the maintenance of the public peace was the object of all his views and negotiations, and that he was proceeding, and should continue to act, on the principles hitherto pursued." His Majesty also repeated his congratulations on the good disposition of foreign powers, and expressed his hope, that the precautions taken in different parts of Europe, would give additional strength and solidity to the peace.

He informed the Commons, that no aid would be necessary, beyond the ordinary supply, which was requisite for the security of the nation, and the support of its commerce. He, at the same time, recommended them not to intermit their attention to the reduction of the public debt, the improvement of the revenue, and the increase of the sinking fund.

He concluded with expressing a hope, that the laws enacted for the suppression of vice and disorder, would produce a salutary effect; and exhorted both Houses to take such farther precautions, as should appear necessary, that as peace prevailed abroad, so good order and tranquillity might reign at home.*

In the House of Peers, the address was moved by the earl of Marchmont, who had recently seceded from opposition, and seconded by lord Archer. It expressed entire concurrence in all the topics of the speech; applauded the cares and labours of his Majesty, for the maintenance of public peace and domestic tranquillity; and, after assurances of cordial support, concluded with a warm effusion of gratitude and loyalty.

The address in the House of Commons was moved by Mr. Charles Yorke, second son of the Chancellor, and seconded by Mr. Tracy. The sentiments conveyed in it, were so similar to those of the Lords, that only one expression merits particular notice, as constituting a subject of debate. In reference to the king's communication, respecting the system of foreign affairs, the address proposed was, to acknowledge "the wisdom," as well as the goodness of his Majesty, in pursuing such measures, as might best contribute to maintain and render permanent, the general tranquillity of Europe. In objecting to this clause, lord Egmont said, "Instead of a prudent and discreet speech from the throne, I find it improper and vain-glorious. I believe that the measures to which his Majesty refers, are well-intended; but they

---

* Journals of Parliament.—Continuation of Rapin, vol. xxi. p. 459.—Hansard's Parl. Hist. vol. xiv. p. 1272.

will prove unsuccessful. The college of princes is averse to the election of a king of the Romans; and the proceedings of the king of Prussia, though outwardly referring to the Silesian loan, are, in reality, prompted by his disapprobation of our conduct, in promoting the election. I am anxious to avoid petulant opposition, but I cannot applaud measures as wise, in which no wisdom has appeared; and I, therefore, propose to omit the word wisdom." Several other members repeated the same objections, and inveighed against the whole system of foreign affairs.

Mr. Pelham argued, that the approbation conveyed in the contested term, referred merely to the maintenance of peace. The goodness of his Majesty in this was readily admitted; and, therefore, he contended, that goodness so acknowledged, implied wisdom; for bad measures were inconsistent with goodness.* The address was carried without a division.

The navy estimates seem to have created no discussion; but those of the army were, as usual, disputed. In a committee of the whole House, January 26th, Mr. Fox, as secretary at war, moved that the number of land forces should be continued at 18,857 men; but Mr. William Northey, having proposed, as an amendment, that 15,000 should be inserted, instead of 18,857, a warm debate ensued. The original motion was opposed, by arguments against standing armies, too trite to merit repetition. Lord Egmont, however, adopted a new mode of reasoning, which was intended as a censure on the inconsistency of the Whigs, in supporting a system, incompatible with the principles of the Revolution.

"I am really surprised," he said, "that some gentlemen, professing, as Whigs, to act upon those principles, should vote for so numerous a force of mercenary troops. Every one knows, that both the Revolution and our present happy establishment, were founded on the principle of resistance; yet, by maintaining such an army, they will make resistance not only ridiculous, but mad. Nor can the mildness of his Majesty's government, or the security derived from his justice and moderation, be made an argument in favour of such a measure. On the contrary, they furnish a strong argument against it; for he, like queen Elizabeth, may point to the people in the streets, and say, ' These are my guards ; upon these I can depend for defence, against all my enemies, either foreign or domestic.' The old pretence of danger from Jacobitism has ceased to afford a reason for

---

* Hansard's Debates, vol. xiv. p. 275.—Lord Orford's Memoires, vol. i. p. 258.

maintaining a large force during peace; for the Jacobites met with such a repulse on their last attempt, that I am sure they will never make another, while his Majesty continues to possess the hearts and affections of all others of his subjects, convinced as the malcontents must now be, that however France may encourage them to rebel, she will never give them any effectual assistance."

Mr. Pelham, in repelling this attack on the party, with which he was identified, developed the doctrine of resistance, in a manner that reflected equal credit on his judgment and patriotism.

He observed, "When the noble lord spoke of resistance, as being the Whig principle, and the principle on which the Revolution and our present happy establishment are founded, he should have distinguished between a constitutional, and a factious resistance. A constitutional resistance is that made against an administration, which advises the sovereign to incroach upon the liberties of the people, or the privileges of parliament, and to pursue measures, evidently subversive of the constitution. A factious resistance, is that which is offered to a just and wise government, and a sovereign who has ever made the law of the land the rule of his conduct; and this resistance has never any other origin, than private, or party interest, or resentment. Constitutional resistance is the true Whig principle. In this respect, I am still, and shall always be as much a Whig as ever; and shall constantly hold myself bound, in duty to my country and to posterity, to join with those who unite, even in forcible measures, when such become absolutely necessary, for removing evil counsellors from our sovereign, and for punishing those who have given him wicked advice. But while a government pursues right measures, and attempts nothing that can be deemed inconsistent with our constitution, it shall always be my principle, so to strengthen the hands of that government, as to render any factious or seditious resistance, not only ridiculous, but mad.

"The measures of government, therefore, form the only criterion, by which we can determine whether resistance be constitutional or factious, just or unjust; and in this case the decision must be left to the public voice. Legislators in either House of Parliament may differ in opinion, on this or that particular plan; and they ought to vote, I hope they always do vote, accordingly. But when a measure is adopted by the king, and approved by a majority, in each House, surely I am not to resist the execution of that measure, because I am of a contrary opinion. On that principle no government could be conducted; no society could subsist for twelve months. Therefore I conclude, that while we have a parliament, regularly and duly assembled, there can be no such thing as a constitutional resistance; because if, during the interval of parliament, the government should pursue any scheme, which some persons might deem hostile to the constitution, those who disapprove it, may wait and apply for redress, the ensuing session; and if parliament should differ from them, they ought in modesty to consider their own judgment erroneous, or at least they ought to submit.

" But when the king seems resolved to govern without a parliament, or manifestly employs illegal means, for the choice of such a parliament as shall be devoted to him, the case becomes very different. The people have no resource but in arms, and resistance becomes constitutional. In this light, let us consider our regular army, and we shall find, that in such a case, it would be a safeguard for our liberties. Both officer and soldier would then be free from every sort of legal restraint, and would certainly act like the military in the time of king James. They would either join the people, or refuse to fight against their countrymen, to support a tyrannical government. I admit, that king James left his army very abruptly; but why did he leave it? Certainly not for want of courage, as we may judge from his conduct in the wars with the Dutch, but because he plainly perceived, that the greater part of his army would refuse to engage against the Prince of Orange, and their Protestant brethren; for, though very few of them had actually joined the Prince of Orange, yet it is well known, that many of the king's principal officers had declared, that they would not fight against a prince, who was come to secure their religion and liberties. This result, indeed, his Majesty might have anticipated, from the acclamations of his army at Hounslow, on the acquittal of the bishops, which drew from Louis the Fourteenth, the severe, though just sarcasm, that 'he could not but laugh at his brother James, for attempting to establish Popery with a Protestant army.' Any prince would merit equal ridicule, who should attempt to establish arbitrary power, with an army trained in the principles and spirit of liberty.

" As to the army, in the time of Charles the First, it was raised with a purpose of subverting the constitution, in church and state; therefore we cannot wonder at the conduct of its leaders. They turned the pretended parliament out of doors, because they were disposed to proceed in a different method. That army consisted, not of men trained in the principles of our constitution, but of men nurtured in enthusiasm, and ready to sacrifice every thing, sacred or divine, to the fanatical cause which they espoused. The conduct of that army, therefore, cannot be urged as an argument against the maintenance of our present military establishment. But in contemplating the history of those times, we may discover a very efficient reason, for strengthening the hands of a just and legal government, with a certain number of regular troops. Let every gentleman consider, whether he would not chuse that parliament should ensure the freedom of their debates, and the order of their proceedings, by a few regular troops, chiefly commanded by their own members, rather than that we should be over-awed, and many of us deterred from attending, by a lawless and unruly mob, instigated by factious men, and inflamed by knavish or enthusiastic preachers.

" I hope it is now manifest, that not one of the arguments, or rather declama-tions, against a standing army, in general, would be applicable to our present army, were it much more numerous ; and, as to its actual amount, I am much inclined to concur in opinion with the gentleman who spoke last (Mr. Fox), that, were it not for the expense, we ought to maintain a much greater number of troops, because we should thus avoid the frequent inconveniences of augmenting, and afterwards diminishing our force. We should acquire greater influence with the amicable powers of Europe ; and should deprive the hostile states of all hope of success, from any sudden attack on us, or any of our allies. The expense can afford no argument for reduction, since by the wise retrenchments of his Majesty, our present military establishment does not cost so much as that of 15,000 or 16,000 men, formerly imposed on the nation ; and we should ill express our gratitude to the king, if we lessened his security, by diminishing the number, when he had reduced the expense. Let due consideration be given, to the force which must always be maintained about London ; the numbers to be constantly employed on the coasts, in the preventive service ; and the large armament requisite in Scot-land, to overawe the disaffected : let these exigencies of the state be con-sidered, and I am sure no gentleman will conclude, that it would be prudent in us to reduce our army. When the auspicious time shall arrive, at which we may abolish or diminish many of our high duties, and cease to appre-hend danger from the disaffected, we may consistently deliberate on such a reduction. That time, I hope, is not far distant ; for our sinking fund will shortly enable us to diminish some of our taxes ; and the disaffected party will soon be extinguished, by the wise laws lately made, for preserving the rising generation from all taint of disloyalty.

"In reference to the disaffected, I must observe, that in the interval from 1715 to 1745, during the greater part of which I was in parliament, I remember that in all debates concerning them, the Jacobites were represented, by gentlemen in opposition, as a dispirited, contemptible party, which had for ever ceased to be dangerous; and yet, in 1745, we found this party again in rebellion, defeating our troops, and advancing on our capital with such rapidity, that if the reinforcements from the continent had been detained but a few weeks, by contrary winds, we could not have defended London against the rebels, with so great a regular force, as that which they afterwards defeated at Falkirk. With this observation, I shall conclude, in the full confidence that every gentleman, who has the security of our present happy establishment at heart, will admit the necessity, that we should maintain, for the ensuing year, the number of troops proposed by my honourable friend."

This constitutional speech being cordially approved by the real friends of the country, the question was carried in the affirmative, by 253 against 65;* and though it was again discussed on the 29th, it does not appear to have produced another division.

Tolerant in character, as well as anxious for the increase of national wealth, and the improvement of national industry, Mr. Pelham gave his sanction to a bill, introduced at this period, for permitting the naturalisation of the Jews, who had hitherto been precluded from availing themselves of that privilege, by the condition exacted, of the previous reception of the Holy Sacrament. The bill for removing this impediment passed through the House of Lords almost without notice, even from the bench of Bishops; and it was supposed, that the stigma, which England had so long affixed on that excluded race, would be readily effaced, by a solemn act of the legislature. This result appeared the more probable, as for above a century,† the

---

* Hansard's Parl. Hist. vol. xiv. p. 1277.—Cont. of Rapin, vol. xxi. p. 460.—Journals of the Commons, Jan. 26th, and passim.

† The first public toleration of the Jews was granted by Oliver Cromwell, for which concession he received £.60,000, as appears from a curious account of the transaction, in Spence's Anecdotes, p. 215.

"When the Jews desired leave to have a synagogue in London, they offered him, when Protector, £.60,000. Cromwell appointed a day for giving them an answer. He then sent for some of the most powerful among the clergy, and some of the chief merchants of the city, to be present

Jews had tacitly enjoyed toleration, and the prejudices so long fostered against their religion and character appeared to be gradually subsiding.

Before the bill was brought into the Commons, it had excited such general alarm, that the opponents of ministers determined to resist it with the utmost vehemence and pertinacity. They were encouraged in their purpose by the approach of a general election, when the impression likely to be made on the public mind, by the discussion, would render the opponents of the bill highly popular. It was also ascertained, that some members, though well affected towards the government, were, from principle, adverse to the naturalisation of the Jews. While the country was in this state of agitation, the bill was sent on the 17th of April, from the House of Lords to the Commons, and read a first time.

On the 7th of May, the question for the second reading called forth the spirit of opposition ; and a long debate ensued, in which most of the principal

at their meeting. It was in the long gallery at Whitehall. Sir Paul Rycaut, who was then a young man, pressed in among the crowd, and said he never heard a man speak so well in his life, as Cromwell did on the occasion. When they were all met, he ordered the Jews to speak for themselves. After that, he turned to the clergy, who inveighed much against the Jews, as a cruel and accursed people. Cromwell, in his answer to the clergy, called them ' men of God,' and desired to be informed by them, whether it was not their opinion, that the Jews were to be called, in the fullness of time, into the church. He then desired to know, whether it was not every Christian man's duty, to forward that good end, all he could. Then he flourished a good deal on religion prevailing in this nation, the only place in the world where religion was taught, in its full purity. Was it not, he said, then our duty, in particular, to encourage them to settle where they could be taught the truth, and not to exclude them from the light, and leave them among false teachers, Papists, and idolators? This silenced the clergy. He then turned to the merchants, who spoke of their falseness and meanness, and that they would get their trade from them. ' And can you really be afraid,' said he, ' that this mean and despised people should be able to prevail in trade and credit, over the merchants of England, the noblest and most esteemed merchants of the whole world?' Thus he went on, till he had silenced them too, and so was at liberty to grant what he desired, to the Jews."

In the reign of queen Anne, the Jews even made an attempt to gain a settlement in England, of which the following account is given by the same author, p. 215.

" The Jews offered my lord Godolphin to pay five hundred thousand pounds (and they would have made it a million) if the government would allow them to purchase the town of Brentford, with leave of settling there entirely, with full privilege of trade, &c. The agent from the Jews said, that the affair was already concerted with the chief of their brethren abroad, that it would bring the richest of their merchants hither, and of course an addition of more than twenty millions of money to circulate in the nation. Lord Molesworth was in the room with lord Godolphin, when this proposal was made ; and, as soon as the agent was gone, pressed him to close with it. Lord Godolphin was not of his opinion. He foresaw that it would provoke two of the most powerful bodies in the nation, the clergy, and the merchants. He gave other reasons too against it, and in fine it was dropped."

speakers took a share. Recourse was had to every argument, likely to produce an effect. It was said, that if the British nation thus bartered their birthright, they would incur a greater curse than was inflicted on Esau, as the patrons of this bill professed to surrender the birthright of Englishmen and Christians, for no compensation whatever; that in past times the Jews had offered vast sums for this invaluable privilege; and as no such offer now appeared, the scheme must be ascribed to some clandestine bargain; that the Bill of Naturalisation would attract to this country multitudes of rich Jews, who would purchase lands; colonize them with Jew settlers; obtain advowsons and ecclesiastical patronage; and finally force their way into parliament, and into administration. ·Precedents were sought on both sides; and no historical fact was overlooked, which might reflect odium on the Jews, or represent the proposed law, as likely to subvert the Christian faith, to which they were inveterate enemies by education, habit, and religion. The Holy Scriptures were cited, for instances of their rancorous and cruel spirit; and it was declared impious, to afford political existence and settlement, to those whom Providence had scattered, as vagabonds and outlaws, without country, or fixed habitation. All the penal enactments against them were commended; and even those of Edward the First, extending to confiscation and perpetual exile, were noticed in terms of approbation. Every mark of favour shewn to them, in the lapse of ages, was stigmatised as a national calamity; and, from the time of William the Conqueror, to that of Oliver Cromwell, who first granted them a public toleration of worship, every indulgence was ascribed to the policy of an usurper, or to the self-interest of some unprincipled monarch, who wished to employ their wealth and influence, in the oppression of his liege subjects. Although an act of parliament was passed, in the reign of William the Third, decreeing that all Jews, who resided seven years in our colonies, or had carried on certain kinds of manufacture for three years, within the realm, should be considered as natural-born subjects, and couse-quently capable of purchasing lands; yet it was argued, that by the common law, which had not been, nor could be abrogated, except by an express act of parliament, they could hold such lands only during the king's pleasure.

To the arguments deduced in favour of Naturalisation bills, from their tendency to increase population, wealth, and industry, little attention was paid. Such regulations were treated as mere empirical expedients, perni-cious to the health of the country; in preference to which the reduction of expense, and the abolition of onerous taxes, were recommended as the genuine and salutary means of promoting national prosperity, without the aid of naturalised Jews, or even of foreign Protestants.

Against objections so accordant with popular feeling, and ancient usage, urged with all the eloquence of enthusiasm, and supported by strong legal arguments, it was difficult to contend ; but Mr. Pelham and his friends did not shrink from the struggle. We may adduce his speech, in particular, as an able and perspicuous summary of the reasons on which the bill was grounded, though some of his arguments were rather specious than solid, and were certainly liable to strong objections.

After observing, that he would not contend with the opponents of the bill, about what was the common law, or how that law was to be altered, he added, " but in the vulgar acceptation of the word, I have always understood common law to be common custom; and I cannot see why an old custom may not be altered by a new one. If this be so, whatever was the custom under our arbitrary monarchs, for some reigns after the Conquest, it has been altered by a late contrary custom ; for the Jews have been deemed, for this last century, as much under the protection of the law, as any Christian in similar circumstances. Without insisting on this point, however, I shall suppose the common law to be, that Jews may purchase landed property, but cannot hold it longer than the king pleases. I do, therefore, still maintain, that it is absolutely necessary not only to pass this bill, but to introduce and enact another, for securing to such Jews, as are willing to live among us, the possession of every part of their estate, as well as their property in the public funds. If the Jews be still liable to the treatment, to which they were subjected, in the reign of king John, even their property in the funds would not be safe, though they resided within the realm ; for the king might demand from any of them, what sum he pleased, on pain of torture until it were paid. What could an unfortunate Jew do in such a case ? If he could not otherwise raise the sum demanded, he must sell his property in the funds for that purpose. In such circumstances, would any rich Jew reside in the British dominions? They might, perhaps, possess themselves of a great part of our public funds, but none of them would live here. They would all reside in Holland, France, or Italy, or in some place where they could find personal security ; and thus perhaps, an annual sum of one or two millions might be drawn from the country, in payment of interest or dividends to fundholders, forced to live abroad, who would otherwise expend their incomes among us.

" Such would be the consequence, if this doctrine, deduced from the common law should be established ; and, in my opinion, the very mention of it will constrain many rich Jews to emigrate, as soon as possible, unless by the present enactment we confirm the toleration extended towards them, by custom, for these last hundred years. According to this custom, a Jew born in the king's dominions, is in every respect as much his natural-born subject as any Christian. The term I have mentioned, of one hundred years, would, in any other case, constitute a right ; but, if the contrary doctrine should prevail, it might be contended, that the children of Jews, who had resided seven years in our plantations, could not be deemed natural-born subjects, though they were all natives of those colonies, unless they declared themselves Christians ; because the act * does not say that such persons, ' *and their posterity*,' shall be deemed his Majesty's natural-born subjects of this kingdom, notwithstanding any law or custom to the contrary. But if, by the existing law or custom, a Jew, born in the king's dominions, be deemed a natural-born subject of this kingdom, what mighty favour are we to grant to the Jews, by the present bill? Except, that the father may, by an act of naturalisation, to be passed by some future parliament, which that parliament, however, may refuse, if so disposed, enjoy those privileges, to which his children would of course be entitled, if born in the king's dominions, and to which even the father would also be intitled, by residing seven years in our plantations, or by engaging in certain kinds of manufacture, in Britain, for three years. Is this a favour, which can be attended with any dangerous consequence? Is it not rather a favour, which ought to be granted ; as it may, and, in my opinion, certainly will, induce several rich foreign Jews to reside here, and thus tend to increase, not only our manufactures and commerce, but our public revenue?

" The objection, that, as Christianity is part of our establishment, we ought not to allow its professed enemies to live among us, any more than we should grant the same favour to the enemies of our civil establishment, is an argument that extends too far. Christianity, as professed and practised by the Church of England, is a part of our establishment ; but will any gentleman say, that we ought not to allow any person to live among us, who will not in every particular, conform to the profession and practice of the Church of

---

* Stat, 12 Will. III, c. ii.—Blackstone's Commentaries.

England? Surely, I am not to deem every man my enemy, who differs from me on a point of religion! This would be a most unchristian principle. Considering Jews, then, much in the same light as other dissenters, we ought to regard them, not as enemies of our ecclesiastical establishment, but as men, whose conscience will not allow them to conform to it. Therefore we may, and in charity should, indulge them to an extent, not inconsistent with its security; and we have less danger to apprehend from them, than from any other dissenters, because they never attempt to make converts, and because such an attempt would be peculiarly difficult. The strict tenets of their religion exclude every man who is not of the seed of Israel; and, as they cannot intermarry with a strange woman, we need not fear that they will have any success in converting our countrywomen.

"Our ecclesiastical establishment, therefore, is in no danger from them; and, as to our civil establishment, the Jews are sufficiently excluded from all participation in it, by existing laws; for, unless they become Christians, they cannot even be excisemen, or Custom-house officers. Thus excluded, they may be permitted to live among us, and enjoy the protection of our laws over their persons and property, without offence on our part, to any prophecy relating to them, or interference with the curse pronounced against them. This curse is plainly confined to the impossibility of establishing themselves as a people, in a country which they can call their own; and from this curse they can never reasonably expect to be exempted, until they have acknowledged Christ to be the Messiah, and have embraced his religion. If the indulgence proposed for them, in this country, could, as I think it will, contribute to that desirable end, I hope that every gentleman will admit this to be a strong argument in favour of the present bill.

"As to our foreign commerce, and the export of our manufactures, the very reasoning that has been employed against the Jews, is, in my opinion, strongly in their favour. It has been said, that by the agency of Jew brokers in foreign countries, they may engross our whole trade, to the exclusion of all other English merchants. If those agents can procure a preference for one merchant over another, they may obtain a similar preference for the manufactures of one country over those of another, and will obtain that preference, for commodities sent from this country by their brethren. And, as we have now foreign competitors, in all kinds of manufacture, our Jew merchants will always be deterred from exacting too high a profit, even supposing that they could engross the exportation of all our manufactures. Hence the true deduction is, that the residence of a great number of Jew merchants would increase our commerce, and the export of our manufactures; and, though I do not admit that their brokers possess the influence in foreign countries, which has been ascribed to them, I think it would be highly to our advantage, that the Jew brokers, in all countries, should be interested in recommending our manufactures. It appears equally indisputable, that this bill, if enacted, will excite such an interest, generally, among those agents.

" But, supposing the residence of Jew merchants to be in no way conducive to the improvement of our foreign trade, it will certainly contribute to increase our domestic consumption, and consequently encourage our home manufactures, and improve our revenue. If, on the passing of this bill, for instance, a Jew, worth £.100,000, should settle with his family, and expend his whole income, £.3,000, annually, in this country, can we suppose that less than £.300 of this yearly expenditure would be laid out on articles of British manufacture? Would not this be an increase of our home manufacture, in nearly the same ratio? Then, admitting that out of every pound sterling, expended by a man in affluence, ten shillings are paid in taxes, would not £.1,500 per annum, be thus added to the gross produce of our public revenue? And if, by this enactment, forty or fifty such opulent Jews should be induced to settle here, with their families, the consequent encouragement of manufactures, and improvement of revenue, is easily to be calculated ; and the advantage is so demonstrable, that I am astonished at the opposition to the bill, offered by gentlemen, who complain of the decay of trade, and the burthen of taxes. I am still more surprised, when I consider the chimerical apprehensions, upon which this opposition is founded. As if the naturalisation of a few Jews would subvert our constitution, destroy our liberties, and extirpate the Christian religion ! I should deeply regret, if any gentleman seriously thought that our religion and constitution rested on so unstable a foundation ; but, as I am convinced that such apprehensions cannot be seriously entertained by any man of sense, and that this bill will certainly be of some advantage, and may prove greatly beneficial, I shall vote for its enactment."

Considering the strong repugnance manifested against the bill, it is remarkable, that, in a very thin House, the question for the second reading was carried by 95 against only 16.

The opponents of so unpopular a measure were, however, far from being

2 κ 2

discouraged ; for they found an increasing support in public opinion. A petition was indeed presented in its favour, by certain merchants and traders of London ; but the attempt injured, instead of promoting the cause ; for, on inquiry, the petitioners were found to be mostly foreigners, or descendants of Jews. A counter-petition was therefore offered from the Corporation of London, seconded by a similar application from the most respectable persons in the commercial interest. Counsel were heard, and witnesses examined, and this scrutiny still farther awakened the attention of the public.

A motion of adjournment having been proposed, lord Egmont seized this opportunity to make a powerful appeal against the bill. He inforced the principal arguments advanced by its adversaries, and placed some of those objections in a new and stronger light. He particularly questioned the commercial advantages anticipated from it, urging that the Jews were neither manufacturers, labourers, nor merchants ; that their wealth was principally derived from usury, brokerage, and commission ; and that their very habits and prejudices unfitted them for assimilating with any Christian people ; that the act was in itself nugatory, as the Jews already enjoyed greater privileges in this country, than in any other part of Christendom, and consequently could want no new inducement to settle in England.

He strongly expatiated on the folly and danger of doing violence to public opinion ; taunted the Whigs with their persecution of Dr. Sacheverell ; declared that this act would be equally fatal to them ; and predicted, with truth, that its advocates and patrons would experience, at the approaching general election, the full force of that national feeling, which they now affected to disregard. " When that day comes," he exclaimed, " I shall not fear to set my foot upon any ground, as a candidate, in opposition to any one man among you, or any new Christian, who has appeared or voted for the bill ; and so, I verily believe, may any other gentleman, who this day, in this House, shall act and vote with me.

" The last argument, which I shall urge against it, is not the least important. This bill frustrates a general naturalisation, which was very daringly attempted, but happily defeated, not more than two years ago. The same spirit now animates those who moved you then, to attempt that hateful scheme. They dare not openly avow their purpose, but artfully employ this expedient to revive it, well knowing with what force, if now successful, they may hereafter expostulate—' What! will you, who have consented to naturalise even the Jews, boggle at allowing the same privilege to foreign

Protestants, professing the Christian religion, like yourselves !'—But the nation will see through this design, and, by some means or other, I am confident, will defeat it now, as they did then.   I conclude my objections, in reference to the Jews, with the common adage, 'there is no rule without exception;' and, if ever an exception existed to a general principle, surely we must object to the naturalisation of a people, the very essence of whose character and religion, consists in their abhorrence of Christianity, and their rancour against the whole Christian race."

The question for adjournment having been negatived by 96 against 55, the bill continued its progress, and finally received the royal assent.*

---

* Journals.—Hansard's Parl. Hist. vol. xiv. p. 1365.—Continuation of Rapin, vol. xxi. p. 462, 465.

CHAPTER XXX.

1753.

Accusation of Jacobitism, preferred by Mr. Fawcett, against the Bishop of Gloucester, and Messrs. Stone and Murray—Promoted by lord Ravensworth—Inquiry into the subject, before the Cabinet Council—Discussion in the House of Peers, on the motion of the duke of Bedford, for a communication of the proceedings—Negatived—Debates on the Marriage Act—Favoured by Mr. Pelham—Strenuously opposed, particularly by Mr. Fox—Misunderstanding between the lord Chancellor and Mr. Fox—Supply—Aversion of the Duke of Cumberland to the Pelhams—Measures of domestic and commercial policy—Amendment of the act relative to the Discovery of the Longitude—Establishment of the British Museum.

IN the midst of the session, considerable embarrassment was occasioned by a transaction, evidently arising from the disputes in the household of the Prince of Wales. It proved, that the obloquy cast on Mr. Stone and Mr. Murray continued unabated; and that the Pelhams had given serious offence to the Whig party, by patronising and supporting those persons, and tolerating for their sake, the continuance of Scott and Cresset, in their important offices. That effect was shewn, by the eager pertinacity with which a trifling and vague conversation was disseminated, and magnified into a public charge, for the purpose of discrediting Mr. Murray, and procuring the dismission of Mr. Stone.

Fawcett, an attorney of Newcastle, and Recorder of that borough, had been in habits of friendly intimacy with the rev. Dr. Johnson, and with Messrs. Stone and Murray, and had often joined their convivial parties. Dining, on the king's birth-day, at the house of the dean of Durham, with lord Ravensworth, and a small company, he inquired who was to be promoted to a prebend of Durham, then vacant; and being informed that it was to be given to Dr. Johnson, who had recently been appointed bishop of Gloucester, he exclaimed, "That man is very lucky; for I remember, some years ago, that he was a Jacobite. I often met him at the house of my cousin, Mr. Vernon, a mercer on Ludgate-hill, a notorious Jacobite, where the Pretender's health was frequently drunk."

No notice was taken of this remark at the time; but some of the guests having imparted it to their correspondents in London, it was rapidly circulated, and became the theme of general conversation. Mr. Pelham was much concerned at the report, as he had concurred with his brother in recommending Dr. Johnson,* for ecclesiastical preferment, and in placing him on the bench of bishops. At his request, therefore, his friend and relative, Mr. Vane, wrote to Fawcett, whom he had usually employed as his attorney at Newcastle, desiring to know whether he had made the imputed remark, on the bishop of Gloucester, and if he had, whether he could vouch for its truth.

Fawcett having returned a prevaricating denial, Mr. Pelham summoned him to town. In the interval, Fawcett held several conversations with lord Ravensworth, and partially retracted his assertion respecting Dr. Johnson; but added, that he had heard Messrs. Stone and Murray drink the Pretender's health at Mr. Vernon's table. On his arrival in town, he was examined by Mr. Pelham, in the presence of Mr. Vane, on the subject of the bishop of Gloucester; when he continued to prevaricate, without making any specific accusation, and without alluding to Messrs. Stone and Murray. Such was the state of this affair, when lord Ravensworth came to London. Though strongly solicited by Fawcett, not to make his disclosures public, lord Ravensworth, in several conversations with many peers, and with some of the ministers, repeated the accusation against Murray and Stone, and declared his opinion, that Stone ought to be dismissed from the office of sub-governor to the Prince of Wales. The affair accordingly took a new turn. On the demand of the bishop of Gloucester, Fawcett expressed a full conviction of his lordship's innocence. In a subsequent interview with the duke of Newcastle and Mr. Pelham, lord Ravensworth also declared, that Fawcett could not substantiate the charge against that prelate: but persisted in asserting that he, Fawcett, had heard Messrs. Stone and Murray drink the health of the Pretender, and that of the earl of

---

* In a letter from Mr. Pelham to Mr. Stone, dated Nov. 8th-19th, 1748, he observes, " I very heartily congratulate you on Dr. Johnson's preferment, and the more so, as my brother tells me, the king was so gracious as to say, he did it the sooner, as it was agreeable to me."

Dunbar, his principal minister. Hence, the conduct of the bishop was no longer included in the inquiry, which was confined to that of the other persons accused.

The charge against Mr. Murray, the Solicitor-general, and the sub-governor, was too serious to be concealed from the king; and, at the request of the ministers, his Majesty referred it to the cabinet council.

Fawcett was consequently summoned, and formally questioned; and, when a letter was shewn to him, which he had written to lord Ravensworth, he betrayed great agitation. Being sworn, he said he could not declare upon oath, that any, or either of the persons whom he had denounced, were present at the meetings, in which the health of the Pretender was drunk; and, though he believed it was so, yet he could not vouch for the truth of the fact. At the same time he was reminded, that he had made such an accusation against Mr. Stone and the Solicitor-general, to lord Ravensworth. This he owned to be true, though he would not confirm it upon oath. Indeed his agitation was so great, that he was unable to return any con-sistent reply to the questions which were put to him; and the council accordingly adjourned.

On his second examination, Fawcett was more calm and composed; but offered no satisfactory apology for his former strange behaviour. He only said, he thought he had heard treasonable healths drunk at Mr. Vernon's, when Messrs. Stone and Murray were present. He thought so still, but could not swear it. Being interrogated, as to the time of the meetings, he could not exactly specify the year; but believed, to the best of his recollec-tion, that they occurred in 1731 or 1732.

After this scrutiny, the Solicitor-general and Mr. Stone were admitted to make their defence; and exculpated themselves from the malicious charges of Fawcett, to the entire satisfaction of the council, who declared, in their report to the king, that the accusation was malicious and scan-dalous. It was, however, distinctly admitted, that Fawcett had told lord Ravensworth all that his lordship had related.*

Mr. Pelham took a warm interest in the inquiry, not only from feelings of duty as a minister, but from attachment to Mr. Stone and Mr. Murray, the former having long enjoyed the confidence of his brother and himself,

---

* The account of this singular transaction is taken principally from Dodington's Diary, from Lord Orford's Posthumous Memoires, and from a MS. letter of Mr. Fox to Sir C. H. Williams, March 16th, 1753, in the Hanbury Papers, MS.

and the latter having been his principal auxiliary in the House of Commons. He doubtless thought, that the decision of the cabinet council, after so minute a scrutiny, would have satisfied the public mind, and extinguished the malicious rumours, to which the charges gave rise. They afforded, however, too plausible a topic to the Opposition, to be passed over in silence ; and the duke of Bedford called the attention of the House of Peers to the transaction.

The formal notice of his motion excited great public interest ; and a numerous and eager audience attended below the bar, on the 22nd of March, when he entered upon the subject, in his usual impetuous and energetic style.

" I am not surprised," he said, " at the multitude I see assembled to hear the discussion, and to obtain some light on an affair, which, though it touches the public so nearly, has been enveloped in such mysterious secrecy ; and concerning which, after so many councils held, on treasonous informa tion, so little is known, either of accusation or process. The effects, indeed, of the acquittal, and the continuation of confidence, are divulged and notorious. My difficulties on this occasion are peculiar ; and, after such repeated obligations, I feel extreme delicacy in mentioning the name of his Majesty : therefore, if I should suggest a doubt, let it be understood as applying to his Majesty's ministers. It is the very spirit of the constitution, that the king can do no wrong ; and this is the language, not only of the law and of parliament, but of my heart. My knowledge of the king's character has taught me this truth ; his Majesty cannot err, but when facts are not fairly stated to him. Those who state them unfairly, may also misrepresent me.

" The notorious fact, that an inquest of treason had been in agitation, led me to conclude, that it must and would be brought hither, for our advice. Could I doubt that it would ? What other judicature is there for crimes and criminals of this high nature ? The incompetence of the Lords, who have been assembled for this trial, is evident. Can the cabinet council condemn ? Can they acquit ? If they cannot condemn or acquit, can they try ? Who, that is accused, is innocent, until he has had a more solemn purgation, than their report can give him ? But if no character can be purified by their verdict, what becomes of their own ? My lords, what a solemn trust is reposed in the cabinet council ! Can they be at peace, until their opinions are sanctioned by our sentence ? But why do I talk of their satisfaction? The nation has a right to be satisfied. Here is an accusation of treason brought against men, in such high and especial trust, in whom the counsels of his present Majesty, and the hopes of the nation in the successor, are reposed. This charge, (appealing impressively to lord Ravensworth,) is brought by a lord of parliament, now present, from whom I have received a communication; and I call on his lordship to give the necessary information to the House."

Lord Ravensworth, with evident embarrassment, strove to obviate any surmise, that he had instigated the duke of Bedford to make his motion; professed his unwillingness to prosecute the affair; and apologised for having named the bishop of Gloucester, whose character, though he had been fully acquitted, was implicated in the charge. After succinctly detailing the conversation with Fawcett, and the different proceedings to which it had led, he particularly adverted to his own interview with Mr. Pelham; and, rather in tone than in words, expressed his dissatisfaction, at not having been apprised of the letter written by Mr. Vane to Fawcett. He adverted to the known Jacobitism of Vernon; instanced the bequest of his property to Mr. Murray, a person not related to him, as giving colour to the accusation; and hinted, that Fawcett had been induced to prevaricate, by the suggestions of Mr. Murray, and of the bishop of Gloucester. He did not fail to remark, that the letter of exculpation, which Fawcett delivered to the bishop, was written at his lordship's request, and in his presence; and that Fawcett refused to add the concluding expression, dictated to him, " this is all I can say, consistently with truth." Lastly, lord Ravensworth, after complaining of the unjust accusations raised against himself, solemnly declared, that he had interfered from duty and zeal, and not from motives of friendship to the late governor.

Some remarks being made by the duke of Bedford, on the particulars of the communication between Fawcett and lord Ravensworth, and on Fawcett's account of the proceedings in council, the lord Chancellor interposed, by declaring that it was unparliamentary and informal, to repeat a hearsay account of what had passed elsewhere.

The duke seized this opportunity to renew his attack on those lords, by whom the inquiry had been conducted. Protesting against the supposition, that it had been brought before the council, he exclaimed, " I deny that it was the council; it was only a private meeting of certain lords. Were they a committee of council? Was it in that capacity that they arrogated the power of tendering oaths, and listening to voluntary evidence? If they were a committee, the lord President of the Council should have presided. But here were no forms, no essence, no authority of council. Indeed, a cabinet council is not recognized in our constitution; it is a state-expedient borrowed from France. In their own persons only, these lords are respectable. The Secretary of State cannot even act as a justice of peace. An attempt is made to erect a jurisdiction, unknown to this country, and derogatory to the authority of this House. Before this revived Star-chamber, this Inquisition, different indeed from the "Holy" Inquisition, in one point, for the heretics of this court are its favourites; before this court, I say, the accused are admitted to purge themselves on oath, and thus a leading step is taken to the introduction of perjury. What is the whole style of their proceedings? Mysterious, secret, arbitrary, cruel! The minutes were secreted; the witnesses held in durance! Lord Ravensworth was required to deliver up letters; orders were given for filing informations against Fawcett; or said to be given, for I doubt the intention of carrying them into execution; though, if they be pursued, the hardship on Fawcett will be the greater, as he is already prejudged.

"The report, concise as it appears, is three-fold: it pronounces Fawcett's accusation to be false and malicious; it declares the accused innocent; it justifies lord Ravensworth, the accuser! How many powers are thus assumed! Fawcett, though a lawyer, was terrified at such a court. Their proceedings I blame. I have a great regard for the majority of the lords concerned; yet I must say, they have erred greatly, if their proceedings were any thing more than preparatory. To me, however, these transactions are not more striking, than the high rank of the accused. Mr. Stone stands in as public a light as any man in Britain. There are other points, on which the nation should be satisfied. For my part, I have never conferred with the right reverend and noble lords, who have lately retired from that important, turbulent scene; yet I own that their resignations have filled me with suspicions. They have been dismissed for no misbehaviour. I hope they will vouchsafe to lay their motives before the House, and that in this *acquitting* age, they also may be exculpated. Nay, the council too should be exculpated: it should be manifest that they were not biassed, and that their report is fit to see the light. Seen to be sure it will be; it cannot be meant to be secreted. Till it is produced, the public will be perplexed with conjecture. In this state of suspense, the mind will be apt to advert to the uniformity of Fawcett's behaviour, on four different occasions. No deviation, no inconsistency, appears in his narrative, until after his interviews with the bishop of Gloucester and Mr. Murray. Then it grew retrograde : then he faltered in his evidence. This change excites suspicion ; it provokes a revision of the whole proceedings. How to institute that properly, I do not know. You all wish that the accused may be cleared : assist me, my lords, in dragging into light every testimonial of their innocence. It is a business that naturally devolves on us ; nor could any have occurred more arduous, on which to give the king advice. Here his Majesty may want it : sinister counsel may have rendered the offer of our honest unbiassed opinions the more welcome.

" The noble lord, who lately superintended the education of the prince, has been as well replaced as possible. The choice was the more acceptable, as it was his Majesty's own choice. He can do no wrong ; he always acts rightly, when he acts for himself. The present is the proper season for such an inquiry ; the affair is no longer under examination, nor can I now be told, as I often have been told, ' we have a clue ; do not stop us ; these are the king's secrets.' No inconvenience can now result from the investigation ; and it may be productive of good. The king desires to have the accused persons cleared. As to the papers that are withheld, they must be produced in Westminster Hall, if Fawcett be prosecuted. There the king's secrets must come out. This, therefore, is the only proper time, for inquiring into the character of the person, intrusted with the education of the prince. Should a minority ensue, and sorry I am that I was not present, to oppose so pernicious a precedent as the Regency-bill, might not they, who are possessed of the person and authority of the king, shelter themselves, however suspected or accused, under the clause of *præmunire*, a clause calculated for protecting from danger, not the person of the prince, but the persons of his governors ? "

The duke of Bedford then moved an humble address, requesting his Majesty to give orders, that there should be laid before the House, the several examinations of lord Ravensworth, the dean of Durham, and Mr. Fawcett, with such other examinations, on oath, as had been taken before the lords appointed by his Majesty, to inquire into informations of a very material nature, relating to a person in the service of the prince of Wales.

and of prince Edward, and to the other persons mentioned in the examinations; likewise all letters and papers relating to the affair, including the report made to his Majesty.

This captious speech abounded in assertions and inferences, which were certainly questionable, but which could not be contradicted without a disclosure of the proceedings of the cabinet council. The king, therefore, dispensed with the oath of the lords of the council; and permitted the lord Chancellor and the duke of Newcastle to acquaint the House with the whole proceeding, which they did, in the most satisfactory manner.

The lord Chancellor answered the vehement appeal of the duke of Bedford, with great calmness and moderation. After adverting to the solemn avowal, which Mr. Stone had offered of his innocence, by oath, he justified the legality of the cabinet council, and vindicated its proceedings. He affirmed that, instead of being borrowed from the institutions of France, the cabinet council was a body, whose existence was on record in the Journals of Parliament. He then declared that the oaths had not been imposed by authority, but administered, at the desire of the accused themselves, as a matter of grace; and that the inquiry had been instituted for satisfaction, not for prosecution. He exposed the inconsistencies and contradictions of Fawcett; applauded the zeal and good conduct of Mr. Stone, during the rebellion; and spoke in warm terms, of the meritorious and irreproachable behaviour of Mr. Murray, since his first appearance in the court of Chancery, in 1742.

He urged the king's undeniable right to govern his own family; and emphatically asked, "Will you wantonly invade this prerogative? Have you any distrust of the lords, who have sifted the matter? And to what good purpose will farther inquiry tend, without condescending to scrutinize the truth or falsehood of charges so vague and obsolete?" He concluded with a moving appeal to the judgment of the House. "I reflect with pleasure, on the many converts that have been made from Jacobitism; and hope that you will not, by inquiry into old stories, prevent and discourage a change of principle. Do not deter, by the alarm of parliamentary inquiry, those who are willing to re-enter the pale of loyalty. They would never deem themselves safe; and it would be ungenerous and cruel, to exclude men of any principles, from enjoying the sunshine and blessings of such a reign and government. For myself, I hate party names and distinctions;

and, for the purpose of stifling any attempt to revive them, will give my entire negative to the motion."

Lord Harcourt then made a brief address to the House, in which he cautiously declined to divulge the motives of his resignation, which he said he had confided solely to the king.

The bishop of Norwich, while he professed his unwillingness to appeal from the king, declared that he had been cruelly obstructed in the performance of his duty, and avowed his readiness to state the reasons of his conduct. By oversight or design, the duke of Bedford did not avail himself of an offer, so favourable to his purpose; and the debate proceeded.

The bishop of Gloucester next explained the particulars of his interview with Fawcett, and entered into some justification of the letter, written by Fawcett, in his presence, to free himself from the imputation of tampering with his accuser.

The duke of Newcastle earnestly vindicated Mr. Stone, commended his loyalty and fidelity, spoke with warmth on his anxiety to have the accusation scrutinized, and applauded his spirit, in requesting to be suspended from his official duties, until he should be fully acquitted. He treated the charges as originating in cabal and intrigue, and as founded on the anonymous Memorial,* which had been so industriously and insidiously circulated.

The principal peers, who had assisted at the council, severally expressed their concurrence in the report. Lord Waldegrave handsomely commended the principles and conduct of Mr. Stone; and declared, that he would act as governor, no longer than while he should find that person to be a man of honour and integrity. He was followed by the bishop of St. Asaph,† who made an eloquent appeal in behalf of the accused. Lord Granville reprobated a prosecution of the inquiry, as inquisitorial, and applauded the reserve with which lord Harcourt had acted.

Lord Bath objected to the farther examination of Fawcett, who had so shamefully prevaricated before the cabinet council. He maintained that the council itself was perfectly constitutional, and that its proceedings were not unprecedented. To prove this assertion, he mentioned, that he himself, in conjunction with Sir Paul Methuen, and Mr. Cholmondeley, had been

---

Alluding to the " Memorial of several Noblemen, &c." see chap. xxix. p. 239.

† Dr. Drummond, afterwards translated to Salisbury, and to York.

examined before a similar council, in the reign of queen Anne, relative to a charge made against Mr. Lewis, secretary to lord Oxford, who, being mistaken for one Levi, a Jew, had been suspected of carrying on a correspondence with the court of St. Germain's. He added, that they had all three undergone a separate examination; and, after some farther remarks, concluded by opposing the motion.

The ill-judged accusation, aimed by the duke of Bedford against the cabinet council, produced a manifest injury to his cause, and probably deterred many Whigs, whose zeal might have prompted them to favour the inquiry, from sanctioning a motion, which bore so strongly the character of a personal attack. Towards the close of the debate, the bishop of Worcester* endeavoured to recall the attention of the House to the primary object, by an indiscreet philippic against Mr. Stone, whose appointment, he contended, had been obnoxious to men of the best intentions, and whose dismissal was necessary, to satisfy the public mind. This attempt, however, made little impression; and lord Ravensworth himself closed the discussion, by declaring that, as his own honour was vindicated, he had no wish to prosecute the investigation, or to see it prosecuted by others. He then abruptly quitted the House; and, after a few minutes' pause, the duke of Bedford went below the bar for a division; but, finding himself followed only by lord Townshend, lord Harcourt, and the bishop of Worcester, he relinquished his purpose, and the question was negatived.†

Thus ended a transaction, which excited much temporary interest, and from which a different result was probably anticipated. It was justly ridiculed by the wits of the day, as a counterpart to the Mountain in Labour; and the Pelhams had the satisfaction of seeing it terminate in the full exculpation of their friends, the Solicitor-general and Mr. Stone.

During this session of parliament, a sensation, scarcely less memorable than that which attended the bill for naturalising the Jews, was produced by the act for preventing clandestine marriages, an act which lord Orford, in the violent spirit of its opponents, has termed "the bane of society, and the golden grate, separating patricians from plebeians."‡

* Dr. Maddox.

† The account of this debate is principally taken from lord Orford's Memoires, vol. i. p. 269–271, with some additional circumstances, from Mr. Etough's manuscript narrative, and lord Melcombe's Diary. For the dates and terms of the motion, we have consulted the Journals of the Lords.

‡ Lord Orford's Memoires, vol. i. p. 311.

The neglect and abuse of the laws relating to marriage, had given rise to the greatest licentiousness, and the most alarming mischiefs; and had tended, both to render the succession to property insecure, and to relax or dissolve the most sacred bond of society.

Numerous appeals were continually made to the court of Chancery, and often from thence to the House of Peers, to establish or annul the validity of clandestine marriages; and it frequently happened, that the offspring of such connections was declared illegitimate, after a long cohabitation, consequent on a *bonâ fide*, but informal marriage of the parents. Although either the proclamation of banns on three successive Sundays, or intervening holidays, or a licence from the archbishop or diocesan, was required by the existing laws, as indispensable to matrimony; yet these formalities were evaded, especially in the metropolis, and marriages were solemnized in the Fleet, in May Fair, and in other unlicensed places, by unprincipled clergymen, who derived a scandalous revenue from the abuse of the privilege attached to their holy orders. Hence men and women of infamous characters, had opportunities of seducing the sons and daughters of great and respectable families; and of ensnaring minors, intitled to property, into indissoluble connections, to the ruin of their interests, and the destruction of their happiness.

A remedy for such deplorable evils had long been deemed necessary; and, accordingly, the House of Peers, at the suggestion of lord Bath, commissioned the judges, on the 31st of January, to frame a new act for that salutary purpose. A draught was prepared by them, and laid before the lord Chancellor, who disapproving its provisions, framed another himself, which was presented, by the Lord Chief Justice, to the House of Lords, on the 19th March, and was warmly approved by a considerable majority. But, in consequence of the opposition it encountered, from the duke of Bedford, and a few other peers, and the numerous amendments introduced, the third reading did not take place until the fourth of May.*

The bill was brought down to the Commons, on the 7th of May, and was warmly attacked in its progress, particularly by Mr. Nugent, and Mr. Charles Townshend, the latter of whom did not spare the lord Chancellor, as the framer of the bill. But its most vehement opponent was Mr. Fox, who not only assailed the provisions of the act itself, but exceeded Mr.

* Journals of the Lords.—Lord Orford's Memoires, vol. i. p. 293-307.

Townshend, in severe and personal reflections on the lord Chancellor. Mr. Pelham warmly promoted the bill, and was supported by the Attorney and Solicitor General, as well as by lord Hillsborough, Mr. Hampden, and even by lord Egmont.

In the committee, the discussion was renewed with increased acrimony; and much warm language passed between Mr. Pelham and Mr. Fox.* The latter reprobated the chicanery and jargon of the lawyers; censured the pride of him whom he termed their Mufti; and complained of the arbitrary manner in which so obnoxious and cruel a regulation was enforced. Every clause furnished new topics for argument or sarcasm; and that for empowering the lord Chancellor to consent to the marriage of minors, in the second resort, presented a pretext for cavils, too favourable to be neglected. Mr. Fox drew a severe character of that great lawyer; and, in allusion to his pertinacious support of the bill, coarsely compared him to an unskilful surgeon, who, rather than retract an opinion once pronounced, chose to sacrifice the limb of a patient, which a more skilful operator might have saved.

Mr. Charles Yorke vindicated the character of his father with equal spirit and ability; and concluded by a threat, which Mr. Fox repelled with aggravated sarcasm and indignation. Notwithstanding the interference of Mr. Pelham, Mr. Fox did not desist from his invectives. He declared, that the whole proceeding was cruel and absurd; that if he could be but partially heard within the House, he would speak so loud as to be heard without doors; and that, from the beginning to the end of the act, no principle predominated but pride and aristocracy.

During these acrimonious debates, every successive clause underwent some alteration. Several judicious amendments were added, particularly one to exonerate clergymen from ecclesiastical censure, for solemnizing a marriage without consent of guardians, when both or either of the parties were under age, provided the banns had been regularly published, or licence obtained for the purpose, and provided also that the clergyman was ignorant of such want of consent. Another amendment of equal importance, said to have been introduced by Mr. Fox, declared that a proof of the previous residence, required by the act, should not be necessary to establish the validity of a marriage once solemnized. Other provisions specified the forms of the

* See Horace Walpole's letter to Mr. Conway, dated May 29th, 1753, in lord Orford's Works, vol. i.

registers to be kept, and declared the forgery of registers or licences, and the destruction of registers, to be capital offences.* But these improvements did not mitigate the acrimony with which the bill was opposed ; and, on the third reading, the discussion was resumed with unabated violence.

Mr. Fox now took the lead, and, in an animated speech, again scrutinized every principle of the proposed law. He complained that, by the abrogation of precontracts, it exposed young women to all the arts of seduction; that it tended to throw all the property of the kingdom into the hands of a certain number of opulent or noble families, who would never intermarry out of their own pale ; and that it facilitated the sacrifice of minors to the interested views of unfeeling parents, or avaricious guardians. In another view, he denounced it as an obstruction to the happiness of the lower ranks, and a preventive to the increase of the best and most useful part of the population; adding, that the restraints thus imposed on the poor, would lead to the extension of licentiousness, debauchery, and crime. Lastly, he solemnly denied the right of any human assembly, to annul by its provisions, that contract which every human being was free to form, by the laws of God and nature. In the course of his harangue, he held up a copy of the bill, in which he had marked the alterations with red ink. On the observation of the Attorney-general, " how bloody it looks !" he retorted, in the language of Macbeth to the ghost of Banquo,

> " Thou cans't not say *I* did it."

He then parodied, very aptly, the lamentation of Mark Antony, over the mangled robe of Cæsar. Pointing to the Attorney-general, he exclaimed,

> " Look what a rent the *learned* Casca made ;"

and then, alluding to Mr. Pelham, added,

> " Through this, the well-beloved Brutus stabbed."

After making a tardy apology for his vehement attacks on the Chancellor, he concluded with a merely ceremonious disavowal of any personal feeling, in his reflections on that noble lord.

During this debate the Solicitor-general, in particular, defended the bill, on the ground of its necessity. He pathetically appealed to the feelings of

---

* Journals of the Commons, June 6th, 1753.

parents, who, amidst their laudable anxiety for the happiness of their children, were too often overwhelmed with the afflicting intelligence, that they had been inveigled into clandestine marriages, the sons united with prostitutes, and the daughters with sharpers, thieves, and felons. He contended, that the female sex were secured, instead of being exposed, by the provisions of the bill, which superseded all the ambiguities of former acts, by the substi. tution of one plain and certain rule. He denied the inference, that it would lead to the accumulation of property in a few hands, even if the richest heiresses were married only into opulent families ; and argued, that an ample opening was still left for matches of affection, by fixing the age of majority at twenty-one. He also maintained, that this law would not prevent marriages among the poor, alleging that the actual proclamation of banns, which was customary in the country, had not produced that effect ; and, on the other hand, he declared that the short delay, now interposed, would prevent many unfortunate and precipitate connections, even in that humble class of society.

Although it appears, from the hints given by lord Orford, in his Memoires, that Mr. Pelham frequently spoke during the progress of the bill, yet we do not find any account of his speeches, in the narrative of the debates, published in the periodical journals. But we learn from a contemporary historian,* worthy of credit, that it was at length regarded as a personal object of the minister, and was carried principally through his influence ; and that many of his friends, who were unwilling to concur in its enact- ment, abstained from voting against it, from delicacy towards him. The third reading was at last decided by 125 against 56.†

The bill was not returned to the Peers, before the 6th of June, the day preceding that fixed for the prorogation. It was again attacked by the duke of Bedford, who renewed his objections, and expatiated on its deficiencies, even in its amended state. He bitterly regretted, that a law so faulty and obnoxious, should have been forced through parliament. His arguments were combated by lord Sandys, and also by lord Bath, who, in

---

* The reverend Dr. Birch, who wrote the Reign of George the Second, which is published, as a Continuation of Rapin by Tindal. He was a particular friend of lord Chancellor Hard- wicke, of his son Mr. Yorke, and of Mr. Horace Walpole, senior, from whom he received much historical information.

† The account of this debate is principally taken from Lord Orford's Memoires, vol. i. p. 293-307.—Hansard's Parl. Hist. vol. xv. p. 1-84.—Debrett's Debates.

defending the principle of the bill, declared that a similar law had pro. duced no ill effect in Ireland ; and that the opposition which had been manifested, proceeded solely from factious motives.

The lord Chancellor then rose, and expressed his concurrence in the amendments, though several appeared to him of a tendency to weaken the bill. He observed, that a regulation of such moment ought not to be abandoned, on account of these objections, particularly as its defects might be subsequently remedied. This had been the case with the Act of Succession itself, which, though purposely clogged with amendments by the Commons, to prevent its enactment, had been adopted by the Lords, who reserved for some future period, their intention to retrench the objectionable passages. He denied that the bill had been forced through parliament; and expressed his surprise, that a regulation so necessary, so long called for, so maturely deliberated, a regulation prepared by the judges, improved by the concurrent efforts of the whole House, and sanctioned by the right reverend bench, should be so wantonly stigmatized as absurd, cruel, scandalous, and wicked.

Yielding, then, to the impulse of wounded feelings, he repelled the attacks which had been levelled against him in the House of Commons. The conduct of Mr. Charles Townshend he ascribed to youth and inexperience, and directed the whole force of his invective against Mr. Fox.

" It is not indeed surprising," he said, " that young men, in the warmth of their constitution, should be averse to regulations, which seem to interfere with their impassioned and sanguine pursuits ; but it is extraordinary, to see grave and solemn persons convert a law, so essential to the public good, into an engine of dark intrigue and faction, and into a pretext for forming a party, and trying its strength. Their opposition, however, has produced a result, which they little expected ; for it has raised a zeal in favour of the bill, which has ensured its success."

He then indignantly animadverted upon the profligacy of the principles avowed by the enemies of the measure, and on the unbounded contempt and reproach cast on the whole system of law, and on its professors, as well as on the administration of justice: Alluding to the apology of Mr. Fox, he said, " With regard to my own share in this torrent of abuse, as I am obliged to those who have so honourably defended me, so I despise the invective, and I despise the recantation. I despise the scurrility, for scurrility I must call it, and I reject the adulation. These candidates for power give a sufficient warning to the public, of what may be expected from them; for, as there are but two schemes of government, that of law, and that of force, and as they have declared their contempt of law, they leave their preference of the contrary principle to be inferred. Indeed this open contempt of the law is but one step short of a design to overthrow our constitution, by abolishing the law, which would, in fact, deserve to be abolished, if it were, as they have described it, a heap of inconsistency, confusion, perplexity, and absurdity."*

For the reasons urged in this able vindication, the Peers gave their hasty assent to the bill, which, on the following day, received the royal sanction. It is, however, remarkable that, notwithstanding the eminent and learned judge, by whom it was principally framed, admitted its deficiencies, it has since undergone no change;† and a candid consideration of its provisions must also warrant the admission, that although liable to some objections, it has falsified the predictions of its opponents; for the evils, of which it was represented as a fruitful source, have proved mostly imaginary.

The animosities excited by these discussions, did not readily subside; and between the lord Chancellor and Mr. Fox, the war of words might have been long and actively waged, had it not been abruptly terminated by the close of the Session. Mr. Pelham, who dreaded a new feud in the ministry, earnestly interposed, and laboured to reconcile two colleagues, whose talents and services he highly appreciated. He not only defended the Chancellor in public, but expostulated with Mr. Fox in private, and probably extorted from him the tardy apology which he had made in the House of Commons. The minister subsequently continued his mediation; and, though neither appeared disposed to bend, he at length succeeded in suspending the progress of their quarrel.

It cannot be denied, that conviction, or personal feeling, may have prompted Mr. Fox to oppose the bill, as his own marriage with lady Georgiana Caroline Lenox, eldest daughter of the duke of Richmond, was clandestine. But we can assign no motive for his personal invectives

---

* The abstract of this speech is principally taken from a letter of Dr. Birch, who was present on the occasion, to the Hon. Philip Yorke, dated June 9th, 1753, (printed in Hansard's Parl. Hist. vol. xv. p. 84.) compared with Lord Orford's Memoires.

† It is true, an attempt was made to remedy the supposed deficiencies, in the year 1822; but the bill passed by parliament, for that purpose, contained such vexatious and absurd enactments, that it was repealed in the following year; and the original act, without any amendment, is still in force.

against the lord Chancellor, unless it be sympathy with the feelings of his patron, the Duke of Cumberland, who could not forget that the Chancellor was principally concerned in framing the Regency-bill, and was pleased with the hope of directing against him the tide of popular resentment.

The conduct of Mr. Fox towards the Chancellor, did not escape notice in the closet. The king gently expressed some dissatisfaction to him on the subject, and received from him a solemn disavowal of any factious or improper motive. This excuse, aided by the influence of the Duke of Cumberland, and the favourable representations of Mr. Pelham, soon pacified his Majesty.

Before we close the account of the proceedings relative to the Marriage Act, we deem it necessary to observe, that the Peers were inclined to extend its operation to Scotland, in consideration of the facility, which the laws of that kingdom afforded, to clandestine marriages. An order* was accordingly passed, for the Lords of Session to frame a similar bill, for that part of the United Kingdom. But, in consequence, either of the opposition, which the measure subsequently encountered, or of the reluctance of the lords of the Court of Session, and of the Scottish peers in parliament, to introduce a change so contrary to the usages, as well as to the religious principles of their country, this purpose was silently abandoned.

In preparing the supplies for the year, Mr. Pelham was very desirous of continuing the land-tax at 3s. in the pound, in order to prevent the farther imposition of any permanent tax. But, as he was apprehensive that it would be opposed by the landed gentlemen, whose influence predominated in the House, he thought proper to submit his proposition to the consideration of the members, without presuming to dictate his opinion, In a calm and conciliatory speech, he observed, that if the land-tax should be continued at 3s. in the pound, there would be no occasion for any farther impost; while, if reduced to 2s. it would be necessary to make up the deficiency, not only by applying the unappropriated money in the Exchequer, amounting to £.230,000, and an additional sum to be drawn from the Sinking-fund,† but also to render permanent the salt duty, which had hitherto been only temporary. Finding, however, that the sense of the House was for the reduction to 2s. in the pound, he relinquished his pur-

---

* Journals of the Lords, April 17th, 1753.

† The two sums taken from the Exchequer and the Sinking-fund, amounted together to £.420,000.—See the parliamentary grants, in the Gent. Mag. for 1753, p. 259.

pose; and accordingly the deficiency was supplied from the Exchequer and the Sinking-fund; and, to his great concern, the duties on salt were rendered perpetual.* The other supplies were voted without difficulty, and are exhibited in the following table.†

SUPPLY.

NAVY.—Charge of 10,000 seamen; Ordinary, &c. ....£. 810,206		
		....£. 946,133
ARMY.—Charge of 18,857 men; extraordinary expenses; half pay, guards, and garrisons, &c. 1,131,314		 579,374
Subsidy to the Elector of Bavaria.. 20,000		 100,489
————————— Elector of Saxony.. 32,000		
For the Forts and Settlements on the Coast of Africa.....		 79,812
		54,580
For the colony of Nova Scotia ..		 420,000
For the colony of Georgia		
For Westminster Bridge		
For loss of horned cattle ...		
Extraordinary expenses of the Mint		
Road from Newcastle to Carlisle		
For making good deficiencies, and payment of Interest 71,012		£.2,180,381
	Balance.........	10,098
£.2,190,479		£.2,190,479

Among the proceedings of this session, we cannot omit to mention the introduction of a bill, for registering the numbers of the people, which was proposed by Mr. Potter, son of the late archbishop of Canterbury. But, although such a census was calculated to furnish most important data in political economy, the public mind was not sufficiently enlightened to appreciate its advantages. Mr. Pelham supported it with his usual liberality of sentiment; but, after struggling through the House of Commons, it was thrown out by the Lords.

The attention of parliament was also directed to the high price of sugar, imported from Jamaica, which was attributed to the neglect or avarice of the planters, in suffering so large a portion of their land to remain uncultivated. A laborious inquiry took place, and the House of Commons passed

* Continuation of Rapin, vol. xxi. p. 460.
† Taken from Postlethwayte's History of the Public Revenue.

a resolution, declaratory of the advantages which would result from peopling the island with white inhabitants.

A bill founded on this principle was introduced, which, from a deficiency of information, was not enacted ; but the inquiry led to many essential ameliorations in the sugar colonies.

Among the regulations for improving the police, may be noticed, a bill for reforming public houses, by restricting the magistrates in the issue of licences, and subjecting the keepers of such houses to severer regulations. A bill was also passed, for preventing the depredations committed on wrecks, and the cruelties inflicted on shipwrecked persons, which, to the disgrace of the nation and of humanity, had increased to an enormous degree, on various parts of the British coast.   Another regulation of importance to the public health, was the law for the more effectual enforcement of quarantine.

Nor will it be deemed trifling to advert to a measure of substantial utility in an agricultural and commercial country.   This was the act, called the Broad-wheel-waggon Act, which required a width of nine inches on the fellies of wheels, belonging to carriages conveying a certain weight, and thus tended to augment the durability of the public roads.

As the French had gained considerable advantages over the British, in the trade to the Levant, Mr. Pelham endeavoured to restore that branch of commerce, by extending the privileges of the Turkey Company to all British subjects, on payment of the small sum of twenty pounds, for the use of the said Company.*

The act passed in the former session, for permitting the importation of Irish wool to the ports of Lancaster and Great Yarmouth, was now extended to the whole kingdom, to the mutual advantage of the Irish grower, and the English manufacturer.   Another expedient for the encouragement of national industry, was an act for allowing bounties on the manufacture of Scotch linens.   Of a similar character were the acts for the farther encouragement of the White Herring fishery ; for preventing evasions of duties on tobacco, to the detriment of the fair trader ; for encouraging the silk manufactures of the country ; and for allowing interest on the debentures, issued for bounties, on the importation of corn.

Two other measures deserve particular notice, from their connection with

* Anderson on Commerce, vol. iii. p. 291.

science and literature. The first was a bill for enlarging the powers vested in the commissioners of longitude, by the act of the 12th of queen Anne, in order to enable them to pay the sum of £.20,000 to the celebrated Harrison, who had recently so much improved his chronometers, as to become intitled to the reward originally offered. The commissioners were at the same time empowered to hold forth farther encouragement for improvements so beneficial to navigation.

The other act was of the highest importance, in a literary view. Its object was to unite in one repository, the Royal and Cottonian Libraries, the Library and Museum of Sir Hans Sloane, and the Harleian Manuscripts. In the Royal Library were preserved many books and documents of our princes, from the time of Henry the Seventh, to that of Charles the Second. The Cottonian Library contained the curious manuscripts, records, and tracts, on the British constitution and History,* which were collected by the celebrated antiquary, Sir Robert Cotton, who died in 1631, and were presented to the Crown, for the use of the public, by his grandson, Sir John Cotton, under an act of the 12th and 13th of king William the Third. The Sloane Library and Museum consisted of the books, manuscripts, and curiosities, both natural and artificial, which had belonged to Sir Hans Sloane,† and which he bequeathed to the nation, on the condition that the parliament should consent to the payment of £.20,000 for the use of his family. The Harleian Collection comprised the interesting series of historical manuscripts, formed

---

* This valuable collection, called, from the name of its founder, the Cottonian Library, was vested by Sir John Cotton, in trustees, consisting of the Lord Chancellor, the Lord Chief Justice, the Speaker of the House of Commons, and four other persons, to be nominated by his family. It was placed under the care of the king's librarian; and remained, together with the Royal Library, in Cotton House, Westminster, where the family resided, until 1706, at which period it was purchased by the Crown. In 1712, the collection was removed to Essex House, in the Strand, and in 1730 was transferred to a mansion in Little Dean's Yard, Westminster, which was purchased from lord Ashburnham. In 1731, a fire broke out in the house, which destroyed many of the manuscripts, and damaged others. For its better preservation, the remainder of this valuable collection was then placed in a building, designed for a dormitory of Westminster school, where it remained until it was removed to Montagu House. This account of the donation of the Cotton Library is derived from the communication of Mrs. Harriet Bowdler, a lineal descendant from Sir John Cotton, the last baronet.

† An enumeration of the principal articles in this valuable collection, which contained no less than 50,000 volumes, including 3,516 volumes of manuscripts, and 347 of drawings, together with a vast number of natural and artificial curiosities, estimated at no less a sum than £.50,000, may be found in the Continuation of Rapin, vol. xxi. p. 471, and in the Gent. Mag. for 1753. p. 52.

by Robert Harley, earl of Oxford and Mortimer. It was offered to the public, by his grand-daughter, the duchess of Portland, for £.10,000, a sum considerably below its intrinsic worth.

Fortunately, a suitable receptacle for these accumulated treasures, was found in Montagu House, which, on the death of the duke of Montagu, in 1749, without male issue, was offered for sale. Mr. Pelham zealously concurred in the necessary arrangements, and promoted the passing of an act, empowering the Crown to raise a sufficient sum, by lottery, to purchase the Sloane Collection, and Harleian Manuscripts, together with Montagu House. The value and importance of the British Museum, by which title the establishment was distinguished, sufficiently attest the public spirit which actuated the projectors and patrons of so grand and patriotic an undertaking.

On the 7th of June,* the king prorogued the parliament. After thanking both Houses for the zeal which they had manifested towards his person and government, and for their assiduity in advancing the commerce and manufactures of the kingdom, his Majesty continued, "The state of foreign affairs has received no material alteration since your meeting. You may depend on my steadily pursuing the same principles and ends, which I then declared unto you. To preserve the peace, to consult the real prosperity of my people, and, at the same time, to assert and maintain the honour and just rights of my Crown and kingdoms, are the fixed objects of all my measures."

Having testified his acknowledgments to the Commons, for granting the necessary supplies, and for adopting efficient arrangements to augment the Sinking-fund, his Majesty concluded with this address to both Houses: "My lords and gentlemen, I have nothing to desire of you, but what I am persuaded you wish for yourselves. Do your utmost endeavours, in your several counties, to promote the true interest and happiness of my people, to propagate industry, and to preserve good order and regularity amongst them: make them sensible of the blessings they enjoy; and, by these means, the quiet and security of my government will be best established."

Journals of the Commons, June 7th, 1753.

CHAPTER XXXI.

1753—4.

Indisposition of Mr. Pelham—His visit to Scarborough—Discussions with France, relative to Dunkirk, the limits of Nova Scotia, and the West India Islands—Contests in the East Indies—Firmness and pacific views of Mr. Pelham—Hostile conduct of the king of Prussia—Ineffectual negotiation with Austria, relative to the Barrier Treaty, and the tenure of the Netherlands—Prosecution of the attempts to procure the election of a king of the Romans—Obstructed by the Court of Vienna—Abandonment of the design—Scheme of the duke of Newcastle, for a subsidiary treaty with Russia—Sentiments of Mr. Pelham on the subject—Party feuds in Ireland— Attacks on the Royal prerogative, in the Irish House of Commons.

THE health of Mr. Pelham, at this period, was in such a precarious state, that he found it necessary to visit Scarborough, for the benefit of the waters. During his stay at that place, in the month of July, we find in the family papers, a correspondence between him and his brother, on different topics, foreign and domestic; and, in particular, we trace great anxiety on the part of both, relative to the pending discussions with France.*

The aspect of foreign affairs was unfortunately of such a character, as to threaten a renewal of those hostilities, which had been suspended by the treaty of Aix-la-Chapelle; and, indeed, the tenour of its stipulations could scarcely fail of proving a fertile source of new contentions. Some indirect attempts to renew the fortifications in the harbour of Dunkirk, excited the alarm of the British cabinet, and produced earnest representations to the court of Versailles. The lively interest which Mr. Pelham took in this question, is shewn in the correspondence between the two brothers; and, however

---

* See these letters in the Illustrative Correspondence.

2 N 2

desirous not to rouse the jealousy or resentment of the French court, yet he was by no means disposed to submit to any serious incroachment. In one of his letters, he observes, " England must speak strongly and act firmly ; and nothing can be allowed, which in any degree tends to the restoration of the port and harbour of Dunkirk." He therefore approved the forcible remonstrances employed by his brother, in the hope, that the wish of the pacific part of the French ministry, to preserve tranquillity, would lead them to thwart the machinations of those, who were desirous of provoking a rupture.* This hope was realised ; for the court of Versailles, in reply to the remonstrances of the British cabinet, declared, " that no repairs of the fortifications were intended, and that in giving orders to dig a canal, behind the barracks, their sole object was to carry off the filth of the streets, which infected the air, and injured the health of the inhabitants ; adding, that they never imagined this innocent precaution could give any cause for the smallest complaint.   Nevertheless, to afford the Maritime Powers a manifest proof of his Most Christian Majesty's religious regard for treaties, and to remove every ground of uneasiness, the king of France not only had ordered the said works to be stopped, but had given directions for laying before their High Mightinesses a plan of Dunkirk, that they might themselves judge of the true state of its fortifications."

In the East Indies the contending interests of the French and English commercial companies, and their interference in the quarrels of the native princes, involved them in a bloody struggle, though under the character of auxiliaries. . The fortunes of this desultory warfare were at first various, until the military skill and bravery of captain Clive gave them a new aspect.   By his spirit and enterprise, and by the exertions of major Lawrence, the French and their Indian allies were repeatedly defeated.   So effectually, indeed, were their means and resources abridged, that, towards the close of 1753, a commissary was dispatched by the French East India Company, to Pondicherry, to negotiate an accommodation ; and reinforcements were at the same time sent to the support of their principal governor, Dupleix.

Had no other cause of animosity existed, it is probable that the respective

---

* It appears that St. Contest, the French Secretary of State, the count d'Argenson, the Secretary for the War Department, and their adherents in the cabinet, had been long desirous of exciting a war between England and France, but were prevented by the influence of the marchioness of Pompadour and her party.—See the letters of the duke and Mr. Pelham, in July and August 1753. Illust. Corres.

courts might have interposed, to prevent a farther feud, between the rival companies, whose power in so distant a region, had increased chiefly by the sufferance of the native princes. In another quarter, however, the two governments were directly at issue. By the peace of Utrecht, Nova Scotia, or Acadia, which had been so repeatedly a subject of contest, was ceded to Great Britain, " according to its antient limits ;" and this cession was confirmed by the stipulation in the peace of Aix-la-Chapelle, that all things should be restored to the same footing as before the war. This remote district had, however, risen in importance, in proportion to the anxiety of the two nations to improve their colonies, and augment their commerce in America. The value attached to it in England, was manifested by the recent foundation of Halifax, and by the exertions made to extend the British settlements in that quarter. Disputes, therefore, arose between France and England, as to the real limits of the colony, which had never been accurately defined by any treaty. The British court claimed the whole district, bounded by the river St. Lawrence, the Penobscot, ʻand the Atlantic Ocean ; while the French insisted, that the designation of Acadia, or Nova Scotia, applied only to the south-eastern part of the peninsula, comprehended between Capes St. Mary and Canso. Although the two Courts had appointed commissaries to settle the boundaries, and had also discussed the affair through their respective embassadors at London and Versailles, yet pretensions so contradictory could not easily be subjected to any arrangement. Accordingly, both evinced a resolution to maintain their rights with equal pertinacity ; and the question was still in suspense.

In the midst of this dispute, another subject of altercation had arisen, in a different part of America. From the first establishment of the French, at the mouths of the Mississippi, they had formed the design of connecting that settlement with their colony in Canada, by means of a chain of forts, which should give them the command of the Ohio and Mississippi, and consequently enable them to circumscribe the trade and population of the British colonies within the line of the Alleghany mountains. To oppose this project, a plan had been formed, by one of the British colonial governors, as early as 1716, for the formation of a company, to establish settlements beyond the Alleghany mountains, and secure the trade of the nations inhabiting the vicinity of the Ohio, which flows to the west of that chain. The design had been defeated, either by the representations of the French, or by the jealousies of the colonists themselves ; but, in 1749, it was resumed, under the patronage of Mr.

Pelham; and an arrangement was concluded with several merchants of London, for the formation of a settlement and a company, to trade with the Indians, under the name of the Ohio Company.

This scheme was not regarded with indifference by the French ; and complaints were soon transmitted, of the intrusion of British traders on their territories, or on those of their native allies. Such contending views brought the two parties into immediate collision ; each striving to defend its position by military works, and engaging the natives in its interest, until at length outrages were committed, and hostilities ensued, on different points of the frontier. At the same time, reinforcements were sent, and military stores dispatched from both countries. But, in this respect, the French had decidedly the advantage, having realised their plan for forming a great line of military posts and communications between Canada and Louisiana, and for collecting a regular army of 11,000 men, besides a numerous and effective militia ; while the British colonies, divided in religion, habits, and interests, were neither able to give equal effect to the exertions of the mother country, nor so well prepared to defend their distant, extensive, and broken frontier.*

Amidst these conflicting claims, other questions, arising from the recent treaty, were equally unsettled ; for, notwithstanding the evacuation of Tobago in 1750, the French still retained their settlements in the neutral islands of St. Lucia, St. Vincent, and Dominica, contrary to their repeated promises.† In furtherance of their schemes of aggrandisement in distant quarters, they seemed to be actively preparing for an approaching rupture in Europe, by the augmentation of their marine, the movements of their troops towards the Netherlands, and their unceasing efforts to embroil the affairs of Germany.

The diplomatic relations of the British and French courts, indeed, still preserved a friendly character ; but new subjects of irritation continually arose. Demands of redress and satisfaction, were either evaded, or imperfectly fulfilled ; and it was evident, that although the pacific principles of Mr. Pelham had induced him to connive at many petty vexations, and to exert his influence, in soothing the rising jealousy between the two countries, their incompatible pretensions, and jarring interests were likely to be eventually decided, by an appeal to the sword. In the mean time, he encountered a painful share of

---

* Cont. of Rapin, vol. xxi. p. 499.   † See Gent. Mag. for 1751.

blame, for the apparent tameness with which he submitted to the aggressions of France; and he found no ordinary difficulty in preventing the introduction of many irritating topics to the cognisance of parliament.

During these disputes between England and France, the violent conduct of the king of Prussia also excited apprehensions, lest the peace of Germany might speedily be broken. We have already observed, that the seizure of some ships, belonging to the subjects of his Prussian Majesty, for conveying corn, and other contraband goods to France, during the war, had provoked his displeasure; and that he had issued a decree, suspending the payment of the interest due on the Silesian loan. Although he was induced to forego his purpose, by a spirited memorial from the duke of Newcastle, yet he still insisted on deducting £.30,000, as a compensation to such of his subjects, as had suffered by the confiscation of their ships; and it was apprehended, at the beginning of the year, that France would support his pretensions. But, in this instance, the firmness of the British cabinet, aided by the influence of the pacific party at Versailles, again prevailed; for we find, that in a conference with the duke de Mirepoix, a compromise was proposed, by which, the demands of Frederic were to be reduced to £.15,000, and his Prussian Majesty to engage to revoke his decree. Mr. Pelham made no objection to the sum, candidly admitting that some compensation was due; yet both he and his brother insisted, that no payment should be made, antecedent to that revocation.*

Notwithstanding this apparent accommodation, the proposal of the duke de Mirepoix was rejected by Frederic; and we find, in a letter from the duke of Newcastle to the Chancellor, that the Prussian monarch was still considered as the principal, if not the only support of the Pretender, and of the Jacobite cause.† This conduct, and the continuance of the contest relative to East Friesland, prevented all immediate and direct approach to cordiality between the courts of London and Berlin.

In consequence of this disagreement between Prussia and England, and the pending contentions with France, the British cabinet were anxious to strengthen their connection with the court of Vienna, by renewing the

---

* Cont. of Rapin.—Smollett.—See also, letters from the duke of Newcastle to Mr. Pelham, dated July 17th and 27th; and one from Mr. Pelham to the duke of Newcastle, dated July 13th. Illust. Corres. for 1753.—Gent. Mag. for 1752.

† See letter from the duke of Newcastle to the Chancellor, dated Sept. 21st, 1753. Illust. Corres.

friendship which had formerly existed between the two powers. But the attainment of this object was rendered difficult, from the change which had taken place in the views and principles of Maria Theresa.

In emulation of Prussia, the empress queen had reorganized her finances and military establishments; and, by a rigorous and persevering reform, since the peace, had rendered Austria more powerful than at any period, subsequent to the accession of Leopold the First. In the ministry of the court of Vienna an essential change had also taken place, by the elevation of count Kaunitz to the office of Chancellor, with the supreme direction of foreign affairs.

Anthony, count Kaunitz, a nobleman still in the prime of life, had already distinguished his diplomatic abilities, in the negotiations of Aix-la-Chapelle, and the embassy at Paris. Profound, imperious, and aspiring, ambitious for the glory of the House of Austria, and entering deeply into the feelings of his sovereign towards the Maritime Powers, it was not to be doubted that his administration would be marked by a decisive and vigorous line of policy. Nor was this anticipation erroneous. In resentment for the imputed abandonment of the empress by England, during the late war, and her compulsory accession to an ignominious peace, he had already tampered with the court of Versailles;* and, although the discouragement which he had at first experienced, in the prosecution of his scheme, had rendered him cautious of proceeding to extremities with the Maritime Powers, yet, in time, they had reason to expect from him, a still stronger opposition to their commercial views, and peculiar interests, than they had already encountered, even from the spirit and temper of his imperial mistress herself.

The promotion of Kaunitz had been announced, as the period, when a final arrangement was to be effected, of the long pending negotiation relative to the Barrier treaty, and the tenure of the Netherlands. The event, however, was far from answering the expectations of the Maritime Powers; for, instead of evincing a disposition towards an adjustment of the dispute to their satisfaction, the new minister started other difficulties; and asserted the rights of his imperial mistress to the uncontrolled sovereignty of the Netherlands, in a still more emphatic and peremptory manner, than the Austrian cabinet had hitherto assumed. Hence, notwithstanding the British government had pressed this negotiation with unabated perseverance, they were unable to

---

* Mr. Keith's dispatches, passim.—History of the House of Austria.

extort from the empress queen the slightest concession, with respect to her new tariff,* or any promise to continue the usual payments, for the main-tenance of the Dutch garrisons. On the contrary, she strenuously urged her indisputable right to support the commerce of her subjects in the Netherlands; and to all the remonstrances and representations of the British minister, she repeatedly and proudly exclaimed, "Am I not sovereign in the Low Countries, and is it not my duty to protect my people, who have been too long oppressed by the Barrier Treaty, and deprived of the advantages which all other nations enjoy?" She also contended, that an efficient defence of these territories could be derived only from an Austrian force, and not from foreign mercenaries.†

In the midst of this irritating discussion, the king of England pursued his plan for the election of a king of the Romans, with a degree of earnest-ness and perseverance, which disgusted, instead of gratifying the court of Vienna. In fact, the communications on this subject, so far from bearing the friendly tone of two powers united in the same cause, were marked by complaints and threats on the part of England, and by evasion or remon-strance on that of Austria.

Notwithstanding this collision of sentiment, George II. persisted in his purpose; and hoped, by firmness, to extort the acqui-escence of the Austrian cabinet in the terms which had been adjusted, at the close of the preceding year, with the elector Palatine. But all his efforts were ineffectual; for the court of Vienna laboured rather to entangle England in alliances against the king of Prussia, than to promote the election, to the accomplishment of which they appeared perfectly indifferent.

Mr. Pelham was not surprised at the turn this affair had taken. In fact he was now fully confirmed in his opinion, that the Austrian ministry never heartily wished success to the project; and his conviction was strengthened by the insidious conduct of that court, which, after drawing England into subsidiary expenses, in time of peace, not only continued to refuse the smallest sacrifice to facilitate the election; but, on the contrary, rather threw such obstacles in the way, as evinced a purpose of indirectly defeating the design. Accordingly, although he approved the king's resolution, to abide

---

* See chap. xxiii. p. 118.
† History of the House of Austria, chap. cix.

by his actual engagements, he strongly dissuaded his brother from entering into any new scheme, however insignificant.*

Adverse, on all occasions, to an indefinite expenditure of the public money, in pursuit of an uncertain aim, Mr. Pelham derived consolation in his disappointment, from the consideration, that no farther sacrifices would be required, and that the delusion which had so long prevailed, was likely to be dispelled by the conviction, that the design was impracticable. His views were verified by the event ; for, though the duke of Newcastle still continued his negotiations with the court of Vienna and the elector Palatine, he encountered so many obstructions, that he was finally compelled to relinquish his chimerical hopes.†

The conduct of the court of Vienna furnishes an additional proof of the instability of the political relations between England and Austria ; although both Maria Theresa and her minister still continued to profess unabated zeal for the maintenance of the antient alliance, as a counterpoise to the power of France and Prussia.

The violent conduct of the Prussian monarch, and the attempts of France to incroach on the settlements in America and the West Indies, induced the duke of Newcastle to form the plan of an union between England, Austria, and Russia, combined with a subsidiary engagement, for a considerable body of Russian troops. The court of Vienna acceded to the overture, and the consent of the empress Elizabeth being obtained, a detachment of her forces was preparing to march towards the Prussian frontier. The duke accordingly submitted to the cabinet council, a proposal to give a subsidy to the empress of Russia for two years. In the deliberation on the subject, Mr. Pelham stated the arguments on both sides, with great temper, calmness, and moderation, but gave no decided opinion. He did not appear to object to the subsidy, which, he said, might be raised by retrenchments, in some of the military departments ; but he did not disguise his apprehension that it would provoke a rupture with Prussia, and, consequently, with France. He was also afraid, that the subsidy would be continued, after the expiration of the term ; and that then it would be imputed to the effects of Hanoverian

* See letter from Mr. Pelham to the duke of Newcastle, dated July 28th, 1753.—Illust. Corres.

† The breach between England and Austria, in 1755, prevented all farther negotiations on this subject ; and, after the peace of 1764, the court of Vienna obtained the election of the archduke, without obligation to any foreign power.

policy, as if the troops had been engaged merely to defend the electoral territories.

The duke of Newcastle met his brother's objections with equal moderation. He observed, that a reasonable subsidy might be granted for two years certain, the first advance not to be paid until the end of the first year; and that he was not without hopes of obtaining a proper security for the troops to remain in their position four years, without any farther grant, which he trusted would produce the intended effect. As to the second objection, he denied that it was a Hanoverian measure. He urged that the situation of Europe required it, and that it was necessary, unless England would yield to the incroachments of France upon her trade and possessions in the East and West Indies, in America, and every where else, and tamely submit to the insults of the king of Prussia.

These arguments, however, did not prevail with Mr. Pelham; and no decisive step appears to have been taken. But the march of the Russian troops towards the Prussian frontier, and the conviction that England was assuming a respectable posture of defence, restrained the king of Prussia from any overt act of aggression; and thus Mr. Pelham was relieved from his apprehensions of a continental war.

We here deem it necessary to advert to the affairs of Ireland, which we have hitherto refrained from noticing. Since the accession of the House of Brunswick, the Irish had gradually improved in arts, manufactures, and all the advantages of social life. But, in proportion as they improved, to use the expressions of a contemporary historian,* they seemed to forget their dependency upon England, and the constitutional ties by which they were bound. Hence, at various times, attempts had been successfully made to extend and consolidate the national resources, and to emancipate the country from restraints imposed by Great Britain.

In fact, at this period, from the indulgence of the British government, few proofs remained of their legislative dependence on the Crown, excepting the acknowledgment of the previous consent of the king, in the preamble to their money-bills, and the revision of their acts of parliament, by the privy council of England, before they could be carried into effect as laws.

Still, however, the high and untamed spirit of the people, broke out into frequent tumults and disorders; and the tranquillity of the country

---

* Continuation of Rapin, vol. xxi. p. 488.

essentially depended on the popularity of the lord lieutenant, or the influence of the lords justices, who, in his absence, directed the affairs of government. After the tumultuary and successful opposition to Wood's patent,* in 1725, the nation appeared satisfied with its triumph; and an unusual degree of tranquillity had prevailed, not only during the remainder of the Walpole administration, but even during a considerable portion of that of Mr. Pelham. The popular governments of the duke of Devonshire and lord Chesterfield, assisted by the judicious choice of lords justices, had preserved the good will of the natives; and, at the time of the rebellion in 1745, the Irish had manifested equal zeal and loyalty, in support of the Protestant establishment.

From 1734, the chief direction of the domestic government had been confided to Mr. Henry Boyle, chancellor of the Exchequer, Speaker of the House of Commons, and one of the lords justices, in the absence of the lords lieutenants. He was a man of illustrious family,† popular manners, and commanding eloquence, and naturally proud of the influence which he had acquired. He had been treated with great consideration by the duke of Devonshire, lord Chesterfield, and lord Harrington, in their successive governments; and, under his guidance, the Irish House of Commons had evinced the utmost docility towards the British crown.

In 1747, however, the promotion of Dr. George Stone,‡ brother of Mr. Stone, the confidential friend of the duke of Newcastle, to the primacy of Armagh, led to a change of interests in the administration; as he was constituted one of the lords justices. During the government of lord Harrington, he was compelled to act a secondary part; and Mr. Boyle continued to retain the same degree of consideration, which he had hitherto enjoyed. But the appointment of the duke of Dorset, as lord lieutenant, brought a new actor on the stage, in the person of his son, lord George Sackville, who held the office of Secretary of State for Ireland. With him the primate formed a close connection; and in consequence of his brother's influence with the duke of Newcastle, aspired to a higher degree of authority than he had hitherto been permitted to exercise.

* See Memoirs of Sir R. Walpole, vol. ii. chap. xxvi.

† His father was Henry Boyle, of Castlemartyr, in the county of Cork, whose father, Henry, was the younger son of Roger, the first earl of Orrery.

‡ He was promoted in 1731, at the early age of twenty-eight, from the deanery of Derry to the bishoprick of Ferns; in 1733 to Kildare; in 1743 to Derry; and, in 1747, he was raised to the primacy of Armagh.

From the satisfaction which the duke of Dorset had formerly given, as lord lieutenant, it was hoped, that his second administration would prove as peaceable as the first. But the struggles of the new candidates for power, created a feud as violent as. it was unexpected. In consequence of the union between the primate and lord George Sackville, the influence of Mr. Boyle was diminished, and he evinced the utmost mortification on perceiving the decline of his ascendancy. He was completely alienated from the British government, by the attempt of the new secretary to induce him to relinquish his post of Speaker, in favour of Mr. Ponsonby, though it was gilded with the offer of a peerage, and a pension of £.1,500 a year. He not only repelled the proposal with contempt, but succeeded in exciting a spirit of opposition, in the House of Commons. He was vigorously aided by many of his colleagues in administration, and by some of those restless spirits, who were jealous of British influence, and sought to raise their consequence by provoking intestine feuds. The effect of their manœuvres was speedily felt in the Irish parliament, where the opposition, which before could scarcely number more than twenty-eight votes, was suddenly increased to such a strength, as to embarrass the proceedings of government.

The disputes on the almost forgotten subjects of privilege and prerogative, afforded an opportunity to commence a struggle. In 1749, under the government of the earl of Harrington, a surplus of nearly £.205,000 having accumulated in the Exchequer, a bill was introduced into parliament, for applying £.120,000 of this sum, to the discharge of the national debt; and, though it was drawn up by the Attorney-general, and the chancellor of the Exchequer, the usual clause "by the previous consent of his Majesty," was omitted in the preamble, as if the Commons of Ireland had an undoubted right to apply the surplus of their own revenue to national purposes, without the royal consent. The advocates for prerogative in England, affirmed that the Irish Commons had no such right, nor even that of taking such an affair into consideration, without the previous sanction of the Crown, conveyed in the most explicit terms; and the bill was not sent back to Ireland until the session held towards the close of 1751, under the administration of the duke of Dorset. In announcing the return of this bill, his Grace declared that he was commanded by the king to acquaint them, that his Majesty, ever attentive to the ease and happiness of his subjects, would graciously *consent* to their proposal, respecting the application of the surplus revenue, and recommended them to apply such surplus towards the farther reduction of the national debt. This declaration was resented by the party in opposition; and in their address of thanks, the Commons made no mention of his Majesty's consent, but only acknowledged his gracious attention to their ease and happiness, in recommending to them the application of the surplus. They also again ventured to omit all reference to the sanction of the king, in the preamble to the bill. The ministry in England were highly offended at this second omission, which they justly construed into a wilful encroachment on the prerogative; and the bill was sent back with an alteration in the preamble, signifying his Majesty's consent, as well as recommendation. The Irish opposition were not yet prepared to offer a more direct affront, and the bill was passed in the usual form.

These feuds in the Irish cabinet affected the duke of Newcastle and Mr. Pelham, in a very considerable degree, and they exerted all their influence to restore harmony. They disapproved generally the conduct of the duke of Dorset, the primate, and lord George Sackville, towards Mr. Boyle, and other considerable persons of his party. At the same time, they were inclined to favour the primate, in consideration of his brother, Mr. Stone; and were fully disposed to check the attempts of the Irish opposition, to circumscribe the prerogatives of the Crown.

Although they at first thought that the removal of the duke of Dorset would be necessary, if he did not conciliate Mr. Boyle and his adherents, yet, on serious reflection, they considered that such a step would be attended with dangerous consequences. They therefore continued their efforts to soothe the contending parties, and effect an adjustment. In fact, their interference commenced with the fairest prospect of success; as the Speaker seems to have made some concessions, and the duke of Dorset adopted a more complacent demeanour towards him. This reconciliation, how- ever, proved but temporary; for, to mortify the primate, the opposition made an attack upon Mr. Neville Jones, one of his creatures, and member for Wexford, who, as engineer and surveyor, had been intrusted with the erection of barracks. He was accused of misemploying the funds confided to his management, and of constructing many of those buildings in un- healthy situations. In consequence of the proofs alleged against him, he was not only expelled from the House of Commons, in November 1753, but a bill was brought into parliament, to render his estate answerable for all deficiencies.

This triumph over the new administration was signalised, generally, by the most clamorous rejoicings; and followed by other incidents, in the highest degree mortifying to the lord lieutenant and his two counsellors.

Before the meeting of parliament, new overtures of accommodation were made by the primate to the Speaker, but disdainfully rejected ; and a menace was indirectly held forth to the lord lieutenant, that the usual compliment to him, as chief governor, would be omitted in the address. Although this threat was not carried into execution, yet the parliament still continued to manifest an untractable spirit.

When the duke of Dorset opened the session, he repeated the expressions of his Majesty's gracious consent to a farther appropriation of £.130,000, the surplus produce of the revenue, towards the payment of the national debt. But the opposition were now grown bolder, and the clause, announcing the consent of the king, was again omitted in the address, as well as in the preamble of the bill. In consequence of this infringement on the prerogative, the clause was not only supplied, but a letter was written to the lord lieutenant, signed by eighteen English privy councillors, intimating that his Majesty could not dispense with such an essential recognition of his authority. The question was thus brought to an issue ; and the opposing party, confiding in the general support of the nation, ventured to make a decided manifestation of hostility ; for the amended bill was rejected by a majority of 122 against 117, though the public creditors were reduced to the utmost embarrassment, by the failure of this expected supply to the circulation. The triumph was celebrated with all the enthusiasm which marks the Irish character; and the Speaker was every where welcomed with those proofs of popular approbation, which signalised the victory of Dean Swift over Wood and his obnoxious patent.

In consequence of this refractory spirit, the duke of Dorset, by order of the English government, adjourned the parliament for three weeks, and dismissed some of the individuals, most active in opposition, particularly Mr. Carter, Master of the Rolls, and Mr. Malone, the Prime Serjeant ; but he did not venture to remove the Speaker from his office of chancellor of the Exchequer. These dismissions, while they roused the resentment of the disgraced parties, and their adherents, were far from affecting their popularity, or allaying the irritation of the public mind. On the contrary, the feelings of the people were displayed in that barometer of public opinion, the theatre, on the refusal of an actor to repeat some lines from a speech, in the tragedy of Mahomet, which were considered as reflecting on the lord lieutenant and his dependents ; for all the furniture and decorations of the place were instantly demolished, and the house reduced to a mere shell.*

It is difficult to conjecture to what extremes this spirit might have led, particularly when urged by the embarrassments, arising from the deficiency of circulation. But, fortunately, at this moment the British government interposed, and by dispatching a royal order for the payment of £.77,000 to the public creditors, removed one active cause of irritation, and gave a temporary turn to public opinion.†

Mr. Pelham had contemplated the rise and progress of this feud with the deepest concern, in the unsettled state of foreign affairs; but he was attacked by his last and fatal illness, in the midst of his efforts to promote a reconciliation ; and the state of Ireland, for a considerable period, continned to cause anxiety and embarrassment to the British ministry.‡

---

* See Gent. Mag. for 1754, by which it appears, that the riot took place on the 2nd of March in that year.

† Lord Orford's Memoires, vol. i. passim.—Rapin, vol. xxi. p. 488.—Smollett, vol. iii. chap. iii. Gent. Mag. for 1754. Correspondence of the duke of Newcastle and Mr. Pelham, in Illust. Corres. for 1752, also letter from Mr. Pelham to the duke of Newcastle, dated May 21, and from the duke to Mr. Pelham, dated June 12-23, 1752.

‡ During the remainder of the duke of Dorset's administration, the dissensions continued in the Irish cabinet, and were not allayed until the marquis of Hartington was created lord lieutenant, in 1755. The influence of the primate was then so much diminished, that he was omitted in the appointment of the lords justices. In April, 1755, Mr. Boyle was created a peer, with the title of earl of Shannon. When the duke of Bedford was lord lieutenant, in 1757, the primate was reinstated in his office, as one of the lords justices, but he never recovered his former influence.

CHAPTER XXXII.

1754.

Meeting of the Parliament—King's Speech and Addresses—Proceedings on the repeal of the Jews Naturalisation Bill—Ineffectual attempt to procure the repeal of the clause, in favour of the Jews, in the Plantation Act—Extension of the Mutiny Act to the troops in the East India Company's service—Financial arrangements—Illness, death, and character of Mr. Pelham—His descendants—Proceedings of the duke of Newcastle for the formation of a new Administration.

IN the midst of these difficulties, both foreign and domestic, the period for the session of parliament approached. Mr. Pelham, still flattering himself with the hope of a satisfactory accommodation with France, and dreading from past experience the renewal of war, appears not to have meditated any increase of the military or naval establishment, and to have apprehended no serious or immediate disturbance of the public tranquillity.

The speech from the throne was delivered on the 15th of November, in language calculated to convey an impression of the stability of the peace. The king assured the parliament, that he should steadily pursue the most effectual measures, for preserving the blessings of tranquillity, to which the general state of Europe seemed favourable. After announcing to the House of Commons, that he should require only the ordinary supplies of the year, he testified his concern at the increase of the horrid crimes of robbery and murder; and recommended the members of both Houses, to cooperate with him, in effecting a reformation of the public morals.

No opposition was made to the addresses in either House, which conveyed the warmest assurances of loyalty, applauded the cares of the king for the preservation of public tranquillity, and the improvement of the national morals; and expressed, not only a full approbation of the proceedings of the crown, but a readiness to afford his Majesty a cordial and efficient support.

Indeed, this session was remarkable for its general tranquillity. The candour, economy, and uprightness of the minister had disarmed many of his antagonists, and made others his friends ; and the concord which reigned between the sovereign and the Princess of Wales, obviated one great and fertile source of dissension.

Such was the weakness of opposition, that no amendment was even offered to the addresses of both Houses; and motions, which were usually the source of strenuous discussion, were permitted to pass, without a debate or division.

The earliest event of the session, was the repeal of the law for the Naturalisation of the Jews. Although this bill had been carried so triumphantly through both Houses, the popular prejudices against it were not only undiminished, but greatly aggravated. The arguments advanced by its opponents, in the heat of debate, had made a deep and general impression ; and the question still continued to be agitated, with increasing warmth, through the medium of the press.

Violent expressions of public indignation occurred, in many parts of the country. The bishops, in particular, were exposed to contumely, for suffering the bill to pass, without opposition, in the House of Peers. The degree of irritation which prevailed against their order, was shewn in the insults offered to the bishop of Norwich, in every part of his diocese. At Ipswich, the very youths whom he was about to confirm, called out for circumcision ; and a paper was affixed on the door of one of the churches, stating that his lordship would confirm the Jews the next day, which was their sabbath, and on the Sunday would perform the same function for the Christians. Nor did the laity escape a similar share of public execration. In particular, Mr. Sydenham, member for Exeter, vainly endeavoured to reconcile his indignant constituents to his support of the bill, by circulating printed declarations of his attachment to Christianity. In every other part of the country, the ferment was equally alarming. The pulpits re-echoed with censures against the patrons of this obnoxious law ; the subject was toasted and discussed at convivial and political meetings ; and one uniform sentiment of dissatisfaction seemed to possess the great mass of the people, against the ministry, and particularly against the Pelhams, who were regarded as the authors of the bill. Indeed, when we consider, that at this period, the Roman Catholics were still subject to penalties and disabilities, greater even than those of the Jews ; and that Protestant dissenters were regarded with jealousy, and threatened with the terrors of the law, we cannot but acknowledge that there was a culpable degree of imprudence, in thus attempting to extend important privileges to a class of men, who by their tenets and habits, must be considered as natural adversaries to the Christian religion.

This conviction operated on the minds of the ministry with double force, when they contemplated the approaching dissolution of parliament; and they did not hesitate to yield to the tide of popular opinion. Mr. Pelham, in particular, however anxious for the continuance of the bill, was too prudent to oppose the national feeling; and observed in a letter to his brother, that, if it gave disturbance to weak minds, it was right to indulge them. He added, that if such was the opinion of his brother and the Chancellor, he would readily acquiesce in their determination, as the repeal could be of no consequence, not being a measure of government.*

In order, as much as possible, to exclude from the discussion all irritating topics, the ministry were induced to adopt the resolution of bringing forward the subject in the House of Peers, where, by the rules of proceeding, no previous notice was necessary. Accordingly, the question relative to the address was no sooner decided, than the duke of Newcastle rose to offer the bill of repeal. He grounded the proposal on the national ferment, which he declared had been artfully raised against the Naturalisation bill, and represented it as the fruit of a disaffected spirit. Professing still to maintain the same sentiments, with respect to the original measure, he treated it as a point of mere secondary importance; and argued, that on such considerations, it would be imprudent to risk the disturbance of the public tranquillity, particularly as the prejudice entertained against it would defeat its beneficial effects. The bill which he then offered, did not however comprise a simple repeal; for, still farther to satisfy the country, he proposed to retain the clause, incapacitating Jews from acquiring any advowson or interest, in any ecclesiastical establishment, hospital, or school; because he considered it unseemly to give a person professing that religion, a right to any sort of estate, appropriated for the propagation of Christianity

The bill did not, however, pass without severe animadversion. The duke of Bedford, although he approved the repeal, on the same grounds which had produced his dissent to the original bill, yet strongly objected to the

* See letter from Mr. Pelham to the duke of Newcastle, dated July 20, 1753. Illust. Corres.

retention of the proposed clause, on the plea, that it would interfere with
that principle of the common law, which rendered the Jews the property of
the king; and, by restraining them from the acquisition of ecclesiastical
interest or property, would countenance the inference, that they were legally
entitled to acquire property of any other description. He even urged the
necessity of repealing that part of the Plantation act, which related to the
Jews, declaring that the clause had been introduced either by surprise or
inadvertence.

Dr. Secker, bishop of Oxford, justified the acquiescence of his order in
the original measure, as the effect of that Christian benevolence, which is
inculcated by the Gospel. He treated it as no way connected with
religion; and consented to the repeal, as a necessary sacrifice, to quiet
the alarms of the people. He opposed, however, the arguments of the
duke of Bedford, for a simple repeal, on the ground that the excepted clause
was necessary to secure the integrity of the church.

Dr. Drummond, bishop of St. Asaph, adopted the reasoning of the
bishop of Oxford, and declared that the prelates could not have opposed
the bill, without indulging a spirit of persecution, contrary to that of the
Gospel.

The Chancellor took the same course of argument as the duke of Newcastle; and adduced, as an additional reason for the repeal, the antipathy
which it had raised among the populace, against the Jews, and which might
lead to outrages that no law could repress. Indeed, he expressed his conviction, that such excesses had been prevented, merely by the general
expectation, that the obnoxious measure would be speedily revoked.

Lord Temple, with his accustomed warmth, complained of the arts which
had been used to mislead the public mind; protested against the legislature,
for listening to the popular outcry, which was less intended to serve the
Protestant religion, than to wound the Protestant succession. He treated the
movers of the opposition with contempt, and pronounced the clamour to be
disaffection, clothed with superstition. He trembled lest the Plantation act,
which granted Naturalisation to the Jews who resided seven years in the colonies, should be repealed. He trembled also, lest fires should be rekindled in
Smithfield, to burn Jews; and declared, that the persecution of the Jews
would infallibly lead to the persecution of the dissenters. Finally, he
conjured the peers, as a permanent and independent body, not to be swayed
in their deliberations, by that popular clamour, which had alarmed the

members of the lower House, on the eve of a general election. But these and idle declamations were heard with indifference, amidst the general feeling of the legislature and the country.

In the committee, the excepting clause, proposed by the duke of Newcastle, was struck out; and the bill, being thus reduced to the state of a simple repeal, was sanctioned by the House on the 23rd of November, without a division.*

In the lower House, the question for the address having been decided, Sir James Dashwood rose; and, after reprobating the bill for the Naturalisation of the Jews, moved for a speedy call of the House, to discuss the necessity of its repeal. But, as it was not usual to propose such a call, for any particular purpose, he framed the motion in a general shape; and an order was accordingly passed to summon the members on the 4th of December. He was seconded by lord Parker, an adherent of the ministry; but before the period appointed for this call, the bill introduced by the duke of Newcastle was sent down from the Lords, on the 23rd of November.

The debate which took place on the second reading (November 26th), turned on a new point. As the preamble asserted, "that occasion had been taken, from the late act, to raise discontents and disquiet in the minds of many of his Majesty's subjects," the opponents of the bill, vehemently stigmatized these expressions, as false in fact, injurious to the dignity of parliament, and conveying an unjust reflection on the people; and proposed to substitute the simple declaration, "that great discontent and disquiet had arisen, in the minds of his Majesty's subjects." The favourers of the motion imitated their friends in the Upper House, by representing the bill as a matter of minor importance; and, though they did not venture to object to the repeal, yet they warmly concurred in vindicating the language of the preamble.

Mr. Pelham could not conquer his mortification, at the compulsory abrogation of a law, which he had so zealously, but imprudently promoted; and his chagrin and disappointment are evident, in his defence of the preamble, as well as in the unguarded language, which he applied to the original authors of the opposition in the city.

" It is an old observation," he said, " which almost every day's experience

---

* Journals of the Lords.—Hansard's Parl. Hist. vol. xv. p. 91 ; and lord Orford's Posthumous Memoires, vol. i. p. 310, 315.

confirms, that great events often spring from trivial causes. From the act which is now to be repealed, we might have seen a new confirmation of this observation; for though itself of very little importance, yet from the opposition it encountered in its progress, and the use to which it has since been applied, it has become an affair of great moment, because, should it remain in force, it might produce some fatal event, as it has artfully, and most industriously, been converted into a religious question. It is this, and this alone, that inclines me to vote for its repeal; because I have always observed, that when religion is brought into any dispute, reason is from that moment laid aside; and it becomes on both sides a sort of enthusiasm, the effect of which has been fatal to this nation, and but a few years ago was fatal also to Europe. Many gentlemen among us must remember, and all, I believe, must have read of the trial of that otherwise insignificant person, Dr. Sacheverel.* Could any one, at the beginning, have imagined that the prosecution of such a low, insignificant person, was an affair of any importance? Yet from thence, occasion was taken, to raise the cry, that the Church was in danger; and this soon propagated such a spirit among the people, against our then excellent ministers, as gave their enemies the courage to supplant them; through which, the war, that had been so gloriously, so successfully carried on, by the great duke of Marlborough, terminated in a most inglorious, I may say, a most infamous peace, when our armies were approaching the very gates of Paris. This has since cost us, as well as our allies, much blood and treasure. I wish it may not, at last, cost us our independence; but, whatever may be the consequence, it is another proof, that the most signal events, may sometimes spring from the most trivial causes.

" The case now before us is of the very same nature. Who could have imagined, when the bill for permitting the Jews to be naturalised, was first brought into the other House, that it was an affair of any importance, or that religion was concerned in the question? Could any one imagine this, who reflected, that the bill for naturalising all such Jews, as shall reside seven years in any of our colonies or plantations, had passed through both Houses, without the least opposition, and has now subsisted for several years, without causing the least murmur among the people! Surely, if any danger could arise, either to our religion or liberties, from the residence of a great

* See Coxe's Memoirs of the duke of Marlborough, chap. lxxxvi.

number of Jews among us, that law would be more dangerous than the law which is now to be repealed, were it to subsist to the end of the world ; because either House of Parliament may, when they please, prohibit the naturalisation of any more Jews, by virtue of the law which is now to be repealed ; whereas both Houses together cannot put a stop to the naturalisation of more Jews, by virtue of the Plantation act, without the consent of the crown, which no prince would grant, who had a design against our liberties, and who thought that the Jews might be useful to him, in carrying on that design. I do not mention this, from any opinion I entertain, that the act for naturalising all such Jews, as shall reside seven years in our plantations, can ever be of dangerous consequence to our religion or liberties. I mention it only to shew, that occasion must have been taken, by some persons, to mislead the people, with regard to the law passed last session, and to possess them with a conceit of its being inconsistent with their religion ; otherwise they would have interested themselves as little about it, as they did about the preceding act. Consequently I must think that the preamble, as it stands, is not only true in fact, but the most proper preamble that could be prefixed to the bill, now before us ; because, to prevent, if possible, the people from running into any religious dispute, either with or without foundation, is so far from being inconsistent with the dignity, that it is the duty of parliament ; since from experience we know that in such disputes, even the parliament cannot make either side attend to reason. On the contrary, the parliament itself is usually hurried away with the stream ; and, therefore, when any such dispute begins to rise, it ought if possible, to be crushed in the bud, which I hope will be the effect of the repeal now before us.

"Having mentioned the dignity of parliament, I cannot conceive how any gentleman, who has a regard for that dignity, can find fault with the treatment given last session to the petition from the city of London. Whilst I have the honour of a seat in this assembly, I shall always be ready to hear, and to give due attention to the petitions of any man, or set of men, who think that their private rights may suffer, or that they may be injured in their property and lawful employments, by any bill depending in this House. In such cases they have a right to petition, and they ought to be heard against it. But in matters of a public concern, no body of men, how respectable soever, have a right to tell us what we ought or ought not to do. To attempt it, is an attack upon the dignity of this House ; and when that dignity is attacked, every member ought to shew a becoming warmth. The opposition that was made within doors to the bill, then depending, though inconsiderable, was carried on with great temper ; and the petition presented by the merchants against the bill was decent. Accordingly, they were heard ; and several witnesses were examined. But the petition of the city of London, which raised the warmth of the House, was so like the famous Kentish petition,* that if its framers and subscribers had been treated in the same manner, they would have met with their deserts ; for I am persuaded it was that petition, which first gave a religious turn to . the dispute, and was the foundation of the seditious spirit, afterwards propagated with so much industry through the whole kingdom.

" Yet, notwithstanding all the pains that were taken, to misrepresent that law, it had little effect among the better sort of people, so far as I could find, or have been informed ; for though I had, last summer, occasion to be present at numerous meetings, I never heard any gentleman express a dislike to it, or signify any apprehension of its bringing upon us an inundation of Jews. No man, indeed, of common sense, could have any such fear ; for as no Jew was naturalised by that law ; as the Jews were only thereby enabled to obtain their naturalisation, by particular acts of parliament ; and, as such acts are so expensive, that poor men cannot bear. the charge, it was not to be supposed, that any but the rich would or could take the benefit of such a statute ; indeed, very few of them, but such. as are fund-holders, or are resolved to carry on an extensive trade, and thereby increase both our navigation and manufactures. The clamour was therefore chiefly among the vulgar and ignorant ; and among them, it is true, it was in some places, and upon some occasions, likely to become riotous, which disposition, if it should continue, might occasion the death of some of his Majesty's subjects. This the parliament ought surely to prevent, as it may be done without any mischief to the public ; for though these poor people have been misled, yet they deserve at least our compassion ; and, as I am convinced that no man would, upon this occasion, have become an object of our compassion, if he had not been misled, I agree to this preamble as it now stands."

---

* The celebrated petition of the juries, grand jury, and freeholders of Kent, against the tardiness of the Commons, in seconding the foreign policy of king William, when a prince of the House of Bourbon was placed on the throne of Spain. The petition was denounced as scandalous, insolent, and seditious, and the petitioners were imprisoned.

The debate was continued by other speakers, but as their arguments offered no novelty, we shall merely observe, that Mr. Pitt, after an absence of several months from the duties of parliament, in consequence of indisposition, again distinguished himself, by defending the preamble. He treated the question as entirely foreign to the interests of religion, and maintained that though the parliament consented to repeal the bill, in compliance with the wishes of the people, yet they would compromise their dignity, if they revoked it without publicly expressing their disapprobation of what was required. A division on this subject took place, and the preamble being approved by 113 against 47, the repeal was finally decided.*

The enemies of the Naturalization bill, having thus attained their object, prepared to carry their aggressions still farther, by attempting to deprive the Jews of the advantages, assigned to them under the Plantation act, which allowed them, after a period of seven years' residence, in any of the American colonies, to be entitled to the privileges of a British born subject. Accordingly, on the 4th of December, the day appointed for the call of the House, lord Harley moved for the repeal of such parts of this act as related to the Jews, and was seconded by Sir James Dashwood. The arguments adduced on this occasion were, that the privileges conveyed by the act would still continue to operate, and render the recent repeal nugatory, by favouring the establishment of Jews in this kingdom, as naturalised subjects.

Several members did not hesitate to oppose this persecuting system, and among others Mr. Pelham. He said, "To repeal the Plantation act, will be to tell the people we repeal this law, not because it has made, but because it ought to have made you uneasy. To part with those who hold our wealth, will be to divest ourselves of our strength. To pay attention to mere clamour, will produce the most serious consequences; but a repeal will revive the intolerant principles of the High Church, which have produced such pernicious effects, and encourage that spirit, which can only be gratified, while it is thundering forth its ecclesiastical anathemas."

Mr. Pitt spoke with still more energy than Mr. Pelham. "I did not expect," he observed, "that this would have been the first return for the

---

* Journals.—Lord Orford's Posthumous Memoires, &c. vol. i. p. 312 to 315.—Debrett's Debates.—Hansard's Parl. Hist. vol. xv. p. 91, et seq.

recent condescension of parliament. A stand must be made, or our authority is at an end. I consider the late clamour to be a little election art, which has been judiciously humoured. The bill was not a toleration, but a preference given to Jews over other sects. My maxim is, not to grant more consideration to the church than it actually enjoys; for if a High Church spirit should revive, the fate which threatens the Jew to day, will menace the Presbyterian to-morrow, and the country will be agitated by a septennial church clamour. We are not to be influenced by laws passed before the Reformation. Our ancestors would have said, ' a Lollard * has no right to inherit lands.' We, on the contrary, do not fear to indulge Jews. They are not likely to become great purchasers of land; for they love their money, and can employ it to much better advantage in trade."

The proposal was rejected by 208 voices against 88 ; and the people, satisfied with the exclusion of the Jews from greater privileges, acquiesced in the decision without murmur.

Except the discussions connected with the Jews' Naturalisation bill, the proceedings of the session were of little importance.

On the 12th of December, a motion was made by Sir John Barnard, for the repeal of the acts prohibiting the wear and importation of French lawns and cambrics, on the ground of their insufficiency ; but it was opposed by the members of administration, and negatived without a division.

Another debate of temporary interest, arose on certain mismanagements committed, in regard to the late lottery, for the purchase of the Sloane Museum and the Harleian Manuscripts. Mr. Pelham had generally expressed his disapprobation of this financial expedient, as tending to foster a spirit of gambling among the people; and he felt the greater repugnance to resort to it at this period, when the vice was peculiarly prevalent. No other resource, however, equally available remained, for the attainment of a national object so important; and, therefore, in framing the act, especial care was taken, to introduce provisions for repressing the spirit of specu-lation, by restricting the number of tickets to be sold to any single person, to twenty. Notwithstanding these precautions, the usual specula-tions prevailed ; and Mr. Le Heup, an officer of the Treasury, and one of the receivers of the contributions to the lottery, glaringly contravened

* Memoires of lord Orford, vol. i. p. 317.—Journals of the Commons, 4th December, 1753.

the act, by disposing of tickets to a considerable amount, under fictitious names.

This abuse was too public to escape notice, and the subject was brought before the House of Commons by Mr. Cook, on the 4th of December. After a slight opposition, a series of resolutions was passed against Mr. Le Heup, accompanied by an address to his Majesty, for the prosecution of the offender; and the law was ultimately vindicated, by his conviction in the Court of King's-bench, and a consequent fine of £.1,000.*

The last debate worthy of notice, took place on a motion made by the Secretary-at-War, for extending the operation of the Mutiny act to the troops in the service of the East India company. This question was strongly combated, on constitutional grounds, as conferring on a trading body, powers which ought to be viewed with jealousy, when vested even in the head of the state. But being supported by the influence of government, as necessary for rendering the military power in the East Indies efficient, it was carried in the affirmative, on different divisions; and finally passed the Commons on the 25th of February.† It received the assent of the Lords, without amendment.

The different branches of supply were granted with little difficulty, and the general establishments of the country were continued on the same footing as before. The only debate which appears to have occurred on the subject, related to the usual topic of the army; and, on the report of the committee of supply concerning this branch, which was delivered on the 26th of February, a division took place. The continuance of the military establishment at 18,000 men was, however, sanctioned by 143 voices against 53.

The financial scheme for the current service of the year, as proposed by Mr. Pelham, is shewn in the subjoined table.‡

---

* See Cont. of Rapin, vol. xxi. p. 484.—Hansard, vol. xv. p. 192.

† The division on the second reading was 245 against 50. On the report of the committee, a motion was made for rendering the bill temporary, which was negatived by 84 against 46.—Hansard, vol. xv. p. 250.—Journals of the Commons.

‡ By favour of T. W. Brereton, esq. of the Exchequer.

SUPPLY.   WAYS AND MEANS.

NAVY.—Charge of 10,000 seamen;
Ordinary; building, and repairs   ......£.1,018,949
Greenwich Hospital......... £.908,747   750,000

ARMY.—Charge of 18,850 men;
garrisons in the Plantations;   15,000
Gibraltar, Minorca; Ordnance;   700,000
Half-pay, Chelsea Hospital, and
Extraordinaries 1,141,390   7,937
Subsidy to the Elector of Bavaria . 20,000
———————— King of Poland .. 32,000   23,562
Charges incurred for the Colonies
of Georgia and Nova Scotia.. 76,575   32,652
For the Forts, &c. on the Coast of
Africa 10,000   30,195
Road from Newcastle to Carlisle 6,000
Westminster Bridge............ 2,000
Expenses of the Mint.......... 15,000   499,600
Purchasing and rebuilding the
King's Bench Prison 18,300
Deficiencies of the Duties on
Sweets 6,792
——————— Half-Duty
on Tonnage and Poundage 61,505
Exchequer bills, charged on the
produce of the Duties on Sweets 499,600
                                         —————————
                                          2,797,909
Balance.................. 279,986

                          £.3,077,895   £.3,077,895

At this period, Mr. Pelham had the gratification of witnessing the
beneficial effect of his grand financial schemes, by which the whole of the
unfunded debt was discharged, the interest on the public funds gradually
decreasing, and the current expenditure of the year placed on the most
economical footing.[*]

The questions relating to the supply were not finally disposed of before the
28th of February, and, till then, Mr. Pelham appears to have been unre-

———————

[*] In fact, although the national debt had, in consequence of the continuance of the war, and
the discharge of the unfunded debt, increased from £.51,043,347 to £.73,075,687, during his
administration; yet, by his wise reductions, the interest did not exceed £.2,615,101, which
was an increase of only £.642,626, the interest being, in 1743, when he became first Lord of
the Treasury, £.1,972,475.

mitting in his attention to the duties of his office. Indeed his speeches display no symptom of decay, either in mind or body ; and his activity as a minister, was in no degree diminished, in the prosecution of those arrangements, which related to the business of the state, or the preparations for a general election.

But his constitution had received an irreparable shock ; and symptoms of erysipelas had induced him, in the summer, as before mentioned, to take a journey to Scarborough, for the benefit of its waters and salubrious air. He returned in a state of health apparently improved, and, in a letter written in the beginning of January to his brother, declares that he was never better in his life.

Still, however, the cause of the disease was unconquered ; and a sudden relapse occurred, which produced carbuncles on his back, and brought on a fever, that in three days terminated his life, at six o'clock in the morning of Wednesday the 6th of March, at his house in Arlington Street. His disorder increased so rapidly, that his brother had but just time to attend him in his last moments.

In finishing the character already sketched of Mr. Pelham, we encounter few of those conflicting opinions, which render it difficult to pronounce a satisfactory judgment, on the merits or demerits of a statesman. Towards him, even political rivalry seems scarcely to have engendered either prejudice or animosity ; and, in the estimate of the principles, by which he was guided, the ends which he pursued, and the means which he employed, both his opponents and friends, with little exception, cordially agree.

His knowledge was rather useful than extensive ; his understanding more solid than brilliant. His abilities did not burst forth with that splendour which has distinguished the opening career of many statesmen, but were gradually developed by experience and practice, and seemed to grow equal to the occasions, by which they were called into action. He was slow and cautious in deciding, yet firm and persevering, when his resolution was once formed ; though he knew the proper time and occasion, to bend to popular prejudice, or public opinion. Instead of declining under the weight of years, his energies continued to increase ; and, at no period did he better assume the spirit and authority of a great minister, than in that which immediately preceded his dissolution.

His temper was naturally equable and conciliatory ; and his disposition candid and unassuming. He was cautious in raising expectations, but faithful in the performance of his promises. These qualities, instead of being deteriorated by the exercise of power, distinguished to the latest period, the minister as well as the man ; and to them he owed more friends, and a stronger attachment, than the most profound and refined art could have acquired. Even his opponents felt the value of such merits ; and, however disposed to question the propriety of his measures, they seldom failed to render justice to his sincerity, disinterestedness, and integrity. Indeed, a better proof cannot be given, of the suavity of his manners, and the impression produced by his manliness and candour, than the treatment he experienced in his intercourse with the sovereign. Notwithstanding the irritability of temper, and pertinacity of opinion, which marked the character of George II, his Majesty invariably behaved towards Mr. Pelham with kindness and attention ; always listened to his advice with complacency ; and, in numerous cases, yielded to his representations, though frequently opposed to his favourite plans of continental policy. When he was informed of his death, he testified his regret by the exclamation, "Now I shall have no more peace !"

In manner, Mr. Pelham united dignity and ease. Though naturally grave, yet no one was more free from affected reserve or repulsive austerity ; and, in his social hours, no one could more gracefully unbend, and mingle in the playfulness of conversation.

In his public character, he was uniformly moderate and disinterested ; and, it is mentioned to his honour, by almost the only author who has treated him with obloquy, that he lived without abusing his power, and died poor.* In a word, Mr. Pelham may be ranked among the few ministers who enjoyed at once the esteem of the sovereign, the confidence of the parliament, the respect of opposition, and the love of the people.

Without the natural gifts of a great orator, he always spoke with good sense and effect ; and his speeches, though rarely marked with bursts of eloquence, or decorated with rhetorical graces, were remarkable for judgment and perspicuity. Though occasionally too colloquial and redundant, they were delivered with such candour and simplicity, as to convince his

---

* Lord Orford's Posthumous Memoires, vol. i. p. 322.   By this expression of lord Orford, the reader will be reminded of a curious coincidence in the concluding lines of the eulogium inscribed on the base of Mr. Pitt's statue, by his friend and pupil, the Right Honourable George Canning ; " Dispensing, for more than twenty years, the favours of the Crown, he lived without ostentation, and he died poor."

hearers that they directly conveyed the real sentiments of his heart; and were rendered still more effective, by the general conviction which prevailed of his honesty, economy, and patriotism.

By his well known attachment to true liberty, and the respect he ever preserved for the principles of the constitution, he dispelled all suspicions of the slightest intention to extend the royal prerogative beyond its due bounds, or in the least degree to incroach upon the rights of the people. He may indeed be classed among those sound patriots, whom Mr. Burke distinguishes by the name of the Old Whigs, who were equally free from faction on the one hand, and servility on the other.

In the development of his financial arrangements, he is said to have proved himself a worthy pupil of Sir Robert Walpole; and, in many instances, is admitted to have been scarcely inferior to his able master. As a minister, however, he was certainly deficient in a knowledge of the general system of European policy. Indeed, he seems to have limited his cares and ambition to his own peculiar province, the finances and domestic economy of the country; and when he did venture to interfere with the management of foreign affairs, it was rather from necessity than inclination. From this principle, he felt all the sensibility of a financier, with regard to the state of public credit; and gave cause for the complaints of his colleagues, that he sometimes manifested too much despondency and alarm in the House of Commons.* Sometimes, also, like Sir Robert Walpole, he was carried by his love of peace to too great an extent of concession. As the head of the financial department, he was a frugal steward of the public money; and, having experienced the difficulties and embarrassments attending protracted and unsuccessful hostilities, he was led to consider even a doubtful peace as preferable to the most successful war; and to think no sacrifice too great for the preservation of national tranquillity.

To the agriculture, manufactures, and commerce, of the country, he was vigilantly attentive; and not only rose superior to the narrow principles of preceding times, but suggested or promoted a greater number of useful and practical regulations, than any other individual, in a similar period of time, since the Revolution.

The great feature of his administration, is the reduction of the interest

---

* Lord Hardwicke's Parliamentary Journal.

on the national debt, and the consolidation of the public funds. This important operation was not only accomplished with peculiar prudence, but with equal justice towards the public and the fundholder ; and no better proof can be adduced of its merits and effects, than the ready acquiescence with which it was attended, and the general satisfaction since expressed in its favour.

In his private life, Mr. Pelham was equally moral and regular. He had, as lord Chesterfield observes, many domestic virtues, and no vices. He was a tender husband, an indulgent father, and a kind master ;* and though peculiarly liberal in his religious opinions, he was a zealous member of the church of England.

It may not perhaps be improper to notice in this place, a singular felicity which attended Mr. Pelham during his whole administration. While all other ministers have been exposed to the censures of party writers, and the lampoons of satirical poets, he escaped the shafts of ridicule, and the small artillery of party warfare. His genius was not of that sublime character which might call forth enthusiastic eulogies ; but his tried integrity, and the purity of his private life, his fondness for retirement, and his attachment to his family, obtained a more affectionate, though less splendid homage. He was fond of stealing away, as often as possible, from the fatigues of office, to solace himself in the bosom of his family, in his favourite seat at Esher, near Claremont, the mansion of the duke of Newcastle ; and his love of this retreat, which he embellished under the direction of Kent, our first landscape gardener, is pleasingly mentioned by the two principal poets of the age.

Pope, in his epilogue to his Imitations of the Satires of Horace, observes,

> Pleas'd let me own, in Esher's peaceful grove,
> Where Kent and nature vie for Pelham's love,
> The scene, the master, opening to my view,
> I sit and dream, I see my Craggs anew.

---

* A traditional anecdote, preserved in the family, and communicated by the present duke of Newcastle, will afford a pleasing instance of the easy and kind condescension with which Mr. Pelham behaved to his domestics. He had sent for his coachman to give him some orders ; whilst he was speaking, the man suddenly drew out his watch, and glancing a look at it, abruptly broke off the conversation, by exclaiming, " Sir, it is my time, and I must go and drive *my* children in the carriage." " Richard," said Mr. Pelham, " the *time* may be yours, the carriage may be yours, and so may the horses and other things ; but, my good Richard, do let the children be my own."

Where in the sweetest solitude embrac'd,
By the soft windings of the silent Mole,
From courts and senates, Pelham finds repose:
Inchanting vale! beyond whate'er the muse
Has of Achaia, or Hesperia sung!
On which the power of cultivation lies,
And joys to see the wonders of his toil.

The decease of a minister, so beloved and respected, produced a deep sensation of regret, and the concluding stanza, in Garrick's celebrated Ode on his death, was frequently quoted with feeling and approbation. Alluding to the publication of Bolingbroke's works by Mallet, which appeared on the day of Mr. Pelham's decease, he thus strikingly contrasts the characters and principles of the two ministers:

The same sad morn to church and state,
So for our sins 'twas fixed by fate,
A double stroke was given:
Black as the whirlwinds of the North,
St. John's fell genius issued forth,
And Pelham's fled to heaven.

Mr. Pelham espoused, in October 1726, the lady Katharine, eldest sister of John Manners, third duke of Rutland; and, on his marriage, his brother, the duke of Newcastle, generously assigned to him half the property which he inherited from his father. By this lady he had two sons and six daughters. Thomas, his first son, was born in 1729, and Henry, the second, in 1736, but he had the misfortune to lose them both, in the same week of November, 1739. Their disease was an ulcerated sore throat, the nature of which was at that time imperfectly understood, and which created such a sensation, that it was for a time termed the Pelham fever. Lady Katharine, their mother, caught the disorder, by her anxious attention to her children; and was saved by Dr. Wilmot, who resorted to the then novel expedient of lancing her throat.* Of his six daughters, only four survived. Katharine, the eldest, espoused his nephew, Henry, ninth earl of Lincoln,

---

* Nichols's Literary Anecdotes, vol. iv. p. 738. On the reappearance of the disease in 1748, Dr. Fothergill distinguished himself by a pamphlet on the subject.

afterwards duke of Newcastle, on whom, as we have before observed, the king conferred the valuable post of auditor of the Exchequer. This beautiful, amiable, and accomplished lady, died in 1760, in the 33rd year of her age. Frances died unmarried in 1805. Grace espoused, in 1752, Lewis Watson, esq., who was created baron Sondes, of Lees Court, Kent, May 20, 1760, and for whom, a few days before his death, Mr. Pelham had the satisfaction of obtaining the place of auditor of the Imprest and Foreign Accounts. Mary, the fourth daughter, died unmarried.

As Mr. Pelham left no male issue, and the duke of Newcastle himself had no son to inherit his possessions and honours, the latter obtained, by a new patent, the ducal title of Newcastle-under-Line, comprising a reversion in favour of his nephew, the earl of Lincoln.

The name and honours of Pelham are continued in this line; for the male issue of the earl of Lincoln consisted of four sons. George, the eldest, died unmarried. Henry Francis Pelham Clinton, the second son, left by lady Frances Seymour Conway, daughter of the earl of Hertford, an only daughter, Katharine, who espoused lord viscount Folkestone, son of the earl of Radnor, and died in 1804, leaving one daughter, Katharine. Thomas Pelham Clinton, the third surviving son, succeeded his father, as duke of Newcastle, in 1794, and dying in 1804, left by his wife, lady Anna Maria Stanhope, daughter of William, second earl of Harrington, Henry Pelham Clinton, the present duke of Newcastle, in whom flows the united blood of the noble families of Pelham and Clinton. The fourth son was John Pelham Clinton, who died in 1781, unmarried, at Lisbon.

The loss of no minister was ever more deeply felt; for Mr. Pelham may be said to have formed the cement of a heterogeneous administration, composed of discordant parties; and by his preponderating influence, to have repressed those ambitious and active spirits, who under him were content to fill secondary stations. The calm which generally marked the period of his administration, is strongly contrasted with the trouble and confusion by which it was followed. On the day of his death, the House of Commons met, and after dispatching the pending business, adjourned to the 12th of March, in order to afford sufficient time for the ministerial arrangements, rendered necessary by that fatal event.

The duke of Newcastle was deeply affected. The following letter to his particular friend, lord Albemarle, will evince his Grace's affection and regard for the memory of his brother.

" Newcastle House, March 28th, 1754.

" I have the greatest loss that man can have; and now have no view, but to endeavour to pursue his measures, serve his friends, and particularly to do every thing that can best comfort his poor family.

" The king's charity, goodness, and confidence are not to be expressed; and I have no comfort so great, as that of following my dearest brother's example to the best of my power; to do the king the best service, and give him the greatest satisfaction. It is for that reason, that his Majesty has commanded me to go to the head of the Treasury, as thinking (and in that the king shall not be deceived), that nobody could so punctually observe all that has been intended, as myself. I shall endeavour to have the same friends, by doing my best to deserve it." ·

Having relinquished the seals of Secretary of State, to accept the management of the Treasury, a post which intitled him who held it to the denomination of prime minister; the duke of Newcastle proceeded to select his immediate colleagues, and devise the means of insuring their attachment. His choice for a Chancellor of the Exchequer was immediately directed to Mr. Legge, from a conviction, that in him he should find a dependent, neither ambitious in himself, nor likely by influence or abilities, to aspire to a higher share of power.

Mr. Legge, however, being ill calculated to act as leader in the House of Commons, no other resource remained, than to consign the seals of Secretary of State to a member of that body, who by his abilities or influence, might manage the House, under his Grace's direction. Three persons were more particularly adapted for this post, by their oratorical talents, and personal qualifications : Mr. Pitt, Mr. Fox, and Mr. Murray, the Solicitor-general.

The duke of Newcastle was well aware that the royal dislike against Mr. Pitt had not wholly subsided; and even if this objection had not existed, he was fearful that his independent and commanding spirit would not long submit to control. Mr. Murray, besides the prejudices entertained against him, as a native of Scotland, had been exposed to obloquy, during the feuds in the household of the Prince of Wales,* which, however unjust, yet rendered his

See Chap. xxviii. p. 2.

principles suspected, and drew on him the jealousy of the Whigs. In fact, he himself was too sensible of the unpleasant situation in which he was placed, to covet a post exposed to so much additional responsibility; and therefore he took the earliest opportunity to announce his resolution of adhering to the profession of the law.

Mr. Fox was indicated by the public voice, as the person best calculated to fill so important a situation; and his pretensions were strongly supported by a powerful body of friends, not excepting even the leaders of opposition. He himself also regarded it as due to his services; and the protection of the Duke of Cumberland operated to his advantage with the king. But the affronts he had offered to the Chancellor, during the debate on the Marriage act, his doubtful fidelity to the interest of the duke of Newcastle, and his attachment to the Duke of Cumberland, were objections of the most weighty kind. As, however, he could not be passed over, the duke of Newcastle adopted the resolution of offering him the seals, under such restrictions, as should either render him wholly dependent, or induce him voluntarily to withdraw his pretensions.

An overture was accordingly made to him, through lord Hartington, offering the seals, with the management of the House of Commons; and when he had announced his acquiescence, a reconciliation was effected, in a personal interview, between him and the Chancellor. The arrangement was considered as complete; for on the 12th of March, the sanction of the king was obtained, and the new appointments were announced in a circular letter. But the next morning, when Mr. Fox waited on the duke of New-castle for more specific explanation, he found to his disappointment, that he was not to be acquainted with the disposal of the secret service money, to share the patronage, or even have a voice in the arrangements for the approaching elections. The interview was therefore cool and unsatisfactory; and as Mr. Fox was unwilling to assume the character of leader of the House of Commons, without the powers which he considered necessary to be attached to it, he took the resolution of declining the seals, and communicated his intention on the 14th, in a letter to the duke of Newcastle, in which he indirectly charged him with duplicity, and a breach of promise.*

If the duke of Newcastle was secretly desirous of avoiding an engage-

---

* This letter is printed in the Memoires of lord Orford, vol. i. p. 334.

ment with Mr. Fox, he thus gained his object, in a manner which was likely to raise a prejudice against him, in the mind of the king.

The Duke hoped, at the same time, to break the phalanx with which Mr. Pitt was united, by raising Sir George Lyttelton to the post of Cofferer of the Household, and Mr. George Grenville to that of Treasurer of the Navy, which was vacated by the advancement of Mr. Legge. But he was mistaken in his calculations. Mr. Pitt was highly offended, because he was not offered a post which he disdained to solicit. At the same time Mr. Fox considered himself as insulted and betrayed. These two rival orators, therefore, united against the administration of the duke of Newcastle, and found a formidable support in the new court of Leicester House. Nor was the choice which his Grace finally made, likely to obviate the effects of this powerful coalition; for Sir Thomas Robinson, to whom the seals were at last confided, though an able diplomatist, and intimately versed in the details of office, and the system of foreign policy, was an indifferent and confused debater; and from his long residence abroad, ill fitted for a commanding post in the House of Commons.

Such an arrangement was therefore evidently but temporary, and ill adapted to obviate the dangers and difficulties of an approaching war. The successive revolutions which rapidly occurred in the administration, furnish ample proof of the loss which the country sustained in the death of Mr. Pelham; and the breach it occasioned in that party, of which his brother was now considered as the head.

In consequence of the judicious arrangements made by Mr. Pelham before his death, the public business, during the short remainder of this session, met with no obstruction. We shall therefore merely observe, that the king dismissed the parliament on the 6th of April, preparatory to a dissolution, with a speech, the conclusion of which may be considered, as comprising a brief eulogy of the administration of the deceased statesman.

"The time draws near, when the present parliament must determine by law, and it is my intention very speedily to call a new one; but it would be unjust to this, not to give It a public testimony of my approbation. The many eminent proofs which you have given, of your duty and affection to my person and government, of your zeal for this excellent constitution, and for the security of the present establishment, can never be forgotten by me. By your vigorous assistance, under the protection of the Divine Providence, I was enabled to put an end to an expensive, though necessary war, by an honourable peace, which you have greatly contributed to preserve, by readily and uniformly supporting my measures. You have gone farther; and, whilst the difficulties arising from the war were scarcely over, seized the first opportunity to perfect one of the greatest works of peace, by concurring in the most proper means for a gradual decrease of the national debt; and, at the same time, raising the public credit. You have also, by several new laws, laid a foundation to strengthen and advance the trade and commerce of my kingdoms. Such a series of wise and steady conduct, cannot fail to recommend you to the good will and esteem of your fellow subjects, as well as mine. For my own part, I securely rely upon the loyalty and good affection of my people, and have no other aim but their lasting happiness."

ILLUSTRATIVE CORRESPONDENCE.

CORRESPONDENCE.

MR. PELHAM TO THE DUKE OF NEWCASTLE.

Approves the conduct of Du Theil, and thinks that France means peace—Is not satisfied with the Court of Vienna.

Sept. 13*th*-24*th*, 1748. * * * * *—" THE letters which came from Aix, yesterday, look well. I own I like Du Theil's manner of speaking and acting. He seems to me to know more of the matter than all of them put together ; and, as I am satisfied the court of France at present mean peace, the more sense a man has, and the more knowledge of business, the more likely he is to bring it to perfection. I wish I could see that good disposition in the court of Vienna, you speak of. I can assure you when it comes it will rejoice me exceedingly. In these doubtful circumstances, how can his Majesty's servants here, determine, either upon the time of meeting, or measures to be opened to the parliament, when they do meet. We must, therefore, wish for the king's return, some time before the day fixed for the meeting of parliament. How can any one form a speech, without receiving his Majesty's particular commands, and talking thoroughly with you ? I can assure you, I do not wish to hurry you over, before the time that shall be thought agreeable ; nothing but necessity will drive us here, to the disagreeable office of calling you before your time ; but you must be sensible affairs are now upon their crisis, and it is too material an æra, for people to act upon uncertainties. I doubt not but this and much more has occurred to you. When I can see the lord Chancellor, I shall desire him to think seriously upon this, and write to you his sentiments."

THE DUKE OF NEWCASTLE TO MR. PELHAM.

The King will be justified in signing without Austria, should the Empress continue obstinate— Not satisfied with the conduct of lord Sandwich and count Bentinck.—P. S. Conversation with the King, about his return to England.

"DEAR BROTHER, *Göhrde, September* 19*th*-30*th*, 1748.

" Though I am just setting out for Hanover, I could not avoid most sincerely congratulating you upon the good prospect of our affairs at Aix. I think there is great probability, that the peace will now be soon made, with the concurrence of all parties : at least, I think the peace certain, in all events ; for, should the court of Vienna be so obstinate, as to stand out now, after all the confidence and regard that has been shewed them, and the attention that has been used in forming this project, so as to make it palatable to them, the king would not only be justified, before God and man, in signing without them, but, I believe, nobody could be against it. I think that cannot happen; for Kaunitz is too cautious a man to have declared he thought his court would accept these conditions, if he had not had good reason for it. I know the joy this will give you, for the sake of the public; and, believe me, dear brother, I am fully persuaded you will have as much, on my private account. I am sure I have no greater satisfaction, than in thinking, that public affairs will now go to your mind; and that we, in all events, can, I think, no longer differ about them. I will say nothing of myself, but that I have happened to judge right.

"I must send you a copy of Sir Thomas Robinson's private letter to me; I think those facts cannot be contradicted. You will not wonder, that I think he has had as much merit in this transaction, as man can have. He has judged right of Du Theil; I pray God he may do the same, as to the court of Vienna. I hope you will approve my letter to the plenipoes, and to Keith. I am not much pleased with the conduct of my friends Sandwich and Bentinck.

"I shall settle every thing for the poor duchess of Newcastle's journey. She is, I thank God, tolerably well. As I can have no business here, till answers come to the letters, that go away this day, I have got the king's leave to stay at Hanover till Monday next. I beg my compliments to my lady Katherine, lord Lincoln, my nieces, &c. and am," &c.

"P.S.—I spoke yesterday to the king again, about his return to England. All I could get was, that he proposed to be in England about the 10th or 12th of November; why might not he keep his birth-day here, and again in England; as he used to do? I urged the necessity of his being in England, some time before the meeting of the parliament, which he agreed might be the end of November. He said a great many things upon that occasion, which I need not repeat; but, at last, concluded with saying, his presence was not necessary; that I might go a month before him; stay one week at the Hague, and then go over to England, and settle things with you for the parliament. I told him that was impossible; that I could not leave him alone; and besides, that my presence would be of no consequence whatever. He said, I should come from him. I persisted in my opinion, and so it ended. I beg to know, immediately, your thoughts upon this whole affair; and particularly, whether you think it will be of any use for me to come before the king. His Majesty said, Stone might stay with him. I doubt there is *now* no chance for his returning before his birth-day. Ever yours," &c.

MR. PELHAM TO THE DUKE OF NEWCASTLE.

Wishes the Treaty could be signed, that he might proceed with his plans of reduction.

"DEAR BROTHER,   *September 20th-Oct. 1st.* 1748.*

"I have just received your kind letter of the 12th-23rd, and am glad to find by it, that you continue in good health, which, by care and pretty severe discipline, I

* Pelham Papers.

am pretty well satisfied I shall do myself. The mail came in this afternoon. I have not seen the letters, nor heard much of them; but I understand Du Theil's project is come; I heartily wish it may prove a good one. I have some hopes of it, as I am told Kaunitz likes it, and talks of signing. If so, for God's sake do not let us delay: every day is material, and, I think, experience shews us, we are not likely to better our terms by standing out.

"I have written to the lord Chancellor, eventually, to beg he would come up as soon as he can; for every hour is now of consequence. I think we ought, and I hope we shall, give our opinions freely, and speedily; for I look upon this as the crisis of the whole. You know my sentiments in general; I will not, therefore, recapitulate them now. When I have seen the project, it will be time enough to speak. You said, in your former letter, that you longed to hear from me, after I had seen the Duke. I think I have not failed writing one post, and have told you, as near as I could, the result of all our conferences. I hope his Royal Highness is satisfied I am right: I know he wishes it could have been otherwise; but indeed I am right, for his sake, as much as the public's.

"I wish we could get this Treaty signed soon, that we might proceed to our reduction. A month gained, of this year, is material for the next; and, I can tell you, not a little so for your residence abroad. How could we go upon a plan of expense, and you not here?

"I most heartily wish all may end well. My spirits rise and fall, as the pacific plan gains, or loses ground. I think we are now brought to such a point, that we must determine; and whatever that determination is, it is better than to remain in the uncertain state we have been in of late. The post stays for me, and I have not much more to say to you at present; though, probably, my next letter may be of greater moment."

THE DUKE OF NEWCASTLE TO MR. PELHAM.

Approves the conduct of Du Theil—Thinks the French sincere, and that Austria will ultimately accede.

"DEAR BROTHER,   *Hanover, September 21st-Oct. 2nd,* 1748.

"I doubt that, to save appearances, it will be necessary for me to go to the Hague, though I shall do no good there; things are so altered there since my last visit. That poor government, that cannot govern one great town of their own, expects to govern us. For Mr. Bentinck, in his letter to his brother, after this reasonable proposal of Du Theil's had been delivered to us, in very bad humour, says, he hopes our plenipotentiaries will receive orders to act agreeably to the instructions he had received, or rather given himself, which instructions the Greffier had acquainted me with; though the Greffier never mentioned, or perhaps knew of the project of Du Theil, which must be the rule for us to go by, and must be, in the main, supported by us. I know you will say, this weak government in Holland does not begin now to think of governing us. That may be; but then they followed, what I own I thought right; but now it is to me evident, they are purely guided by passion and prejudice. However, it will signify little, for we shall all agree, I think, upon what is to be done.

"I entirely agree with you, with regard to Du Theil, both as to the cause, and now as to the success of his mission. I have said it fully, in a letter to my lord Chancellor; and, if I have not done it to you, it was only because I would avoid entering upon that disagreeable subject, of the late behaviour of my lord Sandwich. I always said to Stone, that the French ministers saw the loose unintelligible manner that St. Severin and my lord Sandwich were carrying things on in; every day over-turning what the former had produced; declaration after declaration; to day the provisional possession would meet with little or no difficulty; the day after, no consideration would make France agree to it; and yet going on in the same way, as if that was a trifle, and made no variation in the state of things. In these circum-stances, the court of France, determined to have peace, sent Du Theil to make it in a reasonable, open, clear way; and he has succeeded. The same considerations induced the king to send Sir Thomas Robinson; and that has equally succeeded, and both combine to shew how right it was, to put things out of the method they were in, when St. Severin went to Compiègne. What a difference is there to an English ear, to treat with a French minister, Du Theil, whose whole discourse tends to reconcile our difficulties with our own allies, to make the peace general, as that is the only way to make it lasting, and with St. Severin, whose whole scheme was built upon separate negotiation and separate signatures, force upon our allies, and retaining for a time, at least, Flanders to themselves! And yet poor Sandwich still says, St. Severin is the man; and adheres to his old opinion!

"Kaunitz has told you he thinks his court will accede. Wasner seems positive of it; but what weighs most with me in that question is, whether they accede or not, though I am firmly persuaded they soon will, we have left them without excuse, by our confidential communications, and friendly advice, and early notice. We have got several alterations in the project, to make it to their taste. The article about charges, benefices, and pensions, entirely omitted: the annulling of their reservations, protestations, &c. is omitted also, which will flatter Bartenstein's vanity, and some other less material points; and if we should be obliged (which I hope we shall not) to sign, at first, without them, we shall not sign in a passion. We shall not sign in a hostile manner; but with expectation, and almost a moral certainty, that the court of Vienna will immediately accede, which, in the former case, I am persuaded they would almost have run any risk rather than do. I have a letter from my friend the duke of Bedford, upon his absence this week. He seems to think, he has been a most constant and diligent attender. You know that best."

MR. PELHAM TO THE DUKE OF NEWCASTLE.

The Lords Justices find Du Theil's project better than they could expect—Remarks on the convention between Austria and France, for withdrawing part of their respective forces—Hopes peace will not be delayed—Anxious for reductions, as the country is exhausted.

"DEAR BROTHER, "*Sept.* 23rd-*Oct.* 4th, 1748.*

"Last night we met at Powis House, where were present lord President, lord Privy Seal, lord Chamberlain, the duke of Bedford, lord Chancellor, and myself. We carefully read over all the letters which came by the last mail; and, as well as we could, in so short a time as four hours, went through Du Theil's *Contre-Projét*, article by article; and, upon the whole, we found it, in our opinions, much better than we expected. The duke of Bedford drew up a letter, which he read to us, and altered, and added what was thought necessary. You will therefore have from his Grace, so particular an account of what was the opinion of the Lords upon this plan, that I shall not trouble you with a repetition, or a minute detail of the several observations that may be made upon it. I shall content myself with repeating what our friend, Sir Thomas Robinson says, in a private letter to me, 'that this gives us more certain hopes of the approaching peace, than we have hitherto had.' He says also, 'that the Austrians have, with their usual skill, by agreeing to withdraw their troops, put us under a justifiable necessity of closing at once with France.' I own, my thoughts go farther than that, being satisfied, that the whole of the French project that relates to the cessions in Italy, has been carried on, and concerted with Kaunitz.

"I shall make no observation upon the indecency, to say no worse, of the Austrian minister, in making and signing a treaty, for withdrawing those very troops from the Low Countries, for which we have, not only this year, but almost every year during the war, paid the greatest share of their expense, without even consulting, or asking the opinion of the king's plenipotentiaries then upon the spot. For myself, I am glad of it. It tends to bring about the end I have always thought absolutely necessary; and it will naturally lead the court of Vienna to sign with us, or immediately accede, which is in effect the same thing.

"The article I dislike the most, is that which stipulates the exchange of the ratifications, with all the parties interested, before the restitutions are to be made. Does not this put it in the power of the king of Sardinia to suspend the whole for a time? And, as I think the least delay in the execution, of the greatest consequence, I could have wished, that restitution and cession might have been made by those powers, and to those powers, who should respectively exchange the ratifications in the times limited. I conclude some expedient for this will be chalked out; and, as the French ministers mentioned a secret article for that purpose, our plenipotentiaries may take that handle to accommodate this affair.

"The Assiento is renewed for four years only. We formerly agreed to that; and I

* Pelham Papers.

hope the omission of the treaty, called Doddington's Treaty, will not be of any ill consequence. For, as every thing is left open, with regard to Spain and us, excepting the renewal of antient treaties, and that we do make peace, I presume you will think of sending Mr. Keene to Madrid soon, to settle and adjust many points with that court, which have not been touched upon, either in the preliminaries or Definitive Treaty.

"I now come, dear brother, to the point, which is the particular reason of my troubling you so much by this messenger. I must recommend to you with earnestness, and so do all the Lords that met last night, that you will expedite your orders to the plenipotentiaries for signing, as much as you can, and that you will not hamper them with conditions or restrictions, which may prevent the speedy conclusion of this work. I have made the best inquiry I can, amongst all the men of business in the city, and I can assure you, they are all of opinion, that peace is absolutely necessary. They think also, that the terms of the preliminaries are so advantageous for us, considering our exhausted state, that they can scarce believe France will come into them. You see now, France has herself proposed a project nearer to them than any we have yet seen; and all the material alterations, that are made from our own project, tend to the accommodating the queen of Hungary, our first and principal ally. Credit was sinking, and the stocks falling, upon hearing nothing from Aix, that looked like a finishing; but, as several private letters by the last mail, brought over an account that a project was formed, which all the parties had sent to their respective courts, for approbation, a spirit returned immediately, and the stocks rose two per cent, which is a great deal, at this time of day, when circulation is so cramped.

"I hope, also, that his Majesty will give orders for the immediate reduction of the troops, so soon as the treaty is signed, or, at farthest, when ratified. I think the marines may be reduced immediately. I presume, his Majesty will also order his own troops back, and give the regular notice to the other subsidiary troops, that no time may be lost, in getting rid of that burthen also. If these things are done in time, I am of opinion, we can carry on the public service, without a Money Bill, before Christmas; and then the parliament need not meet to do business, till after the holidays, which will undoubtedly be much more convenient, if it can be made practicable. His Majesty continuing abroad till some time in November, will then be of no moment, with regard to the interior of the government here. Our only concern then will be, that we ·are so long deprived of the happiness of his Majesty residing amongst us; and our fears, from the season of the year, that his journey and passage may be difficult and dangerous.

"But if these things are not finished soon, and the measures taken, which I have presumed to mention, it will be impossible for us to supply the demands of armies, subsidies, and fleets, without meeting the parliament so early in November, as will enable us to pass a Money Bill before Christmas. You will but awkwardly lay those demands before parliament, when you can neither say that you have, or you have not concluded. And I must, with all duty and submission lay before you, for his Majesty's information, the utter impossibility there will be for the king's servants here, to prepare a speech, and form the plan of the next session, without either personally receiving his Majesty's commands, or talking upon them with you, who must necessarily be acquainted with many circumstances, material for consideration, which we here are totally ignorant of.

" I shall send to Mr. Stone the warrant for payment of another fifty thousand pounds, for the Hanover troops, as usual. I will also send him a paper, which will explain the mistake made by Mons. Reiche, for I am very certain the account was made up with baron Steinberg, according to what was demanded in parliament.

" I have now taken a liberty beyond what I thought I should, to lay before you the whole of my thoughts, relative to his Majesty's affairs under my particular inspection. His Majesty and you know best, whether what I propose is practicable. If it is, I am sure you will follow it, because you must see the ease and convenience that attends all parties, in my project. But if you judge it otherwise, I will do the best I can ; but I hope you will not expect I should equally answer for success, as if my own idea could be followed.

" Sir Thomas Robinson writes word, that his appointments and plate are to be on the same foot as lord Sandwich's. I own I think they should, but the orders must come from you, both as to the warrant for the privy seal, at £.100 per week, and the directions to the lord Chamberlain for the plate. I am glad to hear the duchess of Newcastle is better. My family are all well, and much yours, but none more sincerely and affectionately so, than, dear Brother, &c. &c."

THE LORD CHANCELLOR TO THE DUKE OF NEWCASTLE.

Motives which induce the Lords Justices to admit the project of Du Theil—Remarks on the article in the treaty, concerning the hostages—The exorbitant demands of the king of Sardinia should not be complied with.

" MY DEAR LORD,   " *Powis House, Sept. 23rd-Oct 4th,* 1748.

" As I have not received the honour of one line from your Grace, since your letter of Aug. 21st-Sept. 1st, I fear you are still angry with me. But as I know the fidelity and attachment of my heart to your interest and service, I will venture to trouble you in this important crisis of affairs. The new French project of a definitive treaty, together with the dispatches from Aix, occasioned a meeting at my house, last night, of such of the Lords who are usually consulted on secret affairs, as are in town. They were my lord President, lord Privy-Seal, the dukes of Grafton and Bedford, Mr. Pelham, and myself. The dukes of Richmond and Devonshire were both in the country. I found that, for the sake of despatch, the duke of Bedford had, as my lord Harrington used to do, brought a draught of his letter, which underwent some alterations and additions, as your Grace will receive it by this messenger. Your Grace having seemed so desirous to receive early the sentiments of the king's servants here, the Lords thought his Majesty would have the goodness to excuse their forwardness, in transmitting their first thoughts on these papers, before they had received his Majesty's commands upon them. If they have erred, it has proceeded from their zeal for his service, and an opinion, that the saving so much time in this conjuncture, would be agreeable to his Majesty. I must acquaint your Grace, though it will sufficiently appear by the letter itself, that there was shewn the greatest ardour to finish the work of peace, and nobody more eager for it than your brother Secretary. Indeed, I believe the delay of that work, and the manifest danger that will arise, if it miscarries, have made that disposition very general in the country. This, you may be sure, inclined the Lords to admit the present project, as far as can possibly be done with any safety. In support of this opinion, they laid their weight on the following considerations :—

I. The strong representations made by both our plenipotentiaries, that France has delivered this as her ultimatum, and that it is come to the point, that we must either conclude or break off.

" II. The impracticability of renewing the war, and the imminent danger, nay, almost ruin, that may probably attend the breaking off the negotiation.

" III. The evident proofs that the empress queen has, in effect, made her peace with France. And, I own, I think this does plainly appear, by her convention about withdrawing her troops, made without the privity of our plenipotentiaries, notwithstanding she receives our subsidies for them, and from the turn of the whole project, in favour of the court of Vienna, though some things are expressed less favourably, not only to the king of Sardinia, but also to Great Britain.

" IV. That, as France has entirely regained its influence over Spain, and is entered into this extraordinary connection with the court of Vienna, things will probably grow every day rather worse than better.

" As to the disposition and state of the court of Vienna, your Grace must know more, and consequently judge much better of it, than we can. But it seems to me, that they have made this convention with France, to inforce more strongly upon us the necessity of agreeing to this project. They will pretend to justify it, by the example of our convention with the Russians, which, however, differs widely in the circumstances and reason of it ; and, perhaps they will allege the non-payment of the last £.100,000. But I take the true ground to be, to oblige us to swallow the advantages, they think they have gained over the court of Turin ; for now we shall have a very small army in the Netherlands ; and their convention is so loose, that they have not stipulated for any reduction ; and, if France retires her troops just within her own frontier, she is under no farther obligation. I will make no observations on this conduct of an ally, who owes so much to the king and to this nation.

" I am not able particularly to observe upon the variations of this draught from St. Severin's first project, and the last which was delivered by our plenipotentiaries ; but I have sent to the office for them, and if anything material occurs, will trouble your Grace with it by Tuesday's post.

" It is impossible, in my opinion, to agree to the description of hostages, to be two peers of Great Britain. I doubt it would not be legal to insert such a clause in a formal treaty to be ratified. But, however that may be, your Grace will immediately suggest to yourself, what a flame it would raise in the House of Lords, that his Majesty should bind himself, by a solemn act, to send two peers, an order of men vested with greater privileges than any other subjects, to be, possibly, they will say, in the event, prisoners for life. The trying at some expedient, is hinted in general, by the duke of Bedford's letter; but if that will not do, might not this be a proper case, in which the expedient of a letter, signed by the plenipotentiaries, might be made use of, especially if the letter about Dunkirk is out of the question. But if peers should in any event be sent, here not specified, I should think it would be most advisable to send Scotch peers, not members of the House of Lords; because, as to such as are part of that body, a cavil may be raised, that the House has an interest in their members, and a right to their attendance. I throw out this for your Grace's consideration only; but no stone should be left unturned by our plenipotentiaries, to induce France to accept of the general words only.*

" We hope the words relating to the king's possessions in Germany are sufficient. It did not occur to us, that any part of his Majesty's dominions on that side, are out of what is properly called Germany; but if there are any such, the words should be extended.

" It is odd that Du Theil should leave out the express renewal of the guaranty for his Majesty's dominions and possessions, as king of Great Britain; but as the Quadruple alliance is expressly renewed and confirmed, in all its tenour, as if inserted word for word, that comprises the substance.

" The great struggle and difficulty will probably now be made by the king of Sardinia. I am sorry M. Ossorio was not arrived at Aix, for I think Chavannes has hurt his master's affairs, as well as ours, by his too great refinement and minuteness. However, I think the article, as it stands, gives that prince sufficient security. Count Kaunitz's draught would not have done it; because it recited and referred to the empress queen's previous declaration, and her ratification of the Preliminaries. But this, containing a new stipulation posterior to the Preliminaries, and to the empress queen's ratification of them, and entirely independent of it, will invalidate her former protestations, as effectually, in sense and substance, as if express words were inserted for invalidating them. This seems to be the strength of the argument, to be urged to the Sardinian ministers.

" Your Grace sees the extent of the whole much better than I can. I know you are convinced of the necessity of peace. That necessity is grown stronger than ever, and I suppose we may now have the empress queen along with us. She is the principal ally; and I fear the nation will not bear the losing of it, for the sake of niceties regarding his Sardinian Majesty, who, of all the allies, is the only gainer by the war, provided the treaty be admissible in other parts."

* In conformity with this advice, the hostages were to be of rank, but not peers. See Art. IX. of the treaty.

THE LORD CHANCELLOR TO THE DUKE OF NEWCASTLE.

Approves in general the project of Du Theil—The Duke of Cumberland is much mortified
at the Convention between Austria and France.

Powis House, Sept. 26th, 1748.

After acknowledging letter of the 17th-28th, with the accompanying packet, he continues :—"Since I wrote, I have, as well as I could by myself, compared Du Theil's
projét and *contre-projét*, with St. Severin's first *projét*, and upon that comparison, I like
it better than I did at the first sight. I do not mean by this, that it is all I wish for ;
far from it ; but it seems to be the performance of a man who has a mind to make
peace ; and, considering our success, our remaining strength, and our allies ! it is
better than I expected from France. May not the renewal and confirmation of the
Triple alliance greatly help the article about Dunkirk ? for that expressly recites and
confirms the convention of 1716. But pray, my lord, examine whether there is not
an omission of some words, in the king of Sardinia's act of cession, as it stands recited
in this *contre-projét ;* for, if my memory serves me right, the case of Don Philip, or
his descendants, coming to the crown of the two Sicilies, by the death of Don Carlos,
without issue, is not stated in the clause of reversion, according to the copy transmitted hither. Possibly I may be mistaken.

" I find his Royal Highness, the Duke, is much hurt with the convention between
the empress queen and France ; and indeed he has reason. To use, in this strange
manner, a prince who has been so firmly, so generously, and so much upon principle
their friend, is abominable and unpardonable. As things now stand, if we do not
conclude, marêchal Saxe may pick up his Royal Highness and his diminutive army
in detail. I heartily wish they were on this side of the water."

THE DUKE OF NEWCASTLE TO MR. PELHAM.

Is disappointed that he has received complaints from his friends, instead of congratulations—
Difficulties about the king's return.

"DEAR BROTHER,   Göhrde, October 1-12th, 1748.

" It is now late, and the messenger must be going away, so that I shall not trouble
you with near so long a letter as I intended. I must own I never was so much
mortified in my life, as with the last letters from England. You will imagine, from
what I have lately wrote, that I expected congratulations and some compliments, upon
the late great success of our endeavours for a general peace. Instead of that, my lord
duke of Bedford sends, for the first time, a long office letter, descanting upon each
article of the project, mentioning the long delay of the negotiation (owing entirely to
his friend Sandwich), and concluding with a most kind and charitable reflection, that
all this proceeds from some private bargain and treaty, between the court of Vienna
and France. And this last notion was put into his head by my lord Chancellor ;
whose learned letter upon that point I shall answer the first moment I have leisure.
In the mean time, I must content myself with refuting those visionary notions, in
my several public dispatches.

" Dear Brother, this is hard. My fate is extremely so. Peace you all wanted, and I as much as any of you ; but such an one as I could justify. Who has got it you ? I am sorry to be forced to ask the question. I am more sorry to be forced to answer it, myself ; and the other method would have destroyed it. See whether every thing does not tally. If ever consequences followed premises, this event is the natural and single consequence of the measure persisted in here ; and the orders sent to Vienna and Aix conformably thereto. When I was sent abroad, I expected favour and partiality from my friends. I now only desire justice and examination. I really do not mean you ; I know why you blamed me. I cannot conceive why others did. Why did not they, why do not they, publicly, give and avow their opinion, and they will have a public answer.

" As I found by your letter of a former date, that some orders must be sent about the parliament, the king readily consented to the end of November ; but I am sorry to say, though I gave very little opposition, his Majesty was much more uneasy upon that subject, than ever I have seen him : and I much fear, had he not thought it necessary for the parliament to meet before Christmas, it would have been near that time before he would have stirred from hence. I yet do not know the day of his setting out. He was pleased to tell me, that he would not go till the middle of November, O. S. ; but, however, agreed to order the yachts for the 1st of November. He again proposed, and I am apprehensive will repeat it, my going to England some time before him. I see no use in it, and it may have an odd appearance. However, I hope I shall soon know your opinion upon it. I think you will approve all my letters that go by this messenger. Pray read and consider, whether there is argument in them or not. I send you one from the Duke, which I received this morning, and my answer, which I think you must like. Consider me in the light of a disappointed minister, not as to the success of his measures, but the interpretation of his friends. I again repeat I do not mean this, or at least very little part of it, to you."

" P. S.—I hope the duchess of Newcastle will set out on Monday or Tuesday."

THE LORD CHANCELLOR TO THE DUKE OF NEWCASTLE.

If Austria will not conclude, England must sign without her—Anticipates an agreement in opinion, between Mr. Pelham and his brother.

Wimpole, Oct. 4th, 1748.

* * * * " I observe that the convention, signed by count Kaunitz, about the 30,000 men, has given his Royal Highness the Duke much uneasiness, and I think with reason. I long to see the extent of that separate negotiation, and in what conse·quences it will open itself. However, after that transaction, I cannot suffer myself to doubt the court of Vienna's joining in a definitive treaty, either as an original con-tracting party, or by an immediate accession. If they should not do it, my opinion is now more clear than ever, that we must conclude without them ; and if we should not, I think it is plain the Dutch will. In case we should be laid under that unhappy necessity, then the time will come to determine what is to be done with the Hano-verian and Hessian troops.

" Never doubt, my dear Lord, of my most sincere and zealous endeavours, to keep you in good humour, by doing every thing in the compass of my poor abilities, for your honour and service. I dare be confident that your brother will do the same, provided a little indulgence and yielding are shewn on both sides. You know his burthen is the expense, and his great aim is to lighten that, as far as can possibly be done consistent with security."

MR. PELHAM TO THE DUKE OF NEWCASTLE.

Is anxious to begin the reductions—Takes it for granted that the queen of Hungary will accede immediately ; and then Flanders may be restored—Is sorry that the Duke of Cumberland wishes to keep his regiment of Dragoons.

Oct. 4th-15th, 1748.

After acknowledging the receipt of his letter of the 25th of September, he expresses his satisfaction at the appointment of Mr. Arundel to some official situation, and desires his brother to thank his Majesty for his kindness on this occasion. He then continues :—" I am very glad to hear they go on so well at Aix, and at Vienna. I have wrote to you so much on that head, by the three former posts, that I will not trouble you with a repetition now. You say, sure our reductions will now go on. You know my opinion on that head; and I promise you, the moment you give us authority, there shall be not an hour's delay in the execution ; but I suppose you know nothing of that kind can be done, but by orders directly signed by the king, or the lords justices, and I presume, they will not venture to do it, without particular orders from his Majesty.

" I should think, the marines and additional companies might be reduced imme-- diately ; that would be doing something, and the rest might follow, after the treaty is signed, or at farthest when it is ratified. For, I take it for granted, the queen of Hungary will accede immediately, and then, I hope, Flanders, and the Low Countries, will be restored. I am sorry to find, by your letter, that the Duke thinks of saving his own regiment of Dragoons. I had a good deal of discourse with his Royal Highness upon that subject, and I thought he was convinced ; I am sure, he acquiesced. It is, in my opinion, a wrong measure for the public, to keep up that regiment, but I am certain much wronger for himself. I took the liberty to tell the Duke so, and therefore, I am certain, he will not be offended, that I represent it as such to you. As to the other point, of breaking Briggs and saving Conway, that is nothing to the public. I do not know his Royal Highness's reasons, and therefore can say nothing to it. It is not usual in this country, and I believe not in others, to break older corps and keep up younger, unless for some military reproach. That will, therefore, principally affect the Duke, as Captain-general. It is worth his while to think of it, and I hope his Royal Highness will determine as shall be thought right by the military people, before he proposes it to the king."

*   *   *   *   *

THE DUKE OF NEWCASTLE TO MR. PELHAM.

Observations on the approaching signature of the Definitive Treaty—Justifies his own conduct, in the course of the negotiation, and complains that his friends in England undervalue his services. Difficulty of settling with the king the time of assembling the parliament.

"DEAR BROTHER,   *Hanover, Oct. 9th-20th,1748.*

"I have received the favour of your letters of the 27th and 30th of September, the first at Gifferne, the last at my return here on Thursday. I hope and believe you will receive, before you have this letter, an account of the signing the Definitive Treaty, and the accession of the court of Vienna; upon which near prospect, I most heartily congratulate you and my country. I feel the joy of an honest man upon it. I have the secret comfort of thinking that I have not only greatly, not to say almost singly, brought it about; but that if I had not resolutely, and in a manner that has been disapproved by you all, taken upon me to overrule my lord Sandwich, in the way he was going, things would, must, have been now in the greatest confusion; perhaps no treaty signed at all, or at best, one that would have had no effect, but to destroy the old alliance. This being my firm opinion, supported, I think, by reason before, and justified and proved by every event since, you may imagine, that it goes to my heart, to find by every letter from you and my lord Chancellor, not only a determined resolution to think otherwise, but doubt whether I would still clog this Treaty with difficulties; and a kind of silence, upon what is past; an unwillingness to assign the cause of our present good luck, I suppose; strained reasons suggested, of secret negotiations, connections, and concerts with France, which never existed, but in the minds of my friends in England; and, in short, a very different return from what I expected, and was vain enough to think I deserved.

"I could not forbear writing fully upon this subject, to my lord Chancellor. I suppose he will shew it to you. I thought I owed it to myself to do it, or perhaps, more justly, I was too much hurt to avoid it. But you shall hear no more of it, at least by letter. Sure the procuring the immediate accession of the court of Vienna, and the letting the other parties first declare the unreasonableness, and impossibility of insisting upon the demands of the king of Sardinia, is some justification of the late orders; and some excuse for not allowing my lord Sandwich to sign without Kaunitz, till the king knew the state of the case, and what orders it might be proper to give upon it. Though in all this, I differ extremely with you, I entirely agree in every thing you say, relating to the withdrawing the troops, and the immediate reductions, though I own the shewing resentment to the court of Vienna, for recalling their 30,000 men, is no part of my reason. You will have seen the orders sent to his Royal Highness the Duke upon it, and inclosed in my letter to the duke of Bedford, of 1st-12th Oct.; and I now send his Royal Highness's letter to me, and my answer. I must own, as you will see by my answer, that the Duke's letter extremely surprised and concerned me. I have never taken any notice of it to the king; and, as all the letters and orders for his Royal Highness were agreed by the king, and ready to be sent away, when I received the Duke's letter, I did not make any alteration in them, but wrote the private letter I now send you.   Decency, deference, and that consideration, which is due to his Royal Highness on all accounts, made it necessary to submit, in the manner it is done, these things to his Royal Highness's consideration: and I own, I had then, and have still, some little doubt about recalling *all* our troops, till the evacuations are made; except France will, as I suppose they will, agree to withdraw all their troops, but the necessary garrisons, till the towns are given up.

" I think this point must end to our mutual satisfaction; though I have not yet received an answer from the Duke.   Your letter will probably fix him, which he will have about the same time with mine.   I am extremely sorry to find, by your late letters, that you wish the parliament might not meet before Christmas.   I suppose you know the natural consequence of that.   But, if it had not that certain consequence, sure it would have an odd appearance, that we should so long defer the communicating to the parliament a peace so necessary, and so much desired by every body.   Was that to be the case, I am sure the whole nation would assign but one cause for it; and then consider how you would open your parliament upon that foot! As I always love to deal fairly with every body, and consequently with the king, I am considering whether I am not under a necessity of telling him your present thoughts, as to the time of meeting the parliament; or, otherwise, he may have just cause to be angry with me.   If I do, it shall be time enough to send you notice of it by the 19th inst., that you may still regulate the farther prorogation according to what his Majesty may then determine.

" I am very sorry to acquaint you, that I see a most sensible alteration in the king's behaviour to me, ever since my return to the Göhrde.   To what cause to assign it I am entirely at a loss, except it is to the fixing the meeting of the parliament, and the sending for the yachts; though the first was agreeable to what he had always said to me, when I have talked upon the subject.   I go on doing him the best service I can, and with as much cheerfulness as one can do, who has this late mortification to add to the continual ones I receive from England.   I believe the king intends to set out from hence, the 10th of November, O. S.   That is very late, as the parliament is now to meet, the 29th.   But it is no fault of mine.   Formerly all opinion and applications relating to the king's return, came from England.   I entirely submit to her Royal Highness's judgment; which, indeed, was my own.   I shall, therefore, form my schemes upon staying here the birth-day, setting out for the Hague a day or two after, and meeting the king at Helvoetsluys."

MR. PELHAM TO THE DUKE OF NEWCASTLE.

Thinks that his brother has no reason to be dissatisfied with his friends in England, and intreats him to use his influence with the Duke of Cumberland, and persuade him to give up his regiment of Dragoons.

"DEAR BROTHER,   *Oct.* 11*th*-22*nd*, 1748.

" I was very sorry to see, by your letter of the 1st. Oct., which I received on Sunday, that you were very uneasy with your friends in England, and that you took amiss their speaking their thoughts upon the late extraordinary event at Aix-la-Chapelle. Upon my word I do not think you have reason. I am certain, that what was said on that occasion, did not proceed from a desire, or even an opinion, to lessen your merit, for the share you have had in procuring peace for Europe. It was the natural thought of us all, founded on the conditions contained in Du Theil's project, and the convention for withdrawing the Austrian troops, coming over just at the same time, antecedent to any letters which came from you upon it. Nor, indeed, do I see, were our reasonings just, in what degree it lessens your conduct: 'the Austrians were unreasonable; you and all the world thought them so, but you were determined they should have no reason to lay at your door any misconduct of theirs, and therefore communicated to them every thing that had passed between the French minister and ours; and, at the same time told them, we must have peace, but are desirous to have it with you; nothing but absolute necessity shall drive us to sign without you; but if you will, by your unreasonable obstinacy, force us to it at last, we must.' What is the consequence of this, in our way of thinking? Why, that the court of Vienna, seeing that they must have peace, and having no disputes as to the terms of peace, but with the allies of England, thought they should easier get their difficulties removed, by corresponding with the French minister, than by leaving their interests entirely in the hands of England, who had attachments, and some obligations to the other powers, with whom France had none at all. If this be so, the measures taken by the king equally brought about this good end, as if it came any other way. I do not design to argue the point with you, but only to shew you that the inferences you draw from the opinions of the king's servants here, are not so clear as you apprehend them. For my part, I am, for the sake of the whole, so glad of the thing, that I shall be disposed to give merit to any one that has had any share in it; and I cannot persuade myself it can enter into your head, that I should not be more desirous to give it to you than to any, or all the parties concerned. I know you do not love advice, and therefore mine shall be short; but I beg of you not to look upon yourself in so low a light, as to think the personal compliments or flattery of a few private friends, in their private letters, is the praise you should look for. No; you are now in too high a station, and too conspicuous a light, to be paid with such chaff. It is the success of the whole, that will make your character and administration considerable. I told you, in a former letter, that was the touchstone we went by; and that, I thank God, you are now secure in. I could say, if I would, something on my part. I have borne the burden of measures I did not approve of; for God's sake, let me have the comfort of seeing you easy and happy in measures we both approve of.

"I was a little vexed, that you gave me no answer to the business part of a long letter, I wrote to you. I thought it of great moment, or else I should neither have troubled you, nor myself, in writing so much upon it. I found, however, by your letter to the Duke, which came in the duke of Bedford's packet, that you had written to his Royal Highness upon it; and, by a letter from his Royal Highness yesterday, I see he is proceeding upon a plan of reduction, in which his own regiment of

Dragoons is intended to be kept up. I have wrote an answer to his Royal Highness, full of duty, but, at the same time, with my usual freedom, representing to him, in the strongest light, the ill consequences of it, which the more I think of, the more I am convinced will happen. I must, therefore, intreat you to use your good offices with the Duke to give it up. I could say many things, not proper to put in a letter, which would convince every honest man, that wishes this family well, that a debate on that point should by all means be avoided. Remember the debate on the noblemen's regiments, which were raised for public service. Such a one, I am convinced, did more to suppress the rebellion than any other that was taken; yet suppositions and jealousies had great weight, even in those times, and in that necessary measure; à fortiori;—I will say no more. You will find, by the duke of Bedford's letter, that the lords justices had ordered the prorogation of the parliament, to the 17th of November only; but we, having since received his Majesty's commands for the 29th, that will be ratified, and the king's commands obeyed. I doubt, we shall have but little time together to form a speech, and the plan of a session. I was in hopes, therefore, that matters might have been ordered so, as not to meet the parliament till after Christmas. You not having taken any notice of that to me, I suppose you have your own reasons for calling it sooner. I wish we may have time to pass a money-bill before Christmas, as it is. If we have not, I am sure you had better take time before you open the session; but, as we shall, I hope, see you all in England, early in the next month, it may be time enough to determine, then. Undoubtedly, it will make it more difficult after a proclamation is out."

THE DUKE OF NEWCASTLE TO MR. PELHAM.

Doubts not that he will be pleased with the signature of the Definitive Treaty—Has acquainted the King with Mr. Pelham's opinion, that the Parliament need not meet before Christmas, and displeased his Majesty by pressing his return to England.

"DEAR BROTHER,   *Hanover, Oct.* 13th-24th, 1748.

" I need not wish you joy of the Treaty. I am sure, you have enough; at least, all you have desired is obtained, a peace, an immediate reduction, and the recalling all our troops. I am sure, you do not like the peace the worse because it is general, or because it leaves it in our power to keep our old Allies if we please. Whose measures those are, which have produced this peace, I need not say; I am sure we should before this, have felt the fatal consequences of the contrary extravagant measures that were pursuing. I have kept my word with you, as I always shall; for I do not speak so lightly as some imagine. I promised you to do my utmost to conclude a general peace, and to reduce our expenses as soon as possible, and I hope I have done it. As you have repeated so often your desire, that the parliament should not meet till after Christmas, and your opinion that it was not necessary, I thought it incumbent upon me to acquaint the king with it, which I have accordingly done. His Majesty immediately ordered me to countermand the yachts. I told him, that his Majesty must countermand the meeting of the parliament, also; that I thought it very possible that directions might be given for the parliament, before the counter orders could come; that I owned I differed with you; that I thought it would have a very odd appearance, that after his Majesty had concluded a peace, so agreeable to the nation, he should defer acquainting his people with it, for three months, and that it was easy to see to what reason they would ascribe it. He said, he was easy here. I told him, at last, I must receive his orders; and he dismissed me, without giving me any.

" This, I believe, has finished my credit; and I shall return to England, possibly much in the situation, though I hope not quite so bad, as the last minister that was here, now is. But, however, I have done my duty to the king, and my country, I have not concealed from him the opinion, though I was not of it, that the public business did not require the meeting of the parliament before Christmas ; and there is an end of it. I must take the rest for my pains. The king would have had reason to be angry, if I had concealed your opinions from him.

" I am very sorry for the article about the hostages. I doubt, my lord Chancellor will be uneasy about it. It should have been foreseen. It is now about three months since it was proposed : it has a bad look, but there is nothing else essential in it. Prince Louis of Wolfenbuttel the general, is come hither, this night. His Highness, with many others, dine with me to-morrow, to celebrate the peace. We are all as pacific as any of them, but we are glad to have our friends so, with us.

" The duchess of Newcastle, thank God, was pure well on Monday morning, at Deventer. Ever yours."

MR. PELHAM TO THE DUKE OF NEWCASTLE.*

Congratulates him on the signature of the Definitive Treaty—Disapproves the secret Article Anxious to obtain the Duke of Cumberland's consent to the reduction of his regiment of Dragoons.

"DEAR BROTHER,   *Oct. 14th-25th* 1748.

" Though I have no letter of yours to acknowledge, I cannot help writing to congratulate you most heartily upon the signature of the Treaty, which Mr. Levison brought here on Wednesday night, and we understand Mr. Wortley carried the original to Hanover. So very short a letter came with it, that I can scarce take notice of any particulars, as to who will or will not immediately accede. But if the young gentleman knows any thing, he tells us all the powers are ready to sign immediately, but the Piedmontese. I did always fear we should have difficulties in pleasing all our allies at the same time; you have therefore undoubtedly managed well to secure the most material one. I doubt not but the king of Sardinia will soon come in also. He must see the honest and friendly part the king has taken; he must also see, disagreeable as his case is, that he is the only power that is a

* Newcastle Papers.

gainer by the war; and besides, he must be sensible, that such great powers as are now agreed, and are all of them interested in finishing this work soon, since it has gone so far, will find out some expedient for composing their own differences, and leave him possibly alone. I now see the article,* I mentioned to you in my letter of the 23rd of last month, operate unfortunately. It was the only material objection I had to Du Theil's plan; and, as you gave very proper instructions to the plenipoten-tiaries upon it, I am curious to see what they have said upon it, to the French. The secret article is a foolish one, and, I find, very disagreeable to lord Chancellor. I wonder the French insisted upon it, for it might easily be shewn to them, that the king can keep strictly to that article, and yet send them two hostages that no power in Europe would give half a crown to redeem. It will be necessary to keep it quite a secret, as it has no relation to the national conditions of the peace. I think it very well may; and I presume you will immediately pitch upon two persons, possibly not lords of parliament, but officers in the army, who will be glad to pass half a year at Paris, when they will be, as I suppose they must, pretty well paid for it.

" I doubt you think I insist too much with the Duke, upon the reducing his regi-ment of dragoons. I have considered it, and am convinced, it is of vast consequence to him, and not a little to us all. I am sorry to see the king has fixed his return to England, just as the light nights are over. He must either stay a fortnight longer than we hope for, or run some risk, in coming over in the dark nights. We have heard nothing as yet of the duchess of Newcastle. I hope she is upon the road, and that we shall soon see her in England. I find people much surprised at Sherlock's taking London. I am," &c.

THE DUKE OF NEWCASTLE TO MR. PELHAM.†

Accession of Spain, Austria, and Sardinia, to the Definitive Treaty.

Oct. 16th-27th, 1748.* * * *—" Last night we had the pure and simple accession of Kaunitz; the day before, that of Spain; and I find nobody doubts of that of Sardinia; so this great and glorious work is now finished, and the peace of Europe finally settled, notwithstanding the confusion it was in, in as few months, as some of my predecessors were years in doing it. To what, or to whom that is owing, I shall no more say; but send you inclosed a copy of a letter, to shew you how all people think proper, on this side of the water, to talk, when they talk to me.

" Your savings and reductions are put in the way you wish. I hope some method will be found, to oblige the queen of Hungary in the £.100,000. It is a trifle at the end of an account, and for such an end ! The affair of the hostages is the only point that vexes me. We shall come off tolerably well, if this expedient succeeds; sure, the thought of lord Sussex was right. He is a very sensible, discreet young man, and will do well any where. He is just disposed, as I would have him. The king does not talk of making any alteration in his journey. He told M. Mun-

---

* Namely, the article relating to the ratifications of all the parties interested.
† Newcastle Papers.

chausen. ' He heard, it was not thought necessary for the parliament to meet before Christmas; but that he did not know, what he should do.' Ever since, his Majesty has seemed in very good humour, and extremely pleased with the happy and unexpected conclusion of our great affair. I conclude, I shall set out the day after the birth-day, and go to the Hague, or not, according to the day the king goes from here."

MR. PELHAM TO THE DUKE OF NEWCASTLE.*

Objects to the payment of the £.100,000 to the Empress Queen—Congratulates his brother on the conclusion of the definitive Treaty—Is gratified by the Duke of Cumberland's intention not to retain his regiment of Dragoons.

Oct. 25th-Nov. 5th, 1748.

After acknowledging the receipt of his letters of the 9th, 13th, and 16th, he proceeds :—"¡I had yesterday your letter of the 19th, in which you seem still to keep up some suspicion of your friends here; but the latter part of it is so full of kindness to me, that I would rather overlook the little upbraidings, and remember only the cordial, and essential expressions of kindness.

" I come now to the most essential part of our correspondence; and I shall have difficulty to write my opinion upon that, without being liable to some observations, which I wish to avoid, because in this, we truly differ; I mean the finding out an expedient to pay the whole, or any part of the remaining £.100,000 to the queen of Hungary. *You think, their late behaviour deserves some consideration; I protest I think the contrary.* What merit have they to us in making peace, any more than we to them? We all wanted it; the king has stood firmly by his allies; and the only difference, all along, has been, which of the two, he should prefer. I own my opinion is, you have done right, in pleasing the pride of the greatest, since the lesser† does not, in substance, lose any thing by it; but are we to give her £.100,000 for that? How can it be supported? And what appearance is there of her having fulfilled her engagements, in any degree?

" Add to this, have we not paid her Imperial Majesty £.75,000, and the Dutch I suppose £.25,000, for regiments of horse, that never stirred from their quarters, nor to our certain knowledge ever existed. This will be called wantonness of expense; and give me leave to say, dear Brother, what you call a trifle, at the end of an account, will, with the vast expenses of this campaign, break our backs next winter.

" I told you, my whole scheme depends on bringing the expenses of the next year, to be raised within the year. Several such sums as these, which I foresee, will make that impracticable; and if it should be so, our peace will do us less service than you think for. It is a long and tedious subject to write upon; but believe me, a very material one to consider well. I must intreat you, therefore, not to encourage this demand. The prince of Wolfenbuttel may be a very honest gentleman; but his

---

* Newcastle Papers.   † The king of Sardinia.

2 U 2

being in a good or a bad humour will not pay our public debts. Holland is a bankrupt country. They owe us £.50,000 for two advances we have made for them already, and then desire us to go on, advancing farther. Charles Bentinck is, I dare say, a very good-natured man; but he knows nothing of our constitution; and by what I perceive, has not wherewithal to learn it.

" I received by the last mail a most obliging answer from his Royal Highness, to the letter I wrote to him, upon the subject of his regiment of dragoons. Whatever his Royal Highness's opinion may be upon that subject, he seems so convinced, that what I say proceeds from conviction, duty, and regard for him, that he has assured me, I shall hear no more of it from him. I cannot but be exceedingly rejoiced at this; as I think it very essential, both to his own credit, and the success of the king's affairs in parliament. I must also confess to you, I am much affected with his great condescension in this affair; and the expressions used in his letter, will remain with me to my last hour.

*   *   *   *   *   *

" I must, also, from the bottom of my heart, congratulate you on the happy conclusion of a definitive treaty of peace. That this has been brought to perfection, during your ministry, and immediately under your eye and inspection, must give me a double satisfaction. To have the thing I most wished for, brought about by the man I love best, and who is so near to me, must very much add to the pains and industry, which I should otherwise use, to convince mankind, not only that the terms are honourable, but that the manner of negotiating, has also been agreeable to the dignity of the king, and the justice with which he has always acted towards his allies."

MR. PELHAM TO THE DUKE OF NEWCASTLE.

Hopes that Lord Sandwich and Sir Thomas Robinson will be recalled from the Hague—Again urges the necessity of diminishing the public expenses.

" *Nov.* 1*st*, 1748.

" At night I found a letter from you of the 25th-5th, which brought me no certain account, either of your setting out from Hanover, or of the time you propose to be here. But as, probably, you have before this time, heard of the arrival of the yacht, I flatter myself we shall see you all sooner than you have given us hopes of: the next post will, I conclude, bring us a certainty.

" You send me a copy of a letter from lord Sandwich, which only confirms what I have for some time heard, from his friends here, that he longs for nothing so much as to get back to England. For God's sake take him at his word, and Sir Thomas Robinson too, who amused me; he desires nothing so much as to see his native country and friends again. They are a vast expense to the king; and if the other ministers, I mean those of France and Holland, go, I do not see what ours should stay for. I hope you understood my letter by the last messenger. My meaning was to give as little jealousy as was possible, and, at the same time, save as much money for the king as I could. You cannot conceive how poor we are, and what vast expenses have been of late. The Chancellor told me he had wrote you a long letter; but I assure you I have never seen one word that he writes. I could get very little from the duchess of Newcastle, of what passed at Hanover. Her principal topics were upon her own journey, which by her account must have been a very pleasant one. * * * * * *

THE DUKE OF NEWCASTLE TO MR. PELHAM.*

The Duke of Cumberland approves Mr. Pelham's economical plans—Is happy to hear his brother intends to bring the expenses within the current year, and to reduce the interest of the funds from 4 to 3 per cent.

Nov. 15th-26th, 1748.
On board the States Yacht, between Utrecht and the Hague.

* * * *—"I had a most agreeable interview with the Duke; except as to roads and lodgings. It gave me the greatest pleasure to find how kindly, affectionately, and respectfully he talked of you, upon every point; and I really think you are as well with him, as ever you was in your life. I find, by him, you hope to bring the current expenses, this year, to the malt and four shillings land tax, and in subsequent years to two shillings, paying off every year a million of debt, by the Sinking-fund. I find, also, by the king, that you are not without hopes of reducing the interest of the national debt, even this year, to three per cent. God grant you success! It will be the greatest work that ever was done; and will complete my political wishes and happiness, to have it done by you.

"Believe me, you never were higher in esteem with the king, than at present. He has talked us over, in a way we should both like. The Duke mightily likes my draught of the two paragraphs in the speech. He would have some addition about the army being at liberty to set up trades, as after the peace of Utrecht. His Royal Highness has strongly recommended to me, to live well with lord Sandwich. I have no thought of the contrary. His lordship intends to offer to return to the Hague, but the king has no thoughts of that. I shall see whether sir Thomas Robinson staying at the Hague for a month or six weeks only, will be most likely to do good or hurt there. I will not make comparison of men. The one, after two years' service, returns to one of the first offices in the kingdom, and, as he has always said, the most to his taste. The other, after twenty-five long laborious years, returns to nothing, with a wife and seven children."

MR. PELHAM TO THE DUKE OF NEWCASTLE.

Conversation with the duke de Mirepoix on the affairs of Sweden, and with count Fleming, the Saxon minister—Duke of Cumberland dreads the admission of lord Granville into office—Expresses his resolution to support the administration of his brother.

April 26th, 1750.†

"I had yesterday my conference with the embassador,‡ who seems in high spirits, from the answer he has received from his court,§ which, that I might

---

* Newcastle Papers. † Ibid.
‡ Duke de Mirepoix, the French minister. § Relative to the affairs of Sweden.

not mistake, I desired him to dictate, and Roberts took it down in his presence, from his own mouth. You have the paper inclosed, which will explain the whole to you. His desiring that this overture might not come through Holland, but directly from France herself, I like; because then there can be no chicane. I sounded him, as well as I was able, whether their intention was, to have any separate negotiation with us, but found it far otherwise. He concluded, the king would act in concert with his allies, as France was doing with hers; but hoped for good offices and dispositions on both sides. I told him then, that as this was likely to take up some time, I should be glad to know how you were to correspond with him. He said, through the channel of the person that was to reside at Hanover, from Paris.

"That led us to talk on the subject of M. Valory, and occasioned what is mentioned, in the paper concerning your billet. He said, if Valory was not publicly declared, he verily believed your interposition would prevent his being sent. But at the same time, I could see he thought it too late to prevent his going, and then asked how lord Albemarle was with you. I told him he was bred up under your patronage, and that I doubted not of his acting honourably by you. But as he had been employed, of late years, in the military way, and of consequence been for many years out of England, that had naturally extended his acquaintance, and made your intimacy less; though your regard for him, and his for you, was not at all lessened by that. Upon the whole, I saw he was willing to have trusted Albemarle, as the *porteur*, and I did not decline it; but told him I would write to you upon it.

"I must now take notice to you, that Klingraff's * letters all mention this secret negotiation; and he has very correct accounts of all particulars, though not from M. Mirepoix. It is a pity, the embassador should remain ignorant of his being betrayed; and yet, to tell, might discover our secret, even when it is too late to prevent this mischief. Alt has got the account also from the Prussian minister, and wrote it to his court; so that it will be impossible to keep it from the duke of Bedford. Would it not be right, therefore, for you to mention it to him, in a confidential way, as a thing the embassador just hinted to you, the day before the king went, and has been confirmed to you since you have been abroad? Such a communication may stop our mouths for the present; and, without it, it will be impossible to keep things quiet here, when his Grace returns to London. You are, however, the best judge, and will do in it, as you think proper.

"I talked strongly to Mirepoix, upon the behaviour of Mr. Caylus. He has endeavoured to clear it up, but I think he cannot. I doubt they picked a German quarrel with governor Matthews, in order to avoid the execution of the orders received from Paris, for evacuating the several islands.† If so, that will be a great thorn in our sides, in our future negotiations.

"Upon the whole, my opinion is, that as Mirepoix has gained to himself the merit

* The Prussian minister.
† Probably Tobago and St. Lucia, neutral islands, which the French were suspected of endeavouring to occupy.

of first suggesting this, and procured the confidence with you, which he desired, the court of France has no longer an inclination to keep this affair a secret; but are willing in its future progress, to negotiate with you at Hanover, and Albemarle at Paris, in the several and regular forms. The embassador talks of leaving this country, in ten days or a fortnight; and I shall of course be freed from what I am so very little fit for, a secret negotiation. I understand they go to Ligonier to-morrow, and I shall have the honour, not pleasure, of their company at Esher, on Saturday.

"Count Fleming * was with me this morning, and talked over his foreign system. He was well instructed, and I endeavoured to return his civilities as well as I could, without committing myself or you, in any future transactions. I find, the burthen of his song is, assistance for his own court, the consequence of which he magnifies, placing the House of Saxony in the third degree of the Electors, that is, next to the Queen of Hungary and the King of Prussia. I touched with him gently upon the extravagance of his court, and shewed him how little benefit any subsidy we could give his master, would be to the elector, whilst twice that sum was thrown away in unnecessary expenses. He allowed the weakness of his court, but, at the same time, claimed some acknowledgment, as due to them by way of *dédommagement* for their losses, and in consequence of the seventh article of the treaty of Warsaw. You may be assured, I did not dwell long with him upon that subject, but got off as civilly as I could. I believe Villiers † is the better with this court, for allowing, as I suppose he does, their construction of the treaty.

"I have seen the Duke ‡ once, and but once, since you went. I flatter myself my discourse with him would not have displeased you. I cannot repeat it even in the most private letter, but I will give you the key. He dreads Granville.§ I shewed him, it was not your thoughts; and threw out from myself, the supposed way to prevent his coming into council.

"I have also had a long conference with Dorset. I talked my mind freely and friendly to him. He seemed satisfied; and, in endeavouring to satisfy me, talked a language quite different from what I believe he held with you. I told him, I understood what was done to be an inviolable secret, at least it was so for me. I should not understand it as done, and wished I had not been trusted with it; that I did not think it worth a farthing to him, but it might do mischief if it transpired. He agreed with me in the latter, and said he should never mention it; but to my surprise, when I came to court, I found he had notified, to the Duke and the Princess, the king's goodness to him, in declaring him Lord Lieutenant of Ireland. He did not say, any thing was signed; but they concluded more was done than is. I said, I knew little of the matter, but concluded, when one ‖ went out, the other would come in."

* The Saxon minister.

† The honourable Thomas Villiers, son of William, second earl of Jersey, successively minister at the courts of Dresden, Vienna, and Berlin. He was afterwards created baron Hyde, and earl of Clarendon.

‡ Of Cumberland.

§ Lord Granville, whom the king wished again to take into his service.

‖ Lord Harrington, at this time lord Lieutenant of Ireland, whom the duke of Dorset was to succeed.

DUKE OF NEWCASTLE TO MR. PELHAM.

On the negotiations with France relative to Sweden—Considers their joint administration as one and the same—Complains of the cruel conduct of the Duke of Cumberland and the Princess Amelia.

"*Hague, May 9th-20th*, 1750.

After applauding Mr. Pelham's dexterous management in the conference with Mirepoix, he adds :—"The only point of difficulty will be, the withdrawing the Russian troops :* that will go down heavily every where, and certainly cannot be complied with, unless some security be given, in regard to the present form of government. As the duke of Bedford must now be informed of the affair, in some shape or other, I purpose writing to him, on arriving at Hanover. I am glad that Fleming has opened his budget to you. He is an honest sensible man, wishes well to the common cause, but is naturally rather partial to his own court.

"In regard to domestic affairs, I am highly gratified with your cordiality. I consider our administration to be one and the same ; and observe, that an agreement in general principles of business, and a concurrence with regard to persons, which, with a little mutual concession, may easily be accomplished, will perpetuate our harmony, and facilitate all our affairs.

"I think it a little hard, that the Duke of Cumberland, and the Princess Amelia, should use me so cruelly as they have done : excommunicate me from all society, set a kind of brand or mark upon me, and all who think with me, and set up a new, unknown, factious young party,† to rival me, and nose me every where. This goes to my heart: I am sensible, if I could have submitted, and cringed to such usage, the public appearances would have been better, and perhaps some secret stabs been avoided ; but I was too proud, and too innocent, to do it.

"I am persuaded that you said all that was kind and respectful, in regard to me, when speaking with the Duke ; and I would be glad to know his Royal Highness's reply. I know his Royal Highness's dread is, and always has been, lord Granville ; and yet for the last two years, he has taken the direct way to bring him in, thus suffering his passions to get above his reason.

"I have learned from Stone, that the king is in very good humour ; prodigiously civil to him, and gracious in his expressions concerning me. They have not yet touched upon English domestic politics ; that being reserved for my arrival. I think that you have done perfectly right, in regard to Dorset: but that affair must remain dormant for the present."

*

---

* From Finland. These troops were intended to act against Sweden, if an accommodation had not been effected between the two powers.

† Meaning lord Sandwich and the duke of Bedford.

MR. PELHAM TO THE DUKE OF NEWCASTLE.

On the silence of the duke of Bedford—Laments the situation of lord Harrington—Thinks that his brother may regain the favour of the Duke of Cumberland.

"DEAR BROTHER,   *May* 18*th*-29*th*, 1760.

"As a messenger goes to Hanover this day, I trouble you with this private letter, according to my promise, though I have nothing very particular to say, excepting the renewal of my thanks to you, for your very kind and affectionate letter of the 9th instant. The embassador went early the morning after I received it, so that I had no opportunity of saying any thing to him upon the subject. The duke of Bedford has said nothing to me, concerning the secret negotiation, and though he certainly must have some knowledge of it, yet he appears in very good humour. I have seen him only at the regency, excepting once, that I met him for a short time in a third place. It will be therefore very imprudent in me, to begin the conversation; and drawing myself into a scrape very unnecessarily. If he begins the subject with me, I will get off as well as I can; and, at all events, turn the affair as much off from you as I can. In my opinion, it will come naturally to light, as a proposal from France; and any farther secrets that you shall think necessary, may be carried on between you and the embassador, either through Albemarle or Yorke, as you shall think proper. I own, I do not myself see any subject for a secret; and if they are not necessary, it is always best to avoid them.

"The greatest trouble I have, is satisfying lord Harrington upon the several home questions he puts to me. The whole town tell him he is out. I parry, as well as I can. He desires to know the reason of his disgrace. I tell him no new reason, that I am acquainted with; but do not disguise from him, that he is ill with the king. He desires to know whether he is to be totally laid aside, and turned adrift, without any provision at all, which he says his circumstances can very ill bear. I assure him, it is not your desire that he should be so; but I cannot, knowing what I do, give him much hopes. In short it is a melancholy sight to see him, and the best answers I can give, are the chances of time, that it is six months before the king will think of returning, and nobody can tell what may happen, before that time.

"The Duke has not been in London, since the time I had the conversation with him, I wrote to you about, nor is he expected till Sunday. I design to have a conference with him next week; and, if I can extract any thing, you shall be sure to know it. You desire to know his reply. It is impossible to write particulars; and you will permit me to say, you are so lively upon that subject, that I am afraid of false constructions. Upon the whole, I can with truth say, he never speaks to me on your subject, but with respect, and as much kindness, as your late conduct to him, and his to you, can permit. In short, I am satisfied you may, if you please, make all things right with him; but we are also too proud, to submit first; and perhaps we think, too innocent to plead guilty. As to the other branches of the royal family, every thing remains in *statu quo;* the same favorites, and the same pleasures.

" I dare say you do not expect me to write any thing upon the latter part of your letter ; I am heartily sorry you are so much affected, as you seem to be. I do not in my conscience think there is foundation for it ; but rather look upon the whole as *amantium iræ*, which, by a little good humour on both sides, and some yielding on yours, would end in as much love as ever."

DUKE OF NEWCASTLE TO MR. PELHAM.

Angry with the court of Vienna, for persecuting the Protestants, and for suspecting the sincerity of the Electors of Bavaria and Cologne.

Hanover May 20th-31st, 1750.

" We found the king in perfect good health and humour. He has been extremely gracious to us both ; and remarkably so to the duchess of Newcastle, who has supped once at court, and dines there to-day. All my friends seem really pleased and happy to see me here.

＊   ＊

" I am not quite pleased with the politics here, which I find are very strong against the court of Vienna. They complain, and may be, with some reason, that they persecute the Protestants every where ; and have had offers from the king of Prussia to join with them, in support of the Protestants, against the emperor's decree, which offers will be accepted. They also lay to the charge of the court of Vienna, that they oppress the little princes, contrary to the capitulation and laws of the empire ; and that I am afraid is the sore. Though I am as much as any body for supporting the Protestants, in a proper manner, yet I know too well the general influence arising from particular prejudices in politics ; and I wish we may not feel it, in the affair of the king of the Romans. However, I shall go on, my old way ; do, in that, and every thing else, my duty, and what I think is right ; and it must take its course.

" You will see by the inclosed papers, which I send you from Holland, that the affair of the king of the Romans (which the prince of Orange means by the **Grand But**), is made a kind of a *sine quâ non :* and you will see by Keith's letters, they have some doubts about the electors of Cologne, and Bavaria, which the king is angry with them for, but which, however, must be cleared up."

DUKE OF NEWCASTLE TO MR. PELHAM

On the persecution of the Protestants by the court of Vienna—Persuades the German ministers to promote the election of a king of the Romans.

May 22nd-June 2nd, 1750.

＊ ＊ ＊ ＊ " Since my last I have had very full conferences with the two Munchhausens, Steinberg, and Richecourt.＊ The resentment to the court of Vienna

----

＊ Envoy from the court of Vienna.

for their usage of the Protestants, and the emperor's assuming to himself a power, which they pretend he has not, by the laws of the empire, continues very great; whilst I find, by Richecourt's hints, the emperor thinks his authority is attacked, and rendered almost nothing. I am yet apt to think the court of Vienna is greatly in the wrong, with regard to the Protestants, and perhaps does not act up in every thing, according to the capitulation; but, on the other hand, I doubt we are pretty alert on our part, and I find there is now a *conclusum*, as it is called, of the *corps evangélique*, which is to be executed, in opposition to the emperor, and to be supported by the king of Prussia, the king, the landgrave of Hesse, the margraves of Anspach and Bareith, and the landgrave of Hesse Darmstadt. This may create great coolness, if not more, with the court of Vienna; but I am endeavouring all I can to prevent it.

"I have talked strongly to Richecourt; and shall write strongly to Keith, and to Bentinck at Vienna. I have yet heard nothing of Haslang. Count Richecourt began his conversation with me, on the subject of a king of the Romans; and, as I thought that very delicate, I took down in writing before him, what he said, and send it to you inclosed. It is, I think, a good circumstance. You have here the opinion and wish of the court of Vienna; and though it is mixed with an ill-grounded suspicion, about the imperial authority which they seem to fear is meant to be abridged, by a new capitulation, upon the election of a new king of the Romans, yet the court of Vienna must be bound down by this to be for it; and it will be more difficult for others to get off from it, if there was any such intention; which, as far as relates to the king, I am persuaded there is not. Steinberg tells me, the elector of Cologne makes no difficulty upon this point. The Grosvoigt is the person I am labouring at. He says the king has not said one word to him upon it; nor indeed scarcely upon any thing. He has promised not to speak against it to the king; on the contrary, to be for it, and to shew how glorious a work it would be, for the king to bring about. But to me he says there will be great difficulty in the execution. But with all his abilities, I think his difficulties proceed more from his dislike of the thing, than from the thing itself; and I hope to have influence enough over him not only to bring him into it, but to put us in a way really to effectuate it; and that is now my great point. The Grosvoigt thinks, and in that I agree with him, that in order for it, we should have here a person from the court of Vienna, who is not only in confidence with his court, but who is also perfectly master of the laws and constitution of the empire. Kevenhuller is the man he most wishes for; but I fancy it will be general Breitlack, who is in Russia. He will do very well. Every body here thinks Keith a mere cipher at Vienna, and indeed I have always thought so. He approves all that they say and do, and one knows nothing but good from him. Hyndford is the man they wish; but I think Villiers would do much better than he.

"The king is in haste to send Hanbury Williams to Berlin. He is here with Mr. Digby, and Sir William Yonge's son. They are both very pretty young men. Yonge goes to Leipzig to-morrow, and Sir Charles will set out for Berlin, in a few days.

"I now send you a copy of an intercepted letter of the king of Sweden, which I do not know what to make of. It is plain, they do not like Mirepoix's proposal, and I own I always thought that France made the proposal, because they thought it was agreeable to Sweden. If so, things will remain as they are : the Czarina will certainly begin nothing, and France cannot reproach us, when we and our allies were so ready to come into their own proposal. I send you copies of my letter to lord Albemarle, and Monsieur Mirepoix. His to me was only a letter of compliment about Claremont. Fleming is extremely pleased with his conference with you. He says you talked very reasonably, and as a *ministre d' état*. Though you know my thoughts and intentions about the Secretary's office, I would not, however, during my stay here, do any thing that should be improper, or the least uncivil towards the duke of Bedford.

P. S.—" I am just come from court, and am better pleased than I have been yet with what passed there. The king told me that the great affair about the *conclusum* relating to the Protestants was over. That the emperor had submitted. You may imagine I made the best use of it I could. I then told his Majesty that he had made an emperor ; that if he could make a king of the Romans too, it would be the greatest honour to him in the world. He replied " and that of my own proposing, without being asked."

MR. PELHAM TO THE DUKE OF NEWCASTLE.

Difficulties attending the election of a king of the Romans—Cautions his brother on the subject of subsidies—Alludes to the parties at the Duke of Cumberland's.

May 25th–June-5th, 1750.

After acknowledging the receipt of his kind letter of the 20th-31st by Cleverley, the messenger, with the usual papers inclosed, he adds :—" I see very plainly the difficulties you are in, at Hanover. The election of a king of the Romans is your great object, and ought to be that of the court of Vienna ; but the object of the electors and lesser princes of the empire, I fear, is, the receipt of subsidies, and redressing their own grievances with the house of Austria. They will therefore be unwilling to come to the election, till they have secured their own points. As to France, I do not believe she would concern herself about it, one way or other. She may have her wishes ; but there is no instance wherein that crown ever interfered in the election of a king of the Romans, when there were male successors to the emperors of the house of Austria. This makes me conclude, as I always did, that the difficulty as to that election, will lie in the stiffness of the imperial court, and the internal views of the several electors.

" I am glad to hear things remain, at the court where you are, as you left them. They cannot be in better hands. I think the parties mean well. I am sure they wish you well, and are, if I judge rightly, of unenterprising geniuses. You will have seen by my letter of last week, that nothing has passed here, upon the subject of the French negotiation, nor do I see any necessity that there should. The embassador is gone ; and possibly when he comes to Paris, he may find affairs upon a different foot. If he does not, his correspondence with you will, as you observe, give you a fair opportunity to open your correspondence here.

" I have seen little of the duke of Bedford. We have had no calls to meet, on account of business, and his life and mine in other respects are spent differently. He seems in good humour, though I find by lord Gower, he now and then complains of want of confidence, and that he is kept a stranger to every thing that is doing, both at home and abroad. You may be assured, I do not let that pass without making my reply ; and lord Gower is so honest and good-natured a man, that I never leave him with any prejudice to our side of the question.

" You say we have begun our parties ; I told you of one ; you will possibly hear of more. That upon the water I was invited to by the Princess, but having a good excuse, on account of company I had with me at Esher, I got off ; but our friend Arundel and his grace of Grafton were there.

*   *   *   *   *   *

" The chancellor has seen all your letters, and shall have those I received this day, when I have done with them. Nobody else sees the most private ones. I shewed the duke of Grafton your long letter, with the account of your travels. He thought with me, that it was so entertaining a letter, and in many respects so instructive, that I could not do better than to shew it to the Duke. I had a mind to do it on many accounts. He will see it was not wrote with a design for this perusal, and yet there was something so handsome on his subject, that I was willing he should be acquainted with it.

" I have not seen his Royal Highness since I sent the letter to him ; but I am certain he must be pleased with it. I hope you do not disapprove of this. If you do, I shall say nothing, for the future ; but it will appear extremely odd, that I should never communicate any thing I receive from you now, when I had orders the last time you were abroad to shew all. You may be satisfied, I shall do this with discretion, and take care not to commit you, in any thing.

" I must now only beg of you to be aware of what subsidies you enter into. You see how the prince of Orange wants to load this country, even with their own engagements. I doubt, the court of Munich do not intend to separate themselves from France, in the manner you expect.

THE DUKE OF NEWCASTLE TO MR. PELHAM.

Sends a list of the grievances of the German princes against the emperor. The insidious conduct of the king of Prussia—Anxiety of the king to promote the election of a king of the Romans.

Hanover, May 30th–June 10th, 1750.

*   *   *   * " I come now to what gives me much more satisfaction. You will see, by my secret letter to the duke of Bedford, that count Richecourt has explained himself tolerably well, upon the great point of the king of the Romans ; and I am sure you will approve the handle I have taken from thence, to push this point to an immediate execution, as far as the nature of the thing will admit. I also inclose to you a copy of my private letter to Bentinck ; which, I hope, you will think, is as strong as possible, to shew the court of Vienna, the necessity of their doing their part, to bring about this great measure, which is so essential to the establishment and interest, of the house of Austria. I must do the king justice; he seems at present for it, as much as possible, and seems to value himself upon being the first proposer, and promoter of it. I really think it will succeed; and if it does, it is, in my poor opinion, as great, and as matérial a work, for the preservation of peace, and for the honour of England, as ever was undertaken, and carried through, in time of peace.

" But, to conceal nothing from you, I send, in the greatest confidence, a paper of the Grosvoigt Munchausen's upon it. He states all the difficulties, and, I think, great and able as he is, they are not so great as they seem to him. Was he in better humour, I am persuaded, he would see this thing in a different light; but my good friend, his brother, assures me, *mon frère pense comme vous ; je le ramenerai.* The king has not yet said one word to him, upon this great point, and, I believe, very little, upon the treaty with the elector of Bavaria.

" Haslang * is the greatest loiterer that ever was. He is not yet come. His secretary has been here, with his last orders, above this week ; and by what he says, all will go well, and I do not perceive by him, that the affair of the king of the Romans will create any difficulty. The security for the payment of the Dutch proportion, will be the material point, and that, I think, we shall get over; so that, if the article about the king of the Romans, goes down, and the elector of Bavaria will previously concur, I look upon that treaty as concluded. By all the appearances here, we shall have the Elector Palatine also. If so, the king of Prussia will not stand out, and then, dear Brother, the collecting and uniting all the different princes and electors, of the empire, in one same system, either actively, or passively, is a great work, deserves to be attended to, and will be a sufficient reward for all the pains that can be taken to bring it about. I am afraid you will be tired with my German politics, and the voluminous papers I send you upon them. I deal fairly with you ; I send you all, *pro* and *con.* Read what you like, and send them all to my lord Chancellor, who, as he reads every thing, may, perhaps, not dislike to read them.

" You will see, by the letters this messenger carries, that I have taken your hint, in communicating every thing that can be communicated, to the duke of Bedford. I do, I will endeavour to do every thing that shall be agreeable to you, as far as is any ways consistent with my own foreign system ; and I think, and hope, in that we shall not differ."

MR. PELHAM TO THE DUKE OF NEWCASTLE.

Thinks that his brother may mediate between the emperor and the empire—Recommends caution in pecuniary engagements—Hopes the affairs of Sweden will be amicably adjusted— Unpopularity of the Prince of Wales and the Duke of Cumberland—The Stock subscription.

" *June 1st-12th,* 1750.

After saying that he had acknowledged in his last, the receipt of his brother's letter of May 22nd-June 2nd, and alluding to the illness of lord Clinton, he con-

---

* Bavarian minister.

tinues :—" I have read your papers over, and so has lord Chancellor. We both agree, that though your situation may be an unpleasant one, yet you have it so much in your power to stand middle man, between the emperor and empire, that you may possibly be enabled to bring them together, upon more just and advantageous terms for the common cause, than either party would yield to of themselves. It is plain our subsidies will have little weight with regard to the great point, if the court of Vienna does not satisfy the electors and lesser princes of the empire, in their just demands ; and I am also of opinion, that the electors will make higher demands upon the emperor, in proportion as they imagine, we will, or will not support them. I think, therefore, when we have retained these electors in our pay, it may tempt us to look bigger ourselves.

" I must beg of you, dear Brother, to be cautious in your pecuniary engagements, not only with regard to the powers you agree with, but the quantum of the subsidy also. The French, by lord Albemarle's letters, continue in exceeding good disposition ; and if our friend Mirepoix has not overshot himself, I doubt not they will bring Sweden to preserve the peace of the north, upon their own terms. I am every day more convinced of the necessity of keeping things quiet there ; for, besides the natural consequence, being a general war, which neither we nor our allies are yet in a condition to carry on, I am satisfied, any disturbance there, would immediately be followed by domestic troubles here. I have reason to think the Jacobites expect it, even depend upon it ; and I fear this country is not so well disposed to some branches of our royal family, as they were upon the late rebellion. The eldest loses esteem and confidence, more and more, every day ; and the youngest does not conduct himself so prudently, with regard to the temper of this country, and constitution, as to be able to make up for the unfortunate turn of the other. Our whole dependence, at present, is upon the king ; and, as I am a well-wisher to all of them, I pray God things may mend, before Nature calls him from us. I trust in God, that fatal event will not be in my time ; for, whenever it comes, I see a melancholy prospect.

" Our subscription is ended, and there are but £.3,168,871* unsubscribed. I mean exclusive of South Sea capital ; † and, considering the numbers of people abroad, who could not send powers, the ignorant, and the obstinate, it is to every one surprising it has gone on so well. I like it as well, or better than if all had subscribed ; for we have now something to work upon, in case our Sinking-fund should furnish a surplus after what is anticipated for the supplies of the year."

* This sum differs from that given in Postlethwayte, who states the amount to be as we have given it in the narrative, chap. xxii. p. 107.

† A settlement was afterwards made with this Company, who agreed to accept the terms proposed ; and it is included by Sir John Sinclair, in his table, in the list of the subscribers.

MR. PELHAM TO THE DUKE OF NEWCASTLE.

Project for the election of a king of the Romans very popular—Disapproves the views of the Dutch, on the proposed alliance with the two Empresses—On the disputes with France relative to the boundaries of Nova Scotia.

Arlington Street, June 5th-16th, 1750.

" Your foreign politics, I protest I do not understand. I see you are uneasy, which I am heartily sorry for, but cannot find out why. Your great point is the election of a king of the Romans : every body is for it, even France herself ; what, then, have you to do, but to forward the work, whilst there is no objection ? The several princes of the empire want to make their own terms with the court of Vienna ; could that ever be doubted ? or was it ever doubted ? What have we to do then ? Why, support them with our good offices, when they are in the right, and overrule them, if we can, when they are in the wrong. I cannot say, I am sorry to see any intercourse opened between the two great powers,* who are neighbours and relations, though I am no more than you for forming another Hanover treaty, nor another quadruple alliance either.

" For God's sake, let us keep as we are. If you make a king of the Romans, it is, as you say, a great thing ; and if the people you converse with abroad will not spoil it, nobody will be against it. You say the king is right ; that is the whole : and I should hope his majesty and his family may find their account, in doing this great work for the house of Austria, better than by any lower and more expensive managements, with the inferior princes.

" I conclude, the duke of Bedford has sent you an account of the letters from Nova Scotia, I do not like them at all. I am far from being well informed, as to the merits of the question, but I think it is generally understood, that we are in the right, and they grossly in the wrong. If so, I wish Cornwallis† were strong enough to do himself justice ; for I am of opinion, if we get the better without any previous concert with France, she would not break with you on that account ; but if we enter into negotiation, and at the same time act hastily, I fear we shall hardly get off well. But, as lord Chancellor is out of town, and I go to-morrow for a fortnight, I conclude nothing will be resolved upon, till they hear from you, and by that time we shall be all returned. The duke of Bedford has, as yet, said nothing to me about it ; what I have, is from Halifax only. I think I must now have sufficiently tired you, as I have myself. I will only just beg of you not to enter into any engagements, for the securing the payment of the Dutch proportion, in the Bavarian, or any other treaty ; such an article will not, cannot go down, here.

" I propose setting out to-morrow, after the regency, for Euston, and shall return to London in about a fortnight from that time. If any thing comes from you which requires an answer, I shall take care to receive it in a day after it comes to London, and will send my answer to Roberts, who will carry it with secrecy into the messenger's hands."

* Spain and France.
† Honourable Edward Cornwallis, son of Charles lord Cornwallis, and governor of Nova Scotia or Acadia.

THE DUKE OF NEWCASTLE TO MR. PELHAM.*

Thinks that the elector of Cologne is sure, and the election certain—Wishes to gain the electors Palatine and Saxony, but supposes his brother will not approve any farther subsidies— Affairs in America render it necessary to secure the peace of Germany.

Hanover, June 9th-20th, 1750.

* * * *" As to foreign politics, I really think, things look well every where, but in the West Indies. Haslang begins to talk very reasonably; and I believe a small matter will satisfy his master, by way of indemnification for Mirandola, Concordia, &c. He desired me last night, that their affair might be concluded first, and not be incumbered with the Palatine, &c. The elector of Cologne is sure, and the scheme, of chusing a king of the Romans, is universally known, and generally approved, and I begin to think, we shall find little difficulty in it. * * * *

" I extremely like your notion, of the king's mediating between the emperor, and the princes of the Empire. His majesty is certainly, at present, in that situation; and it is a great one. But he must continue to have weight with both, in order to be able to do it effectually. When we have the electors in our pay, you say very right, we may, and we will, look and talk big. Do not imagine by this, that I have any new subsidy in view. You know the extent of my wishes; I should be glad of Saxony. They may, I am convinced, be easily and cheaply had; and they may be necessary, to fix, and secure the great object; but the king will not have them, and I do not suppose, you are inclined to it. I have desired Stone, to explain the hint; he has only done it, in general. I shall not take a step, in any pecuniary engagement, without previously consulting you. I know of no new one. Possibly, the elector Palatine, but, yet, his minister has said nothing of it to me, may ask the remaining part of his demand.* * * *

"The scheme of making a king of the Romans, is, as I said before, talked of, though covertly, as a solid system for the empire, and as what will *eterniser* the king's honour. It is, certainly, nearer being executed than the most sanguine of us all, could have imagined. Sir Charles Williams says, do that, and Harry Fox will approve of subsidies; no subsidies are proposed, but upon that principle; and I really think, the news from America shews the necessity of making ourselves as strong in Europe, as possible. I can never think, that all this is by chance; that Caylus, and La Jonquiere, equally, act without orders, and contrary to the inclination of their court.

"I hope, you will approve my letter to the duke of Bedford, in answer to his upon this subject; and I must beg of you, to give attention to this affair. It is much the most difficult, and most dangerous, of any, now depending. If you do not act with vigour, and support what you have done, and our right to the extended boundaries of Nova Scotia, you may not only lose that province, but, from what I have heard from Halifax, and governor Shirley, endanger all your northern colonies, which are inestimable to us. If you do, you may run a risk of a rupture with France. But I

* Newcastle Papers.

think that is to be run ; for, if we lose our American possessions, or the influence and
weight of them, in time of peace, France will, with great ease, make war with us
whenever they please hereafter : and, as long as we stick to our treaties, the French
may talk big; and, at a distance, their officers act hostilely, or, at least, impertinently ;
but they will not enter into a serious war. I should be as sorry to see that, as you
can be. I hope the spirit of Jacobitism is not much increased. One branch of the
royal family has lost its popularity ; but that, I hope, will not affect the whole. The
king still preserves the esteem and affection of the people in general ; and that, I am
persuaded, will be seen, whenever there is occasion, which, God forbid, should again
happen. As to the other part, I suppose it is pretty much as it has been for many
years."

THE DUKE OF NEWCASTLE TO MR. PELHAM.*

*Is dissatisfied with the duke of Bedford, for writing secretly to lord Albemarle about Nova
Scotia, of which he inforces the necessity of settling the boundaries—Has withdrawn the
Memorial, which he intended to send to the court of France—Aspect of foreign affairs
not favourable.*

Hanover, June 17th-28th, 1750.

* * * * " The material point of business, now immediately depending, is that of
Nova Scotia. I hope you will approve my letter to Albemarle : I could not write less ;
and I think more, at present, might have been unnecessary. I had ordered him to
present a Memorial ; but, upon your letter, altered it. It may be time enough to do
that, when we find they are disposed to support what has been done. I hope the
turn I have given, with regard to M. Puisieulx, will please you. I hope the lords
justices will examine our right, and determine what are the limits we should abide
by, and insist upon. If the French prevail in their construction, Nova Scotia will be
of little use to us. If we carry our point, Cape Breton will not be of great advantage
to them ; at least in the opinion of Halifax and Shirley.

" I am sure if you was here, and thought in the least with me, you would not
wonder at my being uneasy at the present situation of our foreign politics. Nothing
is so bad as inconsistent views and measures, and that, I am afraid, is our case at
present. The court of Vienna (I suppose, as I am told) gives too much handle for
the dissatisfaction of the princes of the empire. We seem at present to be taking
part with them, for redressing their grievances, in opposition to the emperor ; when
we are, at the same time, endeavouring to perpetuate the House of Austria, by the
election of the arch-duke to be king of the Romans. This is the case ; and how it
will end I know not. I have not yet had one word from Vienna, in answer to my
letters, about the king of the Romans, and our negotiation with the elector of Bavaria.
I hear they are much out of humour, upon the execution of the decree of the *Corps
Evangélique.* The king of Prussia will blow up this point, as far as he can : but we
are much to blame to be catched by that. The best and most consistent way of
supporting the Protestants in the Empire, is by shewing the emperor, in an amicable
way, that he ought to do it, by the laws of the Empire ; and must do it, for his own

* Newcastle Papers.

interest : but *voyes de fait* should be well considered. I am as much as any body for encouraging and supporting the Protestants in the Empire ; but, in conjunction with the king of Prussia, I say with Mr. Hopkins, *timeo Danaos ;* it is not so easy, dear Brother, to support people in the right, or overrule them in the wrong. Prejudice makes it often difficult to judge what is right, and what is wrong. I am glad to see, in the main, that you agree in my notion of the utility of making a king of the Romans ; and, allow me to say, you see I act according to yours, in making that a *sine quâ non* of our Treaty with Bavaria.

" I agree with you, a substantial connection with the House of Austria is preferable to any expensive management with the inferior princes. But this substantial work for the House of Austria, cannot be done without those inferior princes. Neither is the House of Austria, alone, of that weight and use, for preventing a war, that it is, when it is supported and joined with the princes of the empire. * * * *

" Nothing can give me more pleasure, than the latter part of your letter, wherein you approve my letter to Bentinck. I wrote it with great attention ; and I hope it will have an effect. I see, as you do, the Dutch want to draw us into expenses ; but I do not think you see me inclined to be drawn in. I find, you have great objection to our being security for the Dutch proportion, in the Bavarian Treaty. I think it would cost us nothing ; but I will do nothing in it, without your previous consent. Russia has not cost us one single farthing ; and that was a much stronger, and more difficult point, considering the extent of it, and the circumstances, then, of the Republic. Our accession to the Russian Treaty seems at a distance ; there can be no thoughts of our paying for it.

" One word more, as to Nova Scotia. I heartily wish we were strong enough there to defend our rights, and beat off the enemy. I am afraid we are not. My letter to Albemarle is wrote so, as to go as far as you please, and no farther : though, I own, I think we must support this affair of Nova Scotia, and its extended boundary, whatever is the consequence."

THE DUKE OF NEWCASTLE TO MR. PELHAM.[*]

Answers for the sincerity of the Court of Vienna—Has secured the vote of Bavaria—Antici-pates the success of the election—Proposes to subsidise Saxony—Augurs favourably of the negotiation with Spain.

Hanover, June 23rd-July 4th, 1750.

" I hope you will be very well pleased with the letters which you will receive by this messenger, whenever the duke of Bedford sends them to you. I think those from Vienna are as good as could be expected. It is impossible to shew more gratitude than the empress queen does, upon this occasion ; and I think they are determined at Vienna, not only to give all proper facilities to bring about this great measure, but also to push it as effectually, and as speedily as possible. The king, as you may imagine, is highly pleased. His Majesty sees the honour and advantage of chusing a king of the Romans, at this time. At present, no power will take umbrage at it. How long that will be the case, nobody can tell ; therefore now is the

* Newcastle Papers.

time for pushing it, and bringing this to a point ; and I hope you will think my letter to Keith not ill calculated for that purpose.

" The two things you seemed to fear when I left England, were, first, that we might make our treaty with Bavaria, without having a sufficient security for his vote. Secondly, that though we had the Bavarian vote, we either might not be desirous, or might not be able, to effect the election of a king of the Romans. As to the first, you must do me the justice to own, that in all that has passed with the elector of Bavaria, and with the court of Vienna, I have declared that our treaty with Bavaria depended, absolutely, upon our having a sufficient security, that the electoral vote should be given for the king of the Romans, *en tout cas et en tout tems ;* and I did that, not only with a view to those two courts, but also that every body might see, that without that, the treaty could not be made; and this, I think, fully comes up to what you wished in that respect. As to the second, viz. the inclination and ability to do the thing, the last letters from Vienna, and my answer, I think, in great measure, prove both. There can be no doubt but we shall go about it in earnest. Haslang thinks himself sure, that the paper sent to his court will be accepted. And Keith must be mightily mistaken, if the court of Vienna will lose this great object, for a small sum of money. I am sure you will approve my pinning down the court of Vienna to give the money, and insisting that Hop should be authorised to satisfy the elector of Bavaria, as to the regular payment of the Dutch proportion.

" The king is so fond of this thing, at present, that he has already told me who shall be his electoral embassador at the Diet ; and has hopes of being able to finish it during his stay in Germany. His Majesty is not a little pleased with the conclusion of Keith's letter; where he assures us that justice shall be done to the Protestants : the affair of Hohenlohe decided in their favour; and we do not agree what has brought this about. Sometimes the king brags that his steadiness and resolution, in the affair of Hohenlohe, and intention, jointly with Prussia, to execute the commission of the *Corps Evangélique,* have greatly contributed to it, as well as the strong orders I sent to Keith. Monsieur le Grosvoight Munchausen is willing to think in this way. I have always said, that the proof the king gave of his affection for the House of Austria, by this offer, about the king of the Romans, with the proper representations, made at the same time upon other points, softened, convinced, and gained their Imperial Majesties. But since they are gained, it is immaterial whether one or both, or what is more likely, both together, and coming at the same time, did it. My friend Steinberg says, *mais c'est un grand ouvrage.* My able friend, the Grosvoight, has engaged his assistance to carry it through ; and that is the most material. Honest English Munchausen answers for his brother. I will enter no farther into the particulars of this affair. The letters sent to the duke of Bedford, and those I shall inclose in this letter, will explain the whole.

" I had really almost forgot to tell you one circumstance, that I had from Haslang, a few days before our answer came from Vienna. He seemed to despair of getting any equivalent for Mirandola, Concordia, &c., and told me that, if we would give the subsidy for six years, instead of four, he hoped that would do it at once ; and, upon discoursing with him, I found, that on taking leave, the prince of Wales had said to him, that he wished the treaty had been for six years, instead of four. But if a small sum of money will satisfy, this is out of the question. I believe you will think upon the whole, that this great work is brought nearer to perfection, than you, or indeed any body, thought it could be, in the time ; and, I hope, you think that, if it is perfected, it will do honour to the king, and to all, who in any shape have a hand in it. For I really am of opinion, no one measure could be, in the present circumstances, suggested by human understanding, so likely to secure and maintain the public peace upon a right foot, as this : not only, as I hope it will put the contending parties more upon a level, but also, as it must take away from one party one great object for disturbing the peace hereafter, which, by late experience, we know was the sole cause of the last war. But should this affair be delayed, another accident may happen, which may make the attempt unadvisable, and the success impracticable ; and, therefore, let us strike while the iron is hot ; whilst there is a disposition on one side, and no appearance of molestation on the other.

" Upon this principle, I would suggest it to your consideration ; and this I do, I can assure you, without the knowledge of the king, or any, the least hint from Fleming. I think there is no doubt, but we shall have six electors ; viz. Bohemia, Bavaria, Mayence, Treves, Cologne, and Hanover. That is enough, and more than enough, to make the election ; but, by the Grosvoight's paper, and, I hear, by Valory's discourse, there is a notion that there may some question arise about the *urgens casus*, the pressing necessity. If, therefore, Saxony would come in, and put this whole affair out of doubt, and bring on the election immediately, would you, on such an account, and on this condition only, think it advisable to join with Holland, in the same subsidy to Saxony that is given to Bavaria ?

" I only fling this out for your consideration. I shall be so far from entering into any engagement, or negotiation, of this kind, that I shall not say one word of it. The king would be very angry if he knew I had any such thought. Pray do not be angry with me, or form ideas to yourself, for which there is not the least foundation. If you think the thing not practicable, there is an end of it at once. * * * *

" I hope you will have attended to the affair of Nova Scotia. Monsieur Puisieulx's answer is certainly as favourable as we could expect ; but yet, when it comes to the point, I am afraid we shall not agree about the limits ; and that, in the reality, is the cause of the present violences ; though, even on supposition, that those countries were really disputable, the proceedings of the French are not to be justified. I must beg that you would look a little to these material points of business."

MR. PELHAM TO THE DUKE OF NEWCASTLE.*

Agrees to subsidise Bavaria—Hopes that no money will be paid for the coadjutorship of Osnaburg—On the affairs of Nova Scotia—Farther remarks on the negotiation for the election of a king of the Romans.

Greenwich Park, July 2nd-13th, 1750.

* * * * " I shall begin with assuring you, no one can have a greater satisfaction than myself, in seeing your mind at ease upon your foreign affairs. I saw by your whole

* Newcastle Papers.

correspondence, that it has been otherwise till now, ever since you have been abroad ; and, whatever my own notions may be, either with regard to the consequence the several disputes you have had, were to this country, or the greater or lesser difficulty there was in surmounting them, yet, as they made impression upon you, they affected me. I doubt not but you have acted with ability, in bringing the court of Vienna to a proper way of thinking, for their own interest ; and I believe the firmness of the king, in shewing that court that he would not be dictated to by them, and that he had resources, even in the Empire, to compel them to do right, has had a good effect also. I agree with you, this is the time to push on the election of a king of the Romans ; nobody, whose interest it is to oppose it, is in a disposition of mind, or perhaps of ability to traverse your negotiations now : it is plain, a proper conduct, in the court of Vienna, may bring it about ; and, I should hope, without much difficulty. But I cannot see any reason for our being brought into more pecuniary engagements : that of Bavaria you were all engaged in, and therefore I yielded, but not from a conviction that the thing was · right. I have, and do wish, therefore, that the sum may be moderate. You have hitherto said nothing of that ; and I shall be glad, for the sake of gilding the pill, that the affair of the king of the Romans may be settled at the same time.

"Haslang mentions the continuation of the subsidy for six years, and quotes the prince of Wales for that. If I remember right, his Royal Highness's proposal was to take half the subsidy for six years, rather than the whole sum for three. I agree in that, but I fear Mr. Haslang has no such thoughts or instructions. You will see by my last letter, how little I approve of a subsidy for Saxony ; and I am glad to find by yours, which I am now answering, that the great northern minister, Sir Charles Williams, is gone to Berlin, where he has my good wishes for a long continuance. His fertile genius can do no hurt there ; and if he writes as many odes as the king of Prussia can read, I shall grudge him neither his wit nor his applause.

' The managements with the elector of Cologne, I have always understood to be for the sake of procuring the coadjutorship of Osnaburgh, for the Duke of Cumberland. I can see through that very well : if that is not done now, his Royal Highness will never be bishop. I do not see that it is our concern ; if the king and he wish it, I wish it too ; but it does not seem reasonable to me, that we should pay for it. I think, therefore, you did very right in avoiding to give any answer to Mr. G. Bourke. These things are to be done when we want to make our court ; but, as I do not see that turns to any account, especially in my particular, I am unwilling to run the civil list more and more in debt, for nothing but moonshine.

"I conclude Albemarle has said nothing of the secret affair to the duke of Bedford ; I have crossed upon nothing of that kind ; and, as you truly say, the whole thing is now under suspense, I see no occasion of mentioning it at all here. It can do no good ; it has not now even the appearance of confidence, and, if I judge right, confidence is not expected. Whatever is done of that kind, must be by frank and open eclaircissement, when you meet. I do not recommend this to you ; you will do as you will ; I only say, that is the only method to be taken now, if any is to be taken at all.

" I have said and done all I can in the affair of Nova Scotia ; the duke of Bedford is scarce ever in town, but on a Regency day ; and then there is so much to do, and so little done, that I˙cannot pretend to answer for consequences. I have always foreseen, our great efforts for settlements there, would create some misunderstanding with our neighbours. I wished, therefore, it might h'ave been done gradually : but, you know, in that, as well as most other things, I was overruled. M. Puisieulx's answer is, undoubtedly, all we could expect from a French minister ; and I am satisfied he is sincere in blaming La Jonquiere, for what he has done, or suffered to be done ; but, at the same time, he clearly understands a neutrality in the disputed parts of that continent ; and if we go to settle any of those parts, I suppose we shall be called the aggressors. By all I can learn, we have an undoubted right to the whole. I am every day, therefore, pressing lord Duplin to finish the instructions for Mr. Shirley, which I understand will take up a fortnight's time. I did suggest, that Cornwallis should be told, that notwithstanding the fair words contained in the French answer, yet if they or their Indians presumed to disturb the English, in the uncontroverted part of Nova Scotia, he should use force to repel them ; and, that he might be enabled so to do, I thought he might be trusted with a power to augment Lascelles's regiment to the number of the other corps, which would give him an additional strength of four or five hundred men. This seemed to be relished, but how it was executed, or whether it is executed at all, I do not know.⁕ * *

" I think I have now answered every particular of your dispatch, that comes within my knowledge. You say, in your postscript, we shall make a great figure at the opening of the next session of parliament ; I heartily wish we may. The chusing a king of the Romans, if we do not pay too dear for it, will undoubtedly strike all those who have any turn to foreign systems ; and, if you can close well with Spain, every individual will feel the benefit ; and no ill humour will then remain in the mercantile part of this country, at least not among the honest and sensible part of them. I am at work upon that affair, in my way, and have some hopes an expedient may be found to satisfy the South Sea Company, and at the same time make them useful, towards the reduction of the unsubscribed part of the public debt : this is as yet in embryo. Bristow, who must do it, is in France ; and Sir John Barnard will, I believe, be rather against us in it : I beg, therefore, nothing may transpire till we are farther advanced.

" P. S.—Since I wrote the long letter which I now send you, I have seen your public dispatch ; and do not find any thing in Mr. Keith's, but what your private letter had informed me of before. Indeed, in your letter to lord Holdernesse, you mention the subsidy to the elector of Bavaria to be £.40,000, two-thirds of which his Majesty is to pay. I do not remember exactly what it is we pay now, but it will seem odd for us to pay as much for no troops, or at least when we want none, as in the heat of war, when soldiers were a scarce commodity.

" You will, I doubt not, be surprised to find the duke of Bedford's name not inserted in the minutes of this day. I knew nothing of his grace's intention to stay in the country, till last night ; and cannot conceive what could induce him to do it, after the several inclosures he received from you. I think it was the first post that brought any thing of business to the Secretary's office here, since his Majesty's arrival at Hanover; but we distinguish little between real and nominal business. I own it grieves me to see such a farce in government; but how it can be remedied, I do not comprehend."*   *   *   *

THE DUKE OF NEWCASTLE TO THE LORD CHANCELLOR.

Regrets an alteration in his brother's conduct—Speaks of the countenance given to the duke of Bedford, by some of the royal family—Laments the king's reserve and coldness—Is much dissatisfied with his situation—Is determined to resign, and accept the place of President of the Council.

Hanover, July 3rd-14th, 1750.

After referring, for all public business, to his dispatches to the duke of Bedford, and his secret letters to Mr. Pelham, he continues:—"I shall confine this letter singly to myself; and must begin with what most nearly affects me, viz.: a great alteration of style and manner in my brother's late letters. I do apprehend this change arises from my private letter to him, about the late royal parties, of which letter I sent your lordship a copy. But I send you a copy of one I wrote to him last post, in answer to the three there mentioned; and of one which I received from him this morning, and of a letter * which I now send to my brother by this messenger, containing my firm resolution relating to myself, from which I think no consideration will make me depart. And therefore I am now most earnestly to desire your lordship's advice and assistance, in the execution of it. It is now I summon all your friendship; and, as a mark of my firm dependence upon it, I shall acquaint you with some circumstances, that I have not mentioned to my brother, and which confirm me in my present resolution.

"I have mentioned to my brother no considerations but what relate to the duke of Bedford, &c.; and the support and countenance given to him, by part of the royal family, with the acquiescence, at least, of some of my best friends. There is another, which weighs with me as strong as any of them, and to which your lordship is not altogether a stranger, though not fit to be known by any body but yourself. I have found a visible difference in the king's behaviour to me, from what it was the last time I was here. And though he is at times very gracious, and, as to English affairs, does what I wish and propose, yet there is an indifference; a sort of reserve; an assuming to himself, with all the ministers here, the sole merit of the measure of the election of a king of the Romans (which, by the bye, you know the true state of), and seldom sending me the material part of his intercepted correspondence, and particularly, not Haslang's last letter, until the Grosvoight spoke to him to do it, and an equal change of behaviour to the duchess of Newcastle. All which I attribute to insinuations from our great lady † here, who thinks that if I were to have the merit of all that is

---

* This letter is dated July 4th-15th.   † Lady Yarmouth.

now doing, and likely to succeed, and the king had not his drawbacks, nothing could withstand that alteration,* which she knows I will insist upon, and which, I fear, she has promised to prevent.

" As to the duchess of Newcastle, she was, at first, extremely civil and agreeable to her. But, I believe, now, she has the demerit of a French embassadress, viz. that of taking the *pas,* where she now presides absolutely. As to myself, she is extremely civil to me. But I have not been alone with her one quarter of an hour, all the times put together since I have been here. I have lamented my never having an oppor- tunity of seeing her alone, to her friends ; to Mons. and Madame Wangenheim, and to her mother, Madame Wendt ; but it produces nothing ; so, I must conclude, she avoids me. I am afraid, I am thought to be too well with the two Münchhausens, and especially the Grosvoight, whom she will never forgive, and who, until within these two or three days, that Mons. de Steinberg has been in the country, has not seen the king alone, three times since he has been here, and never until within these three days, has had any talk with his Majesty upon material business. He is too able a man for the king absolutely to part with, and that is his hold : and I think (though I am not sure), he will not much longer bear very hard usage. Should his brother be hindered from returning to England, I think that would make him fly out ; and that he thinks the security against it. In short, there is no doing business here without him. He is firmly attached to me ; and I have brought him off from all his resentment to the court of Vienna, and his prejudices against a king of the Romans. He now works heartily for it ; and it is by his means, that I shall carry it through. It would therefore be unpardonable in me, to break with such a man ; and nothing else can be laid to my charge.

" Having given your lordship this sketch of our Hanover administration, you will not, I believe, wonder that it is no inducement to me to make a third visit here. When I see what impression my letter by this messenger makes upon my brother, and when I know your lordship's thoughts upon this and that, I must then consider when it may be proper to open my scheme to the king. I shall defer it as long as I can, lest it should make my stay here afterwards more disagreeable. But do it I will, in some shape or other, before our return to England.

" I must beg to know your opinion, whether I should speak directly, first, to the king, or through the medium of lady Yarmouth. I own I am most inclined myself, to the first. I shall have no assistance from her ; she will endeavour to carry me back to England, as she brought me to Hanover, without any decision. She fears, I shall talk to her upon this subject ; and yet, perhaps, if I should speak first to the king, she might think it a slight, and resent it accordingly. I own I had flattered myself, that my brother began to be convinced of the necessity of an alteration ; that he was pleased with my manner and matter, and with my unreserved confidence in him in every thing. I was led into this opinion by most of his own letters ; by two very remarkable ones from my lord Lincoln ; and by one which I have had from Mr. Pitt, who wrote in the handsomest and most

* The removal of the duke of Bedford.

friendly manner imaginable upon the subject; took notice of my brother's great
satisfaction with me, and concluded with the strongest wish for success, to all that I
was doing abroad, and to every thing that I might think necessary for my own ease,
when I came home. This conclusion, though very kind in him, did give me hopes,
that he had known or thought my brother not so averse, as, by the tenour of his late
letters, I must suppose him to be. Read my letter to my brother of this day's date,
and then say, as a friend, whether it is possible for me to do otherwise. That, if ever
it was practicable, is now too late. The king makes it necessary. The Duke and
the Princess Amelia make it necessary. In short, all my own friends have made it
necessary; and they must take the consequences for their pains. I am much easier
in the event than they imagine. I know, my lord, you have often thought me too
vain. But one in my station must sometimes speak for himself. I think a Secretary
of State, who, in the then circumstances, made the peace, with the consent of
every one of our allies; has preserved it upon the same foot; has united most of
the considerable princes of the empire; and, if it shall so happen, has *sans coup
férir*, or much money spent, chosen the Archduke king of the Romans, may retire
to be President of the Council, with some satisfaction to himself; and now, I fancy,
you begin to think me in earnest.

"You see how much I depend on your friendship, or I would not write to you in
the manner I do. I write to nobody else so. I only expect an unreserved letter
in return, which I shall ever value, and am most sincerely and unalterably, &c."

THE DUKE OF NEWCASTLE TO MR. PELHAM.

Threatens to resign if he cannot remove the duke of Bedford.

"DEAR BROTHER,   *Hanover, July 4th-15th,* 1750.

"I shall confine this letter to my private situation; and repeat to you, shortly, my
thoughts and resolution upon it. You know how impracticable I think it is, for me
to go on, in the Secretary's office, coupled as I am at present; and every post, and
every incident of late, confirms me in that opinion. The experience of this summer,
must convince every man that has seen it, how totally unfit, on all accounts, the duke
of Bedford is, for his present employment; and the experience of this summer, and
the last winter, sufficiently convinces me, how totally I am unfit to be joined with him
in it. His Grace's great quality, and greater supports, make it impracticable for any
one in my station, to use that freedom with him, that would certainly be used towards
another, who executed his office in the manner he does : and the daily opportunities
that are taken by the Duke of Cumberland, and the Princess Amelia, to mortify and
depress me, by the countenance shewn to the other, and the little satisfaction, only,
of complaining to my friends, and expecting their advice and support, being absolutely
taken from me, I have no party left to take, but to go on in this disagreeable
situation, which must daily grow worse, or to get out of it in the best way I can : and
that is the present consideration.

" I see, as well as any body, the difficulties that must attend the forcing the duke of Bedford out. I know where they will all be laid. And I know who will be charged with them, upon every slight incident that happens. And, therefore, that is what I am determined shall not be the case. And, indeed, I am very uncertain whether, considering the several late operations, it would be in my power to do it, if it was in my inclination. My present intention, therefore, is, (if no better way can be suggested by you, or my lord Chancellor), to acquaint the king, some time before our return to England, that the situation of the Secretary's office is such (from causes easily to be guessed by the king; and, indeed, stated by his Majesty above two years ago, in a strong, but true light), that I would desire his leave to retire to the office of President, or Privy Seal, which would be vacant by the duke of Dorset's removal to Ireland. But that, if means could be found (which, indeed, in the present humour, every body is in, I think it idle to imagine), to dispose the duke of Bedford to accept, in good humour, the President's office; and his Majesty would be pleased to appoint a Secretary of State, upon whom I could entirely depend ; and who would have a proper deference for one, who has been in that office above six and twenty years, I should then very readily continue where I am ; but that, without it, it was impossible. I have another motive, which weighs strongly with me, to adhere to that resolution. My years (though, I thank God, no other decay), sufficiently tell me, I grow old. This is the second Hanover journey that I have made, at fifty-seven. I find the second not so agreeable (to say no more), as the first. The third must necessarily be less so ; and, therefore, I can have no thoughts of making it. I would, therefore, desire any friend in the world, of mine, to consider what a figure I shall make, Secretary at home, at the bottom of the Regency, with the duke of Bedford Secretary at Hanover, and the duchess, something there also. That cannot be. But, had I one, I could entirely depend upon (and I will have no other), I should be easy at home ; and easy, with regard to every thing abroad. If this is the case, the inference is clear, that this is the time to settle this affair, for me either to be President, or Privy Seal ; or to have another colleague in the Secretary's office.

" The consequence of my being President will be more proper for others to consider, than myself. I can, however, see three persons that may properly succeed me. The first (and most likely, in my opinion, to do), is Sir Thomas Robinson. The duke of Bedford would, then, have the parade, and exterior, of the Secretary's office, and that, I believe, would content him; and the business would be well, and solidly done, by the other. Lord Chesterfield might also go on, some time, with the duke of Bedford ; and drop him, with the approbation of every body, when he thought proper. Lord Granville, to be sure, would supply the place well ;. and, I think prejudices to him are now pretty well got over ; and, in that case, that might do. But, however, this is not my business. It is sufficient for me to know, that persons are so made, that there must be some alteration. And, if there had ever been a possibility of going on, in the present shape, the intrigues carrying on by men and women, great and small ; the public demonstrations of resentment, and irreconcileable hatred, make it altogether impracticable. Those things should have been stopped sooner, by those who think the remedy dangerous." *   *   *

THE DUKE OF NEWCASTLE TO MR. PELHAM.

Is sanguine in his hopes of securing seven electoral votes, and of obtaining the election.

Hanover, July 4th-15th, 1750.

* * * * " I am now to acquaint you, in great confidence (which you will communicate to nobody but my lord Chancellor), that count Haslang has received instructions from his court, to endeavour to get the treaty of subsidy forthwith concluded, upon
the foot of the verbal declaration only, transmitted in my letter of the 6th-17th of June,
to the duke of Bedford; and leave the obligation of giving the electoral vote, to
depend, afterwards, upon the court of Vienna's satisfying the elector, upon his several
pretensions.

" Mons. Haslang was with me, to endeavour, pursuant to his instructions, to get
the treaty immediately concluded upon that foot. I told him, very plainly, that the
electoral vote was a condition *sine quâ non.* That, if the elector, his master, would
give the king sufficient security upon that head, I should have his Majesty's orders,
to sign the treaty to-morrow; and would give him a Declaration, engaging the king's
good offices, for the adjusting all his (the elector's), pretensions upon the court of
Vienna, according to justice and the treaties; but, that it was to no purpose, to be
taking up time in negotiation, except the elector would consent, positively, to give his
vote; and, that upon this the whole depended.

" Count Haslang has since told me, that he had made such a report of what had
passed, to his master, as, he was persuaded, would do the business. And I have
reason to think, that he has represented what I said to him so fairly, and so strongly,
that his court must now determine, whether they will have the Treaty upon these
terms, or not at all.

" M. Haslang endeavoured to shew me, that, by getting the elector of Bavaria's
vote, we should have both that of Cologne, and Palatine; and strongly asserted, that
the elector of Cologne had not engaged his vote, and would not do it, without the
elector of Bavaria. I answered as strongly, that the king was secure of the elector of
Cologne's vote; as major-general Borck, who made the treaty, had assured me.
And I send you what his Majesty has thought proper to direct major-general Borck
to write to M. de Metternich, the elector of Cologne's minister, in order to clear up
this point. * * * *

" I have also the satisfaction to acquaint you, that baron Wrede, the Palatine
minister, has opened himself very fully to the king, the Grosvoigt Münchhausen,
baron Steinberg, and myself; and has given the strongest reason to hope, that the
elector Palatine will concur in this, the king's great object; and, immediately enter
into an alliance of friendship with his Majesty, as elector; and, also into an engagement, with regard to the election of a king of the Romans. And I send you a sketch
of a treaty, which the Grosvoigt has prepared for that purpose; the substance
of which Mons. Wrede has sent to his court, and expects a favourable answer
upon

" Mons. Wrede has made no mention of subsidies to me ; and has been told, both by his Majesty and his ministers, that that is impossible. He has only seemed to wish that those guaranties (relating to the succession of Juliers, and Berg, and the treaty concluded between the present king of Prussia, and the late elector Palatine, for that purpose), which his Majesty may think ·proper to give, as elector, may afterwards be confirmed by the king, as king; to which, I should imagine, there would be no objection, as they relate only to the performance of engagements already entered into with the king of Prussia, by the Treaty of 1741 ; and to the securing the rights belonging to the Duke of Deux Ponts, when he should succeed to the elector Palatine. The support of a Protestant elector Palatine, in his just rights, would certainly be very proper in itself, and highly popular, in all Protestant countries. But, nothing can be said particularly, upon these points, till the treaties are seen, and the guaranties desired, in consequence of them, considered.

" Count Stadion, the elector of Mayence's minister, makes no difficulty in answering for the elector, his master. The elector of Treves is too zealous for the common cause, to be at all doubted. So that if these negotiations, now on foot, should as is very probable, all succeed, and that soon, you see there will be seven of the nine electors secured, for the election of a king of the Romans ; and that with no farther expense to the public than a subsidy of about twenty-eight thousand pounds per annum to the elector of.Bavaria ; and, I believe you will think that this is an object of the utmost importance to the peace and tranquillity of Europe, and the maintenance of that system, which alone can be agreeable to the true interests of the Maritime Powers." * * * *

THE LORD CHANCELLOR TO THE DUKE OF NEWCASTLE.

Mentions a conference, which he has had with Mr. Pelham, with whom he concurs, in persuading the duke to relinquish his intention of resigning.

Powis House, July 13th-24th 1750.

    *   *   *   *   *   *   *

" I had a long conference on Wednesday night with Mr. Pelham, on the subject of your letters to him ; and produced your short one to me, and no more. In this I obeyed your Grace's commands ; though if he should come to the knowledge of my having received a large. packet by that messenger, which is not impossible, it may give him jealousy, and be attended with disagreeable consequences. From hence you may be sure I was perfectly silent upon the alteration of the king's and lady Yarmouth's behaviour to your Grace, though I found your brother had at least suspicions of the former, and ascribed the positiveness with which you declared your resolution in your letter to him, to some such cause. He collected this from what you say of the second journey not being so agreeable (to say no more) as the first, and from expressions of the like tendency, in some of your former letters.—I suffered him to make use of his own inferences, without discovering the least appearance of my knowing any more ; but affirmed, that what you had now written, was no more than what you had often said to me before you left England : viz. that if in some shape or other you could not be delivered from your present colleague, you would yourself retire to the President's place.

*   *   *   *   *

" We next discussed the grand point of the resolution which your Grace has declared.   He professed himself entirely of opinion against it :—that it could not be ; apprehended the worst consequences both to yourself and the public ; wished the other scheme of your colleague's changing his office could take place ; that he had tried at it, both with the duke and princess Amelia, but could not find he had made any impression ; and repeated, what he had formerly said, that it was his opinion, that it could be brought about no other way but by direct removal.   I find he is every day more and more dissatisfied with the duke of Bedford ; blamed his manner of doing business as much as your Grace can do ; that his behaviour in this regency had shewn it in a stronger light; and wished for a more diligent useful secretary in his place.   But how to bring this about he did not know.   That he was convinced the duke of Bedford would change his office to-morrow, in favour of lord Sandwich, but that was going from bad to worse.   We reasoned upon this a good while, and I pressed him to make farther efforts ; but without coming to any conclusion, it ended that he would write to you in his way, and I should write in mine.

" Here it is that your Grace is pleased to summon all my friendship.   It was unnecessary to do it in so solemn a manner.   My best advice, and most faithful service are ever at your devotion ; and when I presume to give it, you may be sure it is always sincere and well meant.   But I am to the last degree sensible, that it is above my ability to advise you upon this nice and delicate question, which is rendered more delicate, by the circumstances added in your letter to me, which are not disclosed to your brother.   But though I am really unable to advise, one cannot help having an opinion about it; and my sincere opinion is, against your Grace's attempting to carry this scheme into execution whilst you are abroad.

" In forming this opinion, I do assure your Grace, that I have laid myself entirely out of the question.   After having drudged in the laborious office of Chancellor near fourteen years, I have no fondness to keep it longer, especially at near three-score. It is a constant round of the same fatigue.   The incentive of ambition is quite over. The profits of it I do not now want or value; and if I cannot have the satisfaction of serving with my friends, I can have nothing to make it tolerable.   My reasons are entirely drawn from the consideration of the public, and of yourself.

" As to the public, you know my opinion, that it will suffer prodigiously, by losing your service in this office.   On that head I will not say all that I think, because I would in this letter, avoid even the appearance of flattery.   If your Grace was in the late earl Sunderland's situation, and could remove from one office to another, still retaining the character and influence of prime minister, the case would be different. But your own scheme, and the motives to it, speak the contrary to that.   In this situation, I think it will be impracticable for your Grace to name your own successor. Those you leave behind will not take Sir Thomas Robinson.   Among other reasons, it would be looked upon, as a mortifying stroke to lord Sandwich.   The king would not take my lord Chesterfield, neither do I think he would serve with the duke of

Bedford. It is therefore my firm opinion, that the king would immediately send for my lord Granville. How could you serve as President under him, or how could the party endure it. For I cannot agree, that the prejudices of your friends against his lordship are got over.

"As to yourself, your Grace must give me your indulgence to speak freely. It is my duty, especially as you summon me to it. I think it would be represented in the world, as your quitting the field, and leaving a complete victory to your adversaries. This reflection you would not easily bear. For your Grace to continue at court, in the President's office, and see all the business and power, the access to the closet, as well as to the other branches of the royal family, in other hands :—suppose also they should happen to make their court so well, that for some time the appearances of favour and countenance on that side should increase,—would not this be a scene of perpetual uueasiness and dissatisfaction to you, and keep your mind in constant agitation? I protest for my own part, I would much rather quit the court entirely, than be in such a situation.

" If you take the President's place, you must either make yourself a mere cause-hearer, or else be a party at political conferences and meetings. The first I take to be impossible. In the latter you would find more contradiction and uneasiness, without the power you have now.

" Do not flatter yourself, my dear lord, that after having been twenty-six years in the office of Secretary of State, you shall find any relief, in retiring to that of President. It never did happen ; and never will.

"In this consideration, what you say of an alteration in the king is certainly very material. But of this, it is impossible to judge, without knowing the nature and extent of it. If it proceeds from any real *alienation*, you will not be more easy in the President's office. But from your own account, this alteration seems to be of another kind.

" Your Grace owns, that he does what you wish and propose, both as to English and foreign affairs. That takes in the whole circle of real business. His reserve or want of good humour, now and then, may proceed from different causes. May it not have proceeded now from his illness ? Pain—apprehension of such a distemper as the gout returning, and giving him frequent vexations ? Your Grace knows the king much better than I do ; but I should think him of a make, likely to be affected by such incidents, especially when they come upon him, at a time, and in a place, where he had promised himself nothing but amusement and pleasure.

" But you say, he assumes to himself the sole merit of the measures of electing a king of the Romans, &c. For God's sake, my dear lord, let him do so ; and flatter him in it. A prince cannot make a minister a greater compliment than by making his measures his own. I have heard it has been no unuseful art, in some ministers, to give things that turn to their masters.

" As to the great lady, your account of her behaviour is indeed surprising. It has been for some time a mystery to me. Your Grace knew long ago, what was my way of thinking about suffering some other persons* to fall off from you, and depending

* The Duke of Cumberland and the Princess Amelia.

entirely upon her. But it is hard for me to persuade myself, that she can be in the same system with the Duke and the Princess. Possibly your Grace's connections with the Munchausens may be in the case. Is that so necessary, that you cannot abate of the appearances of it? But still I do not think, this will go far. However, it is a good reason not to open hastily to her your present scheme, lest some ill use should be made of it.

"To all this your Grace will be apt to retort—'But what is to be done? Am I to go on for ever thus yoked, and have no passport of deliverance?' I think not; and I think farther that there is a prospect of deliverance, not very remote, though not immediate.

"Your Grace mentions your resolution not to take another Hanover journey. God knows, that is a very remote consideration. You are a much younger man than the king. Look forward to his Majesty's age two years hence, and consider what is the probability of another Hanover journey, especially if infirmities should increase. Surely such a *distant possibility* can furnish no reason for taking a present measure.

"But your Grace will still ask what is the prospect of redress? As to that, I really think that the duke of Bedford's manner of executing business, whatever it may be for the public, is the luckiest circumstance for you, personally, that can possibly be. I am thoroughly convinced that your brother is now heartily tired of him; and would be glad to find a method to get rid of him, consistent with his own way of thinking. The experience of this regency must have convinced every lord, who attends that board, of the same thing. His unpopularity increases every day; and he is sensible of it.

"Add all these together, and consider whether at the foot of the account, it does not appear that he is doing his own business for you; and I really think, that with a little patience, the thing will be brought about, in no long time after you come home, provided you keep your hold of the king; whereas if you should prematurely propose your present scheme at Hanover, I cannot pretend to foresee what may be the consequence. It will give new spirits, and minister new cause of triumph. Neither is there any necessity for it, for the President's office may be kept open, as long as you please, without inconvenience.

"Your Grace thinks this a favourable time to retire to be President of the Council, after making the peace with so much advantage, and the other instances of conduct, which you have just reason to be proud of. My dear lord, whenever you retire, it will be, *satur gloriæ*. Nobody can have more real concern for your honour and fame, than I have. Posterity will do it justice; but nobody ought to rely upon their contemporaries for such retribution. Besides, I imagine you would wish to finish the affair of Spain, whilst you are in your present situation. I fear I have tired your Grace; I am sure I have tired myself. Whatever I have said, proceeds from the sincerity of my heart. I will revolve this important question over and over again in my mind; and when any thing farther occurs, will submit it to you. I understand that your Grace has not written to the Duke* since you left England.

Of Cumberland.

You may remember I was humbly of opinion, that it was right for you to seek an occasion of doing it, and I really think so still. It is impossible to want topics."

MR. PELHAM TO THE DUKE OF NEWCASTLE.*

Rejoices that the negotiation for the election is likely to prove successful—Finds it difficult to introduce economy into the public offices.

"DEAR BROTHER,   *Arlington Street, July* 13*th*-24*th*, 1750.

" I am very glad to find you have so good a prospect of coming soon to the election of a king of the Romans. It will certainly be a great work well executed ; and if no more expense is to attend it, than what you mention, I should hope, the very material advantage it is to this country, and to all those who are properly jealous of the power of France, to have the imperial Crown secured to the House of Austria, would, as I have often said, gild the pill, in the instance of the Bavarian subsidy ; though were it to go farther, I cannot say my opinion would be for it.* * * *

" The *ébauche* you sent me of an electoral treaty with the Palatine, I conclude is very proper. It engages us in nothing : and if afterwards, any proper measures are proposed for England's accession, it will be time enough then to consider of them ; and I doubt not, but we shall all agree in what his Majesty shall propose, as I see no possibility of any future expense arising from that quarter. I have now said all that occurs to me, on the subject of your letter ; and most heartily congratulate you on the prospect there is of every thing ending to your wishes, and so far coinciding with my own, that I do not at present suspect any prince in Europe desirous of beginning a new war ; and I believe we shall not invite them to it, if they do not call upon us.

" I take the liberty of inclosing to you a warrant for his Majesty's signature, for the allowance of certain expenses incurred by lord Loudon during the late rebellion in Scotland. I cannot say I much liked this demand, and therefore did, by his Majesty's order, refer the whole account, not only to the auditors of the imprest, but also to the Paymaster General, and the Secretary at War. They examined it carefully, and made strong and reasonable objections. I then took the liberty of speaking to the Duke upon it, who could not answer for the whole demand ; but, as lord Loudon has been years out of his money, and as we have abated all we could, and he is ready to take his oath, that this sum and much more was expended by him, during his command in the Highlands, the Board of Treasury thought we could not any longer defer laying this before his Majesty, and humbly desiring his royal approbation ; for I do truly believe, unless this money is paid, the man is absolutely undone.

" After what I have said in this letter, upon the subject of economy, you will perhaps be surprised, that I am going to offer to his Majesty a small expense myself. The inclosed letter from lady Jane Douglas, sister to the duke of Douglas, who is mad, though not proved so in form, will shew you the case ; I believe you have heard something of her case before ; she is married to an officer of low rank, in the

* Newcastle Papers,

Dutch service, by whom she has children. Her brother used to allow her three hundred pounds a year; but he, in some freak, has withdrawn that allowance, and the poor woman, though of the highest quality, and heiress to her brother's estate, has not clothes to her back, and can hardly keep her children from starving. These circumstances, I own, moved me; and though I have not the least acquaintance with her, I should hope his Majesty would permit me to pay her privately £.300 a year, till her brother comes to his senses, or she comes into a fortune, to be able to support herself. I doubt this long letter will tire you in reading: I am sure it has me in writing. I shall therefore say no more at present, but to desire you to make my compliments to all that I know, or know me, at Hanover.

THE DUKE OF NEWCASTLE TO MR. PELHAM.*

Is not easy upon foreign affairs, though he thinks they will end well—Again complains of the silence of the duke of Bedford—Urges the necessity of an united administration.

"DEAR BROTHER,   *Hanover, July 18th-29th,* 1750.

" I shall now return a more particular answer to some parts of your long letter, than I had time to do by the last messenger. I must begin by saying, my mind is very far from being at ease upon our foreign affairs, I think things will do at last, notwithstanding the many rubs they may still meet with; but they would do better, if we had not people, who through ignorance or worse motives, are constantly flinging in things to set us against those who are, and must be at the head of this affair, and whose conduct, however blameable it may have been formerly, I will affirm is irreproachable at present. You may easily see I mean the court of Vienna; and in this light both the *disputes* and the *disputants* are of consequence to our country. But though I despair ever to convince you of that, I am thoroughly convinced, that as far as my ease, and much more, my reputation, may be affected by them, you take a most kind and affectionate part in them.

" You will see, through this whole transaction, that I deal plainly and sincerely with you. I send you all I know ; I endeavour to lay the fault (where there is any) where it ought to be ; and I keep up, in the strictest manner, to my declarations,. and do not suffer myself to be diverted from them ; and if you recollect some appearances last winter, and the apprehensions you had from those appearances, you will think there is some merit, in insisting, with the elector of Cologne, that he is obliged to give us his vote, by the fifth article of his treaty, now made ; and that no treaty should be made with the elector of Bavaria, without a positive assurance in writing that he will do the same.

" As to the first, I have reason to think that some of the German ministers (not the Grosvoight) were not well pleased with my preparing the *Mémoire Instructif* for general Borch, and no less so with the draught of the declaration ; and though the king had approved both, and made a small alteration to both, with his own hand, in my presence, I do know, that by order of one of the ministers, another draught of a declaration was sent to the king, and signed by his Majesty. This appearing at their

* Newcastle Papers.

meeting, Meyer was ordered to tell the king, that they thought my draught was better than that, which his Majesty had signed; upon which the king cancelled that and signed *mine*. The person principally concerned in ordering the other, said indeed, that I had sent my draught to him; but that he had not had time to read it. This is what I meant by saying, that the putting the king's business (I may add either here, or any where else) into ignorant hands, must necessarily affect the success of it; and this, with many things of this kind, makes me go on here always heavily, and sometimes very unpleasantly. I know, a more discreet man than myself, would not mention these things, but I know also, to whom I mention them.

" I send every thing that is fit to be sent, to the duke of Bedford; but, by the by, was there ever an instance, since Adam's days, as Jacob said, that the Secretary of State has not yet said one single word, upon all these secret confidential communications? To prove my assertion about the court of Vienna, I send you Keith's private letter to me, wherein it appears, that Vorster is directed, not only to *follow,* but to *ask* my advice; and authorised to go all reasonable lengths, in the money asked by the elector of Bavaria, for the equivalent, &c. To prove that my preference of the present behaviour of the court of Vienna, to that of the court of Munich, is well founded, I not only refer you to what I send the duke of Bedford, but in great confidence send you some of his Majesty's *intended* correspondence, by which you will see the declaration made to the king of Prussia, with regard to the election of a king of the Romans, and the not stipulating a body of troops to be furnished; and you will also see, what I said to Haslang upon both. I easily see the evasion of the first, by there being nothing in the treaty. The obligation is proposed to be by *déclaration verbale* though in writing; but as to the troops, I fear he may have more difficulty, though I think we must insist upon it, in order for parliament; and indeed the Dutch will scarce agree without it.

" This last letter of Haslang's, however, shews the palatine minister is sincere; and that is a great article. In a long conversation I had with Haslang, I found he thought, the difficulty about the electoral vote, would be got over, by the money to be given for the equivalent for Mirandola, &c. I told him, they must ask a moderate sum; he said he had given his opinion, by which I might see what sum he thought would do; that was, the prolongation of our Treaty for two years longer, which amounted to £.80,000; for I thought it had always been understood, that, as by the last Treaty, the elector of Bavaria received, I think, £.60,000 per annum, viz. about £.43,000 from us, the rest from Holland, he was to have by this only £.40,000 in all, viz. about 27 or £.28,000 from us, the rest from Holland. I told Haslang, this would be flinging the load of the equivalent upon us and Holland, which we could never consent to; he said we might settle that with the court of Vienna. I find Hop does not dislike this proposal, and thinks that his masters will come into it, as it engages the elector two years longer. For my part, I think, if the elector of Bavaria will be contented with this, we may find a way to make the court of Vienna pay all, or at least the greatest part, of this additional expense of £.80,000, in the course of six years. And this I shall insist upon, when it comes to be settled with Mr. Vorster. I have always laid down, that they must pay something. Keith, at first, gave us good hopes, but now says positively, that Vorster is authorised to go all reasonable lengths. I should think £.80,000, in some shape or other, might be had in the course of six years.

"The Prince of Wales's proposal, first, to Haslang, was £.20,000 for eight years; but Haslang says, at taking his leave, the Prince said, he wished the Treaty was for six years. If every thing else was agreed, I think we should come well enough off upon this point. I send you Borch's instructions, signed by the king, from his German Chancery. You see they have adopted my notions, and my draughts. Whatever may have been the original view of the Treaty of Cologne, you see to what view it is now applied. I hope you will be under no alarm from Sir Charles Hanbury Williams's journey to Warsaw. I think, what you fear is guarded against, by my letters, which I send to the duke of Bedford. I shall also write him a private one, from myself, in answer to one from him, upon the subject of subsidies, in which I shall tell him plainly, that whatever my own private opinion may be, it is not to be attempted. I will never deceive you, or act contrary to what I publicly profess to you, whatever my private sentiments may be.* * * *

"I extremely approve what you say and do about Nova Scotia. That affair is not over. I took an opportunity to hint to the king, from whence the late proposals at the Regency, relating to it, came. I think with you, M. Puisieulx understands a neutrality in the disputed part of Nova Scotia. I am not master enough of what we have done, or are doing there, to know whether we can submit to that, or are acting upon that principle. If we do, I verily believe the French would evacuate all the rest, and perhaps stipulate a neutrality for the controverted part, till the dispute is decided. But I doubt, that will not do our business. We should, I am afraid, be by that obliged to undo a great deal of what we have done; and, therefore, your advice to hasten the instructions, and dispatch the commissaries, is the main thing to be done at present. And I think your measure and orders to Cornwallis will, in the mean time, keep things upon a tolerable foot there.

"I do not at all despair of our being able to open the Session (if we are to open it) successfully, in point of business, both at home and abroad. It must amaze and please every body, if, at a time when it was universally thought that we were reduced so low by the last war, Holland so totally exhausted, and the House of Austria so near it, that we had scarce any thing left but prayers and tears, we should be able to connect such an inoffensive strength together, as to chuse an archduke of Austria king of the Romans, with only one dissentient voice (and perhaps not even that), of Brandenburg. This, added to your glorious thought, which, though only in embryo (for I know your embryos) has given me the greatest joy, of perfecting our great work with Spain; and that, with the consent of the South Sea Company, must make our foreign affairs appear in a great light, and, as you wisely say, please every mercantile man in England, and no man in England is more for pleasing them than myself. This, coming upon the back of your great work of the reduction, coinciding also, as I understand, with the general good humour of the farmers, occasioned by a most immense exportation, and farther demand of corn, must, of itself, make every public measure easy, and his Majesty make a figure, which the most affectionate and the most sanguine of his subjects could not expect, in the present circumstances.

" But this, though the best foundation is laid for it, cannot be carried into execution, without an administration that has solidity, resolution, and experience, linked and united together, void of jealousy and suspicion of each other, supported by the same common friends, and actuated by the same principles and interests ; and, above all, not dependant upon cabal, but favoured, countenanced, and protected by the king. Where this is to be found, I know not : where it is not, I know. But, however that may be, let you and I, and my lord Chancellor, finish, if possible, what we have begun this summer. Do your great part with Spain ; I will do the best I can, towards what I think great here, and let us make our successors ashamed of not following us, if they can ; or those who may bring them there, ashamed of bringing people, who are incapable of doing it ; and this is all I will say at present, upon the subject of the administration, till I receive your answer to my letter, which I wrote a fortnight ago. I shall remain of the same opinion ; and, however you may dislike my manner of expressing it, I am sure you will not the motives, upon which it is founded. I never in my life was more than I am at present, dear Brother," &c.

MR. PELHAM TO THE DUKE OF NEWCASTLE.*

Repeats his censure of the duke of Bedford, for neglect of business, but dissuades his brother from insisting on his dismission—Exhorts him to lay aside his suspicions of his friends.

"DEAR BROTHER,   *July 25th-Aug. 5th,* 1750.

" I can as well sit down to answer your two private letters of the 18th-29th now, as wait till Friday, and possibly not have then so much time to spare ; if any thing worthy your notice happens between this and then, I will add it by way of postscript. But as the duke of Bedford is out of town, and, as I understand, means to continue so, it is not likely that I shall have much to say in addition. I must own, that total neglect of business which has appeared in him, ever since the king went abroad, surprises me much. If I did not see and know, from other circumstances, that he is as fond of his office, and is as desirous to continue well at court, as he ever was, I should conclude he had given every thing over, that he was resolved to quit, but intended by this behaviour to draw you into some overt act, which he flattered himself might hamper, and inconvenience the king's affairs in your hands. But it certainly is not so : it is all jollity, boyishness, and vanity ; he persuades himself that riding post from London to Woburn, and back again, once in a week or fortnight, is doing a great deal of business ; and that nobody has any more reason to complain of his absence, almost the whole summer, than at your going to Claremont, once a week in the winter.

" This is the state of our case here ; but I do not see the great reason you have to dislike it personally ; there is nothing, you write to him about, requires any answer, with regard to government. It would undoubtedly be more agreeable and more

* Newcastle Papers.

becoming an administration, if we were all upon such terms as we could communicate our thoughts to each other, without jealousy, and with friendship and attention ; but that has not been the case a great while, and when it will be so, I agree with you, is very difficult to foresee. What does the king say ? Does he make no observation upon that silence on all business, in the duke of Bedford's letters ? I am sure he sees it, and, if he does not take notice of it, it proceeds from the apprehensions he has of another rupture ; and, as I have long seen, quiet is what he loves better than all of us put together. If the idleness or ignorance of any one does not give him personal trouble, he will take no notice of it. So much for his Grace ; but as you again desire my advice upon your former private letter, relating to yourself, I can only repeat what I have said before ; if you can command yourself, so far as to wait for the chapter of accidents, content yourself with the known superiority you have, both in the court and in the kingdom, as a man of business ; if you will avoid personal altercations and the making comparisons which nobody will make but yourself, and not be perpetually fretting your friends with unjust suspicions of them, or tiring of them with continued communications upon what does not always appear very material : if you can and will do this, I am satisfied every thing will fall into your lap, and ways may and will be found, to prevent any cabal amongst those at present in the king's service, from taking an effect to the prejudice of the whole, or any material part of the present system. But if we are publicly to quarrel, when the king comes over, I very much fear, as I once said before, which ever side gets the better at court, neither will be able, alone, to carry on the king's affairs in parliament.

"You have now my thoughts, and, upon mature consideration, my advice : you will however do as you think proper. I can assure you, and I believe you think it, I have no partiality for any of those gentlemen ; for some of them, perhaps, I have a more fixed dislike than you yourself. I am sorry you do not like the situation of your foreign affairs, so well as you did some time ago. I ever thought it depended on the court of Vienna, whether we should have a king of the Romans chosen or not. If you can persuade them to do what is proper and necessary, for so material a work for their future grandeur and security, you will do greatly ; but I fear the evil genius of that court will follow them to the end of the world, and that some punctilio, pride or avarice, will prevent their doing at this time for a little, what some years hence they may possibly give up another Silesia for.

"Haslang's paper is nonsense : does he think the maritime powers will give a subsidy of £.40,000 per annum for four years, to any German prince whatever, merely for their good words, without either stipulating the electoral vote, or even the furnishing of a body of troops ? You talked incomparably well to him ; and believe me, dear Brother, a little of that language to the highest of them, will now and then do good ; I mean, you may be assured, your favourite court of Vienna. Notwithstanding these rubs, I hope and believe, all will end well. You say, one of the ministers,* not the Grosvoight, gave orders for another paper of instructions, to be drawn up for general Borch, and got it signed, but upon consideration, yours was taken ; I conclude, I must understand who that is, but it surprises me most exceedingly. I not only took

---

* See the duke's letter of the 18th-29th July.

that person to have had the greatest submission to your opinion, but I thought he had also modesty enough, to prefer almost any opinion to his own. I must, therefore, conclude, this goes somewhat farther than I can at present unravel.

THE DUKE OF NEWCASTLE TO MR. PELHAM.*

Is concerned for the situation of lord Harrington, and will endeavour to procure him a pension.

"DEAR BROTHER, *Hanover, August 1st-12th,* 1750.

" As the king will be going to the Göhrde in three weeks, and as it is generally said and believed, that his Majesty will be returning to England, about the 4th-15th of October, it may soon be necessary to consider what to do with the duke of Dorset's warrant for lord lieutenant of Ireland. I should be very sorry that any thing shocking should be done to lord Harrington, at least as to the manner ; and, indeed, the state of his health is such, that he cannot be surprised, if after four years enjoyment of it, another lord lieutenant is appointed. I should think that he might be acquainted, and that soon, that the duke of Dorset (who thought himself ill used by his nomination), had always applied to succeed, after the expiration of three years, and renewed his instances this last winter, that he might be appointed before the king went abroad, and actually found a way to apply to the king, who was not averse to granting his request ; that out of regard to my lord Harrington, that was not then done ; but it was impossible to avoid giving the duke of Dorset hopes of succeeding towards the end of the summer, as new lords lieutenants always are appointed some considerable time before they go over ; that by this means my lord Harrington was appointed of the Regency, and any disagreeable event upon his immediate return avoided; that the king had declared he would appoint the duke of Dorset, at or immediately before his return to England, and that therefore it was to be expected, orders might come from Hanover for that purpose. If you do not care to talk in this way, yourself, to my lord Harrington, or as having had this account from me, upon the receipt of your answer to this letter, I will write to him a letter to this purpose. There is one thing more I would suggest to you. To be sure the bad state of his health makes it impossible for him to continue, or be removed to any place that requires attendance or exertion ; and therefore a pension is the only thing that can be given him. Though I know how it will be received by the king, yet if you think proper, I am very ready to propose, in your name and my own, a pension of £.1,500 or £.2,000 per annum for him. Probably, poor man, he may not enjoy it long. Possibly the king may say, he has given him, and that is true, a very valuable pension of £.2,500 per annum, and that for a term of years. But great as that favour was, it was done during his being in service, and, therefore, when he is to be removed out of every thing, it might, and would, be thought hard, to give him no sort of consideration after so many years service. I have now suggested all I think upon this subject, and beg your advice and opinion. You must see my reasons, and I am sure you will approve them."

* Newcastle Papers.

THE DUKE OF NEWCASTLE TO MR. PELHAM.*

Is disappointed at the change of conduct in the electors Palatine and Cologne—The king blames the court of Vienna, whom the duke of Newcastle justifies—Will follow his brother's advice, in suspending his designs against the duke of Bedford—Explains the motives for his silence respecting lady Yarmouth.

"DEAR BROTHER,   *Hanover, August 1st-12th,* 1750.

" I wanted the cordial of your letter, to support me, upon the disappointments, that I have had this week. When I wrote last, I thought our affairs in an extreme good way ; and till yesterday, had been confirmed in that opinion. I send you little notes, that you may see, my hopes were not ill grounded. Monsieur Wrede, the Palatine minister, not only said, that he had received a letter from their minister, at Munich, that the elector of Bavaria had told him himself, that he had taken the resolution to conform to what we desired, and finish (which letter Munchausen saw), but that the elector Palatine had wrote to him, that he approved all Wrede's ideas, and that he should have full power to finish what he had begun. Notwithstanding all this, I know, and have seen, a letter from Wachendorf, the elector Palatine's minister, quite in a different strain, insisting upon great concessions, from the court of Vienna, and a subsidy of £.40,000 per annum, at least, from us, in consideration of arrears, due to the House of Palatine, in queen Anne's war. His Majesty has neither sent this letter to me, nor owned it. On the contrary, he has this morning railed, for the first time, of late, against the court of Vienna ; and has pitched upon the present time to blame them, though he was, the other day, so well pleased with them, and they are disposed to do every thing, that can be expected from them.

" You will see, from the inclosed letter from major general Borch, that things are far from going well at Bonn. The king makes slight of all this ; will fancy all will do ; or, perhaps (what he may like as well), fling the whole blame on the court of Vienna ; but that will not do. We are here disturbed at some new decree of the empire. Vorster is to be with me to-morrow. We are in great rage, and therefore think, Bavaria, Cologne, Palatine, and all the world, in the right, against them. In short, I hope to send you a better account, by the next messenger, and will conclude this, by a copy of a letter, which M. Haslang received this day, from count Seinsheim, and would make me believe, it comes up to what I wish. I told him, positively, otherwise ; that this supposed we were to give two years more subsidy, and an equivalent also, which was impossible ; and Haslang agreed it was so. Indeed, you are mistaken in the court of Vienna, and a little in thinking, I do not talk to them, as strongly as to any other power. I do it, I have done it, and I will do it ; and it has had its desired effect. Already Vorster offers (as it were), 500,000 florins, for the Bavarian vote, and that is more than any mortal ever thought they would give. They will also satisfy all the elector's just pretensions ; but the unfortunate court of Vienna can never be in the right. The king says, *a Beggar, a Stranger,* put at the head of the empire ! and, shall *he talk and act, so ? I will make them eat their words.* It may, perhaps, cost us dear

* Newcastle Papers.

to do it. But enough of these politics. Now to answer your kind letter, which I received this day.

" As to the behaviour of my colleague, either in London, or the country, towards those in town, or towards those who are out of the kingdom, I will say no more upon it : it does, it must, speak for itself. I have, most sincerely, desired your advice, and I will, as sincerely, follow it ; I mean, till I see you, and can talk the whole over with you. I will command myself; I will wait, I do not say, for the chapter of accidents, but for the concurrence of my friends. I will cherish those, that are my friends, and endeavour, if I can, to increase them ; but, above all, I will go on, steadily and firmly, in the pursuit of what is right. If it succeeds, very well ; if not, it does not miscarry through my fault.

MR. PELHAM TO THE DUKE OF NEWCASTLE.*

Approves the mode of conducting the negotiations with the court of Vienna—Thinks Sir Charles Hanbury Williams will not succeed in his embassy to Warsaw—Difficulty of appointing a secretary of state, in the room of the duke of Bedford.

" DEAR BROTHER,   *August 3rd-14th,* 1750.

" I shall now acknowledge the favour of yours of July the 25th, and the several inclosures, all which I have read, as well as the dispatches you sent to the duke of Bedford. You must not expect any answer from his Grace, as to the opinion of the lords to whom you refer business ; because he has never given any of us an opportunity of informing him what our opinions are. He sends the letters, indeed, round to us all, sooner or later ; but he never produces himself but on a Regency day, as I have told you before ; and he might almost as well not do it then, for we can never fix him to any business or place ; however, I fancy no great mischief arises from this. The common acts of government go on. We make, indeed, partly a ridiculous figure, but his Grace more. I hope and believe, your affairs abroad will end well ; that is, if any thing is done, good will be done, and if nothing, no harm will come of it. You have done your part ; the king has made a great effort ; and if either the court of Vienna cannot, or will not, come up to the terms of the several electors, it cannot be said we have not done our parts ; and, in my conscience, I think you have both ably and honestly shewn the respective parties what are their true interests, and given them such an opening to arrive at a good end, as they never will, if now neglected, have offered to them again. Your account of the Austrian minister is a good one, and what he offers is handsome for that court ; but give me leave to say, well worth their giving.

" I doubt, Sir Charles Williams goes to Warsaw upon a sleeveless errand : to endeavour to persuade the court of Saxony, not to renew a treaty of subsidy with one power, without giving them expectations of an equivalent somewhere else, I fear will not do. However, I am glad he is returned from offering any thing from us ; if he can procure the other, I shall be glad of it, but do not expect it. I see a great deal of management in Guy Dickens's † letters ; I wonder you do not at once give that over, and order him

---

* Newcastle Papers.   † British envoy at the court of Petersburgh.

tell the Chancellor,* it was at the request of the two empresses, his Majesty was induced to accede to their treaty of 1746; but if either of them do not like it, it is the same thing to the king; he has engagements with both those powers already, which he will religiously keep, and that he doubts not, but they will respectively do the same by him.* * * *

"I have had a long discourse with Pitt. He seems mighty happy with an opinion, that his interposition, and his truly friendly offices, have had a good effect in bringing you and me nearer to one another. I let him think so; it may probably keep him nearer to us both; but I would not have you think so, for I should be sorry that it was your opinion, that the interposition of any one, especially of so new an acquaintance, could influence me in your cause, more than my own reason or natural affection for you would do. However, I most sincerely desire you to go on in your correspondence with him, with all the frankness and cordiality you can; I do so, in all my conversations with him; I think him besides, the most able and useful man we have amongst us; truly honourable, and strictly honest. He is as firm a friend to us, as we can wish for; and a more useful one there does not exist. He seems entirely of my opinion, as to what is to be wished;† and hopes you will endeavour to conduct yourself so as that nobody shall be able to lay it at your door, if a rupture should become unavoidable; in that case, which I hope in God will not happen, a great deal will depend on what, as well as who, is your colleague; and I must tell you, that amongst the various difficulties I foresee, there is one insurmountable; it must not be a member of the House of Commons, and out of the House of Lords, it is not easy to find one. In the House of Commons, there are several who put themselves, and indeed are near upon an equality, all greatly above any one you think of. Nature will operate in such a case, and ill humours and discontents, though smothered for a time, will at last burst. I should not have said so much to you, but to shew you my thoughts are at work all ways to serve you, if I can; but when I do endeavour to reduce them to practice, it all ends in difficulties, and confirms me more and more, that, if possible, we must keep as we are.* * * *

THE DUKE OF NEWCASTLE TO MR. PELHAM.‡

Sentiments of the king on the subject of the duke of Bedford—Apologises for not having before communicated the change of behaviour in lady Yarmouth—Intends for the future to act in concert with his brother.

"DEAR BROTHER,   *Hanover, August 12th-23rd,* 1750.

"I am now to return you thanks for your very kind letter of the 3rd, which I received on Thursday last, and which gave me as much satisfaction as it is possible for a letter to do. There is so much real affection, and so much good sense, through the whole, that I must have a very bad head, and a very bad heart, not to be truly sensible of both. I begin by telling you, that it has made such an impression upon me, that you shall hear no more of complaints, upon the late subject of our letters;

---

* Count Bestucheff.   † Probably the removal of the duke of Bedford.
‡ Newcastle Papers.

and that I entirely put myself into your hands, to be directed by you. And, that you may be the better able to judge, I will acquaint you with every thing that I know or suspect, that has any relation to the great question.

"In the first place, till within these few days, the king has hardly ever taken any notice, or made any observation, upon the total silence, and neglect of business, in the duke of Bedford. On the contrary, he said once to Mr. Stone, before I came, 'What would you have him write about? There is nothing to do.' It is true, I have but seldom, very seldom, flung any thing out, upon the subject; the few times I have, he seemed not displeased, but made no answer. I remember particularly, about a month or six weeks ago, talking of our foreign affairs, I said, 'I only write upon the secret part of them to my brother, and my lord Chancellor; the others know nothing of the matter.' The king answered, 'No; they two are the only ministers; the others are for shew.' I did not dwell upon it, but left it. The other day, when Mr. Stone went alone, on account of the duchess of Newcastle's illness, Mr. Stone said, as he did before, 'There were no letters from the duke of Bedford.' The king answered, 'No, he does not much trouble his head about business; never man had an easier office than he has.'

"I thought that very remarkable, and that things began to work. Upon the coming in of the last messenger, without one single line from his Grace (for he very seldom writes at all by the messengers); talking a little upon his Grace's subject, the king said of himself, 'It is not to be borne; he never writes;' and then repeated, 'he has an easy office indeed,' or, 'He receives his pay easily,' or to that purpose. I made no reply, but left it there. But I am persuaded, by the manner, I could that morning (last Thursday), have got any orders I pleased; but I chose to say nothing, not to seem pressing, and would not take any step in this affair, without your advice; and that is my resolution, however things turn out here.* * * *

"I will now give you an account from the beginning. My suspicions began, immediately upon our return from Kensington, the beginning of last winter. All that mickmack about the French embassadress, had its rise here. On a sudden, we were invited to my lord Sandwich's; and I was told, in some confusion, that lady Sandwich (whom she scarce knew), had been there, and had left a card for her. What was the party? Was I to be there? &c. And this party was that with the French embassadress, where the dispute happened.

"Soon after that, I found the duke of Bedford and lord Sandwich very intimate there. But that which confirmed my suspicions, was advice to me, not to attempt removing the duke of Bedford; that the king was uneasy about it; that his Grace was not a man, *de chasser du jour au lendemain;* that this was the advice of a friend, &c.; that I could fear nothing; that my own brother was always present; he would take care; that she knew nothing of the cabals, &c.; and at last, after having told me, '*Votre frère ne le permettra pas,*' I asked her, how the king came to think so differently upon the duke of Bedford's subject, from what he did, when he, in effect, proposed the removing him? Her answer was this remarkable one, '*Le roi ne savoit pas alors, que votre frère ne la permettroit pas.*'

"When I took the resolution of coming hither, without bringing the great question to a point, I acquainted her with it, and then every thing went on smoothly, and she left England in as good humour, and seemingly, as well satisfied with me, and I in as much confidence with her, as ever. Many intermediate incidents, during the winter, you may imagine, must have happened, to strengthen those suspicions. Whenever I lamented the part some of the royal family had taken, she was always silent; sometimes knew nothing of the matter, at other times could not believe it, and was always very reserved upon their subject, which had not been the case formerly, when, perhaps, I had not been so willing to speak.

"Thus things were, when we left England, with strong assurances of friendship, and seeming good disposition of doing every thing agreeable here. After this, you will be surprised, that since my first arrival, to this hour, which is now above three months, I have not had one quarter of an hour alone with her, putting all together. I have lamented to my friends the Wangenheims who, by the way, are grown very shy, and to her mother, madame Wendt, that I have had no opportunity of seeing her in private, as I used to do, every day, in England. That produced nothing; and though, at our first coming, she shewed all possible civility and friendship to the poor duchess of Newcastle, that went off, and she was barely civil; and I sometimes thought, as in the case of the French embassadress, she did not like any body, especially here, who accidentally took place of her. That indifference appeared, more and more, to every body, when all the ladies were named for the Göhrde, and not one word said of the duchess of Newcastle.* * * *

"I told you in one part of my letter, that I should judge to day, what was the cause of the ill-humour yesterday. It was certainly something amongst themselves, in which I had no concern. The king was extremely gracious, and good humoured; wished me joy of the signing of the treaty, and seemed highly pleased. I called at lady Yarmouth's; she was most extremely courteous; thanked me for having wrote to Holland for her son, who had a mind to go into the Dutch service, but has altered his mind, upon some promotion that he is to have here. She then told me, for the first time, that she wanted to have some discourse with me, in private, upon many things, and Tuesday is fixed. I told her, I hoped nothing bad. She answered, *au contraire, bon.* I really thought, at first, she was ordered to speak to me about the duke of Bedford, considering the king's manner the other day; but I now think, it is about the king's return to England, which Le Chaux says positively, to day, will be the first week in October, our style. Whatever it may be, the appointing a private conference, after a cessation of so many months, is extraordinary, and looks as if it were to have things, upon our return to England, as they were when we were last there, and not as they have been since we have been here. That is a good sign.* * * *

"Your own observations, upon the duke of Bedford's conduct, are so just, and so full, that I can add nothing to them. All I will say upon the subject is, that, if it were necessary (as I believe you will find it), to have another secretary in his place, there may be very good ones found in the House of Lords. Lord Holdernesse would fill the place very ably, and well, and lord Waldegrave very agreeably, and to the king's taste, and either of them make good Hanover secretaries. But I have promised not to trouble you upon that subject, and say this only in answer to your letter.

"I am extremely sensible of your affection, and kindness, in turning these things in your thoughts. I shall be glad, if you can bring them to any consistency, in your own mind. You see, I leave all to you. Your account of Pitt gives me great pleasure, and the more, as it is accompanied with the kindest reflection, from yourself, imaginable. Nobody can, nobody ought to help us, with one another, but ourselves ; and, when once that is the case, we shall want nobody. I wish you would shew Pitt my letter, about our foreign affairs ; I believe it would please him. I shall write him two words, by this messenger."

THE DUKE OF NEWCASTLE TO THE LORD CHANCELLOR.*

Conversation with lady Yarmouth on the subject of the duke of Bedford.

Hanover, August 19th-30th, 1750.

After deploring the loss of the duke of Richmond, he adds,—"I desired Stone to acquaint my brother by the last messenger, for I was not really then able to do it, that my lady Yarmouth had told me she must speak to me, and took an opportunity to do it last Tuesday, in the great dining-room at the window. 'It is,' she said, '*par rapport au duc de Bedford ; le roi veut faire quelque chose.* He never writes, and indeed he does nothing,' says she, 'but ride post from Woburn. This I have from the Gazettes.' I asked if the king thought of doing any thing immediately. '*Oui, je le crois comme cela.*' But said she of herself, 'will not this *fâcheux accident* furnish a means of finding an accommodation,' meaning the office of Master of the Horse. I said, there were two vacancies, that and the President. 'No,' said she, '*cela il ne veut pas prendre.* I will talk to the king,' says she, 'and we will talk farther of it, at the Göhrde.' Since that she has told me, the king did not like the duke of Bedford to be Master of the Horse ; but she believed he would give it to him, if he would take it." * * * *

THE DUKE OF NEWCASTLE TO MR. PELHAM.†

Thanks him for his affectionate concern and friendship—Traces the progress of the negotiation with the court of Vienna, and the electors, and augurs favourably of its success— The king communicates through lady Yarmouth, his consent for the removal of the duke of Bedford, and for appointing him master of the horse—Will do nothing without his brother's approbation.

Hanover, Aug. 23rd-Sept. 3rd, 1750.

*   *   *   *   *   *

"You are very kind in carrying me into topics of business. I know the use of them ; I have been unavoidably forced into it and can assure you, have not declined it. I remember too well, what you say, with regard to your dear self. To convince you, I do as you wish, I forced myself (and it was a force) to dine in public with the king the day after, because it had been appointed before. I have gone through the Spanish affair, as you will have seen : but, had not the Bavarian treaty been

* Newcastle Papers.   † Ibid.

finished, and signed, two days before, I verily believe, I should not have been able
to go through what was necessary to conclude that. I hope the treaty and declarations
have spoken for themselves. I do not know whether, otherwise, I have yet sufficiently
explained them. I saw the difficulty you mention, and did once think of making the
queen of Hungary a party, which the Austrian minister would have liked : but that
would have created so much confusion, as to the troops, the requisition of them, and
the other parts of the treaty ; and, particularly, the article about the Diet, which is
the ostensible article for the king of the Romans, that I laid that thought aside, and
have, as I hope, effectually done the business without it. The court of Vienna engage
to pay one fourth part, by a declaration signed by their ministers ; and the court of
Munich not only accepts that fourth part from the empress queen, but discharges, in
the most authentic manner, England and Holland from it : and this declaration must
be ratified, and the ratifications exchanged, at the same time that I shall exchange
the ratifications of the treaty with the elector of Bavaria. So that the declaration for
the electoral vote, and these other declarations, must all be looked upon as part of the
treaty, and will, in effect, be so ; as we shall not pay the half of the subsidy, which
is our proportion, unless all these conditions are performed by the elector of Bavaria :
and the discharge will justify our not paying more than the half of the subsidy.
I was determined, never to make us liable for the whole, to the elector of Bavaria ;
and to have our remedy, afterwards, upon the court of Vienna. No ; the court of
Bavaria should accept them, as paymasters, and discharge us, as they have done. I
hope you will approve this. Every body here that has yet heard of it, are amazed, how
I could bring it about. They say, it is the first time, that ever the court of Vienna
acted in this manner : but the object was great ; and I can assure you I took your
advice, in talking very strongly to them ; and I had reasonable men to deal with.

" You mentioned in a former letter, that I had copied the last treaty with Bavaria ;
and that, from the circumstances of the war, must be very different from the present.
You say very right, and you will see, I have referred to the old treaty, only in the
preamble, and some few articles of course ; and that I did, to introduce the affairs
of the empire, and ground upon them, the absolute promise of the electoral
vote : for it appears, that our last treaty had a relation to the affairs of the empire,
and was not, singly, a convention for troops ; and that has helped us, in our present
negotiation. As to the article about the troops, I was much puzzled : Hop was
as dull as a post ; but I got Haslang to accept the Hessian treaty, which is the
old standard ; but have expressly excluded the levy money. I told him, that could
not be given ; and therefore you see, have referred to the Hessian treaty, only as to
what concerns the pay, the form of requisition, and the decrease of the subsidy,
when the troops shall be in actual pay.

" I did indeed, ask your opinion, upon these points, as I thought then, we should
have time to receive it ; but when I found, I was able to get every one of them determined, in our favour, as, I hope, you think they are, I was resolved to sign immediately. I hope, and believe, all the courts will ratify ; though certainly I made all
the ministers sign, without orders, and Hop directly contrary to his. But you see,
how highly and universally, this bargain is approved in Holland ; and sure it is a

good one; and I must repeat, what I have said before, that it is the first time, I believe, that ever the court of Vienna paid the fourth part of a subsidy, (and that payment accepted, and the other powers discharged from it,) stipulated by a treaty, to which they were no otherwise parties.

"If I have done well in this, as I hope, you think, upon the supposition, that the treaty was to go on, I am sure you will approve what I am doing, or have done, every where else, which is giving an absolute negative to all demands of subsidies from other powers. The Palatine, and Saxon ministers have both renewed their applications, since the conclusion of the treaty of Bavaria; and I have given them both the same flat refusals. They were at first, disappointed, and angry; and my friend Fleming, said, I could do it, if I would. He founded some expectation upon the appearance there is, that the long depending dispute between the king, and the elector of Saxony, about the money due to his Majesty, and the proposal for advancing more upon new and better security, was likely to be finished, and settled, to satisfaction. But this will make no alteration. I see no disposition to it, in the king; and however I may privately think upon the subject in general, I should not like the appearance of having refused it before, and of doing it just now, when the other affair is settled to the king's mind; which however is not yet done; but I believe, it will do. I have talked to them both so roundly, and have shewed them the difference between their situation, and their merit, from that of the elector of Bavaria, that I am inclined to think, both the elector of Saxony, and the elector Palatine will concur with us, though we do not give any subsidy. Cologne, I think, is sure: so we shall proceed immediately to the election, as soon as the forms will admit.

"I send you the minute taken at our last meeting, and also a copy of my letter to major general Borch in consequence of it: and I send you also the last letter from Borch; which shews the good disposition, the elector was then in, and from whence I conclude, that when Borch receives my letter, and Königsegg that from Richecourt, and Vorster, the elector of Cologne will immediately give his consent. If I am mistaken in thinking, that hitherto, I have conducted this negotiation successfully, and that the terms of the treaty with Bavaria, and declarations attending it will not be disagreeable, I am sure I am not, in depending upon the most favourable interpretation from you, and a kind acquiescence upon my account, in what I have done. I shall, certainly go no farther in expenses.

"Whatever little difference of opinion there may be between us, as to our German affairs, I am glad to find we quite think alike, as to what is come from Spain; though I cannot agree that our friend Keene, to whom I am as partial as any body, has acted with his usual ability, upon this occasion. He seems to think, he has got something; and in reality, he has got nothing but a temporary limitation for those rights and privileges, which, in all common sense, were before perpetual. You see, I reason just as you do. The affair of the money is a trifle compared with the other. If the exclusive clause was only meant, that might do well enough, as you say, and as I have said in my letter to the duke of Bedford: but it is plain, Carvajal means the whole, the treaty of 1715; and that carries with

it, the eighth article of the treaty of Utrecht, also : and it is plain, Keene understands it so. It is plain, by Keene's letters that this is so. It is plain, by general
Wall's discourse, that it is so. But you will see, I have suggested, in my letter
to the duke of Bedford, the bare possibility of its being otherwise.

 " In my present situation, and in every situation in which I could hope to be, in business, it is the greatest pleasure to me, to see, that if I had read your letter before those
I sent, upon this subject, to the duke of Bedford and Mr. Keene, I could not have
followed your opinion more exactly in every point, than I have done in those letters ;
and I hope you will take care to have it carried into execution, and something done
upon it. I send you my private letter to Keene ; and the paragraph I omitted of
his private letter to me, in the copy sent to the duke of Bedford. But, my dear
Brother, is it not amazing, that letters of this importance should come to England,
and the Secretary of State there, in whose province that is, should not call the
lords together upon it, or say one word upon it himself, to the Secretary of State
attending the king here ? And, had I not heard it from you, and my lord
Chancellor, I should not have known that you had had the letters.

 " And this brings me to touch upon the great point to you. You say very
rightly, that it is of the utmost consequence to fill up well the three or four
vacancies in the cabinet council ; though that of the Ordnance I look upon as
settled. My lord Chancellor has wrote to me, to the same effect, and wishes
the duke of Devonshire could be induced to come again into the king's service.
I am sure I should like that, better than any thing, and would do any thing to
bring it about ; though, I own, I myself have no notion that it is practicable ;
that is, that he will, on any account : and I am greatly at a loss for proper
persons to fill up any of them. I have had an application from the duke of
Leeds, and from my lord Poulet, besides that from the duke of St. Alban's. You
may be assured I will do nothing, I will resolve nothing, even with myself, without
previously knowing your thoughts.

 " I do suppose, the communication, or rather message, brought me by my lady
Yarmouth, of the king's intention, relating to the duke of Bedford, will have greatly
surprised you and my lord Chancellor : I own it greatly surprised me, notwithstanding what the king said to Mr. Stone, and afterwards to me, that it could not be borne ;
to which I made no reply, but immediately went out of the closet. I verily believe
the king expected an answer from me, and not having one, sent my lady Yarmouth
to me. When I come to the Göhrde, I shall see farther into this affair. I do take
it, it arises absolutely from the king himself, who, to be sure, feels the indecency and
disrespect to him, from the absolute silence upon all the communications that have
been made upon the Bavarian negotiation, and that for the election of a king of the
Romans, and, indeed, upon all affairs in general. The king says, he never writes.
Mr. Stone, who knows the king's ways very well, thinks he has taken his resolution,
and will not be got off from it. It is too much to expect, that I should endeavour
that ; it is enough to leave it to the king, and to execute nothing here. To believe
the words of lady Yarmouth, the king's resolution, as to the removal, is over ; and
the only difficulty that remains is, whether the duke of Bedford shall be Master of

the Horse, if he will accept it; which, I think, she flatters herself with, much more than she has grounds for. If that should be the case, the king would certainly do it. I have always thought the Duke of Cumberland, the duchess, and my lord Sandwich, could govern the duke of Bedford, in this point.

"If the Duke of Cumberland thought, that is, really believed, that this was the king's firm resolution, arising from himself, and from which the king would not depart, would not his Royal Highness do every thing that depended on him, with the duke, the duchess, and lord Sandwich, to prevent it? For, what a situation will the Duke of Cumberland be in, if the duke of Bedford goes absolutely out of the king's service, after he has, by his conduct, given the king so just reason to propose an exchange of his employment, for any of the most honourable ones in the king's service: and this when the Duke cannot lay the blame upon me, for having even proposed it to the king, much less insisted upon it?

"Whether Mr. Stone is in the right or not, as to his notion, that the king has taken his resolution, and will not depart from it, the message, brought me by my lady Yarmouth, puts it in our power, undoubtedly, to carry it into execution, whenever we please; and rather recommend ourselves by it, to the king, than otherwise, as may have been the case formerly; and upon which, perhaps, there may have been some dependence. I hope, by the next messenger, to hear your thoughts upon Mr. Stone's letter; I shall be much at a loss till I know them: I am persuaded I shall conform myself entirely to them; I will promise you to do nothing contrary to them." * * * *

MR. PELHAM TO MR. STONE.*

Is surprised at the proposal made by lady Yarmouth to the duke of Newcastle, relative to the dismission of the duke of Bedford—Exposes the difficulty of appointing his successor—Recommends his brother not to make any changes in the cabinet, till the King returns to England.

"DEAR SIR,   *August 24th-September 4th,* 1750.

" I shall proceed to answer your private letter of the 15th-26th. I chuse to write to you, as I have been obliged to write a very long one to my brother, on other points; and I thought he would like as well, to have the subject of this quite separate, and addressed to you, rather than himself. I own I am much surprised at the abrupt proposal that was made to his Grace; the time and place, to me, were odd; but, I believe she saw some coolness in my brother's behaviour, and therefore resolved to take the first opportunity of saying what she thought would please him. I fancy also, that something had, at different times, dropt in conversation, which led her to think, an alteration, now, would not occasion the same disturbance it would have done, a year ago. I must own, so far, I agree with those that are of that opinion. Many things are now cleared up to the world, which before were only conjectures. The total negligence, or inability in office, was far from being known to mankind, in general, till this year; but still I do not see with whom his Grace can fill that post, easy to himself, and creditable to the service. I have no partiality or prejudice to any one. The two my brother names, I fear, will neither of them stand the test. He that is abroad,* is very trifling in his manner and carriage : he does well where he is ; but he has advantages there, that we know not what use he makes of. The other† is as good-natured, worthy, and sensible a man, as any in the kingdom, but totally surrendered to his pleasures; and I believe that mankind, and no one more than himself, would be surprised to see him in such an office.

"I own, if my brother could away with it, I see nothing so safe, as to continue as we are, provided the other vacant offices are filled up by men of weight in this country, and such as by themselves, or family, will give strength and credit to the administration. That is the way, in my humble opinion, to mortify the young gentry. Shew them to be useless, and they will grow cheap ; and when they are so in office, we shall have less to apprehend from them out. But if nothing can either persuade the king or my brother to keep things as they are, then I would suggest to his Grace, whether Halifax, amongst the young ones, has not much the most efficient talents. He heartily hates the duke of Bedford, and his friend. I do not take that to be the case of the other two. I see many objections to them all ; and some to this latter, that are in neither of the former; but, then, there is something to set against these objections, which we shall have a difficulty to find in the others.

" Notwithstanding what I write now, I beg to be understood, that I am neither an admirer of the measure, nor of the man. You see I take for granted, any proposed change will end in a breach, but if not, where do we stand then ? The duke of Bedford will, it is true, be out of an office, in which he makes a bad figure ; but he, his family, and friends, will be nearer court than ever. He will come there with the grace of obliging the king ; and, if intrigues are what we fear, and nothing else do I see, that is to be feared, how many more opportunities will they have for that purpose, and with what advantage will they pursue such a scheme, when they have complied with the commands of the king cheerfully, and are in situations, where they cannot offend, unless they desire it, but may, by obsequious and steady attendance, ingratiate themselves every day more and more.

" These are, upon reflection, my thoughts. I have some reason to think, the office of Master of the Horse would not be disagreeable to his Grace : he cries it up as the properest for a man of great quality, of any but Lord Chamberlain, and in some respects preferable to that. He talks much of the nearness it is to the king's person, and endeavours to make people think *that* is his principal view. But you will be surprised, after all this, when I tell you this is his scheme, provided Sandwich is Secretary of State ; but, without that, he will undergo any thing, rather than divide the administration, and distress the king's affairs. As I came to the knowledge of this but very lately, I could not acquaint my brother with it till now, and I must insist that it goes no farther than him and you ; for, if it does, I shall never be able to gain him any more intelligence of this kind.

---

* Lord Holdernesse.   † Probably lord Halifax.

" He knows what reflection to make, on my coming to the knowledge of what I now write. I know what I wish he would make ; for to me it is a strong symptom, that he is not desperate if he has a mind not to be so. I must, above all things, recommend it to my brother to stop any hasty step. Who is it can make the proposal ? If any of us, it is the same as if my brother did it himself, and then the answer is easily known. Not a friendly one to be sure, if it comes directly from the highest powers, without any intervention of the ministry. What an opportunity does it give, if people knew how to make use of it ; and some few there are, capable of giving advice, to ingratiate themselves with the king, to lay a foundation of ill blood elsewhere, and to obstruct the future progress of business, even with the assistance and consent of the court.

" Perhaps I may refine too much, but I have reasoned myself into thinking what I write ; and, of consequence, my brother will forgive me, though he differs with me. I think it very material, in this whole scheme, whom the king makes President of the Council ? I take for granted he will not make Harrington ; and if lord Chesterfield would take it, and the king would give it to him, I am confident such a step would lay these young gentlemen on their backs, more than twenty removals.

" You have now not only my thoughts, but my reasonings upon this subject. Whether there is any thing solid in them, I do not pretend to determine, but sure I am they convince me. I acknowledge the situation unpleasant, but I think the remedy worse than the disease.

" Let his Grace consider how he stands now, not only at the head of business, but without a rival, successful, fortunate, and in the eyes of the world, greatly able, in having alone brought about so great a work, as we hope now is in a fair way of being soon completed. This I say with truth, for whatever objection I have to subsidising treaties, if the king can bring about the actual election of the archduke to be king of the Romans for £.20,000 per annum for six years, no one will say that it is not a pur chase cheaply made, and that the great end, when obtained, is national. How does the other stand ? Contemned as a man of business by all sorts of people ; and, though I believe most men think him honest and well-intentioned for the public, yet his childish conduct this summer, and his total neglect of all sort of business, when he was, more particularly than any one, called upon to be watchful and attentive, has lost him exceedingly in the world. If we start a new hare, and change the scene, the sense of mankind may alter ; and that great predilection that the world has now for my brother, may, in case the king's affairs should suffer from divisions amongst his servants, turn another way.

" You see, upon the whole, my wishes are, that we may keep, for a time at least, as we are at present ; that the offices may be filled by men of credit and weight in this country. But if none of these things can be, then I do most earnestly wish, that any other scheme may be postponed, till the king comes over ; that every one may bear his share in counsel and advice ; and that the whole may not be laid at my brother's door, which it certainly will be, if these great points are determined, and put in execution abroad, where no one is near the king but himself. As I am excessively happy, at my brother having understood all my letters of late, as I truly meant them, I hope in God he will not judge this wrote with any other view than the rest were, justly and impartially to lay before him my thoughts, which, in the present times, are far from clear; for I can look no way with satisfaction, and when I speak to a friend, I hope he will understand my advice, not as an option, but as a lesser evil."

MR. PELHAM TO THE DUKE OF NEWCASTLE.*

Opinion on a change in the ministry—Conversation with lord Harrington—Hopes some office will be conferred upon him—Remarks on the death of the duke of Richmond.

Aug. 24th-Sep. 4th, 1750.

? * * * * " I will now own to you, that my opinion as to your situation abroad, the alterations, if any, and the occasions of them, have by your explanation, turned out just as I thought. As to what passed in the winter, you forget it; but you told me every thing you have now written, not indeed owning a suspicion, but endeavouring to satisfy me, that other people were making their court in a certain place. That I could never doubt; but you do not think me such a novice, I believe, to suppose you could be very uneasy at people trying, if you did not at the same time think they made a little way. I never thought that went to any great degree, nor do I yet. But I always thought that person† would be very uneasy at any measures being taken, that might occasion disturbance to the king, and I conclude the making any change in the administration was thought to be productive of that.

" Pitt has been with me. We have talked all those points over, which concern a change; and he seems of my opinion, mighty desirous, that you should be made easy, but very doubtful, whether any violent stroke would produce that good effect.

" I must now give you an account of a conversation I had yesterday with lord Harrington. He came to me full of anxiety and trouble. He has at last found out, that he is not long to continue in the post he now enjoys. He fears a sudden stroke, and thinks that if he is removed, before any thing else is allotted to him, he shall be left without any thing at all! I did not, nor ever have denied to him, that I thought the duke of Dorset would be his successor, and that I concluded the time would not be long before his fate would be determined. He then asked me, if I thought he should succeed Dorset? I told him, by what I saw of the king before he left England, I feared it much. He then said, ' If the king do not care to see me, why cannot lord Gower be president, and I succeed him as lord Privy Seal?' My answer was, Gower was so broke in spirit and constitution, I feared his ability of going through that office, and really thought he would not undertake it. ' Why, then,' says he, ' what is it I am to expect? I desire you will write to the duke of Newcastle; tell him I desire to know my fate, and that I hope the king will not reduce an old servant to want, for no fault he is sensible to have committed.' He asked me whether he had offended the king, in any thing he had done as lord lieutenant. I told him I knew of nothing; that perhaps he might have recommended people, now and then, whom the king did not,

---

* Newcastle Papers.　　　　† Alluding to lady Yarmouth.

like, but that I thought that did not go far. I owned sincerely to him, that I took the old affair* to be the sore which I never saw healed, with regard to him, since the thing happened. He said he believed that was the case; but then, sure those for whom he suffered, would think themselves obliged in honour to stand a little by him, who had lost his all by standing firmly by them. I saw what and whom he meant. I told him, therefore, he was sensible of my friendship, and that I could assure him you were as desirous of accommodating him as I could be.

"I promised to write to you by this post; and told him I would communicate your answer as soon as I received it. I find the world begins to compassionate him; and it is talked about, as if we were, in honour, obliged to do our best for him, since he suffered for standing so thoroughly by us. I have been thinking, though I never mentioned it to him, whether the old story of General of the Marines might not do. His friends, I have reason to believe, will be satisfied with that, though I dare say he himself will not be pleased. I should not, according to my principles, recommend a farther expense on that head of service; but when I consider he will not last long, and that the opposition would probably be stopped from attacking him, I had rather venture that reproach, than the other, of suffering a man to drop, for an offence which we drew him into, and in which we were as much concerned as he. I wish, dear Brother, you would think of this. You may be assured, I will do the best I can, to make him easy; but if nothing is done for him, or proposed to be done, I will not attempt so vain a thing as to try at excuses; for when a man is sorely hurt, that rather irritates than assuages his resentments. At present he is calm, but very anxious as to his fate. I shall write to Mr. Stone a full answer to his letter.

"I have thought of it seriously, and own I am concerned at the abrupt manner in which it was broke to you. I doubt we do not see this administration in its true light. Death or retreat has taken away all our old friends and fellow-servants, the duke of Grafton, lord Chancellor, and yourself excepted. In a little while there will be but one man in the cabinet council, with whom we began the world, or carried on business till within these very few years. I own this reflection often strikes me, and makes me greatly fear new experiments. Perhaps my spirits are the lower for what has lately happened. It is extraordinary, that three† of our own ages, pretty near all old and intimate acquaintance, should die out of that body in less than a year. I shall say no more on these subjects, but refer you, for what I have farther to say, to my letter to Mr. Stone.

---

* The refusal of lord Harrington to desert the Pelhams in 1746, when the king wished to form a new administration. See chap. ix.

† Henry, Ninth earl of Pembroke, who died Groom of the Stole, Jan. 9th, 1749; John, duke of Montague, Master of the Ordnance, who died in 1749; Charles, duke of Richmond, who died, 8th of August, 1750.

THE LORD CHANCELLOR TO THE DUKE OF NEWCASTLE.*

Conversation with Mr. Pelham on the subject of the duke of Bedford and the appointment of his successor—Mr. Pelham proposes to make lord Harrington General of Marines.

Powis House, Aug. 31*st*, 1750.   *   *   *   *   " As to the grand domestic point, I have not time now to enlarge upon it.   I am very glad your Grace has found that I was not mistaken in my notion, that *the experience of this summer* would naturally bring about something, that might tend to bring about what you so much wished. Your brother shewed me your long letter, last night, before I received the copy ; and I find he thinks from appearances, of which you will hear more particularly from him, that the duke of Bedford will accept the Master of the Horse, and that they will trust to events as to lord Sandwich.   His reasoning upon it is, that he apprehends the measure is taken to form a party in the court, to push their point that way, and become popular (if it may be so called) there ; and he seems to think they may be able to create more trouble that way than in foreign business, in which their great man has shewn himself unable, and in which they could not give trouble without risking themselves, by obstructing the king's affairs.   This is a speculation of which I am no judge ; but I agree with him, that it seems right for your Grace, not in fact to execute any thing, until the king's return.   As to a successor in the secretary's office, though I have a great regard for the persons who have been named, I agree with him also in the objections that occur against them ; and that lord Halifax, notwithstanding some objections, will be much more approved by the public than either ; and one good circumstance in his case is, that he is quite cut off from any connection with other people.

" Lord Harrington desired a private conference with me yesterday, which, not having happened for several years, surprised me.   I met him, and must own, some part of it was a moving scene.   His whole business was upon his own subject, in which he related what he had heard, of his being to be removed from his present office as soon as the king returned, which he took for granted to be resolved upon.   He hoped that after so long service, he was not to be left upon the pavement, without any provision ; that his circumstances were so very moderate ; that it would reduce him to *great* inconveniences.   And here he burst into tears, and could not go on.   He could not recollect that he had ever given the king any offence, but by being first in resigning in Feb. 1745-6, which he said was a measure in conjunction with us all.   He reclaimed your Grace's friendship, which he hoped he had never forfeited ; for as to any difference of opinion on political measures, at a particular time, he relied on your candour not to think that any forfeiture of it, and therefore hoped for your powerful interposition and assistance, that if he was to lose the lieutenancy of Ireland, he might at the same time be provided for, in some other way.   I told his lordship, I pretended to no power, but had no scruple to declare my real opinion, as well as wish, that he should be honourably provided for.   That I had good reason to think it was also your Grace's opinion ; and promised to write to you, as I am now doing.   He desired me to let Mr. Pelham know that he had spoken to me ; which I did, and need not tell

* Newcastle Papers.

your Grace, that he is strongly in that way of thinking. He is for making my lord, General of Marines, as Peterborough and Stair were. He says he can, in this instance, stand the doing of it, and thinks the king may be brought to give way to it, as it will cost his Majesty neither place nor pension. I cannot help concurring with your brother in this idea, and also in thinking, that if his Majesty's displeasure is supposed to be founded on the resignation, which was a common measure, then thought right even for the king's service, it will be a reproach to those to whom lord Harrington then adhered, to leave him quite unprovided and destitute. Be so good, my lord, to enable me to say some words of comfort to him as soon as you can." * * * * *

THE DUKE OF NEWCASTLE TO MR. PELHAM.*

Conversations with lady Yarmouth and the king on the proposed removal of the duke of Bedford, and on the nomination of his successor—The duke of Newcastle objects to the appointment of lord Halifax—Will not propose Sir Thomas Robinson, and strongly recommends lord Holdernesse—Desires his brother to write an ostensible letter, to be shewn to the king, recommending the removal of the duke of Bedford—Has no objection that lord Granville and lord Chesterfield should come into administration—Repeats that nothing shall be done without his brother's approbation.

"DEAR BROTHER,   Hanover, Sept. 2nd-13th, 1750.

" I received, by Watson, the messenger, on Wednesday night last, at the Göhrde, all your letters of the 24th of August; and, as you very rightly have confined to your letter to Mr. Stone, all that you say upon the subject of his letter to you, I shall give you my thoughts in this, fully, upon all that has passed here, relating to the present situation of the administration, either before or since Mr. Stone wrote, and upon the contents of your several letters to him, and me, upon this subject.

" That you may see this whole affair, in its true light, I will inform you of some material circumstances, that have passed since the first overture, which will fully convince you, that that neither arose from me, nor was suggested, or occasioned, by any regard for me, or any supposed uneasiness, that might have been observed in me; but purely, and solely, from the king himself, from the impression, that the insufficiency and indecency of the duke of Bedford's late behaviour, by his total neglect, both of the king, and his business, had made upon his Majesty; and the lady was, and is, so far from contributing to it, that all her *embarras*, and abrupt manner, of breaking it to me (of which you take very proper notice), proceeded only from her concern, and confusion, that a measure, which she had been able, so long, to prevent, seemed now to be out of her power, by proceeding solely, and originally, from the king. And that this was, and is the case, is plain, by her behaviour at the time, and, indeed, ever since. She then said, the resolution was taken (and still persists in that) as to the duke of Bedford's not remaining Secretary of State. She then told me (and has repeated the same since), that she understood, the king meant to do it, immediately; *d'abord, je le crois, comme cela.* She then (and ever since has) endeavoured to hinder me from speaking to the king, upon the subject, and did not imagine,

* Newcastle Papers.

then, that the king would have begun it with me himself, as he has now fully done ; and the manner of his doing it, shews the weight of her impressions and influence.

" And I must here observe, dear Brother, that had it not been, singly, out of regard to you, and your single opinion, and that this great and unexpected proposal came from the king, at a time when I was very little able to think, or digest things of that kind, this affair would, then, have been put out of doubt, and neither the king himself have had an opportunity of retracting (which, however, he is far from doing), nor the lady, of creating difficulties in it, which she is doing every day. I am sure, you know the king well enough to know, that what I say is, and must be true. The proposal was his own ; no one word said, from that time to this, by me, or to me, of my having ever had any such thought, or of any disagreement, between the duke of Bedford and me, much less of any impracticability of our remaining Secretaries of State together. She thought, therefore, the thing was over ; but upon the late fatal acci‑ dent, she wanted to compound for the Master of the Horse, which, she has since plainly told me, the duke and the duchess (*qui n' est pas peu de chose*), would like better.

" The great dislike the king has (as you will see hereafter) to his Grace, in that office, has hindered him from putting his other resolution, immediately, in execution, which, however (had he been disposed to do it), you may be assured, I would, accord‑ ing to my promise, in all events, have prevented.

" I think, I have said enough, to prove, that the lady's first view is, to keep the duke of Bedford where he is ; if that cannot be, to remove him to the Master of the Horse, and, in all events, to keep things open.

" After having herself referred me to the Göhrde, for our talking, and settling this great affair, I gave her some opportunities of beginning with me ; but not one word ; and as I had received a letter from my lord Poulett, for the Master of the Horse, which I was obliged to shew the king, as well as to acquaint him with the duke of Leeds's application for it, I thought she would have reason to take it amiss, if I did not tell her of it, beforehand, which I did.

" I found her embarrassed, not at all disposed to talk upon the subject though she had, herself, as I told you, proposed to do it, at the Göhrde. She told me, short, ' Give my lord Poulett a refusal.'—' But,' says I, ' madam, I must have the king's order, for it.'—' But pray,' says she, ' do not press your brother-in-law.' *—' That,' answered I, ' you may be sure, I will not.' She certainly feared, the king might give it him. And then I asked how the other affair stood. She said, the king would do nothing here. He would talk to my brother and the duke of Grafton. As to the Secretary of State, she said, that was resolved, or the king thought the same, about that ; for the king said, *cela ne pouvoit pas être autrement ;* that is, the duke of Bedford must be out, that he would make the duke of Bedford Master of the Horse, to quiet things ; and thus things stood, when, the day after, I saw the king, and began by telling him, that I was obliged to shew him a letter from my lord Poulett, though I knew the answer beforehand.

* Earl Godolphin.

" And now I will tell you, as near as I can recollect, every word that passed, faithfully and truly; and give me leave, by way of parenthesis, to say, that when I tell you so truly, every thing that passes with the king and lady Yarmouth, let it make for or against my point, I should hope you would do the same, as to all that passes between you and the Duke of Cumberland; for I am convinced, by what you have said, that something, very material, must have passed in your last conversation there.

" The king read my lord Poulett's letter without much emotion. I said, his lordship was never one I greatly admired; but that he had formerly been much cried up, which put him upon all these demands. Now to the point: the king said, in very good humour, (as he was the whole time of this material conversation) ' I see (says he) your brother sees, that things cannot continue as they are; and he will be proposing disagreeable exchanges to me, in order to prevent a rupture, or to keep things quiet.' (You see, by this, what turn the lady has given to her proposal of the Master of the Horse). I replied with great astonishment : ' My Brother, Sir, I am persuaded, has no thoughts of proposing any disagreeable exchanges to your Majesty. All that he has said to me upon the subject of the vacancies is, that there are now (and will probably be) three or four vacancies in the cabinet council; and he doubts not, but your Majesty will fill them up with such persons as may be most for your service. But my Brother has not so much as named one single person.' As was then true, for I had not received your last letters.

" The king then grew in very good humour; and entered into the character of the duke of Bedford, and the nature of the office of Master of the Horse. He said, the duke of Bedford was proud, obstinate, haughty; and some epithets of that kind; that the office of Master of the Horse, and that of Lord Chamberlain, were very particular; that he could never replace the poor man that is gone : what should he do, if an accident happened to the duke of Grafton? and, then, many personal kind things of the dear duke of Richmond, and the duke of Grafton.

" He ran out into great encomiums of my lord Waldegrave; that he should be more than he was (in which I entirely agreed); that he would have sent Waldegrave to Aix la Chapelle, when I prevailed upon him to send Sandwich; that he yielded to it, out of regard to my lord Waldegrave, thinking it a very difficult, and hazardous commission; and I thought a great while, that he meant Waldegrave, either for Secretary of State, or Master of the Horse. He said, that the duke of Bedford was absolutely governed by my lord Sandwich, in which I agreed. The whole conversation supposed the duke of Bedford was to be out; and (to make the king easy, about the Master of the Horse, for your sake, and my own) I shewed him the president's place, for the duke of Bedford. That he liked extremely, and said, it had business enough, and not too much; it was four thousand pounds a-year, &c.

* * * * *

" ' I see very plainly,' says he, ' my lord, how lamely things go on; and do not think, that I have not seen it for some time, (which, by the bye, was an excuse for having kept the duke of Bedford in so long), but,' says he, ' things in parliament went well;' and then, or in talking of the duke of Bedford's removal, he said, ' but, my lord, you

and I cannot do it alone; we must have the council with us :' and named no particular person to consult; but, to be sure, the whole meant yourself. He said once,
very significantly (I think upon my lord Sandwich's subject), ' they are caballing;
I know, or you may be sure, that they are caballing at this very time.' Though he
spoke this, by way, rather of apprehension than resentment, I am, from this, as well
as from the king's whole conduct in this affair, fully convinced myself, that the Duke
of Cumberland's parties with the duke of Bedford, and public and open support and
predilection for my lord Sandwich, and the duke of Bedford, is one, if not the chief
cause of the king's present intention of removing the duke of Bedford from the office
of Secretary of State; and though the king has never let drop one word like it to
me, if you will give him the least handle to talk upon it, I am persuaded he
will own it to you, and talk fully upon it to you. This is only my own suspicion,
from my knowledge of the king, without having any other grounds for it. The king
asked me, whom I had thought on, for Secretary of State; or, who should be the man ?
(when I state things in two ways, it is because I cannot positively say, which the
king said; you see by this, my care not to mislead you), I replied, ' I think your
Majesty has choice enough.'

" He then said, of himself, ' I have been thinking of Holdernesse.' I said, he had
named the man that I should have named to his Majesty, if I had taken the liberty
to name any body. He then said much, and, indeed, I think with great justice, in
favour of Holdernesse; how well he behaved in Holland; and I told him, for I had
not then your letter, that you was very well satisfied with lord Holdernesse's behaviour in Holland, and had owned, it was better than you had expected. And then,
says the king, ' Albemarle shall come to England; and Waldegrave go embassador to
France; and then he will be qualified to be Secretary of State.' And his Majesty
hinted to me, that if I had let him send Waldegrave to Aix la Chapelle, he might
have been Secretary of State now. I objected to lord Albemarle's leaving Paris,
whilst it was necessary to have an embassador there, and chiefly on account of the
great expense of a new embassador. ' Oh !' says the king, ' that is but a trifle; £.1,500
or £.2,000.' I told him, you had told me, £.7,000; but he seemed determined that
Albemarle should come home; and I think that is another scheme of the lady,* * *
and that I know, and am, therefore, for keeping him where he is. *   *   *   *

" I wonder you reason upon it as you do. As to Halifax, I love him and esteem
him, and think he has very efficient talents; but he is the last man in the kingdom,
except Sandwich, that I should think of for Secretary of State. In the first place,
the whole council, all of us put together, could not make the king do it. In the
next place, he is so conceited of his parts, that he would not be there one month,
without thinking he knew as much, or more of the business, than any one man; and
I am sure it would be impracticable to go on with him. He hates the duke of
Bedford and Sandwich, I know; and I know also, neither of the others do, but they
are both honest men, and I own I do not desire they should hate the duke of Bedford.
All I desire is, that they should not list under him, or cabal with him. Besides, if
this change is ever made, as it solely arises from the king, so it shall, for me, end with
him. That is, as the king cannot reproach me with having said one word to him,

since I have been here, relating to the removal of the duke of Bedford (as I told him very plainly the other day) and as, therefore, (if it is done) it arises singly from his Majesty himself; so the successor shall be his own choice, that I may have no reproach, from him at least, about it.

" You know very well, if I was to chuse for the king, the public, and myself, I would prefer Sir Thomas Robinson to any man living. I know he knows more, and would be more useful to his country and me, than any other can be. But for the reasons you mentioned in your late letter, I have entirely laid that thought aside; and I find also, the king is aware of the objection to having one in the House of Commons; and therefore, I believe, himself thought of Holdernesse. I wonder you dislike that so much. He is, indeed, or was, thought trifling in his manner and carriage; but believe me, he has a solid understanding, and will come out, as prudent a young man, as any in the kingdom. He is goodnatured; so you may tell him his faults and he will mend them. He is universally loved and esteemed, almost by all parties, in Holland. He is very taciturn, dexterous enough, and most punctual in the execution of his orders. He is got into the routine of business. He knows very well the present state of it. He is very diligent, and exact, in all his proceedings. He has great temper, mixed with proper resolution. He has no pride about him, though a *D'Arcy*. It is true, he has his advantages in Holland, by his relations there; but you are much mistaken if you think they help him in the execution of his business. On the contrary, with the instructions which he has, he has the upper hand of them, and rather directs than follows them. I will risk my reputation with you, and that is not saying a little, if upon trial you do not find every word of this to be true. This is what has got him his credit in Holland; and I wish you would ask Dayrolle, or my lord Chesterfield, whether that is not as I have stated it to you. If, therefore, I am in the right of this, can there be a properer man than my lord Holdernesse? And the consideration of the king's having named him, of his own mere motion, is not an inconsiderable one, upon this great question. * * *

" You are apprised of the king's thoughts, that the duke of Bedford cannot remain Secretary of State. You are also acquainted from me, that the king will do nothing here, and even, not without the opinion of what he calls the council, which is, in other words, yourself. Might not you, therefore, write a letter to me, to the following purport: that you was extremely glad to hear from me, that the king had been so gracious as to declare, that he would not fill up the great employments vacant in the cabinet council, till his Majesty returned to England; that as I had acquainted you with the king's thoughts, as to the present state of his administration (meaning by this, the removal of the duke of Bedford) you could not be surprised, however concerned you might be, that his Majesty should think some change in the present form of it necessary; and that when the king came over, and informed you of his thoughts and commands, you should be very glad to contribute to make him easy, and put his administration upon a foot agreeable to his Majesty; but that great care should be taken to do it in a manner, that might not create difficulty to his affairs. This would please the king, put us upon forming our schemes, and would probably end in the duke of Bedford's being Master of the Horse, and every thing else going on quietly.

As to the other vacant offices, which, I think with you, should be filled up with the best men that can be found, and of the greatest weight in the kingdom; lord Albemarle, I take it for granted, must be Groom of the Stole, the Duke either master of the Ordnance, or there will be none. There then remains only the President, and the Master of the Horse. If the duke of Bedford accepts the President, as the king would have him, there is only the Master of the Horse, and that the king will then certainly dispose of himself; I do not know to whom. If Waldegrave does not go to Paris, I believe he will give it him; if he does, I believe he will put it in commission, as he once told me he would. But if the duke of Bedford is Master of the Horse, and the President is vacant, it will be very material whom to give it to. If my Lord Chancellor's notion has any foundation, to be sure the duke of Devonshire* should have it, before all the world; but I am afraid he will not think of it; I wish he would, for a million of reasons. I own I have my doubts about Chesterfield; and, as I write to you every thing, I think I will tell you plainly, why my lord Granville is certainly worth managing : he is extremely with us, at least with me, in our foreign politics, and it is to that chiefly that we owe our having no opposition to them. I am afraid the taking in Chesterfield in this manner, would make him fly out; and then I see more inconvenience from thence, than advantage from Chesterfield. If any way could be contrived, which I do not see at present, to take them both into these great offices, one would be a check upon the other, and we should have nothing to fear from either, but have assistance from both. My lord Granville is no more the terrible man; *Non eadem est ætas, non mens.* Believe me, I do not say this from any concert with my lord Granville; I have no ministerial correspondence with him, nor ever will, but by your consent and knowledge.

" As to my lord Harrington, I will write a letter directly upon that subject : it is now near seven o'clock, I am afraid I shall not be able to do it by this messenger, but you shall have it by the next. In the mean time, you said every thing I could wish to say upon my account; I will do my utmost to get some equivalent for him; the General of Marines I should hope would go with the king. I wonder you have never thought of the blue regiment. That, perhaps, the king might give him, and it is a noble thing, and a proper one for him.

" I am sure I must have tired you; I have tired myself. I have been all day writing this letter, which must make me short upon all other points to you, and to the rest of my friends. However you may dislike my reasonings, the great point you so much pressed is secured; nothing will be done here of any kind, and what is more, nothing will be done in England, but what you approve; but I hope you will not condemn me to a state of constant inquietude and uneasiness, as long as I remain in the ministry. I must again repeat to you, that I have the truest sense of your affection to me, in every thing you do, and line you write. I hope you will think the same of mine towards you. It cannot be greater, and equal I am sure it is."

* The duke of Devonshire resigned the office of Lord Steward, in 1749.

MR. PELHAM TO THE DUKE OF NEWCASTLE *

Complains that his sentiments have been misrepresented to the King—Declines writing an ostensible letter to his Majesty—Hopes the duke of Bedford will take the place of President—Does not pay his court to the Duke of Cumberland, and strongly objects to the introduction of lord Granville into the Cabinet.

"MY DEAR BROTHER,   *September 7th-18th,* 1750.

" I have received your several letters of September 2nd-13th, and have very carefully read over your very voluminous one, on the subject of the administration. I dare say, you do not either expect or desire, that I should enter into a detail on that subject. You have my thoughts already, honestly and affectionately told you. If I were to say more on the subject, I do not suppose I could convince you ; and if you do not convince me, it is better for me to say nothing at all. I shall, therefore, only take notice of some few things, wherein you are totally mistaken, and clear myself from some notions, relating to myself, in which the king has been made to believe quite different from the truth. I do not mean you in this, I can assure you ; but as little as I may be supposed to know of courts, I think I know mankind enough to determine, that almost all of them, particularly courtiers, when they are to say or do disagreeable things, to the person they wish to please, chuse to lay the burden on some other shoulders, in order to lessen the weight on their own. I mean that part of your letter in which you tell me, the king said ' your brother sees that things cannot continue as they are, and he will be proposing disagreeable exchanges to me, in order to prevent a rupture, or to keep things quiet.' I never said, things cannot keep as they are : I mean with regard to office ; much less have I proposed any disagreeable exchanges ; and I desire you would tell the king so. I have promised the king, and I will keep my word, that I would never enter into any cabal again, to prevent his Majesty from either removing, or bringing into his service, any person he had either a prejudice to, or a predilection for. I do not look upon it, that my telling you my thoughts, when required to do so, over and over, can be deemed departing from that declaration. I have told you my thoughts ; I never meant they should be told the king as mine ; and I see plainly they have not, because the king takes my thoughts to be totally different from what they are. I did not even design that you should tell the king it was my opinion, nothing should be determined, till he came to England. I know what construction his Majesty will put upon that ; for I know what the king has thought, and does think of me, as well as if I was a favourite, and saw him every day.

" The whole turn of your letter is to convince me, and you conclude that will convince the rest of mankind, that this measure of removing the duke of Bedford, solely arises from the king himself, and that you have no share or concern in it. I am satisfied what you say at this time, is strictly true ; but when all the world knows you have been wishing this for two years together, and when they see no English minister or servant of the king's at Hanover, but yourself, can you deceive yourself so far as to imagine, any one, but those with whom you privately correspond, and to

* Newcastle Papers.

whom you give that assurance, can believe you have nothing to do in the measure? And will the king himself like that your friends should give out here, that it is entirely his Majesty's own act, and that you have never mentioned it to him, nor in any manner led him to think of it?

" Believe me, dear Brother, there are things we may wish, but they are not in nature to be credited by the world. You seem in one part of your letter to think, that I have had some material conversation with the Duke of Cumberland, the subject of which I have kept secret from you? I can assure you, your suspicions are totally groundless. I have, I desire to have, no secret from you; but so totally mistaken are you in the *carte du pays* here, that, as a man of truth I declare, I have not seen his Royal Highness often, for he keeps out of town almost as much as the duke of Bedford, and, when I have seen him, nothing has passed that might not be wrote up at Charing Cross. He scarce ever mentions the name of the duke of Bedford, or lord Sandwich; and with regard to business, I have as little of his confidence as any one. I keep up that attention to him, and that respectful beha- viour to him, which my natural affection leads me to, and which I will do to all the Royal Family, that will permit me, as long as I continue at court; but no farther I can assure you. If I am to judge of His Royal Highness's thoughts, they are pretty much the same as the rest of the world; and I do verily believe, he rather wishes a change in the Secretary's office than not; but that I only guess, because I think all lord Sandwich's friends do; and I dare say you will have very little trouble in bringing that about, when you have a mind to it. But I must desire nothing may come from me; and I hope you will not take it amiss, that I decline writing an ostensible letter upon the subject. When I see the king, if he speaks to me, I shall certainly tell him my thoughts honestly and fairly; but as to beginning with him, I am determined not to do it, and I hope you will not take it amiss that I decline it; for, coming in at the last hour, and having nothing to offer but what is disagreeable, is not an office which, upon reflection, you would put me upon.

" You say, the great point which I desire, is determined as I wish; that is, to do nothing in the disposition of the great offices, till his Majesty's return. You could not, my dear Brother, think I meant the formal appointments of these people: if the measures are taken, and the persons agreed upon by the king and you, I had just as soon they were nominated in form at Hanover, as at St. James's. You say, if I approve of it, the duke of Bedford will be removed with ease and pleasure; and desire that I will not condemn you to a constant inquietude and uneasiness, as long as you stay in the ministry. That is putting things a little hard upon me, first to say I am the person that keeps in the duke of Bedford, if he is kept in, and then that the keeping him in, is condemning you to a state of inquietude and uneasiness, as long as you remain in the ministry. I have not vanity enough to think the first, but possibly rather imagine, my frank correspondence with you, may have tended towards his removal; and the latter I am certain you cannot think I shall contribute to. I look upon the duke of Bedford's removal, by what you say, as determined. All I desire is, that I may have nothing to do in it. I look upon the disposition of the other offices, to be pretty nearly so too; *entirely*, if the duke of Bedford takes the President.

What then, is there more for me to say or do, but to make the best of a bad market? which I shall certainly do, as long as I keep open shop. * * * *

" Upon the whole, therefore, I shall only make this observation: if the duke of Bedford takes President, you will strengthen yourself by lord Holdernesse's being Secretary of State, lord Albemarle Groom of the Stôle, and lord Waldegrave Master of the Horse. If he goes to Master of the Horse, I do not find you have any body for President, but lord Granville: you know what I think will be the consequence of that measure; and as to poor Harrington, I think he is fairly cut, by a President's being proposed, and nothing said of him at the same time. By the king's answer, he certainly expected he would have been named; though I believe it would have been difficult, if not impossible, for him to have succeeded." * * * *

THE DUKE OF NEWCASTLE TO THE LORD CHANCELLOR.*

On the subject of the duke of Bedford and lord Harrington.

Hanover Sept. 8th-19th, 1750.

After commenting on the late diplomatic transactions, and on his own share in them, which he doubts whether the duke of Bedford would have had either ability or spirit to undertake, he adds—" And that brings me to the great domestic point mentioned in your letter, Aug. 31st. I have written my thoughts fully to my brother, in a long letter, that went from hence last Sunday, which I have begged him to send to you, and in one that will go by the messenger to morrow. I hope the great point of all is over; viz. that the duke of Bedford is not to remain, in any event, Secretary of State. After that, the easier he is, in accepting any other employment, or his having that which is the most agreeable to him, the better I shall like it. Allow me to say, ' I do not comprehend what my brother means, ' that the measure is taken to form a party at court, to push their point that way, and that they may be able to create more difficulty there, than in foreign affairs, in which that great man has shewn himself unable.' And your lordship says, this is a speculation of which you are no judge. My dear lord, is the measure now beginning, of forming a party at court? What has been doing all this last year? Where have we been? Or do I see things which nobody else sees? What has been the conduct of the Duke and princess, all last winter and this summer? I verily believe, their conduct has greatly influenced the king's present resolution. But, to the other point:—what harm can this young fry, as courtiers, do to us, when none of them are in the ministry, and in the secret, which they cannot do to us, when one of them is in the ministry, necessarily in the secret, and when, as experience ought to have shewn you all last winter, I can do nothing without him, nor the king (though ever so well disposed to it) have one single conference with me alone, without giving an alarm to all the world? To sum up all, if I am any thing in this question; if I am wanted either in foreign affairs, or my concurrence be of service to my friends in domestic ones, I am, I must be, an errant cipher (and that of the worst sort) if the duke of Bedford remains coupled

* Newcastle Papers.

with me as Secretary of State.   What hurt can he do as Master of the Horse?   Can he persuade the king to make him Secretary of State?   If he does, we are but where we are at present.   Can he make Sandwich Secretary?   Or in short can he turn me out?   Would not he do any of these things more easily when Secretary, than when nothing in business?   Will the Duke and princess support him more then; or can they do it; than they do now?   No, my lord; from that moment there will be an end of all *éclat*.   This measure is the king's and the king's own; and no one will dare to censure it, that belongs immediately to his Majesty.   If it is treated as the king's (and I am sure his Majesty will treat it so himself, by what he said to me upon it viz. ' you and I cannot do it alone ; we must have the council with us,') this is his own motion arising from what every body must have seen, and from his own sense of the indecency and indignity that had been put upon him and his government.

"I have given my brother such a circumstantial account of all that passed here, that I hope he will have sent it to you, and consequently that it is unnecessary to repeat it, for indeed I have not time to do it.   The lady has certainly long seen the king's uneasiness, and feared this would end as it is likely to do.   It is possible that she may have given notice of it in England, and that that has produced, as my brother suspects, an inclination for the office of Master of the Horse.   I know, she received lately a great packet from England, which made her very serious and thoughtful.   This accounts for her pressing so much that particular office ; and this accounts also for his Grace's particular declaration for it.   As to the successor, I love my lord Halifax as well as any body; but I am amazed you can think of him for Secretary of State.   First of all, all of us together cannot make the king do it. Secondly, to fear court intrigues, and to put it in their power to be telling the king, every hour, that we have recommended the most odious man in the kingdom to him, because he is related to my brother and me; thirdly, a man of his life, spirit and temper, that in a month will think he knows better than any body!   This would effectually determine the king to keep the duke of Bedford; and upon my word, I doubt whether I should myself not be for it.   The king has himself named a suc- cessor—my lord Holdernesse.   He can never reproach me with the choice, afterwards, and take it from me.   He is as prudent, as honest, and as practicable a young man as ever came into the world ; he has ability enough, and will go through the office with dignity and reputation, will give no uneasiness to his companions, and will make an admirable Hanover secretary in 1752.

" I have now said all that I have time to say, and, I hope, all that is necessary to say, upon the subject of the Secretary of State.   More particulars you will have from my brother.   As to the other points, first, what relates to my lord Harrington, I am much obliged to your lordship for sending me an account of what passes, and for what you said to his lordship upon my subject.   I send you a copy of a letter which goes to-morrow to my brother, singly upon this affair.   I desire you would consider it as written to yourself, and answer my lord Harrington from it, as if it had been written to you, with regard to the part I am ready to take, for procuring the general- ship of marines for his lordship.   As I therefore look upon these two points as in a manner settled, though the execution of what relates to the duke of Bedford will certainly be postponed until the king comes back to England, if my brother and you continue to think it necessary, (for I cannot imagine that the king will refuse to make his Grace Master of the Horse, since that will quiet every thing,) the next consideration, and that a very material one, is, to whom the President's place shall be given? I entirely agree, that if the duke of Devonshire would take it, he would be the best of all; but of that I have no notion. But my brother has suggested lord Chesterfield. My chief objection to that is, that it would highly offend my lord Granville, and make him desperate, who certainly has no intention of being so, and who by his discourse and friends is of use in our foreign affairs. If any thing could be found out for them both, I believe they would be useful and innocent assistants. But I do not see how that can well be. I fling out what I think; but, as I said to my brother, I am open, very open to conviction.* * * *

" Since I have been writing my letter, Haslang's courier is arrived with the ratifications. He brings great complaints of Haslang, but he brings the ratifications. Haslang is ordered to insist upon my giving a declaration that the king would equally conclude with the elector Palatine upon reasonable terms, which, as it may imply subsidies, I shall certainly not do; and that the king would use his good offices with the court of Vienna, in favour of the elector Palatine's pretensions. That, if confined to the treaties, and the Austrian ministers agree to it, I may consent to. In short, I will finish, if I can; but be assured I will not suffer a squint at subsidies.

" I send your lordship, inclosed, a minute, which I wrote last night, to the king, giving an account of the present situation of this affair. It is all a *paroître* on the part of the elector of Bavaria. He will seem to be very zealous for his cousin the elector Palatine; but he will not lose his own bargain for it.

" P. S.—We shall exchange to-morrow night."

MR. PELHAM TO THE DUKE OF NEWCASTLE.*

Approves the Bavarian treaty—Repeats his hopes that the king will confer the office of General of Marines.

"DEAR BROTHER,   *Greenwich, half-past nine, Sept.* 14*th*-25*th*, 1750.

" I have this moment received your several letters of the 5th 7th and 9th of this month; but have scarce time to read them, before the messenger must return to London. I hope you will therefore excuse my answering them with any exactness to night. That which you intend I should shew to lord Harrington, I fear will scarce give him satisfaction; as indeed I do not see how it can. You tell him that the duke of Dorset's removal to Ireland has been some time determined, and seem to give some reasons why it should be so, and at the same time own that nothing has, as yet, been said to the king, as to what is to become of him. You seem to intimate even that he may be out before the king returns; and no reason can be given for that, but

* Newcastle Papers.

that the duke of Dorset will have it so.   I fear he will not think that a sufficient one.   I should hope, therefore, that the king will do something for lord Harrington, at the time he appoints the duke of Dorset; and I cannot think his Grace can with any decency expect his promotion should take place of all others, even to the detriment and discredit of one, whom mankind think deserves as well as himself.   Sure it is enough for the duke of Dorset, that he has every thing he asks for, with the joint consent and approbation of all the king's servants.   I say more upon this subject, because I hear more from various quarters every day.

"As to the other parts of your letter, you will have had my thoughts and resolution before this can come to your hands.   I must now, dear Brother, thank you most heartily for your kind and cordial expressions of friendship to me.   Believe me, mine are as sincere to you, as they can be; and shall continue the same, in whatever situation of life we are.   I have had a very obliging letter from count Bentinck; it is too late for me to answer it by this messenger; I must desire you therefore to make him my compliments.   I do not know what I wrote, that could deserve the compliments you are pleased to make me: I know I wrote my mind, and that mind has been always the same.   If you can carry the election of a king of the Romans, it is worth the subsidy we are to pay the elector of Bavaria; and if you cannot, considering what I know to be the disposition of many people abroad, and some at home, it is a good composition to prevent those measures going farther.   Your part in that scheme, I have always approved, and your perseverance in it, deserves my thanks.

"P. S.—If the king should ask what I think about lord Harrington's being general of the marines, you may with truth say, that if his Majesty is determined to do nothing else for him, I would rather stand the reproach of having given my consent to that measure, than see an old servant of the king's, in the decline of life, turned adrift for no public misconduct, that I know of, and for no private one, that you and I can decently find fault with.

MR. PELHAM TO THE DUKE OF NEWCASTLE.*

Hopes that the Election will follow the execution of the Bavarian treaty—Farther remarks on the removal of the Duke of Bedford—Is cautious not to deceive Lord Harrington with false hopes.

"DEAR BROTHER,   *Sept. 21st- Oct. 2nd*, 1750.

"I have very little to add, either of amusement or intelligence, to what I have sent you in my former letters.   But, as a messenger goes regularly this day to Hanover, I will not suffer him to depart without most heartily congratulating you upon the finishing your great work, by the actual exchange of the several ratifications.   I own I was surprised, as well as you, at the delay of the court of Munich;

* Newcastle Papers.

but when I read the Elector's letter .to Haslang, which you was so kind to send me, I thought I then understood the meeting; and never doubted but that it would go as you wished. I hope and believe, the great end for which you have laboured, will also be brought about soon. I hope it will at least be put in motion, and possibly be in such a forwardness as to leave no room for doubt, before you leave Germany. If so, you may come with a light heart and cheerful countenance. I have taken the best care I could about the yachts: I believe they will be very soon ready after your orders come; at least lord Anson assures me so. I find the king will have dark nights after the 22nd, but our Admiral does not think that much; however, it is proper for you to remind the king of that, lest it should be said we hurried him over, for the sake of being at his birth-day, when it was not safe for him to come. I do not suppose he will alter his intention upon this; and then you will have discharged your duty, and we shall at the same time, not be deprived of the happiness of seeing his Majesty here. I have mentioned nothing to you of the parliament's meeting, because I think we need not call them together till after Christmas, unless your foreign affairs require an earlier meeting. The country gentlemen never like to come up before the holidays; and if any alterations are to be made in the administration, sure it will be right to have a month or two, to see what turn that will take before the people are called together.

" You see by this, what my thoughts are. I wish you would consider of it, and let me know the king's intentions, if you can, before his return to England. I was asked the other day, whether I had heard of any body's being named for Master of the Horse? My answer was ready; no particular person whatsoever, only I understood from you, that the king would probably take one into that office, with whom he was well acquainted, and who was agreeable to him. I was asked again, has nobody been named? I answered, not by you, nor did I in the least think any one had been named seriously to the king; that possibly it might have been said abroad, that if the duke of Bedford left his present office, that of Master of the Horse might be agreeable to him; but that I really knew nothing of the matter. The reply to me was, 'however agreeable that might be to the duke of Bedford, I am sure his Grace will not be agreeable to the king; and I cannot believe he will ever consent to it;' in which opinion I agreed, and confirmed it by saying, I thought it was your opinion also, though I had heard very little from you upon the subject.

" I hope you approve of my way of treating these questions: I am sure I have done no harm, nor made any discovery. You desire to know my thoughts as to the manner and time of this being done, if it is to be done at all. You cannot expect me to give advice in an affair of so great consequence, when I know not the disposition of any one, or either of the principal persons concerned. If it arises from the lady, and her only, who so proper to put it in motion as herself? And can that be done before you come to England? Who can answer to any of you, how this will be liked? Who is there that has acquaintance or intimacy enough with any of the parties, to sound them, before they are authorised so to do? and who is there on this side of the water, that has had any correspondence upon the subject but myself? and I hope and believe you will not send me on so disagreeable an errand.

" You mention lord Holdernesse as successor to his Grace of Bedford again, and seem to think, I have some particular dislike to him. I can assure you I have none; on the contrary, I wish him personally well, but I cannot possibly see him in the light of a Secretary of State. Nor, indeed, do I see any other; I named Halifax, not as thinking that ran upon all four; I saw the objection the king would have, and was no stranger to what you would apprehend yourself. I threw it out, only to say something, and in reality to demonstrate to you the difficulty of a change; and above all, if a change must be, to shew you the absolute necessity of strengthening the administration, in the disposal of the President's place. I had Chesterfield more in my view than any one else, because I am satisfied he would bring with him the opinion of the world; and I knew him so made, and so acquainted, as to take off a great deal of the intrigues of the town, which might possibly operate to our disadvantage, if we had no new supports. I must own I was not afraid of lord Granville's resentment; and I cannot but own to you, it gave me great concern to read what you said and do say upon this subject. You know my thoughts on that, I shall therefore say no more about him.

" I wait with impatience for your reply to my letter of this day fortnight. I hope you do not take it amiss; I am disposed neither to act nor think differently from you, but I cannot act different from my own thoughts; and I should little deserve the many affectionate expressions in your several letters, if I hid from you my serious thoughts, or suffered you to go away with an opinion, that I approved of what you say, when both my past and future conduct must contradict me.

" I have done well with Harrington as far as relates to yourself; but have been very cautious of leading him into false hopes. I cannot but repeat my wishes, that he may not be totally forgot; and believe me, dear Brother, when we cannot satisfy people in essentials, there is a great deal in treating their ill fortunes with decency and concern."

THE DUKE OF NEWCASTLE TO MR. PELHAM.*

Expresses his concern that their misunderstanding should continue—Speaks favourably of Sir Thomas Robinson—Will not press the appointment of Lord Holdernesse—Gives up Lord Granville, and wishes to act in conformity with his brother's sentiments.

"DEAR BROTHER,   *Hanover, Sept. 29th- Oct. 10th, 1750.*

" Last night I received your letter of the 21st, by Price, the messenger. I am sorry to find you continue to write still in the same strain. I hope, though I do not expect it, that the fair and undisguised answers, that I have given to all your objections, will remove your uneasiness.* * * *

" As to the alterations to be made in the administration, I begin to be every day more uncertain what they will be, or whether there will be any at all.

" There is not one word said about them here. All is referred to the king's return to England; and though every thing is settled, I once more affirm, no one single thing is settled, or any thing like it; and I believe there never was a time, when any one here dared so little to talk about English business, as at present.

* Newcastle Papers.

" I conclude I know *the great lady* * that asked you about the successor to the Master of the Horse. I am sorry you said it was my opinion, that the king would never consent to the duke of Bedford's being Master of the Horse. I am afraid *that lady* will make a bad use of it, and endeavour then, to make his Grace never consent to quit the Secretary's office. If you will look back upon my *famous* letter of the 2nd-13th of September, you will find my opinion was otherwise. In that letter there is this paragraph

" ' I took very great notice of the intelligence you had of the duke of Bedford's way of thinking about the office of Master of the Horse; and I conclude by that, that his Grace will take it, if the king will give it him, which he certainly will do, rather than let him remain in the Secretary's office.'

" And in another place of that letter, 'This would please the king, put us upon forming our schemes, and would probably end in the duke of Bedford's being Master of the Horse, and every thing else going on quietly.'

" When I desired to know your thoughts about the manner and time of putting things into execution, I own I thought them very different from what I now find them. I do not see, now, that any thing is to be executed; the consequence of which will be, that nothing, that no business, will be done.

" The whole, I think, reduces itself to this. Those who think the duke of Bedford should remain Secretary of State, should tell the king so, and advise my lord duke to continue; for the worst way of all, of keeping the duke of Bedford in, is by suggesting that there is no proper person to succeed him.

" If the person (lord Holdernesse) who has been accidently dropt by the king, be not thought proper, let the king know it; I dare say the king will, in that, most readily yield to the opinion of his servants. But let it never be said, that there is no man proper to make, when there is one † who has been bred in foreign affairs for near thirty years; has been concerned, and principally, in all the great foreign transactions of Europe; has singly made the great treaty of Vienna, twenty years ago; had a principal share in making the late treaty of Aix la Chapelle; and has all the amiable and valuable qualities, that a private man can have; attached from his childhood to the king's present ministers, and of undoubted principles for his Majesty and his government; not dangerous to those he loves, but able and steady against those who would give disturbance, either to the public or his friends.

" As to lord Holdernesse, I think he would do very well, and the best of any, since the other cannot have it. But if a more proper man can be found, one need not think twice about Holdernesse; he will not, he shall not, stand in the way.

" As to lord Chesterfield, I do not absolutely agree, 'That he would bring with him the opinion of the world;' but if he brings your opinion, it is enough for me, to be for him, at least not to be against him. Lord Granville's resentment may be to be despised; but opposition will not at present be to be feared, except he is at the head of it. My Lord Chancellor is personally hurt by him, and with reason; you have your prejudices, and so have we all. But, however, lord Granville from this time

---

* Princess Amelia.   † Sir Thomas Robinson.

is out of the question. Whatever I have said about him, is from myself only. I suppose my Lord Chancellor suspects the king, or my lady Yarmouth; I do not know that I have heard her name him once, since we have been here; and I think the king only once, and that very slightingly; indeed his Majesty has no intention to combat for my lord Granville. He paid him off with the Garter, and I thought that would be, as it has been, the consequence of it.

"As to lord Harrington, I will hope upon reflection, you will think, not only that I am determined to do all I can, but all you wish. I hope I have never shewed an inclination to have him totally forgot, or not to treat his ill fortune with decency and concern.

" The king was much pleased with what I said from you about the Cologne subsidy. The messenger goes on purpose for the ten thousand pounds in bank bills. Pray send them as soon as possibly you can, that I may not be detained here in expectation of them, and that we may go from hence in good humour." * * * *

MR. PELHAM TO THE DUKE OF NEWCASTLE.*

Disapproves giving subsidies to other electors.—Thinks the duke of Bedford has changed his resolution, and will not accept the mastership of the Horse, unless lord Sandwich is appointed Secretary of State—Hopes his brother will continue to act with the duke of Bedford—Exposes the danger of turning him out, but will at all events give his assistance—Conversation with the duke of Dorset on his appointment to the government of Ireland.

Oct. 5th-16th, 1750.

* * * * " As I conclude this will be the last messenger that will go to Hanover, whilst you continue there, I shall just trouble you with a few thoughts, upon the present situation of affairs, which I hope you will take as I mean them, friendly and impartially; and if they do not in every respect coincide with your own, impute it to a different information of things, and a real difference of opinion, which cannot be avoided, and not to any inclination of my own, or any perverseness or peevishness in my temper; for I can with truth declare, no man in the world has endeavoured to divest himself of all those improper influences, more than I have done, and I think I have succeeded in my endeavours. First then, as to your foreign affairs; you know how well I think you have done, in every thing hitherto transacted by you abroad; I am sensible of the difficulties you have had, and therefore admire more your being able to surmount them. But the last paper of the Elector of Cologne's is the strangest thing I ever read in my life; does he think the Maritime Powers will, or can come into any of his propositions? He stumbles at the very threshold, which I do not think you are enough aware of. England has no treaty with that elector at all, and I hope it is not understood that we have; for it would be a very difficult task to defend that, upon the foot of the Bavarian treaty. I cannot think the court of Munich will suffer him to go off; if they do, they want to get off themselves. I hope

* Newcastle Papers.

therefore, you will stand as firm there, as you have done in other subsidiary applications.

" I think you mentioned in one letter to lord Holdernesse, a proposal for applying the elector of Cologne's subsidy to the king of Poland, and the Elector Palatine. If the king approves of that, and it is done in the same way as the treaty with the elector of Cologne, I do not see how this country can have any objection to it, because they have nothing to do with it. But I believe those two courts will scarce enter into engagements upon the foot of such a treaty, without England is specifically mentioned. This is all I have to say upon these subjects. You see what I wish to avoid, and, I doubt not, will do every thing you can, to prevent our being involved in any farther engagements, particularly where money is concerned. I say the more on this subject, as you are going to the Hague, where you will be pressed very much for something of this kind ; and I can easily see, our friend Bentinck will not be the least warm in driving these measures. Believe me, at the same time, I have as much confidence in you as I can have in any body. I sent your letter as desired to Lord Chancellor, who reasons upon the conduct of the electors, just as I do.

" As to our interior here, I really do not know what to say to it. I have learnt, and not from bad hands, that the scheme is changed ; that the duke of Bedford will on no account change his office, that is, unless he can name his successor, which even he cannot be wild enough to think possible. The view in this resolution must be, either to keep where they are, and rub on in the same awkward manner, which they must know will be disagreeable to you, or put you under the difficulty of advising the king to turn His Grace out, which they know will put us under great difficulties, and possibly, by disuniting, break the administration. Lord Bolingbroke talked in this manner, pretty publicly at Battersea ; and, as was represented to me, with some sort of satisfaction, which I can account for, no otherwise than from a kind of correspondence, which has lately been struck up between his lordship and Leicester Fields. When I see you, I shall be able to explain this farther to you ; but possibly you may know a good deal of it already. Lord Bolingbroke quoted me as having said there must be a change in the Secretary's office, and then made the inferences, which are natural.

" You see, therefore, dear Brother, what is thought of me here.

" If you cannot bring yourself to be easy with having a troublesome, insignificant, colleague, I see no way there is to get rid of him with tolerable safety, but for the lady to undertake the change, with Master of the Horse ; and then, if Harrington can be President, your affairs, for the present, will be settled according to your mind, and we shall rub on pretty tolerably. If the king will not make Harrington President, I do not know where you will find a man to fill that office, with any kind of dignity. The person I proposed, I see is not agreeable ; and as he is now gone to Bath for some time, it is impossible for me or any one else to sound him upon the subject ; and Dayrolles, I know, says that he can assure every one, that lord Chesterfield will take no place on any account whatever. He may possibly be mistaken, but I am far from thinking he is. You see, therefore, how very material it is to look out for a President. I dare say you agree with me, that it will be very ridiculous for the duke of Dorset to hold both; and I dare say he does not think of doing it but for a time; or till some proper person can be thought of.

" I have seen His Grace this morning, and had, I think, a full conversation with him. He told me he thought it was understood that he was to be appointed before the king's return. I told him I understood you so, and that I knew you intended and desired it should be so, and if it was not, that it arose from what I had wrote to you; and repeated to him, as well as I could remember, what I had wrote. He then said, if he was to go to Ireland, and not with the good will of the king's ministers, he would much rather stay at home. I soon made him easy on that head, by shewing him that you and Lord Chancellor he could not, and he owned he did not, distrust. And then as to myself, I declared there was no one I wished to succeed lord Harrington, but his Grace; I did, and always did, wish it might be done with decency there, and also that the fall might be broken by some emolument; that I had suggested one to you, which I hoped would do, and that I thought neither king, royal family, nor minister wished, or thought of any one for Ireland, but himself; and that the vacancy, if not made before the king came over, would, I presumed, be settled very soon afterwards; and so we parted seemingly very well satisfied.

" You see by the minutes of the regency, that we were but just a quorum yesterday. The Chancellor, I hope, will be in town, before the next regency day, for it is very necessary that we should have some discourse together before we all meet.

I have now, dear Brother, told you every thing I can pick up, and laid before you, as well as I am able, my thoughts upon the whole. I own the case as it now stands, is a difficult one. I heartily wish you could reconcile yourself to the letting things remain as they are for some time at least; but if you cannot, consider well what you would have done; and when you have determined, I promise you I will make no complaints, but endeavour to qualify every thing as far as I am able."

THE DUKE OF NEWCASTLE TO THE LORD CHANCELLOR.

The King persists in his resolution to remove the duke of Bedford, but it is expected that Mr. Pelham should interfere.

Hanover, Oct. 14th-25th, 1750.

* * * * " I had a very satisfactory conversation yesterday with lady Yarmouth. She still says, the king continues his resolution about the duke of Bedford, but my brother must speak. I told her, positively, he would not. At last she promised me to send for him, to tell him that the king had taken that resolution; that I had never mentioned one word of it, since the king was here, till *she* informed me of the king's intention; that she desires my brother to make things easy, by getting something for the duke of Bedford (viz. Master of the Horse), that may be agreeable to him. I think this will operate in all the ways I can wish it, and is a proof of her sincerity. I asked her if she had mentioned Chesterfield for President? She said she did, last year; but the king rejected it.

" Let me hear from you at the Hague. I hope, in three weeks, to have the pleasure of assuring you in person, how much I am," &c.

" P. S.—I suppose the lords justices will appoint the meeting of the parliament after Christmas. The king expects that it will be so."

THE DUKE OF NEWCASTLE TO MR. PELHAM.*

The duke of Bedford will accept the Mastership of the Horse—Hopes that his brother and the Chancellor will form a scheme of administration.

Hague, Oct. 23rd-Nov. 3rd, 1750.

* * * * " I had a short, but very satisfactory conversation, with lady Yarmouth, upon the great point, two days before I left Hanover. She still says, the affair of the Secretary's office remains determined, though that of the Master of the Horse will meet with difficulty. If we all agree, I think they will both go as we shall wish, and settle amongst ourselves. I hear, his Grace of Bedford grows very unpopular, which does not surprise me. He will certainly take the Master of the Horse, if he cannot keep the other; and that is the secret of the whole: and the king will certainly give him the Master of the Horse, if he finds every body will agree that he should not remain in the other. I told lady Yarmouth what I had done about the duke of Dorset's warrant. She told me plainly, neither party would be pleased with me; that the duke of Dorset would not like it, (and that, indeed, I find; for his Grace has not done me the honour to answer my letter,) and that lord Harrington's friends would think I *might* have done more.

" Every thing, you see, is in fact suspended, till we come to England, which, I hope in God, will now be soon. The king has declared his intention of leaving Hanover next Monday, and will be at Helvoetsluys on Friday se'ennight. I pray God the present wind may last. I go to-morrow to Moordyke, ... by water, under the command of admiral Knowles; and I hope to be at Calais on Tuesday next, and shall contrive to come to London as soon *after* the king as possible. I wish lord Chancellor and you would form a scheme of administration, that may, as far as can be, answer all our views. Be in good humour, and let us *really* forget. Your last says nothing of lady Lincoln. My compliments," &c.

THE DUKE OF NEWCASTLE TO THE KING.†

" Your Majesty's known goodness and generosity to all your servants, induces me to hope, that you will pardon the presumption I am now taking, in expressing to you, in this manner, the deep concern and affliction I am in, to find myself under your royal displeasure. I should have been totally ignorant of the cause of it, had not your Majesty been graciously pleased to mention it to my lord Chancellor, and my brother.

* Newcastle Papers.

† The original of this letter is without date, but it is evident from the contents, that it was written soon after the resignation of the duke of Bedford, when the king was so much displeased with the duke of Newcastle; probably towards the end of July, 1751, as the lord Chancellor, in a letter to the duke of Newcastle, dated July 28th, 1751, congratulates his Grace on the change in the closet.

" Allow me, Sir, with a heart devoted to your Majesty, to assure you, that the least signification of your displeasure is sufficient to make me alter any mistaken behaviour I may have had, or avoid any that your Majesty may seem to apprehend. The only thing I cannot support, is the thought of losing that gracious acceptance of my best and most zealous endeavours for your royal service, which can alone enable me to go through it, with any hopes of success to your Majesty's affairs, or any possibility of ease, quiet, and reputation to myself. The experience that I have had for many years, of your Majesty's royal favour and good opinion, makes me know too well the value of it, not to do every thing in my power to obtain or recover it.

" It would be the highest presumption in me, to suppose, that any misrepresentation of my conduct can have made any impression upon your Majesty; whilst I must, at the same time, be unjust to myself, did I not know that I am incapable of doing anything knowingly, that could offend you. The differences which have lately, or may have been formerly, between any of your Majesty's ministers, I should humbly hope, your Majesty would not impute singly to me.

" Your Majesty's great goodness to me, and the rest of your servants, in passing over what happened when my lord Granville was last in your service, I always looked upon as the greatest mark of generosity to us all; and the particular marks that I have since had of your royal favour and confidence in me, I shall always remember, in all situations, with the utmost duty and gratitude.

" The resignation of my lord Harrington, which was neither known nor expected by me, above four and twenty hours before it happened, I have ever thought, proceeded singly from my having had the honour to pursue your Majesty's plan for peace and war, in which his lordship entirely differed, and which plan has since been so happily accomplished, for the interest of your Majesty's own kingdom, and all Europe. I cannot presume to enter into the reasons of my lord Chesterfield's resignation, having never been authentically informed of them; but I have heard that they were far from being confined to one single object, and were also chiefly founded upon public considerations and public measures.

" Whatever my private opinion may have been, with relation to the duke of Bedford's remaining in the office of Secretary of State (for I never could have any objection to his Grace's having any other employment in your Majesty's service), it was always my intention, as it was always my duty, most humbly to submit it to your Majesty. Agreeably to that resolution, I have never but once (and that many months ago), troubled your Majesty upon the subject, since your last return to England; and, in answer to what is laid to my charge, I humbly beg leave to appeal to my lord Chancellor, and the rest of your Majesty's servants, whether my personal behaviour to his Grace has not been at least as unexceptionable as his to me. And in the confidence and communication upon your Majesty's business, and particularly the secret part of it, I have been entirely guided by what I apprehended to be your royal will and intention. But, if in that I have been mistaken, I most humbly ask your Majesty's pardon, and that you would have the goodness to believe that I have erred by mistake, and not by inclination. As to the removal of the earl of Sandwich, which I humbly presume has alone occasioned the resignations that have followed (all other reasons, if grounded, having equally existed, long before that), I never presumed, once in my life, to trouble your Majesty upon that point, but when I was ordered to receive your commands for his lordship's dismission.

"Could your Majesty vouchsafe to consider what an old faithful servant must feel, who having been honoured with his royal master's favour and good opinion, finds himself at once in danger of losing it, and is not conscious of having done any thing knowingly that was either disagreeable, or disserviceable to your Majesty, your Majesty's great justice and humanity would pardon any, even improper attempt, which my duty, fidelity, zeal, and (if I dare mention it) affection to your Majesty, may prompt me to take to prevent it.

"Your Majesty will always command whatever service I can do you : I only wish to be enabled to use my best endeavours with a probability of success; and that if through mistake I may have done any thing that your Majesty has disapproved, I may have an opportunity of shewing by my future conduct, that even that shall be most carefully avoided.

"If, in any thing else, which has not yet come to my knowledge, I may have acted contrary, or have omitted to act agreeably to your Majesty's inclinations, the least mention of it, by any canal your Majesty shall think proper, will be sufficient to make me alter my conduct in that respect. The only favour I have now to beg is, that your Majesty would have the goodness to suspend your judgment of me, before you absolutely condemn me,* and that

or that you would allow me to retire, and you would believe me to be, with the in my private capacity to shew the sub- utmost submission, gratitude, and duty, mission, gratitude, and duty, with which your Majesty's most faithful, most de- I shall ever remain, &c. &c. voted, and most obedient subject and servant,

(Signed)   HOLLES NEWCASTLE."

THE DUKE OF NEWCASTLE TO THE LORD CHANCELLOR.

Communicates voluminous dispatches on foreign affairs—Mission of the late Lord Marshal Keith to Paris from Berlin—On the negotiations with Spain and Saxony—Calculates on the concurrence of the two Empresses, of six electors, and of Holland, in counteracting the designs of France and Prussia—Parties in Holland, and weakness of the government —Maritime Powers interested in supporting the Barrier Treaty—On the birth of a duke of Burgundy, and the unfavourable changes in the French cabinet—Good effects of the late changes in the British cabinet—Is satisfied with the conduct of lords Holdernesse and Albemarle.

"MY DEAR LORD,   *Newcastle House, Sept. 6th, 1751.*

"Your lordship, I am afraid, will have been surprised that you have had no account from me of what has passed here since you left London.

* This copy is taken from an original draught in the handwriting of the duke. At the conclusion of the letter is a marginal variation, as above, but cancelled.

" I was absent, you know, a fortnight in the country. · Since that time, I have been answering the arrear of business,· and such fresh letters as have come in ; and I was unwilling to send the messenger till I could give your lordship some light into what may probably be the event of our several negotiations ; and for that purpose I send you all the material letters that have passed in both provinces. They are very voluminous, but you will read them at your leisure, and either send them back by your own servant, or order this messenger to return for them to Wimpole, by the time you may think you shall be able to get through them.

" The most important transactions are, those with the courts of Spain,· Vienna, Dresden, and Petersburg.

" There is an affair which may be more material in its consequences than any of them; I mean the king of Prussia's· sending the late Lord·Marshal, as his public minister to Paris, and the court of France's receiving him as such.

" Your lordship will see by my lord Holdernesse's letters, the orders· sent· to colonel Yorke to represent against it. I have talked, very strongly, to M. de Mirepoix upon it ; and, to do him justice, he entered into it in the rightest manner possible, and not only promised to write to his court, but did in fact send for Michel, and advised him to do his utmost to stop it ; who told him it was too late, and that the late Lord Marshal was absolutely set out from Berlin. Before these orders could arrive at Paris, colonel Yorke had of himself mentioned it to M. Puisieulx ;· and nothing could be more harsh and offensive than his manner of receiving it, and his discourse upon it ; and I own I think· the king of Prussia's sending the late Lord Marshal, the court of France's receiving of him, and M. Puisieulx's extraordinary and offensive manner of defending it, have a very bad appearance, and shew a design of really coming to a rupture with us, or a desire, at least, that we should think they are indifferent about it.

" M. Puisieulx's reproaches, that they have not met with a suitable return to their offers of friendship, and his declaration, that ' the king his master would not concern himself in these matters' (viz., the affairs of the Pretender and the Jacobites), were as bad symptoms as possible; and I should not be much surprised, if they were to be followed with extravagances in North America, Africa, or somewhere or other.

" One may easily see the views with which the king of Prussia has taken this offensive step; first, for the sake of doing an impertinence to the king, then to deter us from going on with our negotiations in the Empire, for the election of a king of the Romans, and to encourage the Jacobite party, that we may apprehend disturbances from them, if a rupture should ensue, in consequence of the measures we are taking abroad. I wish your lordship would consider, and let me have your thoughts, whether any thing more can be done at present, than the representations Mr. Yorke is directed to make, and what it may be proper for lord Albemarle to do or say, upon the bluff refusal that has been given by M. Puisieulx, and probably will be repeated (though perhaps not in so rude a manner), upon the instances that are to be made now by the king's order.

" It has been suggested, to send away Michel, the Prussian minister. I own I think any measures of that kind (which would totally break off all correspondence with a court of consequence), ought to be weighed before they are executed; because, when that is once done, it is difficult to set it right again, without perhaps the intervention or mediation of a power to whom one would not care to be obliged. But it may be worth consideration, whether it might not be proper to make some strong declaration to Michel, upon such an offensive step, after the service the king had done to the king of Prussia, not only by his Majesty's own guaranty of Silesia, but by that of the empire afterwards ; and M. Michel might be given to understand, that these provocations might weaken the force of those guaranties.

" But in my humble opinion, these incidents from France and Prussia confirm the necessity of our establishing some solid system of security and defence, and a constant powerful sea force at home; and that is the best and only use we can at present make of them.

" I send you a very kind letter which I have had from Joe : * I shall send him as kind an answer. Lord Albemarle returns to Paris on Friday fortnight. He is extremely Joe's friend, and desires to carry him the news of his being appointed minister in Holland. I shall desire he may come away, immediately upon lord Albemarle's arrival ; return hither for about a week ; and then set out for Holland, where he will be very welcome, and is much wanted.

" You will see that the Spanish negotiation goes on very well. The queen of Spain is so much of. an Austrian, that she seems to have the cause of the empress queen extremely at heart. That has flattered the folly and vanity of the court of Vienna so much, that that is the true cause of their silence and neglect of us. However, I think we are now pretty sure that the negotiation for the security of Italy, at least, will succeed, and a treaty for that purpose be made between the empress queen and Spain, and I hope we shall get the king of Sardinia included. Carvajal is certainly for it, but I am not sure whether the court of Vienna may not have a view to be at liberty, with regard to the cessions of the treaty of Worms, or at least so far as not to enter into any new, or renewal of the old engagements, with relation to them. You remember the language they held upon this head, before the treaty of Aix-la-Chapelle ; and I am afraid, the same spirit, and the same views, may make them averse to the king of Sardinia's being a party to the present arrangements. However, they will have a difficulty to avoid it, when we propose it, and Spain comes so readily into it.

" Your lordship will see M. Carvajal's reasons upon this treaty pretty much as I did, in my first letter to Keith upon it ; viz., that it should be the base and foundation of a more extended alliance. I own, however, I wish we could hook in the king to be a party even to this treaty; and for that purpose, I have drawn the article inclosed in lord Holdernesse's letter to Mr. Keene, and in mine to Mr. Keith. That will be a foundation for our becoming a party to this treaty ; and is drawn intirely upon Carvajal's plan : viz., the guaranties contained in the treaty of Aix la Chapelle. My last private letter from Mr. Keene, gives, I think, great reason to hope that Ensenada is in earnest, to put an end to the depredations. I cannot pretend to make any posi-

* Colonel Joseph Yorke, son of the lord Chancellor, afterwards successively Sir Joseph Yorke, and lord Dover.

tive judgement of the proposal of establishing an English factory at Honduras for cutting of logwood, as I do not yet know the particulars of it. But, sure, it looks well, and has the appearance of sincerity and fairness; and Keene's referring me to my project of a treaty in 1738, looks as if he thought he might be able to do something solid, for preventing the depredations for the future.

" I must refer you to the letters themselves and the answers returned to them. I know your lordship will make better observations upon them than I can. If you think any thing is omitted, I beg you would suggest it. You see our great view is effectually to detach Spain from France, and afterwards to get the king to be a party to this first treaty, if we can.

" Our Saxon negotiation, I think, must do at last; though, I believe, that steady court is knocking at two doors at once, and de Loss at Paris is negotiating, as well as Fleming here; but the natural interest of the king of Poland, and his connection with Russia, will at last determine him on our side of the question.

" As to Russia, I like much Guy Dickens's account of the reception of the answer I sent in writing to their two papers relating to subsidies; and I like also the design of making a reply, to set right some pretended mistake of their real meaning. For, if that reply is reasonable (as I hope it will be), that is, shall reduce their demand to a moderate subsidy, and a positive proof of the reality and utility of the force intended to be kept constantly on foot, both as to the real existence of the troops stipulated, and their actual quarters on that part of their frontiers which may impose most, I should hope we should all agree here to comply with it.

" Prussia has now thrown off the mask, and that (considering his near relation to the king and our succession), in a scandalous manner. There is no way of parrying the stroke, and preventing the ill consequences of it, but by keeping him in awe, and by shewing France that his Prussian majesty will not be in a condition to begin a war, or to support them in doing it, for fear of being attacked himself, which will be his first consideration. This can be done no way but by Russia; and by Russia it will be effectually done. If, therefore, after we have secured Saxony, we should give such a moderate subsidy to Russia, as should enable them to have such a body of troops constantly on their frontiers, as would keep the king of Prussia in awe, he would not be able to stir a step, and France and all the world would see and own, that he had brought this upon himself, by his wild extravagant appointment of the late Lord Marshal, and the countenance thereby given to the Pretender and the Jacobites. That alone will make the Russian subsidy as popular here, as I, in my conscience, think it makes it necessary.

" I think I can find, that *those* who are the most averse to subsidies, begin to see the necessity of this measure, or, at least, that it will not be withstood. *They* talk of things becoming *necessary* which are not *practicable*, at least for them; but they say, at the same time, that some little concessions, with regard to the number of regiments at Gibraltar and Port Mahon, might enable them to do it.

" This you will understand; and I dare say, agree with me, that it is an indication of what I have said above.

" Those who have been very conversant with the person whom I mean, think they really see an alteration in opinion, with regard to the necessity of forming such a system upon the continent, as, your lordship knows, I have so strongly recommended; and that though there may be a backwardness to own the conviction, arising from the experience and consideration of what has passed since the peace, yet that real conviction has produced the facility we have of late seen, with regard to some subsidiary treaties. And, my dear lord, if ever my doctrine and system ought to take place, it is now, when we have so fair a prospect in Spain; for, though this first treaty should not, perhaps, be just what we could wish, yet the knot is broke; the French union and dependency are dissolved; the queen is an Austrian; the queen governs all; and both the ministers are in appearance (and I believe in reality) good Englishmen, that is, well inclined to us, and disposed to shake off the French yoke.

" What an encouragement is here, to go on, and what a foundation to build upon ! I think we may be sure of the concurrence of the two empresses, of six electors, and of the Republic of Holland; and, on the other side of the question, all these powers may be connected, and that at a time when France and Prussia shew you what you are to expect from them: either absolute or servile dependence; or opposition, even to the very foundation of our government, whenever their ambition or caprice shall enable them to give us disturbance.

" I think I have now gone through every part of foreign business, except what regards our American disputes with France, and the present situation of Holland. As to the first, it is extremely to be wished, that they might be forthwith accommodated; and that all differences between France and us (that is, nation and nation) might be adjusted. That can be done no way but by concessions on both sides. Mr. Mildmay, the commissary (who is now in England), has a notion that France would consent to a proper boundary to Nova Scotia and Acadia, which would secure to us the bay of Fundy, and be sufficient for us; and even give us Tobago, on our yielding to them Sta Lucia in property, to be inhabited and possessed by them. I find, also, our right to Sta Lucia is not so clear as that to the province of Nova Scotia, &c. Lord Albemarle says, there was a time when France would have consented to something like this. I beg you would turn it in your thoughts how far this expedient may be practicable and advisable. I think we should go any reasonable lengths (at least where our title is at best doubtful), to get quite rid of these constant pretences for quarrel; and that, upon a foot where we shall be engaged alone, and perhaps the case of our defensive alliances either not exist at all, or be very doubtful.

" These considerations ought to have the more weight, from the late evident marks of ill humour in France and Prussia.

" As to Holland, you see how readily they come into our Saxon treaty. I doubt not, but they will do the same as to Russia. This is, therefore, a great card in our hands; but it will require great attention and ability to manage it well. Never was a country so divided as that of Holland. Divisions within divisions ! Nobody knows where the chief power is, nor where the credit is with the chief power.* * * *

" We had yesterday morning the great news, of the birth of a duke of Burgundy; of the appointment of M. de St. Contest to be Secretary of State; and of the promotion of M. de Mirepoix to a dukedom.

" The first event will greatly add to the pride, if not to the power of France, and ought consequently to make us press the conclusion of our important negotiations in Spain and the Empire. I wish it do not make the Court of Saxony raise the more difficulties.

" As to M. Puisieulx, we certainly cannot gain by any change in that office, for we shall never have so good a minister for us, as M. de Puisieulx was.* * * *

THE LORD CHANCELLOR TO THE DUKE OF NEWCASTLE.

Observations on the king of Prussia's mission of the late Lord Marshal to Paris, and on the retirement of M. Puisieulx from office—Conduct to be observed toward the Court of Berlin —The two main points of British policy, are the negotiations with Spain and Russia— Proposition of a British factory at Honduras examined—Russia must not be lost; but her terms are excessively high—England cannot keep pace with France in subsidizing foreign princes during peace—Greatly dislikes Count Bruhl's manœuvre—Hopes that Sir Charles Williams will not sign, sub spe rati—Begins to wish that the election of a king of the Romans had never been started—Expects no good from promoting the negotiation between Den- mark and the Grand Duke of Russia—Observations on a proposed treaty at Brussels concerning the Barrier, and the commerce of the Austrian Netherlands—Difficulty of advancing commercial interests by negotiation—Summary of policy to be observed in the present juncture.

"MY DEAR LORD,   *Wimpole, Sept.* 10, 1751.

" I have now, under various interruptions, gone through the many voluminous packets, which I had the honour to receive from your Grace on Saturday last. I could have wished that such numbers had not come at the same time; for the crowding one's head with such a variety of matter, on so many different subjects, is apt to create confusion; and makes it difficult for a mind so little formed for political considerations as mine, to arrange one's ideas with precision and distinction. However, as your Grace has laid your commands upon me to answer your letter, (which is a most clear and able one) I sit down to endeavour it as shortly as I can.

" I will begin with the latest event, because it is the most surprising; I mean the king of Prussia's mission of the late Lord Marshal, as his minister to the court of France; a measure inconsistent with the spirit of his engagements; indecent and uncombinable with his obligations as a prince in the succession of the Protestant line; and not only a monstrous impertinence to the king his uncle, but an indignity and affront to the nation, to which he has hitherto pretended to make a sort of false court. I think it, also, as impolitic as it is offensive; for his present Majesty must be very ignorant, if he do not know that the bringing the Pretender upon the scene in our foreign affairs, has always given an advantage to the king and the adminis- tration.

" The suddenness of Lord Marshal's departure after his nomination, and the hasty reception of him at the French court, shew a concert, in order to avoid any representa- tion from hence; though possibly, France might think they had less to object against it after they had sent Tyrconnel to Berlin; and yet it is plain the latter is under very different circumstances. It is difficult to determine what shall be said to France upon this subject, after he has been actually received, and had his audiences. I am glad Joe ventured to say what he did to M. Puisieulx, since it has been approved by the king; for I think he would hardly have been excusable if he had not. M. de Mirepoix is of a civil complaisant turn, and I believe well-intentioned; but from the little effect I have already seen of his personal propositions to his court, I do not expect more from it than from his application to Mr. Michel.

" I cannot but attribute M. Puisieulx's offensive and peevish behaviour on the occasion, partly to his then disagreeable situation; under the distress of ill health and low spirits; just going to quit his high office, and be stopped short in the career of his ambition; prompted by *that* still to drudge on, and continually teased by *madame* * to do so, though he died for it.

" As I shall take France and Prussia together, I will speculate one word upon this change. I agree with your Grace, that we shall hardly have so good a minister in France for us. And may there not have been another ingredient in this dismission besides ill health? I mean a resolution in his court, to hold a conduct with regard to England, not quite consistent with the many declarations and professions he has made, nor perhaps with his pacific plan. He came much more roundly at first into engaging for the evacuations, than I expected from any French minister. Your Grace knows how that engagement has been *contre-carried* and evaded since. Whether that may not have proceeded from some opposition and contradiction which he has met with in the council, and how far that opposition may have extended to other points, your Grace can conjecture better than I. However, all these things put together, have a bad aspect on the side of France, and are reasons to be much upon our guard, though not unnecessarily to provoke. They are certainly reasons for making an end as fast as you can, of the disputes about Nova Scotia and the four islands, by some reasonable compromise. It is in vain to expect to end them in the way it is, by a discussion of the strict mere right. If some such accommodation could be made, as your Grace mentions to have been suggested, so as not to leave any of our colonies insecure, I should think it happy. The principle should be, to leave both sides their proper *defence*, and to give neither any advantage for *offence*.

" But to return to the king of Prussia. Your Grace is pleased to ask my opinion, whether any thing more can be done with regard to the late Lord Marshal's mission, besides the representations already ordered to be made to the court of France. Your Grace knows, I wished those representations had been made much earlier. I own I cannot come up to the sending away Michel till you have heard farther from France, and most maturely considered it. But surely it will be right to make some declaration, if any thing at all should be dropped *about the weakening of guaranties*. I think it should be only insinuated in the most tender and covert manner, and rather be left to be inferred, than expressed.

" The two main points for Great Britain in foreign affairs, are the negotiations with Spain and Russia. I think France lays more weight upon them, than upon all the rest. The first seems hitherto to have been very ably conducted; and your Grace has

* Marchioness of Pompadour.

stated it so fully, and reasoned upon it so justly, that I can add nothing. to it. The principal thing is, to hasten to a conclusion as fast as possible, lest it should undergo the same fate with the affair of the election of the king of the Romans. And·yet I dread the intractableness· and dilatoriness of the court of Vienna. You have. certainly done right to endeavour .to introduce the king of Sardinia as a party ; but I apprehend, *there* will be the stumbling-block with them ; and I am persuaded that their leaving his Majesty out of the negotiation, and their reserve to him, has chiefly proceeded from their conviction that his Majesty would insist upon it, as becomes him. The clause of general guaranty, as limited by your Grace's draught, is very dexterously proposed, and for very wise reasons. As to the proposition of an English factory at the Bay of Honduras, for cutting logwood, let it be fully examined by those who understand it. May it not tend to a monopoly of that commodity, so essential to our manufactures ? May it not have some consequences like those of the annual ship ?

" As to Russia, we must not lose her ; and yet how can we come up to her terms ? For I understand that you have learned, by the return of Lambe, that my brother Bestuchef * has pretended to explain his *first memorial,* by insisting specifically on his *first demand.* It is impossible for Great Britain to pay such subsidies in time of peace. This is our misfortune. Almost all the princes of Europe are become venal and pensionary, and England cannot keep pace with France in that expense. This is the case of Prussia. I have been long convinced that nothing we can do, could detach him from France, because he cannot keep up his great armies *without their subsidies.* I believe he now receives from France more than £. 400,000 per annum. I am sure he did so in 1749, and have not heard it has· been reduced since. · He knows Great Britain cannot do this. However, I think this *pourparler* with Russia should be kept alive to a certain degree ; and their own interest and connections, together with the Czarina's aversion to France and Prussia, will restrain them from doing any thing wrong that way very soon. For I take what Bestuchef threw out to Guy Dickens, of the offer of a subsidy from France, to be a *fanfaronade.*

" As to Saxony, I dislike count Bruhl's manœuvre as much as possible. The intercepted letter of M. de Loss of the 4th Sept. N. S. proves to me, not only that he is knocking at two opposite doors at the same time, but that he would take with both hands ; for what else can be the meaning of de Loss's expression of running a risque, by embarking themselves in a new *embarrass.* I think, this accounts for M. Bruhl's so absurdly insisting upon leaving out both the article about the troops, and the secret declaration about the electoral vote ; for then he can swear to France, that he has only taken our money, and engaged for nothing. And their now so late agreeing to accede to the treaty of 1746, whereby certain contingents of troops are, by reference to former treaties, stipulated in certain events, is, I believe, meant to enable him the better to parry the article about troops. I know you must conclude this treaty, but when it comes over (as it will now, signed *sub spe rati*) for God's sake, my dear lord, make count Fleming agree to something in writing, in some shape or other ; . for otherwise it will be a subsidiary treaty on our part, without any reciprocity at all, and what

* Grand Chancellor of Russia.

will you say to this in Parliament? By the way, will Sir Charles be so wild as to sign, *sub spe rati*, without any thing in writing, either about the troops or the vote? If he does, it must be for the vanity of signing a treaty, though he puts you here under the greatest difficulty.

" As to the affair of the election of a king of the Romans, prudent as it was at first, and as much as I was for it, I begin almost to wish it had never been started. It has been spoiled by somebody; not by the English *ministers*. The coldness and supineness of the Court of Vienna, have been one great ingredient; and the long dependence of it, has, as I always thought it would, produced much mischief; for I believe it has been a great instrument in the hands of Prussia, to stimulate France to dip so deep in subsidies to the German princes. And your Grace knows, his Prussian Majesty has hinted that a war may possibly break out on that occasion.

" It is certainly right to try whether any good can be done by assisting Denmark in their negotiation with the grand duke of Russia. But I expect no good from it. That king is certainly one of the weakest of princes, and his favourite, Molck, one of the falsest of men. I am persuaded, Tyrconnel's observation is right, that Denmark is trying to get the present *possession* of Holstein by that treaty; and if it succeeds, will endeavour to make that possession secure *in futuro*, by concluding the marriage with Sweden, and the treaty with Prussia.

" The only remaining part of your Grace's letter, relates to the negotiation for entering into a treaty at Brussels, concerning the barrier, and the commerce of the Austrian Netherlands. I have read over the copy of the Dutch instructions to M. Burmannia, which comprise the draught of instructions for their commissaries. There are some expressions in that paper, viz. pages 7, 8, and 10, which seem to be a little equivocal and captious, as to the burden of repairing the fortifications of the barrier towns; for that is involved under the general description of *what is to be made a common cause between Great Britain, the Empress Queen, and the States*. If those expressions were rectified, or the prince of Orange given to understand that we still adhered to our former declaration, I should see no harm in Mr. Keith's joining in the instances to the court of Vienna, as the States desire. We are certainly greatly interested in the support of the barrier, and we have paid dear for it, when the Dutch have thrown it away. But bishop Hare's book is not entirely to be relied on throughout; for it is a book of controversy in politics, and every thing pushed to extremities.

" The Dutch, also, want you to join with them in representing against the new canals, now making in the Austrian Netherlands, under acts of the States of those provinces. How can one word of sense be said against their making those canals in their own country!

" But there is one thing that more immediately concerns England than all the rest; I mean the fixing a new treaty of commerce, and the duties of export and import, which, the court of Vienna insists, should be settled at the same time. Your Grace knows, that commissaries were sent over for three years together; and broke off, *re infectâ*. You cannot refuse to treat about it, because the Barrier Treaty stipulates that you shall; but all the instructions to those former commissaries should be

3 G 2

looked out; and before you conclude any thing, either particular, or even general, it should be thoroughly considered by those who are competent judges of that commerce. Trade is a very delicate, as well as popular point. I have heard that my lord Bath, (then Mr. Pulteney) came one day to the House of Commons, with a resolution to complain of those former commissaries having cost so much money and time, and done nothing; and so formed some motion upon it; but was convinced of his mistake by one of his own friends, who understood better, and told him, the best thing they could do for England, was to do nothing. However, I do not expect to see such a negotiation finished before another war; and it is unfortunate that this commercial point cannot be separated from the rest.

" I am no judge of your alderman's talents for such an employment. He may possibly have some that are proper for it, but I fear that he has others not to be desired in a negotiation.

" The sum of my way of thinking is.: conclude immediately with Saxony, in such a manner as to make it *decent*. Finish as fast as possible with Spain, though what is done should now be restricted only to Italy; if you can get farther, so much the better. Keep Russia in good humour, without subjecting yourselves hereafter to reproaches, for not agreeing to give her a greater subsidy. As to some of the other princes with whom you have to do, indeed they are not *powers*.

" I fear your Grace will think I have made good what I set out with, the apprehension of writing with confusion; but the numbers of pacquets I have now before my eyes, will, I hope, be some excuse for me. I submit the whole to your Grace's superior lights, and am, with the most perfect respect and truth," &c.

THE DUKE OF NEWCASTLE TO THE LORD CHANCELLOR.

The King gives to Mr. Pelham a paper relative to the affairs of Scotland.

"MY DEAR LORD,   *March* 21*st*, 1752.

" Mr. Pelham told me yesterday that the king had sent for him in the morning, and gave him a packet, put into his Majesty's hands by the Duke of Cumberland, containing I suppose a sort of state of Scotland, and all the names of Jacobites employed by the king; chiefly I presume, in the revenue.—As a specimen, it is said, —" Lord Milton, a Jacobite; a place of £.1500 per annum; his son a place for life. Lord Justice Clerk, Mr. Areskine, said by the earl of Albemarle to be a Jacobite," and so on. The king directed Mr. Pelham to go to the Duke, and go through every case; which he is to do, this morning.

" Your lordship may imagine that Mr. Pelham is much affected by it; but seemed determined to act by himself, and without advice. He said it was an attack, and a strong one, against him; and he would not say to any body, even to me, his thoughts upon it; and I think will conceal great part of what shall pass. I told him, I had long thought an inquiry necessary;—he rejected that thought, and said he would not set up a *Si quis*, for people to come in to give him a box on the ear. He is certainly much embarrassed, and told me, the king was very civil to him, but he did believe the king thought it an attack against him. I think he judges wrong. His right way would be, to go into the inquiry; and these papers should be the foundation of it. I did not tell him that I had proposed a reference to those I named to your lordship; but I send you a draught of a letter for that purpose. I also send your lordship a list of the business for our consideration, before the king goes : both which papers I beg you would send back, with your observations upon them. I hope I shall receive a draught of a speech, on Monday morning at farthest. The king begs it may be of the shortest, as he shall have such a number of bills to pass.

" P. S.—What is to be done, at our conference with the Commons, upon the bill against thefts and robberies ?

" Mr. Pelham said the attack against him, was for being for the constitution, against military power, or a military government."

MR. PELHAM TO THE DUKE OF NEWCASTLE.*

Severely censures the conduct of the court of Vienna—Lords Breadalbane and Cathcart candidates to be nominated of the sixteen peers—Is making inquiries into the affairs of Scotland.

April 17th, 1752.

After sending some warrants for secret-service money, to be signed by the king, and expressing his satisfaction at his Majesty's safe arrival at Hanover, he adds :

" Firmness to the court of Vienna, as you say, becomes now absolutely necessary. I may say, their behaviour is abominable. I hope it has no other view than a little mean saving, in the satisfaction to be given to the elector Palatine ; but I fear it goes farther; and if it does, they will expose themselves and their friends, in a most unaccountable manner. I am sure you will do all you can, to prevent the ill effects of their pride and madness. I know also the king's views are great and generous. I will dwell no longer on this subject, but wait for farther information.

" I have begun my correspondence with Scotland ; when I have any thing to send essential in that point, you shall hear fully from me, but informations by halves only fret and confound. Nothing, you may depend upon it, shall be wanting on my part, to come at the truth, in the manner I think most for the king's real service.

" Poor lord Dunmore is in a miserable situation ; he does not die, nor can live, but in great torture, which I am told, he endures with great resolution. Lord Holdernesse tells me, you will have applications for a successor to him, as one of the sixteen. Lord Breadalbane is the king's servant, and has a great estate in that country. Lord Cathcart belongs to the Duke, has a regiment, and is a very honest young man. I conclude it will lie between them two, though others, I am told, are talked of. They have, in my poor opinion, the best pretensions ; but you will be the best judge, what and whom to recommend to the king. I only thought, as I was told you would have application, it was proper for me, just to hint to you my own thoughts. We have nothing material stirring here. I shall, when I have matter, trouble you more at large." * * * *

* Newcastle Papers.

THE DUKE OF NEWCASTLE TO MR. PELHAM.*

Speaks of the duke of Argyle's conduct—About securing the Electors of Treves and Palatine.

Hanover, April 29th-May 12th, 1752.

After informing him that he had, though not without much difficulty, pre-vailed on the king to give his consent that lord Breadalbane should be created a peer, instead of lord Cathcart, he continues :—" The king renewed the discourse of what had passed last session in the House of Lords. He said, though it was in a very wrong way, yet the thing was true ; and that if it was not properly inquired into, it would be strongly renewed, next session ; and that he had told you so that indeed that attack was not against me ; that I had done right, and he had told you so ; but that if the duke of Argyle was suffered to do wrong, it would fall upon you, or me. I then told the king the inquiries you are making, as he might see by your letter, which I had shewed him ; that I had also left advice and instruc-tions with lord Holdernesse to make inquiries into what had passed in the Secretary's office, for your's must be confined to the office of the revenue ; that I would answer for you, that he might depend upon it, the inquiries should be made. His Majesty really seemed satisfied upon this head, and particularly with what you were doing in it.* * * *

" The sooner you can send me some account of the inquiries, to be laid before the king, the better. I am heartily glad they are likely to come out well. Nothing will be so happy as that, provided the proofs carry conviction with them.

" In return to what you say of the greatest, I will only beg you would consider, from whence the scene I have related to you arises. But, however, I hold my tongue, am patient, and do the best I can. We have a letter from M. Spannenlins, the elector of Treves's minister, who has filled us here with all the ill notions of Vergennes, that since his return to Treves, in his way, he has quite changed his language ; says the king of France will not obstruct the election, but rather co-operate in it ; hints that he is agreed with the king, that satisfaction must be given to the elector Palatine ; and in short we might have had the election two years ago, if we had acted then, as we do now. In that I differ *toto cœlo.* I am amazed we hear nothing of this from Albemarle. I do not think his Excellency very alert."

MR. PELHAM TO THE DUKE OF NEWCASTLE.†

*The Dutch will never listen to a proposal which would render a new Barrier Treaty necessary
—Accounts from France more favourable.*

London, May 1st-12th, 1752.

* * * * " I have read over all your dispatches to lord Holdernesse ; and yesterday, after the Regency was up, lord Chancellor, lord Granville, lord Holdernesse, and myself, read them over together. His lordship will give you the result of our conference, which was, in general, an entire approbation of the orders you had sent to Vienna, and a

thorough acquiescence in your opinion, upon the proposal* made by M. Bartenstein : indeed it was impossible to be of another opinion. It cannot be conceived the Dutch would hearken to any such proposition ; nor can we take upon us to advise them to do it, without totally unravelling the Barrier Treaty, and making, as it were, a new one. These are not times, in my opinion, to look out for new systems, or new expedients ; if we can keep the old ones upon a good footing, it is all we have to expect, or desire. Nothing but the firmness with which the king spoke to Vorster,† and the very judicious part you have taken, in both the present negotiations, can preserve that. I fear you will have greater difficulties in your negotiations at Brussels, than upon the point of election.

" You will have seen, long before this time, that the letters from France are rather more encouraging than we had reason to expect ; and, if I am rightly informed, the confusion of their own interior affairs will confirm them in their present peaceable disposition. I do not doubt your address in managing M. Vergennes,‡ when he comes to you ; good words may do a great deal : I am sure they have with the duc de Mirepoix ; possibly this gentleman may not be so frank and so honest as his Excellency. Your next letters will probably open that scene a little. I heartily wish you good success ; keep but firm with the court of Vienna, and I shall fear nothing."

* * * *

THE LORD CHANCELLOR TO THE DUKE OF NEWCASTLE. §

On Scottish affairs.

Powis House, May 5th-16th, 1752.

* * * *" Since his Majesty's departure, lord Holdernesse, Mr. Pelham, and myself, have spent several hours in considering the state of Scotland ; and, among other things, in relation to what was thrown out in the House of Lords, last session. God knows that we have no partialities, nor have reason to have any, for any wrong managements that may have crept in there ! Mr. Pelham produced to us the strictest and properest orders, which he had sent, for inquiries to be made into every thing relative to his department. Lord Holdernesse shewed us the strongest, and most particular and explicit instructions, which your Grace had left in writing with him, and had before-hand apprized me of, relating to yours. They are now carrying into execution ; and I will myself get what information I can for his Majesty's service. It was also agreed, that orders should be forthwith sent to the Lord Advocate, to prosecute those two notorious crafty villains, the Macgregors, who are now in custody, with the utmost rigour of the law ; and that directions should also be given, both to him and the justice clerk, to make strict inquiry concerning the revival of nonjuring meeting-

---

* To exclude the Dutch garrisons from the Barrier towns.

† Envoy from the Emperor to the court of Hanover.

‡ Afterwards so well known as prime minister of France. He was at this time envoy to the court of Treves ; had detached the elector from his connection with the Maritime Powers, and had also persuaded him to withdraw his promise of voting for the election of the archduke Joseph, as king of the Romans. He soon after went to Hanover. § Newcastle Papers.

houses, and to put the new acts of parliament, made since the Rebellion, for suppressing them, into the most rigorous execution.   As the new act, relating to the forfeited
estates in the Highlands, is to commence at Christmas next, some things were
suggested for consideration, in order to the most effectual carrying it into execution.
The more I reflect, the more I am convinced, that that bill is founded upon the justest
principles, and that the provisions of it are, in general, very right.   As to the execution of it, more is left to his Majesty's power and discretion, than is generally thought;
and, if any thing is wanting, it cannot fail to be supplied in the new bill, that must
necessarily pass, for granting and applying the money to discharge such just debts
as shall be finally allowed upon those effects."

MR. PELHAM TO THE DUKE OF NEWCASTLE.*

*Continues his inquiries on the Scottish affairs—Again congratulates his brother on the
prospect of happily concluding the affair of the Election.*

May 8th-19th, 1752.

* * * *" We are going on with our inquiries in Scotland. Some disaffected persons
are already found out, and removed from his Majesty's service ; particularly one Mackinnon, an officer at Glasgow, that I had intelligence of, by the means of the collector
there, and some hints from the duke of Argyle.   The collector is an Englishman, and
an exceeding good officer ; he was sent by me to that port, particularly, for the care
of the revenue, and to have an eye to the persons recommended to employments
there.   Mackinnon is succeeded by an Englishman, sent from the port of London ;
and as the execution of the new Tobacco-act requires able and honest officers, I have
sent three of the best I could hear of, from hence, which I look upon to be the surest
measure of securing both loyalty and integrity, for the service of the king and the
public.   I know this must not be carried too far, for very material reasons ; but when
it can be done, without giving any reasonable disgust, you may be assured I shall,
and have followed that plan.

 "The complaint of the duke of Bedford against one Cumming,† supervisor of the
Excise at Aberdeen, seems to me to be without any foundation. Certificates to his
character are come from the Presbyterian ministers, wherever he has resided ; and as
he was taken prisoner by the rebels, when at Montrose, there was some information
against his behaviour, during the time of his imprisonment, which he himself desired
might be thoroughly examined ; this was accordingly done in the year 1746, before
lord Ancram, and one colonel Jackson, whose letter and acquittal I have seen, a copy
being sent to me of the examination, signed by those two officers, as well as the
superior officer of the revenue in those parts.

 "As to the information of one Alexander, a notorious Jacobite, being appointed
one of the receivers of the bishops' rents, I was sure that could not be so, in its full

* Newcastle Papers.   † See Speech of the duke of Bedford, chap. xxvii.

extent, as those officers are appointed by the Treasury here; and in looking over our books, I find no one has been appointed in my time, or long before, excepting a relation of lord Tweeddale's, who was recommended to me by his lordship, when he was Secretary of State, and this gentleman has continued in the office ever since. I wrote, however, to inquire after that man; and no such person is as yet found to be concerned in that office.

" There is another Excise officer, one Home, of Menderson, who was mentioned in the papers delivered to his Majesty, as well as the preceding people. The charge against this man is found to be true in all its particulars; he is discharged. The commissioners deny their having ever heard the least syllable of this accusation, till I sent it down to them; but the description of the man is so notorious, that I can scarce believe they could be totally ignorant of his character. I cannot yet learn who recommended him to the commissioners of Excise, but I shall endeavour to find that out. I suspect he is a friend, personally, to one of the Board; but that I cannot pretend to affirm as yet.

" I believe pretty strict orders are given, from all quarters, to look into the characters of those employed by the government. I hope it will come out better than is suspected; but be that as it will, his Majesty may depend on justice being done to his service, and no facts disguised, or concealed, that come to my knowledge, upon fair and honourable grounds. Such a scrutiny as is now on foot, I believe was never tried in Scotland, since the Union. If it had, I am satisfied, by what I see already, there was no period of time, let who would be ministers there, that the officers of the revenue would appear so little liable to the charge of Jacobitism, as the present; notwithstanding which, I fear there will be too many found faulty in that particular.

" You desired I would send you some account of what I had learnt. This is as clear a one as I can send at present, without I was to send you all the letters and papers, which have passed forward and backward upon this subject; copies of which I will give orders to have transcribed, and send them to you, if you think they can be of any service to his Majesty.

" I will trouble you no more on this subject at present, but pass to a more agreeable one, which is the prospect you have of finishing the long wished-for election of the king of the Romans, in an amicable way, and possibly by the consent of all parties. I cannot think France will depart materially from what she has already said; and, though M. de Vergennes has no particular instructions on that head, yet by your letter, he seems pretty well furnished with materials to discuss the point, and, I hope, when you have agreed on preliminaries, will be furnished with powers to act up to what we have had reason to expect. You are undoubtedly in the right, when you say the sure way to bring France in, is to convince them that you can and will do it without them. I hope, therefore, the court of Vienna will not undeceive them, in that point, by their own behaviour.

" I see, the court of Prussia are pretty well informed of the reception lord Hyndford met with at Vienna, when he first came there; but it is with pleasure that I see, at the same time, they do not expect France will avail herself of that misconduct. In short, if you can keep France quiet, which I think you will, your business is done; and when done in this manner, I flatter myself, I see peace established for as many years, as you and I can hope to see, unless some unforeseen event should cause a general disturbance. The military commissioners, I hear, are all arrived, so the curiosity of the town is now pretty well satisfied." * * * *

THE DUKE OF NEWCASTLE TO MR. PELHAM.*

Will persevere in encouraging the present favourable disposition of France—The court of Vienna must promote the election, and execute the barrier treaty.

Hanover, May 9th-20th, 1752.

* * * * "I have this opportunity of thanking you for your very kind letter of the 1st instant. Your approbation of my conduct makes me very happy; and if you have any suspicions left, I am sure my future behaviour will quite remove them; for I am as much determined, as you can wish me to be, to encourage France to continue in their present good disposition, and firmly and unalterably to convince the court of Vienna, that if they will have our assistance, they must do their part, in promoting the great object of the election, and in consenting to a reasonable execution of the Barrier Treaty. I like Vergennes very well; and what is more material, I think he likes me very well; though his Grace of Grafton says, that I think every body loves me. My point is, to tie down France to what St. Contest has declared to my lord Albemarle, and to insist with the court of Vienna that they must agree to that proposition.

"I could wish we heard a little oftener from his Excellency at Paris, and from our ministers at Vienna. I should also have been glad, that Vergennes had received his instructions. It is a great while since St. Contest spoke to lord Albemarle; but I conclude they wait for answers from Berlin, Manheim, and perhaps Bonn; and for that reason, I lose no time in accepting their proposition, and getting it accepted at Vienna.

"I shall shew your letter to the king. It is wrote in a style that makes me conclude you intend I should; especially what relates to the assistance you mention from hence, which I think you put in that general way, on purpose that the king might see it, as well as several other parts of the letter."

THE DUKE OF NEWCASTLE TO MR. PELHAM.†

Doubts the sincerity of the Elector Palatine—But still thinks, if the court of Vienna would be reasonable, they might at last do well with France.

"DEAR BROTHER,   *Hanover, May 13th-24th, 1752.*

"Though I have no letter from you to answer (the messenger being not yet arrived), and though I have been writing all this morning and last night, as you will see by my

---

* Newcastle Papers.   † Ibid.

letters to lord Holdernesse, &c., I would not let this messenger go, without saying one word to you upon the present situation of our affairs, which seem much altered for the worse since my last. The unaccountable turn taken by St. Contest in supporting the extravagant demands of the elector Palatine, and even those upon England and Holland, does make one fear that they are not so sincere as we did imagine. But still, I think we should do well enough at last with France, if the court of Vienna was disposed to be reasonable; but by a letter which is now deciphering, I think we are to expect nothing material from thence, but reproaches for presuming to talk in the strong manner we have done to Vorster. You will see, that I have my full share of their resentment. That will not make me alter my conduct in the least; it will neither make me desist from that language, nor fling me, from resentment, into another system or different measures. I have told Vorster plainly, that the king had taken his party, and that he would consider the consequences. Poor man, he does; but I much fear he cannot help himself, or us. I hope you will approve my several letters, and particularly that to Mirepoix. I come as near there, as I can, to your way of thinking, without departing from my own.

" I received yesterday a most manly letter from lord Chancellor upon lord Breadalbane's affair, in which he took an occasion to return his thanks to the king, and to enter very largely into a full justification of our conduct upon Scotch affairs; the pains you were taking; the orders you had sent; the instructions I had left with my lord Holdernesse; his, my lord Chancellor's, own concurrence and assistance; the principle and effect of the late Highland bill. In short, it was as strong, as wise, and as honourable a justification and *confutation* as could be wrote. I sent it, though I did not know what might be the effect; it has certainly had a very good one; for, though I have not had any discourse upon the subject, the king has been in remarkable good humour with me ever since; and that, notwithstanding our last disagreeable accounts from Paris and Vienna." * * * *

MR. PELHAM TO THE DUKE OF NEWCASTLE.*

Approves the conduct of his brother—Hopes that the affair of the election will soon be determined, and that the annual expenditure may then be diminished:—On American affairs.

May 14th-25th, 1752.

* * * * " We all approve of what you did upon the receipt of lord Albemarle's letter, but I fear the accounts you have since had from Paris, have lowered your spirits and expectations. I hope, however, all will end well. I know the consequence it is to the king and his servants, that the election should be forthwith determined; and the utility it would be to Europe, as well as to this country, to have that election unanimous, is evident to all mankind. One particular interest I have in it is, that I think it pins the basket; and when this great affair is finished, I hope we shall all turn our thoughts a little to the interior of this country, and try if we can abate the immense annual expenses, without which I am afraid we shall have a severe account

* Newcastle Papers.

3 H 2

to make up, and greivances with ill humour will grow amongst the people, though at present they are very patient and well satisfied.

" This letter of lord Albemarle's, which has given you such just satisfaction, we had here near three weeks ago ; and you will see in one of my letters, I referred to it, in what I wrote to you ; but undoubtedly you judged right of what the court of Prussia would do, by what I fear they have done ; for St. Contest adopting the demands of the elector Palatine, certainly comes from thence. I think, however, France will not stand extremities ; and if you can get the court of Vienna to do what you think they should do, I am in hopes France will try on her part to lower the demands of the Palatine.* * * *

" We had, last night, a meeting upon the American affairs. We all agree. Lord Granville, particularly, thought, what was thrown out by St. Contest was all we could expect or desire ; but as the granting a line to the French, as the limits of their Canada, seemed to be in some measure yielding to them what, we thought, was undoubtedly our right, though of little utility to us, I mentioned the trying, in such case, whether we could obtain the demolition of Crown Point; a very material circumstance in our favour, if it can be gained, and what we have a right to, as that fort is erected on our ground, and taken possession of by the French since the peace of Utrecht. Lord Holdernesse will give you a more exact account of what passed; which makes my saying more, useless."* * * *

THE DUKE OF NEWCASTLE TO MR. PELHAM.*

The king approves Mr. Pelham's inquiries in Scotland.

Hanover, May, 15th-26th, 1752..

" Cleverly arrived here early yesterday morning, with your two letters of the 8th ; and I would not let the post go away without returning you my thanks for them. I shewed the letter upon the Scotch affairs to the king ; he seemed very well pleased with it. I said, 'your Majesty sees, they go on very fast with their inquiries. One charge seems without foundation, two examples are made.' The king replied, in very good humour, 'your brother is very active; and will do right when he is rightly informed.' I told him Scotland had never been so inquired into before. He seemed very happy, and said it was right. 'The attack, this year, was only against the duke of Argyle. If this had not been done, it might have been otherwise, another session. It is right to get rid of these people ; they only comply seemingly' (meaning the half Jacobites) ; 'and would turn against me upon occasion.' Finding him so well satisfied, I did not push the discourse ; but I shall take occasion to observe how groundless many of the accusations were ; which he saw by your letter."* * * *

* Newcastle Papers.

THE DUKE OF NEWCASTLE TO MR. PELHAM.*

Censures the ingratitude of the court of Vienna—The king proposes to recall lord Hyndford, and considers the affair of the election at an end.

Hanover, May 20th-31st, 1752.

* * * * " You will not be surprised, that I am as much dissatisfied with the news this messenger will bring you, as I have been the contrary, on former occasions.

" Nothing can parallel the impertinence, I had almost said the impudence and ingratitude, of the court of Vienna, in the two written answers given to lord Hyndford and Mr. Keith, or the little low way of acting of M. St. Contest, by the declaration made me this day by Vergennes. As to the court of Vienna, I can say nothing more than what I have suggested in my letter to lord Holdernesse. I think we should let them cool; shew as much indifference as they do, about their own interest: and, if we can bring France to act reasonably upon the elector Palatine's demands, make then one last effort, with the court of Vienna. Perhaps it may not be amiss to make a short strong answer in writing, shewing our sense of the manner in which the king is treated; insisting upon the protocol to be the rule, whereby this is expressly declared, that as soon as we are sure of *Bavaria* and of a majority, measures should be taken for proceeding to the election, and in consequence, again to renew the demand of assembling the diet for that purpose. I think the court of Vienna will still be unwilling to let this affair drop, which it must do, if they do not soon take this step of assembling the diet; and when once that step is taken, France, notwithstanding what they now say, will find some way of making the elector Palatine reasonable. Vergennes says positively, that not one word passed with St. Contest, to the purport of what we took to be lord Albemarle's meaning. I have read his letter over and over, and I can make no sense of it, if it does not mean to refer the elector Palatine's pretensions to the king, and to abide by his Majesty's determination. I own, I always feared that his lordship had a little misunderstood St. Contest, or made a stronger representation of it, than perhaps my lord Albemarle himself designed; for it was hardly possible to imagine, that so very material a conversation, and formal proposal, should have been made, and the French minister here have no notice of it. But yet, sure we were right to take it in that sense, with the knowledge and concurrence of Vergennes; and I am now persuaded, that if the court of Vienna would have understood it so, and accepted of the king's mediation roundly, we should have found out some way of bringing back St. Contest, who would have been ashamed of putting a negative upon the king's decision. However, as to France, we must wait till we hear from lord Albemarle.

" The king, as you may imagine, is, with the highest reason, extremely offended with the court of Vienna, and is for recalling my lord Hyndford immediately, and looks upon the thing as over. But I hope by gaining a little time and shewing au indifference, the court of Vienna may still come to their senses. It is pride and vanity that occasions all this behaviour. They are unwilling to have the

* Newcastle Papers.

obligation to the king; and are even sorry to see, that his Majesty can help them with France, when they cannot help themselves. This I am persuaded is at the bottom. Some fear of giving something to the elector Palatine may also have its share. But if that had been all, they would have talked in a different manner, and had themselves recourse to the protocol, where it was agreed to proceed to the election with six voices; or, if they would not have done that, they would in all events, have turned their answers in a different manner. But pride and impertinence have blinded them. I own I am hurt; but I will not act from passion. I do not think the game desperate yet, though clogged with most unreasonable difficulties, from both sides.

" " Jones will send you a letter, whereby you will see that the king of Prussia gives in, and only wants to have it seen, that France and her allies act in concert in this affair. This takes up so much of my thoughts, that had I any thing else to send you, I should really wish to defer it to the next messenger." *   *   *   *

MR. PELHAM TO THE DUKE OF NEWCASTLE.*

Is concerned that the favourable aspect of affairs relating to the Election is changed.—Conversation with Haslang—Approves his brother's letters on the subject of the Election—On Irish affairs.

"DEAR BROTHER,   *May 21st-June-1st*, 1752.

" I received your letter of the 13th-24th, and have carefully read over all the letters and papers, which you sent to lord Holdernesse. I wonder you had not received any from me, since your former letter; for I have never missed writing once a week by every messenger that has gone from hence, since your arrival at Hanover. I can assure you it concerns me greatly, to find those affairs, which you once thought reasonably in so good a way, change their faces, almost from every quarter. The behaviour of the court of Vienna is abominable; and I fear they are of natures incorrigible; but, as you say, we must not be influenced by their conduct. I agree with you in the present case; but I hope, for the future, this will be a lesson to you, not to engage so warmly in the service of those, who either do not know their own interest, or if they do, will not contribute any thing to the advancement of it, but on the contrary, run the risk of exposing their best friends, rather than yield to advice given to them in the most affectionate and respectful manner. This France sees and knows, and of consequence makes her use of it. We are to expect chicane from that quarter; for though some of the individuals are men of great honour, as I really believe the duc de Mirepoix, yet the nation has never been famous for frank and open dealing; and I cannot say, our friendly dispositions to them have entitled us to more than ordinary good treatment from them. However, I believe they do not mean to quarrel, and you have certainly in your whole behaviour to that court, acted with so much frankness, and address, that they can have no opportunity of cavilling upon what you have either said or done. I am glad you like Vergennes; and whenever that is the case, I do not fear a French minister's liking you. Mirepoix's letter is cordial, respectful, and like a gentleman; your answer is the same, and I am satisfied he means as sincerely as you do. I must own the interpretation he gives to St. Contest's words, is the same as I did. The orders promised to be sent to Hautefort were, as I understood them, upon the court of Vienna's promising to put in execution what should be the king's determinations, not upon the acceptance of the mediation only; and I believe you were of that mind also, but was willing to try whether, for expedition's sake, you could not obtain the other construction.

"Haslang asked me last night, how things went? I told him, I hoped all would end well; some rubs there were; but if his master, and the other electors, stood to their promises, as I did not doubt but they would, our great affair must end well. He said, does France continue to act well? I said, I hoped they would, but France, like other powers, was sometimes obliged to talk the language of their allies, but in the end their allies must come to them. I hope you approve what I said. I am always afraid of saying too much; and by that means appear a little mysterious, when I do not mean to be so. He agreed with me in what I said; which, I believe, is generally the method of ministers, from inferior courts. I hope I have not tired you; I was willing you should know all I had said or thought.

"Lord Chancellor is still in the country. I have not therefore had any opportunity of talking with him: I have wrote to him; and lord Holdernesse tells me, he has sent him an abstract of all that came from abroad by the last messenger. I can assure you, I think all your letters proper upon the occasion, and most heartily wish they may have the good effect they deserve. I see by our little intercepted letters here, every court imagines we are likely to be disappointed, and most of them agree in laying the fault upon the court of Vienna. Prussia thinks, or says at least, that it is an artifice to make us pay dear, for what the court of Vienna are to reap the benefit of. I do not mean, by this, to insinuate that it is not our cause, but to guard against yielding too far in that point. I know you will be cautious; but the behaviour of the court of Vienna will make those things go down heavier, than a more grateful and a more frank behaviour would have done.

"I hope you approve of what the lords said upon our American disputes. Your orders to lord Albemarle seem to correspond entirely with our ideas here. I shall trouble you no more with foreign politics, and have but little to say to you upon domestic ones, in which there is at present a dead calm." * * * *

THE DUKE OF NEWCASTLE TO MR. PELHAM.

Hopes that Mr. Pelham will approve what he has done, and that the Court of Vienna will agree to the meeting of the diet.

Hanover, May 24th–June 4th, 1752.

* * * * " You will have seen by my last, that I was in great distress and uncertainty, what to do. I hope you will not disapprove the party I have now taken, as it seems the

* Newcastle Papers.

only practicable one at present. In the temper that France, and the court of Vienna are in at present, nothing was to be done with going on with the Palatine negotiation. One asked so much, and the other would give so little, that we should only have entangled ourselves, and amused ourselves, with what must have ended in nothing at last. France has given us a fair handle to go on upon our present majority. They have departed from the reference, proposed by themselves, to the king. They insist upon demands, never dreamt of by us, when we began the negotiation with Mirepoix ; and they have declared, that though the three electors would not acknowledge the election, France would not have the least hand in countenancing or supporting any troubles, upon that single point.

" It will be hard for the court of Vienna to avoid agreeing to the assembling the diet, after what they have themselves declared about the Protocol, where it is so expressly said, that as soon as we shall be sure of Bavaria, and a majority, we shall proceed to the election, &c. And how my friend Stadion will go from his own act, because we do not give new subsidies, I have no notion. So that upon the whole, I think we shall bring it about. And the perseverance of France, and the Elector Palatine, in the extravagant demands, may enable the court of Vienna to do the business without giving any thing. Though I am apt to believe, when once the Requisitorial Letters are issued, and the day fixed for the assembling of the diet, France and the Elector Palatine will become reasonable, and we shall again endeavour to do something for them. For, after all that has passed, and what you will continue to see from the extracts, it is clear that we can have no open opposition ; grumbling, protesting, and perhaps menacing for the future, in order to obtain some immediate advantage from the court of Vienna, may very probably happen. But that will end in nothing, at least, at present ; and time will set it all right. If future disturbances arise, it will be from other causes, and not from this." * * * *

MR. PELHAM TO THE DUKE OF NEWCASTLE.*

Again reproves the proud and inconsistent conduct of the Austrian Court.

"DEAR BROTHER,   *May 29th*, 1752.

" Your letter of yesterday gave me as much pain in reading as it did you in writing, though I have expected little better for some time past. I feel for the king ; I feel for you ; and what is more, I feel for those that do not feel for themselves. You had a fine field before you ; the desire of peace had brought France nearer than you could have expected ; and a proper conduct in the court of Vienna, would, I am persuaded, have brought both her and her allies as near as we could wish. But I doubt, it is now over. As little a friend as I am supposed to be to the court of Vienna, and as I really am to their pride and ingratitude, I am not, however, for desperate measures with them, and of course should be sorry to see a strong acrimonious reply in writing, to their two very extraordinary papers, the matter of which is as offensive as possible, though they have artfully dressed that matter in respectful language to the king.

* Newcastle Papers. .

Honour, therefore, does not call for a reply in writing ; and policy, I think, should make you avoid it; the more you say, the more you may perhaps condemn yourself ; for if I remember right, you have nothing to show in writing but the Protocol."

After some farther animadversions on the conduct of the court of Vienna, he continues :—" You see, my wishes are, that cool reasoning and reflection may bring them to their own interest. I own, I have some selfish view in it ; I mean for your sake also ; for unless this matter is made up, and that by them, I do not know what we shall have to say for ourselves ; since I conclude we are resolved not to blame them, so as to make our future union impracticable. Your thoughts seem to me mighty right upon this occasion ; and you see, I agree with them in every thing but the paper. At the same time, I hope you will not lose sight of France ; for if the court of Vienna will not hearken to the king's friendly counsels, you will be neces- sitated to act in some degree of concert with them, mutually to preserve the peace, by checking the wrong measures of the respective allies. Will not the king of Prussia triumph, when he sees how the empress Queen uses us ? And if that triumph should put him again upon any mad project, who, when we are divided, can stop the execution but France ? I hope, therefore, you will guard against both events ; the one by endeavouring to reconcile the court of Vienna to their own interests, and the other by not losing your hold of France, in their present passion for preserving peace."

Alluding to a conference with lord Granville and the Chancellor, he says :—" The Chancellor seemed fond of the measure of driving the emperor to convoke the diet ; but lord Granville, with whom I must own I agreed, thought it absolutely necessary to know whether the court of Vienna would do as they should do, before that measure was taken ; for if the electors should break up in confusion, and that by the obstinacy or wrong conduct of the House of Austria, what mischiefs might not ensue !"

THE DUKE OF NEWCASTLE TO THE CHANCELLOR. *

On Irish affairs.

EXTRACT.—*Hanover, May 31st, 1752.*—* * * * * " I have had two very kind letters from my brother. I have endeavoured to answer them in the same style. I find, he fears, as I do, that the duke of Dorset's administration in Ireland cannot last ; and in that case, that we shall have a candidate, at least, that will puzzle us, if he do not succeed ; and puzzle them where he is to go, if he does. Surely, the duke of Dorset ought to be pressed to make up with those he has lately quarrelled with."

THE DUKE OF NEWCASTLE TO MR. PELHAM.†

Agrees with him on the affairs of Ireland.

Hanover, May 31st-June 11, 1752.

* * * * " I agree quite with you about the affairs in Ireland. I have long thought, those most concerned did not, or would not see their situation ; and that I believe

* Newcastle Papers. † Ibid.

chiefly from a most mistaken notion in politics, that if they did not own their own situation, others perhaps, would not see it; the contrary of which I take to be true. I have talked to Mr. Stone in this way; sometimes he has agreed with me, but always with reserve. Mr. Stone has not mentioned one word of Ireland, in the letter that came by the last messenger. I received a very long one from the Primate, before I left England, which I answered just before I went. I have desired Mr. Stone to bring you that letter and my answer; and I inclose one I had the other day from the Primate, by which you will see that temporising and making up, is by no means their present scheme. I wish you would send for Stone, and read this letter to him. It is of infinite consequence, that the duke of Dorset should set himself right again in Ireland; at least, so far as to make it practicable for him to stay, which, think what they will, his Grace will not be able to do, if what we hear be true, that they have quarrelled with all the considerable people, and the men of business. I doubt you will think my answer to the Primate too favourable; I now think so myself, but I was in hopes things would not come to these extremities; and, as I take the young ministers in Ireland to be the sole actors in this affair, I was not willing to say any thing that could personally displease the Primate, for whom, on many accounts, I have a great esteem and friendship.

" The thoughts of the successor, makes Dorset's stay in Ireland absolutely necessary; but he must make it practicable, and so I beg you would tell Mr. Stone from me. I conclude you know, the fat, little, round, great man, would like it. I should think so from his make, that is, from his absolute resignation to those who will certainly like it for him. There is, I own, something glaring in the proposition; but I am afraid very dangerous in the consequence. We have now nothing to do in the English army. We shall then have as little in the Irish one. I beg you would inform me of every thing you hear on this subject, and I will act in every part of it as you shall advise. I am not in opinion for it; and that not for any reason that immediately affects myself, that is all over : if that should happen, I am afraid there would be again, two administrations. For all these reasons Dorset must stay ; and in order to make that practicable, the Primate and lord George must make up in reality with the Speaker, &c.

" Let Stone once see it in this light, and he will bring it about. Lady Yarmouth has not yet succeeded to get it.* * * * Williams is here. I am sorry for it; he will be much mortified; it has a strange appearance, and must be disagreeable to me. But you know we cannot prevent these things."

THE DUKE OF NEWCASTLE TO MR. PELHAM.*

Farther proceedings on the affair of the election.

Hanover, June 3rd-14th, 1752.

* * * * " There is nothing new in our foreign affairs since my last ; except that Vergennes and Wrede both seem pleased with my having sent Wrede's papers to

* Newcastle Papers.

Vienna. Vergennes said, his satisfaction was from the manner he concluded I had sent it in. Vorster talks sanguinely, that his court will do right; and that he had wrote before, that they should make some offer in money. You will see by the extracts (which I beg you would always send to the Chancellor) that the court of France are under great difficulties at home, and I dare say plagued by the king of Prussia, upon the affair of the election; which must be the reason that St. Contest talks, at different times, in such a very different manner. I think our friend Albemarle does not push him home enough, or put him in mind of what he had said.

*　　*　　*　　*　　*　　*

" However hurt I may be, I am entirely against desperate measures ; and, though I have given an answer in writing, except two or three hints, I have avoided answering the papers, and giving any mark of discontent. I take up the point, where they themselves desire to place it. I join issue upon the Protocol, and in consequence of that, desire the assembling the Diet. The Protocol is avowed by count Stadion, and the sense I put upon it admitted ; and I do not know any one word in it which might not be produced. As to what you propose, I shall tell the minister of the court of Vienna, I have done it with great truth—I am not sure with so much management ; for injured people cannot always keep their temper. I have stated to him what we have done for their sakes ; how unusually we have given subsidies in time of peace ; and I have in strong terms declared to him, if they would not do their part (that is, if they would neither convoke the Diet, and depend upon their *eminent majority ;* or give a little, a very little, to the Elector Palatine, to procure the unanimous consent of France, and all the electors) then the election was at an end ; and the present system with the House of Austria, dissolved.

" I shall never be an actor in any other system ; but I am sure this will not subsist, if the court of Vienna does not take one of these two methods ; and in taking one, I think they may take both. I see your wishes, that this may be made up with the court of Vienna. I know you wish it for the public ; but I am vain enough to think that your real concern for me has a great, a very great share in it. I think I have, in the main, acted pretty agreeably to your way of thinking. I have kept measures with the court of Vienna ; I have given them two ways of saving themselves ; and yet, I think, they are both combined to answer your object.

" I see, lord Granville and you are against pressing the convocation of the Diet ; I fancy, for different reasons : his lordship, for fear his friends, the court of Vienna, should not behave well ; you (and that is a reason which occurred to me) for fear France should be offended at it, when we had a negotiation depending with them, upon another principle. As to lord Granville's apprehension of the electors breaking up in confusion, and that by the obstinacy, or wrong conduct of the court of Vienna, I do not apprehend any danger of that kind. In the first place, this Diet cannot, and is not intended to be called, without the free previous consent of the court of Vienna. In the next, it will not necessarily follow, that when the Diet of the electors is assembled, they should proceed to the election, if any unforeseen reason should arise, to shew that the election would be attended with ill consequences. But I think, if we give up the point of proceeding to the election, with our majority of six voices, we

3 I 2

lose all the ground we have to stand upon. Upon that principle we set out; and upon that principle alone, can we defend all that we have done; for, however accident or wise conduct, has put it in our power, (if the court of Vienna knew its own interest) to have the concurrence of all the electors, and even of France, nobody can pretend to say, that this measure of the election was originally begun, or has been carried on, upon that foot. After the extraordinary answers given by the court of Vienna, and before I took the measure of proposing the assembly of the Diet, and depending thereby (if prudent) in all events, upon our *majorité eminente,* I did consider what effect that might have had in France. I thought, and do think, it would be the most probable way of bringing in the Elector Palatine, when he sees we can and will proceed without him. St. Contest could never reproach us, when they had adopted the demands of the Elector Palatine, which were not comprehended in our negotiation with them; and which we had always since declared were inadmissible; and when he, St. Contest, had departed from the reference which he had himself proposed to the king's decision. But, if the convocation of the Diet should displease them, the part I have taken since, to send Wrede's papers to Vienna, and so strongly to insist upon their enabling us to make some proposal to the Elector Palatine, is returning to the negotiation with them (notwithstanding all the inconsistency on their part) the moment I saw any appearance of reducing the Palatine's demands to what was, or could be thought by us, reasonable and admissible. And I think, if the court of Vienna will do any thing, they will combine these two objects together; and if they assemble the Diet, they will make something like an offer to the Elector Palatine.

" You say very right, the king of Prussia will take his advantage of this behaviour in the court of Vienna; but at present, he will be contented if he can effectually prevent the election; and therefore, I am of an opinion, if we can carry it through, his Prussian Majesty will be quiet. The extracts of this day, are very bad. Podewilz's letter to Wrede, and Wachendorf's, tend to encourage Wrede to stand out; and Vergennes has told the Grosvoight this day, that nothing but *terres* would satisfy the Elector Palatine; notwithstanding the same Vergennes told me the other day, that if the Elector Palatine would be satisfied with Pleissen only, they should be contented. The king of Prussia has certainly engaged France to insist upon the satisfaction for the Elector Palatine, and is now endeavouring to make that satisfaction as impracticable as is possible.

" We must wait for our answers from Vienna. I own I do not despair; I think I have puzzled Bartenstein. He cannot well get off the Protocol; and if that Protocol takes place, for their own sakes they will endeavour to satisfy the Elector Palatine, that they may have nothing to fear, when the election is made, and when they see they cannot avoid coming to it. I own, in the present distress, I did think this was a happy thought; I must repeat it, I think it answers both objects at once; it secures the election, and it makes it necessary for the court of Vienna to try to gain the Elector Palatine, and advisable for the Elector to take what he can get; since without it, he may have the fine words and promises of Prussia and France; but his Highness will get by that, neither land or money.

" I forgot to observe, that lord Albemarle's question to St. Contest, which is the best thing he has done, what would be the consequence of our proceeding to the election with our *eminent majority*, and St. Contest's answer; have prepared them for what we may do, and shew us, that no ill consequence will arise from it. I can assure you, I have not, and will not lose sight of France; but yet I am sorry to say, that the turn St. Contest takes in the Palatine affair; Mirepoix's silence upon our territorial affairs; and the alteration of Vergennes' countenance and manner here, do not look well. The king of Prussia has a mind to frighten us; and France will let him, if he can. But all this would signify nothing, if the court of Vienna had, what they have not, common sense, and, I might say, common gratitude. We shall soon know what part they will finally take."

THE DUKE OF NEWCASTLE TO MR. PELHAM. *

The Emperor has the election very much at heart—Conversation with the king on Irish affairs.

"DEAR BROTHER,   *Hanover, June 12th-23rd*, 1752.

" I have sent a short account to my lord Holdernesse by the post, of the answer which I received yesterday from Vienna. It is much more satisfactory than the last; and I think they will be entirely governed by what shall be advised from hence, upon the point that was the subject of my letter, to which this was an answer. The emperor has talked with great freedom to lord Hyndford; has shewed as much regard and deference to the king as possible; and has undoubtedly, the election very much at heart.

" I should hardly have troubled you by this post, if it had not been for a conversation which I had this day with the king. His Majesty asked me (for the first time) whether I had heard any thing of ill humours and uneasiness in Ireland. I told him, yes, that I had had some account from you; that I had had a very long letter from the Primate † relating to it; that the Primate stated it as an opposition to the power of the crown, the authority of the Lord-lieutenant, and the English interest, from those, who with their places and employments, would be independent of the Lord-lieutenant, and govern themselves; that I believed the Speaker was the person chiefly meant; that it was thought, they were jealous of the ability and credit which lord G. Sackville had got, in the carrying on business there. The king said, ' I have heard that it was thought lord G. Sackville was covetous, and loved getting money;' I asked him whether he had ever had any complaint or fact of that kind. He said, ' No.' I told the king, that I had sent the Primate's letter to you, that you might talk to the duke of Dorset and Mr. Stone upon it; and that when I knew farther your thoughts, and what should have passed, I would acquaint his Majesty with it; that I did not think it proper to trouble him upon the subject, before I could make some certain judgment upon it. I told him I understood from the Primate, that this ill humour, or opposi-

---

* Newcastle Papers.   † Dr. George Stone, brother of Mr. Stone, and Archbishop of Armagh.

tion, began first from the duke of Dorset's support of the amendment made in
England, with relation to the king's gift of the overplus of the revenue to the public.
‘ In that they did right,’ says the king ; ‘ it was Harrington who put that in a wrong
way.’   I then told the king very sincerely, that of all men living, the duke of Dorset
was, from his nature, the last whom I should suspect would be capable of any thing
like violent measures ; the king replied upon my lord G.,* but without the least
discovering any displeasure with the duke of Dorset.   On the contrary, when I told
him, that the Primate said the Privy Council, the House of Lords, and all the people,
were pleased and satisfied with the duke of Dorset, the king mentioned, himself, the
accounts in the newspapers, of the regard shewed his Grace upon his leaving the
kingdom.   As I am obliged to shew the Primate's letter, I beg you would talk this
matter fully to the duke of Dorset, Mr. Stone, and my lord Chancellor ; and let me
know what I shall say upon it.   What the king said relating to lord G. I beg may
not be told the duke of Dorset.

THE DUKE OF NEWCASTLE TO THE LORD CHANCELLOR.†

*Anxiety of the duke of Newcastle to promote the success of the election, and to procure the con-
sent of the Chancellor and his brother, to the subsidy for the Elector Palatine—Ill consequences to be apprehended should the negotiation be discontinued.*

!“ MY LORD,   *Hanover, June 18th-29th, 1752.*

  “ As I am afraid the subject of this letter will not be quite agreeable to my brother,
I address it to your lordship, though it is for the consideration of you both.

  “ I have deferred as long as I could, the mentioning any thing of this kind ; and
have endeavoured, by all the means which I could suggest to myself, to engage the
court of Vienna to give that satisfaction to the Elector Palatine, which might procure
the concurrence of France to the election ; and I have never given the Palatine
minister the least reason to think, that we could, or would contribute any thing
towards this satisfaction ; as you will particularly see by the copy of a letter from
M. Wachtendonck to M. de Wrede.   But I own, I cannot now in conscience avoid
laying the state of this question before your lordship and my brother, for your consideration ; and I can assure you that the king does not, or shall not know one word
of my writing to you.

  “ Whether it was right, originally to engage in the affair of the election, is not now
the question.   You must know my thoughts upon that.   But things are gone so far,
abroad and at home, that I will venture to say, that if the thing is now dropt, or
should miscarry, the king's credit abroad will be totally lost ; and his influence at
home greatly lessened ; as well as the reputation of his servants, and of those particularly, who have the most to do in the foreign measures, and in the support of them ;
and I am afraid also, of such consequences, with regard to the future proceeding in

---

* This passage is unintelligible : something appears to be omitted ; but it is so in the original.
† Newcastle Papers.

foreign affairs, and to the system that will and must be then adopted, as may greatly entangle, and affect the ease of his Majesty's reign.

" If then, the election is to be carried, it must be considered in what way it can be done. There are two which now offer, and I think, if we persevere, one of the two must be brought about. The convocation of the Diet, I take it for granted, will now soon be agreed upon; and though we shall have difficulties, I think we shall get through the election, and carry it, with our *eminent majority;* though France frightens our friends, as you see; and what effect that will have, one cannot positively say. But I rather hope we may get over all that, if we ourselves will abide by our majority, as I own I shall be for doing, if the other method fails. For, to be sure, we entered upon this affair, singly upon the principle of the majority; and upon a presumption (which I think is every day still more strongly to be relied on) that France would not begin a war, on account of this *legal constitutional act,* let them pretend to call it whatever they please; and St. Contest's present behaviour, of which I have an account in my lord Albemarle's letter, which I received this day, confirms me in that opinion. But then we must expect *protests* from the three electors; ill humour from France; and perhaps some reproaches, though in my conscience we do not deserve them.

"The only way, therefore, to avoid all this, and crown the king's measures with success, and I hope with universal applause, would be, to get such satisfaction for the Elector Palatine, as should be approved by France. You see, in my letter to my lord Albemarle, of this day, I have endeavoured to find out what would do. I am sure nothing can be invented to induce the court of Vienna to do this, more than I have done. But it would be deceiving you, if I did not give it as my opinion, that it will not be practicable to bring them up to what will satisfy the Elector Palatine, and France. And this, your lordship may remember, I saw, before I went out of England. And I did venture to talk to the Princess Royal at the Hague, upon this supposition, though I never mentioned it, lest it might be thought, that I would not do my best with the court of Vienna. That I have done, and I send you a copy of a letter, which I hope the king will suffer me to write to the emperor. After that, I can do no more. The most that I can possibly hope to bring the court of Vienna to, would be to yield Pleissen, and to give a sum of money, of 500,000, perhaps 600,000 florins; fifty, or at most sixty thousand pounds sterling. And from what Vorster (whom by the bye I cannot believe two days together) has said, I should hope that might be done. And to say the truth, a considerable fief as Pleissen is (to which the Elector Palatine has no more right than I have) with fifty or sixty thousand pounds out of their pocket, is as much as any one of us could ever have thought they would do, or indeed as was reasonable to ask. For as to the Elector Palatine's pretensions upon the court of Vienna, I will be bold to say, they are not better founded than those upon England and Holland. The least which I can ever get the Elector Palatine to accept, is Pleissen, and one million of florins; about £.112,000 sterling. The question therefore, is, shall the election be lost, or shall we carry it with our *eminent majority,* and risk the consequences, for the sake of fifty or sixty thousand pounds? I own very freely my opinion, that it would be the worst judged economy in the world, if we were to do it; and I verily believe, the very people who may oppose us in doing it, would think so, and say so, if we lost this great object for the sake of such a sum.

"I never heard any objection made to the expense for the election, but that that expense would not do the business. If, therefore, it should evidently appear, that fifty or sixty thousand pounds more would not only do it, but get the concurrence of France and Prussia also in it, I should not think that there could be one word said against it.

"I send by this messenger a load of papers from baron Wrede. I have not so much as given him the satisfaction to think, that I would even take so much notice of them as to transmit them to England. If your lordship and my brother are of opinion, that in the last extremity, and in order to secure the unanimity of the election, and the concurrence of France, fifty or threescore thousand pounds may be given, there are two ways of doing that, either by asking it of the parliament, or by applying the sum, out of the king's civil list, which was intended for the elector of Cologne, for that purpose; and sure, it is as reasonable, and much more useful, to pay that sum out of the civil list, for securing the election (and that unanimously), than it was before the first uncertain step that was taken towards it; but, however, I can say nothing to that. To be sure that is the most to be wished, but that may be the most difficult to be obtained.

"As to the other, I make no doubt but an agreement now made with the elector Palatine, for fifty or threescore thousand pounds (which money should not be asked of the parliament, until the election was actually over), would not only be agreed to in parliament, but most highly applauded. And though I hold quite a different language to the court of Mannheim, and to the court of France, I do think there is a very good pretence for it, upon the foot of their demand, when every body will see that the election is the real object.

*   *   *

"To sum up all in a few words:

"If the election is dropt, or should miscarry, I think the honour and reputation of the king and country will be in a great measure lost, and the most fatal consequences follow from it; if it is carried by a majority, France and Prussia may (though I do not think they will) make such demonstrations of armies, &c., as must necessarily put us to five times the expense; and if a general war should at last ensue, that is a consideration which affects every body.

"I am sensible that it may be said, ' Why, then, was this measure undertaken ?' To that I answer, a measure so right in itself, and which must be attended with so many good consequences, was prudently undertaken, though with some risk. But if all the risk that could be foreseen can be bought off, for fifty or sixty thousand pounds, I will be bold to say that it is the wisest and cheapest measure, considering all the circumstances, that ever was begun or pursued. Though this is my sincere opinion, and by which I shall ever abide, I will engage in nothing, and take no step, until I have an answer from your lordship to this letter.

"It is unnecessary for me to say more. In conscience I could not say less."

MR. PELHAM TO THE DUKE OF NEWCASTLE.*

Is not surprised at any change in France—Approves his brother's conduct, but hopes he will not involve the nation in farther expenses.—Irish affairs.

June 19th-30th, 1752.

After mentioning the affair of captain M'Donald, which is more fully detailed in the next letter, he adds:—" I find by your letter to lord Chancellor, that you apprehend I differ in opinion with you, as to the convoking a diet, more than I do. I wrote you my whole opinion upon it, and in that have not the least reserve; I told you what was Granville's first opinion; his lively transitions do not affect me much. I am mighty glad to find you are in general satisfied with my correspondence; I can assure you I mean it well. To go back to the first beginning of this transaction is of no use, and perhaps my opinion there might not suit with yours; you know it never did; I chuse, therefore, to speak of things as they are, in which I do not foresee we can have any difference of opinion. If I am not so sanguine in my expectations, that is constitutional; I shall be as glad to see that come to pass, which you wish for, as if I thought it never so sure. You say I do not speak out upon St. Contest: it is not from any reserve that I do not, but merely from not knowing what to say, or at least what would be agreeable. I see France, not in the light of a friend, but as one that wishes the same as I do, from necessity : any change, therefore, in their conduct does not surprise me, if I see the necessity removed. If, for instance, they know, as I conclude they do, that the court of Vienna herself does not wish to drive things to extremities, and is cool in this election, what should make France then run the risk of disobliging her own allies, when the mischief she apprehended from their being too tenacious is removed, by the indifference on the other side? This made me say, in my last, if the court of Vienna went to the diet, intending to make any tolerable offer to the allies of France, I thought, for the sake of peace, France would come into it. I wish I may have explained my thoughts to you clearly now. Upon these subjects it is difficult to write one's whole thoughts without trying the patience of the reader, as well as one's own; and especially as the turn of an expression varies the sense totally. I can assure you, my dear Brother, I keep nothing from you. I approve of what you are doing in every respect, and most heartily wish you success. I hope you will take care not to bring any fresh expenses upon us ; for, after the behaviour of the court of Vienna, it will be said, and with great appearance of reason, that she stood out, only till we would be at the expense, which she ought to be at herself. I said, in my other letter, that we waited with impatience for the answer from Vienna; you may easily imagine I do ; for till that comes, it is impossible for us here to make any judgment upon what will be the result of this long negotiation."

* Newcastle Papers.

MR. PELHAM TO THE DUKE OF NEWCASTLE.*

On Scottish affairs—The vassals of the crown do not pay their feu duties—Endeavours to reform these abuses.—Lord Holdernesse has ordered the arrest and examination of one Macdonald of Clanranald—Condemns the want of pliancy in the court of Vienna—Hopes that the French, whose dispositions appear to be pacific, will consent to the proposed limits of Canada.

"DEAR BROTHER,   *June* 19th, 1752.

" I trouble you with this letter, chiefly to transmit a warrant, which I have received from the barons of the Exchequer in Scotland, for his Majesty's signature. I believe the king will remember, that I have for some time told his Majesty, that a great part of his revenue in that kingdom was totally lost, by the Feu-ers and vassals there never paying their feu duty, but constantly, when the arrears came to be considerable, applying for and obtaining a discharge of the whole ; and what is more extraordinary, the officers, who are in several places appointed to collect these duties from under tenants, and are called chamberlains, not only receive considerable salaries, but retain the surplus in their own hands, never pay into the Exchequer any thing, but when prosecutions press hard upon them, apply for, and have constantly obtained, releases for the whole sum. We have now brought them to a composition for the arrears, and fixed regular payments, as they shall become due, for the future. His Majesty may possibly think four shillings in the pound too moderate a composition ; but I can assure you, it is all clear gains ; and I have had some trouble, and was forced to act with some resolution, to procure so much. However, I must submit the whole to his Majesty, and do as he shall think proper ; but it will be necessary to come soon to a resolution, as their several terms require it.

" I see lord Holdernesse has acquainted you, that he has taken up one Macdonald, of Clanranald ; he was stopped at Stevenage, and has, since his arrival in town, been examined once ; nothing very material has been got out of him. We all thought it proper to have the Attorney and Solicitor General's opinions upon the power of detaining him in custody before he was re-examined : in all probability, the whole will be finished by the next week, and then it will be sent to you in form from the office. I heard of this man's being in town, and of his design to go to Scotland ; I consulted, therefore, with lord Chancellor immediately, whether we should not stop him ; who was of opinion with me, that we should. I thereupon sent my informant to lord Holdernesse, who immediately sent Ward, the messenger, with my correspondent, after him ; and, very luckily, he was caught at Stevenage. This gentleman was undoubtedly in the Rebellion; commanded a regiment of eight hundred men there ; but by a misnomer has escaped the forfeiture, upon a judgment of the Court of Session in Scotland. I do not find that the Court did wrong, for unluckily there is another brother whose real name is Donald, which the act of parliament mentions, and this man's name is Ronald. There was great error or neglect in those who sent up the names of the persons to be inserted in the bill of attainder ; but where to lay that

* Newcastle Papers.

blame I cannot correctly say, the king's servants in Scotland having been changed, about that time.

I have just received a return from the commissioners of the Customs, of the supposed disaffected persons employed in the revenue under their management. I find, they have employed the officers of the army, as well as others, to give them what information they could procure; the instances are few, and from very low people; but as general Churchill has transmitted to them a long letter from one colonel Crawford, and another from lord Bury, I have not yet had time to consider those letters thoroughly. When I have perused them, you shall have a full and clear account of all that has passed. * * * *

"We wait here with great impatience for the answer from the court of Vienna. I hope, when it arrives, I shall have as good a reason to congratulate you upon the success of his Majesty's instances there, as I have from the courts of Madrid and Turin. I cannot help observing, that the Austrians are much more pliant in what was demanded of them by the king of Sardinia, where they are not so materially concerned, than in this great affair of the Succession, where they are principally and immediately concerned. I hope, however, all will end well.

" Sure, Albemarle is more sanguine than he has reason to be upon our American affairs. Lord Chancellor, lord Granville, lord Holdernesse, with lord Anson, lord Halifax, and myself, looked over lord Albemarle's letters, and strictly examined the map he sent over, and the several lines he made in it. We all agreed, that, if he can procure such an agreement as that map points out, it is the greatest work for this country, which has been done for many years. And the credit of his Majesty's government, as well as the abilities of those employed in this negotiation, will be transmitted to posterity with the greatest honour. But we fear it is too good; however it is to be tryed : and, considering the present disposition of France, with regard to peace, I am satisfied more is to be got now, than we can reasonably expect another time."

THE DUKE OF NEWCASTLE TO MR. PELHAM.*

Public affairs appear more favourable—Applauds the conduct of the king of Poland—Alludes to the deceitful behaviour of Monsieur de Vergennes.

Hanover, June 24th-July 5th, 1752.

* * * * " I did not trouble you, by the last messenger, upon our public affairs. They certainly have a better appearance than they had : the honourable part which the king of Poland acts, will have its effect, and ought to make (as I told Vorster) the court of Vienna ashamed. Haslang desires to have a copy of the king of Poland's Declaration ; and does not doubt but he shall have the same orders. In short, if Vergennes did not play the knave, we should finish this thing to all our satisfactions. As it is, finish it, I hope, we shall. The king told me this day (for he has not sent me the letter) that Vergennes had wrote to some of his correspondents, that we should amuse his court, and deceive them at last; but that he had apprised the court of it.

* Newcastle Papers.

3 K 2

This is very villanous, and very unlike the duke of Mirepoix; but yet we must scramble through. I hope you approve all my voluminous letters, and especially those to my lord Albemarle. I have wrote him a private one, which I hope will have an effect. Had Mirepoix had the conduct of this negotiation, I am sure all would have gone on well; but this friend of mine, this coxcomb, Vergennes, thinks the skill of a minister consists in jealousies and suspicions. And I suppose his Court has never owned to him how far they have gone with us, lest the king of Prussia should be displeased with it."

MR. PELHAM TO THE DUKE OF NEWCASTLE.*

Strongly reprobates the conduct of the Austrian court, and would do much to extricate the king and his brother from their difficulties.

June 26th, 1752.

After thanking him for his letter of the 18th, and informing him that the marriage settlements of his daughter will be prepared by August, and that all will be concluded by the beginning of September, he continues :—" I do not well understand our friend Granville; he talks forward and backward. I can see plainly, he is struck. D'Abreu visits him and turns his head; he is in good humour, but does not know what to say. The court of Vienna have in good earnest spoiled their own game and yours too. I shall be glad to see the day when you have done negotiating with them, for never any good came of their counsels. You certainly do all you can, in the present circumstances; but an angel from Heaven cannot effectually serve some people against their wills; nor are these kind of political strokes ever successful, when every trifle delays them. You see by our intercepted letters, that little fellow Des Touches† knows every thing that passes abroad, to the most minute and most secret circumstance.

*   *   *

" Believe me, my dear brother, I would do much to extricate the king, and you more particularly, from your present difficulties. I fear it is not in the power of us all, and what is worse, we have not the means allowed as necessary for such measures. If we are to create expenses for some purposes, we should be enabled to lessen them in others; but that is not permitted.

*   *   *   *

" Poor lord Gower is extremely ill; he has had another stroke of the palsy. He will be a great loss to the king, if his Majesty continues those whom he at present employs.

* Newcastle Papers.
† The celebrated author of several excellent comedies: he was at this time the French agent in London.

MR. PELHAM TO THE DUKE OF NEWCASTLE.*

Observations on the private letter from the duke to the Chancellor—Deprecates a partial election, as it may involve England in a war.

July 1st-12th, 1752.

After adverting to the letter intended by his brother for the sole perusal of himself and the Chancellor, he says :—" It appears that there is no certainty as to what the court of Vienna will do. They have taken care, that if by proceeding to the election upon the *eminent majority,* any ill consequences should ensue, they are not to be blamed. They have asked what they shall have, in case of opposition or an eventual rupture; you have said, and I do not see what else you could say, that if any power concerned in this election, should be fallen upon in hatred of that act, all the parties concerned should look upon it as a proper demand, for the execution of our respective defensive alliances, and I look upon that to be understood as *casus fœderis.* Now, dear brother, how do we stand, if that should happen? Engaged in a war, as principals in the first instance, will not the court of Vienna say, and say justly, we would have put off this measure until time should have convinced all the Germanic body, that the measure was right. You insisted upon pushing it now; you obliged us to convoke the diet, and proceed to the election; you have by precipitation brought this war upon us; you are therefore, both in honour and interest, called upon to extricate us out of it, with your whole force. What then is that whole force? And how shall we have it in our power to exert it? You see by my state of the case, I am greatly afraid of a partial election. I own I am; the conduct of the court of Vienna has made that a much more dangerous measure than it would have been, had they acted otherwise. The little regard they have shewn to the king, in trusting their interest into his Majesty's hands, and the difficulties they have thrown in the way of all accommodation, have in my poor opinion, thrown France back into the arms of Prussia, and will enable the king of Prussia to start new difficulties, and new claims with some of the other electors, in case you shall be able, by your own address and management, to procure some reasonable satisfaction for the elector Palatine; your own, I say, because I do not see that you have the least assistance from any court abroad, and by my observation I as little see any considerable assistance you are likely to have from any great genius at home.

" You see, by our intercepted letters, that what Vergennes was supposed to have said to the several ministers now resident at Hanover, is avowed and known to so low a fellow as Des Touches here. Lord Granville told us, in confidence, that D'Abreu asked him whether he had heard of any such intended declaration made, or to be made by the court of France. Granville told him he had seen no letters that mentioned any such thing; to which D'Abreu replied, ' I can assure you, my lord, you will, very soon.' I look upon the intelligence you send lord Albemarle to be true; and therefore your instructions to his lordship are wise and prudent. I hope in God they will have some good effect; for if the consequence of

* Newcastle Papers.

this pacific measure should be the bringing on a general war, though not by our immediate fault, what will be our case; and where will our situation then be? a parliament expiring; a new one to be called; and no fruit of the last peace enjoyed, except the taking from individuals one-fourth of their income, the better, as will be said, to enable us to carry on new and greater expenses!

" You will say, supposing you are in the right, what is to be done? I will venture to throw out to you my bolt, perhaps a weak one. Tell the court of Vienna, if they will satisfy the elector Palatine, and enable the king immediately to negotiate with France for that purpose, you will undertake it; but if they will not do that, it is in vain for Great Britain alone to undertake the support of the House of Austria, in their present possessions, and also without their assistance, and in appearance against their will, to secure the succession in the Emperor's House. The king has done a great deal; the nation has done more; but there must and will be an end some time or other. I was in hopes your plan for electing the archduke king of the Romans, would have drawn the line; but, I fear, if you are not permitted to treat with France, it will rather open the trenches. I was as willing, as desirous, of receiving good news upon this head, as the most sanguine politician I am acquainted with. I was as happy and as full, in giving you all the just eulogiums that properly belonged to you, as any man in this country, or elsewhere; but my love to you, and concern for you, cannot, nor ought not, to make me blind, when I think I see dangers gathering about you. I could say a vast deal more on this head; I fear I have said too much already; and shall now go to your most private letter, sent to lord Chancellor.

" I always foresaw we should be called upon in some shape or other, for a little more assistance, before this affair was finished; and though I think it most unreasonable, and what can scarcely be supported by argument, yet, had the court of Vienna shewn a disposition to do what they could, and reposed that confidence in the king, which they ought to have done, I should not have been averse (when the whole thing was amicably adjusted) to any measure within bounds, that would have pinned the basket, and brought you off with flying colours. But that cursed court has changed, not only the face, but the very nature of business here. To ask a farther subsidy, to relieve them from an expense, which they ought to bear, if it should be borne at all; and that for a service, which they are to receive the immediate benefit of, though they profess indifference about it; after we have been at so considerable expense already, will have a most profuse appearance, and I fear be deemed a weak measure in government. But, however, so sensible am I of your situation, and that of us all in this terrible dilemma, that if you can bring things so to bear, that France shall professedly acquiesce in the election, that the king of Prussia, the electors of Cologne, and Palatine, shall give their voices for the archduke, and that nothing shall be paid by us, till the whole is finished; I will endeavour to turn my thoughts in such a manner, as, I hope, may enable us to furnish some small matter, after the Empress Queen has done what she can be brought to do.

*   *   *   *   *   *

" I might, perhaps, have spared myself the pains of writing, and you the trouble of reading this long letter, without much consequence; for I am of opinion, notwithstanding all we read, and all we write, this matter will not go much farther. The court of Vienna will never venture to proceed to an election, with the opposition that seems now to open itself; and I fear, though I heartily wish the contrary, you will not be able to soften the opposition, upon such terms as you would yourself come into. Lord Chancellor has, or will write to you his thoughts also; he is the only one you can depend upon. I need not say he wishes you well, nor that he would come as far into any measure of yours, *because yours*, as any man in this country. I hope, therefore, you will see by what he says, that I am not to be suspected as backward in your views.

July 3.—" Since writing what is above, I have received your two kind letters of the 19th and 24th of June, which have both of them put me upon considering whether I should send this letter or not. But upon consideration, I have determined to let it go, because I am sure you cannot at this time think I have any reason for writing it, but pure love and kindness to you. If I have false fears, your better knowledge will correct my ignorance: if I should happen to be in the right, I have then done my duty in laying before you my apprehensions. Your public letters vary the case but little; for though I acknowledge the king of Poland behaves very handsomely, yet what will that end in, if the court of Vienna does nothing on her part, and France and Prussia act together in availing themselves of the difficulties we are thrown into, by the conduct of what should be our principal friend. I find you lay a great deal on Vergennes, by which I conclude you mean the court of France; I agree with you; but how can you expect France to assist us, to get out of difficulties, which Vienna, the power we set up against her, has thrown us into.

THE DUKE OF NEWCASTLE TO MR. PELHAM.*

The king is satisfied with Mr. Pelham's inquiries about Scotland, and approves his financial administration—Displeased with the indiscreet conduct of the bishop of Norwich.

Hanover, July 1st-12th, 1752.

* * * *" I had an opportunity to lay your ostensible letter, with the Scotch warrant, before the king; he very readily signed it; seemed mightily pleased with the regulation you had made; and was also quite satisfied, and in good humour about Scotland, thinking every thing was done that was proper.

" I had a good deal of talk upon the arrears in the hands of the Chamberlains. I said, I had often heard Sir Robert Walpole complain of it. ' Yes,' said the king, ' and yet he was always for remitting it for his friends.' Lord Rothes, indeed, (which was a case I had named) he thought was not his friend.

" Though it is very late, and I am quite tired out with writing, I cannot omit giving

---

* Newcastle Papers.

you some account of a conversation I had had, not long ago, upon the subject of Sir Robert Walpole. The king said, ' he managed the money matters very ill; he did not indeed give money abroad, but he gave it away liberally at home; that he was a great man, he understood the country; but that with regard to money matters; your brother does that, understands that, much better;' and said many kind things in that way. I told him, I had often heard you lament that, in Sir Robert Walpole; that I knew you gave great attention to those affairs, and would be glad to be able to bring them into a good situation, or to that purpose. The king repeated, ' he understands it better.'

" I send you a copy of the archbishop's letter : the first part of it is very ignorant, but the character of bishop Trevor very just and proper. The king read it through, and said, ' he was not at all satisfied with the bishop of Norwich;'* upon which I said, I was afraid he had not acted discreetly. The king said, ' You recommended him.' I said, ' Yes, but his Majesty would please to remember that I told him, at that time, that I had very little personal acquaintance with him; it was from the general opinion of the world in his favour.' He looked over the names of the bishops; and in that the archbishop has certainly done Trevor great service."

MR. PELHAM TO THE DUKE OF NEWCASTLE.†

Is proceeding with the Scottish inquiry—Regrets the slow progress of the affair of the election.

July 3-14th, 1752.

  *   *   *   *   *

" The other part of our Scotch inquiries is going on, and several inferior officers are already removed; there does not come out, any thing like what I expected, as to Jacobites in employment. Some there are, and some there ever were; and, undoubtedly, the government, shewing a proper resentment to those who have been recommended to favour, though Jacobites, will do good. I thought I should have been able to send you, before this time, a kind of narrative of our proceedings, for his Majesty's information; but the letters are so voluminous, and frequently contradictory one of the other, that it is impossible to bring the whole into an intelligible paper, without some time and difficulty. The army have been employed, and orders given by general Churchill to all the regiments, to make what inquiry they can, in the several places where they were quartered; a report is sent from them; nothing material appears, excepting some informations of a French captain in lord Bury's regiment. Lord Bury has been come from Scotland some time; I have not yet seen him, nor do I suppose I shall very soon. Lord Holdernesse sends you word of the taking up one Henrich,‡ formerly a clerk in the duke of Bedford's office. We are to examine him, when the papers seized in his house have been carefully perused. Unluckily this man was at Mr. Aldworth's house in Berkshire, when the messenger was sent for him. I doubt not but lord Holdernesse will inform you of all particulars, when he has

---

* Recently appointed preceptor to the Prince of Wales.   † Newcastle Papers.

‡ A Dutchman in lord Holdernesse's office, accused of making improper communications to the French court, of the contents of certain papers in his custody.

been thoroughly examined. I shall trouble you with my thoughts upon him; you may be assured, in this, as well as every other part of government, his Majesty's servants here are, and will be very watchful; we assist each other as much as we can, and I hope the king will find the good effects of our joint labours for the public service. I am sure we ought to do our best here, when you are labouring so hard abroad, where, I doubt, you meet with so much more difficulty, than we, in our little sphere, do here. I am sorry to see so little progress in your great work: the king has done every thing that was possible for him to do; you have also laboured hard; and if it does miscarry, the court of Vienna must thank themselves for it: for how can it be supposed that France will act for *our* measures, when she sees our principal ally does not act for her own. Lord Gower mends, though very slowly. If he lingers on some months or perhaps years more, it will be to him, poor man! a miserable life; but I cannot but say, I wish he may last some time longer, for the sake of the king's affairs; his death would probably make a considerable alteration in many places. I hope lord Trentham would take a right part: I really believe, from himself he would; but I am sure, lord Gower does." * * * *

THE DUKE OF NEWCASTLE TO MR. PELHAM.*

Is of opinion that the court of Vienna will avoid the election.

"DEAR BROTHER, *Hanover, June 22nd-Aug. 2nd, 1752.*

" I troubled you with so long a letter by the last messenger, that I shall be very short this time; and, indeed, I have not materials for a long one.

" The unsatisfactory answer, which was expected from Vienna, came last Friday; and agreeably to the declaration, which the king's ministers were directed to make to the emperor, and the empress queen, I gave the answer to baron Vorster. As I send all those papers, and my letters, to lord Holdernesse, you will there see what we have done, and our reasons for it. I am sure you will approve; for the whole is upon your plan, contained in your long letter. What will be the final end of this affair, I cannot pretend to say. Did I not fear that the court of Vienna did not really wish the conclusion of the election, at this time, for reasons which I have often mentioned, I should think with many here, that this firmness in the king would produce an immediate offer to the elector Palatine. But, as I have my suspicions, as to their real inclinations, I am apt to fear, that they will lay hold of any pretext, to avoid the election. The Bavarian ministers have acted a shameful part, and count Haslang, not a very good one; but, as the elector is an honest man, I think he will go through with us, in spite of his ministers, his confessor, and his ladies, who are all against us, except the empress dowager, his mother, and the electress, his wife.

" The king has talked, very strongly, to the Cologne minister, M. d'Asseburgh, and in most parts of it very well. I really think the whole depends, now, upon a satisfaction for the elector Palatine. * * * * *

* Newcastle Papers.

MR. PELHAM TO THE DUKE OF NEWCASTLE.*

Thinks that the court of Vienna will only make an insidious offer to the elector Palatine, and that the king has acted right in the affair of the election.

July 28th, 1752.

After acknowledging the receipt of his kind letter of the 22nd, O. S., and making some observations respecting the duchess of Newcastle's illness, he continues:—
"I wrote you a pretty long letter from Warminghurst, which will shorten this. I have read your several letters, which came by the messenger last week, and think, in my poor opinion, every thing right. I do not apprehend the court of Vienna will make any offer to the elector Palatine farther than they have done; if they do, I fear it will be an insidious one, to draw us on, but not an effectual one, to do the business. I heartily wish they may do right: you have undoubtedly given them an opportunity; and be it as it will, the king cannot have finished his affair on his side, better than he has done. We must expect that miscarriages, in what the people were led to expect, will occasion some ill humour; but when the whole story comes to be told, no individual in this country can be blamed justly.* * * *

"I hope, upon my return from the north, to find your affairs abroad better settled, than they appear to be at present. I am certain, you will do every thing in your power to contribute to that desirable end; and if any thing should happen disagreeable to you, in the winding up of the whole, you may be certain, your friends here will do their utmost; and I think it will be no hard task, to convince the world, who are not to blame, though it may be somewhat difficult to colour over those who are."

THE DUKE OF NEWCASTLE TO THE LORD CHANCELLOR.†

Dispute between the Emperor and Empress relative to the election.

Hanover, August 5th-16th, 1752.

*   *   *   *

"I have learned from a good hand, that this public, and, I think, particularly advantageous measure of the election, has been considered at Vienna as a point of dispute between the emperor and empress. The former declared violently for it, and said he should not be the poorer, by giving four or five millions of florins for it. Count Colloredo, and all the honest party at Vienna, confirmed the emperor in this. Bar tenstein got wind of it; made it a court intrigue; and blew up the empress to the degree which we have seen; not to buy, not to purchase, and all that stuff; and this is the true occasion of all the delays and difficulties we have met with. It is thought one million of florins would do the whole; viz., £.100,000, of which the court of Vienna pays £.50,000. Wrede asks £.150,000, and answers for Prussia and Cologne, *no purchase no pay.* Is this, in our circumstances, to be lost? Our master told me, he would not give one farthing; 'What will your brother say?' to which I answered, 'I desire

* Newcastle Papers.   † Ibid.

only that it might be referred to him.' I will endeavour to whittle down Wrede as low as I can ; and I believe I shall send you next week a proposal for your consideration and opinion.

THE DUKE OF NEWCASTLE TO MR. KEITH.*

Instructions for treating with the Austrian court, on measures relative to the arrangement with the elector Palatine.

"DEAR SIR,   *Hanover, Aug. 20th-31st,* 1752.

"I am almost afraid to write to you, as I shall now do ; but I think, I may depend upon your making no ill use of the extraordinary confidence I place in you ; and without it you may want those lights, which are necessary for your conduct and success in your present negotiation.

"You have now one last trial to make, after many, for concluding this great affair of the election, in the most honourable manner for the king, and his allies, and thereby establishing the present system with the House of Austria ; for fancy what they will, if the election now miscarries, there will be so many reproaches on both sides, and such resentment in England, for the ingratitude of the court of Vienna, that that resentment will naturally in a short time produce an alteration of system, and an union with France and Prussia. There is no way now of carrying the election, but by immediately agreeing to the Paper of Points in the form in which I send it to you. The court of Vienna may thank themselves, if the demands of the elector Palatine are now too high, and if they are obliged to agree to them.

"I have often observed to you, that the only motive which induced France to acquiesce in the election, on condition of satisfaction to the elector Palatine, was the notion they had, that we could carry the election without them, and that we were determined to try it. The moment they found that the court of Vienna was the first to declare against that, and to engage the other electors to oppose it also, France had the game in their own hands ; and they knew we could not come at the election without them, and therefore whatever conditions they would insist upon for the elector Palatine, we must either grant them, or have no election. That being the state of the case, I had nothing to do but to make those conditions as easy as possible, and to work upon Wrede, the Palatine minister, by shewing him, and having it dinned in his ears, that whatever France and Prussia might gain, the elector Palatine, his master, would be the sacrifice to their views, and never at any time get one single farthing. This reasoning prevailed upon Wrede to wish the thing, and if he wished the thing, he must be tolerably reasonable in his demands ; and that has produced the present *ultimatum;* not moderate in itself, but, considering the circumstances, not otherwise, and the circumstance in particular, that if we do not now accept them, we shall have no election, and if we have no election, France and Prussia will dictate to all the world, and perhaps have England on their side. The great article of all, and upon which I am almost afraid to write, is that of the 1,200,000 florins, of which we have at present only 500,000.

* Keith Papers.

3 L 2

" You see how I have been obliged to write in my public letter; and you will
make use of all the arguments in that letter, and send me an account of the answers;
but I own I have no notion of bringing the empress up to that, that is, to add 700,000
florins more, and therefore you are directed to go as far as you can. To speak out
to you (and if you betray me I am undone) I have long seen that this election could
never be carried this way, except we contributed towards it, though the king says
positively, that he will not give one farthing to purchase votes for the interest of
other powers. I take it, therefore, for granted, (though you must never own it, or mention it but in your public letters) that something we must give; it is, therefore, your
business to make that something as little as possible, and I will tell you my opinion
freely: 700,000 florins are wanting; the court of Vienna gives 500,000; it will
never be supposed that England should give 200,000 florins more than they, for the
election of their son. If, therefore, you could persuade the emperor to add 300,000
florins more, I believe we should very cheerfully pay the other 400,000 florins.
But in the same confidence, I must tell you, that except they will add at least
200,000 florins; I despair of being able to do any thing; but that is what, I should
hope, you might procure. Endeavour to get the whole 1,200,000 florins; haggle long
for 300,000 florins; and do not send away your courier till you have got 200,000.
You see with what confidence and dependence I act with you. I am undone if it is
ever known; but I thought it necessary that you should have this information. Lay
me at the emperor's feet, with the most grateful acknowledgments of all his goodness
to me. Assure him that M. Toussaint has not his imperial Majesty's interest, and
that of his family, more at heart than I have. Assure him also, as the humble and
faithful opinion of a most devoted servant, that the saving these 2 or 300,000 florins,
may occasion more mischief than his imperial Majesty can foresee. Beg him, nay,
conjure him, to hearken to the advice of those, who have his interest at heart, and
who must know, from the tempers and situation of other powers, some particulars,
better than those who are in his imperial Majesty's own service. But you will not
use any of these arguments, or propose or consent to any diminutions, till you have
fulfilled your orders in my public letter, and till you shall see that it is impossible to
obtain the whole 700,000, which, however, you are to endeavour, and to use all the
arguments suggested in that letter to enforce.

" As to the other articles, I may acquaint you, that as they relate singly to affairs
of the empire, I left them to be settled by the king'sGermanministers. My friend M.
de Munchausen, as you may imagine, has had the chief hand in them; and I hear in
the main, that they are pretty tolerable, at least they are such, as should, and will
be passed, if there is an inclination to conclude.

" I suppose we shall have a counter-project. I would advise that you should get
the emperor's answer, and the empress queen's in the margin, to the several articles,
and not let this paper undergo the malicious and boundless pen of M. Bartenstein,
the greatest enemy which the court of Vienna has now in Europe. *To the article
of money so much to the allies as I hope every thing, and then I will answer for it,

---

* A mistake in the copy.

that this affair shall not only be done, but all former dissensions forgot, and we will set out upon a new foot. *   *   *   *   *

" I own I sent lord Hyndford to Vienna, imagining that an extraordinary commission, carried by one of his lordship's character and quality, would have made more impression than it has done. I am very glad to find, that both the court of Vienna, and you, are satisfied with him. I am persuaded he did his best, and that whatever difficulties you have met with, were not occasioned by your fault, or his lordship's. I could have wished you had sent me more particular accounts of the answers made you, to the arguments suggested in my letters.*   *   *   *

THE LORD CHANCELLOR TO THE DUKE OF NEWCASTLE.*

The regency agree to the proposed payment to the Elector Palatine.

Powis House, Aug. 27, 1752.

After acknowledging the letter of the 12th-23rd instant, and rejoicing in the recovery of the duchess, he proceeds :—" Last night the meeting was had between my Lord President, lord Holdernesse, Mr. Pelham, and myself, on the subject of your Grace's important dispatch. There is no difference of opinion, but every body soon concurred both in your reasoning and conclusion. Your brother was not in spirits, as you will easily believe from the unhappy event † that has lately happened in his family ; but notwithstanding that, it was impossible for any body to take a part of more true concern for the success of this great measure, or of more affection to you than he did. And your Grace will see, by lord Holdernesse's letter, that you have our unanimous opinion, that a sum of money, to the extent mentioned in your letter, should be agreed to, on the part of Great Britain, to be paid after the election shall be completed, with an unanimity of the electors, and the concurrence of France, rather than that the election should fail.

" The detail of the German particulars was not entered into ; and I presume, was not expected. In this, however, I think, we all agreed ; that the court of Vienna will never give their consent to some of them ; and that if they should be adhered to, it will be a clear proof of the insincerity of France, and the Elector Palatine himself will be the dupe of it.   *   *   *   *

MR. PELHAM TO THE DUKE OF NEWCASTLE.‡

Congratulates him on the success of his negotiation—Inquiries concerning the mode of paying the sum demanded by the Elector Palatine.

Greenwich, Aug. 28, 1752.

After some remarks on lord Clinton's death, and on the duchess of Newcastle's health, he continues :—" I will now give you as well as I can, and as shortly as I can, my poor opinion upon your foreign affairs. Lord Holdernesse (and I hope Lord Chancellor) will write more copiously to you than I am able to do at present.

* Newcastle Papers.
† Alluding to the death of his grandson, lord Clinton, who died August 19, 1752.
‡ Newcastle Papers.

" On Wednesday afternoon I went to the meeting at lord Holdernesse's, though I found myself very little fit for such conferences.

"I have read over all your letters, and the several inclosures you sent to lord Holdernesse. Upon the whole, I think you have done greatly and wisely in bringing the parties concerned, to their *ultimatum.* I have always thought France, ever since they saw we were so far engaged, wished to bring this affair to a conclusion as well as ourselves; not in an offensive way, but in a manner that might secure the peace with some little éclat to themselves; and our allies have enabled them to do it with dignity, and with considerable advantages to their immediate friends; more than I believe would have been thought on, if you had been suffered by the court of Vienna to have gone on in your own way. I wonder how you could doubt my coming into this proposal, on account of the money, after we had engaged in two considerable subsidies, which would have been thrown away if this had not been done. All I am concerned about now, is the manner of doing it. I see, if all parties agree, this *projet d' accommodement* is to be turned into a convention. Can the king, as king, be a principal contracting party ? Should he, as in Vergennes's paper, be answerable for the whole 1,200,000 florins ? Would it not be better (if you can bring it about) that the empress queen should pay the first 600,000 ? Or, if she cannot be brought to that, at least her 500,000 ? And we, by a separate act, engage to pay the rest, at the time stated in the ultimatum? You say nothing of Holland. Are they not to be at all concerned in this ? I see some objections to the naming of them, upon the foot your paper now stands. But surely as they have been concerned in every trans-action hitherto, it will seem odd to have them totally omitted in the finishing stroke.

" They cannot afford much, I know; but if they were to make up the first payment, it would be but 100,000 florins, and would certainly accommodate us very much. You will easily judge of my way of thinking, by what I have already said to you.

" The king must, and will have the honour of this measure, in whatever way it is turned. Nobody seems to have thought of it, and nobody has pushed it to maturity but himself. At the same time, ought we not to avoid a precedent of our chusing a king of the Romans, by subsidiary treaties, plainly directed for that purpose only ? You understand those things better than I do; and I doubt not but you will act as is right. All I mean by this is, to remind you of some circumstances, which might escape your reflection in your present situation. I am most heartily rejoiced that this long depending affair is likely to end so well, for the public, considering how far we had gone ; for the king's honour, that he might not be foiled in what he had undertaken with so much spirit and earnestness ; for your own ease, credit, and satisfaction, which, though I think, had it failed, I could have clearly brought you off with glory, yet it must necessarily have fallen upon them, whose cause you have so long and so warmly espoused ; which would have been disagreeable to you, and might in its consequences have been detrimental to the public. I have one farther comfort. I think, now, the basket is shut. We can have no more demands of this sort. And we may, if we please, look internally, and put this country upon such a foot, as may enable us truly to hold the balance in our hands."

THE DUKE OF NEWCASTLE TO MR. PELHAM.*

The king disapproves the additional payment to the Elector Palatine, and even seems no longer to favour the election—Condemns the insincerity of France and Prussia, and the equivocal conduct of the court of Vienna.

"DEAR BROTHER,   Hanover, Sept. 19th, 1752.

"I received last Friday at the Göhrde, the most affectionate, and I think best judged letter that ever was wrote. I shall answer the first part of it in a letter apart, but shall, in this, give you an account of all that has passed, in consequence of the last part, relating to our public affairs. I was too vain, and knew too well the effect it would have, to conceal your thoughts and your own expressions from the king. I therefore sent his Majesty an extract of all that relates to the present great question (except the paragraph relating to that wild man in these things, my lord Granville, which I left out) with lord Holdernesse's letter, and a proper extract also of one from the Chancellor.

"I must now acquaint you that the king had constantly assured his German ministers, even after the courier had arrived, and before his Majesty had seen the letters, that I should find myself mistaken, in thinking that you would be, for this additional expense. His Majesty had often said the same thing to me; but I can assure you, dear brother, that I had not acted as I have done, if I had not thought I knew the contrary.

"I met the king and his court next morning at the hunt. In my life the king was never more gracious to me, than when he saw me on Saturday. He began, 'you knew your brother better than I did.' He shewed all the joy and satisfaction in his face and manner that ever I saw. 'You have great reason to be pleased with him; you see the support you will have.' I made the proper answers, applying them to his Majesty. Lady Yarmouth joined in the conversation; and the king said emphatically: 'I think you agree better at a distance, than when you are together.' To which I answered, 'when we agree in essentials, the rest will always follow.' His Majesty kept his good humour the whole day.

"The hunt continued long, and I saw no more of him; but having had a meeting that night with the Grosvoight and M. Steinberg, to adjust every thing as to the *manner*, according to what you proposed, they afterwards saw the king; and his Majesty remained in the highest spirits;-thought now, the thing would do; asked them their opinion, and seemed as happy, and as well pleased, as it was possible for man to be. I made a sketch of instructions for me here, exactly agreeable to your letter, except the guarantying the payment of the 500,000 florins from the court of Vienna, which, the Grosvoight said, Wrede would insist upon, but which is a very immaterial article in itself; for the court of Vienna, by their last answer, offer to pay that money to the king, to be disposed of as his Majesty should think proper.

"I send you a copy of the sketch of instructions which I had drawn for myself. I must interrupt the thread of this transaction by acquainting you, that as lady Yar-

* Newcastle Papers.

mouth had often spoke to me, to mention to the king the sending for the yachts, before I left the Göhrde to return hither ; I told her, upon going in, to the king, on Sunday, that I intended to do it, and I am apt to believe that she apprised the king of it.

" To my great surprise, when I produced the sketch, his Majesty fell into the strongest declarations, against the making up of the 700,000 florins, that ever I heard ; and seemed quite to have forgot the letters from England, which he was so much pleased with the day before.   I soon found the real reason was, that he had a mind to protract this negotiation, in order to have a pretence for staying longer here, perhaps until near Christmas, and that has been confirmed since by lady Yarmouth. He began by saying, that he would not fling away the money of England so ; or to that purpose ; that *I might be in haste, but that he was not ;* that it was the same thing to him, if the answer came in a fortnight or three weeks ; that *I* would give a million for this object, but that *he* had it not so much at heart.   I shewed him that the article about the money was exactly agreeable to the paragraph in your letter, which I read over to him ; that, as to the object, I believed one of that importance had never been so cheaply purchased.   I observed, that the time expired at the end of the four weeks ; and then he had recourse to M. de St. Contest, who, he said, did not think that time sufficient.   In short, so altered a man was never seen.   Nothing was right.   His steadiness had done wonders ; the emperor might pay the whole, and the Elector Palatine would accept less.   The whole calculated for delay.   So that this object is to be risked, in order to give his Majesty some pretence to do so unpopular a thing as to leave his kingdoms in the month of March, and not to return to them till the month of December, and that just before the choice of a new parliament, and when he sees opposition stirring from every quarter of the kingdom.   This is the whole secret ; this lady Yarmouth has confirmed to me, as I said, and for this will he risk every thing.

" I think, some decent but proper notice should be taken from England, of the earnest wishes and expectations of all his Majesty's true friends, that the king would return early this year, especially on account of the approaching choice of a new par- liament.   As I promised, I touched slightly after all was over, that I supposed his Majesty had no orders about the yachts, which took up some time.   He replied, with a laugh, ' What! three months before hand?   It will be time enough when I come back to Hanover.'

" The situation in which I am now placed is so painful, that nothing but your goodness, and that of the rest of my friends, could make me endure it for a week. I have determined to go on upon the principle of the advice from England ; and, if possible, to conclude this great affair, as soon as the answers come from the respective courts.   After that, his Majesty may finally refuse to give his consent, if he thinks proper ; but I believe he will not do it, when nothing but the miscarriage of the election will be procured by it.

*   *   *   *

" I think I see that France and Prussia want delay, to disappoint entirely this affair ; and our master will help them in it, for the pleasure of shutting himself up here until near Christmas.' I cannot but exult in the conviction that I and you are, and ever shall be, of one mind and one heart in every thing, both public and private.

*   *   *   *   *   *   *

P. S. *Hanover, Sept.* 20, 1752.—Mentions a most mortifying letter received this day from Mr. Keith, from which he finds :—" that we must not expect a satisfactory answer on the material articles relating to the court of Vienna. Mr. Keith gives some faint hopes, that they may be brought to give some more money, which is, however, the less material, as that might have been supplied elsewhere. But he says positively, that the article of *non appellando*, and the equivalent for the fief of Ortenau will never be granted; and if this should be the final result, 1 am afraid there is an end of the whole, unless the money which they may give, over and above their 500,000 florins, may be applied as an equivalent to the elector Palatine for those demands."

THE DUKE OF NEWCASTLE TO MR. PELHAM.*

Is apprehensive that the perverse conduct of the court of Vienna will frustrate the election— Thinks the king will proceed to England in October.—Postscript : Conference with baron Vorster on the pending negotiation.

"DEAR BROTHER,   *Hanover, Sep.* 28th, 1752.

" I am here waiting the arrival of the messenger from Vienna. The delay is very extraordinary, and I am afraid promises no great good when he comes. One thing is plain, that they are determined that this answer shall be final, and that no reply shall be made to it, for they industriously keep it back till the term is expired, which, in common sense, it was, last Tuesday, when the four weeks ended; but treaty interpretation, I understand, makes a month mean that day in the month after, which according to that sense is to-morrow; when, or before which, we shall, I suppose, certainly have this long-expected answer.

" I have, however, not altogether lost my labour; for you will see by the inclosed copy of Wrede's letter, which I received yesterday, that there is the most ample approbation, and confirmation, from the elector Palatine, that we could wish; and M. Wrede's offer to sign the necessary declaration, shews that he thinks himself sure of the consent of Cologne, Prussia, and France, for without that he would not have been so explicit. I find by Vergennes, that the answer is gone from the king of Prussia to France. Vergennes would not tell me what it was; but upon my discovering an inclination to know, he said smilingly, ' *I need not make myself uneasy,*' which, 1 think, was an admission that it was a favourable one, so that (as Vorster himself owns) this great affair depends now singly upon the court of Vienna. But 1 am very sorry to acquaint you with a circumstance, which was unknown to me till within these few day

" Baron Vorster told me yesterday, and our Munchausen some days before, when the last *ultimatum* went, a *pro memoria* was given to Vorster, signed by the Gros-

Newcastle Papers.

voight Munchausen, representing to the emperor and empress, that as his Majesty had, upon the occasion of the election, as well as upon several others, shewed his great regard for the interests of their Imperial Majesties, and as other powers were asking expectatives of fiefs, the king hoped their Imperial Majesties would give his Majesty an expectative of some fief, also ; that at present his Majesty did not know of any, but if the king could find out one, he hoped then their Imperial Majesties would give it him.

" What a handle, dear Brother, has the king given by this to the court of Vienna against himself, not to do the thing, and assign that for a reason ! How the merit of all his Majesty has been doing for public considerations, will be (if this is known) lessened, if not quite taken away ; and what a reproach will it be to us, if it should miscarry, and this handle be given for assigning the cause of it !

" The whole will now depend upon this expectative for the elector Palatine ; and to shew how reasonable it is for the court of Vienna to refuse it, his Majesty puts it in their power to say, ' if we give it the elector Palatine, every body else will expect it.' The king of England, who asks it for the elector Palatine, makes use of that very demand to ask the same for himself. But what I most fear, is, they will refuse the elector Palatine, disappoint by that the election, and give the king distant hopes of doing it for him, and imagine by that to make his Majesty easy with the miscarriage of the election ; and in what condition are we then, for these things always come out at last ! It is a most terrible consideration ; and I own makes me quite uneasy. However, I think it is an honour to me, not to have been trusted with the secret. His Majesty, indeed, often has said, that he should expect something for himself ; and I believe once hinted at some fief ; but I am used so much to that sort of vague discourse upon those subjects, that I did not imagine then, that he would seriously attempt it. I remember, also, that one day the Grosvoight at court told me with great concern, that the king would have something, or ask something. He lamented it, and so did I ; but I never heard one word more of it, or imagined any thing had been done in it, till his brother told me, that upon his return from his *terres*, he found amongst the letters of their office, this *pro memoria*. The poor man was struck, and infinitely concerned.

" I told Vorster, that I knew nothing of it ; which I did, in my own justification, that the court of Vienna should not imagine, that I was a party to such a transaction. Vorster said, he believed his court would do all they could to please the king in it, but that I saw, however, that this demand of the elector Palatine had produced them *two solicitors ;* viz., the king, and the elector Palatine, already. My dear Brother, to commit oneself so to such a court, and to a court that we do not love, and are always railing at ! I conceal nothing from you ; I write you the whole ; I am sure you pity me ; but give me leave to say, that this proves how little they will trust to me any view, which is inconsistent with, or may be interpreted a clog upon the measures of England ; and there again is, and has ever been, my pride. Every body that has been at Hanover has not acted upon the same foot, and the same principles which I have done.* * * *

" We flatter ourselves with the hopes of moving towards England about the 23rd,

24th, or 25th of next month; and we must do so necessarily if his Majesty goes in the beginning, or even towards the middle of November; and if the king avowedly stays longer, I hope he will not be against my returning at that time with the duchess of Newcastle, if, as now must be the case, all the public business is finished here, one way or other, before that time. I see you hint at the possibility of an inclination to have an early session. I suppose that is with a notion that the king may want to come abroad next year, as the following one will be the election year. For my own part, I am persuaded he will not: for, as much as one should imagine by his stay that he likes to come hither, he is got into the track of coming once in two years, so that I am persuaded he would not come two years together, even if there was a fair pretence for it.

P. S. *Hanover, Sep. 29th,* 1752.—* * * * "This evening M. Vorster has been with me, and acquainted me that he had received the answer of his court, though he had orders not to produce it, till the elector Palatine had given his, upon the *ultimatum.* He, however, gave me leave to take down minutes of the answer upon every article, which, I own, is infinitely better than I expected, but very different from what poor Keith thought it would be. There is some satisfaction upon every article, and as little upon that of the money as upon any. But I hope to get the whole 600,000 florins to be paid by the court of Vienna, at the same time, and immediately upon the conclusion of the election; so that nothing will be wanted from you till next Spring twelvemonth. Sure, things have a much better appearance than they had ten days ago! We have, I hope, the full consent of Palatine, Prussia, and Cologne; and I think the court of Vienna comes nearer than I imagined they would. I should rectify a mistake which I was myself under. I always thought that the *pro memoria,* signed by the Grosvoight Munchausen, was given to Vorster, at the same time, and went with the last *ultimatum.* But Vorster has told me this evening, that it was given him, and sent by him eight days after, which alters the case a little; and that yet there is no answer upon it. I cannot help flattering myself, that this very great affair, notwithstanding the almost insurmountable difficulties which we have met with, will at last be brought to a happy conclusion. Perseverance and attention in an object which is so undoubtedly right, will generally prevail; but we must go through many most disagreeable circumstances, as I know by experience, before one can obtain it. The difficulty, in some measure, raises the merit. I am sure it does my obligation to you, without whose warm assistance and concurrence this whole great affair must have miscarried at last. You may be assured that the form of the act, wherein we engage for the money, shall be quite agreeable to your way of thinking, and that of my lord Chancellor."

MR. PELHAM TO THE DUKE OF NEWCASTLE.*

Is of opinion it would be imprudent to break off the negotiation with the elector Palatine—Complains of the countenance likely to be given to the duke of Bedford.

Sept. 29th, 1752.

After acknowledging letters of the 20th and 21st,, and justifying his opinions on the late proceedings, he continues :—" I think, having gone so far, it would be absurd to break the whole affair for the additional expense of six or seven hundred thousand florins, to be paid two and three years hence, for I hope you take it for granted the payment of this year was to be by the court of Vienna alone, or by them and the Dutch. This method of payment is very material to us : nothing then will be demanded *this* year ; and if a king of the Romans is chosen, and all the powers of Europe consent to that choice, for the sake of peace, some savings may and will be made in our current expenses, two years hence, which may more than answer the extraordinary charge of this subsidy.   *   *   *   *   *

" I see your mind is still bent upon this election ; and I do not wonder at it. The court of Vienna are abominable. The lord Chancellor knows I always imagined there would be some stop upon the German points, and that for this reason, that I do verily believe the empress queen would rather not have her son king of the Romans, at present ; or at least she would have it to say, that the king forced her into it, and that she had not given up any of the privileges of the emperor, for the sake of securing the succession to her son.

" I have no reserve with regard to lord Granville. I am resolved to live well with him, which I can easily do, if we have no public meetings ; for he takes care we shall have no private ones. My opinion of him is the same it always was ; he hurries forward all these German affairs, because he thinks he shews his parts, and pleases the king ; in both which I think he is mistaken. But, believe me, he lies by ; he has as much vanity and ambition as he ever had ; and he sees the king's personal inclination to his ministers is as it was ; he hopes, therefore, in all these contradictory circumstances, that something may fall out, and then he is sure to succeed ; in which I believe he is in the right. He told the duke of Rutland, his affair would certainly do ; and he told me with an air of triumph, there was a time when the duke of Rutland was not ill with the king ; he could not tell what had happened since ; to which I gave his lordship a proper reply. I send you these accounts, that you may be *au fait* of every thing ; for, notwithstanding this, when we meet at the Regency council, we laugh, and are as good friends as can be.

"There are various circumstances which cause me to apprehend that the answer from Vienna, the behaviour of the court of Berlin, and the existing influence of that court over the councils of France, will prevent the success of all your endeavours for the public good, and the tranquillity of Europe.

" I cannot conceive what the king means by talking in the manner he does, of his return to England. The common notion here is, that he will come sooner than ordi-

* Newcastle Papers.

nary ; and you will see by my letter of last week, that I had my jealousies he would do so, in order to get the parliament up soon, that he may divert himself, in the same way, next year. I was resolved, therefore, to bring that to a test; which, I think, that letter will do.

· " I cannot conceive what objection the king could have to your draught of instructions, after the fourth article was to be omitted. * * * Delay is all that our enemies wish for; decision is the principal thing I wish for; uncertainty cuts us to pieces ; a negative is one day's battle here; but prolongation is perpetual inquietude.
*   *   *   *

" I wrote something upon his (the duke of Bedford's subject) last week, which I intended the king should see ; and, if I know his Majesty, he is more likely to be struck with facts of that kind, thrown in seemingly without meaning, than by a more serious attack. Something the king must do to convince mankind, that he not only employs his ministers, but that he wishes them success also. If what I have so long laboured falls to the ground, an opposition we shall have in the North, and in some places a successful one. If the duke of Bedford is countenanced, the opposition he has begun in the West, and is pursuing at an immense expense, will succeed also. What will be the consequence then? A parliament will be chosen, where half will wish well to the administration, and the other half be composed of their bitter enemies. I wish you would talk this affair over with lady Yarmouth ; and protest, that I am anxious solely for the king, and the tranquillity of his government." * * * *

THE DUKE OF NEWCASTLE TO MR. PELHAM.*

The king seems pleased with the answer of the court of Vienna—Conversation with his Majesty respecting the election, and the time of his departure for England—Interview with lady Yarmouth.

" DEAR BROTHER,   *Gührde, Oct. 3rd, 1752.*

" I arrived here on Saturday evening, time enough to see the king, that night, and was graciously received. I acquainted him immediately with the substance of the answer of the court of Vienna, upon every particular article ; with which his Majesty seemed very well pleased. He thought that the court of Vienna had gone as far upon the articles that relate to the election, as could be expected ; but still, though in very good humour, harped once or twice upon the money. I told him that Mr. Keith had applied all his endeavours to the point; for, as he thought the other articles desperate, he had singly laboured (as appears by his letter) the affair of the money; that M. Vorster had positively assured me, that they would not give one farthing more ; but that I hoped that the whole 600,000 florins, to be paid by the court of Vienna, would be paid immediately after the election was over, and by that means the first payment be made totally by them.

* Newcastle Papers.

"I told the king, if Vorster desired, I would immediately send for some. His Majesty said, in the same good humour, '.but we must try to get the money.'

"On Sunday, when the king had read over the letter, and the minutes taken of the answer of the court of Vienna, I found him in exceedingly good humour. Not one word of the money; and I carried him the draught of my letter to Wrede, which goes to lord Holdernesse. Wrede is, by the king's order, sent for expressly, *pour mettre la dernière main à ce grand ouvrage;* which implies in the strongest manner, the king's acquiescence in the payment of the other 600,000 florins.

"He afterwards talked with great pleasure upon the prospect of this measure being concluded. He would not flatter himself, until the thing was done. I then represented to him, in how advantageous a light this foreign affair would appear in his speech, if the election were fixed, with the consent of all the electors, and the acquiescence of France. The arrangements in Italy, which had been the other source of war and troubles, ever since the peace of Utrecht, were now essentially settled, by the treaty between the empress Queen, Spain and Sardinia; which treaty was certainly greatly owing to his Majesty's weight and interposition. If satisfaction (as there was a prospect) could be procured for the complaints and losses of our merchants, by Spanish depredators.* This had an effect, and the good humour was very great.

"The king then asked me, when I sent a messenger to England? I told him, on the usual day, which, from hence, is this day. His Majesty then said, 'You may order the yachts to be at Helvoetsluys on the 8th or 9th of November; I intend to set out from Hanover on the 8th or 9th.' I received his orders; said not one word, either to confirm or dispute them. I then mentioned the meeting of parliament. What passed upon that, you have an account of, in a letter which the king has seen. Lady Yarmouth is much displeased that the king stays so long, and is not quite satisfied, I believe, with me upon the subject; for she has flung out, more than once, that I was very happy; I had only to   † an affair of four or five hours; that she saw I was easy. 'What would my brother say? what would they say in England?' I told her I had burned my fingers once, in obedience to her commands, and I could do so no more; that she knew it was by her repeated advice, that I even said the little I did upon the subject. She said, 'I advised you well—you did right;' but yet she is uneasy; which arises, I dare say, from the lateness of the season. You will be surprised to hear, after this, that I do know that she told the grand Marshal I had put the king out of humour, by speaking to him upon this subject: that I would do it; that she advised me against it; but that as I would do it, she said, *do then.*

"This would have surprised me, if it had been the first of the kind; which to my great sorrow, I feel to this hour, that it is not. What a situation is mine! in which nothing can make me go on, but finding you think with me upon these points, and determined that we should act in every thing with the utmost and most cordial friendship, and concert, without reserve; of which the following instance will fully shew you the necessity.

* Some words are wanting to render this sentence intelligible, which were probably omitted by the duke, in the hurry of business.

† Illegible in the draught of the letter from which this copy was taken.

" The incident I mean, is a very extraordinary one. On my return hither, the Grosvoight acquainted me with what the king had said to M. Steinberg and him, relating to the 700,000 florins, supposed to be paid by us. His Majesty was pleased to talk very strongly against it ; and, when M. de Munchausen tenderly (I dare say very tenderly) offered to say one word in support of it, the king told them that it was the opinion of a fool, or a madman ; and this in the presence of M. Steinberg. His Majesty then told them both, that he could not open himself to me upon the subject ; that he would do to them ; ' that his true reason for saving the money to the nation, was in order to get a subsidy of £.40,000 per annum for Russia ; that he would *cajole* and *manage* Mr. Pelham, and that he should get his consent to it.' This you may depend upon, is *fact*. If the *cajolerie* promises the Blue Regiment (of which I have some notion, from a circumstance that I will tell you) I shall be most heartily glad of it, for the sake of the public. The circumstance is, that my lady Yarmouth told me the other day, that she had again made another attempt, and particularly of the advantage it would be of to the new parliament (which, you know, was the chief argument I went upon;) that the king said ' *they always represent those things worse than they are ;*' but that she found it made an impression. Combining that with what his Majesty said to Münchausen and Steinberg, I do think there is a very good chance at present. I shall rejoice most sincerely ; you know I have done my best. If I have not had credit to do it, I have at least furnished others with arguments. I did not take the king's orders for my friend Ligonier, when his Majesty told me that he intended to give it him.

" You will see, my dear brother, by these circumstances, what is the *carte du pays*, both with the King and the Lady. I am persuaded, they will not have the least influence over you. I am persuaded also, that you know as much, perhaps more of the same kind, with regard to me ; how we are and have been both played off at each other, though you have been too prudent to mention it. But I tell you the whole ; being thoroughly sure, that what you think, or may hereafter do, you will not let one soul alive (except Stone and the Chancellor) know what I have written to you ; for not only I am undone, but those from whom I have my intelligence are undone also ; and that would be grievous to think possible. I thought it was necessary that you should know all; for, knowing these things, we may, *if we please*, prevent any ill consequences from them ; and the moment it is seen, that we are in concert and without reserve, all this little low game will fall of itself. His Majesty did very right in not trusting me with his true reason against giving the money for the election. I should certainly have told him, that no expense could be justified, or be practicable, if this was neglected. I conclude also, that the king imagined that I should immediately have acquainted you with it. This is the meaning of what his Majesty said remarkably to me : ' *You may have this thing* (the election) *much at heart ; I have it not so much.*' That is, in other words, I have another object in view. I hope, my dear brother, you see the whole extent of what I wish by this communication ; which is, to convince you of the necessity of our acting without reserve with each other. ' I think I have sufficiently done it, on my part. As to the meeting of parliament, be assured, the king has no other view, but what he told me very naturally. I am afraid,

upon the king's plan of not leaving Hanover till the 8th or 9th, there will hardly be
time for it, to give notice, and to prepare the Speech ; but you may be assured, the
king is very indifferent about it.'   *   *   *   *

MR. PELHAM TO THE DUKE OF NEWCASTLE *

*Hopes that his brother will not leave the king alone at Hanover—Farther remarks on the nego-
tiation with the court of Vienna, and the Elector Palatine—On the conversation of
St. Contest with lord Albemarle—Thinks he shews too strong an attachment to Austria.*

Oct. 5th-16th, 1752.

 *   *   *   * " I wrote the letter of the 22nd for the king's seeing ; and I should have
chose to have left him to his own reasoning.   He must there see, that it is absolutely
necessary for him to determine when he would have the parliament meet ; and that
would, in consequence, have opened to you his intentions, as to the time of his return.
What I had to say to you, either as to foreign or domestic concerns, you will see in
my letter of last Friday ;   and I hope you will not think I have said either too much,
or too little.   I can plainly see, by your correspondence with the Göhrde, that things
have not, of late, gone to your mind at court ; and the politeness of your correspondents may palliate, but not cure.   If no more has happened than what you have
sent to me, I acknowledge it to be unpleasant, but of no great consequence, otherwise
than   .   .   .   ,† which you will see by mine, I am as convinced of, as you can be.

" I hope, by the letters which came in last night, that your affair of the election,
will at last end well.   The exchange of fiefs, I do not understand ; but something is
offered by the court of Vienna, in lieu of Ortenau, which it is plain, by all the papers,
France and the Elector Palatine knew the emperor could not, or would not grant.
The 100,000 florins makes up the first payment complete, which will make our
engaging for the remainder, more easy ; but I hope you will never think of placing
that additional sum to the account of the equivalent for Ortenau.   That will immediately be seen through, and make what we are to pay, more subservient to the
particular convenience of the Imperial Court, than I could wish it.

" You had my whole thoughts on this subject in my last letter ; I will, therefore,
trouble you with no more of them now.   You may depend on my keeping secret what
you mention of the *pro memoria* from Hanover ; it does not at all surprise me, nor that
you were not acquainted with it.   I agree with you, that it is greatly for your honour,
that none of those low personal views are intrusted with you ; and I have this farther
satisfaction, that as they are not, they will never come to any thing.   But I believe,
it was this made his Majesty not so much in haste to finish, as you wished him to
be ; and for aught I know, may be the true key to his ill humour in the Closet.

" What does Wrede mean by saying he waits for an answer from Vienna, and
London ?   How came he to think the court of London has any thing to do with the
ultimatum?   I fear, that same 500,000 florins, which are placed, as certain, to our

* Newcastle Papers.
† Illegible in the draft of the letter from which this copy was taken.

account, by the court of Vienna, has some how or other, gained a credit at the court of Manheim also. I say this only by the bye, and that you may see we put things a little together now and then.

"St. Contest's conversation with lord Albemarle is mended; but there is still a loop-hole, and a reserve. Why is not the friendly communication made to the king of Prussia, and the Elector of Cologne? That is easily done, and words cost nothing; but I fear, if it is not done soon, it will at best be cause of delay. Your secret letter to Keith is very natural, and very just; perhaps I think you shew too much personal regard for a foreign power, and perhaps your attachment too strongly, for a minister of this country. But laying down that foundation, your reasonings are all right; and if I thought great princes were, or should be, made like private men, it might do good; but I fear when they have no gratitude for one another, they will scarce think of that duty for a private man.

"Every one of the lords whom the king intrusts with his private correspondence are in the country, except lord Holdernesse. You have my thoughts, therefore, naked, and without reserve. Lord Holdernesse is very good; but I cannot say I am much edified by conferences with him; and when he writes the result of our opinions, he does it rather in the slight manner that he thinks will be agreeable, than as the serious consideration of persons intrusted by the king; which I dare say you saw, by the letter he wrote upon our last conference. I never saw it till after it was gone, nor I believe Lord Chancellor. As I wrote to you myself, I was not very solicitous about it; but to be sure it went much beyond what either Lord Chancellor, or I said, or thought.

THE LORD CHANCELLOR TO THE DUKE OF NEWCASTLE.*

Regrets the king's ill humour—Is glad that his Grace has communicated to Mr. Pelham the supposed attempt to cajole him—Will abide by Mr. Pelham's decision, as to the time when the parliament should assemble.

"MY DEAR LORD,   *Wimpole, Oct. 10th-21st*, 1752.

"Mr. Brown's diligence sent me the honour of your Grace's letter of the 3rd, last night, together with copies of two to your brother. I perceive by them, that the great point of the election, and all other foreign affairs, remain just in the same situation, as when your Grace wrote last; except that there is a return of better humour, and a better disposition to come into the only means that can bring about the end we wish, than appeared before. I never doubted but this affair would happen; though I find we were all out, in our conjectures about that strange sally; and yet I am not quite sure, whether we have the truth yet; or whether what has been given out about Russia, is not a colour thought of since. But this speculation is immaterial. The *manner* of declaring it, and the plan of *separate cajolerie*, which

* Newcastle Papers.

is avowed by it, are the essential interesting parts. Indeed the last is the essential one; for, as to *the words* made use of, though they are to the last degree shocking, and give me real pain to read them, yet they are only the effects of heat and passion, and certain ill humours, to which I do not care to give the true name, and what, in the like temper, would have been said of any body, that ever was about *him*. They are therefore to be neglected; but at the same time, to be known to as few persons as possible; not *merely* for the sake of the persons who have made the discovery. As to the avowal of *cajoling and managing Mr. P—*, your Grace is certainly right in communicating it to him, in the confidence you have done.* The use you made of it is also right; and I think it will have a good effect.

"Lady Yarmouth's turn does not surprise me. Your Grace knows how I have long thought upon that subject; and there I will leave it. But these are useful documents for the future.

"I congratulate your Grace upon having brought his Majesty to a declaration of the time of his leaving Hanover, though it is a late one, and may be the very worst for the dark nights, in case he keeps up to that time. However, I am very glad that something is settled, and the yachts ordered, which will read well in the papers. I need not mention the real pleasure it gives me, in the prospect of seeing your Grace after so long an absence. As to the parliament's meeting before Christmas, the king's indifference about it shews that he has no thoughts of another journey next year; for, if he had, he would be very pressing. For my own part, I think it danger- ous, and impossible to be ventured upon; both on account of accidents that may *delay* his Majesty's journey, and the undecided state of public affairs. The 8th or 9th of November are the days named for his departure; he commonly takes a few days more. The finishing the great affair may occasion a material delay. Contrary winds may delay the yachts getting to the other side; and the king never sets out, until an express informs him that they are arrived at Helvoet. Contrary winds may detain his Majesty there a fortnight. The like delay has, in fact, happened for a much longer time. Suppose the king at Helvoet, and the day of parliament's meeting near approaching; the pressingness of that circumstance may be an ingredient, in his sailing at a time, when in prudence he ought not. If the parliament, should be summoned to meet before Christmas, and then be put off until after Christmas, and the members come to town, what an ill humour will it create, and what a flame upon the inconveniences and unpopularity of the king's long stay! In such circum- stances, I should not wonder to see a paragraph moved, to be added on that subject to your address, on the first day of the session. And all this when you do not yet know what may be the event of the principal point of public business depending; and your Grace says, at the end of your letter, *that you see France will still do all they can to delay it!* The consequence of this is, that you do not yet know, either the plan of your session, or your speech.

"I have written to Mr. Pelham, at large, upon these topics; but, at the same time, have made him the depositary of my conscience on this point. I have told him my thoughts; but have, at the same time, told him, that I do entirely acquiesce in his

* See the duke of Newcastle's letter to Mr. Pelham, dated Oct. 3rd, 1752.

determination, and that whatever shall be his opinion upon it, I will avow and declare to have been mine.

" As my first seal is on the 23rd, I shall be settled in town before your Grace leaves Hanover, and ready to receive your commands, and to embrace you with joy when you arrive. God grant his Majesty a prosperous journey, and the like to your Grace and my lady duchess "

THE DUKE OF NEWCASTLE TO MR. PELHAM.*

On the conduct of France and Prussia—Dissatisfaction of the King on the subject of the Election.

Hanover Oct. 12th, 1752.

* * * * " I refer you to my letters to lord Holdernesse and lord Albemarle, for an account of the present posture of the great affair. The whole seems to depend on B. Wrede's coming ; and I am sure you will approve my letter, which puts an end to the negotiation, if he does not now come. The conduct of Prussia and France is abominable : they approve the ultimatum, and yet fling in all the difficulties to delay the affair ; and my good friends at Vienna are furnishing them materials every day. A little time, however, must now determine this great affair. If the court of Vienna have obstructed this great object, I am sorry to say we here, in our turn, have not done it less. His Majesty is now uneasy when he hears the Election named ; and will scarcely read a letter, either to lord Albemarle or lord Holdernesse, about it. He values himself upon having long thought it over, and says, *he has his answer for Vergennes ready;* which answer I suppose is, that France is governed by Prussia, and will at last be duped by them. Whether his Majesty thinks my attention to the Election carries me from another favourite object, I know not ; but in worse humour he never was, than this day. He had ordered me, when we were at the Göhrde, to write to you, upon a supposition of the king of Prussia's attacking him here. When I received the *intercepted letters,* without any direction from him, I thought, in all lights, it was proper to inform you of them ; and I accordingly prepared the letter, which goes in Jones's hand. I shewed it to the king ; he did not, or could not disapprove it, but was in worse humour afterwards, than I have seen him ; and that is saying a great deal. He observed upon the paragraph about France ; and, whether he was disappointed in finding nothing about a Russian subsidy, I cannot say, but he was as cross as possible."

THE DUKE OF NEWCASTLE TO THE LORD CHANCELLOR.†

Although France, Prussia, Cologne, and Palatine, have agreed to the ultimatum, thinks the conclusion of the affair of the Election is as distant as ever.

Hanover, Oct. 12th-23rd, 1752.

* * * * " I am infinitely obliged to you, for your most kind letter of the 6th. Our great affair is again at a stand, from a new difficulty, certainly flung in from

* Newcastle Papers. † Ibid.

France. Wrede cannot come, until he has been assured from me, that there is, no essential alteration in the answer of the court of Vienna, from the last ultimatum. I have written him a strong letter, upon this indecent refusal; and have told him, in terms, that if he does not come, the king will think no more of this negotiation, in favour of the elector Palatine. I know, to a demonstration, that this idea comes from France, which verifies what your lordship suspected; though, at the same time, I know, that France, Prussia, Cologne, and Palatine, have all approved and consented to the *ultimatum*, and yet, possibly, we are as far as ever from concluding.

" The humour in the closet is rather worse than at the Göhrde. I cannot conceive the meaning of it. We cannot bear to hear the name of the word *Election*. We have given it over a great while; and *we* have an answer ready for *Vergennes*. In short, nothing can be worse there. It is now late; and I have not time to tell you the particulars."

THE DUKE OF NEWCASTLE TO MR. PELHAM.*

Remarks on the conduct and views of the king of Prussia.

Hanover, Oct. 12th, 1752.

" I did not doubt that you would coincide in my opinion on the offensive behaviour of the king of Prussia, in erecting a court of his own, to overthrow the sentences of our Admiralty Court of Appeal, and in appropriating the money due to the creditors of the Silesia loan, to the payment of such sums as shall be adjudged in this unjust and irregular manner.

" I agree with you, that this step of the Prussian monarch is designed to provoke an answer from us, which may authorise his public opposition to the Election, which he is clandestinely endeavouring to delay, or frustrate.

" And, therefore, I think it desirable, that Michel should not make his declaration; since we should not be under a necessity, as yet, to take any public notice of it; and that we should wait until the Election is over.

" Yorke has sent to lord Holdernesse strange accounts of measures adopted by the king of Prussia, as if a number of troops were to be sent from Halberstadt to Wesel. I conjecture that this procedure is intended to intimidate Holland, and cannot imagine that the king of Prussia will venture to attack the king's German dominions. I have ventured to assure the king, that in such a case, the English nation would not fail to support his Majesty.

" I know for certain, but you must not mention it, that Scheffer has written his brother word (speaking of his last conversation with his Prussian majesty, at Berlin, on his way to Stockholm), that the king of Prussia wanted the Swedes to have the superiority at sea, that is, in the Baltic. *Il veut aussi que la France engage la Porte à faire la guerre, dès aujourdhui, ce qu' il croit fut possible, et même aisé;* but Scheffer adds, *il est timide à l' excès,* and without mathematical demonstration, *il ne veut pas se remuer. Je ne blame pas (dit-il) cette prudence; mais avec un allié aussi indolent que la France, il pourrait bien en être la dupe.* I own, the timidity of the one, and the

* Newcastle Papers.

indolence of the other, are happy circumstances for us. But yet cowards may fight, and indolent men may act ; and therefore these advices deserve serious attention.

" I conclude the king of Prussia's scheme is to engage the Turks to begin. In that, he thinks he runs no risk. If the two empresses are beaten, he carries his point. If not, when his Prussian majesty once sees them seriously engaged with the Turks, he will imagine that to be a favourable opportunity to put in execution his views with regard to Poland, which are generally thought to be, not only to make a king of Poland, but to procure Dantzig and Polish Prussia for himself ; whereby he might become a considerable maritime power in those seas, and would be able to distress and ruin all the commerce of other nations there, and particularly that of the Maritime Powers. And this is a very serious consideration for the Dutch and us. He may be willing to have a considerable army on the frontiers of Holland, in order to intimidate both them and us ; and by that means may hope the better to carry on these designs.

" I think that as Spain is well disposed to the king, and to the preservation of peace, a hint should be given to Mr. Keene of these suspicions. May it not be prudent even to sound France in general, with regard to the Ottoman Porte, and the danger of kindling a war in Europe, from thence. I hope the king will permit me, in my passage through Holland, to talk with the princess royal and the well-intentioned ministers, in confidence, on these supposed designs of the king of Prussia ; always taking proper care of the secret. The two empresses, I conclude, will be on their guard. Our ministers at Constantinople, cannot be too much on the alert, on an occasion which may plunge all Europe in war.

" Mr. Porter's letters do not announce any warlike disposition, at present, in the Ottoman Porte. The king of Prussia's designs seem to be formed on the assurance of a revolution in Turkey, which has not yet happened, and which the Porte does not seem to apprehend.

" The king has told me this day, that he has an answer to his inquiries respecting the king of Prussia's supposed design of marching a body of troops from Halberstadt to Wesel, and finds that there was little or no foundation for that report. There was, indeed, an intention of altering the quarters of a regiment or two, but nothing that could give any alarm ; and even that is laid aside.

P. S.—*Oct. 12th*, 1752.—" I hope you will not suspect any mystery in this letter ; I can assure you there is none ; and except one single paragraph, all written of my own head, and without any hint from any body. I do not expect an answer ; so you need not be under any difficulty on that account. I really thought the advices too material not to say something to you upon them, and to suggest what might be proper to do to prevent them from taking effect.

MR. PELHAM TO THE DUKE OF NEWCASTLE.*

His daughter Grace married to Mr. Watson—Hopes the king will soon leave Hanover—Is afraid that France will delay the election—Opinion of the Regency that the parliament should not meet till after Christmas—Regrets the decline of his brother's influence with lady Yarmouth—Parliamentary Elections.

"DEAR BROTHER,   *Oct. 13th-24th, 1752.*

"I cannot help beginning my letter, with what I dare say will give you great pleasure, as it does me infinite; Grace, being entirely recovered of her late disorder, was married last night. Every thing passed off as well as possible, and the new married couple behaved, respectively, as I could wish. I packed them off this morning, at about 11 o'clock, for Lees Court.† Fanny is gone with them; and on Friday next, lady Katherine and I, design to make them a visit for a few days; but not so as to prevent my attendance at the Regency, and doing every thing necessary for his Majesty's service. The only thing we wanted, was the company of lord and lady Lincoln, which I could not desire of them, as they must necessarily put off their mourning, which would have made them uneasy, though I think they every day grow better, and might, if lord Lincoln pleased, be as well as ever they were in their lives. I am now, you may imagine, in my domestic capacity, as happy as I can be; this match, every day pleases me more and more. Mr. Watson is formed as I could wish him for a son-in-law; and Grace's behaviour, and manifest satisfaction, is just as I would have it. Lady Lincoln's two little boys, promise every thing well; the eldest, excepting his cough, which still remains to some degree upon him, is strong and lively, and the little one as fine a child as ever I saw. The loss we have had of poor lord Clinton was, to be sure, at first very afflicting, and ought to be so; but reasonable people should reflect upon their other blessings; and you know how little I flattered myself with the hopes of that poor child's ever coming to maturity.

"I am glad to hear, by Mr. ——, that the duchess of Newcastle continues in so hopeful a way; I heartily wish you may be able to leave Hanover so soon as you propose; but I fear that will be impossible; it cannot be long first, if the king comes away at the time appointed; and the weather has been, and is so fine here, that you may reasonably expect an agreeable journey, which I most heartily wish you.

"Your letter, which I received late on Monday night, prevented my sleeping; but upon reflection, and considering it over coolly, though very unpleasant, I do not apprehend any real mischief arising from it. I thank you for the ample communication you sent me. I can assure you I am as open to you. If I do not say all you expect, it is because I do not know. I have not seen, or conversed with those of the *first rank*, three times since I saw you; and when I did, nothing of consequence passed; and whatever anecdotes I may have hinted at as curious, they related rather to persons on your side of the water, combined with the public actions of some on this side, than as what originally sprung from people here. I beg of you, do not so often call upon

* Newcastle Papers.   † The seat of Mr. Watson in Kent.

me, to act in concert, and to act as one ; 'I have never done otherwise.' If we differ in opinion, *toto cælo*, we cannot act together, in what we differ; but where that has not been notoriously so, and known by you yourself to be so, before you engaged in them, I do not know an instance, wherein either confidence or concert has been wanting on my part. Many trifling official things I do not talk of, because I do not think they deserve it ; and I suppose that is the same, and I desire it should be so, with you. You may depend on my keeping your secret.

" I sent your letter to Lord Chancellor, who had received a copy of it from you. He therefore, is *au fait* of the whole from yourself. I have once seen Mr. Stone, and talked of it to him, as you permitted me, and as I thought you wished I should. We all agree in the same construction of what you sent us, and I believe they are satisfied, as I hope you are, that I am not easily cajoled. · Where I have yielded, as I have often told you, has been where you were concerned, and where the part I must have taken, if I had not yielded, would have been more dangerous than the thing itself. This is what I think you never can be concerned in; and if you are not, I do not mind my neighbour,* who is undoubtedly at the bottom of these politics. If you remember, he almost told me so, when I asked him a question in the king's anti-chamber, to which he gave me a frank answer, that you did not then approve of his doing.

" You know how far I have gone, and why I have done so ; you know also, that I can go no farther, without any new matter arises to make it necessary ; and how little probable it is, that should arise, you also know. I therefore conclude you are firm ; and if you are so, depend upon it I shall not swerve.

" I am mighty glad to hear your reception, on your return to the Göhrde, was to your satisfaction ; and shall be excessively pleased, if the affair you have had at heart so much, shall be finished according to your expectations. I have more hopes of it than I have entertained of late, though I do not like one paragraph in your letter, wherein you say, ' France, *we see*, will do all they can to delay it.' If that be so, I doubt they have it but too much in their power ; for if France does not approve of the satisfaction offered to the Elector Palatine, in the German affairs, that Elector dares not be contented with the pecuniary ones. I hope, however, the desire of peace, will carry even France to an acquiescence. * * * *

" There is one thing I observe, and am very sorry to observe, that a certain person† and you are not so well together as you were : I have thought so by several expres-sions in your former letters ; but by the last I think it is very plain. There was the best ground we had to stand upon ; if that shakes, I doubt we have no resource. I hope, therefore, I am mistaken ; but if not, I cannot but earnestly recommend to you to make up, as soon and as well as you can. You know I never was for placing quite so much confidence there, as you have done ; but now you have begun, it is necessary to go on. The influence in that quarter grows, and will necessarily and naturally grow every year. Do not let us, therefore, quit the hold, when the party

---

* Lord Granville, who lived next door to Mr. Pelham, in Arlington Street.
† Lady Yarmouth.

becomes strong, which we catched at before it was at its full growth. I do not doubt but you understand where I mean; and that you will, on reflection, approve of what I say. * * * *

" I conclude this will be the last letter of any consequence, that I shall have an opportunity of writing you; and therefore you will excuse the length of it. Elections are now the discourse of all companies. Great pains will be taken by the Whigs to get in as many of their party as they can; but of that when done, I am not much afraid. It will be our own faults if we permit others to give us much trouble." * * * *

MR. PELHAM TO THE DUKE OF NEWCASTLE.*

On the difficulty of gaining the consent of France and Prussia to the election—Dissuades his brother from speculative schemes, on account of the public debt.

Greenwich, Oct. 19th, 1752.

* * * * * " You will see by mine of last Friday, that I did not flatter myself much that things would end well, and soon, upon your great affair, that has been in the hands of France and Prussia for some time. My only hopes were, that France, for the sake of peace and quiet, might be willing to have this affair settled, now that she had procured such advantageous terms for her ally. But if mischief is brewing, to be sure they will not allow Germany to be settled; and of consequence you cannot expect this thing will end well; but if these are false reports, and the effects of turbulent minds only, the affair may still end well. And that you will have seen before my letter comes to your hands.

" The conduct of the king of Prussia is astonishingly bold, almost desperate; and I may say, between ourselves, our conduct, with regard to that power, has been ridiculous. We fret, are angry, but cannot hurt. If any real overt act, or even attempt were visible, the king's friends and servants would act but one part; yet so are some people made, that it is dangerous to trust them with their own security. I hope in God, you will engage in no speculative measures. Believe me, dear brother, you do not act upon equal terms; you are frank and disinterested, your allies are dark and selfish, with such a predominant pride, that no one can act with them safely. If your scheme fails, we have, in my mind, nothing to do, but to look to our interior, be faithful to our engagements, and never enter into measures, that can in the least degree aggrandize our great rival; but if, by friendly communication, and an equal conduct with all parties, we can prevent mischief breaking out, we do greatly. This country increases in wealth, every year; but there is such a load of debt, and such heavy taxes already laid upon the people, that nothing but an absolute necessity can justify our engaging in a new war. And that necessity must be very apparent to enable us to carry it on. I am glad the king approves of Sir Francis Drake.

* Newcastle Papers.

MR. PELHAM TO THE DUKE OF NEWCASTLE.*

On the uncertain state and difficulty of the negotiation.

"DEAR BROTHER,   *Nov. 3rd,* 1752.

" I venture this letter by the messenger, concluding he will contrive it shall come to your hands, though I cannot tell where to direct it. I have very little to trouble you with, excepting my thanks for the favour of yours of the 29th of last month, which I have just now received. I most heartily wish you joy of an end being put to all your troubles, and the disagreeable conferences you have been long plagued with. However, that affair shall end, there is some good in there being an end; for whilst that continues in negotiation, nothing else can be thought of, and jealousies will continue.

" I have read over, as well as I could in so short a time, your several letters and papers. I see the pains you have taken, and am sorry to say, I also see how little they deserve it; for when you have given yourself all this trouble, your *projet conciliatoire* does not, by the remarks, seem to be much relished on either side, particularly not by the court of Vienna. Your discourse with Vorster was just, and perhaps he may himself be well intentioned. I have no doubt of the inclinations of your friend Wrede; but I much doubt his power, as well as that of the imperial minister. Nothing could have pinned down France, and by that the court of Berlin, but a literal and thorough acquiescence in the *ultimatum.* That the imperialists seem to avoid, as much as they can, by which I conclude, as well as by many other things, that I hear and read, that they are not in earnest much for the measure.

" I do not doubt their desire that the king would continue his endeavours and negotiations upon this head, but it is our interest to have an end put to it, one way or another, which I am glad to see you think as well as I; and I must own you have taken the most honourable and proper measures for that purpose. I heartily wish the two months may produce what you expect, but I own my fears. France has it in her own hands, and our grand ally is, as you say, furnishing them with reasons for defeating the views of the king every day.   *   *   *   *

MR. PELHAM TO THE DUKE OF NEWCASTLE.†

Mentions the arrival of the king at St. James's, in good humour.

"DEAR BROTHER,   *Saturday Night, Nov.* 18*th,* 1752.

" I did not design to trouble you with a letter, as lord Holdernesse wrote; but as I have received your kind letter from Calais, and Cleverly told me you hoped to have a line from me, I have just time to thank you, to tell you that your friends are all well, that the king came to St. James's about five o'clock in perfect health, and I think good humour. The first thing he said, was asking me whether you were come. I

* Newcastle Papers.   † Ibid.

told him I expected you every day, that there was some circumstance of the yachts getting out of the harbour, or else you would have been here many days sooner. He looked satisfied, neither made a joke, nor shewed the least displeasure. I will certainly be with you to-morrow night, but cannot be sure of the hour, as I have company dine with me. You will, plainly, see the king alone before I shall; if not, I will punctually obey your commands. I have a great many things to say to you, though as we shall meet so soon, I do not think it necessary to tell you now, nor have I time for it, as the messenger stays. The Princess of Wales was at St. James's, and, with her children, met the king at the bottom of the stairs. I am told every thing appeared well there; the children came into the king's room, where we all were, but not the Duke.* The king seemed well pleased with them, but I fear the divisions in that court will give us more uneasiness than any other public event."

* * * *

MR. PELHAM TO THE DUKE OF NEWCASTLE.†

Entirely agrees with his brother, and hopes he shall seldom differ from him.

"DEAR BROTHER, *Esher, April 27th,* 1753.

"I have read over the letters you sent me this morning, and particularly your draught to Mr. Yorke, which, according to my poor opinion, is right in every particular. The 26th article of the Barrier Treaty clears up the matter in dispute, beyond contradiction. I never doubted lord President's opinion, nor that of the other lords you mention in your letter to me; and I am sorry to see what I said from a natural caution, not absolutely to approve what I did not understand, should still make upon you the impression it does. I can say no more than I have done already, that I am entirely of your opinion in this whole affair, and doubt not but I shall be always so in things of this nature, when I understand them; and, until I do understand a question, it is deceitful and dishonest to say, I do, or do not approve.

"I return by the messenger all your papers, and beg you would make yourself easy; for, as to what concerns me or my opinion, you may do it very safely; I have neither desires nor any other call to differ with you, and I hope and believe I never shall. Sir Edward Deering is just come here; we have won a little, and very little. I thought you would like to give him a dinner at Claremont, and have therefore pressed him to stay all night, which he consents to, and will wait upon you to-morrow, with your humble servant."

MR. PELHAM TO THE DUKE OF NEWCASTLE.‡

Turnpike riots in Yorkshire quelled by the troops.

"DEAR BROTHER, *Scarborough, July 6th,* 1753.

"I conclude you will, some of you, expect that I should send you the best account I can of the very extraordinary riot that has happened in these parts, on account of the

---

* Duke of Cumberland.   † Newcastle Papers.   ‡ Ibid.

turnpikes. I know the government has had some information of them, and orders have been sent to the troops to assist the civil magistrate, as usual. Accordingly, colonel Lauren sent a hundred men of Henley's regiment to Leeds, which I believe he was very prudent in doing, for the numbers have been considerable, and the fellows very resolute. They have been assembled to the number of three-score, and, as some say, five hundred, in a place, terrified the people very much, and threatened the recorder Wilson, and all the active part of the magistracy, with pulling down their houses, and even taking away their lives. Young Lascelles, the member for this town, has behaved very resolutely, and in one place drove these fellows away, at the head of his own tenants and followers only. The troops have killed and wounded a good many at Leeds, which has made them quiet there, but they still assemble in other places. I have endeavoured to persuade the few gentlemen I have seen, to be themselves more active. Lord Irwin, I hear, is hurt. This affair seems to me of such consequence, that I am persuaded nothing can entirely get the better of it, but the first persons in the country taking an active part in defence of the laws ; for if these people see them-selves only overpowered by troops, and not convinced that their behaviour is repug-nant to the sense of the first persons in the country, when the troops are gone, hos-tilities will return.

"This is all I can send from hence. Possibly as gentlemen come in here from the western part of this country, I shall hear more ; thirteen of these rioters are sent to York gaol. I hope it will come to the turn of an able active judge to go this circuit. Lord and lady Lincoln came here on Wednesday night ; and lord Ashburnham with Mr. Offly yesterday. We do not, therefore, want much company amongst ourselves ; but without our recruit the place is very void of company, lord and lady Bath being the chief people here, except lord Roberts. I am told writing much is bad with drinking these waters, which must be my excuse for troubling you no more at present."

MR. PELHAM TO THE DUKE OF NEWCASTLE.*

The alarm for the Jew bill has not reached Yorkshire—Will follow the opinion of his brother and the Chancellor—Is sanguine in his expectations that the future elections will meet with no difficulty—Concerned at the situation of foreign affairs—Sorry that France seems inclined to restore the fortifications of Dunkirk, and that Spain threatens, through Mr. Wall, that she will return to her old system, if England will not depart from her just pretensions.

"*Scarborough, July* 13th, 1753.

* * * * "The alarm of the Jew bill has not reached this country, at least not to any degree. I wrote lord Parker word, that whatever was your opinion, and lord Chancellor's, I should acquiesce in; but my own thoughts were, that bargaining with clamour, was a dangerous expedient, especially in a case where the government had no interest, nor could be supposed to have. I sent Mr. Thernagh word, my opinion

was, for an immediate declaration, as you yourself propose, for fear of accidents. He is of another opinion at present; but when your letter comes to him, I am confident he will do whatever you desire.

"I saw in the public papers, our assizes were appointed for the 25th of August. You may depend on my being in London time enough to attend you there, where I hope we shall meet with no difficulties in any of our elections, at least it does not appear to me at present that we can. When your voluminous packet came, I was so unfortunate as not to find one letter to myself, till the very last, and then I found two, for which I give you my thanks; the principal one concerning election affairs &c., I have already touched upon, the other relating to your foreign affairs, is of too much consequence for me to write much upon, informed only as I am. Lord Holdernesse and I ran the material letters over last night, and I fear the attention to so much reading did me little good; for I had no notion of the consequence that much reading or writing produces, when you drink these waters upon the spot.

"I own myself much concerned to see what I think I do, ruptures, or something like it, almost from every quarter. Your letters are undoubtedly very proper in the present situation, but I am very sorry our situation is such as to make them proper : France attempting to restore Dunkirk, the king of Prussia insulting us in the private rights of his Majesty's subjects, and, what is to me the worst of all, Spain insinuating here to her minister, Mr. Wall, by whose instigation, it is plain, she does it, that they must return to their old ways of acting, if we do not depart from what we cannot depart.

"These, dear Brother, are melancholy symptoms. The march of the Russians may be pleasing, and if we are drove to a war, I agree we have no where else to go; but they cannot march without money, and we cannot do in the course of one ministry double what my lord Marlborough and lord Godolphin did, united, without a rival, and with success every year, and an ally in Holland for nothing, superior to all we can get, if we had never so much money to spare. Notwithstanding what I say, I hope you do not think my opinion is, meanly to submit to insults from any quarter : I can assure you, that is the farthest from my thoughts; and to lay before you the present condition I see this country is in, is certainly right, that you may look beforehand, and not dip yourself faster than the necessity of the case requires.

"I will trouble you no more on this subject; it may possibly displease you, as I know it hurts me; but I mean well, and that must satisfy me. All your friends here are well : we have most of us drank the waters regularly; and lord and lady Lincoln, little Mary and myself, have bathed in the sea. I think it does me much good, but nothing can be certain till we have had the experience of time. If you hear of any thing of moment from abroad, a line from Mr. Jones will be as much as I can desire, and much more convenient to us both; for as I told you before, I am not able to read long letters, and perhaps by the style, and incorrectness of this, you will think, not very fit to write them."

SIR CHARLES HANBURY WILLIAMS TO THE DUKE OF NEWCASTLE.*

Account of the Emperor Francis and the Empress queen—State of the ministry at the court of Vienna—Character of Count Kaunitz, and negotiations with him relative to the Barrier Treaty.

Dresden, July 15th, 1753.

"I had at different times several free conversations with his Imperial Majesty, who seems to me to be more formed for what he was born to, than for what fortune has since thrown in his way. Nature designed him to be duke of Loraine, but never to be emperor : his honours sit awkwardly upon him, and he is visibly uneasy under his dignity. The etiquette of the House of Burgundy is the thing in the world the most contrary to his disposition. He suffers, in all the processions and ceremonies with which that court abounds ; but he is happy when he can get privately out of the palace to walk upon the ramparts with his sister, or some of his ordinary companions, without any other attendance ; and I think also his talents much more suited to private life, than to the high station in which he is placed.

"From all the political discourses I have had with his Imperial Majesty, I am convinced that he means perfectly well. France is as odious to him as Prussia is to the empress queen ; and he seems to have just sentiments of the necessity of preserving the strictest friendship with the king. I endeavoured, by every method I could think of, to find out what share the emperor really had in the management of affairs ; and though I discovered that every thing was communicated, and nothing hid from him, by the empress's express command, and though I am persuaded that her Imperial Majesty would take it extremely ill of any minister who should attempt to keep a secret from the emperor, yet I am equally convinced that the emperor's opinion has not the greatest weight at that court, in affairs of consequence, but that the empress does govern, and govern solely. I have other reasons besides experience for this opinion. In the first place, the superiority of the empress queen's talents over his Imperial Majesty's is very great ; and secondly, her jealousy of her own authority has always been too manifest. To these may be added, the principles which Bartenstein inspired early into her Imperial Majesty, against being governed by any person, which he meant should comprehend her rejecting all counsels and advices, however salutary, except those of her own ministers, over whom he himself was an absolute director. His wicked counsels had but too much success, and to them I impute all the unaccountable proceedings of the court of Vienna with respect to the allies, and the different interests, that their Imperial Majesties have had, and still have, in their own affairs. The empress will be supreme in her vast territories ; the emperor is full as jealous in the management of his duchy of Tuscany. The affairs of the empire which are relative to both, often make disputes. But count Kaunitz makes no secret to declare, that he will use his whole power and credit to put an end to all these jealousies ; and if he cannot do it, nobody can, since he is equally well with both their Imperial Majesties.

* Hanbury Papers.

" To carry the proof farther, of the little weight which I think the emperor has at Vienna, I will appeal to your Grace, whether you yourself are not thoroughly con vinced that his Imperial Majesty has not all along been a well-wisher to, and a zealous promoter of, the election of a king of the Romans ; and yet your Grace has been a melancholy witness of the little good his support did to the cause he espoused. I cannot help owning to your Grace, that since my being at Vienna, I am more dis- satisfied than ever with the negligent manner, to say no worse, in which that court has always treated the affair of the election; because I am convinced, that the Imperial dignity is of more consequence to the House of Austria than even the duchy of Silesia, and that if ever that Crown goes into another family, the grass will soon grow in the streets of Vienna.

" I must do his Imperial Majesty the justice to say, that all his expressions that concerned the king, seemed to me to flow from a heart filled with gratitude for past favours, and very desirous to merit new ones.

" I have already told your Grace, that the emperor loves a private life. There are ten or twelve persons at Vienna whom he admits to his familiarity, and with whom he sups in private every night ; but I am sorry to say his companions are all ill chosen; and do him little honour; they are negligent of his favour, because it does not lead to pro- motion. His ministers, whom he employs in his own affairs, serve him but ill, and hurt his character and honour.   Touissant, who is his treasurer, is known to lend money upon pawns at exorbitant interest; and the people say it is the emperor's money; which lessens his Imperial Majesty.   I repeat again to your Grace, that the emperor's talents are of the middle rate, and I do not find that he has any great application to business. Hunting and play take up a great deal of his time ; and both their Imperial Majesties play much deeper with their subjects than sovereigns ought to do.

" This is all that I could remark of the emperor worthy your Grace's notice. I now come to the empress queen. Her person was made to wear a crown, and her mind to give lustre to it. Her countenance is filled with sense, spirit, and sweetness, and all her motions are accompanied with grace and dignity.   She is a person of superior talents, great application to business, and strong passions, which she does not seem to wish to disguise, and which are very visible in the frequent changes of her countenance. Had her education been suited to her situation, and to the part that was designed her to act upon the theatre of Europe, or had she, at her father's death, fallen into the hands of able and honest ministers, she would have made as great a figure as Elizabeth of England, or Isabel of Castile; but during the life of Charles the Sixth she was carefully kept ignorant of all public affairs, and at his death fell into hands that were unwilling, and perhaps incapable, to enlighten her, and give her those ideas and counsels, which were necessary to extricate her out of that turbulent state of affairs, which she was involved in, immediately after her father's death.

" Bartenstein's counsels, which had already proved so fatal to Charles the Sixth, immediately prevailed at her Imperial Majesty's court; and he began his administra- tion by inspiring jealousies into the empress against all her subjects who are men of parts and abilities. He suggested to her, that they aspired to govern and lead her where they pleased ; and this wrought exactly as he wished, of which I will give your

Grace one proof. When her Imperial Majesty gave the seals of Austria to count Uhlfeld, in preference to his competitor, count Frederick Harrach, she declared that she gave them to the person of inferior parts, because she knew the other intended to govern her, and she would be governed by nobody. This step of her Imperial Majesty, was of the greatest service to Bartenstein ; for Uhlfeld, of whom I shall say more by and by, had none of the qualifications requisite for so high an employment, and willingly put himself into Bartenstein's leading-strings, in which he has been from that day to this. Another method which Bartenstein took to extend his power, was to give the empress an aversion to business ; and this he attempted, by sending her more papers to read than he thought she could peruse, though she was to apply seven or eight hours a day. All that the voluminous Diet of Ratisbon, the Chamber of Wetzlar, the Aulic Council, the Chanceries of Austria, Bohemia, &c. could furnish, were sent at full length to her Imperial Majesty, for her perusal ; no extracts, no abridgments were ever made, to save her eyes and her time. But as the empress's application to business is very great, she read every paper that she received ; which took up so much time, that she had but very little left to consider them, and so, in the end, was always governed by Bartenstein's advice ; the effects of which your Grace has but too many melancholy proofs of.

" It is impossible to have a quicker conception, or to decide more justly than her Imperial Majesty does, upon those affairs that she has duly considered. But her want of having been bred to business, which she daily laments, makes her diffident of herself, and yielding to those who have not the tenth part of her understanding.

" The same snare that Bartenstein had used, to prevent the empress from employing the most able of her subjects in her own affairs, was extended by him to take in, and make her Majesty jealous of the best friends and allies of the House of Austria, particularly England. His constant cry was, that the empress was to be governed by nobody ; a friendly office was construed by him into a command ; and the numberless services which the king has rendered to the House of Austria, were constantly said to be equally for his Majesty's own interest, since the well-being of Great Britain depended entirely upon the power and friendship of the court of Vienna. But, to cover and gild these pernicious counsels, it was remarked by observing people, that whenever Bartenstein had any project to execute, that was sure to be ill taken by the court of London, he was then loudest in his praises of the king, and in his invectives against France and Prussia ; and by such mean arts did he circumvent the empress queen, and mislead her better understanding.

" I cannot help believing, from the conversations which I have had the honour of having with her Imperial Majesty, that when things are laid before her in their true light, when she is fairly informed of her true interests, and when jealousy and prevention are banished out of her councils, she will act another part, and make a greater figure. I am convinced, from what her Imperial Majesty herself said to me, and what I have heard from others, worthy to be believed, that she was thoroughly tired of Bartenstein, long before she dismissed him. She told me, that she hoped my court would have no longer reason to complain of the *mauvaises manières et mauvais papiers de la cour de Vienne,* and that she hoped the change of her ministry, would be agreeable to the king. She also told count Fleming in January last, in talking of the last offers which this court made to that of Manheim, that that affair ought to have been finished six months before; and she told Christiani, the Chancellor of Milan, about the same time, that the papers of Chancery were always very ill drawn, and generally ill received by her best friends. It was also well known, that for four months before count Kaunitz came to Vienna, she expected his arrival with the same impatience, as Harry the Eighth did the return of Cranmer, when he was tired of Wolsey; and from all this I conclude, and I fancy your Grace will conclude with me, that her Imperial Majesty is convinced of her errors, in having so long employed such a minister as Bartenstein, and that for the future, he will have no share in the councils of Vienna. Her Imperial Majesty is generous, and sometimes lavish; but either she is not well informed, or has not a just sense of the miseries of her subjects. Their impositions and taxes are very heavy; so heavy, that I am afraid it would be difficult to raise them in time of war; and the people groaning under their weight, begin to lose the remarkable affection, which they formerly bore to their sovereign. I am also sorry to say, that the spirit of persecution still reigns at Vienna, which is pushed on, and encouraged by the empress queen's confessor; for it is known at Vienna, that in a council held upon the affairs of Protestants, in Upper Austria, the emperor's confessor declared, that he knew of no lawful method for bringing the lost sheep back to the flock, but argument and persuasion. On the other hand, her Imperial Majesty's confessor declared loudly for the legality of violent measures, and compelling them to come in by force; and this advice prevailed. What followed upon it is a very melancholy story.

" The spirit of persecution, which is the great blot in her Imperial Majesty's character, is the work of her confessor, as her false politics were the work of Bartenstein. The latter is disgraced, and I wish the former may follow; for I think, the natural bent of the empress's mind, is to do well; but the diffidence she has of herself, makes her adhere implicitly and obstinately, to the advice of those who have her confidence. After what I have now said, and after I have told your Grace, that her Imperial Majesty is daily showering down riches and favours upon the whole priesthood, you will be surprised to hear, that in general the priests are not her friends. They talk loudly and openly against the government; and the pulpits are filled with persons, who daily instil sedition into the people; and this is done in so barefaced a manner, as would not be tolerated in the most free government in Europe.

" It was not difficult to perceive, in the conversations which I had the honour of having with her Imperial Majesty, that her intentions are to live in the strictest union with the king. But I had the misfortune to differ with her Imperial Majesty about the means of cementing that union. Her jealousy of being governed, broke out very often, and particularly in the whole story of the Maritime Powers having signed the preliminaries at Aix without her. Upon this I took the liberty to talk with great freedom to her Imperial Majesty; I recapitulated in the strongest manner, the many obligations she had to the king, and concluded what I had to say, by telling her Imperial Majesty, that I believed she was the only person, left in Europe, who was not of opinion, that the signing those preliminaries, had been the salvation of the House of Austria.

I also told her Imperial Majesty, that besides all the king had already done for her service, he had been at no time more inclined to continue and improve the strictest union with her Majesty, than at present; that the king desired no superiority, but that he insisted upon equality and reciprocity ; and that I was sorry to tell her Imperial Majesty, that all unprejudiced persons were convinced, that it was owing to some jealousy of this sort, and the want of a due confidence, in the best and most powerful friend of the House of Austria, that the great affair of the election of a king of the Romans, had not been long ago completed ; and that it was a melancholy considera- tion for those who were sincerely attached to the House of Austria, to reflect, that while the king was taking indefatigable pains, and expending great sums for attaining one of the greatest benefits that could accrue to her Imperial family, and to the peace of Europe, the court of Vienna had rather hindered than forwarded the great work. The empress queen was warmed by what I had said, and seemed to take it very ill ; but I could not depart from what I was convinced was true.   Your Grace had ordered me to talk with freedom, and I did so.

" Our conversation was still more animated upon the affair of the Barrier.   I had endeavoured to make myself thoroughly master of that point, by carefully considering all the treaties that had been made upon the subject, and diligently perusing the different papers which Mr. Keith furnished me with, and which had passed between the Maritime Powers, and the House of Austria, relative thereto. As I am convinced, that till that point is settled, the connection between the House of Austria and the Mari- time Powers is but precarious, I was resolved to do my utmost, to persuade her Imperial Majesty, of the necessity of her giving the Maritime Powers satisfaction upon that head, and of the injustice with which they had been treated.   This I did with a decent freedom.   But I am sorry to say, that I found her Imperial Majesty so prejudiced in this affair, that reason had very little share in all she said.   The notion of being the independent sovereign of the Low Countries, is so fixed in her, that it will be difficult to eradicate it... I took the liberty to tell her Majesty, in so many words, that she was far from being the independent sovereign of the Low Countries ; that she was limited by her treaties with the Maritime Powers, which I hoped, for the future, at least, would be no more violated.   This her Imperial Majesty seemed also to take very ill ; and insisted loudly, so loudly, that the people in the next room heard her, that she was the sovereign of the Low Countries, and that it was her duty to protect her sub- jects, who had been too long oppressed by the Barrier Treaty, and deprived of the natural privileges, which all other nations enjoy.

" To this I replied, that the Treaty of the Barrier was still in force, though it had certainly been violated by her Imperial Majesty, with respect both to England and Holland ; to England, by the alteration of the old tariff, to which we have an undoubted right, till a new Treaty of Commerce is made, and a new tariff settled ; to Holland, by the non-payment of the subsidy, to which they are justly intitled, and without which, they will not be able to maintain their twelve thousand men in the Low Countries.

" To this her Imperial Majesty said, that we had not complied with the obligations of the Treaty of Barrier ; that a new Treaty and tariff ought to have been made, a

great while ago ; and that it was high time for her to think of encouraging the trade and manufactures of her subjects in the Netherlands ; that the Barrier towns had been so ill defended in the late war, and were at present in so miserable a condition, that it was very unsafe to trust the defence of the Netherlands to such precarious aid : and that, therefore, she was resolved to keep up so large a body of troops in Flanders, as should prevent France from overrunning that country at pleasure ; and that to enable her to keep up that great body of troops, she could not pretend to continue the full payment of the Dutch subsidy.

" I answered, that I verily believed that if a new Treaty of Commerce and tariff had not been yet made, it was not the fault of the Maritime Powers ; that the past and present propositions of the House of Austria upon that head, were such as neither England nor Holland could or would accept ; and that if we were to sign the preliminaries lately delivered by count Kaunitz to Monsieur Bentinck, the second and third paragraph of the first Article, and the whole second Article, would at once deprive us of rights which we had gained at the price of much blood and treasure, and which we would never part with ; that we had no objection to her Majesty's encouraging the trade and manufactures of her subjects in the Netherlands, provided that in so doing her Majesty did not attack and violate the rights and principles which we had acquired in those countries.

" As to the reproach which her Imperial Majesty was pleased to throw upon the Dutch, for the bad defence of the Barrier Towns in the late war, though I had something to say in answer of that, yet I thought it better not to revive the remembrance of past faults on either side. But I desired her Majesty not to forget, that the Dutch barrier was more immediately the defence of the Maritime Powers, than it was of the House of Austria ; and that it was never intended that the defence of that country was to be trusted wholly to the court of Vienna. I then said, that I was glad that her Majesty had so considerable a number of troops in the Netherlands ; that I could assure her that the twelve thousand Dutch were also there complete ; but that if ever by any accident, or any false measure, the States General should be obliged to withdraw out of that country that body of men, I was fully persuaded that, in less than two years, all Flanders would be in the hands of France ; for I could never forget that Flanders had been conquered and always defended for the House of Austria by the Maritime Powers. After this I took the liberty to tell her Imperial Majesty, that I had observed from her discourse, that the two things she chiefly wished for was, the encouragement of the trade of her Flemish subjects, and the diminution of subsidy which she paid to the Dutch. I then desired her Majesty to reflect upon the methods she took to obtain these two ends, which were, by offering us preliminaries to sign, which it was impossible for us to accept, and which, therefore, prevented us from shewing the good disposition we were in, to assist her Majesty in both those points. And to prove the good intentions of his Majesty toward the Empress in this affair, I explained to her the king's great condescension, in treating at all upon this subject, before the new impositions laid upon the English manufactures in Flanders, in direct contradiction to the Barrier Treaty, were taken off.

" I wish I could tell your Grace, that any thing I said upon this subject had made the least impression upon the empress queen; but I shall have farther occasion to talk upon it when I come to count Kaunitz's character.

"The empress queen desired me to recommend to the king in the strongest manner, the fixing Russia more firmly, and rendering that empire more useful to the common cause, by giving an immediate subsidy to the Czarina. In answer to which I replied, that I would do so, but that, in my opinion, any measure to be taken for the security of the peace of Europe, and the good cause, would prove all useless and unnecessary, till the affair of the Barrier was finished, to the satisfaction of the Maritime Powers.

"I again repeat to your Grace, that I think the empress queen a person of superior talents, and of strong passions, born to govern, but wishing to extend that government over her allies as well as her own subjects. The new footing the Austrian troops are upon, and the new regulations made in their finances, have swelled the ideas of her Imperial Majesty, and of that court, about their own power, to a higher degree than they ever were before, which I will prove to your Grace, by one thing which the Empress said to me; and which count Kaunitz, and a person who has his confidence, repeated to me. After talking of the low state of our army, as well as that of the Dutch, they all three told me that the preservation of the tranquillity of Europe, from the time of the Peace of Aix to this day, was entirely owing to the hundred and fourscore thousand men, which her Imperial Majesty had on foot, and of which she had not reduced any since the late war. Your Grace may be sure, that I took the liberty to combat this fatal opinion; and I imagine, in my discourse upon it, I proved very plainly, that it was more owing to their allies than themselves, that Europe had remained in peace for this last five years; and to this I added (because I thought it was necessary to say something of the sort), that if their army did actually consist of a hundred and fourscore thousand men, I did readily agree that, so far from having reduced their troops, they had greatly augmented them since the last war.

"I believe your Grace will now be of opinion, that I might have made my court at Vienna in a better manner; but my chief object there was a due execution of your Grace's orders; and, if I have his Majesty's approbation, I am very indifferent about every thing else.

"I now come to the Austrian ministry, such as I found it when I arrived at Vienna. Count Kaunitz was then absent, and the cabinet council consisted of count Uhlfeld, count Colloredo, count Kevenhüller, and Feld marshal Bathiani; and under, or rather above, them all, Bartenstein.

"Count Uhlfeld was then chancellor of state and of court. For many years he enjoyed the appearance of being minister for foreign affairs; and the weakness of his administration, of which your Grace has had too many melancholy proofs, must give you a just idea of his capacity. His abilities are as confined, and his way of thinking as narrow, as those of any man I ever talked to. He has neither the manners nor the fashion of a gentleman. His behaviour to, and reception of those who had to do with him, was cold and disgusting, so that it was painful to transact business with him. I think I had four conversations with him while I was at Vienna; and the only time I saw him in good humour was, when he acquainted me that the answer

3 P 2

was come from the court of Manheim, and that it was such a one that it was
impossible for their Imperial Majesties to accept. I own I was so shocked at his
manner of telling me, that I could not help asking whether he thought that was a
piece of news to be glad of.

" The empress queen put him in that post by the persuasion of Bartenstein; and
Bartenstein's reason for giving that advice, was such a one, as would have induced an
honest man to have opposed his promotion. Want of abilities was count Uhlfeld's
chief recommendation, and his known insufficiency raised him to that high post ; and
the placing him there was, as it is afterwards proved, very detrimental to her Imperial
Majesty's interest, yet it was very favourable to those of Monsieur Bartenstein.
Uhlfeld had neither knowledge in business, nor parts, or application, to acquire it,
for he was as indolent as he was slow, and these qualifications made Bartenstein
what he wanted to be, absolutely necessary to that chancellor ; and he used his power
in a most arbitrary manner, not only over Uhlfeld, but over the whole cabinet, of
which I shall give your Grace some instances. Bartenstein was *referendaire* of the
cabinet, and no more. His business was, to take minutes of what passed at the
conferences, and, in consequence of them, to draw up the necessary protocols, letters,
and other papers. Instead of which, he often neglected all that had been resolved
in the council, and drew up his papers, according to his own sentiments, which
papers were often issued, without ever having been revised, or even seen by the
ministers.

" This behaviour of his was very notorious in the letters which were sent to the
Austrian ministers in foreign courts ; for I am well informed, that when those
ministers have in their dispatches, quoted and repeated passages out of Monsieur
Bartenstein's letters to them, some of the ministers of the Conference have declared,
that they were entirely ignorant of such orders having been sent, and that they
should never have advised the writing such letters. Upon my asking baron
Wasner whether this information was true, he assured me, that to his knowledge it
was ; that it had been his own case; that Monsieur Bartenstein had been extremely
angry with him for so doing, while he was in England, and in his private letters to
him, had forbid him, in his dispatches, to quote any passage out of his letters.

" But in all these proceedings, Uhlfeld always supported Bartenstein ; in return
for which Bartenstein did him perpetual good offices with the empress queen ; and
his chief argument in Uhlfeld's favour was, that he was a minister that never
pretended to govern her Imperial Majesty, but always submitted his sentiments to
her superior lights. And thus, while he persuaded the empress queen that she
governed her minister, and that her minister did not govern her, his own pernicious
counsels had an absolute influence over them both.

" The seals are at length taken out of Uhlfeld's hands, to his great mortification ;
and he is very uneasy at being placed in an office much higher than either his abilities
or services ought ever to have made him aspire at, or hope for. He is now *Grand
Maitre*, which gives him the first rank in Vienna. He has forty-five thousand florins
a year for his salary ; and, as he is obliged to quit the Chancery, her Imperial Majesty
has made him a present of a large house, which she has purchased for him in Vienna.

Besides all this, she actually pays his debts for him, for the second time ; and his present debts amount to one hundred and sixty thousand florins. He is also continued a member of the cabinet council, which I am sorry for ; because I fear through him Bartenstein will continue to be informed of all that passes there, and will very probably inspire into Uhlfeld his pernicious sentiments, which he will adopt, and make use of in the conference. Uhlfeld is far from being rich of himself, but he loves expense ; and under the figure of as awkward a ploughman as ever you saw, he is as vain as any man. He loves deep play, but he plays ill, and loses large sums of money every year. He has the character at Vienna, of being an honest man ; but his disagreeable behaviour hinders it from being believed.

" It is certain that to all appearance, he has never been a friend to the project for electing the eldest archduke, king of the Romans. I have heard, while I was at Vienna, that it was Bartenstein's intention never to have that election take place, till the king's designs for effectuating it had proved abortive, and then to produce a new plan of his own, which his vanity made him believe would bring it about. But in my opinion, any Austrian minister, that did not contribute every thing in his power towards the success of that great event, must be a very weak man, or something worse.

Having now done with count Uhlfeld, I proceed to count Colloredo, who is a person in a very right way of thinking, and of many good, great, and amiable qualities ; and had he a capacity or application answerable to them, England could not wish to see a better minister at the head of the Austrian affairs. He never had the good fortune to be in M. Bartenstein's favour, and of consequence had but little share of that of her Imperial Majesty. His being properly the emperor's minister, gave room for jealousy to work against him ; and some few amours in which he has been engaged, offended the empress's religion, and added to her dislike of his person ; but the wise and steady part which he has acted for this last twelvemonth, particularly in the affair of the election of a king of the Romans, has very much raised his character, and gained him the esteem of all the well-intentioned party in his court. During count Uhlfeld's absence last summer from Vienna, at the baths of Carlsbad, he lived in a perpetual war with Bartenstein ; and though in their disputes at that time, count Colloredo had not the wished-for success, yet the empress being since convinced, that the measures she then pursued were wrong ones, she must also be convinced that count Colloredo's advice was that which she ought to have followed ; and this has placed him higher in her Imperial Majesty's esteem, than ever he was before. To this I may add, that he is at present closely connected with count Kaunitz ; and if that union continues, as I heartily wish it may, it is not likely that his credit at that court should lessen, as there is nobody there upon a foot to oppose those two ministers.

" I am sorry to say, that count Colloredo loves play, at which he spends a great deal of time, and at which he loses a great deal of money. He is much beloved at Vienna ; for the gentleness of his manners, and his generous heart, have procured him many friends. I could not help observing, that in the many long conversations I had with him, whenever we differed upon any point, he seemed rather pleased to be convinced, and embraced with pleasure any argument, that he thought might be of use, for the carrying on the good harmony between our two courts, and for the benefit of the common cause.

" Count Kevenhüller is great Chamberlain and minister of the conference; he has the character of being a very honest man, and meaning well. He was for a long time a worshipper of Bartenstein; but of late, he has, through conviction, thrown off that yoke, and he now sees Bartenstein in his true light. Count Kevenhüller has no great capacity, and is very diffident of his own judgment. Mr. Keith tells me, he is perfectly well-intentioned to the good cause.

" Feldmarshal Bathiani is also of the conference. He is a most amiable man, but certainly no very great minister.

" These were the persons, who at my arrival at Vienna (count Kaunitz being then absent) composed the cabinet council. But I have already said, that this council was subordinate to the superior credit of Bartenstein, of whom I will here say something ; though not much, because your Grace, during your long administration, has already heard and known too much of him.

" He is the most insolent and presumptuous of all men, fancying that his talents and knowledge, are superior to those of other people. He is either a madman, or pretends to be so ; his manners, and his way of talking, are very surprising to a stranger. They are certainly affected, with design ; and while he was in power, those who had to do with him, were obliged to hearken to all the nonsense he talked, for as long a time as he pleased, or they were sure their affairs would go ill ; and this stuff he talked so fast, that ministers have been with him four or five times running, before they could find the moment to mention the business they came upon ; and whenever the affair was disagreeable to him, he either entrenched himself in his usual nonsense, or declared to them, in a brutal manner, that he was no minister, and therefore was not obliged to make them any answer, though at the same time all Vienna knew that there was no answer given, to any affair, that he did not dictate. He flattered himself, even after the arrival of count Kaunitz, that he should not be turned out ; and thought to intimidate that minister, by throwing out, very publicly, that if there was to be any change in the management of affairs at Vienna, he would continue to serve up the papers as usual ; but that, if any minister pretended to make alterations in any of his performances, they must change the whole, for he would neither make, nor suffer any corrections in what he had once finished.

" But upon count Kaunitz's arrival, he began to shew some fear, which was perceived by his coming regularly for the three first days, to make his court to that minister, without being once able to gain admittance ; and at last he left a card, upon which was wrote, ' M. Bartenstein has been three days following, to pay his respects to count Kaunitz.' But neither his threats, nor his civilities had any effect, and count Kaunitz not only got him removed from his employment, but has already put the office for foreign affairs upon a new footing, in imitation of those of England and France ; and all his *commis* and clerks are persons of his own, very little known at Vienna.

" I believe it is pretty sure, that count Kaunitz will also take four young men of the first quality (besides his *commis* and clerks) to work under him in his office, whose names are Kannegieser, Wirna, Zintzendorff, and Meric ; but what titles they will have I do not yet know. It is certain, that at my departure from Vienna, Bartenstein was totally excluded from any public share in foreign affairs ; and it *it* as certain, that while count Kaunitz has credit, he will have none.

" I now come at last to the person, who certainly is the first in credit at Vienna, and equally in the good graces of the emperor and the empress ; I mean count Kaunitz, of whom all the good I have heard is true, and all the bad I heard is false. His person has nothing left of the fop. He has been cured of that distemper in France ; and he seems to be a person very easy to live with. I studied him to the utmost of my power ; and you may be sure, my lord, that his natural abilities are of the first rate, and that they are extremely cultivated. He studied well, and with great application in his youth ; and since that time, he has been constantly employed in different affairs. He speaks well, and with great precision ; so well, that I suspect he loves to hear himself talk. His phrases are a little too much chosen and studied ; but the multiplicity of business in which he is actually engaged, will soon cure him of this defect. Every body says, that he is an honest man, and that he has the interest of his sovereign at heart. He wishes to see the House of Austria make that figure it ought to do ; and in most things he has just and noble notions, and views, for obtaining that great end.

" He has another advantage, which nobody but himself can have, which is, that the empress queen is not afraid of his talents. She looks upon him as a person trained up to business, under her own eyes and directions, and she reckons that she herself has formed him for affairs, and therefore has no jealousy of the work of her own hands, nor suspicion that her own creature will ever think of governing her.

" On the other hand, count Kaunitz declares that he serves from principle and attachment, and not from avarice or ambition ; that at present he has the happiness and honour of being equally possessed of both their Imperial Majesties' favour, and while that continues, he will serve them with diligence and fidelity ; but the moment he perceives that his credit diminishes, or his favour is declining, he will ask for his dismission, and retire to Rietberg.

" Upon most of the points on which I had orders from your Grace to talk to that minister, I found him filled with as just, and great notions of the affairs of Europe, as any man I ever talked to. He is now convinced (though he was not so when he went to Paris) that the House of Austria had neither friendship nor service to expect from the court of Versailles ; and that her Imperial Majesty ought, in good policy, to be ever upon her guard against the ambitious designs of that crown ; and consequently, how necessary it is for her Imperial Majesty, to tie the knot of friendship still closer, with her antient and natural allies. But this same person, who had talked to me so reasonably, and so wisely, upon all other affairs, when we came to negotiate about the Barrier, talked, in my opinion, as weakly and unjustifiably, as possible.

" I had too much truth and reason on my side, to be in the least afraid of the superiority of his talents. He once or twice began to grow warm, and then I discovered his desire to overbear, where he could not convince. He put on a superiority, which I took care by my answer to bring down to an equality. I also discovered, that for want of a better answer, he sometimes asserted more than he could prove; for he once told me, in the heat of his discourse, that he was surprised to find me insist so strenuously upon the existence of the old tariff, since that point had been already given up by the English ministry, in memorials which had been delivered to the court of Vienna, in the year 1750 : to which I could not help replying, that if that was the case, I should be obliged to confess that I had been ill instructed, and that I had no more to say; but I owned to him, that I doubted very much of the truth of what he asserted; so much, that I would put the whole upon that single point, because I was positive, from the knowledge I had of your Grace's way of thinking and acting, that no such paper had ever issued from your office; and then, turning to Mr. Keith, who was present, I asked him whether he had delivered in any such memorial to that court, and he replied, he had not. * * * *

"I have been endeavouring to reconcile to myself how count Kaunitz, who, upon all other points was so reasonable, and shewed such just and great notions, should be so unreasonable, and, if I may say it, so different a person, in the affair of the Barrier; and I will take the liberty to lay before your Grace what has occurred to me upon the subject.

"I have been told from good hands, that when count Kaunitz was employed in Flanders, under the late archduchess, he had at that time begun to form plans of his own, for extending the commerce, and raising the revenues of that country; and the marquis de Botta, ever since he has been at Brussels, has been working the same plan, with this additional idea of his own, that Flanders was to be defended by an Austrian army; always considering the empress queen as independent sovereign of the Low Countries, and entirely forgetting the Barrier treaty, and the interests, rights, and privileges of those, who conquered and gave the Low Countries to the House of Austria. Any plan for the extension of their trade is very agreeable to the Flemings; and any proposals for the extension of their power and greatness, and the augmentation of their revenues is always well received at Vienna. All, therefore, that Monsieur Botta wrote to the empress queen, upon this subject, was very pleasing to her Imperial Majesty, and the more so, as she found that his schemes were highly approved, and strongly supported, by all her Flemish subjects, and all her ministers at Vienna; and they have made such an impression upon her Imperial Majesty as will not easily be effaced.

"When count Kaunitz was sent from Paris to Brussels, in order, as we hoped, to put a finishing hand to the affair of the Barrier, it is natural to believe (nay it must be the case), that he took all his informations from the marquis de Botta, and those who were employed by him. Of this I have no doubt; because it was easy to perceive, through his whole discourse, that he had adopted all Botta's system; for he talks as wildly about stopping the arms of France in Flanders with twenty-five thousand Austrians, and of her Imperial Majesty's right to encourage the trade of her Flemish subjects, as far as she thinks proper, as Botta himself can do.

"I must here lay before your Grace one of his arguments for insisting that the present tariff had no longer any existence. He says, that by the treaty of 1715, it was agreed that a new treaty of commerce and tariff should be made as soon as possible ; and by the Dutch accession to the treaty of Vienna of 1732 it was farther agreed, that the said treaty and tariff should be made in two years, or, if it could be, sooner. The conclusion that he drew from this was, that it was entirely the fault of the English and Dutch, that such a treaty and tariff had not been made, and that, therefore, the court of Vienna ought to look upon the old treaty and tariff as expired in the year 1734.

" I will not tire your Grace with repeating what I said in answer to this. I will only tell you the conclusion of my answer, which was, if one might judge of the past by the present, it was natural to believe that the propositions of the court of Vienna were much the same then as they were now ; and that such propositions would at no time be accepted by the court of London, till there was a king and a minister in that kingdom, who had no longer the rights and privileges of the British nation at heart, which was far from being the case at present.

" I was surprised at an argument that count Kaunitz made use of, and which he said ought to persuade the Maritime Powers to agree to his preliminaries as soon as possible ; viz., that as soon as ever we had signed those preliminaries, the court of Vienna would begin the payment of the Dutch subsidy, which, by those very preliminaries is reduced to four hundred thousand florins per annum, and which he says the court of Vienna will otherwise not begin to pay, till after the treaty of commerce and the new tariff are settled, which it is said will take up at least six months to regulate. Your Grace sees by this argument, that M. Kaunitz would persuade the Maritime Powers to sign his preliminaries, and consequently leave themselves at the mercy of the court of Vienna for a new treaty, for the sum of two hundred thousand Dutch florins, to be paid to one of those powers.

" The last time I had the honour to see that minister, after I had recommended to him, in the strongest terms, and in the most pathetic manner, the finishing the affair of the Barrier, as the basis of our alliances and friendship with the court of Vienna, I told him, that I believed that no minister had ever entered into his office with the advantages which he was possessed of. The equal confidence which both their Imperial Majesties placed in him was what his predecessors had never enjoyed. To this I added, the high esteem, which the best friends and allies of the House of Austria had conceived for him ; the hopes which they promise themselves from his administration; and the trust they were resolved to repose in him. I also took the liberty to lay before him, a short sketch of the critical period in which he was advanced to his high post, and all the advantages which I thought an able minister might draw from such circumstances. I then added, that the first impressions that were given and taken of a new minister, were always strong ones ; and that, therefore, if he was really of the opinion which he had so often declared himself to be, that it was the true interest of his court to tie the knot of friendship still closer, with its antient and natural allies, I hoped he would begin the administration with giving the Maritime Powers satisfaction with respect to the Barrier, which was the point upon which that union must stand or fall ; of the truth of which I hoped he would be speedily convinced ; for a very small hesitation might, in my opinion, rather unloose than strengthen that cement, dishearten the allies of the House of Austria, lessen the ideas they had formed to themselves of his merit, and cast a damp upon the hopes they had conceived of his administration.

*   *   *   *   *   *

" I remember once, when he seemed a little yielding and attentive to my discourse, I took the liberty to ask him the following question :—Whether his intentions in the present negotiation upon the Barrier Treaty were not, to obtain some new advantages for the trade of her Imperial Majesty's Flemish subjects, and some abatement in the quantum of the subsidy due to the States General?—He told me those were his intentions. To which I replied, that I could assure him, that the king was well inclined to give her Imperial Majesty his assistance in both those points, and would do so, if not prevented by the court of Vienna itself. Here count Kaunitz desired me to explain myself, which I did ; that by his paper, England and Holland would be obliged to give up all their rights, before they came to treat about them, and consequently would be left to the mercy of the court of Vienna, with respect to their commerce, for such a treaty and such a tariff, as that court should be pleased to give them. All I shall say to your Grace about count Kaunitz's answer to this is, that it neither contradicted nor agreed to what I had said.

" I must not here forget to acquaint your Grace, that count Kaunitz insinuated to me more than once, that the affairs of the Barrier should be concluded at Vienna, and not at Brussels ; and I am apt to believe that he is in earnest in this, from the choice they have made in the minister the court of Vienna is sending to Brussels, of whom, I own to your Grace, I have but a very indifferent opinion, and whom count Kaunitz owned to me they sent, because it was very difficult to find any other person who would accept of that post.

" I took care at different times to let count Kaunitz know, that it was the king's sincere intention to live with the empress queen in the strictest union and friendship, but that the union and friendship must be founded upon equality and reciprocity ; that the affectation of superiority would not be borne, but would continue to produce bad effects, as it had done some time past, of which there was no necessity for mentioning some fresh instances.

" Upon the whole I think count Kaunitz a great and able minister, and I could wish that in conferences he did not affect that superiority which has at all times been too much the fault of the Austrian ministers, and which has disgusted many of their friends, and exasperated all their enemies.

" I have now, my lord, finished what I have to say at present about count Kaunitz, and beg your pardon for having been so tedious in my account of him, though I assure you that I made it as short as I possibly could."* . *   *   *   *

THE DUKE OF NEWCASTLE TO MR. PELHAM.*

The Marchioness of Pompadour restored to favour, aided by Machault, the Keeper of the Seals—Baffles the efforts of d'Argenson and the war party in the French cabinet, to provoke a rupture with England—On the attempts of the French to restore the fortifications of the harbour of Dunkirk—On the disputes with the king of Prussia for stopping the payment of the interest on he Silesian loan—On the abusive paragraph in "The Protester"—Public indignation against the Jew bill—Policy of repealing it.

Newcastle House, July 17th, 1753.

" I received late on Sunday night at Claremont, your letter by Blackmore, and I am extremely glad to find that you and your family are in so regular a course of drinking the waters and bathing; and I hope and believe you will find all the benefit that is proposed by it. I would by no means be the cause of your doing any thing that might prevent or interrupt the effect of either, and therefore I shall endeavour to inform you as shortly as I can, of the material events here; and I shall be glad to know, in as short a way as possible, and by lord Ashburnham's, or any hand you like, your opinion, where necessary, upon them.

" I have had an answer from lord Albemarle, that the court being gone to Compiegne, he could not execute his orders until his arrival there. But in a *private* letter he tells me, ' that he hopes for a change in *measures there:* Madame de Pompadour being fully restored to favour, having dismissed the little Irish girl, and obtained many favours for her dependants, having got the king to dine at Machault's† house, a favourable turn, seeming, by her influence, to be given to the affair of the parliament.'

" And lord Albemarle adds, ' that since she has been able to do these things, he makes no doubt of her carrying her views farther, and of pursuing, with the advice of the *Garde des Sceaux*, the pacific steps she has always made the rule of her past conduct, for peace keeps the king her master pinned to her petticoats; it gives time to her favourite minister to follow his schemes of economy; and it overturns those of her enemy D'Argenson, who can pilfer more *impunément* in time of war, than in that of tranquillity.

" Thus far is well; and it is upon this principle that I have ever thought the only way to preserve peace was to shew France (that is, madame de Pompadour and her favourite Machault), that if they suffered D'Argenson or the king of Prussia to insult us, by restoring the harbour of Dunkirk, or refusing proper and reasonable satisfaction upon our disputes with Prussia, they would be exposed to a general war, which was what their private interest made them the most anxious to prevent. Michel has alarmed that worthy man, M. de Mirepoix, that these disputes will not be made up, upon our present proposal; viz., the taking off the *arrêt* and determining the points in dispute by appeal. Upon that I talked to Mirepoix, in the manner you will see, by the inclosed copy of my letter to lord Albemarle. Sir Piercy Brett has been at Dunkirk; has made a most exact plan of the new works; and has informed me so fully of the certain effects of them, that I wrote in concert with Sir Piercy Brett and Sir Thomas Robinson (the man of all England the best informed of these things) the inclosed letter to lord Albemarle upon it. We now wait for answers upon both these

* Newcastle Papers.   † Machault, *Garde des Sceaux*, or Keeper of the Seals.

3 Q 2

heads. I much fear we shall not have satisfactory ones upon either; it is then to be considered what is farther to be done.

" I acquainted the king, in general, with my having had a letter from you upon public business, and only in general with the contents of it, with which his Majesty was very well pleased. The king was for some days extremely uneasy with me, for having let the Prussian ship go by (the only way, his Majesty often said, of doing anything for the support of the honour, &c.), and that he should be told that his regard to his German dominions was the occasion of it, when I knew the contrary. Of late we are a little easier, and very properly are turning our thoughts now to what is next to be done. Sending away Michel, prohibiting commerce with Prussia, &c., have been mentioned by the king. These are all future considerations, but I dare say we shall all be of opinion that something must be done.

" I am more puzzled about Dunkirk. I take it for granted that France will give an evasive answer, and go on with their works; and then will be the great question. I send you " The Protester" of last Saturday, where you will find that they have already begun upon this point. The infamous personal abuse upon me, for serving under all administrations, I really despise. I am sure I never did, nor ever will, serve under his Grace of Bedford's administration. But the paper is serious Jacobitism; a comparison in favour of the Tory ministry in queen Anne's time, against the Whig ministers at all times; a most severe reflection upon the king and his family; and a most strong attack and censure of Sir Robert Walpole and his administration. How this will serve the views of the duke of Bedford and his great friends I do not see. I am sorry, however, that they have got this Pen, for we shall be thus entertained every week. I intend to take an opportunity of talking to the king upon it.   *   *   *   *

" I dread the Yorkshire election more than any thing, there will be such an animosity among the most considerable Whigs in this kingdom, which will extend itself farther, I am afraid. I hear also, the Jew bill is more extensive than you seem to imagine; they will call it an act of the administration; but the worst of all is, that the country is ready to receive a disadvantageous impression. It was the case formerly of the Quarantine bill, which, as the lord Chancellor says, was repealed; and that may become necessary in this case also. There is a messenger from Spain. Keene seems in high spirits and fully satisfied; but still nothing is done about depredations. Keene answers for Carvajal; but he is not the man in this business."   *   *   *   *

MR. PELHAM TO THE DUKE OF NEWCASTLE.*

Is glad that Madame Pompadour has excluded her rival—Does not think that France in pacific hands will support the unjust demands of the king of Prussia—Is more afraid about Dunkirk; but thinks that we must speak firmly and strongly on that subject— Should the Jew bill give real uneasiness to tender consciences, it may be repealed.

"DEAR BROTHER,   *Scarborough, July 20th, 1753.*

" I am much obliged to you for your letter, with the several inclosures, which I received this morning. I am glad to find the marchioness has got the better of her

* Newcastle Papers.

rival, and of the intrigues of her enemies. I should hope, good would come of that. I cannot think France, in pacific hands, will finally support the king of Prussia in his unjust and unreasonable conduct. I am more afraid of Dunkirk; but there we must undoubtedly speak strong, and act firmly, which your instructions to lord Albemarle shew to be your own opinion. If the Dutch minister puts in his word, it will be very well; but I conclude you will order lord Albemarle to speak for himself only, which I am of opinion will have more weight than coupled with the minister of Holland.

" You see by this, I am not for yielding to any encroachments of France upon our treaties already made. By them I would abide; what I have wanted to avoid always, was giving jealousies to one side, or false hopes to the other, by making new ones.* * * *

" I read " The Protester" a few days ago, and saw he was upon Dunkirk, and think of the paper as you do. The more his Grace of Bedford supports such doctrine, the better for us. I have been abused in every paper he has wrote, and you may expect your turn. It gives not me the least concern; though sometimes the fellow hits upon truths, which you know I would rather never have given an opportunity for him to do. I am satisfied, the less notice is taken of him the better: it has been my doctrine always, and I think experience shews I am in the right. I could have had the fellow if I would; but his conduct, when in pay, was such, that I should have been ashamed to have corresponded with him; this I told his friends, and told the king. * * * *

" I am too much, and too well acquainted with unreasonable demands, to be much alarmed at these. I have the same thought of the Jew bill, that I have of " The Protester:" let them take their course, and if you find it gives a real uneasiness, repeal next year, as a matter of no consequence in itself; but if it gives disturbance to weak minds, it is right to indulge them.

MR. PELHAM TO THE DUKE OF NEWCASTLE.*

Thinks that France cannot, and will not, support the unjustifiable conduct of the king of Prussia—Dunkirk gives him most concern—There the French are themselves interested, and we cannot yield—On election business.

"DEAR BROTHER,   *Scarborough, July 27th,* 1753.

" I wrote you a long letter by the last post, and shall trouble you now only with thanks for yours, which I received this morning. I am sorry for the account you send of the last French post, but still flatter myself, France cannot, and will not, support the king of Prussia in his unjustifiable conduct. Dunkirk gives me most concern; there they are interested themselves, and we cannot yield. You will have seen by my last, that it will not be very long before I come to you. Lord Ashburn- ham sets out on Tuesday, and will probably be at court on Wednesday. If you think he stays here, on any account but his health, you do us all wrong: I was for his going immediately, but he was very much pressed by Dr. Shaw, to stay at least three weeks, and his own opinion went with that advice. Your letter gave him some lati-

* Newcastle Papers.

tude also. He did not go with us to Castle Howard, purely that he might not lose
the benefit of the waters one day; his life has been that of a valetudinarian, not of a
man of pleasure or court. I am glad to hear Staffordshire is agreed : the contest would
have cost a great sum of money, and I believe not ended better than it will now. I
understood by lord Chetwynd, when he was in town, that he was sure for his brother
and his son. If Litchfield is compounded, it will save the Anson family a great deal of
money ; but then we lose a member there, for lord Gower would not have set up his
son Dick. It was reported, lord Trentham was to come in there. I hope I shall be
able to reconcile Osbaldiston and Lascelles ; the latter is very reasonable, the former
is honest but stiff. I dine with him to-morrow, and shall then talk plainly to him. I
am, as you may imagine, most heartily tired ; but I think the benefit I receive from
being here, answers my full expectation. My whole family desire their compliments
to you, and I beg to join mine with theirs, to the duchess of Newcastle.

THE DUKE OF NEWCASTLE TO MR. PELHAM.*

*Unfavourable answers relative to Prussia and Dunkirk—Difficulty of arranging the dis-
putes with Prussia, by the mediation of France—Conference with the duke de Mirepoix on that subject, and his attempt to compromise the affair—Spirited behaviour of the
British Cabinet—On a proposal respecting the negotiation with the Elector Palatine.*

"DEAR BROTHER,   *Newcastle House, July 27th,* 1753.

" The occasion of my sending this messenger, is not only to carry you all the
material letters which we have received, but also to give you a particular account of
what passed, yesterday, with the duke de Mirepoix

" You will see by lord Albemarle's letters, that the answers from France upon the
two points of *Prussia* and *Dunkirk*, are as bad as possible ; upon which I had, on
Wednesday night, a meeting with my Lord Chancellor, my Lord President, my lord
Holdernesse, and my lord Anson ; and the inclosed minute and instruction for lord
Albemarle, will inform you of our unanimous opinion, subject, however, to what
might pass with the duke de Mirepoix ; with whom I was to have a conference
yesterday morning, upon a courier he had just received from his court.

" M. de Mirepoix began the conference, by reading a very long dispatch from M.
de St. Contest, in which I observed he often skipped over several passages. The
letter stated, very fairly, the proposition I had made, and the reasons given in
support of it, and for condemning the behaviour of the king of Prussia. M. de St.
Contest then proceeds to answer my reasonings ; to shew the necessity and regularity
of appointing commissaries, to examine into these disputes, and to leave the final
determination to such neutral powers, as might be agreed upon. But as the proposal
in St. Contest's letter (viz. the reciprocal declarations, and the nomination of commissaries) was the same with that mentioned in my lord Albemarle's ; and as all the
reasonings in St. Contest's letter, were in a manner foreseen, and considered by us
the night before, I was strong in declaring to the embassador, that we could not

consent to St. Contest's proposal, or depart from our own.   Sir George Lee happening to be in the house, I called him in ; and he explained some things to M. de Mirepoix. I thought our conference would have ended there ; and Dr. Lee seemed to wish to stay, and talk upon some other business ; but M. de Mirepoix told him plainly, that he had something to say to me.

"The French embassador, when we were alone, asked me, very seriously, whether we could not depart from what we had declared ; that it was not possible for them to bring the king of Prussia to consent to take off the *arrêt*,* and go again into our courts ; that we had asked their interposition, though not mediation ; that we must have proposed something by it.   To which last I aswered, that we thought that the king of Prussia's proceedings were so irregular, that the French king, as a friend, might have advised him to take off the *arrêt*, and proceed as other powers had done, in the usual course of law, for obtaining satisfaction for their real grievances, if he had any. Finding me so determined (and I could not be otherwise) M. de Mirepoix walked about the room, seemed much agitated, and then said to this effect : '*Je ne vois rien que la confusion*,' (hinting as I thought, that they must take part with Prussia) ' but,' said he, ' *vous, mi lord, et moi, nous devons l'empêcher si nous pouvons ;*' and afterwards said, ' I have a thought of my own, which is just come into my head ' (but I believe it was contained in the passages of St. Contest's letter, which he passed over), ' what is. the sum which the king of Prussia asks for satisfaction ?'   To which I answered, ' I think his Prussian Majesty states it at *£*.30,000.'   ' Why, then,' says M. de Mire-. poix, ' the king of Prussia shall take off the *arrêt*, pay, or satisfy the full debt to the creditors, and then half or £.15,000 be given to satisfy his demands.'   I told him, it was not the sum ; the honour of the king and the nation was concerned ; that giving any money was some admission, that the king of Prussia has been in the right ;. that this proposal would be thought dishonourable to the nation ; that I did not know from whence this money was to come ; was it to be paid by the king, or be asked of parliament ?   ' Not asked of Parliament,' says Mirepoix, ' that destroys my intention.   I would not commit the honour of the king ; this money may be paid without being known.'   And once, I think, said, ' *Le roi n'y doit paroître*.'   I told him that I was sure the king would be ready to fling any body out of the window, who should make him such a proposal ; that the payment of this money would be looked upon as the condition of the king of Prussia's taking off the *arrêt* : and that his Prussian Majesty would know and think, that his behaviour had obtained that payment from us.   He said there should be no condition at all ;. that the king of Prussia should do every thing.   I told him the payment would always appear to have been the condition.   Upon finding me so firm (for in all views I thought it right to be so at first) Mirepoix said, ' *Donnez jusqú' au Mercredi qui vient : et peut être je puis alors digérer mes pensées*,' and so he went away.   I immediately made a report of this conversation to the king, who, you may imagine, was very well pleased with this appearance, whatever may be the ultimate issue of it.   It certainly shews

---

* *Arrêt* issued by the king of Prussia, who refused to abide by the decision of the British High Court of Admiralty.

that France is at present afraid of breaking with us ; and the march of the Russians, when known, I am persuaded, will make them more so.

" You now know very exactly, what passed with Mirepoix. I hope Cleverly will be back by Tuesday night; and I must beg to have your thoughts by that time, that I may be the better able to talk to Mirepoix. I have some notion (though without any foundation) that he would propose that the French king should pay the £.15,000, provided he can be assured privately, that we will repay it. To be sure, £.15,000 is nothing to prevent a war. But the yielding to such an insult is something ; and the giving £.15,000 in this summary way, when there does not appear to be the least pretence for it, or right, on the part of Prussia, except that which may arise from power and force ! That may be an objection, which it may not be so advisable to get over. Besides, where shall we get this money? Or how will it be possible to conceal the payment of it? which the king of Prussia's own pride and vanity will make him publish.

" You have also our news from Vienna. If the king agrees to the answers I propose to give to some points, given me by the Austrian Secretary (the chief of which is the engaging for the last 600,000 florins to be paid in two years after the election, unanimously made) I will inclose the paper in this letter. I am glad to hear from all hands, that you have received so much benefit from Scarborough. * * * *

" P. S.—I thank you for your kind letter just received ; will not trouble you with the Paper of Points and my answer. The only material article, Jones will send you inclosed, with his Majesty's note ; and the farthest length he will allow me to go, and that, without any design at present to do the thing. All that I will say is, that it is money the worst spared that ever was. The whole is £.67,000, half to be paid (if the election is over, and not otherwise) the first year of the new parliament; and the other half the second session only. We debated the affair, fully. I alleged all the arguments which I thought unanswerable ; and my brother Holdernesse, very à propos, gave your reason for your consent; as the money given to Saxony and Bavaria would not have its effect without it. I shall not send the answer until next week, so we will try to get a more favourable answer. For my part, I am not sanguine about the election ; but I would not have the loss of it fall upon us. We shall be the ridicule of every body abroad and at home, if it does. The greatest part of the resentment fell this day upon the Hanover ministers, in appearance ; but as they did not deserve it, I am afraid the real blame is laid to the charge of yours, &c.

MR. PELHAM TO THE DUKE OF NEWCASTLE.*

On the dispute with the king of Prussia, and on the affair of Dunkirk—The change of ministers at Vienna has not produced a change of measures—The court of Vienna was never sincere in the affair of the election—Approves two of the points, but disapproves the third.

"DEAR BROTHER,   *Scarborough, July 28th,* 1753.

" Cleverly the messenger arrived here with your several dispatches, at seven this afternoon, which when I saw the date of your letter, surprised me extremely ; and

* Newcastle Papers.

upon examination, I find he has rode two hundred and fifty miles, in twenty-six hours.

" I have read your letter, the minutes of the lords, the instructions to lord Albemarle, and the notes of what passed between you and the duke de Mirepoix, as carefully as I could. I have also read lord Albemarle's several letters upon the two subjects of Prussia and Dunkirk, together with your respective answers.

" I am very little able, at any time, to give an off-hand opinion upon such material points, without any previous conversation with those who are more thoroughly conversant with business of this nature than I can be; but there is this additional difficulty now, which you are not a judge of; the constant drinking of these waters, makes application to business exceedingly uneasy to me. I wish, therefore, I had been excused till I came to London, which I sent you word would be by to-morrow se'nnight; but, as you seem to desire my opinion, I will give it you as well as I can form it, though it is not to be doubted that your resolutions will be taken, as I think they are very wisely already, before my letter can reach your hands.

" The opinion of the lords, upon these points, is undoubtedly right; and your conversation with the French embassador was firm and well guarded, as it ought to be. We all know Mirepoix's good intentions, and we must not, therefore, presume every thing he says, to be exactly the opinion of his court. If I could think it was, I should be easy; for as he supposes we would not go to war, where £.15,000 could prevent it, so I must conclude, France will not take part essentially with a prince, who is to be bought off with such a sum. As true an economist as I am, the sum of money has no weight with me; it is the honour of the king and the nation, that is to be attended to ; and my opinion is, no pecuniary bargain should be made, antecedent to the king of Prussia's revoking his *arrêt* : that once done, sure ways might be found to satisfy the individuals of his country, who may possibly have been a little hardly dealt with by our law; and if such a sum as Mirepoix mentions, can do it, that might be found, either with, or without application to parliament.

" St. Contest's discourse upon Dunkirk is surprising. I do easily believe the court of France do not mean to offend at this time; but the inhabitants of Dunkirk, and possibly one part of their ministry, may avail themselves of orders, given only with a view to cleanse the town as St. Contest says, so as to give great grounds of jealousy, as if more was intended. Whatever the case is, we must abide by our treaties, and nothing can be allowed of, which in any degree restores the Port and Harbour of Dunkirk. The more persons you have to examine these works, the better. I have observed always, that the reports of sea-faring men, are stronger than those of our land engineers. Dunkirk is such an eye-sore to a sea officer, and, if restored, so detrimental to our navigation, commerce, and even security here, that I do not wonder, the least step towards repairing that, gives the greatest alarm to our sea officers and merchants. I hope, and believe, persisting in the firm conduct you have set out with, will in the end, bring the French to ; for they certainly desire quiet, as much, as we, in my opinion, ought to do. But, then, I would not disturb them with new projects, and by that means give the king of Prussia an opportunity of arguing with them, that we are desirous of disturbing Europe, and wait only for ability, and an opportunity.

. " I am now going to read over your letters from Vienna; and hope I shall be able, before I go to bed, to tell you my poor thoughts upon them also. As soon as I opened the Vienna packet, I was frightened at the sight of three long papers, which, if I had read, I am sure I should not have understood. I did read Mr. Keith's letter, and cursorily ran over your paper of comparisons; by all which I very plainly see the bent of the court of Vienna, which has been the same for some time past. The change of hands in that country does not, to me, seem in the least degree a change of measures. They have not for a great while, if they ever did, heartily wished success to the project of electing the archduke, king of the Romans; and I must say, if any thing, this last paper shews it more than all that went before. You will forgive me, if I add, that the Imperial Court, in my opinion, treats us with as much contempt as the king of Prussia. They have drawn us into subsidiary expenses in time of peace, for benefits apparently and immediately for their own family only; and when the time comes that they are to do any thing themselves, to forward the execution, they throw in such a number of frivolous objections, and make such difficulty, as no one would do, that does not wish rather to put an end to the negotiation. This being the case, I am clear for the king's abiding by his present engagements, but not for entering into any new ones, let them be ever so insignificant.

" I do not remember to have talked with lord Holdernesse upon any thing relative to this subject for a great while : I do not see, therefore, how he could quote my opinion. That I was for the engagements you entered into, when you were last at Hanover, is true ; but why? because by them nothing was to be paid till the election was over. Could any one be against that, who had consented to the former treaties, which, unfortunately for us, did take place, though the election, perhaps, by the principal parties concerned, was never thought of.

" I am not afraid, dear brother, that any mortal, at home, or abroad, will think this measure miscarries by our fault. I am much more afraid that the behaviour of the court of Vienna may give willing minds an opportunity of insinuating, that we were drawn into expenses, for obtaining the succession of the Imperial Crown in the House of Austria, without being sure that they themselves desire it.

" You have now my opinion upon the several points mentioned in your letter. In the two first, and most material ones, we agree ; in the latter, we always have differed in opinion, and I believe always shall ; but you will never meet from me, with any obstructions to what you wish. I have endeavoured to promote what you thought right, and shall continue to do so, where I do not see immediate danger. In this I trust to the court of Vienna ; for I am satisfied, whether you do, or do not agree to the security they propose, the money never will be demanded.

" Lord Ashburnham left us this morning. I continue in my design of leaving this place on Thursday, in the afternoon ; and shall certainly be, if I meet with no accident, in Arlington Street, on Sunday, in the evening. We are all here in good health : those that have been kept to the waters and bathing, have received benefit by it ; and the great regularity of our lives has done good to us all. There is very little news here ; what there is, you will have from lord Ashburnham. I hope you will approve of what I write to you, as I do extremely, what you have wrote, to lord Albemarle, and talked to Mirepoix." * * * *

MR. PELHAM TO THE DUKE OF NEWCASTLE.*

Approves his Memorial about Dunkirk, but laments the necessity of it.

"DEAR BROTHER,   *Greenwich, Aug. 18th,* 1753.

" I send you back your draught of a Memorial, and the two plans of Dunkirk, which lord Ashburnham left with me yesterday. The Memorial I have read, and doubt not its being a very proper one ; I am no judge of the propriety of such draughts, especially in French, which language I understand very imperfectly. But that we must speak strong, and abide by what we say, I know very well. I am sorry for the necessity, but cannot help it. Your plans I did not look upòn, having nobody here to explain them to me ; it is impossible for me, alone, to understand them. I hope you will excuse my coming to town on Monday ; my coach goes that day, with Frances, part of the way to Tunbridge, and I design to be in London on Tuesday, and not to return here till I come from Sussex." * * * *

THE DUKE OF NEWCASTLE TO THE LORD CHANCELLOR.†

King of Prussia the principal, if not the sole support of the Pretender and the Jacobite cause. —The Duke of Newcastle defends the Treaty with Russia, as necessary to support the influence of England on the Continent.

Newcastle House, Sept. 21*st,* 1753.

" I must now acquaint your lordship, that we had a meeting at lord Holdernesse's, on Tuesday night, where were present, his lordship, lord Anson, my brother, and myself. I send, inclosed, the short minute of what passed. You will see how we altered the Memorial about Dunkirk, and also that your doubts about the addition, made in Holland, to the second Article of the Barrier project, took place so far, that we determined to leave the whole additional clause out, as you will more particularly see by my letter to Joe.

" As I had an opportunity of taking down, in general Wall's presence, some points relating to our disputes with Spain, they were read and approved. But my brother made a very proper objection to one expression, " *taken on the high seas,*" which I altered to "*molested ;*" and, by Mr. Drake's advice, struck out "*the high seas ;*" and, with some difficulty, have got lord Holdernesse to mention it in his letters to Mr. Keene.

" I come now to give your lordship an account of what passed upon the material affair of the Russian Treaty, which we have determined to consider very maturely on

* Newcastle Papers.   † Ib.

Wednesday next, the 26th inst. ; and, for that purpose, I hope we may depend upon your lordship's being in town, according to your kind offer on Tuesday night; and I have written to my lord Granville (as you will see by my letter to him) to be in town on Tuesday night also. And indeed we have so many points of business, which must necessarily be now dispatched, that we shall have a difficulty to get through them in two meetings, on Wednesday and Thursday.

" To return to the affair of Russia; I am sure you will be glad to hear, that, in all my life, I never knew a meeting of business pass with so much good humour, temper, and proper consideration on all sides, as that did. My brother reasoned with great good sense; did not seem quite determined in his opinion; but stated very fairly the arguments on both sides. His chief objections seemed to me, the almost certainty, that this provisional subsidy would be constantly continued, after the expiration of the two years, and that then it would be argued, that this new sort of expense was occasioned by (perhaps not an improper) attention to the king's Hanover dominions, which might be of ill consequence to his Majesty and his family, and concluded that, if this measure should be necessary, or thought so, some saving on other heads of expense (the army at home, the garrisons at Gibraltar and Mahon) ought to be made; or the whole would be too great a burthen for the circumstances of the king-dom. For my brother was sensible, that the expense of the fleet could not be less than one million a year. When I saw him the day after, I thought him much more determined against the measure, than he appeared to be at lord Holdernesse's.

" I have now very fully, and I think very fairly, stated the objections. I shall say very little in answer, as the point will now come to be seriously and finally considered amongst us. You will see, by the paper I call *Ideas*, two methods for answering the objection of the continuance of the subsidy, or the retiring the troops from Livonia, when perhaps they may be as much or more wanted, than they are at present. The first is the best; and I should not despair of getting that accepted, though Colloredo does; and the last expedient was suggested by him. But, I own, if we can agree upon a proper sum of money, either once for all, or a reasonable subsidy for two years (it being always to be understood, that nothing shall be paid until the end of the first year), I should not despair of getting a security, that the troops should remain there for four years; and that, I hope, would do our business completely, for the reasons mentioned in my letter to lord Granville. Colloredo's expedient also might be made practicable, if necessary; and, either one way or the other, I think the objec-tion to the perpetuity of the subsidiary measure is answered.

" I come now to consider the great and material argument, that the interest of the king's family will be affected by such a measure, which will be looked upon to be entirely calculated for the preservation of Hanover. To that I answer, that in fact it is not so; the situation of Europe in general requires it, except we will give up all pretence of holding the balance, and upon all occasions yield to the encroachments of France upon our trade and possessions, in the West Indies; perhaps both Indies; in America; and every where else; and do determine to submit to the insults and flights of the king of Prussia, now avowedly the principal, if not the sole support, of the Pre-tender, and the Jacobite cause; for, though I think it could not have been otherwise, it is too late to look back, whether it could or not. It is now so ; and upon that foot we must consider it, and act accordingly.

" Our present particular dispute with Prussia will require something to be done. The application to France (a measure thought necessary by us all) has, in the opinion of us all, absolutely failed ; and if nothing is done, and the king of Prussia be suffered to detain the Silesia money, and to go off unobserved, not only the honour of the nation will have an eternal blot upon it, but I will be bold to say, the most fatal stroke will be given to the trade, commerce, and naval influence of this country, that can be invented. For, though we do not in words yield to the king of Prussia, if we avoid any thing that may bring this dispute to an honourable end, we do effectually and essentially give up the point ; and if that be so, I would appeal to the world, whether this measure can be justly called, in any sense, a Hanover measure. And what would be the consequence to this kingdom, if right measures for our own honour and interest should be avoided, for fear of a wrong interpretation being put upon them? Or (what is still clearer) if we are not to act, lest the king's German dominions should be affected by it, or we should be under a necessity of taking measures, which may be, by ill-designing or mistaken men, falsely interpreted? This argument, I own, turns upon a supposition, that the having a strong Russian army on the frontiers of the king of Prussia's country, will be a means of preventing the king of Prussia from breaking the peace, and enable us the better to come to terms with him, by making him desist from his unjust violences, exerted against the rights and properties of his Majesty's subjects. Every body knows, that the king of Prussia acts only from interest or fear ; by interest we cannot gain him, by fear we have no means of doing it but by Russia ; and, as the king of Prussia must be looked upon to be ill-disposed to the king and this nation, and the most likely power in all Europe to stir up a war, whatever contributes to keep him quiet, must contribute also to the preservation of the peace.

" The declaration made to me by the duc de Mirepoix (of which you have a particular account, in my letters to Mr. Keith and colonel Yorke), I take to be the consequence of the king of Prussia's fright. It is possible that France may assemble their troops in Flanders ; but they will strike no stroke ; and we certainly are masters of the Russians. So that, notwithstanding *that demonstration* (if it should take place), I do not apprehend any consequence from it. But if we should take an alarm from it, and drop our negotiation with Russia, or stop the march of the Russians, we shall have *these demonstrations* in Flanders, upon every single measure we may take, which may not be agreeable to France or Prussia. I believe your lordship will think that it was right to acquaint our friends in Holland with it, and the court of Vienna, that they may be upon their guard ; but I have insisted as strongly as possible, that the secret should be kept, and I hope it will.

" I am ashamed of having given your lordship so much trouble, especially as I hope to have the pleasure of seeing you so soon ; the best amends I can make you is, to desire that you would give yourself none in answering it. I have most seriously weighed the many strong and material arguments offered by my brother, all of which have great weight. But as, upon examination, I have seriously and honestly formed, *so far,* my opinion, I was willing that my friends should see the reasons I went upon. I have no objection to your shewing my brother this letter. I hope you will keep the inclosures, and shew them to him ; for those he has not seen. I should, in all events, be obliged to you if you would talk over this affair fully with him, for debates at meetings do not do much, and often produce disagreeable incidents ; but there is no probability of that in this case. My brother and lord Anson will be with you on Sunday : I heartily wish I could have been of the party."

THE DUKE OF NEWCASTLE TO THE LORD CHANCELLOR.*

Enclosing a letter from lord *Granville, on the subject of the counter-project relating to Russia.*

Claremont, Sept. 22nd, 1753.

*   *   *   *   " I have had a good deal of discourse with a very sensible man, who is naturally a great enemy to foreign expenses, and who dreads a war above all things. He thinks this expense cannot well be gone into, unless some saving be made, this next session, either in the garrison at Gibraltar, or in the army in Scotland. But he seems to think there may be great utility in this measure, towards preserving the peace, or enabling us to support our essential rights with France, in the affair of Dunkirk, and our American and West Indian disputes, which he thinks never can be given up. But, as peace is the first point, he reasons with my brother, that this measure, if taken, should be put wholly on the preservation of the peace, the general situation of Europe, and the necessity of being in a condition, in case justice is not done us, as to Dunkirk and the West Indies. He calls it a *fraud* and not an *overt act ;* a private injury, and not a national insult; and thinks the letting it remain as it is, is no departure from our rights, or the doctrine which we must ever adhere to, with regard to captures at sea, in time of war. Though I do not quite agree with him, in this latter supposition, or opinion, I think there is sense in it; and whatever tends to secure peace, without giving up our honour and interests, I shall be for. And indeed I am at present strongly of opinion, that this measure will tend to peace, upon a right and honourable footing. I do most sincerely give the utmost attention to all my brother's objections. I think there is great weight in every one of them. I am very far from driving or forcing the measure : my desire is, that it should be coolly and calmly considered ; and it is with that view, that I have taken the pains to lay every thing before your lordship and my brother, that has either occurred to me, or I have learned from others.

" I hope we shall have the honour of seeing you in town at the council, for the recorder and parliament, on Wednesday, and at dinner that day, at lord Holdernesse's. I am," &c.

* Newcastle Papers.

MR. PELHAM TO THE DUKE OF NEWCASTLE.*

"DEAR BROTHER,   *Richmond, Monday Morning, Jan. 7th, 1754.*

" Fox was here yesterday; told me lord Kildare † was not come to London, which he wondered at, but supposed it was the frost, and possibly the waters out.   He told me almost all that passed between the king and him ; pretty nearly word for word what the king said to you.   He was anxious to know what I thought of his beginning with the king upon the subject; and said if I had been in town, he would have desired me to have done it for him.   I told him I thought it always right, in these cases, for people to speak for themselves ; that had he employed me, I should literally have obeyed his commands, but that I thought it much better as it was.   He made the same professions to me as he did to you, with the addition of personal friendship and personal obligations.   I am easy upon that subject, for I am confident he will act a more honourable part than his governors or his followers wish him to do.   The only remarkable thing he told me (which I do not remember you did), was, that the king desired him to prevent lord Kildare's asking an audience, for if he did, he was determined not to see him, but send him to his ministers.   Fox thinks the king as angry with Kildare as is possible for a man to be, and very much in earnest upon the whole Irish affair.   I fear, the duke of Dorset will remain in a state of uncertainty, notwithstanding your private letter; for I protest, on considering the minute, I cannot comprehend what it means.   The Primate's and lord George's letters are both sensible, particularly the former ; but shew great partiality to the House of Dorset, which indeed is not to be wondered at.

" I cannot finish this letter without thanking you most cordially for the great affection you have in every circumstance shewn to me, during my late illness.   I am now, thank God, as well as ever I was in my life.   They will persuade me to stay here till Friday, which I am almost ashamed of, though I certainly shall gather strength faster here than in London."   *   *   *   *

---

* Newcastle Papers.

† The Earl of Kildare married lady Emilia Lennox, second daughter of Charles, second duke of Richmond, and sister of lady Caroline Fox ; he was created duke of Leinster in 1766.   He seems to have been distantly related to the Pelhams, as his ancestor, Wentworth, eighth earl of Kildare, married lady Elizabeth Holles, second daughter of John Holles, earl of Clare.   His lordship was opposed to the duke of Dorset, and a favourer of Mr. Boyle.

MR. PELHAM TO THE DUKE OF NEWCASTLE.*

Relative to the advancement of lord Barnard and the Lord Chancellor in the peerage Intended visits of lord Kildare.†

"DEAR BROTHER,   *Richmond, Jan. 8th,* 1754.

"I have just received your letter by the messenger, and am heartily glad to hear that you have spoken to the king upon lord Barnard's affair.‡ I never doubted the king's doing it, whenever you thought proper to mention it; and I cannot but say it gives me great pleasure that you have done it. It removes a thousand disagreeable ideas; and a coolness, which I have seen for some time on your side, to as honest, hearty, and friendly a creature as ever was born, could end in no good. You know him as well as I do, and, I dare say, think the same of him. The king's offer to the lord Chancellor is a great proof of his present disposition; and I hope, for all our sakes, the lord Chancellor will not demur in accepting it. I know few things that would give greater *éclat* at present, than this promotion. I hope we shall not lose the benefit of it. I have had a letter from Mr. Fox this afternoon, giving me an account of lord Kildare's disposition, at least what Mr. Fox has a mind should appear so. He tells me lord Kildare expected to be very ill received by ————; that he never thought of desiring an audience, that he came over without any credentials or instructions from his party, but merely to see what was thought and said of himself. He designs waiting upon you, lord Holdernesse, lord Chancellor, and myself; when he supposes he shall be asked some questions by us all: if so, he thinks he can justify his own conduct, and, as Fox represents, does not seem solicitous of what is thought of other people. The letter is a wise one; so much so, that I conclude it is the result of deliberation, since his lordship's arrival, and little thought of when he left Ireland.

"I think I have given you the substance. I thought it necessary you should know to whom lord Kildare designed his visits, and the plan he at present takes in consequence of those visits. I continue to mend every day. I want to be with you, as I know this is a time that requires mutual advice, and steady conduct among true friends."

THE LORD CHANCELLOR TO THE DUKE OF NEWCASTLE. §

Is glad that Mr. Pelham takes in good part the elevation of lord Barnard in the peerage— Alludes to the offer of an earldom to himself, to which he was afterwards promoted.

"MY DEAR LORD,   *Powis House, Jan. 8th,* 1754.

"I return your letter, and join most heartily in the satisfaction you receive in the manner in which Mr. Pelham takes this affair. Your Grace knows how I have

* Newcastle Papers.

† This letter seems to contradict Dodington's statement of the misunderstanding between the two brothers relative to lord Barnard's peerage, although it might possibly have subsequently taken place.

‡ Christopher, created lord Barnard in 1699, married Elizabeth, eldest sister and co-heir to John Holles Newcastle. His son, Henry lord Barnard, who is mentioned in this letter, was created earl of Darlington, April 1754.

§ Newcastle Papers.

always thought about lord Barnard's part in it, and what I have said upon that subject, and for the wishes your brother gives relative to yourself and your own family, I should have taken a sincere pleasure in it, although it had not been accompanied with the other part. Mr. Pelham is very good to me in what he says on that topic, which concerns myself. Your Grace is a witness with what coolness and indifference I have always looked upon that rise in rank ; but I see your brother considers it in a higher light, which, as it regards us all, makes it much the more interesting and agreeable to me. This way of considering it has made me reflect, once more, upon the resolution we took, about the time of my waiting upon the king ; and I beg your Grace would send me your opinion, to-night, in three words, whether, as his Majesty directed your Grace to acquaint me with this his serious intention, I should not go to-morrow morning. Do not imagine that this proceeds from any affectation or forwardness ; for it arises merely from the light in which Mr. Pelham takes it, and from an apprehension that the king may think that you would immediately acquaint me with it, and that I am guilty of some neglect towards him. In every other respect it is indifferent to me, and therefore be so good as to tell me your opinion frankly.

" The account of Mr. Fox's letter is very remarkable ; and I think with him (Mr. Pelham), that it is a new disposition, not thought of when lord Kildare left Ireland. As his lordship intends to come to us separately, we should all agree what language to hold to him ; and the sooner the better.

" I heartily rejoice in the account Mr. Pelham gives of himself, and long to see him perfectly re-established and returned to us ; but I am so much his well-wisher, that I do not wish to see him make too much haste."

INDEX.

THE END.

T. C. HANSARD, Printer,
Paternoster Row,
London.

ERRATA.

VOLUME I.

VOLUME II.

Lightning Source UK Ltd.
Milton Keynes UK
UKOW06f0622190617

303652UK00016B/647/P